OCCUPATION

OCCUPATION:
Israel Over Palestine

Second Edition

edited by
Naseer H. Aruri

Association of Arab-American University Graduates, Inc.
Belmont, Massachusetts, 1989

First published in the United States of America by

 **PRESS**

Copyright " The Association of Arab-American University Graduates, Inc., 1983; Second Edition, 1989

ISBN 0-937694-64-9

Library of Congress Cataloging-in-Publication Date

Occupation : Israel over Palestine / edited by Naseer H. Aruri. – 2nd ed.

    p. cm. – (AAUG monograph ; no. 18)
    Includes bibliographical references.
    ISBN 0-937694-83-5. -- ISBN 0-937694-84-3 (pbk)
    1. West Bank--Politics and government, 2. Gaza Strip--Politics and government, 3. Palestinian Arabs--Politics and government, 4. Zionism--Controversial literature. I. Aruri, Nasser Hasan, 1934-   . II. Series : AAUG monograph series : no. 18.
DS110,W47023 1989
956,9405--dc20   89-38409
                                        CIP

Design and typesetting by Amana Books, Inc.

DEDICATION

Fayez Sayegh

This book is dedicated to the memory of Dr. Fayez A. Sayegh, statesman, scholar, and teacher. The issues addressed herein were of primary and pressing concern to him throughout his life. His devotion to Palestine was legendary; he was eulogized as the "spirit of the Palestinian people."

For more than three decades he worked to compile and systematize a vast collection of specialized information – a sort of archives of modern Palestine. At the same time, he studied, taught, and spoke for the causes of Arab nationalism and Palestine, often seemingly alone during the dark days when Palestinians despaired of world attention to their plight. But Fayez Sayegh had faith in the justice of their cause, and in the dignity of his dispossessed people. He dedicated his life to their service.

Fayez Sayegh began his academic career with degrees in philosophy from the American University in Beirut. He pursued his studies in the United States, and received a doctorate in philosophy from Georgetown University. In the ensuing years, he taught at various universities, in the United States and abroad, and he wrote, with learning and passion, on Arab nationalism and on the question of Palestine. His writings have appeared in sixteen languages.

His devotion to the causes he loved so well was exercised not only in the academic forum, but in the wider world of political activity as well. In 1959, he was elected president of the Palestine Arab Congress; in 1965 he founded the Palestine Research Center in Beirut. He served on the Executive Committee of the Palestine Liberation Organization, and was a member of the Palestine National Council from 1970 until his death ten years later. (It is perhaps fortunate that he did not live to see the looting of the Palestine Research Center by Israeli occupation forces during the last week of September 1982).

Fayez Sayegh was well known in the international diplomatic arena. He was advisor, consultant, or member of various Arab delegations to the General Assembly of the United Nations; his encyclopedic knowledge of UN resolutions on Palestine earned him the respect of friends and foes alike.

He was a man of peace, and felt that a real peace in Palestine could only be achieved through coexistence and cultural plurality. He always felt that Zionism, by its very nature, precluded any such peaceful solution. Prior to the June 1967 war, which more than doubled the size of Israel, he wrote the following prophetic words:

> As an essential ingredient of Israel's very being, Zionism is certain to impel Israel sooner or later to resume the process which gave it birth and to embark upon imperialist, expansionist adventures unto fuller self-realization.

To American critics of his steadfast position, who charged that his insistence on secularism and pluralism was impractical and utopian, he replied:

> I hope I will never cease to want to cling to utopian ideas; . . . besides, I am speaking of a pluralistic society which I think is accepted as a common-day fact of life in this country. What I am asking for my land is that we have a state that is not an exclusively Jewish State with a Law of Return only for Jews . . . [but a] country in my land that will be for everyone, the Jew and the non-Jew. . . . If that is utopian, America's utopia has become a reality, and I hope one day that Palestine will become a reality also.

His firm beliefs led him to reject such proffered solutions as the Camp David accords – in an eloquent and reasoned analysis of those documents he urged resistance to appeals that Palestinians join the Camp David process, appeals "as seductive and destructive as a siren-call," but presupposing "Palestinian readiness to abdicate and renounce the inalienable birthright of the Palestinian people as a whole forever, in return for a partial satisfaction of part of the aspirations of a part of the Palestinian people."

Always, the central concern of Fayez Sayegh was the question of justice for the Palestinian people. Once, after a university lecture, a member of the audience asked why he should share this concern, which in his eyes was nothing more than a problem caused by "tribalistic conflict." Sayegh reminded his questioner of the treatment accorded to the "primitive savages" found by early settlers on American shores, and continued:

> Sir, I bow my head in shame for all the backwardness in my land, but I take pride in the fact that my generation and my children's generation have not accepted this backwardness as a final verdict of history. We are trying to do something about it. . . . However, my backwardness should be no license for someone else to take my land, and this is the essence of the Palestine problem. Now, sir, you asked why you should interest yourself in my problem. You owe it to me; you created my problem. You live in a world no longer capable of compartmentalization. My tragedy will become yours. The whole world order, if it crumbles, will leave no one safe, and the next war in the Middle East, God forbid, will not see you sitting comfortably on this seat, warm and happy, saying why should I care about you.

Fayez Sayegh died on December 9, 1980, but his ideas and his cause live on. And he is remembered by those whose lives he touched, as teacher and friend, as source of knowledge and of inspiration. Dr. William F.

Stinespring, professor emeritus of Old Testament and Semitics at Duke University Divinity School, recalls his first meeting with Fayez Sayegh, on the occasion of a university-sponsored lecture on the struggle between the Arabs and the Zionists over Palestine. The lecture was to have been a debate, to which the Arab information office agreed, but the Zionist office refused such a format. The Arab spokesman was Dr. Sayegh, who, Professor Stinespring learned, was a fellow Presbyterian, but with a

> vast and sympathetic knowledge of Islam, as befitting a person representing all the Arabs. The greatest pleasure and surprise, however, came with the hearing of his lecture. His zeal, eloquence, and command of a massive array of facts and figures were unparalleled. I suspected later, when I was told that no Zionist could withstand him in debate, why the Zionists had insisted that the debate be changed to a pair of lectures on different dates. After that I heard him whenever possible and read everything he had written that I could acquire. He could say what I thought and believed, but say it better and with data to back it up.
>
> It was significant that during the last thirteen years of his life, Dr. Sayegh served as senior consultant to the ministry of foreign affairs of Kuwait.. Kuwait is a predominantly Islamic country, yet was willing to entrust this important post to a Palestinian Christian because of his unique character, ability, and knowledge of not only the Arab and Islamic group of nations, but of the entire world with its need for mutual understanding and recognition.

An American student of Sayegh's, P. Edward Haley, now professor of international relations and director of the international relations program at Claremont McKenna College in California, remembers his teacher's dedicated commitment to his beliefs. Their first acquaintance was in the late 1950s, when Haley was an undergraduate at Stanford,

> basking in what we all thought to be the eternal sunshine of those days. My strongest thoughts of Fayez are thus mixed with the sweet recollections of undisappointed hope, of powers sensed but not yet fully tried, and of an ever-deepening awareness of myself, of others, of my nation, and of the world.
>
> The 1950s have not been given a place in the hierarchy of fashionable times. That is a mistake. For many Americans who came of age then it was a time of moral awakening. We were keenly aware of the richness of our blessings and determined to become better. Some of us were driven by a seemingly irresistible moral impetus into the civil rights movement. Others devoted fervent, sometimes fevered, efforts to understand other nations and cultures. It was this latter desire that led us to Fayez. "Have you taken a course from the Arab professor?" a friend asked. A few of us thought we'd try. Thus began an intellectual adventure and an enduring friendship. Fayez taught us about Zionism, using only Zionist sources! In those days I think he believed that if only he were good enough – if his presentations were meticulously prepared, scrupulously logical, eloquent, thorough, overwhelming – then the truth would become an invincible sword in the cause of his people, the Palestinian people.

He seemed made for us and the times. He was a man with a message: committed, bold, erudite. But he respected our moral wish to know and understand foreign causes and peoples. He never hectored us, never forced his point of view on us. In truth, he had no need, for he had chosen his academic approach so intelligently that he had only to ask us to read the basic Zionist texts to fulfill his mission as teacher and patriot.

As a teacher Fayez shared his learning, his life, and his dreams with us in ways that far surpassed the ordinary notion of student-teacher relations. Early one summer Fayez invited all of us who had taken his spring seminar to come to the little house near the campus where he lived with his wife, Arlene. We had been studying the entire history of the Palestine question at the United Nations. "Bring all your notes," Fayez said. "We're going to discuss the Palestinian problem until we solve it." We stayed up all night arguing and debating and learning. Then it was morning, and as Arlene served us breakfast in the strong California sunshine, Fayez reminded us that it was the day of Algerian independence. That was my last class from Fayez.

We saw one another again in 1968, when I attended one of his lectures in Washington, D.C. With his customary eloquence and logic, Fayez advocated the new uncompromisingly anticolonialist positions of the Palestinian resistance. I came away from the lecture puzzled and hurt, and when I spoke with him after he seemed cold and distant. "He's changed," I said to myself resentfully. "He's not the same man at all." But I was wrong. He had concluded that the goal of Palestinian self-determination could not be achieved without the support of anticolonialists everywhere, including the Soviet Union. Slowly, painfully, I began to realize the impact of the 1967 War on developments in the Middle East and on the lives of my Arab friends. I also saw that what I had reacted to was not simply a harsh, anti-American line but a statement of the new international realities as seen by the Palestinians themselves. Eventually I realized that the Palestinians were not so much eager to turn away from America as they were determined not to shrink from their goal of self-determination. Once again, Fayez had been my teacher.

Although we corresponded during the years, after the 1968 lecture, Fayez and I were not close any longer; perhaps we could not be, while I and my country worked at the lessons he put before us and the world from the rostrum at the United Nations. But I miss him keenly. There's so much I'd like to talk to him about, so much still to learn about him. Sometimes I seem to hear him saying, "Come over tonight, friends, and we'll talk about this until we have the solution." Then I remember that it cannot be. But my sadness passes quickly, and I turn to my own students with new energy and devotion. That is Fayez' last gift to me.

Fayez Sayegh's gifts as a teacher were treasured by his students in the Arab world as well. Professor Hani Faris, of the University of British Columbia's Institute of Asian Research, remembers that

The courses Fayez offered at AUB [American University of Beirut] attracted Arab students of all nationalities. A common bond quickly developed among them, their different backgrounds notwithstanding. They flocked to his lectures to satisfy their search for answers to the many challenges facing the Arab world.

Like many other students, I registered in almost every course Fayez offered during his two-year stay at AUB [1965-1967]. We were captivated by both the philosophy and the methodology that guided his courses. Arab unity, Arab socialism, anti-Zionism, anti-imperialism, and nonalignment offered the first principles in a philosophy which Fayez believed must form the basis of any program for national action and revival. A number of attributes distinguished the teaching style of Fayez Sayegh – structured and highly analytic presentations, encyclopedic knowledge, sharp and witty comments, and impeccable English. Speaking with confidence, he both dominated and involved his audience in such a way that he was able in the same session to move them from laughter to tears.

The teacher-student association went beyond the confines of the classroom, Professor Faris recalls. Students would often gather around Fayez Sayegh in the cafeteria or would continue discussions at his home. His wife Arlene was a familiar figure, and the whole class joined in rejoicing at the birth of his daughter Rima. The private aspect of Fayez the man is also warmly remembered by Dr. Elmer Berger, one of his oldest friends who is now executive director of American Jewish Alternatives to Zionism. He recalls that his home, "enriched with the love and companionship of Arlene, became a sanctuary where friends discovered his warmth and gracious hospitality." Berger also notes his pride and delight in his daughter, and suggests that these aspects of his nature might surprise those who knew him only across the space between audience and lectern, for "in debate, he could be savage – but only with words, never stooping to the *ad hominem,* and reinforced with unerring logic." His style in debate often reminded Berger of that of Muhammad Ali in the prize ring – he could "float like a butterfly, sting like a bee." His ability to dominate an audience, says Berger, came from

an absolute mastery of the facts down to the minutest detail. Except for a few specialized libraries, perhaps no one had more complete files, along with almost every book and periodical having anything to offer on the problem of Palestine. Many were the times he challenged a doubter by reciting not only a general title of an authoritative source, but he would add the chapter, page number, and sometimes even the line for the documentation of his argument.

There is another phase of Fayez' "lectureship" little known except to those who knew him well. It will probably never be known for how many of the interventions by Arab ambassadors to the United Nations Fayez was the speechwriter. He never wanted, for himself, the formal role of diplomat. Despite his apparent ease on the platform, his love of personal privacy accommodated only with great reluctance to the often necessary politesse of diplomatic protocol. But in the speeches he wrote for others and in the wording of United Nations resolutions, for which he often did the first drafts, his economy of words and his mastery of language permitted him to "lecture" vicariously without loss of principle.

All this hardly explains the success and popularity as a lecturer of this quiet, scholarly man. He indulged in few if any histrionics; there was no hypnotic, mellifluous voice. He was of ordinary physical stature, in later years partially bald. He rarely lightened his lectures with amusing anecdotes. But there was no mystery to his success – it was born of his profound conviction and dedication to his cause. The wide variety of his audiences responded to this, because the foundation of his case for the Palestinians was universal in dimension. He asked for them no special favors, but only for recognition of their common humanity; for justice and equality under international law. His plea for compassion, for truth and integrity, was backed with meticulous documentation, the result of a lifetime of dedicated scholarship. The listening world of Fayez Sayegh believed him when he spoke.

Fayez Sayegh, teacher, scholar, statesman. And finally, Fayez Sayegh the man. Hisham Sharabi, professor of history at Georgetown University in Washington, remembers:

Fayez was deeply religious. but in a personal, non-institutional way. His private life and his public life moved in separate spheres, but both were animated by the same passion for transcendence and liberation.

To him Palestine was *the* great passion: he loved it as one could only love a person. His entire life was a continuous struggle for Palestine. The day he died he was preparing an article on the subject for *Arab Perspectives*.

His wit was whip-sharp; for him irony was a normal way of communicating. Yet his sense of life was tragic; the pain and cruelty of the human condition touched him more deeply than did its joys or pleasures. Still he never gave in to bitterness or self-pity.

He had a profound love for the American people, but also a fierce anger against American government policy. He could not understand how the victims of terror could, in American eyes, themselves become the terrorists, or how the Palestinians' demand to recover their homes and land could become almost blasphemous.

He once told me – long ago, walking by the sea – that only a great pain or a great loss can make one really strong. For Fayez, the inner struggle is now over, and with it the pain and the loneliness. But the other struggle goes on. In that struggle Fayez Sayegh will always be alive, he will always be our comrade, and together we shall overcome.

This book is offered in tribute to the memory of Fayez Sayegh, and towards the realization of his vision and dream – the realization of the new Palestine.

The editor wishes to acknowledge with sincere gratitude a grant, which Mr. A. Moshin Qattan made available to the AAUG Press. Acknowlwdgements are also due to Dorothy Stade, who copy – edited and proof–read the manuscript, and to Dr. Samir Abed Rabbo and his staff at Amana Books.

NASEER H. ARURI
February 1989

CONTENTS

PART I: INTRODUCTION

PART II: THE CHANGING STATUS OF PALESTINIAN AREAS SINCE THE 1967 OCCUPATION

PART III: CONSEQUENCES OF THE 1967 OCCUPATION

PART IV: THE INFRASTRUCTURE OF RESISTANCE

THE CONTRIBUTORS

SAMEER Y. ABRAHAM is senior survey director at NORC, a social science research center at the University of Chicago. He is coeditor of *Race, Class and the World System* and *Arabs in the New World.* He has written on the sociology of the Palestinians and the Palestine national movement.

ZIAD ABU-AMR is professor of political science at Bir Zeit University. He holds a doctorate from Georgetown University and has published articles in *Middle East International, American-Arab Affairs* and other magazines. He is the author of *Usul al-Harakat al-Siyasiya fi Qita Gaza 1984-1967 (*The Genesis of Political Activities in the Gaza Strip).

JANET ABU-LUGHOD is professor of sociology at the New School for Social Research in New York. She has written widely about cities in the United States, the Arab region, and the world, and has conducted research on Palestinian demography.

NASEER H. ARURI is professor of political science at Southeastern Massachusetts University, N. Dartmouth, Massachusetts. He is author of *Jordan: A Study in Political Development 1921-1965.*

IBRAHIM DAKKAK is a Palestinian engineer who lives in Jerusalem. He is president of the West Bank Engineers Union and founder of the Arab Thought Forum in Jerusalem.

PETER DEMANT is a historian at the University of Amsterdam. He is author of *Ploughshares Into Swords:* Israeli settlement policy in the Occupied Territories, 1967-1977.

MUNIR FASHEH is dean of students at Bir Zeit University in the West Bank. He has worked in education for over twenty years and has published a number of books and many articles on the subject of education.

SARAH GRAHAM-BROWN is a freelance writer. She was cultural editor of *Middle East* magazine in London. She has written on the economic and social history of Palestine in the nineteenth and twentieth centuries. She is author of *Palestinians and Their Society 1880-1946: A Photographic Essay*, and *Education, Repression and Liberation: The Palestinians*, written for World University Service (UK).

MUHAMMAD HALLAJ is the director of Palestine Research and Educational Center in Washington. He was formerly vice-president of Bir Zeit University and is co-author of *Palestine Is But Not in Jordan.*

ANN LESCH is professor of political science at Villanova University in Pennsylvania. Formerly with the Ford Foundation, she served as program officer for Middle East and Africa. She is author of *Arab Politics in Palestine 1917-1939.*

IBRAHIM MATAR is a Palestinian economist and an expert on Israeli settlement. He was formerly head of the department of business and economics at Bethlehem University in the West Bank.

EMMA PLAYFAIR is an attorney who is currently program officer for the Middle East and Africa with the Ford Foundation in Cairo. She was formerly with al-Haq (Law in the Service of Man) in the West Bank. She is the author of *Administrative Detention in the West Bank* published by al-Haq.

SARA ROY is presently doing research in the Gaza Strip. She received a doctorate from the School of Education at Harvard University and is the author of many articles pertaining to the Middle East, including "The Gaza Strip: Critical Effects of the Occupation."

SHEILA RYAN is a founder of the Palestine Solidarity Committee and co-author of *Palestine Is But Not in Jordan.*

ROSEMARY SAYIGH is a researcher and freelance journalist. She is author of *Palestinians: From Peasants to Revolutionaries.*

RAJA SHEHADEH is a practicing Palestinian attorney in the West Bank. He is founder and codirector of al-Haq (Law in the Service of Man), and author of *The Third Way: A Journal of Life in the West Bank,* and *Occupier's Law: Israel and the West Bank.*

The Association of Arab-American University Graduates, Inc., was established December 1967, incorporated as a nonprofit educational and cultural organization in the state of Michigan in 1968 and obtained tax-exempt status from the Internal Revenue Service in 1970. The Association aims at promoting knowledge and understanding of cultural, scientific and educational matters between the Arab and American peoples. Membership is open to all college graduates who are U.S. citizens or permanent residents and who are of Arabic-speaking origin. Associate membership is open to U.S. citizens or permanent residents interested in furthering the aims of the AAUG.

For further information write to:

Secretary
AAUG
556 Trapelo Road
Belmont, MA 02178
617-484-5483

MAP OF PALESTINE

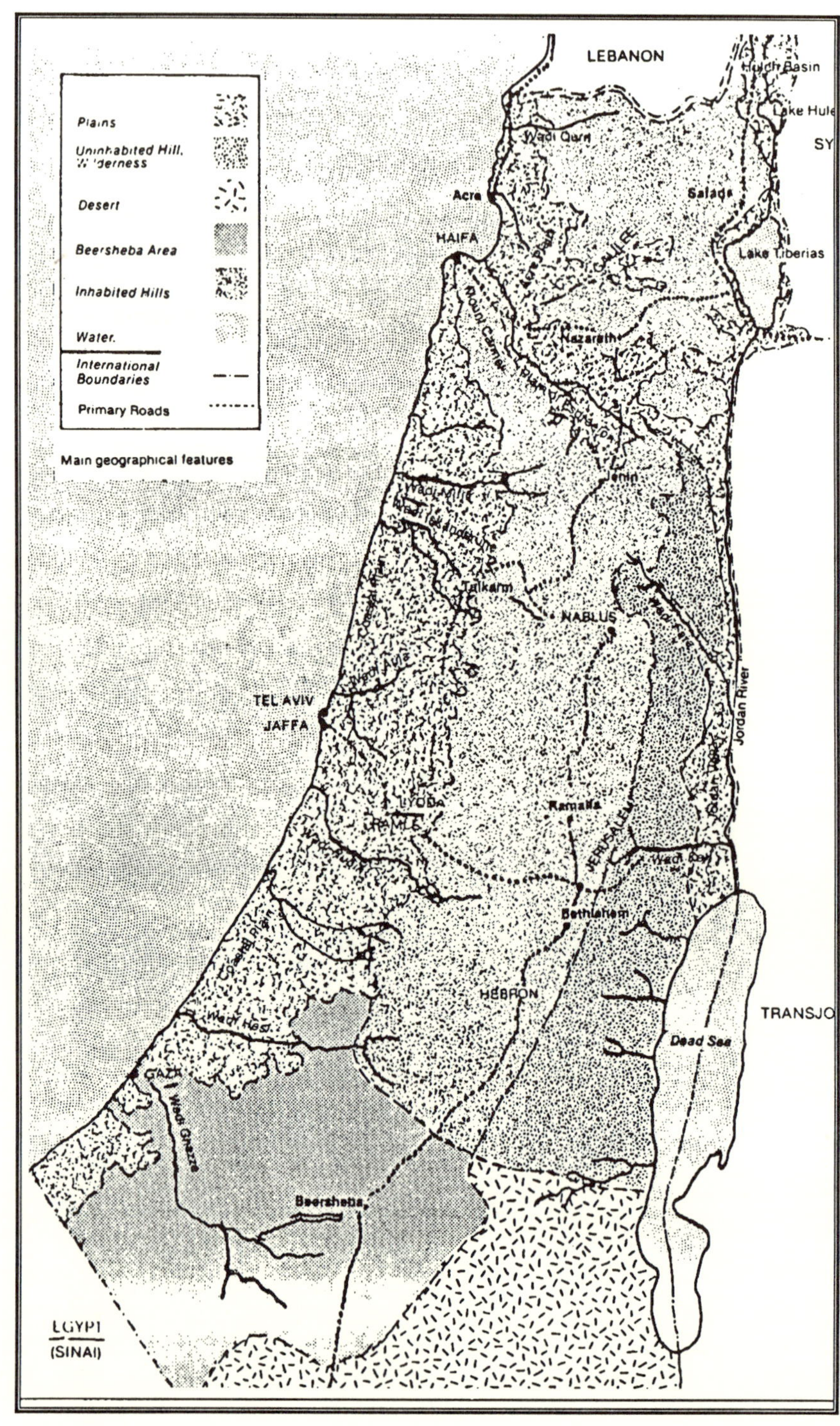

PALESTINE – MAP OF PARTITION
U.N. RESOLUTION 181 (11) OF 29 NOVEMBER 1947

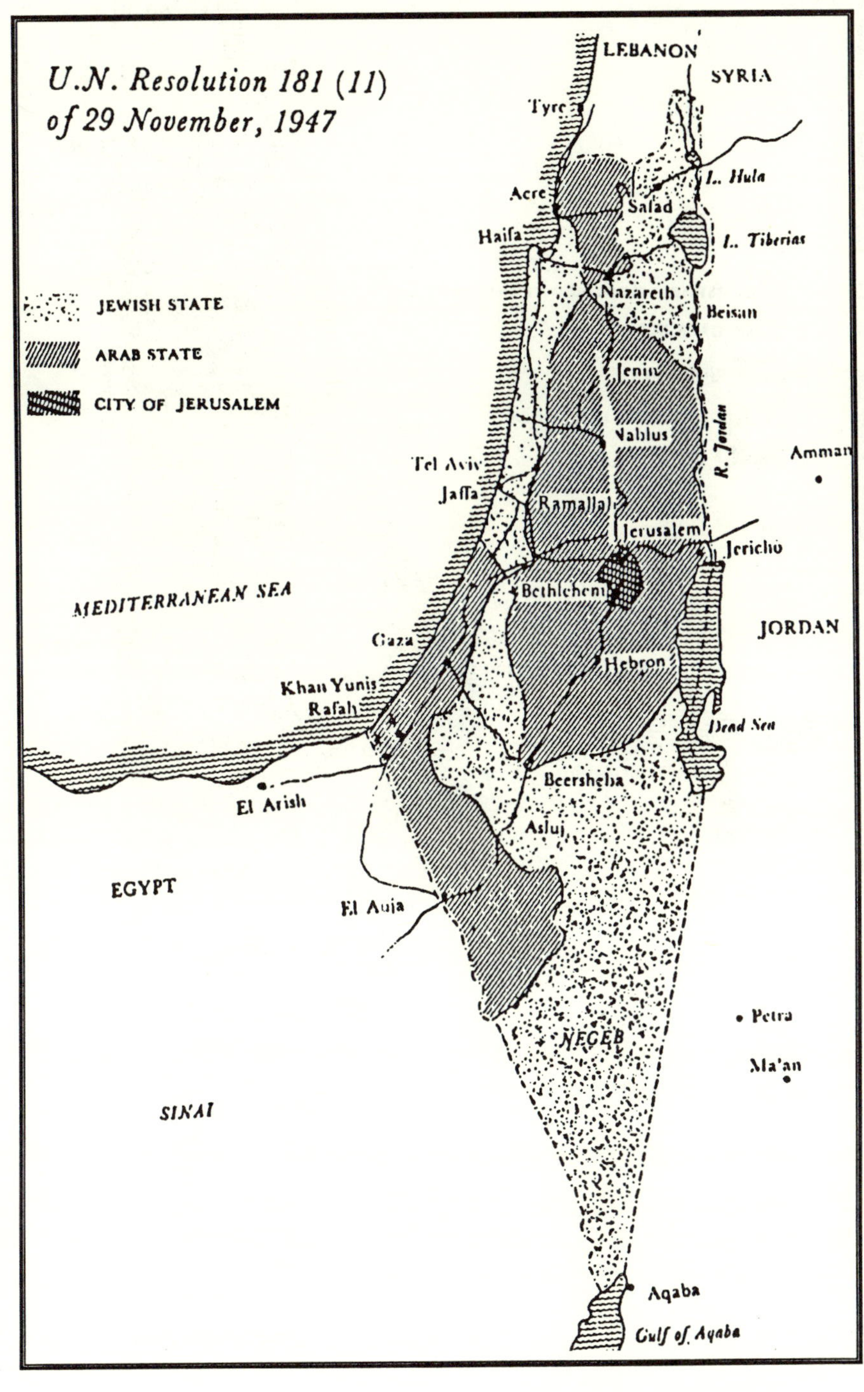

PALESTINE AS A RESULT OF ARMISTICE AGREEMENTS 1949

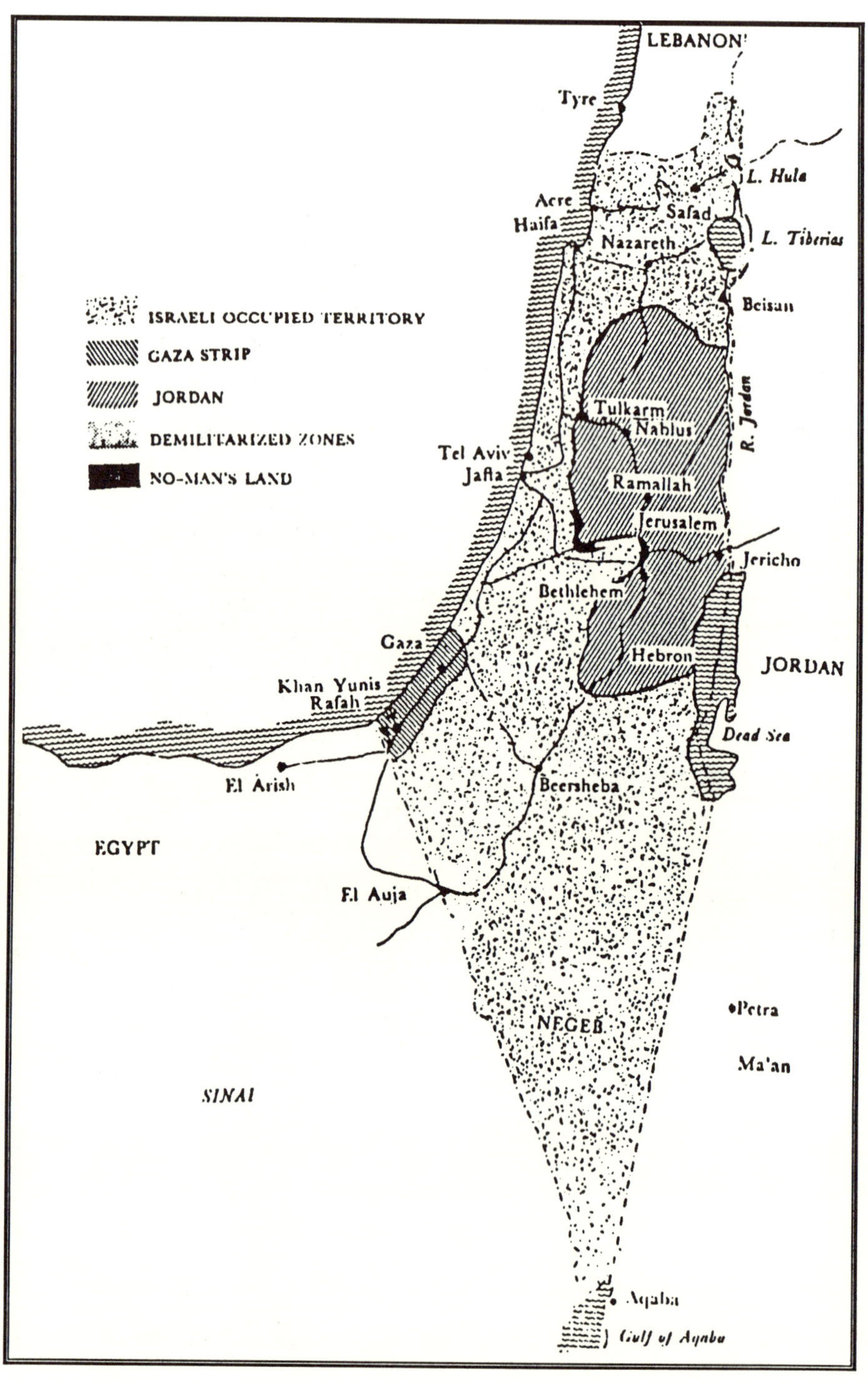

ARAB TERRITORIES OCCUPIED BY ISRAEL IN JUNE 1967

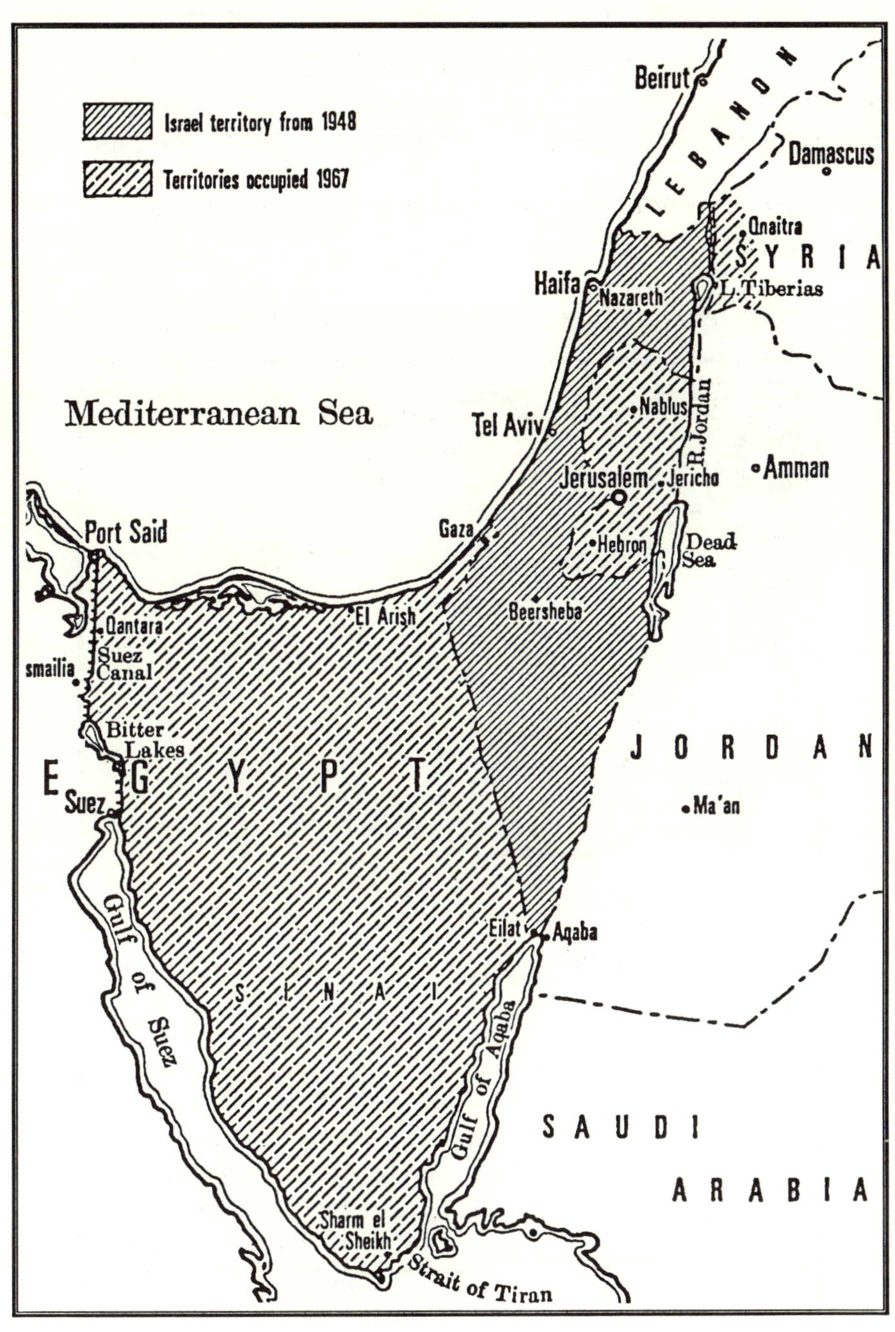

JEWISH SETTLEMENTS IN THE WEST BANK
Estimated Total Population

	May 1967	Sept. 1967	1977	1987
Jewish	–	–	5,023	60,000
Palestinian*	765,000	595,900	675,000**	813,000

*Estimates for the Palestinian population do not include East Jerusalem
**Estimate for 1975

Settlements founded between 1967 and mid-1977

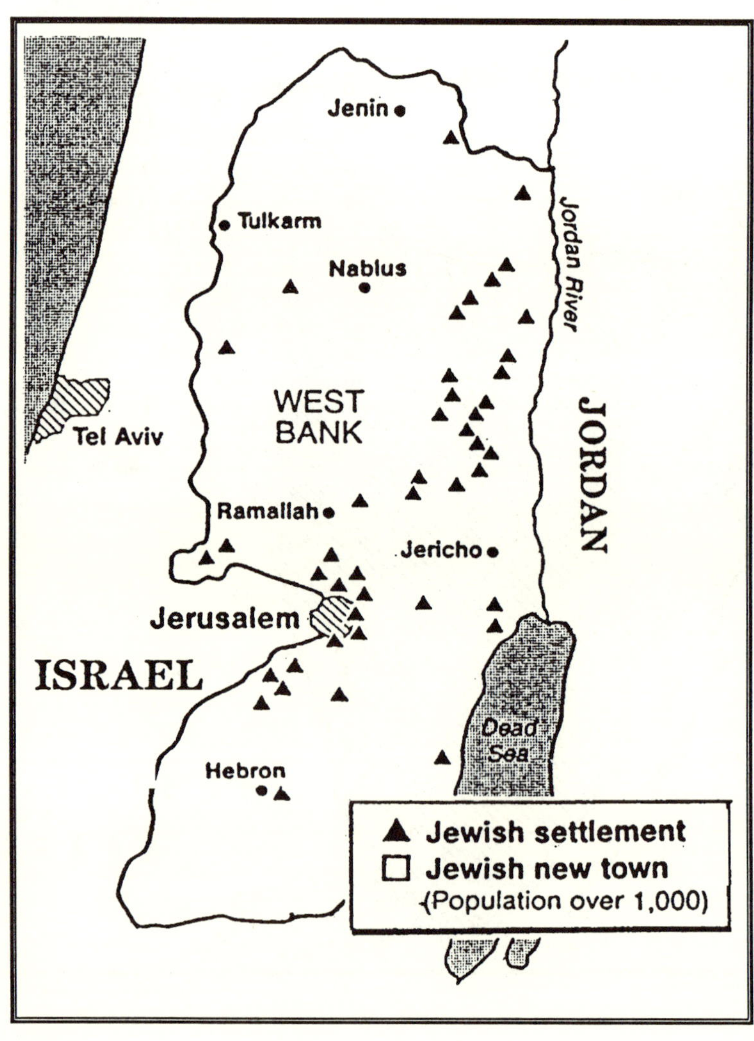

JEWISH SETTLEMENTS IN THE WEST BANK

Settlements as of April 1987

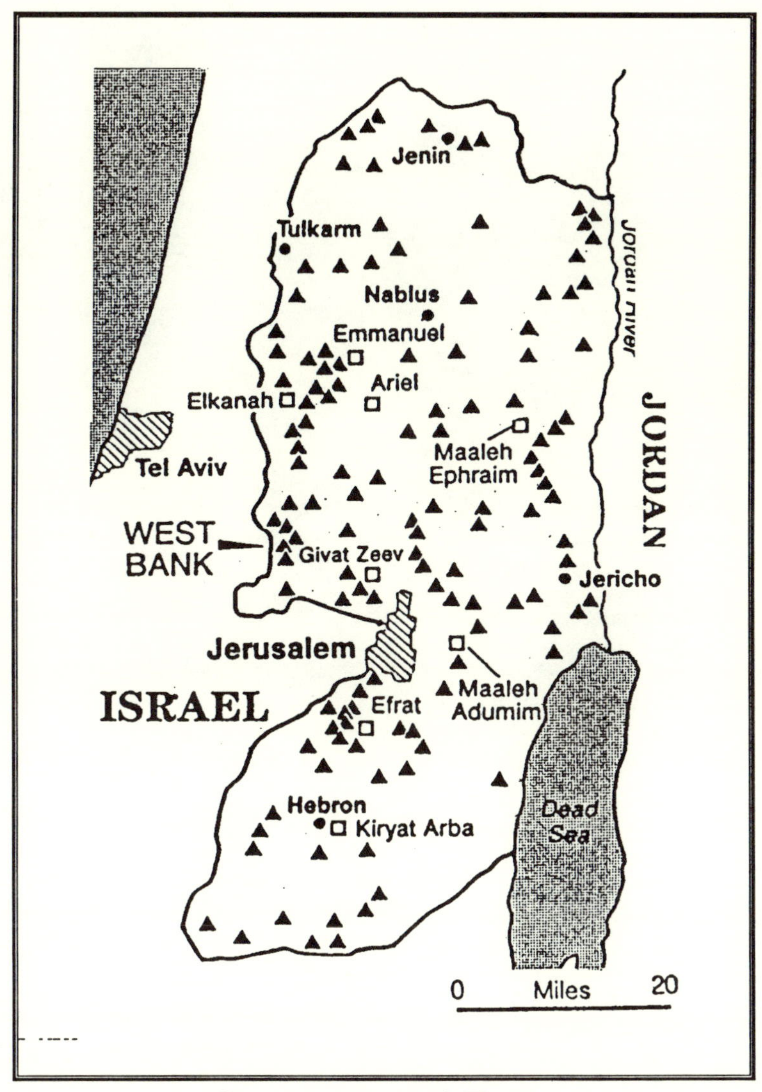

Source: *New York Times*

PART I

INTRODUCTION

CHAPTER 1

Dialectics of Dispossession

Naseer H. Aruri

WHY THIS BOOK?

This collection addresses some timely and significant issues in three major areas: those of theory, of politics and the law, and of human rights. The theoretical issues relate primarily to the dynamics of colonialism and its settler phenomenon in an age when colonialism is considered a relic of the past. With the independence of Algeria, Zimbabwe, and the former Portuguese colonies of Angola and Mozambique, Palestine and Azania (South Africa) remain as the two major areas where segregation of groups is a way of life, institutionalized in such a way that it permeates every aspect of the society. Government programs of apartheid and homelands, doctrines of autonomy, closed areas, and security zones are present reminders of the colonial settler state. In these societies, international law has been adapted to rationalize systematic repression in the political, social, and economic spheres, all under the protective umbrella of the major powers in the Western world. With such protections, none of the threatened embargoes by an incensed third world could harm or restrain the system of institutionalized discrimination. Even so, the struggle of the native populations touched the conscience of the world; recognition of the justice of their cause was enhanced by increasing international challenge, internal demographic changes, and the willingness of the native population to endure a protracted conflict against unfavorable odds.

In this book, the process of dispossession, disinstitutionalization, and proletarianization of an entire people is documented. It shows how a society of people with normal aspirations for a dignified existence has been transformed, within the lifetime of the present generation, to one of people leading abnormal lives. They have become either refugees, stateless without political identity; civilian inhabitants under military occupation in eastern Palestine and Gaza; or remnants of the Palestinian majority turned into minority in Israel, manipulated and controlled by its government. That this entire process was done in the name of "security," "ingathering of exiles," and "divine rights" in a world and an age in which secular and pluralist values predominate, is just as puzzling as is the reappearance of settler colonialism in the era of decolonization.

The political and legal issues addressed in this collection pertain to the relevance of the occupation and colonization to regional politics, international relations, and international law. Not only does the Israeli occupation affect the lives of Palestinians and the future of their society, but it has also affected political developments in neighboring states. Jordan is thus declared a nonstate or a Palestinian state; Lebanon's political system swings between the confessional model, with its communal distribution of power, and the dominance by one group, promoted by Israel and recently defended by United States marines; and Egypt remains on an ambivalent course since Anwar Sadat became a victim of Israeli machinations.

Israel's policies and behavior pose a challenge to international legal principles as developed over the last century, and as codified at the Hague, the United Nations, and at major international conferences. Some of these principles are as basic as those of sovereignty, inadmissibility of territorial conquest, self-determination of people, and extraterritorial jurisdiction. The relationship between the occupying power and the civilian inhabitants of an occupied territory is governed by well-established rules and principles. The rights and obligations of both parties are defined in numerous charters and conventions such as the Hague Regulations of 1907, the London Charter of 1945, and the Geneva Convention Relative to the Protection of Civilian Persons in Times of War of 1949. Yet the very existence of an "occupation" within the meaning of international law is simply contested by Israel. Euphemisms, such as administered territories, are used in an attempt to hide the fact that political rights are denied to the indigenous civilians under occupation.

Finally, human rights issues are addressed. Are the principles enunciated at Helsinki, the United Nations, and by the United States (whose State Department compiles and publishes an annual record of violations of human rights around the world) being upheld by the Israeli occupiers? "No member of the United Nations can claim that mistreatment of its citizens is solely its own business," said former president Jimmy Carter in a speech at the United Nations in March of 1977.

Numerous reports released since 1967 by such bodies as the International Red Cross, Amnesty International, and the United Nations Human Rights Commission demonstrate a pattern of violations of internationally recognized human rights in occupied Palestine.[1]   These include illegal expulsion of residents, detention without charge, confiscation and destruction of property, the use of collective punishment, the use of toxic gas and live ammunition against unarmed civilians, and mistreatment of prisoners. The issue of human rights in occupied Palestine is highly dependent upon national security concerns and superpower strategies. Despite U.S. commitment to the protection of internationally recognized human rights, Israel remains the largest recipient of U.S. military aid and continues to enjoy a special relationship with the United States.[2] A portion of aid funds has been and continues to be used in building illegal Jewish settlements and in bolstering the technology of repression.

Thus, this collection addresses very timely and significant questions in international law, international relations, human and political rights of people – questions that pertain to the very definition of a people and their rights. How the situations that gave rise to these questions came about will be discussed next.

HISTORICAL OVERVIEW

Palestine Occupied

Throughout the present century, generations of Palestinians endured foreign occupations. Four hundred years of Ottoman Turkish rule came to an end during World War I, to be followed by thirty years of British rule,

1. Recent reports that document Israeli violations of human rights include: *Journalism Under Occupation: Israel's Regulation of the Palestinian Press* (New York: The Committee to Protect Journalists, October 1988); Carmel Shalev, *The Price of Insurgency: Civil Rights in the Occupied Territories under the Intifada* (Jerusalem: West Bank Database Project, 18 October 1988); *The Casualties of Conflict: Medical Care and Human Rights In The West Bank and Gaza Strip: Report of a Medical Fact-finding Mission by Physicians for Human Rights* (Somerville, Mass., 30 March 1988); Amnesty International, "Excessive Force: Beatings To Maintain Law and Order," AI Index: BDE 15/32/88 (August 1988); "Use of Live Ammunition by Members of the Israeli Defense Force," AI Index: MDE 15/30/88 (June 1988); "Prisoners Cases – March 1988," AI Index: ME 15/18/88 (April 1988); "The Misuse of Tear Gas by Israeli Army Personnel in the Israeli Occupied Territories," AI Index: ME 15/26/88 (June 1988); and "Oral Statements To The UNCHR," AI Index: MDE 15/03/88 (February 1988).

2. For a discussion of the special relationship, see Naseer Aruri et al., *Reagan and the Middle East* (Belmont, Mass.: AAUG Press, 1983); Noam Chomsky, *The Fateful Triangle: The United States, Israel and the Palestinians* (Boston: South End Press, 1983).

during which the next occupation was planned and executed. No sooner had the British Mandate ended on May 15, 1948 than a new colonial settler regime was declared on 78 percent of Palestinian territory.

For more than thirteen hundred years Palestine was inhabited by Palestinian Arabs. Their presence as a cohesive national group in their own homeland was forcibly terminated when Zionists succeeded in driving them into forced exile between 1947 and 1949. The bulk of the Palestinian Arab population was removed to eastern Palestine (renamed West Bank in 1950) and Gaza, which constituted 20.5 percent and 1.5 percent of the territory of Palestine respectively. About 750,000 Palestinian Arabs were made homeless as a result of the creation of Israel in 1948.[3]

Following the attack of June 1967, Israel managed to occupy the rest of Palestine and to expel some 186,000 additional Palestinians. The Palestinian people had, therefore, suffered a kind of political extermination as their ancestral homeland was transformed into a Jewish colonial settler society during the past four decades. But while Palestine ceased to exist as a political community, it continued to exist in the collective consciousness of its own people. After two decades of futile reliance upon the international community and the Arab states, Palestinians in the mid-sixties seized the initiative and took their destiny into their own hands. With an unwavering commitment to the restoration of their national rights, they opted for armed struggle, and gained international recognition of these rights. Their transformation from refugees to guerrilla fighters was the principal factor that redirected the character of the Arab-Israeli conflict in the aftermath of 1967 to a struggle between Palestinian Arabs and Israeli Jews. The occupation of eastern Palestine and Gaza by Israel is the subject of this book.

The successive occupations of Palestine varied in purpose, nature, and style. Until World War I the tax collector and the army recruiter served as the dominant symbols of the Ottoman rule. The British occupation was rationalized by a League of Nations mandate to promote the "well-being and development of peoples not yet able to stand by themselves under the

---

3. Recent accounts by Israeli writers, based on state, military and Zionist archives, document the use of terror by Zionist militias against Palestinian civilians and its contribution to the creation of the refugee problem. See Benny Morris, *The Birth of the Palestinian Refugee Problem* (Cambridge and New York: Cambridge University Press, 1988); Tom Segev, *The First Israelis* (New York: Free Press, 1986); Simha Flapan, *The Birth of Israel: Myths and Realities* (New York: Pantheon Press, 1987). See also Erskine Childers, "The Other Exodus," *The Spectator* (London), 12 May 1961, reprinted in Walid Khalidi, ed., *From Haven to Conquest* (Washington, D.C.: Institute For Palestine Studies, 1987).

strenuous conditions of the modern world." Although the League covenant recognized the independence of the Arab provinces of the defeated Ottoman Empire, it made that independence subject "to the administrative advice" of the mandatory power. And in the case of Palestine, mandatory Britain added in 1917 the Balfour Declaration, with its promise of a national home for the Jews, as another condition. The relationship between the mandatory power, which assumed the "sacred trust of civilization," and the untutored natives was dictated by British imperial interests and commitments to international Zionism. Palestine was strategically located in territory adjoining the Suez Canal. That geopolitical reality was appreciated by both the Zionists, who dreamt of the establishment of a Jewish state in Palestine, as well as by the British, who wanted to secure the routes of their empire. Following the Palestine War of 1947-1948, a *de facto* partition of the country occurred when Israel was proclaimed a state in approximately 78 percent of the territory. The remaining portion in Arab hands was divided between Egypt, which set up an administration in the Gaza Strip between 1948 and 1967, and Jordan, which annexed eastern Palestine and changed its name to West Bank – i.e. of the Jordan River.

The Jordanian period (1949-1967) was characterized by the fact that dynastic ambitions constituted perhaps the most crucial factor in the merger of eastern Palestine and Transjordan. Arab unity was the principal rationale for the merger of the two banks of the Jordan River on April 25, 1950, but the Act of Union made it clear that the merger did not prejudice the "final settlement of the just cause of the Palestinian people." The merger was therefore considered, in theory at least, neither immutable nor irrevocable.

Although the Palestinians failed to set up a Palestinian state after the 1948 defeat, their participation in the Jordanian political system gained them some access to political power. The opposition forces, however, remained largely outside the political process and were subjected to repressive measures ranging from detention to long-term banishment in distant desert prisons.

The 1967 Occupation and International Law

Under basic rules of international law, the Israeli government is a "belligerent occupant" of the "West Bank," Gaza, Golan Heights and Jerusalem. The Palestinian inhabitants of the West Bank and Gaza are considered "protected persons" and the areas in which they live are "occupied" territories according to the provisions of Article 42 of the Hague Convention and Article 4 of the Fourth Geneva Convention. Article 42 of the Hague Convention states:

> A territory is considered as occupied when it is actually placed under the authority of the hostile army. The occupation extends only to the territory where such authority has been established and can be exercised.

The United Nations views the Fourth Geneva Convention applicable to the Israeli-occupied territories. The Commission on Human Rights and the General Assembly have repeatedly reiterated this view since the Israeli occupation began. For example the General Assembly reaffirmed in December 1978:

> that the Geneva Convention Relative to the Protection of Civilian Persons in Time of War, of 12 August 1949, is applicable to all the Arab territories occupied by Israel since 1967, including Jerusalem. . . .

This occupation, however, is uniquely distinguished by the claim that it does not constitute an occupation. The Israeli government considers the Hague Convention of 1907 and the Fourth Geneva Convention of 1949 (Protection of Civilian Persons in Time of War) irrelevant to the Palestinian areas occupied since 1967. The provisions of these conventions obligate the occupant to respect the fundamental human rights of the occupied population and limit its authority to the necessary administration of the areas until a peaceful settlement is consummated.[4]

Although Israel adhered to the Fourth Geneva Convention of 1949 on April 10, 1951 and on June 7, 1967 (Military Order 3, Article 35), it rescinded that agreement at the end of 1967 by virtue of Military Order 144, which denied the applicability of the Fourth Geneva Convention to the newly occupied territories. It would no longer receive any international commissions to investigate the conditions of the inhabitants of the occupied territories nor allow an Israeli investigation accompanied by an international observer.

The Israeli position is based on the spurious notion that there is an inseparable bond between the Jewish "people" and the "Land of Israel," which includes "Judea and Samaria," i.e., eastern Palestine (West Bank). It is also based on the assumption that the applicability of international regulations governing military occupations is dependent on the "legitimacy" of the sovereign rights of previous "occupiers." This position was articulated by Yehuda Blum, former Israeli ambassador to the United

4. See W. Thomas Mallison and Sally V. Mallison, *The Palestine Problem in International Law and World Order* (New York: Longman, 1986), pp. 485-87; also U.S. Department of State, *Treaties and Other International Agreements of the United States of America, 1776-1949*, compiled by Charles I. Bevans, (Washington D.C.: U.S. Government Printing Office).

Nations, in a speech to the Security Council on March 13, 1979. Blum considered the Zionist conquest of Palestine in 1948 as a form of self-defense against aggression by the Arab armies, which involved the "violation of the international boundaries of Palestine" and the setting up of an "illegal occupation by them" which could not have given rise to "any legitimate claim of sovereignty."[5] Blum went on to discuss a "renewed aggression" by Jordan which resulted in its "loss of control" over "Judea and Samaria":

> Thus, when the Israel Defense Forces entered Judea and Samaria in June 1967, in the course of repelling the renewed Jordanian aggression, they ousted from those territories an illegal invader who enjoyed, at the most, the right of an occupant. However, the rights of such an occupant under the international law of belligerent occupation are self-terminating upon the conclusion of the occupation and no rights survive for him thereafter.[6]

Moreover, Blum asserted that because Jordan and Egypt did not constitute a "legitimate sovereign" in the occupied territories, the fourth Geneva Convention, therefore, did not apply. With regard to Israel's colonial settlements in these territories, he claimed that "Article 49 of the Fourth Geneva Convention bans forcible transfers, not voluntary acts of individuals."[7] His attempt to reinterpret international law was indirectly repudiated by a report of the International Association of Democratic Lawyers:

1. Israel's attempt to exempt itself from the international obligation as an "occupant" is negated by the provisions of the Regulations Concerning the Laws and Customs of War on Land of 1907 (Article 42) and by the Fourth Geneva Convention (Article 2). They are applicable "in all cases of occupation of all or part of the territory of a High Contracting Party," with no reference to the validity or otherwise of titles to ownership and no nice distinction between *de facto* and *de jure* requisition of territory.
2. The Geneva Convention seeks to protect primarily the *population* and not, as Israel claims, the rights of the evicted *states,* irrespective of the

---

5. "Judea, Samaria and Gaza – The Israeli Record," statement by Ambassador Yehuda Z. Blum, Permanent Representative of Israel to the United Nations in the Security Council, 13 and 19 March 1979 (Jerusalem: Israeli Ministry of Foreign Affairs, n.d.).

6. *Ibid.*

7. *Ibid.*

legitimacy of their sovereign claims. As a "High Contracting Party," Israel's obligation under the Geneva Convention is beyond contest. The various United Nations bodies have confirmed this obligation. Moreover, Blum's argument that the Jewish settlers are engaged in a voluntary as opposed to a "forcible" act holds no water, as the broad policy goal of the settlements is to make a temporary illegal occupation permanent.

3. Israel is also in violation of international humanitarian law, which recognizes wars of national liberation as a category of international armed conflict. The United Nations had already declared the Palestinian struggle as falling under that category. The right of the Palestinian people to self-determination, recognized by the United Nations, is considered an integral part of the norms of preemptory law.[8]

Ironically, the United States, whose material, moral, and diplomatic assistance contributed to the continuation of occupation, has taken the official position that the Israeli occupation is governed by international law. The U.S. State Department's *Country Report on Human Rights Practices* for 1987 states:

> The United States holds the view that Israel is an occupying power in these territories and, therefore, that its administration is subject to the Hague Regulations of 1907 and the 1949 Fourth Geneva Convention concerning the protection of civilian populations.[9]

Despite an international consensus that Israel's control of occupied territories since 1967, which has now reached a state of quasi-permanence, is illegal, both sectors of the Israeli political establishment (Likud and Labor) have tried to insure that the *de facto* annexation is irreversible. Yet, Israel's contempt for international law was reinforced by its special relationship with the United States and by the disarray in Arab ranks, which prevented a practical response to that contempt.

8. International Association of Democratic Lawyers, *Territories Occupied by Israel (West Bank)* (Brussels: IADL Mission of Inquiry, October 1984).

9. *Country Report On Human Rights Practices (1987)*. Submitted to the Committee on Foreign Affairs House of Representatives and The Committee on Foreign Relations U.S. Senate by the Department of State, p. 1184.
A perceptive examination and appraisal of Israeli judicial claims under the criteria of international law appears in Mallison and Mallison, *Palestine Problem*, pp. 253-68.

Zionism, Jews, and the People of Palestine

The Israeli occupation of Palestine has another distinction: that of being associated with an ideology which denies the very existence of the Palestinian people. The questions of sovereignty and human rights in occupied Palestine are inextricably tied with Zionist ideology which promoted a colonial settler society in Palestine based on the concept of minority settler supremacy.

Zionism was in essence the offspring of movements, ideologies, outlooks, and practices of the nineteenth century. German nationalism, with its emphasis on the Fatherland, blood, and manifest destiny, equipped Zionism with much of its ideological arsenal. The resurgence of European colonial imperialism in the late nineteenth century served as incubator for the state of Israel; Orientalism, the concept of the white man's burden, and apartheid offered inspiration, theoretical guidance, and concrete models. For example, the colonial character of the Zionist movement was freely admitted by Zionists; in fact the first society established in 1861 in Frankfurt-on-Oder was named the "Society for the Colonization of the Land of Israel."[10] The Twelfth Zionist Congress set up a "Colonization Department;" the villages established by Zionist settlers in Palestine were called "colonies," and the term Yishuv itself, denoting the entire body of Jews in Palestine, meant "settlement." Chaim Weizmann compared his experience with that of the French colons in Tunisia, and Theodore Herzl, the founder of Zionism, viewed Cecil Rhodes as a role model.[11] When Herzl was trying to secure Bismark's blessings for the Zionist project in Palestine, he wrote: "Who will dare to call my plan a pretty dream after the greatest living empire builder has stamped his approval on it?"[12]

Zionist leaders were not unaware of the fact that the "outpost of civilization" which they pursued was already inhabited, but they were confident that native resistance would be overcome by an "assured supremacy" guaranteed by the West. Herzl recorded in his diary that after the Jewish state is established it would be necessary to "spirit the penniless population across the border. . . by denying it any employment."[13] A basic

10. On the colonial nature of Zionism see the excellent study by Fayez Sayegh, "The Non-Colonial Zionism of Mr. Abba Eban," *Middle East Forum* (1966), 42(4): 49-50.

11. Chaim Weizmann, *Trial and Error: An Autobiography* (New York: Harper, 1949), p. 191.

12. Theodor Herzl, *Complete Diaries*, ed. Raphael Patai, trans. Harry Zohn (New York: Herzl Press and T. Yoseloff, 1960), 1:120.

13. *Ibid.*, p. 88.

tenet of Zionism is that the dominant Jewish majority has rights denied to others. Israel is considered legally "the sovereign state of the Jewish people."[14]

The grounding of Zionism in the negative ideologies of late nineteenth-century Europe became a source of concern to Jewish leaders,who had to ponder its effect on Jewish values, traditions, and behavior, as well as on the Arabs of Palestine and the areas surrounding Palestine. That concern began to grow as the Zionist movement ignored the existence of the native Palestinian, declared that people nonpeople, and proclaimed their land "empty" in accordance with the application of nineteenth-century European scientific techniques to the Asian and African continents. Ahad Ha-Am, who was committed to the establishment of Jewish colonies in Palestine, exemplifies that concern. For him, a "return to Zion" was to be seen in the context of developing "a cultural life of Jewry and the spiritual regeneration of Judaism."[15] He cautioned against "national egoism"[16] and was troubled by the violations of the rights of the Palestinians and the impact of these violations on the moral fabric of the Jewish community.[17]

There is a strong indictment of this nationalism, with its German rather than French antecedents, in the anti-Zionist literature. As a philosophy and vision, anti-Zionism is coherent in its opposition to the establishment of an exclusive supranational Jewish state as the only means of Arab-Jewish coexistence. Many Jewish writers, firmly rooted in a nonideological humanist democratic tradition, shunned ghettoism and recognized a kinship between Zionism and its presumed antagonist, anti-Semitism. Their alternative to a world full of regressive, reactionary, and dehumanizing instruments of retardation was an open society in Palestine, or elsewhere, based on the ideal of freedom, of civil and political liberty, of the free flow of ideas as well as the unrestricted movement of people and the mixture of races.

For example, Professor Morris Cohen viewed Zionism as a nationalist philosophy inherently dangerous to liberalism, inasmuch as it promoted

14. See Noam Chomsky, "Against Apologetics for Israeli Expansionism," *New Politics* (Winter 1978), 12(1):15-47.

15. Abdelwahab Elmessiri, *The Land of Promise: A Critique of Political Zionism* (New Brunswick , N.J.: North America, 1977) , p. 59.

16. Hans Kohn "Ahad Ha-Am: Nationalist with a Difference," *Commentary* (June 1951), 11(6).

17. See Gary Smith, *Zionism, the Dream and the Reality* (New York City: Harper & Row, 1974), p. 31.

unreasonable classification based on religion or ethnicity.[18] Morris Jastrow, another anti-Zionist Jew, warned the 1919 Paris Peace Conference against the "reactionary" nature of political Zionism and opposed a Jewish state in Palestine on the grounds that such an "anti-democratic" policy constituted a "plan of segregation."[19] And the eminent scientist Albert Einstein also recorded his opposition to the partition of Palestine and the creation of a Jewish state on the grounds that it contradicted "the essential nature of Judaism."[20] Hannah Arendt saw Zionism, with its uncritical acceptance of German-inspired nationalism, as a philosophy that explained people "not in terms of political organizations, but in terms of biological superhuman personalities."[21] For her, Herzl was the epitome of the reactionary underdog who saw reality not in terms of differences in class structure, in political parties or movements, but in terms of unchanging and unchangeable bodies of people who showered hostility upon Jews. The world's political forces were separated into two categories in accordance with how they related to Jews. This Manichean outlook led the Zionists to seek and develop their own isolated haven. Maxime Rodinson, another prominent Jewish writer, distinguished between the Zionist brand of nationalism and the liberating nationalism that promotes independence and struggle against oppression. Although Zionism achieved its principal objective, the creation of a Jewish state in Palestine, it did not solve the "Jewish" problem.[22] And I.F. Stone described the effect of Zionism's double standard:

Israel is creating a kind of moral schizophrenia in world Jewry. In the outside world the welfare of Jewry depends on the maintenance of secular, non-racial, pluralistic societies. In Israel, Jewry finds itself defending a society in which mixed marriages

18. *Ibid.*, pp. 51-55; see also Morris R. Cohen, *A Dreamer's Journey* (Boston: Beacon Press, 1949), p. 227.

19. M. Jastrow, *Zionism and the Future of Palestine* (Westport, Conn.: Hyperion, 1975; reprint of New York, 1919), Appendix. His statement to President Wilson for conveyance to the Paris Peace Conference.

20. Quoted in Moshe Menuhin, *The Decadence of Judaism in Our Times* (Beirut: Institute of Palestine Studies, 1969), p. 324.

21. Michael Selzer, ed., *Zionism Reconsidered: The Rejection of Jewish Normalcy* (New York: Macmillan, 1970), p. 241; see also Hannah Arendt, "Zionism Reconsidered," *Menorah Journal* (Autumn 1945), 33(2).

22. Maxime Rodinson, *Cult, Ghetto, and State: The Persistence of The Jewish Question* (London: al-Saqi, 1983), p. 112.

cannot be legalized, in which non-Jews have a lesser status than Jews, and in which the ideal is racist and exclusionist.[23]

Even before the establishment of the state, the indigenous Arabs were referred to, in the Balfour Declaration and the Zionist draft which it amended, as the "existing non-Jewish communities." The only safeguards they were given pertained to civil and religious rights whereas any reference to political rights was deliberately omitted.

Today, well over a half-century since the Balfour Declaration, the Arabs of Palestine have neither enjoyed the political rights to which they are entitled as a "people," nor even the civil or religious rights promised them by a former occupier of their land. The ideology of the latest Zionist occupiers precludes these rights for the occupied; in fact the Palestinians are viewed by their occupier as temporary residents. According to the "Homeland Doctrine" enunciated by the Labor government and supported by the Likud, the territories occupied since 1967 form part of the natural boundaries of the state of Israel and are not occupied within the meaning of international law. The Palestinians in these territories are considered as people living on sufferance. The Israeli reporter Yeshayahu Ben-Porat insisted in a newspaper article written in 1972 that "there is no Zionism, and there is no settlement, and there is no Jewish State without evacuation of Arabs and without expropriation and fencing of lands."[24]

Menachem Begin's argument for Jewish sovereignty in the West Bank and Gaza was promoted from a rhetorical slogan of the Israeli right-wing opposition to a negotiable item at Camp David. For more than thirty years the Likud expansionist scheme, laden with a parochial and anachronistic historical perspective, was taken seriously by the very few. The late Israeli historian Jacob Talmon complained that he couldn't really be expected to face sophisticated colleagues abroad and tell them that the Jews have a "divine title deed to the land and that this title deed preempts all other legal claims."[25]

Today, however, thanks to former president Jimmy Carter and the late Anwar Sadat, the context of the Camp David proposals renders imperative the fact that legal sovereignty is at issue in the West Bank. The three chief executives who met at Camp David in 1978 somehow determined that the rights of those Palestinians living under Israeli occupation in eastern

23. Menuhin, *Decadence of Judaism*, p. 210.

24. Quoted in Gay Gonen, *A Psychohistory of Zionism* (New York: Mason/Charter, 1975), p. 196.

25. *Ibid.*, p.198.

Palestine and Gaza were to be confined within the framework of autonomy. Israeli Prime Minister Menachem Begin, however, limited that autonomy to the people and excluded the land. If the autonomy scheme succeeds under those who come after Begin, then the Palestinian people will have been relegated to the status which had been assigned to them by Theodor Herzl and his movement, Settler colonialism would then be legitimized in the age of decolonization.

Life under the Occupation

The most salient feature of the 1967 occupation is the *de facto* annexation of the occupied territories. Israel made a determined effort, beginning in the mid-seventies, to make the ongoing annexation of the West Bank irreversible. A network of highways crisscrosses the West Bank, connecting the Jewish settlements, while severing Palestinian areas one from the other. By 1982, Menachem Begin could boast:

> Gradually we have been managing to erase the physical distinction between the coastal area and Judea and Samaria. . . . We haven't completely succeeded yet. But give us three or four or five years, and you'll drive out there and you wouldn't be able to *find* the West Bank.[26]

The most recent platform of the Likud bloc bars return of occupied areas, and the December 1988 coalition agreement gave Likud veto power over any attempt by Labor to move towards an exchange of land for peace. Jewish settlements already have their own "regional councils" and court systems, and the government has linked the settlements to Israel not only with roads and infrastructure, but also in political policy.[27] The Fourth Geneva Convention's provision that "an Occupying power shall not deport or transfer parts of its own civilian population into the territory it occupies" has been set aside as having no relevance whatsoever. Israel's settlement policy is designed to seal the fate of the West Bank, and to deter the Palestinians from uniting, territorially or politically, into a coherent entity. A further aim is to prod the Palestinians to accept autonomy on Israel's own strictly limited terms. Given this *de facto* annexation and the attempted atomization of the Palestinian community, life under the occupation has assumed the character of legal and social limbo.

26. Ted Nemko, "The Struggle for the West Bank," *Christian Science Monitor,* 19 February 1982.

27. Trudy Rubin, "Israel and the West Bank: What Price Occupation?" *Christian Science Monitor,* 15 August 1983.

Furthermore, the occupation constitutes a web of all-embracing restrictions on the everyday activities of the Palestinians who live under it. There is a total ban on all organized political activity. The 1976 municipal elections were the first and last exercise in electoral politics to be conducted under the watchful eyes of the occupation regime. The concepts of freedom of assembly and association are not recognized by the authorities, who maintain a total ban on organizing political meetings and forming political parties. Given these restrictions, cultural events and meetings of philanthropic, academic, professional, and social organizations are often transformed into political meetings, which lead to such unhappy results as detentions, expulsions, and university closures.

Restrictions also apply to the press, where military censorship often extends beyond those security-related issues that define its formal mandate. Newspapers receive closure orders whenever the censor determines that legitimate expression has been transformed into "fighting words."[28] The distribution of publications in the occupied territories is often prohibited in convenient accordance with restrictive Jordanian press laws that ban all types of "radical" literature. For example, the newspaper *al-Ittihad,* organ of the Israeli Communist Party, Rakah, is prohibited in the occupied territories but not in east Jerusalem, which Israel does not consider occupied.

Freedom of movement is subject to severe curtailment. Palestinians who travel abroad must return within a prescribed period, otherwise they lose their residency status: those who leave the country via the airport must return within a year; those who leave via Jordan are permitted three years. These regulations, which do not apply to Israeli citizens, often result in loss of residency rights for Palestinians, who are then forced to apply for family reunification permits. These are generally issued very sparingly and after long delay; the Palestinians may be considered "visitors" in their own country, subject to visa and consular procedures.

Military justice is applied throughout the occupied territories and the verdicts are usually considered final. The few cases that reached the High Court have seldom resulted in reversals. The jurisdiction of the local Arab courts is limited to civil and criminal cases, but all politically related conflicts or "security matters" are dealt with in the military court system. These cases are often based on confessions obtained during the first few days after arrest, during which detained suspects have no access to legal counsel. Any person, in the occupied territories can be arrested without a warrant and detained for eighteen days before being brought before a

28. Joel Greenberg, "Palestinians Say Tight Controls Force Them To Turn to Violence," *Christian Science Monitor,* 18 December 1987.

military judge. The methods used by the Shin Beth (Israel's internal intelligence service) to obtain confessions include torture. The Landau Commission, a top-level investigative panel, concluded in November 1987 that the Shin Beth had for sixteen years routinely used "physical pressure" to force confessions.[29] Yet the commission might itself have opened the way for legalizing a certain level of torture by stating that the "effective interrogation of terrorism suspects is impossible without the use of means of pressure to overcome an obdurate will."[30] (Incidentally, the inquiry itself and its chilling results followed the death of a healthy twenty-three-year-old Palestinian who was an avid soccer player, only two days after his arrest on July 19, 1987, as a result of what was officially described as a heart attack, then as pneumonia. Earlier in 1984, Shin Beth ranking officers ordered the beating deaths of two Palestinians who hijacked a bus.)

Property rights are almost nonexistent in the occupied territories, where expropriations for "public use" or requisitions for military purposes frequently lead to the establishment of illegal Jewish colonies. Homes are often blown up upon suspicion that a family member was engaged in what the occupation regimes consider a "terrorist murder."

The unrest of the past twenty years, which culminated in open revolt on December 8, 1987, was the Palestinian response to the daily outrages of occupation itself.

Palestinian Resistance

The history of recent decades does not mark a new departure for the Palestinians; it is a continuation of a national struggle which spans most of this century. The Palestinian nationalist struggle did not begin in 1967 or in 1948. As early as 1891 Palestinian leaders urged the Ottoman government not to facilitate land transfers to Jewish settlers in Palestine. They also pressed their concerns about Jewish immigration and land alienation after the coup by the Young Turks in 1908, using the local press and central parliament among other vehicles. They insisted that Palestine remain an Arab country and not be used to solve the plight of European Jewry. The General Syrian Congress, which included a Palestinian delegation, declared after the Paris Peace Conference of 1919 its opposition to the mandate

29. See Israel Shahak, "Report to the Israeli League for Human and Civil Rights," 15 December 1987 (mimeo); also see Felicia Langer, "With Great Regret and Shame," *Zu Haderech,* 11 November 1987.

30. See Juan O. Tamayo, "Torture Scandal Rocks Israel's Secret Service," *Miami Herald,* 6 December 1987.

systems, to the concept of a "Jewish commonwealth" in Palestine, and to the separation of Palestine "from the mother country."

Palestinian resistance to British mandatory rule and the Zionist movement peaked in the 1930s: the six-month general strike in 1936 was followed by a thoroughgoing rural uprising which engaged displaced and landless peasants and unemployed urban workers, supported by urban professionals and merchants, who gathered under the umbrella of the Arab Higher Committee. The nationalist movement resisted the principle of territorial partition or merger with Transjordan. But despite broad support for its nationalist aims, the movement could not achieve the cohesion and strength to withstand the continued pressure.

The struggle was reignited in 1947-48, a period known to the Zionists movement as Israel's war of independence. For the Palestinians, it was a colonial war of conquest, which ended in the destruction of Palestinian society and institutions: for them it was the era of the catastrophe (*al-nakba*). The people of Palestine suddenly found themselves refugees with all the human, legal, economic, social, and psychological liabilities which that naked status implied. Under those conditions, the active pursuit of political sovereignty was not the priority of the day. Existence itself was the priority – to find shelter and a source of livelihood, to readjust and get over the trauma, to provide for children and for the education of those children.

The activists among them integrated their struggle into the Arab nationalist movement, while some went underground. Other more conservative elements hoped against hope that the combined force of Arab armies, Arab diplomacy, and international goodwill would achieve their deliverance and bring them redress.

During the two decades between the 1947 conflict and the 1967 war, the Palestine question was confined largely to the agendas of charitable international organizations. The dispersed Palestinians retained an unwavering commitment to the restoration of their sovereignty over their homeland. At no point did they acknowledge the legitimacy of the state of Israel. They retained their national identity and resisted all schemes of settlement outside their homeland and all attempts at national subjugation and assimilation. Their struggle, however, remained anchored to the Arab states, whose failure to obtain redress induced them to opt for armed resistance. Without doubt they were inspired by the process of decolonization and the success of liberation movements in the third world. They began to learn that one does not address moral and legal arguments to his oppressor. They began to view their adversary as a System – a System that assumes their negation. Resistance to that System thus became an act of self-affirmation and a cogent expression of identity.

Post-1967 Resistance

The reemergence of an awakened Palestinian nationalism spurred on by Arab defeat in six days in June 1967 created new forms of non violent resistance inside Palestine and a militant armed struggle outside, combined with diplomacy. It produced a new type of leadership, and a new class base. The elite families who presided over the Arab Higher Committee were replaced by professionals and intellectuals from the Palestinian mainstream. The new social backbone consisted of the internal refugees in crowded Gaza and the West Bank, the uprooted peasants in Galilee and the West Bank, the merchants and small manufacturers victimized by the occupation, the students and intellectuals under occupation, and the external refugees in Lebanon, who manned the infrastructure of the Palestine Liberation Organization, a state-in-formation.

Faced with a settler regime that asserted divine claims and pressed to acquire the "land without the people," Palestinians in the occupied territories were left with but one option – to resist the occupation. The confrontation is total: the Israeli state is determined to replace the entire Palestinian community; that community refuses to accept its negation. A cycle of violence is implicit in this kind of relationship in which the occupier inevitably defines every single member of the native community as a potential terrorist and a suspect. Palestinian resistance to the occupation, which has been raging almost uninterruptedly since the June War of 1967, has been taken up by all classes in Palestinian society. Socioeconomic conflicts have been subordinated to the national question. Both inside and outside Palestine, the resistance assumed the need for a broad nationalist front. Landowners and businessmen, as well as students. women's groups, and professionals, joined the struggle. All found good reason for doing so: landowners, traditionally a pillar of the *status quo,* because their land has been steadily confiscated; businessmen because they have to endure the highest taxes ever levied in Palestine and operate in a market totally controlled by Israel; professionals because they are subjected to regulations intended to create despair and encourage emigration. And women, who together with relatives are herded to jail or subjected to exorbitant fines after every incident of rock throwing, find very little time to think about "women's liberation." The response of one Palestinian woman to a query by a *Los Angeles Times* correspondent summed it up thus:

> When you are under military occupation, you don't ask for equal rights with your husband because he does not have any rights either.[31]

31. *Los Angeles Times,* 9 May 1976.

Finally, the conditions created by the 1967 War had enabled the Palestinian national movement to evolve into a broadly based, widely representative political body with a sophisticated organizational structure suitable for a nation-building strategy.[32] A military apparatus that dwarfed every single militia in pre-1982 Lebanon stood side by side with a civilian infrastructure that provided health, educational, and social services rivaling those of any state in the area. Possessed with extensive administrative and diplomatic machinery, Arab and international legitimacy, and broad Palestinian support, the PLO was developing from a virtual government in exile to a real state.

The shattering defeat of three Arab armies in but six days in June 1967 galvanized the nascent Palestinian leadership into action. They denounced the unconditional ceasefire that the Arab states accepted as well as Security Council Resolution 242, which compromised their national rights. They vowed to resist the Zionist system and announced their ultimate goal of setting up a unitary democratic nonsectarian state in all of Palestine, for all its inhabitants irrespective of creed, national origin, or language. They resolved to take their destiny into their own hands and to restore the conflict to the original parties. Arab tutelage or guardianship for the Palestinians was to be terminated just as international responsibility for the refugees was to assume new dimensions.

Beginning in 1969, a more representative United Nations has come to recognize the status of the Palestinian people as a colonized people entitled to independence and possessing inalienable rights (resolutions 2535, December 10, 1969; 2649, November 30, 1970; 2672, December 8, 1970; 2787, December 6, 1971; 2792, December 6, 1971). Linking their cause with that of oppressed people in Africa, the General Assembly affirmed the legitimacy of the Palestinian struggle for liberation by all available means, including armed struggle. The high point of this international legitimacy was reached in 1974, when the General Assembly invited the Palestine Liberation Organization to attend the twenty-ninth session. Subsequently, the General Assembly adopted Resolution 3210 on October 14, which recognized the PLO as representative of the Palestinian people and conferred upon it full observer status. This resolution was opposed only by Israel, the United States, Bolivia, and the Dominican Republic. The assembly passed another historic resolution on November 22, 1974. Resolution 3236 reaffirmed the rights of the Palestinians to self-

---

32. See Cheryl Rubenberg, *The Palestine Liberation Organization: Its Institutional Infrastructure* (Belmont, Mass.: Institute of Arab Studies, 1983); also Helena Cobban, *The Palestine Liberation Organization: People, Power and Politics* (Cambridge: Cambridge University Press, 1984).

determination, national independence, and sovereignty, and requested the secretary-general to establish contacts with the PLO on all matters concerning the question of Palestine. Significantly, this resolution preempted the clause in Security Council Resolution 242 of 1967, which treats the Palestinians as merely refugees. Moreover, it raised the question of whether Resolution 242 provided an adequate basis for a Middle East political settlement.

If the war of June 1967 provided impetus for the armed struggle against Israel, the war of October 1973 created a favorable climate for a political challenge *inside* Palestine directed at the occupation regime. The myth of Israeli invincibility was effectively challenged by Arab armies, whose performance in October 1973 revealed a capacity to assimilate modern technology and eventually to bridge the gap. Following the war, the declarations of the Arab summit conferences at Algiers in 1973 and Rabat in 1974 heightened the morale of the captive Palestinian population in the occupied areas and in Israel proper, and reinforced their will to resist. These declarations elevated the role of the Palestine Liberation Organization in the diplomatic configurations of the Middle East: the PLO was declared sole legitimate representative of the Palestinian people.

Other factors that intensified the resistance to the Israeli occupation included a determined attempt by the occupation regime to tighten the reins and to create a new situation in the occupied territories. Rapid schemes of colonization in the West Bank were embarked upon by Yitzhak Rabin's Labor government, and continue to this day. Economic measures designed to weaken indigenous institutions and to further subordinate and integrate the economy of the occupied areas to that of Israel were introduced. The decision to take over the concession of the (Arab) East Jerusalem Electric Company in early July 1980 is a case in point.

Two groups in particular have played the vanguard role in the resistance movement. The Palestine National Front (PNF) was declared on August 15, 1973, in response to the escalation of Israeli repression and colonization and to the setbacks suffered by the Palestinian nationalist movement in Jordan in 1970-71. The PNF adopted the approach of civil disobedience and nonviolent resistance, organizing against land confiscation and sales and publicizing the plight of political prisoners. It campaigned against the Israeli sponsored municipal elections designed to legitimize the Israeli annexation of Jerusalem. The insignificant Arab turnout in these elections was largely credited to the work of the PNF. Furthermore, the PNF foiled Israeli efforts to link Arab labor to the Histadrut (Israeli Labor Federation), encouraged businessmen not to pay taxes to the Israeli authorities, and organized massive demonstrations to protest the expulsion of eight Palestinian leaders from the West Bank in December 1973. By April 1974, the occupation authorities had launched a repressive campaign against the PNF, placing a large number of its leaders under administrative detention without charge or trial.

The crackdown against the PNF was followed by a more stiffened resistance generated by two events in late 1974. The Arab summit conference meeting in Rabat on October 29, 1974 declared the PLO sole legitimate spokesman of the Palestinian people. And Yasir Arafat, chairman of the PLO Executive Committee, delivered his historic address to the United Nations on November 13, 1974. These two events had such an impact on Palestinians in the occupied territories that people made no attempt to conceal their sympathy with the PLO. Soon after Arafat gave his speech, demonstrators filled the streets of Jericho, Ramallah, Bethlehem, and Hebron. The occupation authorities made more than 200 arrests on November 18 – 132 of those arrested were sentenced to up to six months in jail with fines.[33] Three days later five prominent Palestinians, including the president of Bir Zeit University, were deported.[34] And in response to a merchants' strike in the city of Ramallah the authorities imposed economic sanctions and travel restrictions on the entire city.

On the political and psychological levels the occupation regime embarked on a plan to counteract the impact of the Rabat decision and Arafat's appearance at the UN on the minds and hearts of the people. It announced a plan that would offer the population limited self-government under the military occupation. Using the slogan of trying to fill a "political vacuum," Israel proposed municipal elections in cities and towns in the area as a first step toward "home rule." That announcement, however, was greeted with a general protest and almost unanimous public denunciation by mayors and municipal councils. Demonstrations to protest the plan (and to protest as well the second Sinai Accord between Israel and Egypt negotiated by Kissinger in September) and to commemorate the uprising of the previous autumn began on November 8 in Ramallah and Bireh. Soon demonstrations spread to all the cities; they lasted until December 1975. The city of Nablus appeared as an armed camp; hundreds of demonstrators and suspects there were thrown in jail.

The year 1975 witnessed another phenomenon of great importance in the Palestinian sector occupied since 1948. In February of that year the Arab Students Committee of Tel Aviv University issued a declaration protesting nonrecognition of their committee by the university administration and the frequent unlawful searches of their rooms and personal effects by the police.

33. *Washington Post,* 19 November 1974.

34. *New York Times,* 22 November 1974.

A public rally was held in Nazareth on April 30 in solidarity with the students' protest. And in June 1975 the same students of Tel Aviv University issued a periodical which not only criticized violations of civil rights but questioned the fundamental premises of Zionism and the state of Israel. The periodical, called *Sheikh Munis*, was named after the Arab village on whose ruins stood Tel Aviv and the university itself. In the meantime plans for the expropriation, under the pretext of development, of some twenty thousand dunums in the Galilee region were reported in the daily *al-Shaab* on June 27, 1975. The plan was not announced officially until February of the following year, but preparations to oppose it were already under way in October 1975. A public rally was held on October 18 to protest the government's "Galilee Outline Plan," as it was called, and committees were set up throughout the Galilee region for the defense of Arab lands. Shortly after, the Zionist establishment was shocked by the smashing victory of the Nazareth Democratic Front in the city council elections. Tawfiq Zayyad of the communist party Rakah and nine on his list were ushered into office by the Nazareth voters on December 9, 1975, thus ending a long reign of local Arab accommodationists in the largest Arab city in Israel.

By the end of 1975 Palestinians were fighting on three fronts: in Lebanon against right-wing forces determined to neutralize them as an organized political force, in Galilee where the confrontation was beginning to take the shape of a national conflict, and in the occupied West Bank and Gaza where the population had opted for an independent Palestinian state. In the West Bank and Gaza, the struggle was nationalized. By 1975, it had been extended to almost every city and major town in the area and involved most sectors of the population. It was characterized by an unprecedented mobility – an uprising taking place in one city was extended to most of the other cities in a short period of time. A new spirit of defiance was reflected in the attitudes of people in their daily encounters with the occupation authorities, whether in the street, the government office, or the interrogation room.

The year 1976 witnessed an intensification of the struggle throughout occupied Palestine as well as an escalation in the level of repression. Some new issues had arisen in addition to the old ones: A U.S. Security Council veto on Palestine; a provocative march by orthodox right-wing Jews through occupied territory; a court decision on the right of Jews to pray in the vicinity of al-Aqsa Mosque; a tax levy on all sales; the municipal elections of April 12, which swept into office a dominant majority of PLO supporters; and last but not least the Day of the Land.

The refusal of the Israeli court to convict a Jewish group which had been arrested for disobeying a statute banning prayers in the vicinity of the Haram, coupled with the officially sanctioned arrangement for the alternate use of the Tombs Mosque in Hebron, provoked an uprising which was the first link in a chain of events lasting throughout the year. In their attempts to put down the revolt, the Israeli police and border guard units displayed a brutality bordering on state-sanctioned terrorism. The city of Nablus became a battlefield when Israeli soldiers launched an attack on and occupied the Qadri Touqan high school, causing mass resignations of education commissioners, city councilors, and the chamber of commerce. Similar resignations took place in the cities of Ramallah, Bireh, Tulkarem and Bir Zeit, where a mass strike was also declared to protest the closure of a Ramallah school for one month as well as the beating of students in Nablus and Bir Zeit by the border guard.[35]

The uprising continued for seven weeks in the West Bank and it merged with the general protest in Galilee on the occasion of the Day of the Land on March 30. Six Arab citizens of Israel were shot dead at this demonstration in Sakhanin. Their funerals on the next day occasioned a national protest, with more than ten thousand in attendance from thirty-six towns and villages in the Galilee region.[36] The police took about three hundred people into custody, and Prime Minister Rabin charged that the event was communist-inspired.

In April, municipal elections designed to fill the so-called vacuum in eastern Palestine and Gaza were scheduled in twenty-two cities and towns. They were Rabin's answer to the rising international stature of the PLO and its impact on Palestinians under occupation. The venture, however, proved counterproductive.

The municipal elections represented a new juncture in the Palestinian struggle. The former leaders left over from the Hashemite regime were replaced by a new generation of progressive mayors who ran on the National Bloc list of the PLO and PNF. The National Bloc captured 148 seats out of a total of 191 seats contested throughout the occupied territories, despite certain rescue efforts by the Israeli military on behalf of the older group.[37] Two weeks before the elections, the military authorities summoned two candidates in Sheikh Muhammad Jaabari's district at 1:30 A.M. and expelled them conveniently the next day at 3:45 P.M., only 15 minutes before a scheduled judicial hearing. Jaabari was one of the main pillars of Hashemite rule who, subsequently, cooperated with Israel. But despite the expulsion of his two opponents from the National Bloc, he withdrew from the race.

35. *Washington Post,* 11 March 1976.

36. *New York Times,* 1 April 1976.

37. *New York Times,* 14 April 1976.

Commenting on the election results, the Western press openly questioned Israeli contentions. The London *Times* wrote editorially on April 14 that the results confirmed that the "invisible occupation of which Israel boasted between 1967 and 1973 has now completely broken down."[38] And *Newsweek* wrote on April 26 that "after the vote Israel had proof positive that Palestinian nationalism was no longer just a fig leaf for political terrorists but a rallying cry for most of West Bank."[39] Other newspapers and periodicals gave similar assessments. The election results shattered that quiet cooperation which had existed between old municipal leaders inherited from the Jordanian system and the occupation regime and exposed the myth of the benevolent occupation. The new municipal leaders were no longer the brokers and facilitators of occupation policies; they spoke for a nationalist movement unwilling to settle for anything less than a political sovereignty in place of the Israeli occupation.

The elections were followed by a multiplicity of Israeli provocations that heightened the level of tensions throughout the following year. Chief among them was the march organized by the right-wing settlers Gush Emunim on April 18 and 19, which was intended to dramatize their opposition to any withdrawal from eastern Palestine. The march of thirty thousand Jews between Jerusalem and Jericho provoked countermarches in major Arab cities, followed by other demonstrations against Israeli ceremonies marking the twenty-eighth anniversary of Israel on May 15. The total numbers of Arabs killed by Israeli forces since the uprising began in February reached sixteen, including at least two very deliberate assassinations: of a seventeen-year-old girl in Nablus and of the West Bank's weight-lifting champion in Jerusalem. In September, Galilee Arabs staged a protest demanding the dismissal of District Commissioner Israel Koenig, whose notorious report on how to curb the increase of the Arab population in that region was never repudiated by the Rabin government. A sympathy strike of two hours was observed by municipal councils throughout the West Bank and Gaza. In the following month, Hebron was the scene of renewed violence over the right of worship in the Patriarch's tombs. Arab sentiment was so intense that the Israeli authorities felt compelled to close the tombs in the face of Jews on Yom Kippur for the first time since 1967.

A further provocative step was taken by Israel when the 8 percent tax on all sales, permitted to lie dormant since July 1976, was suddenly enforced in December. This was tantamount to economic war against Arab enterprise. Arab businessmen had to open their books to Israeli auditors and thus risk

38. *Times* (London), 14 April 1976.

39. *Newsweek,* 26 April 1976.

revealing their financial position to Israeli capitalists anxious to contain their enterprises. Demonstrations erupted on December 6 to protest this taxation without representation, while at the same time hunger strikes were staged by Arab prisoners in Gaza, Ramallah, and Ashkelon beginning on December 14 and continuing until January 18 of 1977. They were followed by demonstrations in March to commemorate the first anniversary of the Day of the Land, demonstrations that swept the entire West Bank area and the Galilee.

The Iron Fist Policy of Menachem Begin

By 1977, it became apparent to the occupation regime that Palestinian resistance had entered a new stage in the aftermath of the October War of 1973. The rate of escalation on both sides left no doubt that a major response was forthcoming. The "iron fist" policy was put forth almost as soon as Menachem Begin formed the first Likud government in the summer of 1977. It was intended to suppress the dissent increased by the Camp David affair and the Israeli-Egyptian treaty.

With Begin in power, it became increasingly clear that the occupation was here to stay. In fact the differences between Likud and Labor were peripheral but the former was less discreet about its plans for the occupied territories. Begin's symbolic visits to settlements and his assurances to the settlers served notice that the Israeli presence in the West Bank and Gaza was permanent. His plan of self-rule which was announced in the Knesset in December 1977 assumed center stage in the Camp David agreements and was indeed the framework for the so-called autonomy talks between Egypt, Israel, and the United States. The agreements of Camp David that condemned the West Bank and Gaza to a permanent status of subordination, with less real authority than a Bantustan, and that sentenced the Palestinians outside Palestine to a permanent exile, were denounced as a plot against the Palestinian people. A declaration affirming the unity of the Palestinian people under the sole leadership of the Palestine Liberation Organization was signed on October 1, 1978 by the overwhelming majority of mayors and city councils and by many and various civic, professional, and labor organizations in the occupied territories.

The mayors organized themselves under the National Guidance Committee, which acted as the principal "legal" opposition after the PNF was pushed underground. They issued appeals and manifestos, sent protest cables, and sponsored rallies and demonstrations as the occupation regime intensified its repression. The Israeli authorities countered with a series of measures designed to inhibit all political activity, consisting of the following:

1. Warnings to mayors that they were to be held responsible for civil disobedience activities emanating from their district.
2. Restrictions on public meetings and freedom of movement including that of the mayors themselves.
3. Curtailment of the mayors' roles as providers of social and economic services through the use of the military governor's power to issue or deny licenses for municipal projects. The power to block the transfer of funds earmarked for various municipalities from abroad has proven to be a strong weapon in the hands of the military government.

The post-Camp David period witnessed an escalation in repression and violation of human rights including censorship, restrictions on all political activity, interference in municipal affairs, facilitation of land transfers, crack down on universities, collective punishment, expulsion of dissenters, and various forms of terrorism ranging from beatings to murder.

The Begin government made use of a variety of laws and regulations to acquire land for Jewish settlements in the occupied areas. There are lands designated "waste lands," which the government can "return to its ownership" even if they were cultivated in the past and are a private possession of the cultivators.[40] Arab landowners customarily receive "orders to sell" by the custodian of absentee property. The government, moreover, decided on September 16, 1979 to permit Jews to purchase land in the occupied territories. After the High Court of Justice ruled in 1979 that the Elon Moreh settlement near Nablus must be dismantled because private land was confiscated, the settlers moved to a nearby site and the government began to consider altering the legal status of the occupied territories in order to avoid such rulings in the future. Settlements in the midst of Arab population centers were also approved by the Begin government. After the killing of a Jewish student in Hebron on January 31, 1980, the government authorized the establishment of two religious schools in the center of Hebron – today these constitute a settlement. As the opposition to settlements and repressive measures increased, the United Nations General Assembly on December 12, 1979, and the Security Council on March 1, 1980, voiced strong criticism of Begin's settlement policies. Israel's Knesset expressed its-contempt in two resolutions on March 6, 1980, affirming Israel's right to settle anywhere in the occupied territories. Both Likud and Labor were associated with these resolutions, which violate the Geneva and Hague conventions prohibiting the transfer of civilian population into or out of territories occupied in war.

40. Danny Rubenstein, "The Gloves Were Taken Off," *Davar,* 5 February 1979.

Censorship also increased after Camp David and the peace treaty in order to conceal the overwhelming opposition to the Camp David autonomy scheme and the unified posture behind the PLO.[41] Writers and journalists were arrested, books were banned, and students were beaten.[42] Tagrid Butmeh, a student at Bethlehem University, was shot and killed by Israeli soldiers in what was officially described as an accident.[43]

Indiscriminate mass punishments were frequently used by the military to weaken the resistance and discourage dissent. Curfews, school closings, banishment of entire families, and public humiliations were among the collective punishment techniques employed by the occupation authorities. A curfew at the Jalazone refugee camp of four thousand residents was announced through an army bullhorn at 5:30 A.M. on May 6, 1979, following student demonstrations protesting the "autonomy" plan. Everyone was locked inside the camp for twenty-two hours a day with doors and windows tightly shut. The curfew lasted for twelve days. The *Jerusalem Post* reported on May 16, 1979 that no fresh vegetables, fruits, or milk were allowed into the camp. Only flour was delivered by officials of the United Nations Relief and Works, Agency. The *Post* added:

> Sanitary conditions are deteriorating every day the curfew continues. Garbage collection and disposal is difficult, and none of the residents has a refrigerator, limiting the life of fresh food. There, reportedly, are a large number of small children, pregnant women and nursing mothers in the Camp.

The curfew was and still is considered a standard punishment for the smallest acts of resistance, such as throwing rocks at Israeli army vehicles or settlers' vehicles.

Banishment and internal exile is another form of punishment reported for the first time in 1979 as an attempt to discourage dissent. Two families were taken out of their homes and dumped together with their belongings in roofless mud huts in abandoned and scorpion-infested refugee camps in May 1980. The action was a form of collective punishment for rock throwing at military cars by the families' teenage sons. One of the boys was beaten and required surgery. When the families were finally returned home the liberal *Jerusalem Post* boasted:

41. See the *Washington Post,* 6 March 1980.

42. See article in *Davar,* 12 March 1979: "Violent Demonstrations in Ramallah." Also see articles by Yehuda Litani in *Haaretz,* 12 and 13 March 1979; by Y. Zuriel in *Maariv,* 13 March 1979; and *Haolam Haze,* 14 and 21 March 1979.

43. See article in *Christian Science Monitor,* 21 June 1980.

Had this taken place in Kabul [Afghanistan] . . . the young culprits would have been
summarily executed . . . and the entire families would have been lucky to be merely
exiled . . . but Israel is not the Soviet Union and the West Bank is not Afghanistan,
despite allegations to the contrary by a number of countries.[44]

When curfews and collective punishments failed to weaken the resistance
and stem the dissent in the aftermath of the Camp David affair, the
occupation regime began a systematic campaign to get rid of the leadership
in the municipalities. Their efforts to create quislings in Hebron, Ramallah,
and elsewhere yielded few results. The "Union of the Hebron Area
Villages," under the leadership of Mustafa Dudin, was exposed as a fruitless
attempt to weaken the authority of Mayor Fahd Qawasmeh and the Hebron
City Council. Abd al-Nur Jenho, a well-known collaborator in Ramallah,
was assassinated in February 1978.

The confrontation with the mayors took several forms, resulting in the
expulsion of four, the maiming of two and the dismissal of most. According
to the *Jerusalem Post* (11 October 1979) the military authorities considered
mayors Bassam Shaka, M. Milhelm, K. Khalaf and others as members of an
illegal body called the "Preparatory Committee for the Palestine National
Front," allegedly operating under the name of the National Guidance
Committee. They held that committee responsible for the almost complete
general strike of March 26, 1979, the day the Egyptian-Israeli peace treaty
was signed. In a thinly veiled attempt to force them out of office, mayors
Khalaf and Tawil of Ramallah and Bireh were brought to trial in October
1979 on a charge of having scuffled with a policeman a year earlier in
Jerusalem. Mayor Bassam Shaka, another member of the Guidance
Committee, was arrested on November 11, 1979 and threatened with
expulsion simply because he expressed his views on the occupation in a
private conversation with a high official of the military regime. The reaction
in the occupied areas was swift and massive. A general strike was followed
by a meeting in which twenty-three mayors submitted resignations en
masse. The United Nations called on Israel to respect the Geneva
Convention proscribing expulsion from occupied territories. Finally, on
November 23, the High Court surprisingly overruled the minister of defense
and the cabinet and ordered against carrying out the expulsion orders.
Mayor Shaka returned home to a hero's welcome that signaled the
consolidation of the national movement in the occupied areas. That victory,
however, was set back five months later after a group of Jewish settlers was
ambushed in Hebron on May 2, 1980. A few hours later mayors Qawasmeh

44. *Christian Science Monitor,* 30 May 1980.

of Hebron and Milhelm of Halhul, together with Hebron's chief religious judge, were awakened and taken, their heads covered with black bags, for a one-way helicopter ride to south Lebanon. Upon arriving, they were told that they were expelled by orders of the defense minister, on the predictable charge of incitement to violence. On May 8, 1980 the United Nations Security Council called on Israel to allow the return of the expelled leaders, and the Israeli High Court ordered the government to show cause why it should not allow their return. The mayors were returned on October 6th and kept in detention while the High Court was trying to determine whether their expulsion was legal. Only one of the three judges, Haim Cohen, argued that this "deportation" violated the Geneva Convention, which forbids the occupation regime from deporting citizens from their own country. Hence the majority ruled that the deportation was legal. The decision, however, contained a recommendation that the mayors be allowed to return to their towns for a "trial period" to see if they would endanger the peace in the region.[45] Menachem Begin, however, acting in his capacity as acting defense minister, wasted no time in expelling them again to Lebanon on December 4, 1980. Mayor Qawasmeh was assassinated in Amman four years later.

Exactly one month after the expulsion of the two mayors and the chief judge, Palestinians in the occupied areas were awakened to the news that mayors Bassam Shaka and Ibrahim Khalaf were maimed in their own cars as they started for work in the morning. Seven other Arabs were injured in Hebron and Mayor Ibrahim Tawil of Bireh was saved when the device attached to his garage door exploded in the face of an Israeli Druze soldier. The prime minister of Israel, who was himself responsible for much terror in the 1940s as head of the Irgun Zvei Leumi, condemned the assassination attempts at the mayors as "crimes of the worst kind."[46] (However, David Halevy, an Israeli reporter, was subjected to criminal proceedings for having reported that Avraham Achituv, the head of Shin Beth, had resigned in protest of Begin's attempt to obstruct the investigation of the car bombings.[47] Disclosure of the name of Shin Beth is considered a punishable crime.) Begin's condemnatory statement, however, hardly concealed the fact that his annexationist policy created the atmosphere for that kind of terrorism. The private armies organized by right-wing Jewish settlers of Gush Emunim and by members of Rabbi Meir Kahane's racist party Kach

45. See *New York Times*, 6 December 1980; *Washington Post*, December 1980.

46. *Christian Science Monitor*, 3 June 1980.

47. *Washington Post*, 15 December 1980.

were in fact implementing the goals of the settlement policies of the Begin government. The Israeli government has been providing the settlers with economic incentives, protection, and legitimacy, while ensuring that their victims remained defenseless and powerless. This vigilante terrorism is reminiscent of the kind practiced by Begin's Irgun and Shamir's Stern Gang in the 1940s.[48]

The perpetrators of the crimes against the mayors were not apprehended until four years later when Jewish settlers, who were arrested in late April 1984 for planting bombs on Arab buses, also confessed to the car-bombing attack on the mayors. The attack on the Arab-owned buses was planned by a sophisticated network of Jewish settlers tied to the mainstream of the Gush Emunim movement. The *New York Times* quoted the Israeli newspaper *Maariv* as describing one member of the group as a highly placed official in the West Bank and a winner of the "Medal of Bravery for Heroism" on the Syrian front in the 1973 War.[49] After large explosive charges were discovered attached to five Arab-owned buses, it became known during police interrogation that the bus line from Jerusalem to Qalandia refugee camp had been chosen because only Arabs and no Jews would be on these buses.

In the meantime, the indigenous Palestinians continued their struggle in response to new restrictive measures imposed upon them by the Israeli government. In late July, 1980, the Knesset was asked by the cabinet to issue legislation that would make it a crime to carry Palestinian flags or sing Palestinian songs. The request received overwhelming support in the Knesset on July 29, 1980.[50] Arab citizens in Israel were being placed under house arrest in accordance with emergency regulations.[51] The use of torture became common, as verified by the International Committee of the Red Cross, Amnesty International, the Israel League for Human Rights, and many other agencies.[52] During the last week of July 1980 two Palestinian

48. See Lenni Brenner, *The Iron Wall* (London: Zed Press, 1984).

49. *New York Times*, 3 May 1984.

50. *New York Times*, 30 July 1980.

51. *Ibid.*, 7 July 1980.

52. See Naseer Aruri, "Resistance and Repression: Political Prisoners in Israeli Occupied Territories," *Journal of Palestine Studies* (Summer 1978), 7(4): 48-66; also "Israel Tortures Arab Prisoners: Special Investigation by Insight," *Sunday Times* (London), 17 June 1977; U.S. Department of State, *Country Reports on Human Rights Practices* for 1985, 1986, 1987; *Amnesty International Report, 1987* (London: Amnesty International, 1987), pp. 348-52.

prisoners died as as result of forced feeding by prison authorities in Israel. A prison official was quoted by the press as saying forced feeding would continue as long as the hunger strike continued in the Nafha prison. Allowing prisoners to die is rejected, he said, because of "Jewish humanism."[53] Yet prisoners had suffocated after salt water had been pumped into their lungs by guards.

Begins iron fist policy was intensified during the period between 1980 and 1982 as Palestinian resistance to the occupation remained constant despite some ups and downs. On August 11, 1980, three Palestinian editors of Jerusalem-based newspapers were confined by order of the military to their hometown, al-Bireh, about ten miles northwest of Jerusalem.[54] In November, Israeli soldiers shot more than twelve unarmed Palestinian students on the Bir Zeit campus during Palestine Week activities; the University was closed.[55] In the face of mounting student unrest, the Israeli military began to apply measures, under sweeping emergency regulations first drafted by the British in 1945, to prevent firsthand reporting of resistance activities and Israeli suppression, which included the use of live ammunition to disperse unarmed demonstrators. The *London Times* correspondent, Christopher Walker, together with a colleague from the *Washington Post,* were served with a military order in November 1980 banning them from Bir Zeit, which was declared a "closed area" during the unrest. Walker reported that at the same time, criminal charges were filed against the Jerusalem correspondent of United Press International because he was found in Bir Zeit after it was declared a closed area.[56] The government policy towards the covering of events, similar to that in South Africa, was protested by more than two hundred members of the Foreign Press Association. Suggestions by Israeli officials that the foreign news media may have been responsible for the violent demonstrations were dismissed by the association as "unjust and baseless slanders." The regulations of press coverage were issued on December 13, 1980 after the British agency, Visnews, filmed Israeli troops firing live ammunition from a rooftop at Palestinian teenagers during a demonstration.[57]

53. *Boston Globe,* 25 July 1980.

54. *New York Times,* 17 December 1980.

55. *Washington Post,* 20 November 1980.

56. Christopher Walker, "Mr. Begin Asked To Explain Increasing Censorship Severity," *Times* (London), 12 December 1980.

57. William Claiborne, "Israel Limits Coverage of the West Bank," *Washington Post,* 15 December 1980.

The iron fist policy was fitted with a new face in August 1981 when Defense Minister Ariel Sharon ordered soldiers to refrain from breaking into schools to quell demonstrations, to avoid collective punishment, and to be more sensitive at checkpoints and roadblocks. An editorial in the Israeli daily *Haaretz* described the "new policy" by saying "if this is liberalization, it is being offered, for the time being, with pincers."[58] Sharon's strategy was to create an alternative leadership that would negotiate on Israeli terms. To that end, he introduced the concept of a civilian administration and attempted to implement Camp David's autonomy in the strict administrative sense – autonomy for the people but not for the land. Directives were also issued forbidding the mayors from meetings with PLO officials abroad, from expressing any verbal support of the PLO to the press, and from bringing in funds that passed through the joint PLO-Jordanian screening committee in Amman. At the same time quisling groups organized under the name Village Leagues were equipped with funds, weapons, and influence as part of the Israeli strategy to challenge the mayors.

This attempt to foster artificial leaders, considered by the majority of the population as collaborators, ultimately failed and so did the attempt to impose autonomy unilaterally. Sharon's "civilian administrator" Professor Menachem Milson finally resigned his post. The occupation regime violated its own guidelines less than two months after they were issued. By the autumn of 1981 universities had been attacked, protesters had been killed in the streets, and collective punishment, including home demolitions and harsh curfews, had been reinstated. The Sharon plan was in fact stillborn.

The government's policy dictated that the fight against Palestinian nationalism must be total. To that end Israel moved systematically in the spring of 1982 against the remaining nationalist mayors and replaced them with Israeli army officers. There are twenty-five cities and towns in the West Bank, four in Gaza, and three hundred and thirty villages all together. The major municipalities were placed under Israeli military personnel. The pretext for the dismissal of the elected mayors was their refusal to discuss vital municipal issues with the "civilian administration." In fact, most of these mayors ran on a platform of "No to the Civil Administration." In fulfilling their campaign promises, these mayors clearly ran afoul of any Israeli ideas of the nature of autonomy.

A 1982 spring uprising in the West Bank and Gaza challenged the Israeli government to the extent that the Begin government was on the verge of collapse after an opposition no confidence vote had resulted in a tie on

58. William Farrell, "Israeli Shift on Arabs: Real or Mirage?" *New York Times,* 19 August 1981.

March 23. Yet, less than a week later Begin issued an ultimatum to the Palestinians in the occupied territories: either accept the Israeli version of autonomy or risk outright annexation.

Having undone the results of the 1976 municipal elections, canceled the 1980 elections, and dissolved various popular organizations, Begin embarked upon a determined effort to liquidate the PLO itself in Lebanon. His and Sharon's notion of autonomy, manifested in an atomized exploitable reservation in eastern Palestine and Gaza, clashed with the "idea of Palestine,"[59] and that ultimately drove the Israeli military machine to its hysterical assaults in 1982 on refugee camps and civilian quarters in Lebanon, and on universities and municipal councils in eastern Palestine. By applying the iron fist in eastern Palestine and attacking the PLO in Lebanon, Israel had hoped to eradicate Palestinian nationalism and to remove all internationally sanctioned proposals for Palestinian-Israeli coexistence from the agenda of the world community.

The Israeli invasion of Lebanon must be seen in the context of that ongoing and relentless campaign, discussed above, to preempt a Palestinian state-in-formation. Lebanon was the principal base of the social, political, and military infrastructure of Palestinian nationalism; the West Bank was the logical site of the Palestinian state-in-waiting. The momentum had to be sharply interrupted in order to erode international legitimacy, tame the Palestinians under the occupation, and destroy any organized voice that could speak for Palestinian rights.

The Israeli invasion resulted in the partial destruction of the PLO infrastructure in Lebanon and the evacuation of its fighters, which dealt the resistance forces in the occupied territories a severe blow, but by no means succeeded in eradicating it, as had been planned.[60] In fact, the invasion had failed to accomplish most of its objectives, such as redrawing the political map of Lebanon and reducing Syria to manageable proportions. Paradoxically, the Lebanon campaign inflicted damage on the Israeli body politic, as the military and political establishment spent three years trying to extricate itself from the war, which was intended to establish its hegemony over Lebanon.[61] Instead, most of the war gains had been erased, and the

59. See Edward W. Said, "The Idea of Palestine in the West," *MERIP Reports* (September 1978), 70: 3-11.

60. See Tabitha Petran, *The Struggle Over Lebanon,* (New York: Monthly Review, 1987); Emile Sahliyeh, *The PLO after the Lebanon War* (Boulder, Colo.: Westview Press, 1986)

61. The impact of the war on Israeli society was described by Jacobo Timerman in *The Longest War: Israel in Lebanon* (New York: Random House, 1982) and by Israeli Lt. Colonel Dov Yermiya, *My War Diary* (Boston: South End Press, 1983).

armed forces had in effect retreated for the first time in front of Arab guerrillas. The success of the Lebanese national resistance in frustrating Israeli ambitions provided inspiration to the Palestinians under Israeli occupation.

The realignment that the invasion had generated in Lebanon and its implications for the Palestinians in that country constituted another factor influencing the political scene in the occupied territories. The massacres of Sabra and Shatila in September 1982 and the war of the camps in Lebanon between Lebanese Shite forces and the Palestinians contributed to the mood of defiance throughout Palestine. Violent demonstrations raged following the invasion of Lebanon. A pattern of systematic vigilante terror by Jewish settlers against the Arab population began to assume new and ominous dimensions. The summer of 1983 witnessed an attack by settlers (including some highly trained members of elite army units) on the campus of the Islamic College of Hebron. Masked men raced into the campus, threw a hand grenade and sprayed automatic weapons fire into crowds of Arab students and faculty. The attackers were reported to be residents of the Jewish settlements in the center of the Arab city of Hebron. Such incidents continued to plague Arab communities within easy reach of Jewish settlements.

The months of February and December, 1986 witnessed an escalation of violence by Jewish settlers and soldiers. Students were shot dead during demonstrations at Bir Zeit University during the first week of December 1986.[62] A hunger strike by more than one thousand Palestinian political prisoners in Israeli jails inspired a new wave of demonstrations in April 1987.[63] During the same month, hundreds of Jewish settlers set fire to Arab-owned orange groves and houses and rampaged through the town of Qalqilya after a firebomb killed a Jewish woman. Meanwhile another Bir Zeit University student was killed by troops during a demonstration on April 13, which resulted in an Israeli order to close the university for four months.[64]

The convening of the eighteenth session of the Palestine National Council in Algiers in May 1987 generated tremendous excitement among Palestinian

---

62. See *Boston Globe*, 9, 11, and 15 December 1986; *Christian Science Monitor*, 9 December 1986.

63. Mary Curtius, "Palestinian Jail Strike Turns Political," *Christian Science Monitor*, 10 April 1987.

64. Mary Curtius "West Bank Confrontation Heightens," *Christian Science Monitor*, 14 April 1987; also *Washington Post*, 4 April 1987.

activists under the occupation, particularly as it promised to restore a larger measure of unity to a fractious PLO as well as to abrogate the PLO-Jordan accord of February 1985, which called for the establishment of a Jordanian-Palestinian confederation.

Israel, however, intensified the iron fist policy in its continuing attempt to undermine any signs, no matter how small, of nationalist ascendancy. The entire population of Gaza – some six hundred and fifty thousand people – were subjected to severe collective punishment in August 1987 after an Israeli army officer was stabbed to death in a marketplace.[65] Ordinary activities came to a standstill during a total curfew, which coincided with *I d al-Adha*, the most important Muslim holiday, while hundreds of suspects were rounded up and mistreated by soldiers. Violence erupted again in Gaza and in Jerusalem in October after the army shot four armed men identified later as members of the Islamic Jihad movement in Gaza.[66] The occupation regime announced on October 14 that it had uncovered a guerrilla network of the Islamic group and arrested more than fifty suspected members. The incident gave rise to the question of whether religious activism constituted a new dimension of the nationalist resistance.

The December 1987 Uprising (intifada)

The uprising, which began in Gaza on December 8, 1987 and spread to the West Bank, is the most recent major movement in defense of Palestinian rights. It constitutes the third phase of post-1967 resistance to the Israeli occupation. The first phase was characterized by the nonviolent struggle waged by the Palestine National Front (PNF), which planted the seeds of a policy of noncooperation with the occupation regime. As indicated above, that resistance was energized by the October 1973 War, the 1974 Rabat declaration naming the PLO sole legitimate representative of the Palestinian people, and the mounting legitimacy of the PLO that culminated in its admission to the United Nations as an observer. It was further cemented by the 1976 municipal elections that produced a nationalist victory.

The internal resistance entered its second phase after Camp David, when it was reorganized under the leadership of the National Guidance Committee. Two sectors of the Palestinian community under occupation figured prominently during that phase: the new municipal councils and the

---

65. Mary Curtius, "Israel's Collective Punishment of Gaza Palestinians Reaps Bitterness," *Christian Science Monitor,* 6 August 1987.

66. Joel Greenberg, "New Brand of Resistance to Israeli Occupation," *Christian Science Monitor,* 14 October 1987; see also *Boston Globe,* 15 October 1987.

institutions that were a product of the comprehensive institution building by the Palestinian nationalist movement during the 1970s inside and outside Palestine. This phase of internal resistance was largely a response to Likud rule, which was marked by a pervasive domination of the economy and land and water resources and by increased colonization of urban and rural areas.

Although the National Guidance Committee was suppressed under the impact of Iron Fist I, which was formulated in 1979 and executed in 1981-82, preparations for an extended and renewed phase went under way, under the impact of Iron Fist II, this time authored by Laborite Defense Minister Yitzhak Rabin. These preparations culminated in the present *intifada.*

The *intifada* is of historic importance because of its duration, depth, breadth, scope, unifying character, and commitment to the creation of social, political, and economic alternatives to the occupation. The mass resignations of tax collectors and Arab policemen in March 1988 as well as the prolonged strikes in the labor and commercial sectors have seriously impeded the governance process. Businesses now open three hours each morning in compliance with the regulations issued by the Unified Leadership of the Uprising. By spring 1988, the army had to abandon its ongoing attempt to break locks to force stores to open during strikes and closing hours ordered by the Unified Leadership.

The revolt is all-embracing. It encompasses all sectors irrespective of class, age, and gender. It explodes from an entire population for whom the occupation has become one continuous nightmare of physical and psychological coercion. The national unity that characterizes the *intifada* is not forged from above as a result of summit conferences or Palestine National Council meetings; it is dictated from the base. It emanates not from deliberate policy statements issued by realists and skilled politicians, but from the daily practices of an endless variety of people and sectors organized in functional units for creating alternative systems to the occupation. Two organizational levels figure prominently in that endeavor:

First are the popular committees. These grassroots organizations (declared illegal on August 18, 1988) carry out the directives of the underground Unified Leadership: they organize demonstrations, dispense food and medicine to needy families, coordinate underground educational services for thousands of pupils idled by months of school closures, organize patrols, and distribute seeds and plants for victory gardens. These neighborhood committees are viewed by Palestinians as tools for building a sense of community and discipline and for overcoming the previous fragmentation and confusion – they are seen as the catalyst in the process of nationbuilding under occupation.

The second level consists of professional, charitable, and public service organizations, which render alternative specialized services. Together these institutions supplanted the traditional structures of *mukhtar* (selectmen) and family networks and created a new leadership and new forms of social relations. With the breakdown of the traditional hierarchy aided by two· decades of occupation and the termination of the Jordanian system, power has devolved to these organizational networks and public service institutions. The young people who run these structures have, in effect, been inducted into the business of public administration and local self-government. Their inexperience and the hardship under which they operate are counterbalanced by a vested interest in the continuation of the *intifada*. Otherwise their huge sacrifices will have been in vain.

Thus, the uprising has faced Israel with an ungovernable mass of Palestinians realizing their demographic strength and economic power and through their developing self-help organizational network aiming to maintain social order, run the economy, allocate scarce resources, and develop community-based solutions to social and economic needs. The goal of the *intifada* is to out administer rather than outfight the occupation, to meet Palestinian needs by Palestinians and to ultimately create that social reality that would make Palestinian independence necessary and not merely desirable. In fact, the Palestinians have been largely managing their own health and educational systems at all levels. The so-called government hospitals are run entirely by Palestinian staff and the private hospitals are autonomous institutions financed and managed by Palestinians. The Union of Palestinian Medical Relief Committees (UPMRC), which has been rendering voluntary services for ten years in distant communities and refugee camps, using mobile and permanent clinics, comprises one third of the the physicians in the occupied territories.

Its 850 volunteers deliver basic curative and preventative medical and dental services, provides training for emergency services focusing on the rehabilitation of the victims of Army violence and cooperate with local health institutions. The UPMRC, together with other medical groups are effectively the national Palestinian health infrastructure. Other institutions such as the Agricultural Relief Committees provide seedlings and training designed to reinforce self-reliance in the areas of farming and animal husbandry. The Council of Higher Education is virtually a national board of regents for Palestinian higher education.

Palestinian institutionalization which began in Lebanon in the early 1970s gave the PLO the character of a government-in-exile, a military character, but from its broad framework which permitted the aggregation of Palestinian services which rivaled those of any established state in the area. That infrastructure was the real target of Sharon and Begin's invasion of 1982, just as today's infrastructure in the West Bank and Gaza is the target of Rabin, who is entrusted with the task of crushing the *intifada*.

The root cause of this *intifada* is Israeli colonization of the West Bank and Gaza discussed above, reinforced by important factors that have become more and more significant since 1967:

1. The Demographic Factor: The decline of the Arab oil economy since the early 1980s gave the Palestinians a new, more realistic sense of their future: that it was to be found in the towns and villages of Palestine rather than in Kuwait or Abu Dhabi. The oil boom (1973-1980) had siphoned off a significant sector of the high-level manpower in the occupied areas during the 1970s. But when that boom came to a halt, more and more Palestinians returned home and more new graduates stayed put in the West Bank and Gaza. The majority of the annual two thousand five hundred university graduates either joined a growing mass of the unemployed or accepted menial work in the Israeli labor market. Only about four hundred jobs requiring academic training were opening up on the West Bank each year, and in Gaza the situation was worse.

    Israeli statistics show that between 1968 and 1983, the annual rate of population increase in the occupied areas was 2 percent. Since 1983, it has been over 3 percent, a fact that can be attributed to the decline in employment in the Arabian peninsula-Persian Gulf region. Palestinian emigration from the West Bank and Gaza to the Arab states averaged seventeen per thousand between 1975 and 1980; in 1980, it decreased to nine per thousand and by 1983 it was only three per thousand.[67] Moreover, the population of the occupied territories has become an exceedingly young one during the past decade: a majority of the population is under age twenty, and one-third are students. In Gaza,where six hundred fifty thousand Palestinians live, 77 percent of the population is under the age of twenty-nine.[68] Just as in Soweto, every day thousands of vehicles transport Arab workers from the West Bank and Gaza to Israel and back.

2. The Economic Factor: Palestinian access to land and water has been threatened severely, with 55 percent of the land in the West Bank and 30 percent in Gaza having been expropriated by Israel. More than 120 colonial settlements had been built on this land, and control of the area provides Israel with more than one-third of Israel's total water

67. See Danny Rubenstein, "Economic Woes in the Territories," *Davar,* 18 November 1984; and Zio Rabi, "Demographic Update," *Haaretz,* 28 November 1984.

68. Motti Basok and Yitzhak Shor, "Grossman Charges Moderate Palestinians Being Deported," *al-Hamishmar,* 28 October 1987.

consumption, and with $1.5 billion in tourist-related revenue. Beside land, water, and tourist resources, the occupied territories provide Israel with cheap labor, a captive market, and tax revenue. Some 115,000 Arab workers cross into Israel proper daily to perform services in the construction sector, where they constitute 50 percent of the work force, and in the agricultural sector.[69] These workers, who make up about one-third and more than one-half of the labor force in the West Bank and Gaza, respectively, are an exploitable resource who receive lower wages than their Israeli counterparts and no social benefits. The tax collected from these workers is equivalent to the entire budget of the West Bank and Gaza. Moreover, the occupied areas provide the Israeli treasury with $800 million, a sum which Meron Benvenisti, the Israeli director of the West Bank Data Base Project calls an "occupation tax."[70] Much of the revenue collected from workers and generated from value added taxes and custom duties remains in Israel proper rather than being spent on West Bank or Gaza development. The rate of public consumption in the occupied areas is 13 percent of the rate in Israel. Government expenditure for public services inside Israel amounts to $1350 per capita, compared with $158 per capita in the occupied areas.[71]

3. The Regional and International Factors. At the regional level, a shifting Arab realignment in the 1980s favored conservative Arab states, whose dependency on the West in general and on the United States in particular removed their leverage for bringing about a peaceful settlement that would ensure the realization of minimal Palestinian rights. The reintegration of Egypt into the Arab state system and the promotion of a Jordanian role by the Arab states, the Reagan administration, and Israel's Labor Party contributed to a diplomatic course unfavorable to Palestinian independence. The Palestine question was so removed from Arab concerns that it did not merit its normal place on the agenda of the Amman Summit at the end of November 1987. Nor did the question make the agenda of the superpowers at the Reykjavik and Washington summits in 1985 and 1987.

69. See article by Israeli Economic Affairs Minister Gad Yaacobi, "An Economic Stake In Peace," *Jerusalem Post,* 29 June 1988.

70. Yitzhak Ravihal, "We Already Have a Civil War on Our Hands," *Yediot Ahronot,* 13 September 1987.

71. *Ibid.*

The combination of all these factors, coming after two decades of political and cultural repression, deinstitutionalization, and physical integration of the area into Israel's economic infrastructure, helped produce this *intifada*. The sociopolitical significance of these factors is not to be underestimated in view of the revolutionary potential of a rising mass of unemployed skilled elements in the ranks of the intelligentsia and the labor force. Meanwhile twenty years of "armed struggle" had failed to produce any tangible political advantages or to bring the Palestinians nearer to their national goals. A feeling that they had been neglected by almost all actors seems to have convinced the people inside the occupied areas to take their destiny into their own hands. They were undoubtedly influenced by the success of the Lebanese nationalist resistance, which had forced Israel to evacuate Lebanon in 1984. A new generation of Palestinians, free of their parents' complex of defeat and fear of the Israelis, was determined to challenge the occupation irrespective of the cost. Hence, as of June 1989 more than five hundred civilians have been killed by the army and Jewish settlers, sixty-five people have been expelled, about fifteen thousand have been detained, fifteen to twenty thousand have suffered severe injuries, and the property damage has mounted into the hundreds of millions of dollars.

The *intifada's* impact on the landscape of the Arab-Israeli conflict and all actors involved in it, local, regional, and international, has been profound. To begin with, the massive demonstrations and the brutality of repression brought the two politically fragmented Palestinian communities – in Israel proper and in the West Bank and Gaza – together in a unified posture when they observed a complete work stoppage on December 21, 1987.

As for Israel, the *intifada* has accentuated its crisis of governance and of leadership and its economic and moral crisis. It provided the Israeli election campaign of the autumn of 1988 with its pivotal issue: self-determination for the Palestinians and the exchange of land for peace. The result was a polarization worse than that which had created a crippling impasse throughout the tenure of the government of "national unity" from 1984 to 1988. That polarization of Israeli society which pitted Likudist and ultraorthodox and ultrarightist parties, openly calling for Palestinian expulsion, against Laborites, moderate Zionists and leftists, has been reinforced by a polarization within the Labor Alignment: as Labor Zionist parties such as Mapam, Shinui, and the Citizens Rights Movement moved to the left of the Alignment's center, two army generals departed from the Alignment altogether and formed two parties at the extreme right of the broad spectrum – to the right of Likud and Tehiya. This impasse has further eroded Israel's ability to deal with the *intifada* on terms other than those of Yitzhak Rabin's policy of "force, power, and blows."

The *intifada's* impact on the economy of Israel was assessed by the

The *intifada's* impact on the economy of Israel was assessed by the Minister of Economic Planning Gad Yaakobi. He estimated the cost to Israel's economy at the end of June 1988 at 2 percent of Gross National Product or about $600 million – representing about half of the expected economic growth in 1988.[72] In the first three months of the uprising there was a drop of 30 percent in tax revenue and a 20 percent drop in production in the construction industry.[73] There was also a 40 percent drop in Israeli exports to the West Bank and Gaza – these exports had amounted to $1.1 billion in 1987.[74]

As for the United States, which continues to assume the role of chief arbiter and sole conciliator, the *intifada* provided a renewed sense of urgency that led Secretary of State George Shultz to journey to the area three times and to offer a settlement proposal. Although that proposal fell short of meeting even the most minimal Palestinian demands and was met with a categorical rejection by Prime Minister Yitzhak Shamir, it illustrated Washington's concern about the destabilizing potential of the *intifada* in the region. It was also designed to repair Israel's image, which was tarnished by the *intifada*. The public mood had changed in the United States to favor a political settlement; the Shultz Plan was an attempt to bridge the gap between the requirements of public policy and public opinion.

The Arab states, whose November 1987 summit meeting relegated the Palestine question to the sidelines and was dominated by the Gulf War, convened a summit meeting in Algeria in June 1988 and called it the *Intifada* Summit. But perhaps the most visible impact of the *intifada* on the Arabs was felt in Jordan, whose monarch announced a severance of administrative and legal links between his kingdom and the West Bank on July 31, 1988. The legal and administrative system of Jordan had remained intact in the West Bank despite twenty-one years of Israeli occupation. But the *intifada* convinced King Hussein that the time for the United Hashemite Kingdom had passed. Not only did the *intifada* accelerate the deterioration of Jordanian influence in the West Bank, but the June 1988 Arab summit, the *Intifada* Summit, removed Jordan from the process of channeling money to support the uprising, in favor of the PLO. The *intifada* has removed the "Jordanian option" from the political agenda.

The United Nations Security Council convened three times,on December 22, 1987 and January 5 and 14, 1988, and adopted resolutions deploring

72. Yaacobi, "Economic Stake In Peace,"

73. Levi Norav, "The Real Cost of the Uprising," *al-Hamishmar,* 25 April 1988.

74. *Ibid.*

Israeli killing of demonstrators, calling on Israel not to deport Palestinians and to respect the 1949 Geneva Convention Relative to the Protection of Civilian Persons in Times of War.[75]

The *intifada's* impact on Western Europe was best exemplified by Yasir Arafat's speech to the European Parliament on September 12, 1988 in Strassbourg and his official visit to France in April 1989. The invitations to the PLO chairman emphasized a new European readiness to participate in a peace process based on the concept of mutual recognition.

But above all, the *intifada* has set the pace for the Palestinians, reshaped and refined their consensus, and fostered the linguistic and conceptual parameters which culminated in the Palestine National Council's declaration of independence issued on November 15, 1988 in Algiers and Arafat's recognition of Israel's "right to exist" issued on December 14, 1988 in Geneva. After fourteen years of futile diplomacy, the *intifada* came to supply the political struggle that ordinarily leads the diplomatic struggle.

The *intifada* has a new lexicon that features clear, well-defined, and specific categories rather than those ambiguous, boastful, and sweeping terms that connote grandiose schemes and unachievable objectives. The movement itself was declared neither a revolt nor a revolution but simply an uprising, despite the fact that its impact on Palestinian society and social structures has been more profound than that of any other movement in the past. Its ultimate goal is "independence," rather than "liberation." That term redefines the context of the struggle, emphasizes its insurrectionist character, and specifies the objective. The armed struggle has thus been rescued out of its dilemma, which left the Palestinians struggling in diplomatic councils for fourteen years while being judged in the courts of terrorism.

The new emphasis on clarity produced an unequivocal call for mutual recognition: a two-state solution, which had in effect been adopted as long ago as 1974. This program was anchored in the principles of parity, symmetry, and reciprocity. The *intifada* gave the Palestinians a sense of power which they had lacked, and therefor, encouraged them to make concessions. Their new initiative is called a pursuit of peace through strength. Although that initiative, which produced the November 15, 1988 Declaration of Independence and the Political Program, was drawn up by the expatriates who run the PLO, the *intifada* had paved the way, redefined the minimum, and conceptualized the framework.

75. United Nations Security Council resolutions 605 (1987); 607 (1988); and 608 (1988).

The Prospects for Settlement

Although the Declaration of Independence and the Geneva declaration would challenge the world community to make good on its numerous pledges to support Palestinian self-determination, the prospects for an early settlement seem to be still remote. Both Israeli domestic factors and the regional and international realities favor an extended yet more turbulent Israeli occupation of the West Bank and Gaza. The Israeli Labor Party is beset with a leadership crisis, and in any event the most generous offer it has devised is the division of the occupied areas between Jordan and Israel. With Jordan out by choice and by an act of Palestinian will, the Labor Party has been deprived of a cover; its Jordanian option is dead. Similarly, the Likud, which has succumbed to extremist demands by ultrareligious and ultrarightist factions, is likely to be even more intransigent than it usually is. The irrelevance of its "functional autonomy" scheme would simply bolster the present impasse. The Arab world is in severe disarray, torn by internal conflicts and faced with economic difficulties related to oil prices. The United States, which has dominated the diplomatic agenda, has pushed the Palestine question to the background during the eight years of the Reagan presidency. The Reagan administration has accepted the Likud thesis that the Palestine question is a secondary issue which must not interfere with the special relationship of a superpower and an important partner. This special relationship is not likely to be compromised by the defense-conscious Bush administration. Given that there is neither internal nor external pressure on the Likud coalition to reverse its annexationist course, only long-range international factors could change the process.

THE COLLECTION

The following chapters, with two exceptions, were written especially for this volume, and cover the political, social, demographic, economic, legal, and cultural dimensions of Israeli policy towards the Palestinians in eastern Palestine and Gaza. The study is organized into four sections.

The first section includes this overview, a chapter on the land and people of Palestine by Professor Ann Lesch, and a chapter on the class structure and political elites of Gaza from 1948 to 1988 by Professor Ziad Abu-Amr. The transformation of the land and people from the announcement of the Balfour Declaration in 1917 to the Israeli occupation of the West Bank and Gaza in 1967 is detailed. The failure of the Zionist movement to come to grips with the moral dilemma posed by the Palestinian people is shown to be a consistent pattern throughout this period. Zionist leaders from

Weizmann to Shamir rejected the concept of a Palestinian nation and chose instead to deal with the Arab states.

The second section includes six chapters dealing with the changing status of Palestinian areas under occupation since 1967. The first chapter in this section examines the legal aspects of the 1967 occupation in terms of international law and actual practice. Emma Playfair, who worked as a human rights lawyer with Al-Haq in Ramallah until mid-1988, concludes that local laws have been altered by Israel beyond recognition, rendering a wide variety of daily activities subject to the approval of the military government. The next chapter examines the impact of occupation on personal status and individual rights. Lea Tsemel, an Israeli attorney whose practice has been devoted to political and civil rights cases, concludes that the "rule of law" applies only insofar as it does not conflict with the interest of the occupier. The transformation of the city of Jerusalem, both physically and juridically, to suit the territorial and demographic aims of Israel is dealt with by Ibrahim Dakkak in chapter 6. The physical changes introduced in Jerusalem are shown to be part and parcel of the general plan for the integration of the West Bank into Israel. In chapter 7, Raja Shehadeh discusses the phenomenon of land alienation and the various measures used by the military government to "legally" facilitate a transfer of Palestinian land into the Israeli sector. Israel's settlement policy in the occupied territories is discussed in the concluding chapters of section 2. In chapter 8, Ibrahim Matar provides a description and analysis of the colonization strategies of the Labor and Likud governments; in chapter 9 Peter Demant analyzes Israel's settlement policy between 1977 and 1983 with emphasis on the ideological and domestic political factors affecting the entire process of colonization.

Section 3 includes five chapters, each of which examines the impact of the occupation on a specific sector. Sara Roy concludes in Chapter 10 that Israel's "Soweto," Gaza has experienced no economic development during twenty-two years of occupation. Whatever economic benefits obtained from wage labor inside Israel and remittances from Palestinian workers abroad, have been achieved without any structural transformation. Israeli restrictions on most forms of political and economic activity conducive to growth is likely to perpetuate the present state of dependency in Gaza and weaken the ability of the economic structure to sustain itself. Chapters 11 and 12 by Sarah Graham-Brown analyze the impact on the economy and social structure of Palestinian society. These chapters reveal in a succinct manner the relationship of dependency that was created between Israel and the occupied territories between 1967 and 1987. Here the phenomenon of internal colonialism, discussed also in the chapters on settlements, is seen in operation on the social, economic, and territorial levels. The demographic dimension of this colonialism is discussed in the following chapter by Professor Janet Abu-Lughod. The number of Palestinians who lived in the occupied West Bank and Gaza in 1984 is approximately the same as lived there twenty years ago, despite a natural increase rate of 3.5 percent. The Zionist endeavor of a whole century, to have the land without the people, thus proceeds uninterruptedly and at a faster rate since 1967. Chapter 14, by a research team of the Union of Palestinian Medical Relief Committees (UPMRC), examines the present status of health and health care services in the West Bank and Gaza. Not only did the health care structure and services deteriorate since the 1967 occupation, essential services are, in fact, being denied as a measure for suppressing the *intifada*. Professor Emanuel Theodor, the head of internal medicine at Tel Aviv's Belinson Hospital, declared during a press conference on January 1, 1989, "we are shocked to see the extent to which the authorities are using medicine as a stick to beat against people with and I don't mean just against those wounded in the *intifada* , but also against the sick among the civilian population."[76]

Section four includes five chapters that delineate the ongoing attempt to create alternative institutions to the occupation. Professor Lisa Taraki of Bir Zeit University discusses the emergence and proliferation of mass organizations in the West Bank that began in the mid-1970s and continued until the eve of the December 1987 uprising. The success of the *intifada*, which is well into its second year as we go to press, is in large part due to the existence of an infrastructure of mass organizations which predates it and which facilitated the integration of wide sectors of the Palestinian community into the insurrection.

Chapter 16, by Rosemary Sayigh, examines the situation of Palestinian women under occupation, on both sides of the 1967 lines. Measured in terms of political consciousness, the impact of occupation on women is seen as positive. Deterioration in their situation, however, has been caused by "forced proletarianization and the transformation of the indigenous household from a center of multiple activities – social, cultural, economic – into a dormitory of workers and school children." In the following chapter the editor examines the effect on institutions of higher learning with emphasis on Military Order 854 of 1980, which was intended to transfer control of the university from its board of trustees to the military government. The impact of the occupation on the educational sector is dealt with in chapter 18 by Dr. Munir Fasheh, dean of students at Bir Zeit University. In an addendum to this chapter, which was prepared for the first

---

76. Quoted in Elfi Palis, "No Pity for Children," *Middle East International,* (3 February 1989), 343:8.

edition, Dr. Fasheh discusses education in terms of Gramsci's concept of empowerment. He demonstrates the irrelevance of formal education to Palestinian needs and realities and appeals for a new progressive education capable of facilitating the fulfillment of Palestinian needs by Palestinians. Together with Taraki's study, this chapter offers valuable insight into the social and psychological dynamics that made the *intifada* possible.

The last section of this volume includes four chapters structured around the theme "subjugation versus liberation." Sheila Ryan in chapter 20 offers a description and analysis of the various plans proposed to regularize the occupation in order to make it permanent. Dr. Salim Tamari's chapter examines the Israeli search for Palestinian quislings, also intended to regularize the occupation. The Movement of Palestinian Leagues, known as Village Leagues, is seen as no more successful a collaborative base than its ill-fated predecessor, the Farmer's Party of the mid-1920s. The alternatives to the occupation are dealt with in the last two chapters, by Dr. Sameer Abraham and Dr. Muhammad Hallaj. Abraham traces the development of the Palestinian national movement in distinct phases, from 1956 up to the 1982 Israeli invasion of Lebanon. Shifts in political objectives and strategy are linked to the movement's development from one period to the next. This chapter reveals that "as the Palestine Liberation Organization evolved from an uncompromising and militant revolutionary organization to a diplomatic and governmentlike one, Israeli policy became more intransigent." Finally, the Palestinian alternative is discussed in chapter 23 by Hallaj. During the past twenty years, three basic proposals have been presented: the United Arab Kingdom of Jordan, the democratic secular state, and the two-state solution.

Both the first and the last chapters in this collection reach the same conclusion: that the Zionist movement, historically and at present, has been unable and unwilling to recognize the Palestinian reality and seek a political solution that would accommodate the interests and needs of both people. The past twenty-one years opened up the possibility of a radical change in Israeli attitudes and perceptions. Not only did Israel fail to awaken to that challenge, but the prospects of accommodation were further dimmed by the triumph of annexationist tendencies, and by the contemporary political economy with its extensions overseas, a trend accelerated by revisionist Zionists since 1977. The process of undermining Palestinian economic self-reliance, of forging a relationship of dependency, of segmenting and atomizing Palestinian society, of depopulating and proletarianizing, and of neutralizing segments of the Arab world has resulted in a deep Israeli entrenchment in the territories occupied since 1967 – by now so many sectors of Israeli society have so much interest vested in the occupation that a withdrawal would not be a simple task even for the most conciliatory of

Israeli governments. This is not an ordinary military occupation; consequently it cannot be ended by military withdrawal alone. The end to occupation must depend on transformations in regional and international politics, on future developments within the Palestine national movement, and on the changing dynamics of Israeli politics. The *intifada* has already shown that there can be no return to the *status quo,* for what is in question is not a specific policy or a combination of policies, but the occupation itself. Indeed, the events of the past eighteen months have reshaped the dimensions of the conflict, redefined the rules of the game, and raised the possibility that yesterday's constraints may very well be tomorrow's opportunities for the Palestinians.

Palestine: Land and People

Ann M. Lesch

The Zionist movement has maintained a striking continuity in its aims and methods over the past century. From the start, the movement sought to achieve a Jewish majority in Palestine, and to establish a Jewish state on as much of the land as possible. The methods included promoting mass Jewish immigration, and acquiring tracts of land that would become the inalienable property of the Jewish people. This policy inevitably prevented the indigenous Arab residents from attaining their national goals and establishing a Palestinian state. It also necessitated displacing Arabs from their lands and jobs when their presence conflicted with Zionist interests.

The Zionist movement – and subsequently the state of Israel – failed to develop a constructive policy toward the Palestinian Arab presence and aspirations. Although many Israelis recognized the moral dilemma posed by the Palestinians, the majority either tried to ignore the issue or resolve it by *force majeure.* Thus the Palestine problem festered and grew, instead of being resolved.

The fighting in 1947-49 led to the consolidation of Israel on three-quarters of Mandatory Palestine and the displacement of over half of the Arab inhabitants. In 1956-57, Israel temporarily occupied the Gaza Strip, which was tightly packed with Palestinian refugees, parts of Syrian territory on the Golan Heights, and all of Egyptian Sinai. With almost half of the Palestinians living under its control, Israel had an opportunity to deal directly with the issue. However, the leadership chose to sidestep it, preferring to negotiate with the neighboring Arab states rather than with the Palestinians' representatives in the diaspora and in the occupied territories. Thus, Israel sought negotiations with Jordan for the return of parts of the West Bank to its control, and concluded a peace treaty with Egypt that resulted in the complete withdrawal of Israeli forces from Sinai in April

1982. The subsequent invasion of Lebanon forced the expulsion of the Palestinian leadership and fighters from that country and opened up the possibility of neutralizing Israel's northern border. Once again, Israel sought to resolve the Palestinian problem through force instead of political accommodation. The invasion thus served as the latest manifestation of the inability of the Israeli leadership to come to grips with the moral dilemma posed by the Palestine problem and to seek a political resolution that would meet the needs of both peoples.

HISTORICAL BACKGROUND

The Zionist movement arose in late nineteenth-century Europe, influenced by the nationalist ferment sweeping the continent. Zionism acquired its particular focus from the ancient Jewish longing for the return to Zion and received a strong impetus from the increasingly intolerable conditions facing the large Jewish community in czarist Russia. The movement also developed at the time of major European territorial acquisitions in Asia and Africa, and benefited from the European powers' competition for influence in the shrinking Ottoman Empire.

One result of this involvement with European expansionism, however, was that the leaders of the nascent nationalist movements in the Middle East viewed Zionism as an adjunct of European colonialism. Moreover, Zionist assertions of the contemporary relevance of the Jews' historical ties to Palestine, coupled with their land purchases and immigration, alarmed the Arab residents of the Ottoman districts that comprised Palestine. Jewish immigration remained at too small a scale to threaten the Arabs' majority: the Jewish community (*Yishuv*) was six percent of the population in 1880 and ten percent by 1914. Nevertheless, the numbers were significant enough and the settlers were outspoken enough to arouse the opposition of Arab leaders and induce them to exert counterpressure on the Ottoman regime to prohibit Jewish immigration and land buying.

One young Russian Zionist settler wrote in 1882: "The final goal is eventually to gain control of Palestine and to restore to the Jewish people the political independence of which it has been deprived for 2,000 years."[1] This goal, he argued, would be accomplished both by agricultural and industrial development and by military means. These aims were embodied in the political pronouncements of the movement, crystallized at the first Zionist Congress of August 1897. Other institutional developments

1. Quoted by David Ben-Gurion in *My Talks with Arab Leaders* (New York: Third Press, 1973), p. 2.

followed soon after: the creation of the Jewish National Fund in 1901, the opening of the Palestine Office in Jaffa in 1907 to assist immigrants and purchase land, the establishment of an all-Jewish town called Tel Aviv in 1909, and the founding of the first kibbutz (collective agricultural settlement) in the same year.

The Zionists did not try to quell Arab fears, since their concern was to encourage colonization from Europe and to minimize the obstacles in their path. Meanwhile, the Arab community became increasingly aware of the long-term threat posed by Zionism. As early as 1891, a group of Muslim and Christian notables cabled Istanbul urging the government to prohibit Jewish immigration and land purchase. The resulting edicts radically curtailed land purchases in the *sanjak* of Jerusalem for the next decade.[2] When a Zionist Congress resolution in 1905 called for increased colonization, the Ottoman regime suspended all land transfers to Jews in both the *sanjak* of Jerusalem and the *vilayet* of Beirut.

After the coup d'etat by the Young Turks in 1908, the Arabs used their representation in the central parliament and their access to local newspapers to press their claims and express their concerns. They were particularly vociferous in opposition to discussions that took place between the financially hard-pressed Ottoman regime and Zionist leaders in 1912-13, which would have let the Zionist Organization purchase crown land (*jiftlik*) in the Beisan Valley, along the Jordan River.[3]

The only effort to convene a meeting of Zionists and Palestinian Arabs occurred in the spring of 1914.[4] Its difficulties illustrated the incompatibility in their aspirations. The Arabs wanted the Zionists to present them with a document that would state their precise political ambitions, their willingness to open their schools to Arabs, and their intentions of learning Arabic and integrating with the local population. The Zionists rejected this, realizing that they could not make any statement that would satisfy their Arab interlocutors.

At the close of the Ottoman era, Zionism was still a small, struggling movement. It had an increasing number of adherents in Europe and some

2. Neville Mandel, "Turks, Arabs, and Jewish Immigration into Palestine, 1882-1914," *St. Anthony's Papers* (1965), 17:86.

3. *Ibid.*, pp. 101-2.

4. Neville Mandel, "Attempts at an Arab-Zionist Entente, 1913-1914," *Middle Eastern Studies* (April 1965), 1:263; see also Yaacov Ro'i, "The Zionist Attitude to the Arabs, 1908-1914," *Middle Eastern Studies* (April 1968), 4:198-242.

practical achievements in Palestine, but its growth was inhibited by the opposition of the Ottoman rulers and by the absence of a strong European patron. Moreover, the articulation of its aim to transform Palestine into a Jewish state had aroused the opposition of the indigenous Arab majority. Nevertheless, the settlers of the 1900s provided the nucleus for a major political force and worked out political and socioeconomic programs that guided the movement for the following decades, when political conditions became more auspicious.

THE BRITISH MANDATE

The proclamation of the Balfour Declaration on November 2, 1917, and the arrival of British troops in Palestine soon after, transformed the political situation. The declaration gave the Zionist movement its long-sought legal status, by stating the British government's support for "the establishment in Palestine of a national home for the Jewish people" and by promising that the government would "use their best endeavors to facilitate the achievement of this object." The qualification that "nothing shall be done which may prejudice the civil and religious rights of the existing non-Jewish communities in Palestine" seemed a relatively insignificant obstacle to the Zionists, especially since it referred only to those communities' "civil and religious rights," not to political or national rights. The subsequent British occupation gave Britain the ability to carry out that pledge and provide the protection necessary for the Zionists to realize their aims.

In fact, the British had contracted three mutually contradictory promises for the future of Palestine. The Sykes-Picot Agreement of 1916 with the French and Russian governments proposed that Palestine be placed under international administration. The Husayn-McMahon Correspondence of 1915-16, on whose basis the Arab Revolt was launched, implied that Palestine would be included in the zone of Arab independence. In contrast, the Balfour Declaration encouraged the colonization of Palestine by Jews, under British protection. British officials recognized the irreconcilability of these pledges but hoped that a *modus vivendi* could be achieved, both between the competing imperial powers, France and Britain, and between the Arabs and the Jews. Instead, these contradictions set the stage for the three decades of conflict-ridden British rule in Palestine.

During the mandate period, Britain sought to maintain the security of the Empire and to exclude the influence of European rivals from the eastern Mediterranean and the routes to India. In the 1920s France was the main competitor but, by the mid-1930s, Italy and Germany posed the major threat. Initially, many British politicians shared the Zionist assumption that gradual, regulated Jewish immigration and settlement would lead to a Jewish majority in Palestine whereupon it would become independent, with legal protection for the Arab minority. The assumption that this could be accomplished without serious Arab resistance was shattered at the outset of British rule. Britain was thereafter caught in an increasingly untenable position, unable to persuade either the Arabs or Zionists to alter their demands and forced to station substantial military forces in Palestine to maintain security. Moreover, Britain lost its clear naval predominance in the Mediterranean by the late 1930s, when Italy challenged Britain's monopoly. During World War II, Britain was able to use Palestine as the base from which to attack and occupy Lebanon and Syria, held by Vichy France, and it served as a reserve area for the battle on Egyptian soil against Germany's North African forces. At the close of the war, however, Britain was too exhausted to maintain its hold on Palestine in the face of a full-scale Jewish revolt.

In practice, the British umbrella was critically important to the growth and consolidation of the Yishuv, enabling it to root itself firmly despite Arab opposition. When British support diminished in the late 1930s, the Yishuv was strong enough to withstand the Arabs on its own. After World War II, the Zionist movement was also able to turn to the emerging superpower, the United States, for diplomatic support and legitimization.

The Arabs in Palestine had assumed that they would gain some form of independence when Ottoman rule disintegrated, whether through a separate state or integration with neighboring Arab lands. These hopes were bolstered by the Arab Revolt, the entry of Faisal ibn Husein to Damascus in 1918, and the proclamation of Syrian independence in 1920. But they were dashed by Britain's imposition of direct colonial rule and its elevation of the Yishuv to a special status. Moreover, the French ousted Faisal from Damascus in July 1920, and British compensation – in the form of thrones in Transjordan and Iraq for Abdullah and Faisal, respectively – had no positive impact on the Arabs in Palestine. In fact, the action underlined the different treatment accorded Palestine and its disadvantageous situation politically. These concerns were exacerbated by Jewish immigration: the Yishuv comprised 10 percent of the population in 1914, 28 percent in 1936, and reached 32 percent by 1947.

The Arabs' responses to Jewish immigration, land purchases, and political demands were remarkably consistent.[5] They insisted that Palestine must remain an Arab country, with the same right of self-determination and

5. Ann Mosely Lesch, *Arab Politics in Palestine, 1917-1939* (Ithaca, N.Y.: Cornell University Press, 1979), pp. 79-80.

independence as that accorded by the British to Egypt, Transjordan, and Iraq. The Arabs argued that Palestinian territory could not and should not be used to solve the plight of the Jews in Europe, and that Jewish national aspirations should not override their own needs.

Arab opposition peaked in the late 1930s: the six-month general strike in 1936 was followed the next year by a widespread rural revolt. This rebellion welled up from the bottom of Palestinian society – unemployed urban workers, displaced peasants crowded into towns, and debt-ridden villagers. It was supported by most merchants and professionals in the towns, who feared competition from the Yishuv. Members of the elite families acted as spokesmen before the British administration through the Arab Higher Committee, which was formed during the 1936 strike. But the British banned the committee in October 1937 and arrested its members, on the eve of the revolt.

Only one of the Arab political parties was willing to limit its aims and accept the principle of territorial partition. The National Defense Party, led by Ragheb al-Nashashibi (mayor of Jerusalem from 1920 to 1934), was willing to accept partition in 1937 so long as the Arabs obtained sufficient land and could merge with Transjordan to form a larger political entity. However, the British Royal Commission's plan, announced in July 1937, would have forced the Arabs to leave the olive and grain growing areas of Galilee, the orange groves on the Mediterranean coast, and the urban port cities of Haifa and Acre. That was too great a loss for the party to accept, and so it joined in the general denunciations of partition.[6]

During the mandate period the Arab community was 70 percent rural, 75 to 80 percent illiterate, and divided internally between town and countryside, and between elite families and villagers. Despite broad support for the national aims, the Palestinians could not achieve the unity and strength necessary to withstand the combined pressure of the British forces and the Zionist movement. In fact, the political structure was decapitated in the late 1930s when the Arab Higher Committee was banned and hundreds of local politicians were arrested. When efforts were made in the 1940s to rebuild the political structure, the impetus came largely from outside, from Arab rulers who were disturbed by the deteriorating conditions in Palestine and feared its repercussions on their own newly acquired independence.

These rulers gave priority to their own national considerations, and could give limited diplomatic and military support to the Palestinians. The Palestinian Arabs continued to demand a state that would reflect the Arab

6. *Ibid.*, p. 120; Simah Flapan, *Zionism and the Palestinians* (New York: Barnes and Noble, 1979), p. 258; Yehoshua Porath, *The Palestinian Arab National Movement, 1929-1939* (London: Frank Cass), 1977, pp. 229-30.

majority's weight – diminished to 68 percent by 1947. They rejected the UN Partition Plan of November 1947 that granted the Yishuv statehood in 55 percent of Palestine, an area that included as many Arab residents as Jews. However, the Palestinian Arabs lacked the political strength and military force to back up their claims, and the Arab rulers – though denouncing partition – used their armed forces only to protect those zones that the partition plan had allocated to the Arab state. By the time that armistice agreements were signed in 1949 the Arab areas had shrunk to only 23 percent of Palestine. The Egyptian army held the Gaza Strip, and Transjordanian forces dominated the hills of Judea and Samaria. Some 780,000 of the 1.3 million Palestinian Arabs fled from the area held by Israel. Emir Abdullah, who had failed to gain Palestinian territory in 1937, then annexed the zone that his army occupied, renaming it the West Bank.

THE ZIONIST MOVEMENT

What were the policies and actions of the Zionist movement that led to this massive displacement? Fundamentally, Zionism focused on two needs: to attain a Jewish majority in Palestine and to acquire statehood, irrespective of the wishes of the Arab population. The nonrecognition of the Palestinian people "was the cornerstone of Zionist policy, initiated by [Chaim] Weizmann and faithfully carried out by [David] Ben-Gurion and his successors. This policy has been pursued despite abundant proof of the tenacity with which the Palestinians have clung to their national identity in the most adverse circumstances."[7]

Chaim Weizmann, president of the World Zionist Organization, placed maximalist demands before the Paris Peace Conference in February 1919. He stated that he expected seventy to eighty thousand Jewish immigrants to arrive each year in Palestine. When they became the majority, they would form an independent government and Palestine would become "as Jewish as England is English." Weizmann proposed that the boundaries should be the Mediterranean Sea on the west; Sidon, the Litani River, and Mount Hermon on the north; all of Transjordan west of the Hijaz railway on the east; and a line across Sinai from Aqaba to el-Arish on the south. He argued that "the boundaries above outlined are what we consider essential for the necessary economic foundation of the country. Palestine must have its natural outlet to the sea and control of its rivers and their headwaters. The boundaries are sketched with the general economic needs and historic traditions of the

7. Flapan, *Zionism*, p. 12.

country in mind."[8] Weizmann offered the Arab countries a free zone in Haifa and a joint port at Aqaba.

Weizmann's policy was basically in accord with that of the leaders of the Yishuv, who held a conference in December 1918 in which they formulated their own demands for the peace conference. The Yishuv's plan "laid heavy emphasis on the need for Zionist control over administrative appointments, and for a strong and truly 'partisan' Trustee to govern the country during the transition to a Jewish majority. At the end of the transition, a Jewish state was implicit: a constitutional democracy in which the Arabs would be granted the appropriate minority rights."[9] Although the peace conference did not allocate such extensive territories to the Jewish national home and did not support the goal of transforming all of Palestine into a Jewish state, it opened the door to such a possibility. More important, Weizmann's presentation stated clearly and forcefully the long-term aims of the movement.

These aims were based on certain fundamental tenets of Zionism. First, the movement was not only inherently righteous, but also met an overwhelming need among the Jews. Second, European culture was superior to indigenous Arab culture, and the Zionists could help civilize the East. Third, external support was needed from a major power, and relations with the Arab world were a secondary matter. Fourth, Arab nationalism was a legitimate movement, but Palestinian nationalism was either illegitimate or nonexistent. Finally, if the Palestinians could not reconcile themselves to Zionism, *force majeure,* not compromise, was the only feasible response.

Adherents of Zionism believed that the Jewish people had an inherent and inalienable right to Palestine. Religious Zionists stated this in biblical terms, referring to the divine promise of the land to the tribes of Israel. Secular Zionists relied more on the argument that only Palestine could solve the problem of Jewish dispersion and virulent anti-Semitism. Weizmann stated in 1930 that the needs of 16 million Jews had to be balanced against those of one million Palestinian Arabs: "The Balfour Declaration and the Mandate have definitely lifted [Palestine] out of the context of the Middle East and linked it up with the world-wide Jewish problem. . . . The rights which the Jewish people has been adjudged in Palestine do not depend on the consent, and cannot be subjected to the will, of the majority of its

8. Quoted in Sami Hadawi, *Bitter Harvest: Palestine 1914-1979* (Delmar, N.Y.: Caravan Books, rev. ed. 1979), p. 215; also Flapan, *Zionism*, p. 46; and J.C. Hurewitz, *The Struggle for Palestine* (New York: Schocken Books, 1976), p. 20.

9. Neil Caplan, *Palestine Jewry and the Arab Question, 1917-25* (London: Frank Cass, 1978), pp. 24-25.

present inhabitants."[10] This perspective took its most extreme form with the Revisionist movement. Its founder, Vladimir Jabotinsky, inflated "feelings of self-righteousness to the point where the whole, absolute truth and justice were on one side only,"[11] thereby justifying any actions taken against the Arabs in order to realize Zionist goals.

Second, there was a strong feeling that European civilization was superior to Arab culture and mores. Theodor Herzl, the founder of the Zionist Organization, wrote in the *Jewish State* (1886) that the Jewish community could serve as "part of a wall of defense for Europe in Asia, an outpost of civilization against barbarism."[12] Weizmann's views have been described as follows:

> Weizmann betrayed a nineteenth century mentality – a faith in Europe's civilizing mission among backward peoples. He firmly believed that the Zionist cause was a fight of civilization against the desert, the struggle of progress, efficiency, health and education against stagnation. . . .
>
> His image of the Arabs was that of a primitive and backward people who were easily swayed by power. money and success. They were treacherous and shifty, lacked moral values, could not be relied upon to take a principled stand, and did not appreciate European ideals.[13]

David Ben-Gurion, the leading Labor Zionist, could not understand why Arabs rejected his offer to use Jewish finance, scientific knowledge, and technical expertise to modernize the region.[14] He attributed this rejection to backwardness rather than to the affront that it posed to the Arabs' pride and their aspirations for independence.

Third, the Zionist leaders recognized that they needed an external patron in order to legitimize their presence in the international arena and to provide them legal and military protection in Palestine. Great Britain played that role in the 1920s and 1930s, and the United States became the mentor in the mid-1940s. Zionist leaders realized that they needed to make tactical accommodations to that patron – such as downplaying their public state-

10. Quoted in Lesch, *Arab Politics*, pp. 43-44.

11. Flapan, *Zionism*, p. 117.

12. Quoted in Arthur Hertzberg, ed., *The Zionist Idea* (New York: Atheneum, 1969), p. 22.

13. Flapan, *Zionism*, pp. 25, 39.

14. *Ibid.*, p. 134.

ments about their political aspirations or accepting a state on a limited territory – while continuing work toward their long-term goals. The presence and needs of the Arabs were viewed as secondary. The Zionist leadership never considered allying with the Arab world against the British or Americans. Rather, Weizmann, in particular, felt that the Yishuv should bolster the British Empire and guard its strategic interests in the region.[15] Later, the leaders of Israel perceived the Jewish state as a strategic asset to the United States in the Middle East.

Fourth, Zionist politicians accepted the idea of an Arab nation but rejected the concept of a Palestinian nation. They considered the Arab residents of Palestine as comprising a minute fraction of the land and people of the Arab world, and as lacking any separate identity and aspirations. Weizmann and Ben-Gurion were willing to negotiate with Arab rulers in order to gain their recognition of Jewish statehood in Palestine in return for the Zionists' recognition of Arab independence elsewhere, but they would not negotiate with the Arab politicians in Palestine for a political settlement in their common homeland. As early as 1918, Weizmann wrote to a prominent British politician: "the real Arab movement is developing in Damascus and Mecca . . . the so-called Arab question in Palestine would therefore assume only a purely local character, and in fact is not considered a serious factor.[16] In line with that thinking, Weizmann met with Emir Faisal in the same year, in an attempt to win his agreement to Jewish statehood in Palestine in return for Jewish financial support for Faisal's kingdom in Syria.

In 1939, Ben-Gurion, Weizmann, and other Zionist leaders met with prominent Arab officials during the London Conference, which was convened by Britain to seek a compromise settlement in Palestine. The Arab diplomats from Egypt, Iraq, and Saudi Arabia criticized the exceptional position that the Balfour Declaration had granted the Jewish community, and emphasized the estrangement that the large-scale Jewish immigration was causing between the Arab and Jewish residents. In response, Weizmann insisted that Palestine must remain open to all Jews who wanted to immigrate, and Ben-Gurion suggested that all of Palestine should become a Jewish state, federated with the surrounding Arab states. The Arab participants criticized these demands for exacerbating the conflict,

15. *Ibid.,* p. 9.

16. letter to Lord Balfour, quoted in Flapan, *Zionism,* p. 38; the discussions with Faisal are described in Lesch, *Arab Politics,* pp. 132-34, and Flapan, pp. 31-55.

rather than contributing to the search for peace.[17] The Zionists' premise that Arab statehood could be recognized while ignoring the Palestinians was thus rejected by the Arab rulers themselves.

Finally, Zionist leaders argued that if the Palestinians could not reconcile themselves to Zionism, then *force majeure,* not a compromise of goals, was the only possible response. By the early 1920s, after violent Arab protests broke out in Jaffa and Jerusalem, leaders of the Yishuv recognized that the gap between the aims of the two peoples was "almost unbridgeable"[18] and that "the upbuilding of their national home . . . would lead to an unfortunate, but unavoidable, clash with the Arabs." They realized that "the Arab majority in Palestine was unlikely to agree voluntarily to change places with the Jews as majority and minority." In fact, as early as 1919 Ben-Gurion stated bluntly:

> Everybody sees a difficulty in the question of relations between Arabs and Jews. But not everybody sees that there is no solution to this question. No solution! There is a gulf, and nothing can fill this gulf. . . . I do not know what Arab will agree that Palestine should belong to the Jews. . . . We, as a nation, want this country to be *ours;* the Arabs, as a nation, want this country to be *theirs.*[19]

At that time, Ben-Gurion thought that the decision would be made by the Paris Peace Conference and that Britain would tip the scales in favor of the Zionist movement. Later, the Zionist leadership realized that they had to take the initiative and compel the Arabs to acquiesce to their diminished status. Ben-Gurion stated in 1937, during the Arab Revolt: "this is a national war declared upon us by the Arabs. . . . This is an active resistance by the Palestinians to what they regard as a usurpation of their homeland by the Jews. . . . But the fighting is only one aspect of the conflict, which is in its essence a political one. And politically we are the aggressors and they defend themselves."[20] This conclusion did not lead Ben-Gurion to negotiate with the Palestinian Arabs, but to adopt "an even more militant line on the need to build up Jewish military strength in order to coerce the Arabs."[21]

17. Lesch, *Arab Politics,* pp. 152-53.

18. Caplan, *Palestine Jewry,* pp. 3-4.

19. *Ibid.,* p. 41.

20. Flapan, *Zionism,* p. 141.

21. *Ibid.,* p. 142.

Practical Zionism

In order to realize the aims of Zionism and build the Jewish national home, practical steps were taken in many different realms. Political structures were built that could assume state functions. A military force was created, large-scale immigration was promoted, land was acquired as the inalienable property of the Jewish people, and monopolistic concessions were established. Moreover, the labor federation, Histadrut, tried to enforce the employment of only Jewish labor in Jewish enterprises, and an autonomous Hebrew-language educational system was established. These measures created a self-contained national entity on Palestinian soil that was entirely separate from the Arab community.

The Yishuv established an elected community council, executive body, administrative departments, and religious courts soon after the British assumed control over Palestine."[22] When the mandate was ratified by the League of Nations in 1922, the Zionist Organization was given the responsibility to advise and cooperate with the British administration not only on economic and social matters affecting the Jewish national home, but also on issues involving the general development of the country. Although the British rejected pressure to give the Zionist Organization an equal share in administration and control over immigration and land transfers, the Yishuv did gain a privileged advisory position.

The Zionists were strongly critical of British efforts to establish a legislative council in 1923, 1930, and 1936: "At an early stage Zionist observers realized that the constitutional demands of the Arabs were almost totally irreconcilable with their own demands and needs and would have to be considered a 'threat' to be resisted."[23] In 1923, the Jewish residents participated in the elections, but they were relieved that the Arab boycott compelled the British to cancel the results. In 1930 and 1936 the Zionist Organization vigorously opposed British proposals for a legislature. They feared that, if the Arabs received the majority status that proportional representation would require, then the Arabs would try to block immigration, land buying, and other essential policies of the Zionists. Their opposition was couched in the phrase that Palestine was "not ripe" for self-rule, a code for "not until there's a Jewish majority."

To bolster their position, defense forces (*Haganah*) were formed in March 1920. They were preceded by the establishment of guards (*hashomer*) in the Jewish rural settlements in the 1900s, and the forming of a

22. Lesch, *Arab Politics*, p. 46.

23. Caplan, *Palestine Jewry*, p. 148.

Jewish Legion in World War I. Eliahu Golomb, head of Haganah, had felt that the Jewish Legion should be used to garrison Palestine: it "accustoms the Arabs to the idea that we are destined to rule this country and puts a fear among them which prevents them from doing anything against us."[24] However, the British disbanded the Jewish Legion and allowed only sealed armories in the settlements and mixed Jewish-British area defense committees. Haganah was an illegal force, formed during the period of increasing Jewish-Arab tension that led to major Arab assaults on Jews in Jerusalem in April 1920.

Despite its illegal status, Haganah expanded to number ten thousand trained and mobilized men and forty thousand reservists by 1936. During the 1937-38 Arab Revolt, Haganah engaged in "active defense" against the rebel bands and cooperated with the British in guarding railway lines, the oil pipeline to Haifa, and the border fences. This cooperation deepened during World War II, when 18,800 Jewish volunteers joined the British forces and Haganah's special *Palmach* units served as scouts and sappers in Lebanon in 1941-42. This wartime experience helped to transform the Haganah into a regular fighting force. When Ben-Gurion became the Zionist Organization's secretary of defense in June 1947, he accelerated mobilization as well as arms-buying in the United States and Europe. As a result, mobilization leaped to thirty thousand by May 1948, when statehood was proclaimed, and then doubled to sixty thousand by mid-July – twice the number serving in the Arab forces arrayed against Israel.[25]

A principal means for building up the national home was the promotion of large-scale immigration from Europe. The mandate specified that the rate of immigration should accord with the economic capacity of the country to absorb the immigrants. In 1931, the British government reinterpreted this to take into account only the Jewish sector of the economy, excluding the Arab sector, which was suffering from heavy unemployment. Only in 1939 did the British impose a severe quota on Jewish immigrants. That restriction was resisted by the Yishuv with a sense of desperation, since it blocked access to a key haven for the Jews whom Hitler was persecuting and exterminating in Germany and the rest of Nazi-occupied Europe.

Estimates of the Palestinian population demonstrate the dramatic effect of immigration on the Yishuv's status. The first British census (December 31, 1922) counted 757,182 residents, of whom 83,794 (11%) were Jewish. The second census (December 31, 1931) enumerated 1,035,821, including 174,006 (17%) Jews. Thus, the absolute number of Jews had doubled and

24. Quoted in Caplan, p. 34.

25. Nadav Safran, *From War to War* (New York: Pegasus, 1969), p. 30.

the relative number had increased from 11 percent to 17 percent. Two-thirds of this growth could be attributed to net immigration, and one-third to natural increase.[26] Two-thirds of the Yishuv was concentrated in Jerusalem and Jaffa-Tel Aviv, with most of the remainder in the north, including the towns of Haifa, Safad, and Tiberias.

The pace of immigration accelerated in 1932 and peaked in 1935-36, so that the absolute number of Jewish residents doubled in the five years from 1931 to 1936 to 370,000, constituting 28 percent of the total population.[27] Net immigration was considerably reduced in the late 1930s and 1940s, but the government estimated in 1946 that there were about 583,000 Jews out of nearly 1,888,000 residents, or 31 percent of the total.[28] Seventy percent of them were urban, and they continued to be overwhelmingly concentrated in Jerusalem (100,000), the Haifa area (119,000), and the Tel Aviv and Ramla districts (327,000). The remaining 43,000 were largely in Galilee, with a scattering in the Negev and almost none in the highlands of Judea and Samaria.

The Yishuv launched large-scale land purchases in order to found rural settlements and stake territorial claims. In 1920 the Yishuv held about 650,000 dunums (one dunum equals approximately a quarter of an acre). By 1930, the amount had expanded to 1,164,000 dunums and by 1936 to 1,400,000 dunums. The major purchasing agent (the Palestine Land Development Company) estimated that by 1936 89 percent had been bought from large landowners (primarily absentees resident in Beirut) and only 11 percent from peasants. By 1947, the Yishuv held 1.9 million dunums. Nevertheless, this represented only 7 percent of the total land surface or 10 to 12 percent of the cultivable land.[29]

According to Article 3 of the Constitution of the Jewish Agency, the land was held by the Jewish National Fund as the inalienable property of the Jewish people, and only Jewish labor could be employed in the settlements.[30] The result, as a British commission reported:

26. Janet L. Abu-Lughod, "The Demographic Transformation of Palestine," in Ibrahim Abu-Lughod, ed., *The Transformation of Palestine* (Evanston, Ill.: Northwestern University Press, 1971), pp. 142-44.

27. *Ibid.*, p. 150; see also Hurewitz, *Struggle for Palestine,* pp. 27-28.

28. J. Abu-Lughod, "Demographic Transformation," p. 153.

29. John Ruedy, "Dynamics of Land Alienation," in I. Abu-Lughod, *Transformation,* pp. 125-26, 134; Lesch, *Arab Politics,* pp. 68-69.

30. Ruedy, "Dynamics," p. 130; see also Hurewitz, *Struggle for Palestine,* pp. 30-31, 139.

has been that land has been extra-territorialized. It ceases to be land from which the Arab can gain any advantage now or in the future. Not only can he never hope to lease or to cultivate it, but he is deprived for ever from employment on that land. . . . It is for this reason that Arabs discount the professions of friendship and good will on the part of the Zionists in view of the policy which the Zionist Organization deliberately adopted.[31]

This inalienability clause was protested bitterly by Arabs. The moderate National Defense Party, for example, petitioned the British in 1935 to prevent further land sales, arguing that it was a "life and death [matter] to the Arabs, in that it results in the transfer of their country to other hands and the loss of their nationality. . . . [Once] Arab lands are alienated from Arabs to Jews, it is immaterial whether the productivity of these lands is increased or decreased, so long as the Arabs cannot derive any further benefit therefrom."[32]

The placement of settlements was often based on political considerations. The Palestine Land Development Company had four criteria for land purchase: the economic suitability of the tract, its contribution to forming a solid block of Jewish territory, the avoidance of isolated settlements, and the impact of the purchase on the political-territorial claims of the Zionists.[33] The "stockade and watchtower" settlements constructed in 1937, for example, were designed to secure certain areas of Galilee for the Yishuv if the British implemented partition.[34] Similarly, eleven settlements were hastily erected in the Negev in late 1946 in an attempt to stake a political claim in that entirely Arab territory. Yigal Allon, the Palmach commander, stated explicitly:

The planning and development of pioneering Zionist settlements were . . . partly determined by politico-strategic needs. The choice of the location of settlements, for instance, was influenced not only by considerations of economic viability but also and even chiefly by the needs of local defence, overall settlement strategy (which aimed at ensuring a Jewish political presence in all parts of the country),

31. Sir John Hope Simpson, *Report on Immigration, Land Settlement and Development*, Parliamentary Papers, Command 3686-87, London 1930, p. 54, quoted in Ruedy, "Dynamics," p. 130.

32. Quoted in Lesch, *Arab Politics*, p. 72; a detailed evaluation of the effect of Jewish land purchases is provided by Porath, *Palestinian Arab National Movement*, pp. 80-90.

33. Avraham Granott, *Agrarian Reform and the Record of Israel* (Mystic, Conn., 1956), pp. 32-35, quoted in Ruedy, "Dynamics," p. 129.

34. Flapan, *Zionism*, p. 250.

and by the role such blocks of settlements might play in some future, perhaps decisive, all-out struggle. Accordingly, land was purchased . . . in remote parts of the country deep in Arab-populated areas and when possible close to the political borders of the country.[35]

In addition to land purchases, prominent Jewish businessmen won monopolistic concessions from the British government that gave the Zionist movement an important role in the development of Palestine's natural resources. In 1921, Pinhas Rutenberg's Palestine Electricity Company acquired the right to electrify all of Palestine except Jerusalem. Moise Novomeysky received the concession to develop the minerals in the Dead Sea in 1927. And the Palestine Land Development Company gained the concession to drain the Huleh marshes, north of the Sea of Galilee, in 1934. In each case, the concession was contested by other serious claimants, and Arab politicians argued that the government should retain control itself in order to develop the resources for the benefit of the entire country.[36]

The inalienability clause in the Jewish National Fund contracts included a provision that only Jews could work on Jewish agricultural settlements. The concepts of manual labor and the "return to the soil" were key to the Zionist enterprise. This "Jewish labor" (*Avodat Ivrit*) policy was enforced by the General Federation of Jewish Labor (*Histadrut*), founded in 1920 and headed by David Ben-Gurion. Since some Jewish builders and citrus growers were willing to hire Arabs, the Histadrut launched a campaign to remove Arab workers in 1933. Citrus groves were picketed and mobile units evicted Arab workers from construction sites and factories: "The atmosphere of tension and hostility created by the forceful eviction of Arab workers in the cities and by the acrimonious propaganda which accompanied this operation amplified the natural Arab fear of the Jewish majority, and transformed it into a state of panic."[37] An Arab labor leader wrote angrily in 1937: "The Histadrut's fundamental aim is 'the conquest of labour.' . . . No matter how many Arab workers are unemployed, they have no right to take any job which a possible immigrant might occupy. No Arab has the right to work in Jewish undertakings."[38]

35. Yigal Allon, *The Making of Israel's Army* (New York: Bantam Books, 1970), p. 7.

36. See Lesch, *Arab Politics*, pp. 44, 45, and 57 on the three concessions.

37. Flapan, *Zionism*, pp. 206-7.

38. George Mansur (Secretary of the Arab Labor Federation in Jaffa), *The Arab Worker under the Palestine Mandate* (Jerusalem: Commercial Press, 1937), p. 28, quoted in Lesch, *Arab Politics*, pp. 45-46.

Finally, the establishment of an all-Jewish, Hebrew-language educational system was an essential component of the upbuilding of the Jewish national home. It helped to create a cohesive national ethos and a lingua franca among the diverse immigrants. However, it also separated Jewish children entirely from Arab children, who attended the governmental schools, and increased the linguistic and cultural gap between the two peoples. In addition, there was a stark contrast in their literacy levels: In 1931, 93 percent of Jewish males (above age seven) were literate, as were 71 percent of Christian males, but only 25 percent of Muslim males were literate. Overall, Arab literacy increased from 19 percent in 1931 to 27 percent by 1940, and only 30 percent of Arab children could be accommodated in government and private schools.[39]

The practical policies of the Zionist movement resulted in the creation of a compact and well-rooted community by the late 1940s. The Yishuv had its own political, educational, economic, and military institutions, parallel to the governmental system. It minimized its contact with the Arab community and outnumbered the Arabs in certain key respects. Jewish urban dwellers, for example, greatly exceeded Arab urbanities, even though Jews comprised but one-third of the population. Many more Jewish children attended school than did Arab children, and Jewish firms employed seven times as many workers as Arab firms. Thus the relative weight and autonomy of the Yishuv was much greater than sheer numbers would suggest. The transition to statehood was facilitated by the existence of the proto-state institutions and a mobilized, literate public. But the separation from the Arab residents was both exacerbated and ensured by these autarchic policies.

Policies toward the Arab Community

The main viewpoint within the Zionist movement was that the Arab problem would be solved by first solving the Jewish problem.[40] In time, the Arabs would be presented with the *fait accompli* of a Jewish majority. Settlements, land purchases, industries, and military forces were developed gradually and systematically so that the Yishuv would become too strong to uproot. In a letter to his son, Weizmann "compared the Arabs of Palestine to the rocks of Judea, as obstacles that had to be cleared on a difficult path."[41] When the Arabs mounted violent protests in 1920, 1921, 1929, 1936-39,

39. Lesch, *Arab Politics,* p. 56; Hurewitz, *Struggle for Palestine,* p. 36.

40. Caplan, *Palestine Jewry,* p. 203.

41. Flapan, *Zionism,* p. 56.

and the late 1940s, the Yishuv sought to curb them by force, rather than look for a political accommodation with the indigenous people. Any concessions made to the Arabs by the British government concerning immigration, land sales, or labor were contested strongly by the Zionist leaders. By 1936, Ben-Gurion stated that the Arabs will only "acquiesce in a Jewish Erez Israel" after they are in a state of "total despair."[42]

Even the acceptance of territorial partition was viewed as a temporary measure: the Jewish community's right to all of Palestine was upheld, even at the expense of the Arabs. Thus Weizmann commented in 1937, "in the course of time we shall expand to the whole country . . . this is only an arrangement for the next 15-30 years."[43] And Ben-Gurion stated in 1938, "after we become a strong force, as a result of the creation of a state, we shall abolish partition and expand to the whole of Palestine."[44]

One method that was adopted in the 1920s in order to reduce Arab opposition was the provision of financial support to Arab political parties, newspapers, and individuals. This was most evident in the establishment and support of the National Muslim Societies (1921-23) and Agricultural Parties (1924-26).[45] These parties were expected to be neutral or positive towards the Zionist movement, in return for which they would receive financial subventions and their members would be helped to obtain jobs and loans: "The establishment of each branch [of the National Muslim Society] was a very practical affair, requiring an initial investment and regular monthly disbursements for the rental of premises and the payment of 'salaries' to local members and organizers. . . . The sympathy and loyalties of those Arabs who joined became precariously dependent on the flow of these subsidies."[46]

This policy was backed by Weizmann, who commented that "extremists and moderates alike were susceptible to the influence of money and honors."[47] But it was denounced by Leonard Stein, a member of the London

42. *Ibid.*, p. 153.

43. *Ibid.*, p. 257.

44. *Ibid.*, p. 265.

45. Lesch, *Arab Politics*, p. 51; Yehoshua Porath, *The Emergence of the Palestinian-Arab National Movement, 1918-1929* (London: Frank Cass, 1974), pp. 219-21, 229-30.

46. Caplan, *Palestine Jewry*, p. 129.

47. Comment to the British High Commissioner, December 11, 1922, quoted in Lesch, *Arab Politics*, p. 52.

office of the Zionist Organization. He argued that the Zionists must seek "a permanent *modus vivendi*" with the Arabs by hiring them in Jewish firms and admitting them to Jewish universities. He maintained that political parties in which "Arab moderates are merely Arab gramophones playing Zionist records" would collapse as soon as Zionist financial support ended.[48] In any event, the Zionist Organization terminated the policy by 1927, as it was in the midst of a financial crisis and as most of the leaders felt that the policy was ineffective.

Some Zionist leaders, such as Stein, argued that the Arab community had to be involved in the practical efforts of the Zionist movement. Chaim Kalvarisky, who initiated the policy of buying support, articulated in 1923 the gap between that ideal and the reality:

> Some people say . . . that only by common work in the field of commerce, industry and agriculture mutual understanding between Jews and Arabs will ultimately be attained. . . . This is, however, merely a theory. In practice we have not done and we are doing nothing for any work in common. How many Arab officials have we installed in our banks? Not even one. How many Arabs have we brought into our schools? Not one. What commercial houses have we established in company with Arabs? Not even one.[49]

Two years later, Kalvarisky lamented: "We all admit the importance of drawing closer to the Arabs, but in fact we are growing more distant like a drawn bow. We have no contact: two separate worlds, each living its own life and fighting the other."[50] Some members of the Yishuv emphasized the need for political relations with the Palestinian Arabs, either to achieve a peacefully negotiated territorial partition (as Nahum Goldmann sought) or a binational state (as *Brith Shalom* and *Hashomer Hatzair* proposed). But few went as far as Dr. Judah L. Magnes, chancellor of the Hebrew University, who argued that Zionism meant simply the creation of a Jewish cultural center in Palestine. In any case, the binationalists had little impact on the political trends and were strongly opposed by the leadership of the Zionist movement.[51]

48. Letter to the Zionist Organization's political officer in Palestine, June 12, 1923, quoted in Lesch, p. 53.

49. Letter to the ZO's political officer in Palestine, July 2, 1923, quoted in Lesch, pp. 52-53.

50. Quoted in Caplan, *Palestine Jewry*, p. 198.

51. Details on binationalism can be found in Susan Lee Hattis, *The Bi-National Idea in Palestine during Mandatory Times* (Haifa: Shikmona Publishing Company, 1970) and Flapan, *Zionism*, pp. 163-87.

In fact, the leaders felt they did not harm the Arabs by blocking them from working in Jewish settlements and industries or even by undermining their majority status. The Arab residents were considered a small part of the large Arab nation, and thus their economic and political needs could be met in that wider context, rather than in Palestine. Arabs could move elsewhere if they sought land, and could merge with Transjordan if they sought political independence.

This thinking led logically to the concept of population transfer. In 1930 Weizmann suggested that the problems of insufficient land resources within Palestine and of the dispossession of peasants could be solved by moving Arabs to Transjordan and Iraq. He urged the Jewish Agency to provide a loan of one million pounds sterling to help move Arab farmers to Transjordan.[52] The issue was discussed at length in the Jewish Agency debates of 1936-37 on partition. At first, the majority proposed a voluntary transfer of Arabs from the Jewish state, but later they realized that the Arabs would never agree to leave voluntarily and therefore key leaders such as Ben-Gurion insisted that compulsory transfer was essential.[53] An Israeli commentator argues:

> the transfer idea played a much greater role in Zionist thinking in the Mandatory Period than is usually admitted. . . . Schemes for transfer cropped up repeatedly in Zionist deliberations on Arab opposition in Palestine. . . . Weizmann and others rejected the argument that the idea of transfer of populations was immoral. The example of the transfer of populations between Greece and Turkey under the auspices of the League of Nations was offered as a precedent. . . . It is not by accident that the idea of transfer was incorporated into the plan for partition of Palestine in 1937.[54]

The fighting from 1947 to 1949 resulted in a far larger transfer than had been envisioned in 1937. It solved the Arab problem by removing most of the Arabs and was the ultimate expression of the policy of *force majeure.*

THE PALESTINIANS IN EXILE

The Palestinian community was shattered by the war of 1948. Some 780,000 of the 1.3 million Arabs (60%) fled from Israeli territory. The Gaza

52. Flapan, *Zionism*, p. 69.

53. *Ibid.*, pp. 248-50, 260-61.

54. *Ibid.*, pp. 82-83.

Strip was overwhelmed by 280,000 people (of whom only 80,000 were local residents) and 350,000 refugees fled to the West Bank of Jordan, which already had 450,000 inhabitants. At least 100,000 escaped to Lebanon and 80,000 to Syria, the rest scattering to other countries.

The situation facing the Palestinians differed considerably in each country. These varying experiences had an impact on the character of each segment of the Palestinian community. However, there were certain common denominators. First, the traditional elite lost its credibility and legitimacy, as its ineffectiveness was blamed for the disaster. But the village-level leadership remained relatively intact through the 1950s, as the clan and village structures were transferred to the refugee camps.[55]

Second, the refugees suffered similar psychological traumas. They felt lost, disoriented, and uprooted from their way of life. Their landless status exacerbated their sense of alienation and lack of self-respect. The older generation waited numbly for "the return"; the young people grew increasingly impatient.

Third, the authorities in most of the host countries were highly suspicious of the refugees and maintained tight control over them. In Israel, this took the form of the fifteen-year military government, which closely regulated the Arabs' movement, limited access to jobs and education, and circumscribed the exercise of political rights.[56] Palestinians living in Syria were given access to jobs and schools alongside Syrian citizens, and many became army officers. The Lebanese authorities, in contrast, were highly restrictive,[57] denying the refugees the right to study in public schools and making it difficult for them to obtain permanent employment. Lebanese troops entered the refugee camps at will to keep the residents subdued.

In the Gaza Strip, after the short-lived experiment of the All-Palestine Government in 1948-49, the Egyptian military government controlled the local governmental, judicial, and educational system. It limited entrance to and exit from the Strip through dispensation of *laissez-passers* (travel passes), which were vital for the stateless residents. Only after Egypt regained the Strip, following the Israeli occupation of October 1956 to March 1957, did the government ease restrictions. A national assembly was

55. Bassem Sirhan, "Palestinian Refugee Camp Life in Lebanon," *Journal of Palestine Studies* (1975), 4(2):101 -2.

56. The situation of the Palestinians within Israel is detailed in section 2.

57. Sirhan, "Palestinian Refugee Camp Life," pp. 95, 99-101; Rosemary Sayigh, "The Palestinian Identity among Camp Residents," *Journal of Palestine Studies* (1977), 6(3):9-10, 17.

formed that year, but elections were supervised closely. In addition, Gaza became a free port, which enabled it to expand commercially even though employment opportunities remained critically limited.

The least abnormal situation was found on the West Bank, where most towns and villages remained intact and only one-third of the refugees settled in refugee camps. Furthermore, both refugees and indigenous residents received Jordanian citizenship after the annexation of the West Bank to Jordan in 1950. That entitled them to passports, which enabled them to travel abroad for employment and schooling. The Jordanian regime also staffed its rapidly growing administrative and educational systems with Palestinians, and encouraged them to develop commercial and industrial enterprises. But most of these businesses had to be established on the east bank, rather than the West Bank. Moreover, the regime never trusted the Palestinians enough to place them at the top of sensitive ministries or to appoint them senior military officers or pilots. The Transjordan Bedouin soldiers who patrolled the West Bank were alien to the Palestinians and reacted sharply to any protests. Nevertheless, a process of "Jordanizing" the Palestinians was noticeable by the 1960s.[58]

The period from the 1949 armistice agreements to the invasion of Sinai in 1956 was troubled by frequent Palestinian infiltration and raids across the lines into Israel, and strong Israeli counterattacks against Arab villages in the West Bank and the Gaza Strip. Israel also encroached upon and occupied demilitarized zones along the border with Egypt and Syria, and activated a sabotage and spy ring in Cairo and Alexandria in July 1954 in order to damage Egyptian relations with Britain and the United States.

During the early 1950s, Israel absorbed a massive influx of Jewish immigrants. The Jewish population, which numbered 680,000 by 1949, more than doubled to 1,404,400 by 1952, with a net immigration of 666,000. Almost half of those immigrants came from the Middle East and North Africa, particularly Yemen, Iraq, Morocco, and Tunisia. They were housed in deserted Arab towns and villages, transit camps, or new development towns along the borders or in the northern Negev. The Israeli government maintained a defensive posture that emphasized immediate response to any Arab incursion. Although the Israeli army was stronger and better equipped than the Arab forces, the Israeli public felt besieged by hostile states and supported the retaliatory measures and the blocking of the

58. Details on Palestinian politics in Jordan can be found in Naseer H. Aruri, *Jordan: A Study in Political Development* (1921-1965) (The Hague: Martinus Nijhoff, 1972); Shaul Mishal, *West Bank/East Bank: The Palestinians in Jordan, 1949-1967* (New Haven: Yale University Press, 1978); and Avi Plascov, *The Palestinian Refugees in Jordan, 1948-1957* (London: Frank Cass, 1981).

return of Palestinian refugees to their homes.

At first, most of the infiltration across the borders was carried out by refugees who were trying to go home, retrieve property from their houses, or pick their crops and fruit. Later, organized bands engaged in sabotage against Israeli settlements. The Jordanian Arab Legion was primarily concentrated in the highlands, and had little ability to check infiltration across the long, hilly armistice line. The government tried to control the border by confiscating arms from villagers and moving refugees away from the border (except in Tulkarem and Qalqilya) to Jericho, in the Jordan Valley.[59] The National Guard, recruited from residents of the border villages, tried to prevent infiltration and protect the residents against Israeli raids, but its men had little training, no transport, and were issued only a few rifles.

The ineffectiveness of this system was exposed by the Israeli attack on Qibya village during the night of October 14/15, 1953, in retaliation for the killing of a woman and two children in Yahud settlement. Unit 101, under the command of Ariel Sharon, blew up forty-two houses and killed more than sixty residents who were trapped inside. The forty-man National Guard unit in Qibya was helpless against the assault. The newly appointed Israeli prime minister, Moshe Sharett, opposed the operation (which had been approved by his predecessor, Ben-Gurion) and warned the cabinet afterwards: "this stain will stick to us and will not be washed away for many years to come."[60] For Jordan, the Qibya raid was a turning point: "there were fierce demonstrations, Western emissaries were stoned, and the cry for revenge was widespread."[61] An Israeli analyst commented:

The frequency and manner of Israel's so-called 'retaliatory actions,' far from achieving their aim of preventing such activities and stimulating tighter control of law and order along the common border by the Jordanian Legion, were counter-productive in that they harmed a Jordanian regime which itself had a direct interest in a quiet border. Furthermore, these retaliatory actions and especially that against Qibya on 14 October 1953 in which many of the village's defenseless inhabitants were killed, exposed the Jordanian government to violent demonstrations and protests against any . . . [resettlement] scheme [for the refugees].[62]

59. Plascov, *Palestinian Refugees in Jordan*, pp. 72-77.

60. Sharett's diary, 18 October 1953, as quoted in Livia Rokach, *Israel's Sacred Terrorism* (Belmont, Mass.: Association of Arab-American University Graduates, Information Paper No. 23, 1980), p. 16.

61. Plascov, *Palestinian Refugees in Jordan*, p. 94.

62. *Ibid.*, p. 90.

The situation was similar in the Gaza Strip, from which there was continual illegal movement of refugees across Israel to the West Bank. In August 1953, Unit 101 attacked the Breij refugee camp. That autumn, the Egyptian military administration imposed sharp penalties for infiltration and blocked access routes to the border. It forcibly dispersed Palestinian demonstrators who demanded arms and protested Egyptian plans to transfer some of the refugees to el-Arish, in Sinai. In January 1955, the Egyptian government imposed a sunset-to-dawn curfew on movement on the entire Strip east of the Gaza-Rafah road, and ordered its army to fire on any infiltrators.[63]

Nevertheless, as soon as Ben-Gurion returned to the Israeli cabinet as minister of defense, he authorized a major military attack on Gaza. That nighttime assault on February 28, 1955, caused thirty-nine deaths and destroyed prospects for a *modus vivendi* with Egypt. Sharett commented in his diary that the American ambassador believed that fear

> has seized the Arab world due to Ben Gurion's comeback. The Gaza attack is interpreted as signalling a decision on our part to attack on all fronts. The Americans, too, are afraid that it will lead to a new conflagration in the Middle East which will blow up all their plans. Therefore they wish to obtain from us a definite commitment that similar actions will not be repeated.[64]

At the cabinet meeting on March 25, Ben-Gurion proposed that Israel occupy the Gaza Strip after declaring the armistice agreement no longer valid, and then cause most of the refugees to flee from the Strip to Sinai or Jordan. Sharett criticized Ben-Gurion bitterly in his diary: Even if most of the refugees should flee, "we shall still have 100,000 of them in the Strip, and it is easy to imagine what means we shall resort to in order to repress them and what waves of hatred we shall create again."[65] He argued:

> what we succeeded in achieving . . . in 1948, cannot be repeated. . . .Today we must accept our existing frontiers and try to relax the tensions with our neighbors to prepare the ground for peace and strengthen our relations with the Powers. . . . The occupation of the Gaza Strip will not resolve any security problem, as the refugees . . . will continue to constitute the same trouble, and even more so, as their hate will be rekindled by the atrocities that we shall cause them to suffer during the occupation.[66]

63. Rokach, *Israel's Sacred Terrorism*, p. 58.

64. Sharett's Diary, 12 March 1955, quoted in Rokach, p. 43.

65. *Ibid.*, 27 March 1955, p. 48.

66. *Ibid.*, 29 March 1955.

By May 1955 public pressure compelled the Egyptian government to let Palestinian commando units operate from the Gaza Strip, and in September Egypt signed an arms deal with Czechoslovakia. Two months later Sharett was replaced as prime minister by Ben-Gurion, and in June 1956 Sharett lost the foreign minister's portfolio as well. By then, plans were well underway for the occupation of the Gaza Strip and Sinai. Egypt's nationalization of the Suez Canal in July won over France and Britain to the idea of an armed attack, thus providing Israel with international backing for its operation. But the United States deprived the three states of the spoils of their war in October 1956: France and Britain had to evacuate the Suez Canal area and Israel relinquished Sinai and the Gaza Strip. A UN Emergency Force was placed on the Egyptian side of the border to enforce the truce.

The border remained relatively quiet until the mid-1960s. In 1964, Israel's construction of a national water carrier to siphon water from the Jordan River for use in the Negev desert caused an outcry in the Arab world. Not only might the carrier drain water from the Jordanian-controlled section of the river, but it would also enable Israel to consolidate its hold over the Negev by expanding settlements there. The Arab League announced counterplans to divert the headwaters of the Jordan River, parts of which were controlled by Syria on Mt. Hermon and the Golan Heights.

In the meantime, many Palestinians were becoming disillusioned with the Arab regimes, which promised to liberate Palestine but failed to take effective steps against Israel. Moreover, the hope that Arab unity would enhance their cause was dashed when the Egyptian-Syrian union broke up in 1961, after only three years, and Egypt became embroiled in the civil war in North Yemen. In contrast, the Algerians won their independence in 1962 after a lengthy rebellion, which indicated to Palestinians that they should also take the initiative themselves. In fact, underground guerrilla cells were formed in the early 1960s. Fatah, established by young professionals from Gaza who were working in Kuwait, made its first commando strike into Israel in January 1965 – hitting at the national water carrier.[67]

The *fedayiin* (commandos) wanted to catalyze the Arab world into action. But the Arab regimes tried to channel the Palestinian discontent into a less militant form by establishing the Palestine Liberation Organization (PLO) in 1964. Its founding congress in Jerusalem brought together 422 delegates from all the countries (except Israel) where Palestinians resided. The Palestinian mayors on the West Bank and Palestinian representatives of the

67. On the founding and initial years of Fatah, see Abu Iyad with Eric Rouleau, *My Home, My Land: A Narrative of the Palestinian Struggle* (New York: Times Books, 1981), pp. 27-29, 34-37, 41-44.

Jordanian parliament attended, but so did members of Fatah. It was the first time since the late 1930s that the Palestinian elite had been able to meet and articulate a common program. This was a crucial step in the process of reestablishing Palestinian political identity and defining its aims. The PLO adopted an uncompromising charter, wishfully rewriting history and seeking a return to the *status quo* before 1948.

Fatah raids increased in 1965 and 1966: small bands crossed from Syria through Jordan to hit inside Israel. Instead of retaliating against Syria, Israel struck against Jordanian villages. The most massive attack came on November 13, 1966,[68] when Israeli army units entered es-Samu, on the southern edge of the West Bank. The soldiers killed 18 people, wounded 130, and demolished 125 houses, including the school, clinic, and mosque. This triggered demonstrations in Jordan against the lack of effective protection provided by the government, and demands that Palestinians be issued weapons to protect themselves.

In order to deflect attention from himself, King Hussein criticized Syria and Egypt for not assuming their responsibilities in the struggle with Israel. In particular, he accused Egypt of hiding behind the UN Emergency Force. Air raids by Israel in late November against the Syrian water diversion project were followed by artillery and air battles in the spring of 1967, marking a rapid escalation of the confrontation. By June, Egypt took steps that were viewed in Israel as *casus belli*:[69] concentrating troops in Sinai, withdrawing UN forces, blockading the Straits of Tiran on the Gulf of Aqaba (the only access for Eilat), and joining Syria and Jordan in a military union. These challenges precipitated Israel's full-scale mobilization and attack. The June War had a devastating impact: The Golan Heights, Sinai, the Gaza Strip, and the West Bank were occupied by Israel in a six-day blitz. All of the Palestinian territory fell under Israeli control and almost half of the Palestinian people came under Israeli rule. The Arab armed forces were discredited and the *fedayiin* assumed control of the PLO.

CONCLUSION

The land and people of Palestine were transformed over the span of fifty years, from the announcement of the Balfour Declaration in 1917 to the occupation of the West Bank and Gaza Strip in 1967. The idea of a Jewish

68. Shlomo Aronson, *Conflict and Bargaining in the Middle East: An Israeli Perspective* (Baltimore: Johns Hopkins Press, 1978), p. 59.

69. *Ibid.*, p. 57.

majority and Jewish state, seemingly utopian in 1917, became a reality three decades later. Twenty years after that Israel gained control over the remaining portions of Palestine, and extended its reach into parts of Egypt and Syria in pursuit of its elusive goal of security. Israeli leaders failed to perceive that security could not be achieved by military means alone but rather required a serious effort to accommodate the aspirations of the Palestinians and the Arab world. The emphasis on achieving military preeminence in the region turned Israel into a garrison state. The war of 1967, which brought Israel face to face with Palestinian society, opened up the possibility of a radical change in Israeli perception and policy. The failure of Israel to awaken to that challenge and the triumph of the annexationist trend form the core of the following chapters in this volume.

CHAPTER 3

CLASS STRUCTURE AND THE POLITICAL ELITE IN THE GAZA STRIP: 1948 - 1988

Ziad Abu-Amr

This study deals with class structure and its relationship to political power in the Gaza Strip during two successive periods: 1948 to 1967 and 1967 to 1988. This is a complex undertaking: prior to 1967, Gaza was under Egyptian administration, and political authority did not directly reflect the interests of any of the indigenous social classes. At least theoretically, political authority was divorced from the social class structure. The same may be said today of the Israeli-occupied Gaza Strip.

Socially, the Gaza Strip is divided into two distinct communities: the original inhabitants of both the cities and the countryside, and the refugees living in the camps. The original inhabitants constitute one-third of the entire population, with the refugee community constituting the remaining two-thirds. Although the original inhabitants and the refugees at first formed two distinct communities, a gradual process of interaction and integration has taken place. This process has not, however, succeeded in eradicating the unique characteristics of each community.

During the first period (1948 to 1967), the Gaza economy was distorted by two main factors: the sudden and arbitrary separation of the Strip from the rest of Palestine, and the subsequent collapse of local infrastructures, a phenomenon aggravated by the area's limited resources. A major cause of the infrastructural collapse was the acute demographic imbalance that followed the 1948 influx of some one hundred thousand and fifty refugees from various Palestinian towns and villages. Under Egyptian rule, economic conditions improved slightly, but the Gaza economy continued to suffer from overpopulation, scarcity of resources, lack of economic planning and development, and a dearth of productive sectors. Economic distortion during the second period (1967 to 1988), marked by the 1967 war and the annexation of the Gaza economy to that of Israel, ultimately resulted in Gaza's virtually complete dependence on the more well-developed Israeli economy.

All of these factors contributed in retarding the emergence of well-defined social classes. The study of social classes in the Gaza Strip is further complicated by the fact that classical schemes cannot readily be applied to Gazan realities. Because of interrelationships existing among the various modes of production, it is difficult to establish strict lines of demarcation between Gazan social classes. For example, at the same time that small industry, trade, and monetary exchange were carried out in the city, and while large landowners and merchants were establishing connections to the world capitalist market (through citrus export and the import of consumer goods), primitive agriculture remained a major economic activity for village inhabitants. Some forms of barter existed in parts of the countryside until 1967 and even later. Furthermore, a clear interlocking existed between the landowning and the merchant segments; they were involved in virtually the same economic activity.

Yet despite these difficulties in defining strict social class demarcations in the Gaza Strip, four major classes may be distinguished: large landowners and merchants, the petty bourgeoisie, the workers, and the peasants.

LANDOWNERS AND MERCHANTS

This class is comprised of two segments, whose members share common interests and social relationships and are engaged in a duality of economic activities.

Landowners

Most of those with extensive landholdings are original inhabitants of the Gaza Strip. Social conditions and relationships prevailing in the Strip prior to 1967 constituted an extension of semi feudal relationships operating in Palestine's southern province (the Beer Sheba and Gaza districts) prior to 1948. Before 1948, the combined landholdings of twenty-eight individuals in this province amounted to two million dunums (1 dunum=1/4 acre). Eleven of these individuals owned one hundred thousand dunums each; another seven owned between thirty and one hundred thousand each.[1]

---

1. Hussein Abu al-Namil, *Qita Ghazza: 1948-1967* [The Gaza Strip: 1948-1967] (Beirut: The Research Center, the Palestine Liberation Organization, 1979), p. 322; originally quoted from A. Granott, *The Land System in Palestine* (London: Eyre and Spottiswood, 1952), p. 29.

Palestinian feudal lords owned entire villages and their authority extended even beyond these to other villages.

One consequence of the 1948 war was the disappearance of large feudal estates in the southern province. For example, the landholdings of families such as the Shawwa family, which had reached close to one hundred thousands dunums in the 1870s,[2] were reduced to less than one thousand dunums inside the borders of the Gaza Strip.

Despite the loss of many of their feudal estates, the landowning families continued to enjoy great influence. The former landlords have not easily relinquished their feudal mentality in dealing with the other social classes, nor has it been easy for the residents of the Strip, particularly in the countryside, to stop viewing these landowners as masters. However, the disappearance of the material basis for feudalism did contribute to a weakening of existing social relationships. The new situation forced the large landowners to seek to maintain their power by extending their activities to trade and by consolidating relationships with the existing administrative and political authorities.

In the Gaza Strip from 1948 to the present, landholdings of five hundred dunums or more have been confined to about thirty families. These families, mostly orange-grove owners, reside in various areas of the Strip. The landholdings of some of these families amount to several thousand dunums. Combined landholdings of these thirty families range between twenty-five and thirty thousand dunums, which represents about one-quarter of the agricultural land in the Strip. Some landowners do not work in agriculture, but others are both actual owners and capitalist farmers at the same time.

Many changes have affected the landowner class since 1967. New elements have joined this segment, primarily merchants who used part of their accumulating capital to purchase land. At the same time, in the face of deteriorating and unstable economic conditions under Israeli occupation, a number of landowners have been forced to sell sections of their land in order to maintain their accustomed standards of living. Land has also been sold to enable reinvestment in agricultural land or real estate or to capitalize investment projects inside or outside the Strip. The breakup of large landholdings for construction purposes or because of divided inheritances has led to a situation in which few individual holdings today exceed two hundred dunums. And just as many merchants have come to combine two economic activities, a number of landowners have also sought to combine business with the ownership of agricultural lands (particularly citrus).

2. Pamela-Ann Smith, *Palestine and the Palestinians, 1876-1983* (New York: St. Martin's, 1984), p. 13.

Although members of this class have not attempted to confront the occupation authorities, largely because of the need for access to Israeli ports and foreign markets for their products, they live under a constant threat from continued occupation of the Strip. Among other things, the occupation holds for them the possibility of land confiscation, especially with an active Israeli settlement policy. Their interests are further harmed by unfair competition from Israeli farmers, who receive subsidies and other privileges denied their Gazan counterparts. Yet despite threats to its power base, the landowner segment has managed to maintain a relatively secure existence.

Merchants.

The period following 1948 witnessed stagnation in the commercial activity of the Gaza Strip, as commercial relations between the Strip and the rest of Palestine were abruptly broken off. Internal trade was also weakened, owing to a deterioration in the standard of living for refugees and nonrefugees alike. Economic conditions continued to deteriorate until the mid-1950s, when the Egyptian administration opened the Strip for free external trade. The Egyptians believed that opening the Strip for free trade, perhaps even transforming it into a free economic zone like Hong Kong, would help solve some Egyptian economic problems. There was also a wish to "tame" the Strip by allowing it to flourish economically, thereby lessening the impact of conditions conducive to the rise and development of political opposition movements. And perhaps it was hoped that a new social class would emerge that could rival the power of the traditional landowner segment, rendering it easier for the Egyptians to restrain and control the traditional elements when necessary.

Thus, in early 1955, the Egyptian administration established a chamber of commerce in Gaza. Foreign trade was also encouraged, by making Gaza a semifree port. Merchants were granted special import and export privileges. In the period from 1958 to 1967, the merchant class (including landowners engaged in commercial business) flourished, becoming the most powerful and influential social segment in the Strip.

These merchants came from various parts of the Strip, but mainly from Gaza city. Both before and after 1967, citrus export formed the backbone of Gaza's trade. In 1966, citrus accounted for approximately 90 percent of the Strip's total exports.[3] In fact, imports were financed by revenues from the exported citrus; Gaza's importers were none other than the exporters of citrus, the only individuals in the Strip financially capable of engaging in external trade.

3. Al-Namil, *Qita Ghazza*, p. 268.

Merchants in the Strip capitalized on the special relationship between Gaza and Egypt and the related opportunities thereby provided for increased profit. Essentially to satisfy the needs of the Egyptian market, they imported consumer goods, which were then transported to Egypt by various means – either smuggled or hand-carried by "suitcase vendors" (Gazans who traveled regularly to Egypt with suitcases full of consumer items imported from abroad, such as transistor radios, batteries, whiskey and similar items). Another means through which Gaza's goods made their way into Egypt was via Egyptian tourists, who visited the Strip in increasing numbers [4]

The fact that an increasingly large number of Gaza residents were employed abroad contributed to the rise and prosperity of the landowner/merchant class. The merchants acted as middlemen, transferring the earnings of these employees to their families in the Strip. Those working abroad eschewed official means of transferring funds, as these entailed financial loss. The merchants obliged them by exchanging their foreign earnings at black-market rates, though of course skimming off part of the profits for themselves. These hard currency earnings were of further benefit to the merchants when deposited in foreign banks and used in external trade. These merchants, in their role as bankers and money brokers, were indispensible for Gaza money transfers, since no alternative mechanism was available. The money transfer, in turn, increased expenditure and purchase power and consequently stimulated internal trade in the Strip. Landowner/merchants also controlled official banking activity, as they held a majority on the board of the Bank of Palestine, the only local bank in Gaza.

After 1967, a number of changes ensued that affected both the commercial situation and that of the influential merchants in the Strip. The Strip lost its free port, as well as the commercial privileges granted by the Egyptian authorities. The Strip was also denied intercourse with Egyptian markets and with Egyptian tourists visiting the Strip. The volume of citrus exports decreased from 260 thousand tons prior to 1967 to 140 thousand tons at present, owing to the Strip's loss of its traditional markets in the wake of Israeli-imposed restrictions. As a result, the number of citrus merchants decreased. Some have turned to the Israeli market to compete with their better equipped Israeli counterparts, who are subject to fewer restrictions and have a monopoly over trade. The Israeli authorities have imposed heavy customs duties on imports from abroad, as well as what is called the Value Added Tax (VAT) on those engaged in internal trade. A

---

4. In 1958, the number of Egyptian tourists to Gaza was about four thousand, in 1960 twelve thousand, and in 1961 seventeen thousand. Al-Namil, *Qita Ghazza*, p. 271.

number of merchants have consequently been forced to give up trade with foreign countries and have turned instead to imports from the Israeli market. Israeli policies have contributed to the deterioration of commercial conditions in the Strip, which has in turn forced a number of merchants to close their commercial businesses. A number of merchants have emigrated from the Strip – with their capital – to Cairo and Amman, where they have invested in real estate trade and agriculture. And a new segment has emerged from the landowner/merchant class whose members have come to dominate foreign and local trade by becoming agents for foreign and Israeli products and companies. These agents represent such organizations as General Motors, Mercedes, Volkswagen, and Diahatsu; a number of Israeli companies and businesses also have local Gaza agents. A new segment of mid-sized retail and wholesale merchants has also joined this subclass.

Essentially, it was the occupation authorities, using the granting of licenses to co-opt some individuals and to appease or return favors to others, who determined who would constitute the members of this group. The emergence and quick success of this segment, closely linked to the Israeli economy and the occupation authorities, has weakened traditional social classes and laid the basis for the emergence of a middle bourgeoisie class. The favorable position attained by this new segment has induced some landowners and merchants to engage in similar economic activities as the quickest means to profit.

After the occupation, there also emerged another new group, the money changers, which did not exist in the Strip prior to 1967, or at least not in the same number as today. Although the money-changing establishments work illegally, the Israeli authorities turn a blind eye to their activities.

A new group of land and real estate traders has also emerged. Since 1967, the activities of some of these brokers have been characterized by a certain degree of obscurity, due to intense competition and other factors.

In the years following 1967, a number of citrus packing and waxing factories were established, owned by members of the landowner/merchant class. Prior to 1967, there had existed a number of carbonated water factories in the Strip, owned by members of the same class.

The economic activity of merchants of various kinds and sizes has been controlled by the principles of maximum profit with minimum risk and studied avoidance of long-term investment projects. At best, these merchants have invested some of their capital in real estate and in purchasing lands and buildings, particularly in commercial areas.

Since 1967, a relatively few citrus merchants have monopolized the citrus trade, exploiting small producers and blocking their access to international markets. These merchants have sometimes succeeded in obtaining long-term leases on smaller farms, capitalizing on the pressing financial needs of the small farmers. The economics of large-scale production could in most cases effectively shut out the small producer from competition in international markets.

THE PETTY BOURGEOISIE

The conditions prevailing in the Gaza Strip and the limited resources of the Strip itself did not allow the emergence of a large middle class. Nonetheless, there did exist a small class of landowners and merchants with relatively high income (farm owners, store owners, bureaucrats, and professionals such as lawyers, doctors, engineers) who could be said to constitute a small middle class. In the period following the 1967 war, some newly rich individuals joined this class. Yet unless their high income relative to that of the petty bourgeoisie is taken as a criterion for classification, members of this group do not constitute a class per se.

In the Gaza Strip context, it is more appropriate to speak of a petty bourgeoisie, taking into account the different levels of income in its various segments. Both prior to and since 1967, the petty bourgeoisie class in the Strip has been comprised of several heterogeneous social segments; members come from different social and economic backgrounds and from different geographic locations (cities, villages, and refugee camps). Numbered among its members are those who own their means of production, as well as those who are classified as petty bourgeois because of their professions. Generally speaking, this class encompasses three main segments: professionals, small merchants and craftsmen, and small contractors and service workers.

Professionals. This group is made up of such workers as engineers, doctors, lawyers, teachers, and executives working in government departments and the United Nations Relief and Works Agency (UNRWA). It is the largest group among the segments that constitute the petty bourgeoisie class.

Small merchants and craftsmen. The flourishing of trade, exports, and imports in the Strip prior to 1967 led to an increase in the number of merchants of various types. In 1967, these numbered 1550.[5] The number of commercial shops increased from two thousand in 1962 to ten thousand in 1966.[6] Despite a first impression that these figures reflect a state of relative prosperity, there is also a negative element: the flourishing of foreign trade

5. Interview with Raghib Murtaja, head of the Gaza Chamber of Commerce, Gaza, December 1987.

6. Al-Namil, *Qita Ghazza*, p. 271.

impeded the development of local industries and of a working class. After 1967, as a result of the Israeli occupation of the Strip and its consequences, half the commercial shops that had existed prior to 1967 were closed.[7] This, however, did not greatly affect the total number of those working in trade, since peddlers replaced merchants working in commercial shops.

Small contractors and those working in the service sector. Change occurred in this segment due to a decline in work opportunities, resulting from Israeli competition. Members of this segment were therefore forced to join the Israeli labor market as wage laborers.

The petty bourgeoisie class emerged mainly because of the increased availability of educational opportunities in the Strip and because new social forces did not emerge due to the high rate of unemployment among refugees. The absence of a distinct and well-defined social class structure made education a significant criterion for social stratification.[8]

The petty bourgeois class plays a central role in conducting the various affairs of society in the Gaza Strip. Yet the central position of this class has not translated into a significant political role, as the fragmentation of its various segments does not encourage class consciousness or organization. Hence, some senior employees, administrators, and professionals have sympathized strongly with the large landowner/merchant class, whereas others of modest income and humbler socioeconomic origins have sympathized more closely with the working and peasant classes. The petty bourgeoisie class has been further weakened by the ongoing and steadily increasing emigration of its members in search of work abroad. Thus, its role under the occupation has been minimal.

THE WORKING CLASS

Most members of the working class came from peasant origins subsequent to the uprooting of Palestinian peasants following the 1948 war. Yet because of the small area of agricultural land in the Strip, refugees originally from the countryside could not return to the peasant life style. Therefore, many of these refugees were hired as agricultural workers. The presence of a large pool of cheap labor encouraged large landowners to reclaim and cultivate additional sections of their landholdings.

Cheap and abundant labor also encouraged capitalists to develop local industries.[9] Some of the refugees from the cities were technically and

7. Murtaja interview.

8. See also discussion by Sara Graham-Brown, p. 361 of this volume.

9. Smith, *Palestine and the Palestinians,* p. 77.

professionally experienced; they could therefore be described as skilled laborers. Before emigrating to the Strip, these laborers had worked in ports, factories, industrial workshops, and British army camps.

In the period from 1948 to 1967, most workers were employed in building projects, road construction, and services. Yet such tasks absorbed only a small portion of the labor pool; consequently, a large number of laborers were forced to emigrate from the Strip to Egypt, Saudi Arabia, and other gulf states in search of work opportunities.

The working class in the Gaza Strip prior to 1967 can be divided into three segments: skilled laborers, unskilled laborers, and agricultural laborers.

Skilled laborers. Skilled laborers are those workers with certain technical skills or qualifications in the fields of industry, agriculture, and services. There were few such laborers, and most were refugees. Before emigrating to the Strip, these workers had had the opportunity to work in technical areas; while in Palestine, they had worked in industrial centers and British army camps.

UNRWA absorbed a portion of this segment within its institutions. Over the past years, the UNRWA industrial school has also graduated (and is still graduating) technical laborers. Other skilled laborers from Palestine worked in trades such as smithcraft, carpentry, car repair and the like. The segment of skilled laborers also included a small number of original inhabitants of the Strip, who had previously worked in British army camps in Palestine. The segment of skilled laborers also included craftsmen and manual workers employed in spinning, weaving, and handicrafts, such as cane furnituremaking and pottery.

Unskilled laborers. Most members of the working class in the Gaza Strip belonged to this segment; most were refugee camp residents. Unskilled laborers worked in road construction, housing construction, agricultural services, and in seasonal temporary and manual labor. A number also worked on construction projects in the Sinai desert (road and airport construction) with Palestinian contractors and in the Aswan area on the High Dam project.

Agricultural laborers. This segment of workers did not constitute a solid labor force due to its small size and to the seasonal nature of its work. The majority of small landowners in the Strip cultivated the land themselves or with the assistance of members of their families. Therefore work opportunities on small agricultural landholdings were limited. Small farmers could not afford to recruit manpower which entailed additional costs. Their income was limited; after covering expenses, a small farmer did not earn more than a wage worker, and perhaps even less.[10] Workers

10. Al-Namil, *Qita Ghazza,* p. 315.

were recruited only in rare cases, particularly during harvest. Only large landowners (owners of orange groves) regularly hired agricultural workers. Most of the recruited agricultural laborers were refugees, as the majority of refugees in the Strip came from the countryside and were experienced in agricultural matters. High rates of unemployment meant cheap labor.

The size of the working class in the Strip prior to 1967 was small, owing to the absence of productive industrial activities and the high percentage of unemployment among those of working age, refugees and nonrefugees alike. Until 1960, the percentage of unemployment among the original inhabitants of the Strip was 35 percent (23,600 workers) and among refugees 83 percent (64,500 workers).[11]

Since 1967, the working class in the Strip has been subjected to two forms of oppression simultaneously, national oppression as well as social oppression. During the years of Israeli occupation, the working class has undergone a number of structural changes. Shortly after the occupation with the opening of the Israeli labor market, the size of the working class increased. Meanwhile, a large number of individuals belonging to various segments of the petty bourgeois class joined the working class, as a result of a deterioration in their economic conditions. In 1987, the number of those working in Israel reached about 45.9 thousand workers,[12] in addition to the almost ten to twenty thousand workers who were drawn to Israel from the black market.[13] These constitute over 50 percent of the overall labor force in the Strip, which reached 99.7 thousand in 1987.[14]

Expansion in the construction industry and other economic activities inside the Strip, in Israel itself, and in settlements established in the West Bank and the Gaza Strip contributed to the noticeable expansion in the size of the working class.

The dependence of the working class on the Israeli labor market and the fluctuating Israeli economy resulted in a state of uncertainty and anxiety characterizing the conditions of the working class, which expanded and contracted for reasons beyond its control. Furthermore, the needs of the

11. Mohamed Ali Khulusi, *At-Tanmiya al-Iqtisadiyya fi Qita Ghazza: 1948-1962* (Economic Development in the Gaza Strip: 1948-1962). (Cairo: The United Commercial Printhouse, 1967), pp. 22, 64.

12. *Judea, Samaria and Gaza Area Statistics* (Jerusalem: Israel Central Bureau of Statistics, 1987), no. 3, p. 35.

13. Sara Roy, *The Gaza Strip Survey* (Jerusalem: The Jerusalem Post, 1986), p. 33.

14. *Judea, Samaria and Gaza Area Statistics,* no. 3, p. 31.

Israeli market determined and controlled the formation of certain trends within the working class. On the employment level, the need for construction workers in Israel increased the number of this type of worker within the working class. Construction workers comprised 45.1 percent of the total number of workers from the Strip employed in Israel.[15]

The dependency and frustration engendered by the continued occupation fostered certain social, moral, and behavioral trends, until then virtually unknown in the Strip. Strong consumer tendencies, deterioration of moral values, the use of drugs, and frequent visits to brothels in Israel became common among increasing numbers of workers.

Subsequent to the occupation, about half of Gaza's manpower worked outside the Strip for Israeli employers. The Strip's workers (particularly those from the black market) were denied political and trade union protection. Some Israeli employers in fact favored recruitment from the black market, as it relieved them from certain otherwise necessary payments. For various reasons (fear, need, unemployment, ignorance, lack of organization, etc.), the workers themselves also accepted such conditions, believing, for example, that not demanding their rights would exempt them from taxes and other pay deductions such as those for insurance and social security.

The Strip's workers in Israel are paid much less than their Israeli counterparts. One source points out that the average wage of a worker from the occupied territories working in Israel hardly reaches 36 percent of the wage of a comparable Israeli worker.[16]

Laborers from the occupied territories recruited by labor offices, those of the Gaza Strip included, pay up to 30 percent of their wages as taxes and installments for social security, without receiving the same benefits their Israeli counterparts receive, particularly bonuses, sick leave, and unemployment or disability benefits.[17]

Among other structural changes is the entry of increasing numbers of women and children into the labor force. Many are to be found working in Israel. In the Strip, they work on farms and fields, in factories and workshops. Yet, sources indicate that the average number of working women fourteen years and older decreased from 6 percent in 1969 to 3.3

15. Roy, *Gaza Strip Survey*, , p. 33.

16. Taysir Aruri, "Al-Muqtataat min Ujur Ummal al-Manateq al-Muhtalla al-Amileen fi Israel" (Cuts from the Wages of Workers of the Occupied Territories Working in Israel), *al-Katib* (Jerusalem, October 1984), 54:26.

17. Roy, *Gaza Strip Survey*, p. 35.

percent of the same age group in 1984, despite the fact that women constitute 10 percent of the overall labor force in the Strip.[18] These figures, however, do not take into account the thousands of women working on their families' lands (orchards, fields, produce farms, chicken and rabbit farms, etc.). The figures also do not include those women engaged in seasonal work (such as reaping and selling fruits and vegetables) or those working in the area of trade, selling ready-made clothes or textiles. The rate of unemployed women increases as males lose their jobs in Israel, as the latter often return to seek work in the Strip where they are given priority.

As for child workers, these are employed as agricultural laborers in settlements and on Israeli farms in the Strip and in Israel. Sources point out that about 20 percent of the black market workers are 17 years old or younger.[19]

THE PEASANTRY

The peasant class was originally small in proportion to the overall population and was comprised mostly of the original residents of the Gaza Strip, who owned and worked small areas of cultivated land themselves or sometimes with the help of a few wage laborers. About two-thirds of the population, the refugees, did not own cultivable land. This situation led to the emergence of only a small class of agricultural wage laborers rather than to the creation of a peasant class of any considerable significance

The peasant class in Gaza can, however, be divided into four segments on the basis of size and type of landholding.

Peasants with mid-sized holdings. The landholdings of these peasants ranged between ten and fifty dunums. Due to the limited amount of land in the Strip, there were few members of this segment. Whether or not they hired agricultural laborers depended on the use to which their lands were put and on the types of agricultural produce they grew: in intensive agriculture and citrus growing, more agricultural workers were used. In any case, this hiring was limited, as middle-level peasants themselves worked with their families on their lands.

Peasants with small holdings. The landholdings of these peasants did not exceed a few dunums (ten and below). Most of the Strip's original

18. *Ibid.*, p. 27.

19. Musa Budeiri, "Changes in the Economic Structure of the West Bank and Gaza under Israeli Occupation," *Labor, Capital and Society* (April 1982), 15(1):51.

inhabitants in the countryside knew one form of agricultural cultivation or another, no matter how small the area was. This segment, considered one of the largest in the Strip, depended on its small plot of land as a source of livelihood, utilizing this property in seasonal agriculture. Owners of larger properties within this segment turned their land into small citrus groves, using artesian wells for irrigation. A water well would be dug jointly by a number of small landowning peasants to make the project feasible. As for the owners of smaller properties, these depended for their subsistence on their small holdings supplemented by home gardens, which were planted with vegetables to supply the family's needs. These peasant families also raised poultry for home consumption or as an additional source of income.

This segment, the majority of which came from the Strip's original inhabitants, contracted just prior to and after the occupation for several reasons, but mainly because the poor economic conditions in the Strip forced some landowners to sell part or all of their property to provide for daily needs or to fulfill other social commitments, such as building homes or educating or marrying off their children.

Land tenants. Members of this segment rented land from owners for fixed sums of money and cultivated it on their own, or marketed the produce, as in the case of citrus, fruit, and vegetable farms. Members of this segment were drawn from the original inhabitants of the Strip as well as from the refugees.

Sharecroppers. These worked on the land for a certain proportion of the crop. It has become the smallest segment as this form of partnership is disappearing.

Owing to the constant increase in the population, vast areas of agricultural land have been converted into residential areas. The Israeli authorities' expropriation of large areas of land in the Strip for settlement purposes and the issuing of restrictive military orders concerning water use, agriculture, and marketing have prevented the expansion of the peasant class and even prevented this class from maintaining its preoccupation size. Some peasants in the Strip have been forced to quit farming their land or working in agriculture, turning instead to the Israeli labor market. The peasant class was further weakened by the deterioration of agriculture due to such factors as the limited capabilities of farmers, Israeli competition, the high cost of agricultural labor, marketing problems, and the high probability of financial loss.

CONSTRAINTS ON CLASS CONFLICT

A number of factors have contributed to the rather static social situation in the Strip, and have restrained any development of class conflict.

First was the character of the social structure before 1967. The role of the family, the clan, the tribe, and their heads was very prominent; no major socioeconomic transformation had taken place. The traditional social structure remained intact and horizontal integration was very slow. The populations of the city and the countryside remained relatively isolated from each other; social relations and interaction between the urban and rural communities remained minimal. This situation continued until 1967, when the traditional social structure was disrupted by the 1967 war and the Israeli occupation of the Strip, and later by the emergence of Palestinian armed resistance and the spread of political movements.

The nationalist struggle against the Israeli occupation put a damper on class conflict, or at least relegated it to a side burner. The landowner/merchant class, for its part, tried to maintain and enforce existing vertical social relations. During a violent confrontation between nationalist and religious factions in Gaza in 1986, for example, Rashad al-Shawwa, a traditional leader, called upon heads of families and clans to control their followings. He said: "Each clan should have a patron, and all of those patrons should have a patron."

Second, there were few socioeconomic interrelationships among the classes. The landowner/merchant class monopolized all economic activity in the city that was of a commercial nature. The peasants, for their part, were involved in their agricultural activities and were mainly restricted to the countryside. As for the refugee camp inhabitants, they essentially depended on UNRWA for subsistence. Productive sectors were either marginal or did not exist at all. Major contradictions between the employer and the employed did not evolve, and a social class consciousness did not emerge. An additional dimension was added to this situation after 1967: about half the working class in the Strip left the local environment for work inside Israel. These workers became subject to social as well as national oppression.

Third, the need to mobilize all potentials for national liberation played an important role in restraining social class conflict. This tendency was enforced by the nationalist ideologies prevailing in the region, and in the Strip in particular. Even the Communists in the Strip, the political group most interested in class conflict, gave the nationalist issue top priority and relegated class struggle to a secondary position. This attitude was shared by all political groups.

Other factors contributed to social stasis. The continuous emigration from the Strip of young and educated elements in search of employment has deprived the area of a potential political vanguard that could have played an important role in the social struggle. Also, the Strip lacked a socialist ideological tradition; embryonic socialist tendencies were subjected to successive blows, as illustrated by the persecution of Communists dating back to 1948. Finally, the presence of the Egyptian administration and its monopoly on political authority in the Strip until 1967 was an effective restraint on class conflict. This administration was prepared to intervene directly to impede the development of such conflict; it defended the interests of the influential upper class and oppressed the lower classes by banning their political activities. Any criticism or dissent was interpreted as directed against the Egyptian administration, rather than at the social class hiding behind it, which enjoyed the lion's share of political authority and economic influence without being held accountable. Furthermore, the Egyptian administration used the threat posed by Israel as a pretext for restricting political freedom. Political activities and political opposition were weakened by Nasser's overwhelming popularity in the late 1950s and 1960s.

THE POLITICAL ELITE IN THE GAZA STRIP

With regard to political authority in the Gaza Strip, it must be stressed that we are not dealing with a classical pattern. Political authorities usually express the interests of the most influential class or classes in society. Yet, the political authority in the Strip has not been national, but external, and the interests of those in power have not always coincided with the interests of the ruling classes. This of course applies to both the Egyptian administration (prior to 1967) and to the Israeli occupation authorities (since 1967).

In the context of this study, the political elite will be defined not only as those exercising political influence within existing frameworks or structures (i.e., holding office in the government or in political, legislative, and administrative bodies belonging to the government), but also as those who are considered representatives of the political opposition inside and outside the existing official frameworks.

Before 1967

Prior to 1967, most members of the political elite in the ruling apparatus were drawn from the landowner/merchant class. The influence of this class, particularly that of the large landowners, goes back to a period prior to 1948 and has continued with some fluctuation until today. The longevity of the influence the landed families have enjoyed is closely linked to the relationships they have established with successive governments (British Mandate, Egyptian administration, and Israeli occupation), though this is not to say that members of this class are devoid of national aspirations or have failed to play, on various occasions and in their own ways, national roles.

The Egyptian administration promoted the leadership role of both the influential landed families and the large merchants, vesting more influence in this traditional leadership so that it might in turn confront the growing popular trends. That is, the Egyptian authorities were in favor of reinforcing the vertical social structure in the interest of consolidating their own grip on the Gaza Strip.

Both before and after 1948, political leadership in the Gaza Strip was drawn from members of the landed families. Following the Partition Plan of 1947, for example, a National Committee was formed. This committee took control in the Strip for almost six months, until the advent of the Egyptian administration later on. Virtually all members of this committee were landowners inside and outside Gaza.[20] Similarly, the successive municipality heads in the Strip were members of the large landowning families, who compete incessantly for political power in the Strip. From before 1948 until the present time, the Husseini, al-Shawwa, al-Rayyes, and al-Alami families have alternately headed the Gaza municipality.[21]

Prior to 1967, large landowners and merchants, despite their small number, continued to exercise extensive influence toward the top of the political hierarchy, second only to the Egyptian authorities, whose interests usually more or less coincided with those of the landowner/merchant alliance. This political elite was concentrated mainly in Gaza city and most of its members were original inhabitants of the Strip, much to the exclusion of the refugees. Yet, for various reasons, some of these large landowners and merchants failed to achieve prominence or political distinction commensurate with the economic influence they enjoyed. While some settled for smooth and beneficiary conduct of their business and established their relations with the authorities on that basis, others, for various reasons,

20. This fifty-five-member committee included Musa al-Sourani, Abdul-Khaliq Abu-Shaban, Munir al-Rayyes, Hamdi al-Husseini, Rajab Abu-Ramadan, Hasan Khayal, Rushdi al-Shawwa, and Musa Khalil Hillis. Aref al-Aref, *Al-Nakba* (The Disaster) (Sidon-Beirut: Al-Maktaba al-Asriyya, n.d.), p. 377 (Part II).

21. In a few cases and for limited periods of time, municipal committees were formed in place of full-fledged municipal councils. These committees were headed by individuals who did not belong to landed families. The real influence remained, however, in the hands of the large landowning families. The municipal committee of 1951, for example, which was headed by Abdul-Razzaq Qlaibu, had in it both Munir al-Rayyes and Rashad al-Shawwa, both large landowners. And in the 1952 committee, headed by Omar Sawwan, Munir al-Rayyes was the deputy head of the committee.

refrained entirely from engaging in politics. A few large landowners and merchants even had decidedly antagonist relations with the Egyptian administration in the Strip because of political or ideological differences.

In addition to their role in the municipalities, the landowners and merchants played a prominent political role in constitutional and political bodies (the Legislative Council and the National Union). They also occupied senior administrative positions. The first Legislative Council was established by decree of the Egyptian administration in 1958; it consisted of forty members, half of whom were elected and the other half appointed. A large number of the Council's members belonged to large landowner and merchant families.[22] Their share in the National Union, also founded in 1958, was large too. The interim executive committee of the union, which consisted of fifteen members, included nine members of this class. As for the significant administrative positions, these were doled out to individuals, the majority of whom also came from the landowner/merchant class.

This class continued to enjoy political supremacy throughout the Egyptian administration. However, some members of the higher echelons of the petty bourgeois class also managed to make their way into the political elite at this time.

The newcomers were lawyers, doctors, engineers, administrators, and educators. They gained legitimacy through their educational or family/tribal backgrounds, the accumulated experience of their field work, or from their national contributions. Most also enjoyed the sympathy of the Egyptian administration, which did not oppose them. On the contrary, the Egyptian administration was interested in the emergence of a new segment, distinct from the traditional, in the political elite, especially since the political and ideological orientation of the members of this new elite coincided with the new socialist orientation of the Egyptian regime. The new elements were pan-Arab nationalists, either pro-Nasser or members and supporters of the Arab Nationalist Movement and the Ba'ath Party. A number of them occupied high positions in the Legislative Council and in the National Union, including Council Head Haidar Abd al-Shafi, Fayez Abu Rahme, Mustafa Abd al-Shafi, Ibrahim Abu Sitta, Ibrahim al-Sagga, Sayyid Bakr, Ramiz Fakhra, Habib Jarada and others.[23]

A number of the members of the petty bourgeois class enjoyed political influence outside the framework of the existing power structure due to their affiliation or membership in secret political movements and parties, such as

22. Ibrahim Skaik, *Qita Ghazza taht al-Idara al-Masriyya 1957-1967* (The Gaza Strip under Egyptian administration: 1957-1967) (Gaza, 1983), p. 104.

23. *Ibid.*, pp. 98-100.

the Communists, the Muslim Brotherhood, and Fatah. In many cases, these individuals managed to convey their views on various national and social issues to the higher and middle strata in the power structure. They also had access to segments of the population at large.

The working class and peasantry played virtually no political role, despite the fact that these classes were numerically the largest in the Strip. To be sure, some prominent heads of clans enjoyed friendly relations or modest influence in official circles and with prominent figures of the political elite in power, due to earlier family alliances for economics or protection or due to the social influence of some of these peasant families. Yet, as mentioned earlier, the working class was extremely weak due to its small size, lack of organization, and lack of social and political awareness. Thus, the role of these classes remained marginal, despite the fact that most members of the society (original inhabitants and refugees alike) were of peasant origins.

The only new variable was the social mobility enjoyed by the children of peasants and workers with respect to positions within the framework of the petty bourgeoisie. While the traditional leadership gave up a portion of its power to some members of the petty bourgeoisie class, the conditions of the peasantry and working class remained pretty much the same.

After 1967

The political elite continued to include all the segments it had originally comprised, yet under the Israeli occupation, all were weakened. The political influence of the various classes has undergone distinct changes. The political authority of the large landowners and merchants, unmatched and unchallenged prior to 1967, suffered a number of setbacks.

The majority of members of this class lost their positions in the official authority structure because they refrained from participating in it, or because of the abolishment of some of the frameworks within which they had worked prior to 1967 (the Legislative Council, the National Union, and later on the Palestine Liberation Organization [PLO] with its various departments). Some members, however, continued to hold official responsibilities in the municipal councils and in the administrative apparatus.

The emergence of the Palestinian resistance movement in the Strip deprived members of this class of some of their power. This power waxed and waned in accordance with specific variables, such as the intensification of armed resistance (in which this class was in general loath to participate) and the nature of the relationships the large landowners and merchants had established with various factions of the resistance movement inside and outside the Strip. In this context it should be noted that – both before and after 1967 – a number of individual members of the large landowner and merchant families did occupy significant posts in the PLO and in its institutions, such as the Executive Committee and the Palestine National Council.

Another portion of the influence of the large landowners and merchants was given up, this time to a growing segment of newly affluent merchants, agents of Israeli companies in the Strip, contractors, and collaborators with the occupation authorities who occupied posts in the municipalities, village councils and government departments.

Despite these developments, most large landowners and merchants still enjoy some favorable treatment from the Israeli authorities and exert both direct and indirect influence, because this class has avoided participation in any serious confrontation with the authorities and occasionally because of the good relations members of this class have established with these authorities. The interests of this class has determined the establishment of such relationships.

Yet the existence of such relationships should not imply that the interests of this class were not shaken or damaged as a result of the occupation. Landowners and merchants have been denied the traditional markets open to them prior to 1967, either as a result of clear orders from the occupation authorities or as a result of burdensome conditions, such as the imposition of heavy taxes and customs duties. At the same time, the condition of occupation has placed the landowners and merchants in direct confrontation with a stronger class of the same type, i.e., their Israeli counterparts. In addition, the interests of this class have been seriously threatened by an active Jewish settlement policy, which has entailed the possibility of loss of land.

As for resistance to the occupation, the role played by this class is not in any way comparable with that played by other social classes.[24] Most class members are eager to see an end to the occupation, but are not willing to pay the price. They also realize that growth of the resistance movement in the Strip and an increase in the disruption to normal life resulting from that resistance will necessarily affect economic conditions and activities.

These landowners and merchants, whose economic interests have been either threatened or actually damaged by the occupation, have also realized that under conditions of revolutionary political and social change, they will

24. The criterion here is involvement in direct resistance to the occupation and the magnitude of sacrifices and penalties suffered, i.e., the number of members of a given class that have engaged in armed resistance, died, were jailed, deported, had their houses demolished, etc.

be the biggest losers. Hence they have tended to favor political initiatives and solutions to the Arab-Israeli conflict and to the question of the West Bank and Gaza, as opposed to violence or armed resistance. For this reason this class is favored by the Israeli authorities. Rashad al-Shawwa, for example, was appointed in 1971 by the Israeli authorities as head of the Gaza municipality. In 1972, al-Shawwa supported King Hussein's plan for the "United Arab Kingdom." He resigned his post in the same year only to be reinstated in 1975 by a decision of the occupation authorities, this time claiming to want to save "the Arab character of Gaza and not let some crass Jewish officer run our affairs."[25]

Politically, two distinct groups can be identified within the landowner/merchant class. The first group served under the Egyptian administration prior to 1967, the second under the Israeli occupation authorities after 1967. It is worth noting that the group committed to the Palestinian national program is the group that served under the Egyptian administration, while the second group, that which gained prominence during the occupation and is today headed by al-Shawwa, did not enjoy any comparable position during the Egyptian administration. Neither Rashad al-Shawwa nor his brother Rushdi, for example, headed the Gaza municipality under the Egyptian administration. Before 1948, the British Mandate authorities had appointed Rushdi as head of the municipality. Two months after the Egyptian revolution of 1952, Rushdi was removed from the job.

To illustrate, let us compare the role played by Munir al-Rayyes, a representative of the first group, to that played by Rashad al-Shawwa, a representative of the second. When the Israeli occupation authorities deposed Munir al-Rayyes from his position as head of the municipality in 1956 during the Israeli occupation of the Strip, Rashad al-Shawwa was appointed in his place. Prior to that, in the 1950s, Rashad al-Shawwa had called for the transfer of the British forces stationed in the Suez Canal Zone region to the Strip, while Munir al-Rayyes had played a significant role in organizing political resistance to the Israeli occupation of the Strip in 1956.

A "relationship" with Jordan appeals in more than one way to the landowner/merchant class. Members of this class generally believe that a solution in which the PLO becomes acceptable to Israel is not likely to be forthcoming in the foreseeable future. Hence they choose to deal with what they consider "realistic." Their lack of confidence in the Palestinian resistance movement and in its ability to realize its declared objectives is consistent with both the consciousness of this class and its ideological orientation. A situation in which the Palestinian resistance movement

25. Rafik Halabi, *The West Bank Story* (New York: Harcourt Brace Jovanovich, 1981), p. 87.

would enjoy political power and which would bring about social change is threatening to some, who are convinced they have an original claim to authority and representation. In this light, they consider the resistance movement as a traverse movement, and consequently adopt the position that prudence dictates the establishment of an alliance with a regime that shares with this class similar positions and convictions. Many believe that a future relationship with Jordan could lead to such developments as the opening of new markets and the reopening of the Gaza port that would allow the transformation of the Strip into a prosperous economic center from which this class would benefit.

There is also the fear that, should occupation and settlement continue, the Israeli authorities would confiscate land belonging to members of this class. This fear has strengthened as it becomes increasingly clear that the occupation will not spare anyone, no matter how moderate his political stance. Consequently, most members of this class support a political settlement such as the Jordanian option, that would "save what could be saved." Others of this class, however, favor the return of the Strip to the Egyptian administration.

As for the role of the other classes in political power and influence, that of the petty bourgeoisie remained limited prior to 1967 owing to the continuous harassment to which members of banned political organizations were subjected. Even this small role diminished in the period following 1967. Politically active members of the petty bourgeoisie were weakened by the occupation, which attempted to paralyze their role and compromise their national credibility through continuing pressures, harassments, and blackmail, through the imposition of various restrictions, and through forcing certain elements to comply with the wishes of the occupation. Others were overtly attacked, imprisoned, detained, placed under town arrest, or banned from traveling abroad. Consequently this group lost much of its cohesion, and its role in resisting the occupation diminished. Some of its members emigrated, others coped with the *status quo* or retired, while others continued to try to play a national role or engaged in underground work. The influence of those who joined underground work increased in the years following the occupation; at times they managed to exercise considerable political influence over the masses, as they tied their destiny to that of the Palestine resistance movement. But years of the "iron fist" policy of the occupation all but extinguished the political influence of the petty bourgeoisie, either in the open or underground.

As for the workers and peasants, the participation of these two classes in the political power structure has not undergone any significant change since the occupation. Yet large numbers of their members have joined the armed struggle through enlisting in commando organizations.

Members of the working class could have played a more significant role, had they been organized. Those who work in Israel are centered in important economic areas, such as the construction, agriculture, and service sectors. Yet, this class lacks organization and class consciousness. The irony here is that 32.2 percent of the total manpower in the Strip has received thirteen or more years of education.[26] Members of the petty bourgeois class who lost their jobs had to join the working class. They nevertheless carried with them some of the values characteristic of the petty bourgeois, such as the inclination toward consumerism.

During the past four years in particular, a larger portion of the working class has taken part in national activities, such as demonstrations and strikes. Attempts at labor organization were also made and certain concessions were extracted from the occupation authorities. Against the wishes of and in defiance of active intervention on the part of the authorities, labor elections actually took place and new, nationalist labor leaders were elected. In 1987, the trade unions of carpenters, tailors, public service workers, and drivers all carried out elections and reactivated their unions.

In contrast, for reasons of their own, the occupation authorities encouraged increased political power for certain peasant leaders. The role played by this group has become more prominent under the occupation, for some members have directly collaborated with the occupation authorities. It is to the mutual interest of the occupation authorities and these peasant leaders to enforce traditional social relationships and old habits, and to resolve family and tribal feuds. To justify its existence, therefore, this group has an interest in more feuds taking place.

26. Roy, *Gaza Strip Survey*, p. 33.

PART II

THE CHANGING STATUS OF
PALESTINIAN AREAS
UNDER OCCUPATION
SINCE 1967

LEGAL ASPECTS OF ISRAEL'S OCCUPATION OF THE WEST BANK AND GAZA: THEORY AND PRACTICE

Emma Playfair

One of the principles firmly established in the international law of war is the rule, enshrined in Article 2(4) of the United Nations Charter for Human Rights, that no territory may be acquired by force. Thus the state of belligerent occupation is by definition a temporary and provisional one.

Israel has faced a dilemma from the start of its occupation of the West Bank and Gaza in 1967. On the one hand, it sought international acceptance as a state respecting and obeying the rule of law. On the other hand, both Israel's major political parties avowed their intention of retaining permanent control over at least part of those territories – Likud, based on biblical claims and Labor, on strategic security interests – an aim which is clearly incompatible with international law. Israel's dilemma was: How to reconcile its intention to retain part or all of the occupied territories with its desire to comply with international law, which holds that belligerent occupation cannot lead to a transfer of sovereignty or to permanent control.

One option might have been simply to flout international law, as Israel did when illegally annexing east Jerusalem in 1967 and the Golan Heights in 1981. But demographic and political considerations have so far ruled out this option in relation to the West Bank and Gaza, the remaining parts of historic Palestine. Instead Israel has opted to proceed with its aims, but to try to frame its actions within the parameters of international law. How it has done this, and the extent to which its actions actually correspond to international law, is the subject of this chapter.

The international law applicable to Israel's rule over the West Bank and Gaza, and Israel's interpretation of its applicability, form the subject matter of the first part of this chapter. The next section reviews the requirements of international law that govern the administration of occupied territories, and Israel's interpretation of these. The last part is devoted to consideration of

Israel's treatment of one central aspect of the infrastructure of the occupied territories, the legal system of the West Bank, which provides an illustration of the application of its policies.

Although east Jerusalem and the Golan Heights are both territories occupied by Israel, their situation differs radically from that of the West Bank and Gaza, each having been subject to Israeli law since annexation. They are therefore not considered in this chapter. Furthermore, although the chapter is concerned with the West Bank and Gaza, the main focus will be on the West Bank. The treatment of each by the Israeli military authorities has been very similar, but the details are different, due to the different legal systems of each before occupation. Each would require separate discussion, but to deal with both would be repetitious, so most references will be to the West Bank alone. In almost all cases, however, legal developments in Gaza have paralleled those in the West Bank, differing only in detail.

INTERNATIONAL LAW AND THE OCCUPATION

The main provisions of international law regulating belligerent occupation are to be found in the following instruments:

The Fourth Hague Convention Respecting the Laws and Customs of War on Land and the annexed *Regulations Respecting the Laws and Customs of War on Land* of 1907 (The Hague Regulations);

The Fourth Geneva Convention Relative to the Protection of Civilian Persons in Time of War of 1949 (The Fourth Geneva Convention); and

The Protocols Additional to the Geneva Conventions of 12 August 1949 of 1977 (The Geneva Protocols).

The Hague Regulations have come to be considered customary law and as so binding on all states. The Fourth Geneva Convention has been ratified by almost all states, including Israel, Jordan, and Egypt, and is therefore binding on those states; some argue that it too has become customary law, but this view is not widely held, although some individual provisions are probably by now customary. The Geneva Protocols have as yet been ratified by relatively few states and by none of those just mentioned, so will not concern us further here.

Before the 1967 war, according to Israeli sources, the military advocate-general carefully studied and considered conventions and reference books on the law relating to occupation. The army had apparently found itself ill-prepared for an occupation during the Sinai campaign of 1956, and did not intend this to happen again. Israeli military lawyers were reportedly made to attend training programs in administration of occupied territories and were equipped with emergency legal kits with copies of the Fourth Geneva Convention and authoritative reference works.[1]

These preparations were evident in the array of military proclamations and orders issued in the first days of the occupation of the West Bank, setting up a military administration and establishing the framework of rule. The application of certain parts of the Fourth Geneva Convention to the occupation is acknowledged in one of the first of these proclamations, Article 35 of Proclamation No.3. Mention of international law so early on boded well for the occupier's intentions, but it proved to be short-lived. Only four months later, the acknowledgement was revoked and replaced by a provision relating to calculation of prison sentences, which bore no relation at all to the convention.[2]

No Israeli government has since acknowledged the applicability of any part of the Fourth Geneva Convention to its rule over the West Bank and Gaza, although there has been agreement that the Hague Regulations apply. The rationale for this stand has not always been consistent and considerable energy has been devoted by the government and its apologists to developing arguments to support this position and to assert its conformity with international law. The most widely cited of these arguments will be considered here. Other more elaborate theories have been expounded, such as that which holds that Israel's rule over the territories is in the nature of a trustee-occupancy, but such theories have been used more by apologists for Israel than by the government itself or by its courts.

The central argument of the Israeli government is that the Fourth Geneva Convention applies only when sovereign territory of another state is occupied. It argues that, because Egypt never claimed sovereignty over the Gaza Strip, and because Jordan's annexation of the West Bank in 1950 was allegedly recognized by only two states, Britain and Pakistan, no legitimate sovereign was displaced, and thus the convention does not apply. Thus Meir Shamgar, a former attorney-general and later president of the Israeli High Court, argued that:

1. Teveth, *The Cursed Blessing: The Story of Israel's Occupation of the West Bank,* pp. 10-11, 32 (1969) quoted by Stephen M. Boyd in "The Applicability of International Law to the Occupied Territories," *Israeli Yearbook of Human Rights* (Tel Aviv: Tel Aviv Univeristy Faculty of Law, 1971), 1:259.

2. This substitution was effected by Military Order 144.

> The whole idea of the restriction of military government powers is based on the assumption that there had been a sovereign who was ousted and that he had been a legitimate sovereign. [3]

In Shamgar's view, to accept that the convention should apply would therefore be tantamount to acknowledging the sovereignty of each state over the territory in question.

But Article 2 of the Fourth Geneva Convention, establishing the circumstances in which the convention is to apply, states that:

> The convention shall also apply to all cases of partial or total occupation of the territory of a High Contracting Party, even if the said occupation meets with no resistance.

There is no reference in the article to sovereignty. Furthermore, Article 4 defines those protected by the convention as:

> Those who, at a given moment and in any manner whatsoever, find themselves, in case of a conflict or occupation, in the hands of a Party to the conflict or Occupying Power of which they are not nationals.

Contrary to Shamgar's view, the restriction of the powers of a belligerent under the humanitarian law of occupation as it exists today is primarily intended to protect civilians finding themselves in a land occupied by an alien power, not to protect the reversionary rights of an ousted sovereign. This is clear from the very title of the Fourth Geneva Convention, which describes it as being "relative to the protection of civilian persons in time of war." These are territories indubitably occupied by Israel in belligerent action, over which it has no claims of sovereignty, and as such are subject to the provisions of the Fourth Geneva Convention, regardless of the status of Jordan or Egypt's rule over the West Bank and Gaza.

Another reason given by Israel in support of its argument for selective application of the provisions of international law, not only the Geneva conventions but international law regulating occupation as a whole, is that the existing law is inadequate to regulate a prolonged occupation. According to this argument, the existing body of international law relating to occupation was developed with occupations of perhaps a few weeks or months in mind, and so is not equipped to regulate occupations such as those of the West Bank and Gaza, of many years duration.

3. Meir Shamgar, "The Observance of International Law in the Administered Territories," *Israeli Yearbook of Human Rights,* (1971), 1:263.

The danger of this approach is the conclusion that if the existing law is inadequate, the occupier should be entitled to abandon or adjust these rules. Where there is a long occupation, potential for abuse of the powers of the occupier is arguably even greater and protection of the humanitarian rights of the local population becomes ever more important.[4] The law is by no means perfect, but its inadequacies are preferable to allowing the occupying power to decide when these laws can be overridden. Moreover this argument is based on a false premise. Although most – though by no means all – former occupations have been of shorter duration than those of the West Bank and Gaza, this does not in itself mean that longer occupations were not envisaged by those drafting the laws. Indeed Article 6 of the convention makes specific provision for occupations lasting more than a year after the cessation of hostilities.

Finally, Israel claims that, although it does not consider the Geneva Convention applicable in law, it does in practice voluntarily comply with its "humanitarian provisions." But Israel has never defined what it means by humanitarian provisions, nor does international law recognize this distinction, the whole convention being considered to be a humanitarian one. Moreover, it is hard to see what these provisions could be, if not such matters as the prohibition of deportation, destruction of property, or collective punishment, all of which, as we will see, are widely practiced by the military authorities.

This apparent concession, however, has frequently succeeded in deflecting critical discussion of Israel's legal position, on the basis that such discussion is academic. It has also enabled Israel to claim credit for its apparent willingness to comply voluntarily with provisions which it does not consider legally applicable, as in Meir Shamgar's explanation of Israel's position:

> The territorial position is . . . *sui generis,* and the Israeli government tried therefore to distinguish between theoretical, juridical and political problems on the one hand, and the observance of the humanitarian provisions of the Fourth Geneva Convention on the other hand. Accordingly, the government of Israel distinguished between the legal problem of the applicability of the Fourth Convention to the territories under consideration which, as stated, does not in my opinion apply to

4. It is now widely agreed that the existence of a situation of belligerent occupation does not exonerate an occupier from complying with many of the provisions of international human rights law, although there are certain specified exemptions in times of emergency. These laws are not discussed here, but for a full discussion see Adam Roberts, "The Applicability of Human Rights Law during Military Occupations," *Review of International Studies* (January 1987), 13(1):39-48.

these territories, and decided to act *de facto,* in accordance with the humanitarian provisions of the Convention. [5]

Like the state, Shamgar fails to identify which are the "humanitarian" provisions with which the state is to comply, and which provisions are merely "political," and as such do not, in his view, merit compliance.

If Israel were actually complying with the Fourth Geneva Convention in practice, there might indeed be little to complain of in its legal stand, but in fact its violations of the convention are numerous. This is not the place to enter into them in detail, but a few examples will suffice:

Deportations: Article 49 contains an absolute prohibition of deportations, yet Israel deported seventy-five Palestinians between January 1985 and August 1988 alone. Two main arguments have been used to assert that in so doing Israel has not contravened the Fourth Geneva Convention. First, it is argued that the convention does not apply to individual deportations comparable to those carried out by Israel, but only to mass deportations comparable to those carried out during World War II against Jews. This, however, is directly contrary to the express reference in Article 49 to "individual and mass forcible transfers . . . regardless of their motive."[6]

A second response to criticism of deportations to Jordan of West Bank Palestinians holding Jordanian passports is that the expulsion does not constitute deportation, because those concerned are Jordanian citizens. This claim not only contradicts the basis of the entire convention, but also demonstrates the peculiarity of Israel's distinction between humanitarian and other provisions of the convention. Few actions can be considered more inhumane than the permanent exile of a person from his or her homeland.[7]

Settlement of the occupier's own population in the territory occupied is also forbidden by Article 49, which prohibits the transfer of parts of the occupier's own population into the occupied areas. However, there are currently some sixty-five thousand Jewish settlers living in the occupied territories. Israel claims that Jewish settlement does not constitute a

5. Shamgar, "Observance of International Law," p. 266.

6. This stand was recently reiterated in the High Court decision delivered on 10 April 1988 in the case of HCJ 785/87 *Nasser Aziz Affo et al.* vs. *Commander of the Judea and Samaria Region et al.*

7. More detailed descriptions of all these practices can be found in the publications of al-Haq / Law in the Service of Man, Ramallah.

violation of Article 49, since those who settle do so voluntarily. Yet the settlers are only able to live in the occupied territories with the permission of the military government, and those willing to do so are offered substantial incentives by the government.

Collective punishment, or punishment of some for the acts of others, is absolutely prohibited under Article 33. Yet collective punishment is one of the main methods used by Israel in its attempt to deter resistance to the occupation authorities, or to induce cooperation with those authorities. This may take many forms, including the demolition or sealing of the family home of a person suspected of committing an offense, a travel ban imposed against a whole area for weeks or months at a time, the banning of exports from a certain community, prolonged curfews continuing for days or weeks after they have ceased to serve any legitimate security purpose, or the months-long closure of universities and schools. Israel claims that such actions are necessary either for security reasons or as a deterrent. But this prohibition in the convention is absolute and does not admit any exceptions.

Demolition of houses lived in by families of those suspected of some offense involving violence is one form of collective punishment routinely used by the military authorities. Not only is this in violation of Article 33, as mentioned above, but it is also forbidden by Article 53, which prohibits destruction of private property unless absolutely necessary for actual military operations.

Place of detention: Article 76 requires that protected persons shall be detained and, if convicted, shall serve their sentences in the occupied country. Yet, at the time of writing, over two thousand Palestinians from the West Bank and Gaza, mainly internees, are being held in a desert prison in the Negev inside Israel; others are regularly held in other Israeli prisons such as Nafha, another desert prison, Atlit, Ramle, and Abu Kbir.

Administrative detention or internment, meaning imprisonment without charges or trial, is permitted under Article 78, but its use is allowed only if "necessary, for imperative reasons of safety." Furthermore, according to Article 6, internment may only be used during the first year after "the general close of military operations." Israel nevertheless actually used this measure for the first fifteen years of occupation before phasing it out in 1982. It then reintroduced internment in 1985, eighteen years after the close of military operations, and has since placed over three thousand people under administrative detention. This is out of a total population of 1.5 million. Such extensive use, so soon after internment was abandoned as unnecessary, belies claims that it is used only in the circumstances allowed under Article 78, even if the provisions of Article 6 are ignored.

Despite repeated condemnation of these obvious violations, as well as of many others, Israel continues to protest that the "humanitarian" provisions of the Fourth Geneva Convention are respected. It is increasingly isolated in this stand, however, receiving little international support for its actions or for its legal arguments. The United Nations General Assembly, the International Committee of the Red Cross, and almost all states, including the United States of America, have repeatedly held that the Fourth Geneva Convention is applicable and must be applied in its entirety to Israel's occupation of the West Bank, including east Jerusalem, and the Gaza Strip, and have condemned violations by Israel of the convention.[8]

Nevertheless, the arguments continue to be used, and enable Israel to answer criticism of its policies with replies couched in legal terms and apparently based on international law. It requires familiarity with this relatively obscure branch of the law to respond to these arguments.

THE LEGAL BASIS OF THE OCCUPIER'S POWERS AND DUTIES

In recognition of the provisional nature of the state of belligerent occupation, international law governing occupation defines the role of the occupier as similar to that of a trustee. At the end of the occupation, the territories should be restored in whatever manner is agreed, with as little change as possible. Thus a foreign occupying power has no right to make permanent changes unless it is absolutely unavoidable.

The powers and duties of an occupier are laid down in Article 43 of the Hague Regulations of 1907, perhaps the single most important provision relating to occupation, which states that:

> The authority of the power of the State having passed *de facto* into the hands of the occupant, the latter shall do all in his power to restore, and ensure, as far as possible, public order and safety [l'ordre et la vie publics][9], respecting at the same time, unless absolutely prevented, the laws in force in the country.

This is a conservative provision, allowing for only a minimum of change. As has often been pointed out, adherence to this principle can lead to a degree of stagnation in the development of the territories occupied, as it

8. See, for example, UN General Assembly Resolution A/RES/42/160 of 7 January 1988 and the unanimous UN Security Council Resolution of 5 January 1988.

9. The precise meaning of the phrase "l'ordre et la vie publics," rendered inaccurately in the unofficial English translation as "public order and safety," is the subject of much debate. Various alternative translations have been proposed, such as "public order and civil life" or "public order and security," but none precisely captures the meaning of the official French text.

precludes any significant modernization or new planning. This consequence is a price that must be paid to avoid the risks inherent in the alternative, which range from development in a fashion totally inappropriate to the occupied territories to the outright exploitation of the territories by the occupier, under the guise of well-meant improvements.

Article 43 reflects a balance that must be maintained between the occupier's need to ensure its own security on the one hand and respect for the rights and welfare of the local population on the other. It contains firstly a general duty and power to restore and maintain safety and public order, which includes the right to ensure the security of its own forces and the duty to protect and ensure the well-being of the occupied population, and secondly a restriction on the extent to which existing legislation may be altered in so doing. There is not a total ban on permanent changes, but these may only be made if it is absolutely necessary for legitimate security reasons, to maintain law and order, or for the welfare of the population. Other than in these situations, the *status quo* must be respected. The law, the judicial system, the infrastructure, and the land itself must remain unaltered. The occupier's interpretation of what is justified by security needs on the one hand and by the restoration and ensuring of public order and safety on the other is of crucial significance to the way the occupied territories are administered.

Security Concerns

An occupier's paramount concern is inevitably the security of its forces, a concern which is recognized by international law, and Israel has justified many of its actions on the basis of security. Some of these are undeniably legitimate, such as the introduction of new penal law to deal with hostile activities and the temporary requisition of land for essential military needs. But the need for security is also used to justify an extraordinary range of other measures such as restrictions on travel, closure of schools, mandatory burials at dead of night for those killed by the army, restrictions on erection of traffic lights, and the banning of the use of the colors of the Palestinian flag, even on a T-shirt or shopping bag. Security clearance must be established before traveling, before taking a government or white-collar job, before obtaining a telephone, before driving lessons can be taken, and, since the uprising, even before registering a baby's birth. "Security" has become a refrain that runs through the life of every Palestinian living under Israeli occupation, impinging on his or her activities at every turn.

Perhaps most importantly, security or military necessity has been used to justify the expropriation of large amounts of land, later handed over to Jewish civilian settlers. Initially it was argued that the presence of settlers augmented security. Now this point is rarely pressed, it being more often asserted that the settlers are a liability to security, but they are allowed to remain. In a self-perpetuating cycle, the settlers' presence is now used to justify more and more measures to ensure the settlers' own security: they are authorized to carry arms and are rarely censured when these are used against Palestinians; military guards are provided for vulnerable settlements; entire refugee camps are fenced off from main roads with twenty-foot fences to protect settlers from stones, and new roads are planned to link up the settlements and avoid Palestinian population centers. All of these measures, which are in themselves provocative and lead to yet more such measures, are justified by the need for security – the security of those same settlers whose presence was itself supposedly justified by security.

Nor are "security" measures confined to serving the needs of Israel's population within the occupied territories, but are also imposed to serve the security of Israel itself. In the case of *Amira et al.* vs. *Minister of Defense et al.,*[10] the High Court allowed the expropriation of privately owned land on the basis of security needs. The security need served was the strengthening of defense for Ben-Gurion Airport, well inside Israel, by the construction of a line of three civilian settlements inside the West Bank. In this case the military authorities utilized their status and power as occupiers to improve the state's own security system, which is not a legitimate aim in international law.

The Kafkaesque quality of the use of security by the military authority is increased by the near impossibility of challenging a decision purportedly based on security. The Israeli government, its courts, and the public are all equally loath to interfere in or even to question decisions when these are said to be taken for security reasons and based on military intelligence. Perhaps the most extreme example of this practice occurs in the case of deportation orders. These orders are almost invariably said to be necessitated by the threat to security posed by the person concerned. When the deportee asks to know the basis for this allegation he is told that it cannot be revealed for security reasons, and that neither he nor his lawyer can see the evidence, because to reveal this might endanger the security source. To complete the process, the hearing before the military committee is held in secret, for security reasons.

Meanwhile the security of the local population receives scant attention. Senior posts in the police service are held by Israelis, with Palestinians in the junior ranks. Observation shows that the police essentially operate as an adjunct to the military government and the intelligence service. Palestinians

10. HC 337/71: *Falah Hassan Ibrahim Amira et al.* vs. *Minister of Defense et al.*

in the occupied territories are actively discouraged from submitting complaints to the police, and if they insist their complaints are rarely followed up. The role of the police is perhaps best illustrated by the fact that the sign POLICE on the face of the police station in Ramallah is written in Hebrew and in English, but not in Arabic.

Thus the provision in international law that permits the occupier to take action necessary to ensure the safety of its forces has been stretched far beyond its natural meaning. It now covers not only the security of the occupier's forces and that of the original population of the occupied territories, as is permitted by international law, but also the security of the occupier's own civilian population illegally allowed to settle in the occupied territories and even the security of Israel itself. The impact of this is felt daily in the occupied territories.

The Restoration of Public Order and Life

The powers authorized under the terms of Article 43, authorizing and obliging the occupier "to restore and ensure" public order, bear little resemblance to those of a sovereign. The occupier is not urged to take all steps needed to ensure full development of the occupied lands, for the reasons referred to above, nor to treat the occupied land as it treats its own land. It is required only to see that public order and safety are restored and then maintained. But both the military government and the Israeli High Court have taken an increasingly expansive view of the restrictions imposed by international law.

The Israeli High Court, when first called on to rule on the extent to which the military government could alter the law or infrastructure of the West Bank, held that Article 43 placed on an occupier:

the duty to regulate economic and social affairs [of the occupied population].[11]

Ten years later, the court had elaborated on this ruling to authorize the occupier:

to maintain an orderly administration, including all branches existing nowadays in an enlightened society, such as security, health, education, welfare as well as quality of life and transportation.[12]

11. HC 337/71: *The Christian Society for the Holy Places* vs. *Minister of Defense et al.*

12. HC 202/81: *Said Mahmoud Tabib et al.* vs. *Minister of Defense et al.*

Most recently, in 1987, it authorized change to ensure:

> the public order and community life of a modern, sophisticated, democratic state at the end of the twentieth century.[13]

Although the aims expressed may appear laudable, it takes little reflection to realize that this effectively allows the military government freedom to regulate all these aspects of life as though it were a sovereign government, removing all the safeguards intended by the Hague Regulations. As the Israeli jurist Yoram Dinstein has written:

> The concern of an occupant for the needs of the civilian population in an occupied territory is not always genuine, and at times it is imperative to guard the inhabitants from the bear's hug of the occupant.[14]

As early as 1971, in the case of *The Christian Society for the Holy Places* vs. *the Minister of Defense et al.,* known as the *Muqaddsa* case, the court had adopted the principle that the motivation of the occupier was of crucial significance in deciding whether or not an action is contrary to the provisions of Article 43, and had linked this to the welfare of the local population:

> The legislator's motive is of great importance: Did he act in order to further his own interests, in which case the legislation is invalid, or out of concern for the welfare of the civilian population.[15]

Such a test may appear reasonable, although it omits any concept of necessity, but a new twist was to emerge which robbed it of reason. In evidence in the case of *Electric Corporation for Jerusalem District Ltd.* vs. *Minister of Defense et al.,*[16] it became clear that the military government had considered not only the interests of the Palestinian population of the town of Hebron, but also those of the Jewish settler population of Kiryat Arba, in deciding to award the electricity concession, formerly held by the Palestinian petitioner, to an Israeli supplier. The definition of "the local

---

13. HC 507/85: *Bahij Tamimi et al.* vs. *Minister of Defense.*

14. Yoram Dinstein, "The International Law of Belligerent Occupation and Human Rights," in the *Israeli Yearbook of Human Rights* (Tel Aviv: Tel Aviv University Faculty of Law, 1978), 8:104.

15. HC 337/71.

16. HC 256/72.

population" was thus construed to include not only the local Palestinian population, but also the illegal Jewish settler population, whose interests were considered on a par with, and even preferentially to, those of the local Palestinian population. Similarly, when a new road plan for the West Bank, Road Plan 50, was drawn up, it was clear that the settlers' needs were considered before those of the Palestinian population. The roads are primarily designed to link up settlements and connect them with Israel, while avoiding Palestinian population centers, and will involve massive expropriations of land in some of the most fertile areas. The plan transforms the original network of roads whose main axis ran north/south, following the line of the major Palestinian town centers, into one whose main lines run east/west, linking the West Bank with Israel. While many Palestinians do commute to work in Israel, the main benefit is thus clearly reaped by the settlers.[17]

Neither the military government nor the High Court, both being institutions of the occupying power, can be considered appropriate judges of what is in the interests of the local population. The absence of adequate mechanisms for consultation with the local population – and almost all such mechanisms have been abolished – is another reason for requiring absolute compliance with the conservative provisions of the Hague Regulations.[18]

In practice, even when the welfare of the local population is purportedly the motivating factor for a certain measure, decisions as to what is for the benefit of the population rarely appear to be based on a global view of the interests of the local population, but rather on assumptions about their immediate consumer interests. For example, Israel has steadily transferred responsibility for supply of basic services such as water, electricity, and telephones in the occupied territories from local Palestinian enterprises to Israeli ones. It is argued in support of such changes that the Israeli enterprises can supply the services more efficiently. If Israel were sovereign, this might be an adequate justification for deciding in favor of the most efficient supplier, but as an occupier its duty is to shore up the existing institutions and supply systems, not to encourage dependency on, and channel new business towards, its own state's institutions. Again the need to introduce a value added tax (VAT) in the occupied territories was

17. See Fuad Aziz and Raja Shehadeh, *Israeli Proposed Road Plan for the West Bank – A Question for the International Court of Justice* (Ramallah: al-Haq, 1984).

18. For instance, municipal elections have not been held since 1976, and most of the mayors elected then were later dismissed. A requirement that the local population be consulted in planning was deleted from the Jordanian planning law. See Mona Rishmawi, *Planning in Whose Interest?* (Ramallah: al-Haq, 1986).

explained on the basis that the closely linked markets of Israel and the occupied territories necessitated equivalence of tax. This begs the question of whether it is in the interest of the occupied territories that those economic links, imposed by Israel since the occupation, should be cultivated. Because there is no sovereign able to make an independent decision on such a matter, international law requires that no new taxes be introduced.

More recently an even looser test has been applied, one proposed by Yoram Dinstein:

> There is no objective criterion in practice for drawing a distinction between sincere and insincere concern for the civilian population. But to my mind, in most instances the criterion may be simple enough, namely, whether or not the occupier is equally concerned about his own population.[19]

This test was endorsed by Justice Shamgar in a High Court decision in 1983, known as the *Kandil* case,[20] in which he approved the introduction of a new VAT in the occupied territories on the basis, *inter alia,* that it was legitimate since it was done simultaneously with the introduction of a VAT in Israel. This test, however, is quite inappropriate when applied to occupied territories. The powers of an occupier are in no way equivalent to those of a sovereign government, and moreover there is no ground for the assumption that the differing social, economic, and other characteristics of the occupied territories call for similar treatment as those of the occupier's own state.

The provisions of international law are designed to avoid prejudicing the eventual disposition of the territories. This outcome is inevitably prejudiced by the inextricable linkage of their infrastructure and economy with that of the occupier, however efficient or apparently desirable. By not obeying this injunction, Israel is preempting a resolution of the occupation by presenting a *fait accompli,* instead of restricting alterations to those absolutely necessary, as required by international law.

All differentiation between the occupier's powers within its own state and those in the territories occupied was abandoned in a High Court decision in 1983 regarding the new road plan for the West Bank, Road Plan 50, described above.[21] Contrary to all indications in international law, the court

19. Dinstein, "International Law," p. 113.

20. HC 69/81: *Abu Aita et al.* vs. *Commander of Judea and Samaria Region et al.;* and HC 493/81: *Kandil et al.* vs. *Commander of the Gaza Strip Region et al.*

21. HC 393/82: *A Cooperative Association Lawfully Registered at the Judea and Samaria District Command* vs. *The IDF Commander in the Judea and Samaria District.*

held that long-term, basic investments involving permanent change could be made if they benefited the local population, and concluded that these investments could involve planning with outside elements. The outside element, in this case, was of course Israel itself, and the local population included the settlers as well as the Palestinian population. The Court thus authorized Israel, the state, to negotiate with Israel, the occupying power, as though the two were independent sovereign states, each ready to negotiate in its own best interests. This is of course precisely what the Hague Regulations were designed to outlaw, and the results are predictable. The road plan was approved, and indeed overwhelmingly serves the interests of Israel itself, which gains direct and fast access to the Jordan Valley defenses, and of the Jewish settler population. The Palestinians are provided with a road in whose planning they have played no part, whose capacity far exceeds their foreseeable needs, whose orientation does not reflect usage by Palestinians, and whose construction will involve the expropriation of vast tracts of fertile land.

The West Bank is thus being treated not only as though it were the sovereign territory of the military government, but as an extension of Israel itself. The borders are being steadily eroded by interlinking electricity, water and telephone networks, roads, economic systems, and even, as we will see, overlapping legal systems. The question of whether this is really in the long-term interests of a population and a territory whose links with the occupying state are by definition temporary, is rarely given any serious consideration. To the extent that the interests of the local population are considered, these are their immediate consumer interests, not their long-term overriding interest in maintaining the territory in such a way as not to preempt any decision about the future of the territory upon termination of the occupation.

THE LEGAL SYSTEM

The nature of the legal system of a society is a central factor in determining the character of that society. Its proper functioning and the maintenance of its standards is of crucial significance to the functioning of a just and viable society. Furthermore, the existence of an independent judiciary and legal profession and of a properly functioning legal system is an essential requirement for the rule of law to operate. The fostering of such a system should thus be of paramount concern to an occupying power.

Indeed, international law singles out the legal system of occupied territories as particularly in need of protection, adding specific regulations to the general principles discussed above. Article 43 of the Hague

Regulations and Articles 64 and 66 of the Fourth Geneva Convention all contain special provisions regarding the need for respect for the laws and judicial system in force, reinforcing the general provisions. Israel maintains that it has respected these provisions of international law in relation to the legal system: that the Jordanian law remains in force except where legitimately amended, and that the Jordanian courts continue to function.

The treatment of the legal system of the West Bank therefore provides a good illustration of the application by Israel of the principles discussed above.

The Law

Legislative power, as well as governmental, appointative, and administrative power, was awarded to the military area commander on the first day of the occupation by Proclamation 2(3a) of 1967. As already noted, however, his power to effect any permanent changes is very strictly limited by international law. In addition, the second part of Article 43 of the Hague Regulations enjoins him:

> [to] respect . . . unless *absolutely prevented,* the laws in force in the country [emphasis added],

while carrying out his duty to restore and ensure public order and safety. As to criminal law, Article 64 of the Fourth Geneva Convention adds that:

> the penal laws . . . shall remain in force [except] where they constitute a threat to [the occupier's] security or an obstacle to the application of the present Convention

and allows legislation by the occupier only when:

> *essential* to enable the Occupying Power to fulfill its obligations under the present Convention, to maintain orderly government of the territory and to ensure the security of the Occupying Power [emphasis added],

that is to say, in much the same circumstances as those referred to in Article 43.

In apparent compliance with the requirements of international law, the West Bank area commander affirmed in Proclamation 2(2):

> The law which existed in the area on the 7th June 1967 shall remain in force in so far as there is nothing therein repugnant to this proclamation, any other proclamation or order which will be enacted by me, and subject to such modifications as may result from the establishment of the rule of the IDF [Israeli Defense Forces] in the area.

At the time of the Israeli occupation, the law in force in the West Bank was that of Jordan. This was itself derived from the Ottoman law originally in force throughout Palestine, as amended under the British Mandate and by subsequent Jordanian legislation. To this day, Israel maintains that the Jordanian laws in force in Jordan in 1967 are applied in the West Bank, any changes being only those authorized by international law.

In reality, Jordanian law remains only the foundation of the law now in force, altered often beyond recognition by over twelve hundred military orders issued by the military commander since 1967. Far from respecting the local law except where absolutely prevented, these military orders have entered into every facet of life; only religious law has remained relatively unchanged. The laws relating to other areas such as land ownership, criminal matters, legal procedure, tax, finances, commerce, agriculture, and infrastructure have suffered radical change.[22]

The whole body of military orders passed by Israel in the occupied territories is referred to as "security legislation," regardless of content, giving an initial impression that all the orders are indeed justified by security. At first the military commander was indeed cautious in exercising his powers, explaining in the preamble to each order that it was issued for security purposes or in order to restore public order, but as time went by this punctiliousness diminished. Now, the majority of military orders carry no justification, merely being prefaced by a phrase such as: "Based on my authority as Commander of the Israeli Defense Forces in the area, I hereby order as follows. . . . "[23]

Some of the changes made to the law are undoubtedly within the powers of an occupier. For instance, the introduction of certain new offenses relating to resistance against the occupying forces are permissible on grounds of security; changes in fees and in tax rates will inevitably have to be made as the value of local currency alters; some regulations may have to

22. For a more detailed review and analysis of military orders, see Raja Shehadeh and Jonathan Kuttab, *The West Bank and the Rule of Law* (New York: International Commission of Jurists and Law in the Service of Man, 1980); and Raja Shehadeh, *Occupier's Law* (Washington, D.C.: Institute of Palestine Studies, 1984).

23. A survey of the military orders issued between 1980 and 1985 shows the rationales cited as follows:

no rationale given at all	155 orders
public order (or a similar phrase) cited	80 times
welfare or benefit of the population cited	33 times
security cited	18 times

The survey covers the 272 orders issued during this time, but in some cases more than one rationale is cited.

be introduced over time to enable the economy of the occupied land to continue to function. Other quite radical changes, although possibly exceeding the powers of an occupier, are made to conform with current human rights standards, such as the abolition of the mandatory death penalty and the enfranchisement of women. For much of the military legislation, however, no such justification is apparent. No more than a brief review of the effects of some of these orders can be given here, but this may serve to give an idea of the scope of the new legislation and its content.

The most notable of the orders based on security is the massive Military Order 378 concerning Security Instructions, which has been amended over sixty times, and which contains the basis of the penal jurisdiction of the military courts, introducing new offenses, procedures, and penalties. Recent military orders, issued during the popular uprising, impose penalties on house owners who fail to remove graffiti from their walls, and make a father liable to a fine or imprisonment for an offense committed by his child.

For the most repressive measures used against Palestinians, such as demolition of houses and deportation, the military authorities have, however, preferred not to introduce their own military legislation but to utilize the draconian powers contained in the British Defense (Emergency) Regulations of 1945, maintaining that the regulations formed part of the Jordanian law. This is contested by Palestinian lawyers who point out that the British revoked the regulations in 1948 in the last days of the Mandate and that they were not used during the intervening years of Jordanian rule. Faced by this argument, and perhaps concerned that the High Court might find against the validity of the regulations, the military authorities passed a series of military orders altering procedural law so as to invalidate retrospectively the revocation by the British.[24] Such retrospective legislation and manipulation of the law may have lessened the damage caused to Israel's public image by the use of these laws, but it is contrary to the rule of law.

Similarly in the area of land law, already a complex area based primarily on Ottoman law, apparently technical changes enabled the military authorities to increase their control over land. The initial stages of this process are described in chapter 7 of this collection, and the process continues. The land most easily acquired was taken in the early years, so other methods have had to be developed to continue the process. In recent years new military orders have facilitated secret land registration, enabled foreign (including Israeli) juridical bodies to acquire land, and transferred expanded jurisdiction over land issues from local courts to military

---

24. See Andre Rosenthal, "The 1945 Defense Regulations: Valid Law in the West Bank," unpublished paper (1986), and al-Haq *Briefing Paper No. 9*, Ramallah, 1987.

tribunals. This has facilitated the acquisition of land or control over land by the military authorities. None of these measures bears any relation to security or public order or the needs of the population, nor could any be described as necessary.

In other spheres, military orders have closed banks, restricted cultivation of vegetables and fruits and the use of wells, imposed new taxes, exercised control over charitable and social organizations, created nature reserves, declared the protection of archeological sites, and amended planning procedures. They have also been used to establish a separate legal and administrative system for the Jewish settlers, and to extend Israeli law to them, as though the settlements were islands of Israel.

A number of these alterations to the law have been challenged, directly or indirectly, before the Israeli High Court. From the start the Court took a lax view of the injunction that the law should be respected unless absolutely prevented, with the notable exception of a dissenting judgment by Justice Haim Cohn in the early case of *Muqaddsa.* In that case the majority ruled that an arbitration procedure, which had been posited in a Jordanian law though not set up, could be implemented even though not yet established in Jordan. Judge Cohn, disagreeing, said that the authority granted to an occupier was not to institute an ideal order, or the one that seemed best to him, but to maintain the existing order.[25] Ten years later, the High Court ruled, seemingly in total contradiction to the words of Article 43, that:

> ... the "prevention" mentioned at the end of Article 43 is not absolute at all ... the question is one of the preferable and convenient means for achieving the purpose as stated in the beginning of Article 43, namely "ensuring public order."[26]

Perhaps one should not be surprised at the effect of the ruling in this particular case, which was to approve a relaxation of the law's strict requirement as to the notification of a person that his land was to be expropriated.

Yet again, the Court has entirely departed from the natural meaning of the words of international law, to arrive at an interpretation which allows maximum flexibility for the military government, while continuing to give the impression of taking the obligations and restrictions under the treaty seriously.

25. HC 337/71.

26. HC 202/81.

The Courts and the Legal Profession

The courts too are accorded special protection in international law. Article 66 of the Geneva Convention authorizes the establishment of military courts, but limits their jurisdiction to those offenses legitimately introduced by the military authorities under Article 64 of the convention, which otherwise provides that the regular penal courts of the territories shall continue to function as before. These provisions are of course in addition to the general directions of Article 43 of the Hague Regulations. There is no provision for establishment of courts or tribunals regulating civil matters.

During the Israeli occupation of the West Bank, three separate court systems have developed: the local courts based on those that existed prior to the occupation, the military courts and tribunals set up by the military authorities, and the settlement courts, also established by the military government, which regulate some aspects of the affairs of Jewish settlers living in the occupied territories. Only the first of these systems will be discussed here in any detail, as the others are both discussed elsewhere in this collection. The usurping by the military courts and committees, by the settlement courts, and even by courts inside Israel of the functions of the local courts will, however, be apparent.

Prior to the occupation, the administration of justice in the West Bank fell under the Jordanian legal system, and consisted of four tiers of courts: magistrates' courts, courts of first instance, courts of appeal, and the Court of Cassation, which was the highest forum.

Several changes befell the court system at the time of and immediately after the occupation. The highest recourse, the Court of Cassation, was based in Amman and so became inaccessible to West Bank appellants. It was not replaced by the military authorities, and was thus effectively abolished, its duties falling on the court of appeal The court of appeal continued to function, but after the Israeli annexation of east Jerusalem it was made to vacate its new court building, centrally located in the main street of east Jerusalem. This building was then used by an Israeli district court. The appeal court for the whole of the West Bank was sited, with other local courts, in a cramped and ill-equipped building in the chicken market area of Ramallah, where it remains to this day. Perhaps most importantly, except for a period of about a year in 1985, there has been no independent inspector of courts. This is an important post, whose incumbent is responsible under the Jordanian system for inspecting the work of all civil and criminal courts, of the judiciary and of the court staff, and so is crucial to the maintenance of standards in the court. The Jordanian inspector was based in Amman. Instead of appointing a substitute, his powers were entrusted to the president of the appeal court, who was thus required to inspect his own work and that of his court.

The removal of a tier of courts is a severe depredation of a system of justice, as is the absence of an inspector in a system reliant on such an official to monitor standards. Both would seem to offer clear instances in which an occupier could legitimately take steps to replace the missing element in order to help restore a proper system of justice. This the Israeli military government refused to do, despite the requests of lawyers, and instead allowed the court's jurisdiction to fall on the court of appeal and the inspector's functions on its president. The failure to replace these elements vital to the judicial system is symptomatic of the neglect suffered by the local courts.

Although, except as mentioned above, the local criminal and civil courts remain in place, they are radically changed. Their structure has been weakened by the absence of vital elements of the judicial system, their jurisdiction has been steadily eroded by military courts and tribunals, by Israeli courts, and by settlement courts, and their ability to function diminished by neglect.

Military courts were established immediately after the occupation and initially had jurisdiction over "any offense defined by security legislation and over any other offense consistent with what is defined in security legislation" (Military Order 378, Art. 7). So far, this is in accordance with international law, which permits the establishment of military courts to deal with offenses introduced to ensure the security of the occupier. But Military Order 842 gave the military courts concurrent jurisdiction with the local courts over *any* criminal matter, meaning that a military commander can decide that any specific case should be transferred to a military court. Military courts have since taken jurisdiction from the local courts in cases that cannot by any stretch of the imagination be considered security-related. For instance, cases relating to drug abuse, traffic offenses, tax offenses, and even antiquities are now heard by military courts. So at times are common criminal cases in which the Israeli military authorities have an interest, such as the murder of one Palestinian by another when an informant is involved.[27]

The civil courts have not been allowed to retain their jurisdiction either, because military tribunals, whose use for such purposes has no foundation in international law, have taken over a number of their functions, particularly those relating to land and to certain commercial transactions. Objections to expropriation of land by the military government for public purposes, or to declaration of land as state property, are heard by the military Objections Committee, not by a court. Any case involving land on which an application for registration is pending is removed from the local

---

27. See Shehadeh, *Occupier's Law,* p. 85.

courts and heard by another military committee. Appeals against assessment of income tax have also been removed from the jurisdiction of the court of first instance to the Objections Committee. These are only a few examples of many such alterations to the existing system. Such matters obviously have no security significance, but reflect the desire of the military authorities to maintain tight control over disposition of land and regulation of commerce.

The final limitation imposed on the powers of the local courts may perhaps provide the key to the neglect and erosion suffered by those courts. The courts, which nominally have jurisdiction over the entire West Bank, are allowed to exercise that jurisdiction only over the Palestinian population, and even then only over those who are not in the service of the military authorities. Under Military Order 164, permission must be obtained from the military government before legal proceedings can be taken against members of the Israeli government or the Israeli army or any employee of either, and in practice such permission is rarely if ever given to local courts. Furthermore, a whole sector of the inhabitants of the West Bank and Gaza has been partially removed from the jurisdiction of the courts: the Jewish settlers live illegally and armed within the occupied territories, yet have been granted effective immunity from their courts. In theory, in criminal matters, settlers are subject to the jurisdiction of the local Jordanian courts, military courts, criminal courts in Israel and, for certain offenses, courts in the settlements themselves. By a special military directive issued on 16 December 1984, no complaint may even be registered against an Israeli citizen without the prior consent of the officer in charge of judiciary. This means that a Palestinian must wait until the appropriate officer can be located before the police will take any action to restrain a settler at all. In practice, settlers are almost always tried by courts inside Israel, and never by local courts, even in cases of common crimes. This is so even when a West Bank settler is on trial for an offense against a Palestinian committed in the occupied territories.[28]

In civil matters local courts can and sometimes do hear cases involving Israelis, but Palestinian parties receive little cooperation from officials, making the pursuit of such cases costly and often futile. It is commonplace to find that proceedings are not served, witnesses are not summoned, and judgments are not enforced, all these steps being dependent on the cooperation of the police. The outcome is that it is rarely considered worthwhile to embark on such a case.

28. For example, the so-called Jewish terrorist trials of 1984-85 were all held in the Jerusalem District Court, although the crimes were committed in the occupied territories and many of those on trial were residents of the West Bank or Gaza.

How has the legal profession as a whole fared under occupation? Faced with unacceptable interference in the legal system and the extension of Israeli law to east Jerusalem, West Bank lawyers went on an indefinite strike in 1967. The military government responded by issuing Military Order 145, which allowed Israeli lawyers to appear in all West Bank courts, without any requirement that they should be trained in the applicable law or conversant in Arabic. Some Palestinian lawyers in due course felt that, although their complaints remained unanswered, their community could best be served by their return to work, and at the present time the profession is roughly equally divided between "working" and "striking" lawyers. Although there are now over two hundred Palestinian lawyers practicing in the courts, the permit allowing Israeli lawyers to practice in West Bank courts has not been revoked.

In contrast, lawyers from the occupied territories, other than those from east Jerusalem, are not allowed to become members of the Israeli bar and so cannot practice in Israeli courts or even in courts in east Jerusalem. Palestinian lawyers from annexed east Jerusalem are not automatically allowed to practice in Israeli courts, but may only do so after passing strict legal and language tests. Exceptions to this rule are not even made in the case of appeals by West Bank or Gazan residents to the High Court. If a Palestinian who employs a lawyer from the occupied territories wishes to appeal to the Israeli High Court, he or she has no option but to instruct a second lawyer in mid-case, even if the original lawyer is competent linguistically and in law to argue the case. It is obvious that this system is highly prejudicial and discriminatory not only to Palestinian lawyers from the occupied territories, but also to their clients.

Practicing lawyers, already struggling to operate professionally in a complex web of laws and courts, are further hampered by the absence of a professional organization which could maintain the standards of the profession, monitor and report developments in the law, represent the interests and views of the profession in regard to legislation, and advocate reform. Attempts by West Bank lawyers to set up such an association were consistently blocked by the military authorities. A group of lawyers eventually filed a petition in the High Court, but even a High Court ruling that the military commander reconsider the matter has resulted in no progress to date. At the time of writing there is still no professional association to serve and maintain the standards of the legal profession.

One other development relating to the legal system should be noted, which is the decision by Israel to make available its own High Court to the residents of the occupied territories. In this, Israel has indeed gone beyond what is required of it as an occupier by international law; nevertheless, the role of the High Court should not be overstated. It does not function as an appeal court, but as a forum for review of administrative acts of Israeli officials or employees, including the military. Although the High Court does not take the same stand as the government with regard to the applicability of the Fourth Geneva Convention, it has been able to avoid coming into conflict with the government by holding that, as treaty law rather than customary law, the Geneva Convention cannot in any event be applied by the courts.

Evidence in the High Court is given by affidavit, so that there is no opportunity to cross-examine those giving evidence. The Court has proved extremely loath to question those acts that the authorities claim are based on security requirements, and its interpretation of a number of points of international law, such as the legality of deportation of individuals, of demolition of houses, and of imposition of new taxes, has varied from that of the rest of the world. The military government then cites such decisions in support of its contention that these acts are legal.

Perhaps the best indication of the efficacy of recourse by Palestinians from the occupied territories to the High Court is the result of a study by Advocate Mazen Qupti of all published decisions of the High Court from 1967 to 1987.[29] He found that in only two and one-half cases out of the fifty-nine reported cases involving a petitioner from the occupied territories did the Court decide in favor of the petitioner. The High Court does, however, serve one valuable function, which is to grant temporary relief, by delaying the immediate execution of an order until the military commander can show why he should be allowed to proceed with the proposed action. But because the final decision, as has been seen, almost invariably supports the military government, this benefit is limited. Palestinian petitioners faced with deportation, for instance, must thus decide whether to appeal to the Court, perhaps thereby lending credibility by their participation to a system in which they have no faith, or not to appeal, thus foregoing the temporary reprieve and facing immediate expulsion.

Although the formal structure of the local courts still exists, albeit in a truncated manner, the courts have suffered from such neglect and their functions have been so depleted that little of their former character remains, and they struggle to maintain their professional standards and identity. Most importantly they have been shorn of any possibility of defending their constituency from the acts of the military or of the Israeli population illegally settled in the territories. In matters relating to the occupier's security, this is to be expected, but as has been seen above, it stretches far beyond issues of security to practices affecting the future of the land,

---

29. Reported by Mazen Qupti at a conference in Jerusalem, January 1988.

resources, and population. The changes have rendered the courts incapable of preventing or even checking the practices and changes wrought by the military authorities in the occupied territories, and have left them bereft of any powers which might have enabled them to slow the process of land acquisition and economic exploitation.

CONCLUSION

The process of change that has been described above in relation to the legal system has occurred to a greater or lesser extent with regard to every other aspect of the infrastructure of the occupied territories. Each sector has been progressively disempowered or forced to depend on its Israeli counterpart and its ability to function independently placed in jeopardy, if not lost. Attempts to prevent this or to fulfill the functions normally carried out by governmental bodies or professional organizations are systematically thwarted.

These changes are almost invariably framed in apparent compliance with local law, and the pretense has been maintained that local law is still applied, but it too has been altered beyond recognition. Laws have been amended, sometimes as necessitated by inevitable changes, but more often to allow actions or policies of Israel to be framed within the terms of local law, in apparent compliance with international law.

There are four apparent reasons for these pervasive changes. First, Israel wants to establish total control over the population of the territories, for instance by rendering a wide variety of daily activities subject to the approval of the military government, by suppressing all forms of collective social activity such as youth groups, voluntary work committees and professional organizations, and by imposing administrative punishments without trial. Second is a need to repress nationalistic expressions of the population and suppress the ability of the infrastructure to function independently. Third, the occupier wants to acquire permanent control over the resources of the occupied territories, such as water and land. And finally, Israel hopes to further the aims of the settlers, and thus establish a permanent presence in the territories, one inextricably and irreversibly linked with Israel.

All four purposes, except to the limited extent to which control over the population is genuinely necessary for security, are outside the occupier's powers under international law. But international law has itself suffered a similar process of adaptation to suit Israel's purposes. The provisions of international law are repeatedly reinterpreted, either to exclude Israel's own actions, as in the case of the application of the Fourth Geneva Convention or the practice of deportations, or to expand the meaning so as to leave it without meaning, as was seen in the interpretation of the parameters imposed by the Hague Regulations on the conduct of the belligerent occupier.

Although Israel frames its actions in terms of either local or international law, in neither case does Israel accept the interpretations of others of this law, if this would not fit its actions. This is not because the law, as Israel maintains, is inadequate to govern a modern and prolonged occupation. It is because Israel's purposes in occupying the West Bank and Gaza are not those of a simple belligerent occupier, but those of a country with sovereign designs over the land and its resources. The process it has been steadily implementing is that of *de facto* annexation, and the law has been harnessed to disguise and legitimize this process.

CHAPTER 5

Personal Status and Rights

Lea Tsemel

"They slapped an Arab, so what. The military governor is authorized to detain any Arab here for 18 days without warning. So instead, in order to be more gentle with them, they are invited to interrogation three times a week. So it's true that this is very disturbing and a bother, because they have to close their businesses those days. But it still saves them 18 days of arrest," he said, in a tone of great compassion.

(Aharon Domb, *Yediot Ahronot*
Friday Supplement, October 29, 1982)

Aharon Domb, a resident of the Israeli settlement of Kiryat Arba in the West Bank, was speaking to reporters from one of Israel's major daily newspapers about relations between residents of the settlement and Palestinians from the nearby town of Hebron. His comments give only a partial picture of relations between the Palestinian residents of the occupied territories and the Israeli authorities. There are countless cases of settlers and military personnel beating Palestinians for real or perceived misdemeanors. Other measures, such as the repeated calls for interrogation or detention for eighteen days that Domb mentions, are used not only to "find facts," but also as methods of punishment. It must be said, despite all Israeli propaganda, that an occupation is an occupation, and each and every Palestinian in the occupied territories lives under full occupation. (In this chapter east Jerusalem and the Golan Heights will be considered as part of the "occupied territories," as they are in reality, despite their formal annexation by Israel. Except for technical legal differences, the Israeli attitude towards the Palestinian and Syrian populations in these areas is identical.)

Israeli legal experts, particularly those who have served in the administration of the occupied territories, are fond of pointing out to critics that the occupation functions according to the rule of law. I will describe in this article how, whenever necessary, the "rule of law" is recruited in all its flexibility to directly serve the purposes of the conqueror. Thus, while

Israeli statutes do refer to personal status and rights, these are protected only insofar as they do not contradict or conflict with the interests of the occupiers.

LAWS AND THE COURTS

The "civil administration" in the occupied territories, like the military government before it, uses three sets of laws. Primary among these are the regulations issued on a day-to-day basis by the military commander of the occupied territories. These military orders adapt the legal code to the changing situation and serve precisely the growing needs and demands of Israeli policy towards the occupied territories. The military commander is the sole legislator. Over one thousand such orders have been issued since 1967.

Second in terms of frequency of use are the British Mandatory Defense (Emergency) Regulations of 1945. These regulations are applied in the occupied territories under the pretext that they are part of Jordanian law: under an order issued by the first military commander early in the occupation, every law that has ever been applied in the territories, unless formally nullified, remains in force.[1] The government of Jordan, which annexed the West Bank in 1950, has publicly denied that these regulations were ever adopted in the Hashemite Kingdom. So much has been written and said about the Defense regulations that I will not enter into a discussion of them here.[2]

Finally, Jordanian law is invoked whenever necessary.

Two sets of courts operate in the occupied territories: the civil courts, which deal with civil cases when the military government has no interests at stake, and the military courts, which deal with everything that falls under the rubric "security" or involves the interests of the military government. For instance, a straightforward case of murder involving two Jordanian civilians was brought before the military courts because the suspected murderer, a man named Janho, was a well-known collaborator with the Israelis, who did not want to risk his being found guilty by a civil court. He was acquitted by the military court in Ramallah. Land expropriations are generally transferred to the military domain, and are dealt with in special military committees.

1. Order Concerning Interpretation (Additional order no. 3), Judea and Samaria (no. 224), 1968.

2. See, for example, Sabri Jiryis, *The Arabs in Israel* (New York: Monthly Review Press, 1976).

ARREST AND DETENTION

In the areas under Israeli military occupation, every soldier has the right to detain any person if the soldier has "grounds for suspicion" that the person in question has committed an offense. This vague and general condition means that practically anybody can be held in custody. Detention can be extended for up to eighteen days on the approval of a police officer. (The police, it should be pointed out, are totally subservient to the military governor.) During this period a person can be denied, and in fact is almost automatically denied, access to a lawyer. Observers from the International Committee for the Red Cross are also normally denied access for at least fourteen days. A detainee can be held for up to six months without being brought to trial; a lawyer's access to a client can be denied indefinitely, even throughout the client's detention.[3]

Formally it is the prison governor who decides whether or not a lawyer will be allowed to see a client, but in fact it is the security services who make the decision. Almost without exception, a lawyer gets access to a client only after the client has broken down and confessed, or when the security services have abandoned interrogation. The reason for this is simple. The interrogation has one central purpose: to extract a confession. In order to achieve that purpose, the authorities subject the prisoner to isolation, torture, and humiliating physical conditions. Interrogations are carried out by anonymous, unexposable security service interrogators, in special sections in each detention center and prison. The detainee undergoes a preliminary period of starvation, sleep deprivation, and prolonged periods of standing with his hands cuffed and his head covered with a sack. The prisoners frequently complain of physical abuse – being dragged about, beaten and kicked – during this initial period. Often a prisoner is stripped and thrust under a cold shower. Verbal abuse, psychological pressure and humiliation – such as spitting in a prisoner's mouth or forcing him to crawl around a cell – are also frequently reported.

Since the publication in the London *Sunday Times* in June 1977 of a report on torture in Israeli prisons, lawyers have noticed a decline in reports of severe physical torture by security service interrogators. Apparently they have received orders not to "dirty their own hands" with excessive force. Prisoners report that this kind of torture is now being carried out by settlers involved in arrests, the border police (a paramilitary squad attached to the police), and prison guards. This duty has also been given to small groups of collaborators in each prison. At each central prison and detention center special rooms are set aside for collaborating prisoners, known as *asafir*

---

3. Order no. 29, article 11, amendment 2.

("song-birds"). Some of these have been convicted on criminal charges, while others are being held on political charges. In return for their services they are promised special privileges. Interrogation by *asafir* has proved very effective. It generally follows a set pattern. Initially the *asafir* represent themselves to the new detainee as the leaders of the PLO organizations in the prison. There are then two methods of approach. Prisoners report that initially the *asafir* greet the newcomer warmly, praising his courage, offering warm tea (which some allege is drugged), and asking to hear about what he did. If a prisoner does not "open up" in the face of this ruse, the *asafir* turn hostile; they may threaten the newcomer with razors, accuse him of collaborating with the authorities, and threaten to torture or kill him if he does not tell them what he has done. Many prisoners who have faced down their official interrogators for weeks break under this treatment and "confess." Their confession is often written down and they are made to sign. At their next interrogation prisoners are confronted with whatever information they have given the *asafir*. Often prisoners say they "confessed" to *asafir* to save their skins, to maintain their honor, or merely to "save face."

The importance of the confession and its contents has been even greater since 1981. Until that date a person could be tried only if he had personally confessed or, rarely, if there was solid evidence against him. But that year an amendment to the military orders[4] empowered courts to adopt and use as the principal or sole evidence against a defendant, allegations made about him in another person's confession. Perhaps the most notorious case of this type to date has been that of Ziad Abu Eain, a young Palestinian from al-Bireh who was deported from the United States to face trial in Israel on charges of planting a bomb in Tiberias. The only evidence against him was the confession of another prisoner, Jamal Yassin, who in it claimed that Abu Eain planted the bomb. At Abu Eain's trial Yassin maintained that he had only mentioned the former's name to divert responsibility from himself, as he had known that Abu Eain was out of the country. He denied that his confession was true. Nevertheless, and despite the fact that he produced an alibi, Ziad Abu Eain was found guilty and sentenced to life imprisonment.

With respect to confessions, it should be borne in mind that the vast majority of them are written in Hebrew, a language hardly any Palestinians from the occupied territories can read. In court these confessions are considered to constitute totally accurate and irrevocable records. Prisoners frequently complain of mistranslation. For example, these confessions invariably read, "I was a member of a terrorist organization" – a formula

---

4. Law Amending the Evidence Order (no. 4), 1979.

that a Palestinian who really was a member of a Palestinian organization would never use.

In east Jerusalem and the Golan Heights Israeli law applies. People accused of committing a security offense inside Israel are usually tried by a military court in Israel, under the British Defense Regulations. Rarely are they tried in civil courts. In general, the decision whether or not to try an individual in a civil court depends on international interest in the specific case. Archbishop Hilarion Capucci was tried by the Jerusalem district court, and Ziad Abu Eain by the district court in Tel Aviv. But of the thousands of Palestinians who have been tried in the past fifteen years, only a handful have had their cases heard before civilian judges.

For several years Palestinians living in Israel or east Jerusalem could benefit from some of the advantages that Israeli law extends to detainees. Foremost among these was the right to see a lawyer shortly after detention. (This is not to say that the process generally went smoothly.) However, on December 3, 1981, the Knesset passed a bill[5] enabling the security services, acting through the police, to prevent a client from seeing his or her lawyer for successive periods of fifteen days. Subsequently wide use has been made of this new regulation, and the situation in Israel now parallels that in the occupied territories.

Quite commonly detainees are not interrogated at all. Some of these detentions are "preventive" arrests; others are intended as scare tactics, with a political aim. As the quote at the beginning of this chapter illustrates, detention can be used to penalize an individual or a family or, for instance, to "persuade' a certain *hamula* to cooperate with the Village Leagues (see chapter 21). For example, in July 1982 over one hundred residents of the village of Sair in the Hebron district were rounded up and held for eighteen days following an attack on the home of a Village League activist. There are grounds to suspect that some of these detentions are used to provide unpaid laborers to work in the military camps. This is particularly the case when mass arrests are made for a period of eighteen days to a month. The last annual Passover cleaning of military installations suspiciously coincided with mass arrests of people none of whom was ever brought to trial, and who were released once this service was complete.

The large number of people being arrested on such eighteen-day harassment detentions necessitated the opening, in 1982, of two special detention centers specifically for this type of detainee. One of these centers is at Faraa, in the Nablus area, and the other near Jericho. There have been no reports at all of people being interrogated at these centers; they are

5. Criminal Procedure Law, 1965; article 27(a), amendment no. 3, 1981.

merely subjected to a punitive and humiliating regime for eighteen days, then released.

LAWYERS

Besides the major restriction – that of forbidding the detainee access to legal counsel – other aspects of a lawyer's work are increasingly restricted. Lawyers who frequently defend political prisoners have been barred from working on certain political cases. The formal reason cited is "security." But information coming out of such security trials reveals that the authorities are most concerned with keeping from the public eye harsh methods of interrogation and other illegal measures which may have been used prior to detention. Brigitte Shultz and Thomas Reuters and a number of Palestinians were "kidnapped" from Kenya with the probable cooperation of the Kenyan government and held clandestinely in Israel for over a year. Their trial was held behind closed doors; after their release it became clear that the only reason for this was to prevent the lawyer of their choice from representing them and to cover up the illegality of their kidnapping and detention. Under this law the minister of defense can declare any trial restricted to a list of lawyers drawn up by the military authorities. Since the Supreme Court has confirmed this practice, naturally it has been widened: today, a lawyer who is not on the list cannot represent any administrative detainees in Israel whatsoever. The above situation, together with the limitations on lawyers' seeing their clients under interrogation and the virtual impossibility of retracting a confession once it has been signed, are measures of how slight the possibility is of a lawyer giving any meaningful aid to a Palestinian client.

There is no doubt that the authorities try to minimize the involvement of a lawyer and the effect of our profession. Perhaps the only benefit a lawyer can hope to win for a Palestinian prisoner is the mitigation of some of the harsher effects and punishments of the judicial system of the occupation. At the same time there is a fringe benefit for the authorities, in that they can then claim that the trials go smoothly and that prisoners are formally represented. In the case of the Palestinian prisoners taken in south Lebanon during the 1982 war, however, the authorities have decided to eschew this fringe benefit: when lawyers who have been given power of attorney by concerned relatives have asked to visit prisoners of that war, they have been denied access because, say the authorities, the prisoners are not on Israeli soil.

Although formally it is not on Israeli territory, the Israeli army has long behaved in southern Lebanon and all along the Lebanese coastline as if it were on Israeli territory. The first foreigner was kidnapped from Lebanon and brought to trial in a military court in Israel in February 1973. Faik Bulut, a Turk who lived in a Palestinian refugee camp in Lebanon, was tried in Israel on charges of membership in al-Fatah and illegal training with weapons. In 1971, as if predicting this event, the Israeli legislature had amended Article 5(a) of the Penal Law (Offenses against the State) to read: "The courts in Israel are entitled according to the laws of Israel, to try any person who has committed abroad any action that would have been an offense if it was carried out in Israel, [if] the action endangered or was intended to endanger the state of Israel, its security, property, economy or transportation, communications or contacts with other countries." Since then a large number of Palestinians, Lebanese and foreigners have been tried under similar circumstances: after being kidnapped by the forces of either Saad Haddad or Israel, they have been tried for actions that are considered offenses in Israel, even though those acts were committed on sovereign Lebanese territory.

The courts have decided that it makes no difference whether the person came to Israel of his own free will or was brought to Israel by force. Theoretically, a person living in Boston, Massachusetts who supports a Palestinian organization could be taken to Israel and tried as a criminal.

Over the past few years the Israeli navy has become a self-appointed coast guard for Lebanon. The Israelis have taken it on themselves to stop, check and search any ship traveling in the eastern Mediterranean. Many of the people apprehended in these raids have been tried in Israel.

It should be noted that all of these people were first detained administratively, held secretly in military camps, interrogated by military intelligence and only then brought to trial. In many cases they were held for several months without anyone knowing their whereabouts.

NATIONAL IDENTITY

Like any occupier of another people's land, Israel finds itself in a constant battle against any manifestation of national thought or identity. This is a pernicious and unwinnable struggle in which the occupier puts outside the law not only acts against the occupation but, increasingly, virtually any independent expression. It has not yet reached the heights of the ridiculous attained, for example, by the British – who during the mandate outlawed the wearing of the traditional Palestinian head covering, the *kuffiyya* – or by the Nazis in Europe, who fought a losing battle against Norwegians wearing paper clips on their lapels. It is, however, getting close.

Under the Ordinance for the Prevention of Terror, amendment 84, article 4, 1980, any action identifiable with an illegal organIzation is punishable by up to three years in prison. This law has been interpreted to in effect illegalize Palestine. The Palestinian flag is considered in Israeli courts the "flag of the PLO." Hundreds of people, especially youngsters, have been tried for possessing or flying the flag, and even for drawing it.

A pseudo-judicial decision was taken concerning this issue at Ben-Gurion University in Beersheba in May 1982. At a party given by Arab students at the university, some of them danced waving their *kuffiyyas* . One of the students, Mohammed Yassin, was subsequently tried before the university's disciplinary board on charges of "participating in a dance in which *kuffiyyas* in the colors of the flag of Palestine were waved," thus "hurting and insulting the feelings of his fellow students." He was issued a severe reprimand and ordered to apologize in writing, via the pages of the student newspaper, to the two Israelis who were present at the party. Refusal would result in the cancellation of his credits for that academic year. He refused.

In December 1981, Raymonda Tawil and Ibrahim Karaeen appealed to the High Court against the refusal of the Registrar of Companies to register their press office under the name "Palestine Press Services." After the judges agreed with a lower court decision that the word "Palestine" was "offensive to the Israeli public" and had been chosen for "improper reasons," the case was dropped. It is interesting to note in this respect that the Israeli newspaper *The Jerusalem Post* is still registered under the name "The Palestine Post Ltd."

Freedom of assembly is severely restricted. Overt political meetings are impossible. The laws restricting gatherings are also used to prevent cultural events. Anyone who organizes a meeting or parade without a license (a meeting is defined as "where ten people or more come together to hear speeches or to discuss a political subject or any subject that could be interpreted as political"), faces up to ten years in prison and/or a stiff fine.

PUBLICATIONS AND CENSORSHIP

Any material with a political content cannot be published unless it is authorized by the military governor. This is true even of fine arts and literature. The military government frequently issues lists of banned books; the forbidden titles now number more than a thousand. The police frequently raid the homes of intellectuals and journalists, gather up all their books and search for banned titles. It has become general practice to keep individuals charged with this offense in jail until their trial, when they are sentenced to a jail term equivalent to the time they have served, plus a large fine. Hamdi Farraj, a journalist in Bethlehem, was held thirty days and fined I£ 7,500 ($300). The banning of books is particularly problematic for several reasons. First, there is no central register of banned titles to which a person may refer to determine whether a specific book has been banned or not. Some lawyers have partial lists, but there is no comprehensive list available to the public. Then, because of the anomaly of the annexation of east Jerusalem, some publications that are legal in east Jerusalem are illegal in the West Bank. Radwan Abu Ayyash, a member of the executive committee of the Journalists Association, was arrested in Ramallah for possession of a publication legally printed by the association in Jerusalem – only ten miles away.

There are several laws and regulations governing censorship. All newspapers published in Israel must have a license, under which the owner or editor agrees to submit all material to censorship. Most Palestinian-run newspapers are published in east Jerusalem and are thus liable to Israeli laws.

Palestinian newspaper owners charge that they are discriminated against in the way their papers are censored. Primarily they cite an agreement between successive Israeli governments and the major Hebrew- and English- language dailies, under which an editorial committee from these publications and representatives of the administration meet annually to draw up guidelines for censorship. In essence this means that while news stories in Israeli papers are seen by the censor, opinion and editorial material is not. In Palestinian papers, everything is subject to censorship.

HARASSMENT

On the whole there is a campaign against anyone considered a potential leader, in any field, in the occupied territories – reporters, teachers, union activists, mayors, heads of charitable associations and professional bodies such as the Engineers' Union. Most individuals in these categories eventually fall victim to one or more of the authorities' harassment measures; administrative detention and restriction to one's house or town are particularly prevalent. Detention or restriction orders are issued for a period of three to six months which is, however, renewable at the order of the area military commander. No reason other than "security" need be given.

Another means of eliminating potential leaders is to encourage them to emigrate. Many people believe that the frequent clashes between the authorities and the various universities are intended at limiting higher education in the occupied territories and thus forcing as many intellectuals as possible to leave the area to teach at or attend foreign universities.

During academic year 1981/82, for example, the authorities closed down Bir Zeit University, for "security reasons," on three separate occasions, for a total of seven months (see chapters 17, 18 and 19).

Some measures of harassment take the form of military orders. Regulation 854, drawn up by the military government in the West Bank, was aimed at increasing Israeli supervision of institutions of higher education; it enabled the military government to exercise control over foreign faculty and students through the issuing of special permits requiring annual renewal (see chapter 17). The campaign against educational institutions is perhaps the most systematic harassment of a whole group.

Another way in which emigration is "encouraged" is by preventing open and regular passage between the occupied territories and Jordan. What Israel calls the "open bridges" are not really open. Many people are not allowed to leave unless they sign a commitment not to return for three to five years. Dr. Emile Jadallah Abu Dabaat, for instance, a West Bank physician who asked for permission to study in Canada, was given permission to leave only with the understanding that he would not return for at least five years. Evidently the authorities hope that after such a long absence most people will settle abroad permanently.

Once a Palestinian has left the occupied territories, if he cannot prove that his life is still centered there, his residency may be canceled. (When a Palestinian leaves the occupied territories his identification papers are taken from him, and Israel's consular officials often refuse to renew the laisser-passer.)

As I am limiting this chapter to a discussion of the legal aspects of the occupation, I will not go into the thorough and elaborate system by which opportunities for employment are kept in short supply, thus forcing Palestinians to leave the occupied territories in search of work. This is, however, another major factor in the outflow of population (see chapters 11, 12 and 13).

This policy of stifling the cultural, educational, and economic development of the Palestinian community is applied in Israel as well as the occupied territories. Israel Koenig is district commissioner for the northern district of Israel including the Galilee, where the majority of Israel's Palestinian citizens live. In 1976 he drafted a secret memorandum for the authorities suggesting major restrictions on Arab rights and the linking of any concessions to "cooperation" with the authorities. The report was leaked, and caused an immediate scandal. Nevertheless Koenig retained his post, and continued to be responsible for the formulation and execution of policy in the area.[6]

6. "The Koenig Report," *Journal of Palestine Studies* (Autumn 1976), 6 (1): 190-200.

People frequently ask me what it is like to be an anti-Zionist lawyer in Israel during this occupation. I usually answer that it is very sad to see injustice being done under a cover of "legality," while feeling so impotent and having to play a part as a lawyer in this system. But if it enables me to understand the system better and, from time to time, to alleviate its harshness, and if it enables me to bring the facts of the occupation before open-minded people, then it is worthwhile.

CHAPTER 6

The Transformation of Jerusalem:
Juridical Status and Physical Change

Ibrahim Dakkak

JURIDICAL STATUS

With the air of a vacationer coming home after a jaunt of some two thousand years, Israel's Prime Minister Levi Eshkol stated in 1968 that "by the grace of the unfolding of Jewish history," the Israelis "came back to historic Jerusalem and made it one and undivided again, as [their] whole and sovereign capital."[1]

Mr. Eshkol, *prima facie,* had required no moral or legal justification for the Knesset's passage in 1967 of three laws extending Israeli law to east Jerusalem and enlarging Jerusalem's municipal boundaries by government order.[2] Instead, it was Palestinian rights that were made questionable.[3]

Nevertheless, while the controversy over Jerusalem had lain dormant for almost nineteen years, it returned to the fore nineteen days after the Israeli occupation of the city in 1967. On July 4, 1967, the UN General Assembly reacted to the Israeli measures by adopting Resolution 2253 (ES-V), calling upon Israel to "rescind all measures taken [and] to desist forthwith from taking any action which would alter the status of Jerusalem."

1. *Israel Government Year Book, 1968-1969* (Jerusalem: Central Office of Information, Prime Minister's Office, 5739), p. 9.

2. Amendment No. II to the Law and Administration Order, June 28, 1967; Amendment to the Municipalities Ordinance, June 27, 1967; Protection of the Holy Places Law, June 1967.

3. Julius Stone, "Peace and the Palestinians," in John Norton Moore, ed., *The Arab-Israeli Conflict* (Princeton, N.J.: Princeton University Press, 1977), pp. 143-44.

The Israeli foreign minister responded by denying that the city had been "annexed," as the resolution stated, although he admitted that its administration and municipal services had been "integrated" into the authority of the Israeli municipal council.[4] In Resolution 2254 (ES-8) of July 14, 1967, the UN General Assembly deplored Israel's failure to implement Resolution 2253 and reiterated its call for Israel to rescind all measures intended to change the status of Jerusalem.

Whereas the authority of the "unfolding of Jewish history" may have been sufficient argument for Israel's Jewish population, it was not binding on the international community. Furthermore, although Israeli religious and historical claims abounded, counterclaims were also at hand.[5] Israel may not have been seeking bona fide imperatives, but nonetheless, some legal justification was required: while might was already in effect, right had not been established.

The Israeli Argument

Exponents of the Israeli position accepted the challenge and presented their views. Their main thesis rests on the negation of the Palestinian role, and consequently of Palestinian rights. The late Golda Meir summed up this position in a statement to the *London Sunday Times* (June 15, 1969): "There is no such thing as a Palestinian. . . . It was not as though there was a Palestinian people in Palestine considering itself as a Palestinian people and we came and threw them out and took their country away from them. They did not exist." Beclouding Palestinian rights within a misty veil of Arabism, these jurists have found it convenient to refer to an illegal Jordanian occupation of the city and a Jordanian act of aggression in June 1967. The Palestinians, they claim, by accepting Jordanian intervention in 1948 in lieu of their right to establish a Palestinian state, renounced this

4. Report of the Secretary-General on Measures Taken by Israel to Change the Status of the City of Jerusalem, 22 UN SCOR, Supp. July-Sept. 1967 at 73, UN Doc. 5/8052 (July 10, 1967), cited in Moore, ed., *Arab-Israeli Conflict;* see also Ibrahim Dakkak, *Some Aspects of the Israeli Annexation: Policy as Practiced in Jerusalem* (Jerusalem: The Arab Thought Forum, 1977), pp. 3-4.

5. For a presentation of the Israeli claims, see *Jerusalem* (Jerusalem: Kater Books, 1973), pp. 9-37 and 272-306; for counterclaims, see for example *Israel According to Holy Scripture* (Cedar Rapids, Iowa: Igram Press, n.d.); John Allegro, *The Chosen People* (London: Hodder and Stoughton, 1971), pp. 29-39; Mary Ellen Lundsten, "Wall Politics: Zionist and Palestinian Strategies in Jerusalem, 1928," *Journal of Palestine Studies* (Autumn 1978), 8(1):3-27; and Norton Mezvinsky. "Zionist Claims on Jerusalem," *The Search* (April 1967), 2(2).

right entirely; consequently, UN General Assembly Resolution 181-II of November 29, 1947, calling for the partition of Palestine, has been "overtaken by events."[6] Furthermore, this view develops, the newly created Jewish state found itself in a posture of self-defense,[7] and therefore was drawn into a military confrontation with the Arab armies in a "just war."[8] The Arabs by attacking the Jews outside the area of the Jewish state and by forcibly rejecting the internationalization of Jerusalem were themselves responsible for the first Israeli expansion beyond the partition boundaries."[9] In support of their argument, the Israelis claim that the emerging situation proved the existence of a vacancy or vacuum in sovereignty,[10] extending until June 1967. During that period, they point out, Jordan enjoyed the status of a belligerent occupant, but not that of a belligerent sovereign; therefore, Jordan's occupation of the West Bank and Jerusalem gave it neither title nor sovereignty. Further, as the use of force by contiguous Jordan was illegal, the Jordanian presence in Jerusalem constituted a *de facto* occupation.[11] Once Jordan was physically removed from east Jerusalem in a "just war" of self-defense the way was open for a lawful occupant – i.e., Israel – to fill the still subsisting vacancy.[12] As a result, the Israelis argue, Jordan is not entitled to reversionary rights of sovereignty.

In the view of these jurists, the situation is analogous to that prevailing after the conclusion of the armistice agreements in 1949.[13] Israel's land gains then in excess of the area allotted to it under the partition plan find

6. "Testimony of Yehuda Zvi Blum . . ." in *Hearings Before the Subcommittee on Immigration and Naturalization of the Committee on the Judiciary,* US Senate, Ninety-fifth Congress, October 17 and 18, 1977 (Washington: U.S. Government Printing Office, 1978), pp. 27, 29, 33.

7. *Ibid.,* p. 34.

8. Sylvan M. Berman, "Recrudescence of the 'Bellum Justum et Pium' Controversy and Israel's Reunification of Jerusalem," *International Problems* (May 1969), 8(1-2[15]):32.

9. Elihu Lauterpacht, *Jerusalem and the Holy Places* (The Anglo-Israel Association, 1968) p. 45; also Blum testimony, p. 29.

10. Lauterpacht, *Ibid.,* p. 41.

11. Blum testimony, pp. 29, 33, 37-38.

12. Lauterpacht, *Jerusalem,* p. 4; also Blum testimony p. 38.

13. Blum testimony, p. 36.

their legal justification in Security Council Resolution 242 of November 22, 1967, which called for Israeli withdrawal to the boundaries of June 4, 1967 (Article 1[i]). They find further justification in the principle of *uti possidetis.* According to this legal formula, a belligerent victor may, at his discretion, annex all or any part of the subjugated enemy territory if no provisions in any subsequent treaty between the two belligerents provide for a different arrangement.[14]

The Israeli polemic goes on to assert, *ex post facto,* that since title to the territory was based on a claim of relative, rather than absolute, validity,[15] and as no other state can produce a legal claim equal to that of Israel, then Israel's possession of Jerusalem is virtually indistinguishable from an absolute title to be valid *erqa omnes.*[16] (Relevant UN resolutions are included as an appendix to this chapter.)

Counterargument

The Israeli argument is more of a justification and rationalization than a bona fide legal judgment.[17]

In his reply to Professor Blum's testimony before a Senate subcommittee,[18] Professor W. T. Mallison expressed total agreement with the former's arguments with only two exceptions: one to a point of fact, and the other to a point of law.[19] So what were the exceptions?

The Israeli thesis depends basically on the denial of the existence of the Palestinian people, and consequently of the Palestinians' right to self-

14. Berman, "Recrudescence," p. 31.

15. Julius Stone, "No Peace – No War in the Middle East," in Moore, ed., *Arab-Israeli Conflict,* p. 325.

16. Blum testimony, p. 35; also his study *The Juridical Study of Jerusalem,* Jerusalem Papers Peace Problems No. 2 (Leonard David Institute for International Relations, February 1974), pp. 21 and 27.

17. Seth Tillman, "The West Bank Hearings," *Journal of Palestine Studies* (Winter 1979), 7(2):83.

18. Blum testimony, pp. 24-46.

19. Testimony of W. T. Mallison, in *Hearings Before the Subcommittee on Immigration and Naturalization,* pp. 46-56.

determination.[20] The Palestinian people's role is ignored, denied, or amalgamated in a general Arab role. The Jerusalem problem is made yet more complex by historical precedents, religious claims and acts of the Divinity,[21] counterclaims, and last but not least, political manipulation.

Regardless of the claims, religious and otherwise, to the contrary, Palestine in general and Jerusalem in particular have never been devoid of population since the third millennium.[22] Throughout its long history Jerusalem has been a matrix of ethnic metabolism. The synthesis of this continuous process all along the course of its history has produced the people known as Palestinians.[23] This organic continuity, rather than any "quantum" emission or absorption of ethnic groups, is backed by historical evidence. The purity of race claimed by present-day Zionists can find but a shaky basis in fact, or at best a metaphysical interpretation.[24] Joseph Reinart asserts, in his essay in the *Journal des Débats,* that the Jews converted to their religion Greeks, Egyptians, Romans, Asians, North Africans, Italians, Spaniards, Gauls, and so forth, while the great majority of Russian, Polish, and Galician Jews are descended from the Khazars, an ancient Turkic people whose nobility embraced Judaism in the eighth century. He concludes that to speak of a Jewish race, one must be either ignorant, or of bad faith.[25]

Even if the "quantum" change could be accounted for, the net result was nonetheless a continuous amalgamation[26] between the indigenous population and the incomers. Changes in language, culture, and state

20. See, for example, Tillman, "West Bank Hearings," pp. 85-86; Hassan Bin Talal, *Palestinian Self-Determination* (London, Melbourne, New York: Quartet Books, 1981); Henry Cattan, "The Status of Jerusalem," *Journal of Palestine Studies* (Spring 1981), 10(3).

21. Genesis 12:7, 13:15, 15:18, 17:8, 34:12; Exodus 3:17.

22. Kathleen Kenyon, *Digging Up Jerusalem* (London and Tornbridge: Ernest Benn, 1974), pp. 39, 79-81.

23. *Ibid.,* p. 108; M. A. Amiry, *Jerusalem: Arab Origin and Heritage* (London: Longmans, 1978), pp. 32-33, 48-52.

24. Kenyon, *Digging Up Jerusalem,* p. 108; Allegro, *Chosen People,* pp. 15,31-33.

25. March 30, 1979; cited by Henry Cattan, *Jerusalem* (London: Croom Helm, 1981), pp. 94-98, cited originally by Phillip de Saint Robert in *Le Jeu'de la France en Mediterranée* (Paris: Juillard, 1970).

26. Kenyon, *Digging Up Jerusalem,* p. 108.

religion can be acknowledged. But in no way are these changes relevant to the claim against the natural development of the population of Palestine and Jerusalem into the present-day Palestinians. Therefore the Palestinians can claim a bona fide ancestral relationship to the Canaanites, Hebrews, Greeks, etc.

The dialectics of the convergence of the Palestinian identity from its divergent roots is seen, by some, as similar to the dialectics of the emergence of Islam, after Judaism and Christianity, as the final revelation of God's message to humanity.[27] Muslim protagonists confirm this type of relationship by quoting the Quran, in which Abraham is said to have been Muslim before the advent of Islam (Ali-Umran No. 69). Similarly, one could suggest that the population of Palestine has been "Palestinian" since the third millennium, despite the modern connotations of the term. This argument is plausible insofar as it represents the deep organic and dialectic dynamics governing the development of the Palestinian identity.

Whatever its convoluted historical background, the Israeli argument finds no ion in international law. A belligerent victor, according to the law, may not annex all or a part of the subjugated enemy territory. The acquisition of territory by conquest ceased to be acceptable after World War I, and the Covenant of the League of Nations outlawed such acquisition. Accordingly, states do not recognize territorial changes based on title of conquest.[28]

Furthermore, although the nature of the war (just or unjust) that led to Israels' 1967 occupation of the West Bank, Gaza, and Sinai is very controversial, the Israeli negligence in seeking "consent" from the Palestinians contravenes the Palestinians' right to self-determination. Paul J. I. M. de Waart asserts that:

> Legally speaking, Israel has derived its territory as a criterium for its statehood from the mandate system and from having taken the law in general and its membership of the U.N. in particular precludes Israel from changing its boundaries unilaterally.[29]

A scrutiny of the Israeli thesis in light of this argument reveals how Palestinism completely undermines the Israeli argument. The Israeli

27. See for example Frank H. Epp, *Whose Land Is Palestine* (Grand Rapids, Mich.: Eerdmans, 1970), pp. 70-72.

28. Paul J. I. M. de Waart "International Law as a Framework for Peaceful Solution of the dispute between Arab States and israel," informal discussion paper (mimeographed), February 1988.

29. De Waart, "International Law," p. 6.

contention against the existence of a Palestinian identity and Palestinian rights therefore can be seen to hide a malicious aim. By the same token, any argument concerning Jerusalem that deletes the Palestinian factor is equally malicious. Thus the Israeli endeavor to substitute for the Palestinian role an ambiguous Arab or a Jordanian role, serves no justice. In fact, it follows that any agreement that fails to take into account the Palestinians' right to self-determination is *ex injuria jus non oritur* – invalid by reason of its injustice.

It follows from the above that the efforts to discredit the Israeli aggression by justifying Arab intervention in the 1948 war and Jordan's annexation of the West Bank[30] only play into the hands of the Israelis. Thus Arab conduct has served to discredit Palestinian rights, and in fact has helped the Israelis to claim that the land originally allotted for a Palestinian state in accordance with General Assembly Resolution 181-II of November 29, 1947, had become *terra nullius*, and that a vacancy or vacuum in sovereignty existed. However, with the establishment of a Palestinian identity in its own right, the Israeli claim of sovereignty falls flat.[31] In addition, the difficulty encountered by some[32] in accommodating Palestinian rights in the *status quo ante* expressed in Security Council Resolution 242 of November 22, 1967 and in General Assembly Resolution 2253 (ES-V) of July 4, 1967, is resolved by a rereading of General Assembly Resolution 181-II of November 29, 1947 and subsequent UN resolutions, particularly General Assembly resolutions 3236 of November 22, 1974 and 3375 of November 10, 1975, both of which explicitly call for the restoration of the inalienable rights of the Palestinian people, including the right to national independence.

Regardless of the history of the conflict, the status of Jerusalem remained, in accordance with General Assembly Resolution 181-II, that of a *corpus separatum* under international control.[33] No subsequent UN

30. Salem Kiswani, *Al markaz al-quanuni li madinat al-Quds* (The Legal Status of Jerusalem) (Cooperative Printing Press Society, 1977), pp. 291-96; also Henry Cattan, "Status of Jerusalem." See also the text of the cablegram from the Secretary-General of the League of Arab States to the Secretary-General of the United Nations in Moore, ed. *Arab-Israeli Conflict,* pp. 939-43; and Malcom H. Kerr, "The Changing Political Status of Jerusalem," in Ibrahim Abu-Lughod, ed., *The Transformation of Palestine* (Evanston, Ill.: Northwestern University Press, 1971), p. 368.

31. Hasssan Bin Talal, *Palestinian Self-Determination,* pp. 64, 129.

32. Stone, "No Peace – No War in the Middle east," in *Arab-Israeli Conflict,* p. 317.

33. see *The Status of Jerusalem* (New York: United Nations, 1979).

resolution was passed altering that status. Thus the change of status unilaterally effected by Israel – the Knesset's proclamation of Jerusalem as Israel's capital on January 23, 1950; its passage on June 27, 1967 of three laws extending Israeli jurisdiction to east Jerusalem; and Israel's official annexation of Jerusalem on July 30, 1980 – contradicts in letter and in spirit General Assembly Resolution 273-III of May 11, 1949, which admitted Israel into membership in the United Nations, as well as the other resolutions passed subsequently by the General Assembly and the Security Council.

The question remains whether the internationalization of Jerusalem by a resolution of the United Nations conferred sovereignty over the city on the international body. The answer is that sovereignty is vested in the Palestinian people. The UN does not possess the competence to extinguish this right.[34] Furthermore, with respect to Jerusalem, UN Resolution 181-II was a conditional recommendation. Part III, Section D of this resolution stated that the special regime to administer the *corpus separatum* was to remain in force in the first instance for a period of ten years, unless the need arose for a reexamination before the end of that period. A mandatory reassessment was to take place at the end of the ten-year period. The right of the inhabitants to express their wishes regarding any proposed modifications of the city's regime was also guaranteed. It is thus fair to say that the United Nations, acting on behalf of the international community, was competent to rule that Jerusalem be internationalized; but it did not have the authority to divest the Palestinians of their sovereignty over the city. In 1948 the Palestinians were not able to respond freely to Resolution 181-II. They had been deprived of their freedom to act independently since 1936, when the Arab sovereigns had intervened (October 8) to end the Palestinian revolt. After this beginning Arab rulers had continued to falsify the Palestinian will. In 1946 the Arab League had decreed that Palestinian political parties should be disbanded. In view of the inability of the Palestinians to respond freely to Resolution 181-II, the division of the city constituted an aggression against their fundamental rights of self-assertion and self-determination.

The juridical case for the Palestinians does not, however, negate the necessity of a political solution.[35] Notwithstanding the existence of political

34. Cattan, "Status of Jerusalem," p. 9.

35. See, for example, Simha Flapan, ed., *When Enemies Dare To Talk* (London: Croom Helm, 1979), pp. 88-89.

BOUNDARIES OF JERUSALEM AS PROPOSED IN THE "PARTITION RESOLUTION" ON NOVEMBER 29, 1947

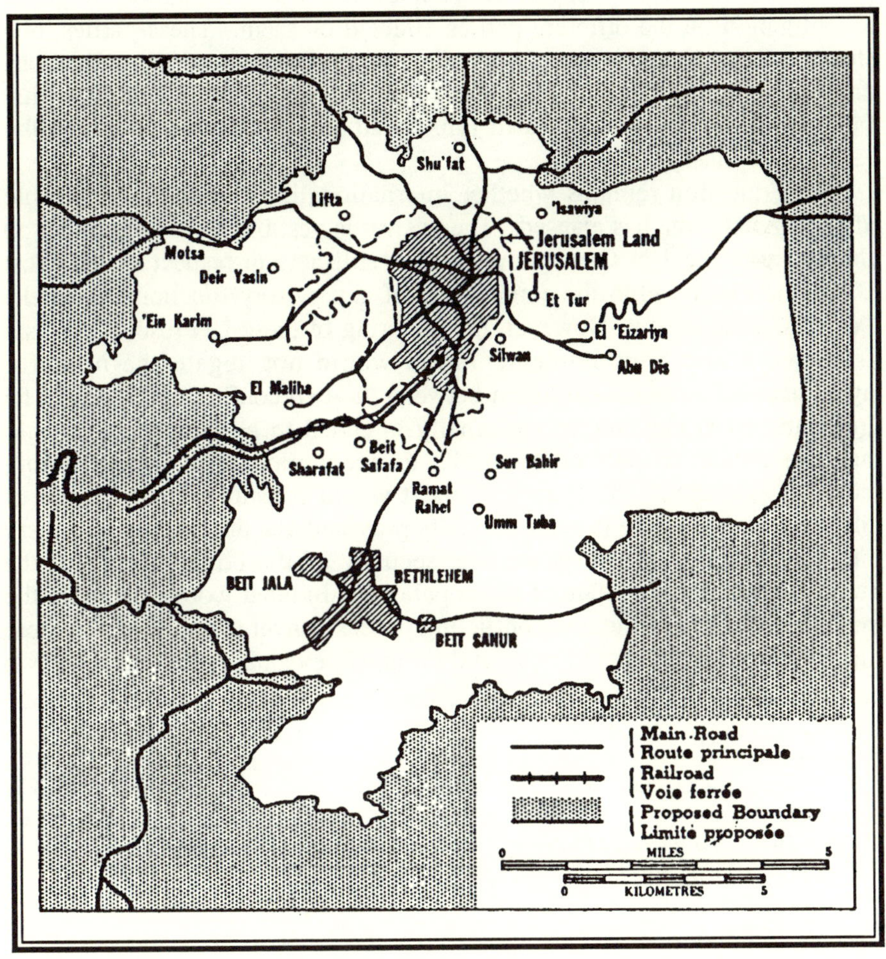

Source: *The Status of Jerusalem,* United Nations, New York, 1979.

and religious external interests,[36] the internationalization of the city, as an expression of the failure to reach a compromise formula between the conflicting parties, provided a common denominator accepted and adopted by the international community.

The injustice contained in the partition plan does not deprive it of its merits. In other words, the resolution, under the prevailing conditions at that time, constituted a rational approach to a political solution.[37] The United Nations, by virtue of its responsibility, was the most eligible body to pass an injunction with respect to this question, and its resolutions imposed an obligation on the different parties affected by them. These parties, one should presume, cannot simply be selective in disposing of the obligations and accepting the benefits. Thus any juridical argument on this issue that fails to honor these rulings also fails to attain credibility, and enters the realm of sophistry.

The question remains whether internationalization is still applicable after so much time has elapsed. The answer is yes, basing my argument on the fact that the UN General Assembly "still acts in respect of the West Bank and Gaza within the competence of supervisory functions under the Palestine Mandate."[38] However, the honoring of these UN resolutions as a framework and their implementation would not negate the need for agreement on a political solution between the two conflicting parties. The international administration, originally intended to be temporary,[39] would have to adjust, in part or in whole, to accommodate any forthcoming bilateral agreement. Such an agreement would constitute the antithesis of the continuation of the present situation, provided that the two parties satisfy the conditions of world peace, the security of the contestants, and the maintenance of the welfare of the population. In other words, the more the national interests of the two conflicting parties converge willfully, the more internationalization should relax and diminish, eventually to vanish.[40] Two

36. See, for example, A. L. Tibawi, *British Interests in Palestine* (London: Oxford University Press, 1961). For the emergence of Christian attachment see also Walter Zander, *Israel and the Holy Places of Christendom* (London: Weidenfield and Nicolson, 1971), pp. 10-14, 72, 74, 171-74, and appendix 2, pp. 175-80.

37. Flapan, ed., *When Enemies Dare To Talk*, p. 89.

38. De Waart, "International Law," p. 8.

39. UNGA Resolution 181-II, Part III, Section D.

40. For another argument concerning a solution see Henry Cattan, *Jerusalem*, pp. 144-48.

conditions should be satisfied. First, whatever the present situation in Jerusalem, Israel should rescind the pseudo-legal status it has unilaterally conferred on its presence. Second, the right to self-determination should be respected and practiced freely by the two concerned parties.

GEOGRAPHIC AND POLITICAL IMPERATIVES

Historical Background

The choice of Jerusalem as a Jewish center in the tenth century B.C. was prompted by more than one factor. As recounted in 2 Samuel 6, external pressures at that time forced the unification of the Hebrew tribes. The centralization of the tribal cults necessitated taking over the Jebusite shrine at Jerusalem in order to avoid arousing tribal jealousies. Thus a state religion based on a single shrine at Jerusalem was established. Consequently, before the Babylonian conquest and during the exile, the notion of Jerusalem evolved to become a symbol of the unity of the Jews and their yearning for reunion after their redemption from bondage.[41]

The evolution of this religious symbolism owes a great deal to the city's central location. Historically speaking, much of Jerusalem's sanctity has derived from the city's geographic and political eminence in the course of the history of Palestine.

The strategic importance of Jerusalem is revealed by the numerous attempts, in different periods, to establish a unified control over Palestine. In the Bronze Age, Palestine was composed of city-states under distant control. The nature of the country's terrain restricted the communications routes within very narrow limits. From the watershed the valleys on either side deepen very rapidly. The summit of the watershed – in which Jerusalem lies – forms the "backbone" supporting the structure of the country. Along this backbone extends the main north-south route.[42]

King David, in his endeavor to unite his kingdom, made Jerusalem his capital because of its dominating position over this main route.[43] Though it lacked commercial prominence,[44] it commanded the approaches to the

41. Allegro, *Chosen People,* pp. 26, 30-33, 37.

42. Kenyon, *Digging up Jerusalem,* pp. 29-41.

43. *Ibid.*

44. George Adam Smith, *Historical Geography of Jerusalem* (Jerusalem: Ariel Publishing House, n.d.), 1:14.

coastal plain and the Jordan rift valley, thus affording the master of the city direct control over both the Via Maris and the King's Way, extending from the Aqaba area to Damascus via Kerak and Amman.[45]

Likewise, despite the eschatological argument, the late Christian and early Muslim attachments to the city may find their explanation within the same geopolitical context. This context, which helps explain the prominence Jerusalem has enjoyed through its history, has found its explicit modern expression in the 1948 conflict and its aftermath.

The 1947 partition plan (Part III, Section B) excluded the area of Jerusalem as a *corpus separatum* not assigned to either party. The division of the city in the wake of the 1949 armistice between the warring parties represented a politically and strategically inadequate *fait accompli,* the demotion of the status of the city and the cessation of its historic and strategic role.

The western sector, controlled by Israel, was connected to the heartland of the state by the Jerusalem corridor, a narrow bottleneck that posed a military headache for Israel. Haim Herzog, then Israel's director of military intelligence, overdramatized this situation when he commented that the Knesset was within light mortar range from the Arab side, while some government offices were within pistol range.[46]

The Jordanians, by keeping the eastern sector of the city, were able to salvage part of the main north-south route. The only dIsruption was at the southern end of the city, where a detour had to be constructed through Sur Baher and around the Israeli enclave to preserve the geographic unity of the West Bank. But this route was incomplete: the southern part of Palestine from Hebron to the Sinai, and the northern part from Jenin to the Syrian border, had fallen under Israeli domination.

In both cases the east-west route was disrupted. The Israelis had to move the north-south route to the old Via Maris, while the Jordanians moved the route to the old King's Way. Thus these historical routes regained their old prominence.

The most dramatic change in this respect, however, was Jordan's conversion of the strategic core area of Palestine into a mere hinterland serving the new economic and political center: Amman, situated astraddle

45. E. Orai and E. Efrat, *Geography of Israel* (Jerusalem: Israel Universities Press, 1964), pp. 225-26, 247-48.

46. Israel Ministry of Foreign Affairs, Department of Information, Press Release no. 176, June 9, 1961, cited by J. C. Hurwitz, "The Role of the Military in Society and Government in Israel," in Sydney Nettelton Fisher, ed., *The Military in the Middle East: Problems in Society and Government* (Columbus: Ohio State University Press, 1963), p. 92.

the newly revived King's Way. By thus demoting Jerusalem to a mere historical and religious shrine, the Jordanians adjusted to the emerging new geographic situation.

Israel, on the other hand, having established its economic and political activity from the outset in the coastal plain, made use of the symbolism attached to Jerusalem to charge the Israelis with religious and political aspirations.

The changing status of Jerusalem brought with it new facts. The annexation of the West Bank by the Hashemite Kingdom of Jordan in 1950 called for the emergence of a new set of economic, social, and political priorities in the new-formed entity. Likewise the Israelis, during the same period, developed their own priorities. As the two sets of priorities were in no way designed to converge, the net result, after nineteen years of occupation, was further alienation between the two sides.

The situation in general was unsettled. Neither party made any secret of its desire to regain full control over Palestine. As a result of these conditions, the status of Jerusalem was not strategically decided.

The Annexation of Jerusalem

With Israel's annexation of east Jerusalem on June 27, 1967, a new situation was created. By imposing its control on the whole city, Israel was paving the way for the total annexation of the West Bank. To put it differently, the annexation of the West Bank by Israel should logically have been decided on concurrently with the decision to annex east Jerusalem.[47]

In retrospect, Israel's decision to adopt the terms of the Fourth Geneva Convention "voluntarily" without any "obligation," was a sign of Israel's intention to treat the area occupied in 1967 as territory "liberated" from alien rule, as was the official decision on December 17, 1967 to change the name of the West Bank to "Judea and Samaria."[48] The Israeli decision on February 29, 1968 to no longer consider the occupied area "enemy territory"[49] was a further indication of Israeli aims.

Taking into consideration the lack of strategic interest the Jordanians displayed with respect to Jerusalem after reviving the King's Way, in

47. Ibrahim Dakkak, *Al Quds Il Ashri Sanawat* (Jerusalem during Ten Years) (Jerusalem: Arab Thought Forum, 1981), p. 23.

48. Blum testimony, pp. 25-26, 35.

49. Nahumi, "Politics and Practices of Occupation," *New Outlook* (Tel Aviv), May 1968, p. 35; cited by Raja Shehadeh, *The West Bank and the Rule of Law* (New York: International Commission of Jurists and the Law in the Service of Man, 1980).

addition to the restiveness of the Israelis during the period when they were prevented from controlling the city and the strategic value of the "backbone" of Palestine, it is easy to understand the euphoria expressed by the Israelis over their strategic gain in June of 1967, and the comparatively cool emotional response of the Jordanians to their corresponding loss.

Whatever the reaction on both sides, the losers were the Palestinians. Israeli control of Jerusalem, under eschatological and other pretexts, virtually ensured full Israeli control of the West Bank. The Israelis' claim that they had "liberated" Eretz Israel faced the Palestinians with an unprecedented challenge.

The restoration of the geographic unity of Palestine under Israel in 1967 allowed the latter to reinstate the strategic position of Jerusalem on the north-south and east-west axes.[50] The extension of the latter axis to the east was maintained by the "open bridges" policy, while the northern and southern extensions were restored through the "good fence" policy (Saad Haddad enclave) in the north, and by the normalization of Israeli-Egyptian relations following the March 1979 peace treaty, in the south.

Plans put forward by various Israeli statesmen called unanimously for the widening of the Jerusalem corridor in the Latrun and Gush Etzion areas.[51] On the northern side of the corridor, controlling its western approach, the three Arab villages of Yalu, Imwas (Emmaus) and Beit Nuba were completely destroyed in 1967 after the fighting had stopped; their inhabitants were forced to leave the area. The Modim and Givon blocs of settlements were established to control the approach and to "thicken" the Jewish presence on that flank. Ramot and the Jerusalem bloc completed the extended northern periphery of the strategic belt by adjoining the Maale Adumim bloc and the southern tip of the Jordan Valley bloc.[52] To the south, the city is embraced by the Gush Etzion bloc, comprised of an urban center

50. J.W.L. Hopkins, *Jerusalem: A Study in Urban Geography* (Grand Rapids, Mich.: Baker Book House, 1971), pp. 16-19; see also Walid Khalidi, "Facts and Fiction," in Institute of Palestine Studies, Beirut; and World Conference of Christians for Palestine, Canterbury, *The Judaization of Jerusalem 1967-1977*, Beirut, p. 15.

51. For details see William Wilson Harris, *Taking Root: Israeli Settlement in the West Bank, the Golan and Gaza-Sinai, 1967-1980* (Chichester and New York: Wiley, 1980), pp. 39-40, 56-57, 147-53, 177-81.

52. The Modim bloc includes the settlements of Mevo Modim, Matityahu, Matityahu B, Shelat, Kfar Ruth and Mevo Horon; the Givon bloc: Beit Horon, Mitzpe Givon, and Givon (urban Givon); Givon B and Givon C are still to be established; the Jerusalem bloc: Kalandia, Neve Yaakov, Ramat Eshkol, French Hill, and Mount Scopus. For details of the Maale Adumim and Jordan Valley blocs, see chapters 8 and 9.

(Efrat), five rural settlements, a regional center and two settlements still on the drawing board. The highway running from the coastal plain through Gush Etzion to Ain Gidi on the Dead Sea marks the southern edge of this belt.

In practical terms, the thickening of the Jewish presence in this belt has created a new Jerusalem corridor extending from Jerusalem to the Jordan River. Thus the east-west axis has been dominated both demographically and strategically.

It is no strange coincidence that the Israeli defense minister stated, in May 1982, that Israel must transfer the bulk of its production centers from the coastal plain to the West Bank within the next twenty years. His warning that failure to do so would undermine Israel's security reflects the country's strategic need to inhabit the "backbone" in order to defend it. His statement fits in perfectly with the present geographic position Israel holds and intends to keep.

Thus the physical changes introduced in Jerusalem by the Israeli administration are part and parcel of the general planning scheme now being applied in the West Bank. The geographic distribution of the settlements and the new transportation network are meant to reformulate the geomorphology of the area to complement the Israeli regional master plan. They are intended, ultimately, to effect the political integration of the West Bank into Israel proper, and to subordinate Palestinian priorities, political and otherwise, to Israeli interests.[53]

"The Greater Jerusalem Area"

The "Greater Jerusalem Area" (GJA) as it figures in the 1982 planning scheme comprises the area surrounding "unified" Jerusalem from the north, east and south. The area affected by this scheme covers roughly one-half million dunums (1 dunum=approximately one-quarter acre – see table for details of land use), or almost 8 percent of the total area of the West Bank. It includes five Arab municipalities (Ramallah and al-Bireh in the north and Beit Jala, Beit Sahour, and Bethlehem in the south), and thirty-eight villages. The plan calls for at least one Arab village, al-Walajah, northwest of Beit Jala, to be razed.

53. For a clear Israeli viewpoint see Saul Bernard Cohen's studies on the geopolitics of Jerusalem, especially "Geographical Basis for the Integration of Jerusalem," *Orbis* (Summer 1977), 20(2):287-313, and "Jerusalem, a Geographical Imperative," *Midstream,* May 1975.

The GJA plan is being presented as an amendment to Mandatory Plan RJ5.[54] Its most prominent characteristics are:

1) The extension of the Israeli road network to the area;

2) its use of land; and

3) the legal and juridical juxtaposition introduced in the text of the amendment order.

The road network proposed almost completely neglects the existing system. Under the circumstances, the new system is bound to win out over the old. This will lead ultimately to a selective integration of the various Palestinian localities into the economic and production systems of Israel proper, thus forcing Israel's strategic needs on the Palestinians' natural right to maintain and develop their indigenous social, economic, and political life. When we add to these negative effects the effects of the other proposed major lateral routes in the West Bank,[55] it is possible to visualize the damaging physical and moral impact these systems will have on the inhabitants and their future.

The "land use" proposed by the scheme in effect freezes the natural expansion of Arab towns and villages, while providing ample room for the expansion of Jewish settlements. Areas without any specific "use" under the plan have been designated "special areas": it has been left to the discretion of the Israeli-staffed Higher Planning Council in the West Bank to decide when and for what purpose these areas will be utilized. Further restrictions against natural expansion have been introduced in agricultural areas and in the building regulations for the villages. Other areas have also been restricted in use. The right of way for the main transportation routes varies between two hundred and three hundred meters.

With respect to the third point, the occupation authorities frequently strain the law with respect to the above-mentioned Regional Planning Scheme No. 1/82. It is common practice for the commander of the West Bank to confer on himself or delegate to others authorities unaccounted for in the original Planning Law (No. 79, 1966). Furthermore, some of the Israeli amendments to Jordanian law have jeopardized proper legal procedures and controls.[56]

54. Israel Defense Army – The Civil Administration in Judea and Samaria, "Partial Regional Planning Scheme" No. 1/82, Amendment No. 1/82 to scheme (RJ5), n.d. The project is based on the Kendall plan of 1948.

55. See chapters 8 and 9.

56. Shehadeh, *West Bank and the Rule of Law,* especially pp. 27-34, 107-112, 117-18.

JERUSALEM'S VIA DOLOROSA

Israeli planning in Jerusalem proper emanates from the same philosophy that has governed the planning of the Greater Jerusalem Area and the West Bank in general.

Within the city, Israel has subordinated Arab Jerusalem to the priorities of west Jerusalem and its society. All that Israel's Zionist heritage has to offer Jerusalem is the Western idea of urban planning, with its good and bad points. This has been applied with emphasis on the Jewish character of the city. Whereas historically the western sector had always been a satellite of the Old City, now the opposite is true: the Israeli sector has become the focus of the city, while the subordination of the Arab sector is being accentuated.

Between 1948 and 1967, planning in the Arab and the Israeli sectors followed two vastly different philosophies. In the eastern sector, the Arab administration succeeded in adapting the planning schemes introduced by the mandate to something closer to the character of the city, in harmony with its civilization and the temperament of its inhabitants. This is not to claim that planning in east Jerusalem was perfect; but it did harmonize with the character of the Old City. Meanwhile, the Old City spread outside its walls so spontaneously that the city inside the walls and its extension outside them were integrated in a genuine and totally natural manner.

At the same time, the western part of the city developed along Western lines, quite unrelated to the atmosphere of the Old City and its cultural heritage, independently of it and quite unintegrated with it.

Probably the fact that the western part of Jerusalem developed in complete isolation from the Old City, and that relations between the two were for nineteen years restricted to visual contact through telescopes set up by Israel in the western part for the benefit of visitors, entrenched the idea of the separation of the two sectors in the minds of the Israeli planners. It may also have entrenched their view of the Old City as an embodiment of archaeology, rather than a living population center. They have ignored the vitality of the Old City and its ability to keep up with the times, and thus have increased the alienation of the western sector from it. This separation between Arab Jerusalem and west Jerusalem was emphasized by the creation of a green belt separating the two parts. The workmen who removed the wall that separated the two cities until 1967 may well have been preparing the ground for a more symbolic separation. This entrenchment of the separation, at the wish of the Israelis, increased the geographical and psychological distance between the focal points of the two sectors, an effect accentuated in turn by the exaggerated prominence given to the walls of Jerusalem and the severance of relations between it and its

THE STRATEGIC SIGNIFICANCE OF JERUSALEM

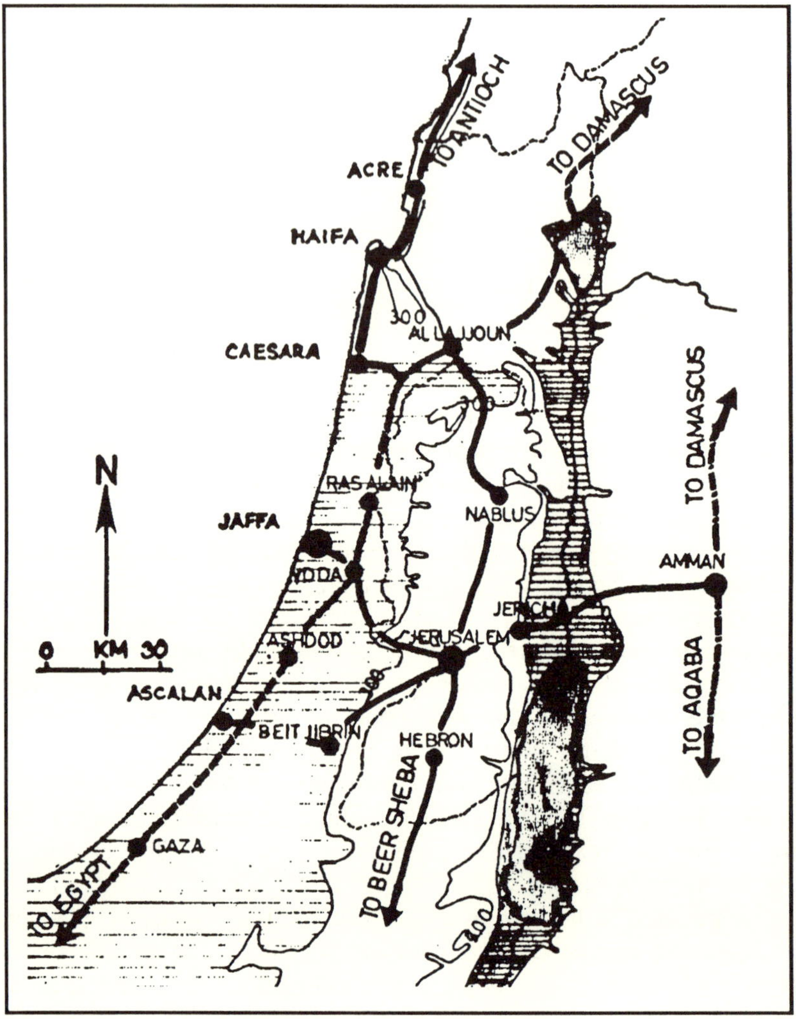

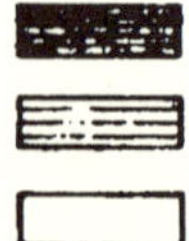

JERUSALEM – LINES BEFORE HOSTILITIES OF 1967

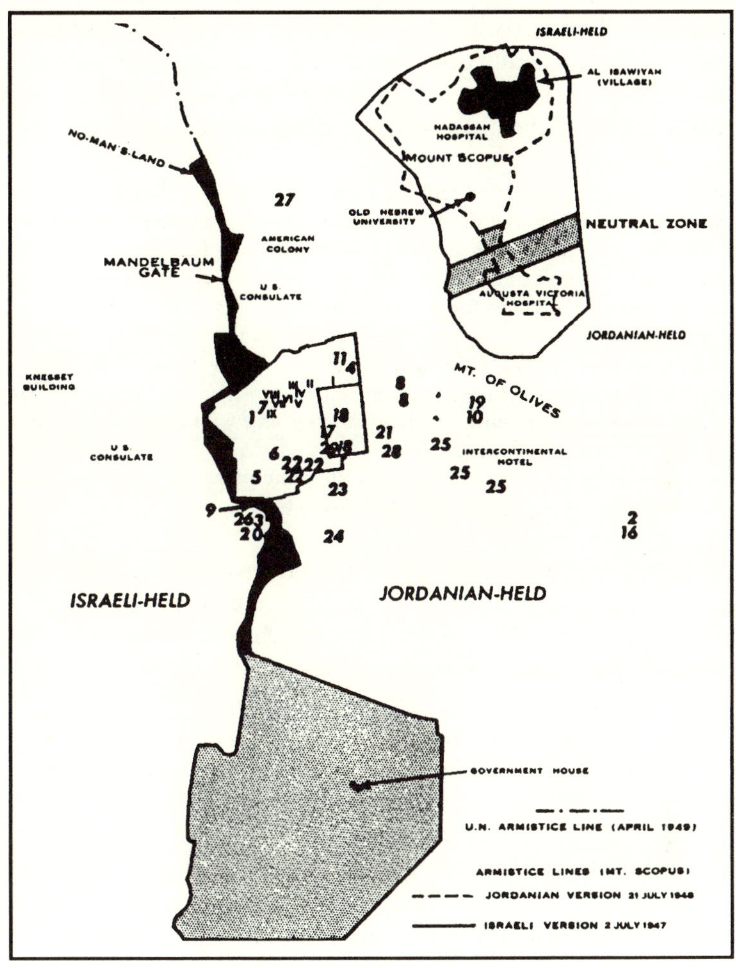

CHRISTIAN	MUSLIM	JEWISH
1. Basilica of the Holy Sepulchre		
2. Bethany		
3. Cenacle		
4. Church of St Anne		
5. Church of St. James the Great		
6. Church of St. Mark		
7. Deir al Sultan *		
8. Tomb of the Virgin * and Garden of Gethsemane		
9. House of Caiphas and Prison of Christ		20. Tomb of David (Nebi Daoud)
10. Sanctuary of the Ascension * and Mount of Olives		21. Tomb of Absalom
11. Pool of Bethesda		22. Ancient and Modern Synagogues
12. 'Ein Karim **		23. Bath of Rabbi Ishmael
13. Basilica of the Nativity, Bethlehem * **		24. Brook Siloam
14. Milk Grotto, Bethlehem * **		25. Cemetary on Mount of Olives
15. Shepherds Field, Bethlehem * **	16. Tomb of Lazarus	26. Tomb of David
I to IX inclusive Stations of the Cross	17. El Burak Esh-Sharif	27. Tomb of Simon the Just
	18. Harem al-Sharif (Mosque of Umar and Mosque of Aska)	28. Tomb of Zachariah and other Tombs in Kidron Valley
	19. Mosque of the Ascension	29. Wailing Wall *
		30. Rachael's Tomb * **

* Holy Place to which the Status Quo applies
** Holy Places in international area of Jerusalem not shown on this map

SOURCE: *The Status of Jerusalem,* United Nations, New York, 1979.

immediate environment. In this way, the Old City is being turned into a place to be visited, while west Jerusalem is a place where people work and make a living. This separation of functions, in addition to the physical separation, has increased the division between the two sectors of the city.

The overall purpose of the plan has been described faithfully by one of the former planners of the city. Arthur Kutcher wrote in 1973:

> The Israeli victory in June 1967 reunified Jerusalem. It also brought contemporary Western culture in a massive dose. The speed and magnitude of the cultural and technological changes which are now occurring are far greater than any in Jerusalem's past. There can be no doubt that the next few years will stamp the city's character for decades, perhaps for centuries to come.
>
> The question is, of course, what sort of values and ideals is Western civilization bringing to the Holy City? As a specific instance of a general case, Jerusalem presents one of the most extreme and hurtful examples of contemporary Western technology and Western values invading and clashing with a city whose form and setting are essentially pretechnological, a city relatively uncorrupted by contemporary urban ills, built according to principles and priorities totally at variance with those of our contemporary Western Civilization.[57]

Given that the politician, and not the professional, handles town planning in Jerusalem,[58] it would perhaps be unrealistic to expect organic and normal planning. And in fact, the imprint of official directives and military thinking is clearly visible in the city.

The encirclement of Jerusalem by "pure" Jewish neighborhoods has turned the Old City into a ghetto. Meanwhile, the evolving grid relationship between Jerusalem, the surrounding towns, and more distant areas has, by subjecting all Jerusalem's requirements as a city to the needs of the politician and the strategist, transformed it into a fortress city.

Seen in this light, the new names given to many of the city's main thoroughfares since 1967 seem less surprising: Zahal (the Hebrew acronym for the Israeli Defense Forces) Square, Paratroopers' Street, Jerusalem Brigade Street. When the Jerusalemite observes the way in which "unification" is being carried out, he cannot help but recall Godfrey de Bouillon's conquest of the city on a summer day more than eight hundred years ago. He feels that the replanning of Jerusalem hides a narcissist and aggressive invasion of the Old City, with its long history and heritage, by the Israeli

---

57. Arthur Kutcher, *The New Jerusalem, Planning and Politics* (London: Thames and Hudson, 1973), p. 9.

58. Kutcher, *ibid.*, pp. 51-52, and Meron Benvenisti in *The Jerusalem Committee: Proceedings of the Third Plenary Session, December 16-19, 1975* (Jerusalem: The Jerusalem Committee), pp. 16-17.

sector, with its Western values. There is no compromise between the two, only the forceful submission of historic Jerusalem to Western values and whims. "The fundamental, commonly shared awareness that Jerusalem's spiritual essence is inextricably bound up with her visual, tangible qualities, an awareness evidenced by four thousand years of building in the City, is now not simply ignored: it is not even recognized. Instead, a new way of thinking about Jerusalem has sprung up: The City is a resource to be exploited, its spiritual and visual qualities are commodities to be bought and sold.[59]

The Old City

The most dramatic change has taken place in the Walled City. The reconstruction of the Jewish Quarter required the expulsion of five thousand Arab inhabitants out of it. The over emphasis on its tourist attractions has likewise, yet indirectly, encouraged Palestinian inhabitants to leave and settle outside its walls. Other factors played an important role in changing its established demographic balance. Such factors include the declining of services and the escalation of insecurity as a result of Jewish-Palestinian friction.

The demographic policy adopted by the Israeli authorities, including those of the municipality, calls for further reduction in the number of Palestinians living in the Old City. There are indications that approximately seven thousand Palestinians are to be removed in order to meet the Israeli target. The present policy calls for a ceiling of twenty thousand inhabitants in the Old City, two-thirds of whom are to be Jewish and the remaining one-third "non-Jewish."[60] The adoption of this policy will require successive removals of Palestinians to maintain the required ratio and keep the population under the suggested ceiling.

Two main factors support the trend toward Israeli demographic control of the Old City. One is the increasing commercialization of the area; the other, the Israeli policy of reinforcing its "security" by encouraging settlement by ultranationalist Jews.

Intentionally or otherwise, the exaggerated focus on the touristic value of the Old City serves the purpose of encouraging some Palestinian inhabitants to leave. This has been brought about in two ways. First, the original functions of religious and historical monuments and the traditional

59. Kutcher, *The New Jerusalem*, pp. 54-55.

60. For details see A. Sharon, *Planning Jerusalem: The Old City and Its Environs* (London: Weidenfield and Nicolson, 1973).

marketplaces (bazaars specializing in specific merchandise, such as spices, copper goods, cotton, meat, and so on) have been partially or totally transformed to cater to tourist needs, To a great degree, this deprives the locals of their services. And second, other services have been redeveloped and subordinated to the needs of the visitors

Neither development brought comfort to the indigenous population of the Old City. To add salt to the wounds, some services that had been available inside the walls either declined or vanished. The government hospital which was closed in July 1985 by order of the Israeli minister of health is a case in point.

Competing services in the Palestinian Jewish sectors of the new city had to be sought. Affluent Palestinians responded by leaving the Old City. Those with fewer assets were left with no alternative but to stay. The net result was a diminishing number of Palestinians in the Old City, and the evolution of slum areas. Bab Hutta area is an example: the average density there is 54 persons living in 9 units on 1000 square meters, and an average 2.95 persons per room. The average annual income per household is eighty-three dollars.[61]

As for security, the move of Orthodox and ultranationalist Jews to settle in the Palestinian Quarter aggravated the situation in the Old City. Tension mounted to the point of fighting in many cases. Events were complicated by the support the settlers received in the form of money and backing from different Jewish and Israeli sources.[62] Ariel Sharon, minister of commerce and industry in the government of Yitzhak Shamir, moved to settle in the Muslim Quarter. His timing was important: it coincided with the first week of the *intifada* (uprising) in the occupied territories and with the Jewish Hanukkah festival (December 15, 1987). Sharon celebrated the occasion with prominent Israeli right-wing leaders and in the presence of Prime Minister Shamir. This was undoubtedly meant to boost the morale of the Jewish settlers in the Muslim Quarter.

The deteriorating security situation was not conducive to normal living in the Old City. Palestinian neighbors of Jewish settlers were molested, and an atmosphere of unrest prevailed in certain areas. Palestinian inhabitants had the option of either surrendering to the settlers' coersions and leaving the area, or of remaining to fight against provocations and aggression.

61. M. Safadie, *The Harvard Jerusalem Studio: Urban designs for the Holy City* (London: MIT Press, 1986), p. 125.

62. For more details, see "Religious Jews Trickling Back to the Moslem Quarter of Old City," *Out of Jerusalem* (Winter 1983-84), 4(1).

These dramatic changes in the conditions of the Old City had three main effects on its Palestinian residents. The more affluent left the city to live outside its walls in a more suitable environment. Those who were unable to leave faced a steady deterioration in their living conditions. And those who were evacuated from the Jewish Quarter moved to slum areas on the outskirts of the new city (notably in Arram and Bethany).

Efforts to solve the problem of the slum area in the Old City failed to reach a satisfactory conclusion. Architect M. Safadie covers the different approaches and proposals, and is quite successful in defining many of the problems, but he fails to grasp two main issues.

First, the proposals are insensitive to the nature of the location to the community and to the historic relationship between the society and the location. It seems these plans were inspired indirectly by what was achieved in the restoration of the Jewish Quarter, but this approach could be considered alien to the area in question.

Second, political considerations have assumed an unwarranted importance in the planning process. Israeli efforts to transfer the Palestinian populations and to build the Third Temple in the place of al-Aqsa Mosque and the Dome of the Rock stand as major obstacles to the establishment of confidence between the Israeli authorities and the inhabitants.

Following this line of thought, it is not surprising that the planning authority has "done over" the city wall, turning it into a model to be appreciated from the outside, and a museum to be visited from the inside. The old Jewish Quarter has been completely demolished by the Israelis, without any proper record being made of its buildings, and rebuilt in a counterfeit mode, in order to provide an archaic setting with modern facilities to attract wealthy immigrants. To meet the demands of the new inhabitants, parking areas, a hotel, a supermarket and so on were planned. A lack of green areas and open space inside the Old City has prompted a proposal to turn the roofs of the adjacent Arab cluster of houses into an interconnected overhead green area to meet the demands of the newcomers. (The municipality of Jerusalem asked the Muslim *waaf* – endowment – to allow the use of the roofs of Islamic buildings for that purpose, in a letter dated March 9, 1982.)

The measures taken since Israel's annexation of Arab Jerusalem have not received such unanimous Israeli support as did the annexation itself. Varying views have been expressed as regards the future of the city and consequently, its planning; some of the individuals involved have resigned or been dismissed as a result of differences on these issues (Arthur Kutcher, Nathaniel Lichfield, and Meron Benvenisti are among those in this category). But the process of Judaization has not stopped, and the haphazard building of residential quarters around Jerusalem has proceeded:

Ramat Eshkol and the French Hill neighborhood were completed even before the Jerusalem municipality issued the building permits. Israeli planning policy has thus followed a pragmatic course determined by the conflict between different pressure groups in Israeli society.[63] Some common denominators do of course exist; those most widely held are as follows:

1. The belief that Jerusalem is a Jewish city and the capital of the state of Israel. It is inhabited by a non-Jewish minority, which must not be allowed to exceed one-third of the total number of inhabitants, living among a Jewish majority of not less than two-thirds of the total.[64] The inhabitants as a whole constitute what is known as a "mosaic" society.[65]

2. The civilizations that have come and gone in Jerusalem were not indigenous. Therefore, the search for biblical antiquities is a necessity dictated by the Jewish character of the city.

3. As a precaution against any security contingency, Arab Jerusalem must be surrounded by a belt of settlements that must constantly grow more dense.

4. The question of the Islamic holy places, and in particular the Haram al-Sharif, and the solution of the problem of building the Temple and holding prayers in the courtyard of the Haram, can be left for the future to take care of. But the Wailing Wall surrounding the Haram is a Jewish holy place.[66]

5. The expansion of Jerusalem to a total population of six hundred thousand in the 1980s, and the provision of the services required by Israeli society and foreign tourists, is a national aim.

63. Meron Benvenisti, "A Review of Progress," in *Jerusalem Committee Proceedings,* p. 19.

64. See the statements of Lichfield and Benvenisti in *The Jerusalem Committee: Proceedings of the Second Plenary Session, June 18-21, 1972,* p. 91. See also Nathaniel Lichfield, "Jerusalem: A Progress Report," in Msgr. John Cesterneicher and Anne Sinai, eds., *Jerusalem* (New York: John Day, 1974), p. 176.

65. See Teddy Kollek, "Present Problems and Future Perspectives," in Peter Schneider and Geoffrey Wigoder, eds., *Jerusalem Perspectives* (London: The Rainbow Group, 1976).

66. Meron Benvenisti, *Jerusalem, The Torn City* (Jerusalem: Isratypsel, 1976), pp. 288-89, 293-94. See also page 314 for the memorandum of Chief Rabbi Nissim to the Ministerial Committee for the Holy Places in which he asked that the entire length of the Western (Wailing) Wall of the Haram be cleared of all adjacent buildings. He also stated in his memorandum that the four walls of al-Haram are sanctified by the Jews.

6. The touristic and religious character of Jerusalem requires, from the economic point of view, planning that gives high priority to the tourist industry.

The main feature of the Israeli view of Jerusalem is its concentration on making Jerusalem a metropolitan city in which the Old City accounts for less than 1 percent of the whole area.

Malcolm Kerr, in a study on Jerusalem,[67] observed that on social and political grounds the consideration that "reunification" is an inherent virtue is a silly mysticism. It overlooks, he suggests, the basic elementary cleavages of identity and allegiances between the two parties.

Social problems among the Palestinian population have been exacerbated as a result of the Israeli measures. The expropriation of land (3,800 dunums in 1968, 13,800 dunums in 1970, 6,000 dunums in 1980), the stringent building regulations, and the biased land use that are central to Israel's plans, have seriously impeded the natural development of Jerusalem's Palestinian community.

In the final analysis, this situation has served the purpose of fostering the heterogeneous "mosaic" society advocated by Jerusalem Mayor Teddy Kollek.[68] The mayor suggests that the ethnic differences among the inhabitants of Jerusalem should be preserved and even encouraged, but under Israeli hegemony. As a result, the Palestinians of the "unified" city have become second-class citizens.

EPILOGUE

The 8th of December, 1987 has ushered in a new era in the history of the occupied territories. The irreversibility theory of Meron Benvenisti (the director of the West Bank Data Base Project and the previous deputy mayor of Jerusalem), which received wide coverage in 1983, proved to be incompatible with the actual dynamics acting in the area. What he thought was irreversible proved to be reversible. Teddy Kollek, the Israeli mayor of Jerusalem, admitted unwillingly that the Arab-Israeli coexistence, in Jerusalem, in which he took so much pride as founder and champion, had collapsed. Yehuda Litani, the Israeli journalist, dramatized the emerging situation as a result of the *intifada* as tantamount to redividing Jerusalem.[69]

67. Malcolm Kerr, "Changing Political Status of Jerusalem," p. 370.

68. Kollek, "Present Problems and Future Perspectives."

69. Yehuda Litani, "A United Jerusalem Is No More United," *Jerusalem Post,* 8 February, 1988.

Irrespective of the rhetoric, the question stands: What did the *intifada* do? My personal appreciation of the situation is that the *intifada* has provided the means and substance to rescind the unilateral measures taken by Israel in Jerusalem against the spirit and letter of international law. Security Council resolutions 605 (22 December 1987) and 607 (5 January 1988) were of noticeable importance in this respect. The two resolutions asserted the Palestinian peoples' identity, and reconfirmed that Israeli presence in the occupied territories (including Jerusalem) was a belligerent occupation. They further asserted that Israeli occupation is subject to the conditions of the Fourth Geneva Convention of 1949.

The demonstration of the Palestinian will to challenge the authority of occupation provided substance to reverse the Israeli process of transforming the *status quo* to *fait accompli*. The *intifada*, by its dynamics and impact, clarified the relationships in the conflict and put names to faces: Israel is a belligerent occupant and the Palestinians are a nation. Therefore Israel has no right to occupy Palestinian territory and to negate the Palestinian right to self-determination.

APPENDIX

U.N. GENERAL ASSEMBLY RESOLUTION NO 181 (II) OF 29 NOVEMBER 1947 – PARTITION OF PALESTINE

The General Assembly:

Recommends to the United Kingdom, as the mandatory Power for Palestine, and to all other Members of the United Nations the adoption and implementation, with regard to the future Government of Palestine, of the Plan of Partition with Economic Union set out below;

Requests that:
(a) The Security Council take the necessary measures as provided for in the plan for its implementation;

. . .

Calls upon the inhabitants of Palestine to take such steps as may be necessary on their part to put this plan to effect;

Appeals to all Governments and all peoples to refrain from taking any action which might hamper or delay the carrying out of these recommendations.

B.
PLAN OF PARTITION WITH ECONOMIC UNION

Part I – Future Constitution and Government of Palestine

A. TERMINATION OF MANDATE – Partition and Independence.

1. The Mandate for Palestine shall terminate as soon as possible but in any case not later than 1 August 1948.
2. The armed forces of the mandatory Power shall be progressively

withdrawn from Palestine, the withdrawal to be completed as soon as possible but in any case not later than 1 August 1948. . . .

3. Independent Arab and Jewish States and the Special International Regime for the City of Jerusalem, set forth in Part III of this Plan, shall come into existence in Palestine two months after the evacuation of the armed forces of the mandatory Power has been completed but in any case not later than 1 October 1948. The boundaries of the Arab State, the Jewish State, and the City of Jerusalem shall be as described in Parts II and III below. . . .

B. STEPS PREPARATORY TO INDEPENDENCE

1. A Commission shall be set up consisting of one representative of each of the Member States. The Members represented on the Commission shall be elected by the General Assembly on as broad a basis, geographically and otherwise, as possible.

. . .

4. The Commission, after consultation with the democratic parties and other public organizations of the Arab and Jewish States, shall select and establish in each State as rapidly as possible a Provisional Council of Government. . . .

9. The Provisional Council of Government of each State shall, not later than two months after the withdrawal of the armed forces of the mandatory Force hold elections to the Constituent Assembly which shall be conducted on democratic lines.

10. The Constituent Assembly of each State shall draft a democratic constitution for its State and choose a provisional government to succeed the Provisional Council of Government appointed by the Commission. . . .

11. The Commission shall appoint a preparatory economic commission of three members to make whatever arrangements are possible for economic cooperation with a view to establishing, as soon as practicable, the Economic Union and the Joint Economic Board, as provided in section D below. . . .

D. ECONOMIC UNION AND TRANSIT

1. The Provisional Council of Government of each State shall enter into an undertaking with respect to Economic Union and Transit. . . .

The Economic Union of Palestine

2. The objectives of the Economic Union of Palestine shall be;
    (a) A customs union;
    (b) A joint currency system providing for a single foreign exchange rate;
    (c) Operation in the common interest on a non-discriminatory basis of railways; inter-State highways; postal, telephone and telegraphic services, and ports and airports involved in international trade and commerce;
    (d) Joint economic development, especially in respect of irrigation, land reclamation and soil conservation;
    (e) Access for both States and for the City of Jerusalem on a non-discriminatory basis to water and power facilities.

3. There shall be established a Joint Economic Board, which shall consist of three representatives of each of the two States and three foreign members appointed by the Economic and Social Council of the United Nations. . . .

4. The functions of the Joint Economic Board shall be to implement either directly or by delegation the measures necessary to realize the objectives of the Economic Union. . . .

PART II – Boundaries

. . .

PART III – City of Jerusalem

A. SPECIAL REGIME

The City of Jerusalem shall be established as a *corpus separatum* under a special international regime and shall be administered by the United Nations. The Trusteeship Council shall be designated to discharge the responsibilities of the Administering Authority on behalf of the United Nations. . . .

C. STATUTE OF THE CITY

The Trusteeship Council shall, within five months of the approval of the present plan, elaborate and approve a detailed statute of the City which shall contain, inter alia, the substance of the following provisions:

1. *Government machinery; special objectives.* The Administering

Authority in discharging its administrative obligations shall pursue the following special objectives:

(a) To protect and to preserve the unique spiritual and religious interests located in the city of the three great monotheistic faiths throughout the world, Christian, Jewish and Moslem; to this end to ensure that order and peace, and especially religious peace, reign in Jerusalem; . . .

2. *Governor and administrative staff.* A Governor of the City of Jerusalem shall be appointed by the Trusteeship Council and shall be responsible to it. . . .

4. *Security measures.*

(a) The City of Jerusalem shall be demilitarized; its neutrality shall be declared and preserved, and no para-military formations, exercises or activities shall be permitted within its borders. . . .

5. *Legislative organization.* A Legislative Council, elected by adult residents of the city irrespective of nationality on the basis of universal and secret suffrage and proportional representation, shall have powers of legislation and taxation. . . .

13. *Holy Places.*

. . .

(b) Free access to the Holy Places and religious buildings or sites and the free exercise of worship shall be secured in conformity with existing rights and subject to the requirements of public order and decorum. . . .

* * *

U.N. GENERAL ASSEMBLY RESOLUTION NO. 194 (III) OF 11 DECEMBER 1948 – U.N. CONCILIATION COMMISSION FOR PALESTINE

The General Assembly:

Having considered further the situation in Palestine. . . .

2. Establishes a Conciliation Commission consisting of three States Members of the United Nations:

. . . . .

5. *Calls upon* the Governments and authorities concerned to extend the scope of negotiations provided for in the Security Council's resolution of 16 November 1948 and to seek agreement by negotiations conducted either with the Conciliation Commission or directly, with a view to the final settlement of all questions outstanding between them;

6. *Instructs* the Conciliation Commission to take steps to assist the Governments and authorities concerned to achieve a final settlement of all questions outstanding between them;

7. *Resolves* that the Holy Places – including Nazareth – religious buildings and sites in Palestine should be protected and free access to them assured, in accordance with existing rights and historical practice; . . .

8. . . . .*Requests* the Security Council to take further steps to ensure the demilitarization of Jerusalem at the earliest possible date;

Instructs the Commission to present to the fourth regular session of the General Assembly detailed proposals for a permanent international regime for the Jerusalem area which will provide for the maximum local autonomy for distinctive groups consistent with the special international status of the Jerusalem area. . . .

11. *Resolves* that the refugees wishing to return to their homes and live at peace with their neighbours should be permitted to do so at the earliest practicable date, and that compensation should be paid for the property of those choosing not to return and for loss of or damage to property which, under principles of international law or in equity, should be made good by the Governments or authorities responsible;

Instructs the Conciliation Commission to facilitate the repatriation, resettlement and economic and social rehabilitation of the refugees and the payment of compensation, and to maintain close relations with the Director of the United Nations Relief for Palestine Refugees and, through him, with the appropriate organs and agencies of the United Nations; . . .

14. *Calls upon* all Governments and authorities concerned to cooperate with the Conciliation Commission and to take all possible steps to assist in the implementation of the present resolution; . . .

* * *

U.N. GENERAL ASSEMBLY RESOLUTION NO. 3236 (XXIX) OF 22 NOVEMBER 1974 – QUESTION OF PALESTINE

The General Assembly:

Having considered the question of Palestine;

Having heard the statement of the Palestine Liberation Organization, the representative of the people of Palestine;

Having also heard other statements made during the debate;

Deeply concerned that no just solution to the problem of Palestine has yet been achieved and recognizing that the problem of Palestine continues to endanger international peace and security;

Recognizing that the Palestinian people is entitled to self-determination in accordance with the Charter of the United Nations;

Expressing its grave concern that the Palestinian people has been prevented from enjoying its inalienable rights, in particular its right to self-determination;

Guided by the purposes and principles of the Charter;

Recalling its relevant resolutions which affirm the right of the Palestinian people to self-determination;

1. *Reaffirms* the inalienable rights of the Palestinian people in Palestine, including:

    (a) The right to self-determination without external interference;

    (b) The right to national independence and sovereignty;

2. *Reaffirms also* the inalienable right of the Palestinians to return to their homes and property from which they have been displaced and uprooted, and calls for their return;

3. *Emphasizes* that full respect for and the realization of these inalienable rights of the Palestinian people are indispensable for the solution of the question of Palestine;

4. *Recognizes* that the Palestinian people is a principal party in the

establishment of a just and durable peace in the Middle East;

5. *Further recognizes* the right of the Palestinian people to regain its rights by all means in accordance with the purposes and principles of the Charter of the United Nations;

6. *Appeals* to all States and international organizations to extend their support to the Palestinian people in its struggle to restore its rights in accordance with the Charter;

7. *Requests* the Secretary-General to establish contacts with the Palestine Liberation Organization on all matters concerning the question of Palestine;

8. *Requests* the Secretary-General to report to the General Assembly at its thirtieth session on the implementation of the present resolution;

9. *Decides* to include the item entitled "Question of Palestine" in the provisional agenda of its thirtieth session.

CHAPTER 7

The Changing Juridical Status of Palestinian Areas under Occupation: Land Holdings and Settlements

Raja Shehadeh

ZIONISM AND PALESTINIAN LAND

Some preliminary observations are helpful as an introduction to the discussion of the legal changes affecting land holdings in Palestine.

Mainstream Zionism has never wavered from the aim formulated early in the history of the movement: to establish in "Eretz Israel" a home for the Jews. There has been a similar continuity in the methods and tactics used by the Zionists to achieve that aim – those same methods are still being employed today in the West Bank and the Gaza Strip to hold the land inalienably in Jewish hands.

Also consistent is the position which Israel has taken regarding the West Bank (not including Jerusalem) and the Gaza Strip – they are "liberated" rather than occupied territories. As a consequence, the military government established there has not been concerned only with safeguarding the security of its members and the state of Israel, but in facilitating the acquisition by Jews of the areas that were occupied in 1967.

Zionism, as Professor Edward Said puts it in *The Question of Palestine*, has a culture of discipline by detail. Whereas it was possible and is conceivable that the military government could have acquired full and total possession of all the lands in the occupied territories by force, this did not happen. Legal methods were found to transfer Arab lands to Jewish hands, ensuring wherever possible that Jews acquired inalienable rights over the land. If that had not been the method used this chapter would not have been necessary.

The Zionists have been concerned with projecting an image of a community ruled by the principles of justice and the rule of law. In order to preserve that image, it was necessary to employ a dynamic and creative approach to law and legal systems and to manipulate existing systems so that Zionist aims could be achieved under a semblance of adherence to the rule of law. The creation, for example, of a military objections committee to function as a tribunal to hear appeals from the acts of the same military power which administers this board is intended to give the impression that the basic principle of the right of appeal is complied with.

The Palestinians have been inflexible in their adherence to formality and in their attitudes and reactions to Israel's policies. The rigidity of the Palestinians' position as a group and as individuals has rendered their reactions predictable. This has made it easier for Israel to plan its actions and has allowed it to take positions which implied readiness for more compromise than it was in fact ready to make. The signing of the Camp David accords is an example of this.

Even so, Zionist policies and aims are based on a conception of the Palestinians and the Palestinians' attitude to their land that differs greatly from the reality. The Zionists have assumed from the beginning that there is no Palestinian nation, that the Arab inhabitants of Palestine are part of the Arab world, and that their tie to the land is weak and can be severed easily. Quite the opposite has proven to be the case, namely, that the Palestinians consider themselves as constituting a distinct national group, and that they have an unusually strong relationship to their lands which has not weakened despite the elapse, in some cases, of more than thirty years. This is evidenced by their general refusal to sell their lands or accept monetary compensation for those parts of it that have been acquired by Jews.

The Zionist movement espoused the physical return of Jews to Zion and the establishment for them there of a national home. The Jewish National Fund was established as "the first instrument for the practical implementation of the idea of the Jewish renaissance." Since its establishment in 1901, it has been dedicated to the acquisition and development of land in Palestine as "the inalienable property of Jewish people.[1] The conviction that Eretz Israel belonged to the Jews was translated by the active Zionists into an attempt to use whatever means available to acquire good legal title to the lands in the physical area of Palestine for Jews. This conviction and aim has, with most Zionists, been consistent and unchanging. The methods employed to realize it were adapted to the changing times.

---

1. Quoted in Ian Lustick, *Arabs in the Jewish State* (Austin: University of Texas Press. 1980), pp. 97-98. (From Keren Kayemeth Le'Israel – The Jewish National Fund, "Who's Who in Israel," p. 416.)

Since this aim was formulated, there have been in Palestine the following powers: First there were the Turks, then the British Mandate, then the state of Israel in part of Palestine, Egypt in another (in the Gaza Strip) and the Hashemite Kingdom of Jordan in what has come to be known as the West Bank of Jordan (including east Jerusalem). At present the state of Israel is in control of the whole area of Palestine.

This chapter will trace the legal methods used to acquire lands for Jews since the Turkish times to the present. In the whole of Palestine, except the Gaza Strip and the West Bank, 93 percent of all the land is owned inalienably by the state of Israel. A substantial percentage of all lands in the Gaza Strip and the West Bank is also similarly owned, although an exact figure cannot be quoted for reasons that will be explained later. Whereas the process for the acquisition of the rest of the Arab lands in both these areas is still continuing, this chapter will focus mainly on the legal methods that are presently being employed. The discussion will be limited to the West Bank, but the same methods, with some necessary adjustments, are being employed on the Gaza Strip.

LAND AQUISITION THROUGH PURCHASE

This method has always been the most favored by the Zionists. There are many indications in the Zionist literature that it was a widely held belief, among both the early immigrants and the rich Jewish establishments in the West who supported the Zionist program, that the Arabs of Palestine could be induced to sell their lands by the offer of large sums of money. Zionists were, in fact, successful in buying large tracts of very fertile lands held by feudal lords who lived outside Palestine. Much lobbying and diplomacy at the Turkish parliament was necessary to allow Jews to register land in their names.

These efforts continued after the transfer of power in Palestine to the hands of the British Mandate. The influence of the Zionists was stronger then, and their efforts conformed in part with the terms of the mandate, which included the creation in Palestine of a Jewish and an Arab state.

In pursuance of this aim the mandatory government passed the Land Transfer Ordinance of 1921, which required that a permit from the mandate government be obtained before any transfer of land could take place. Also the settlement of disputes over land was started in those areas designated as the future Jewish state, so that good title could be transferred to Jewish purchasers. However, despite these attempts and the lucrative purchase price that was offered, by 1948 no more than 6.6 percent of the total land area of Palestine was acquired by purchase.[2]

2. Sabri Jiryis. *The Arabs in Israel* (New York: Monthly Review Press, 1976), p. 77.

After the Israeli occupation of the West Bank in 1967 several changes were made to the Jordanian law (which in principle continued to be in force) to facilitate the purchase of Palestinian lands by Jews.

First, public inspection of the land registers was prohibited. Only an owner or a holder of a power of attorney from the owner could obtain an abstract of the deed of the land owned. In absence of this, permission must be granted by the court, which must state that the inspection is necessary for an existing court case before inspection of relevant deeds can be allowed.

Second, Military Order 25 (1967) was promulgated, which necessitated that permission be granted by the Israeli officer in charge of the judiciary, in his capacity as registrar of lands, for any transaction in land to be carried out.

Third, in order to acquire ownership over land without going through the land registry (which risks public exposure) acquisition of ownership may, under the local law, be through an irrevocable power of attorney. This is an instrument in which the owner names an attorney who is instructed to register the land in the name of a purchaser in consideration of a stated sum of money for which the irrevocable power of attorney is a receipt. As the name of this instrument implies, the principal may not go back on his instructions. Under Jordanian law this instrument lapsed after five years from the date it was executed. Military orders prolonged the duration of the irrevocable power of attorney from five to ten years, and then to fifteen.[3]

Jewish purchasers sought expatriate Palestinians everywhere in the world and attempted to persuade them by various means to sell their lands by executing irrevocable powers of attorney. Israeli consuls were made the only authority empowered to authenticate signatures on these instruments, and the officer in charge of the judiciary the only authority to legalize that signature.[4]

Given the conditions under which the Palestinian population lived, whereby a permit was needed for most vital matters, those in desperate need of permits fell easy prey to the insistent demands of Jews, either directly or through Arab middlemen, to sell their lands. There are also several reported cases of violence or deception being used to force owners into signing contracts of sale or irrevocable powers of attorney. A common strategy has been to convince the owner that his land is going to be (or in fact has been) acquired for the use of a nearby Israeli settlement, and that no building

3. Military Orders 811 and 847.

4. Military Order 264.

permit will ever be granted for an Arab to build on it. He is then induced to sell.[5]

In short, the entire administrative and legal system in the West Bank has been changed to facilitate purchase by Jews of Arab lands and to discourage use and transfer to Arabs. The two latest such changes are the following:

1. Military Order 1025, which authorizes the "head of the civilian administration" (appointed by virtue of Order 947) to allow certain juridical bodies the right to own lands in the West Bank even if the conditions required according to the Jordanian law on the subject are not met. The order also declares all land transactions committed contrary to law, which the above order now declares permissible, as done according to the law in force. The date of this order is October 4, 1982.

2. The increase in fees payable upon devolution of land from the name of the deceased owner to his lawful heirs, from one-half a Jordanian dinar to 4 percent of the assessed market value of the property. The effect of this is to render devolution more costly – the authorities now treat it as a transaction in land.

It is not possible to give a good estimate of the land already acquired by Jews through purchase, but the diligence with which the Israeli authorities pursue other methods for acquiring Palestinian lands indicates that the purchase method has not met with great success.

ACQUISITION OF "ABANDONED" LAND

This method was obviously not used before the establishment of the state of Israel. But the concept of "abandoned" property existed in the minds of the Zionists from early on. Consistent with their belief that the Arabs did not feel strong ties to their land, they were inclined to believe that many had abandoned or were willing to abandon their property if offered property elsewhere in the Arab world. The feudal absentee landowners who lived outside of Palestine were the first targets.

After the establishment of the state of Israel in 1948, the exiled Palestinians left behind immovable property, the estimated value of which was 100,383,784 Palestinian pounds. They also left 19,100,000 Palestinian pounds worth of movable property. These properties included extensive

5. See David Richardson, "West Bank Jews Irked over Land-grabbers," *Jerusalem Post,* 10 February 1982.

stone quarries, forty thousand dunums of vineyards, 95 percent of Israel's olive groves, nearly one hundred thousand dunums of citrus groves, and ten thousand shops, businesses, and stores.[6] Those Arabs who stayed were termed "internal absentees" – 40 percent of their lands were also confiscated as "abandoned" property.[7]

Islamic *wakf* lands (lands dedicated for a pious purpose), which amounted to hundreds of thousands of dunums, were also considered as absentee lands. In 1950 the Absentee Property Law was passed; under its provisions a custodian was appointed to manage this property.[8] The Development Authority (Transfer of Property) Law (also of 1950) established a development authority which was permitted to buy the lands placed by the earlier law under the control of the custodian of absentee property.[9] Lands so acquired may not be alienated.[10] The Development Authority has eight members from the Jewish National Fund and seven representatives of the state of Israel.[11]

The Israeli Absentee Property Law defined an absentee as, among others, someone who departed to a state which is in a state of war with Israel.[12] The military order on the same subject (Military Order 58, passed in 1967 by the military commander of the West Bank), defines an absentee as someone

6. Quoted in Lustick, *Arabs in the Jewish State*, p. 59.

7. Quoted in Lustick, p. 60.

8. *Laws of the State of Israel*, 4:68.

9. *Ibid.* p. 151.

10. Article 1 of The Basic Law: Israel Lands, published in *Laws of the State of Israel* vol. 14, prohibits any form of the alienation of the lands, in the ownership of the state of Israel, the Development Authority, or the Jewish National Fund.

11. See Lustick, *Arabs in the Jewish State*, p. 107.

12. "Absentee" is defined in the Absentee Property Law as follows:

1. A person who, at any time during the period between the 16th Kislev, 5708 [29th November 1947] and the day on which a declaration is published. under section 9(d) of the Law and Administration Ordinance, 5708-1948),[1] that the state of emergency declared by the Provisional Council of State on the 10th Iyar, 5708 [1948]2) has ceased to exist, was a legal owner of any property situated in the area of Israel or enjoyed or held it, whether by himself or through another, and who, at any time during the said period –
   (i) was a national or citizen of Lebanon, Egypt, Syria, Saudi-Arabia, Trans-Jordan, Iraq or the Yemen, or

   (ii) was in one of these countries or in any part of Palestine outside the area of Israel, or

who was not in the area of the West Bank at the time of the 1967 war.[13] This definition renders even a Palestinian who in June 1967 was resident in the United States, for example (which is not a country in a state of war with Israel), an absentee. This definition, however, has not been strictly applied as yet.

The control of the military authorities over the land registers and their successful penetration of Arab society in the West Bank helped them identify which property is (according to the order) "abandoned" property. However, even when the owner of the property has not left the area (and therefore his property does not qualify according to the order to be placed under the control of the custodian of absentee property) and a Jewish settlement is in need of it to establish or develop, the custodian can still acquire possession over it and enter into transactions with third parties who are either individuals or Israeli development companies. In one such incident with which the author is familiar, involving land registered in the name of an Arab who lives in the West Bank, the custodian sold over seventy dunums of land to private Israelis who were living in a settlement adjacent to this land and who wanted to enlarge their settlement. When the owner objected, the custodian invoked article 10 of order 58, which authorizes transactions done in good faith between the custodian of absentee properties and third parties, which the custodian carried out believing the property to be absentee property.

(iii) was a Palestinian citizen and left his ordinary place of residence in Palestine

    (a) for a place outside Palestine before the 27th Av, 5703 [1st September, 1948]; or

    (b) for a place in Palestine held at the time by forces which sought to prevent the establishment of the State of Israel or which fought against it after its establishment;

2. A body of persons which, at any time during the period specified in paragraph was a legal owner of any property situated in the area of Israel or enjoyed or held such property, whether by itself or through another, and all the members, partners, shareholders, directors or managers of which are absentees within the meaning of paragraph (1), or the management of the business of which is otherwise decisively controlled by such absentees, or all the capital of which is in the hands of such absentees.

13. Property of an absentee is defined in Military Order 58 as follows:

The property whose legal owner or possessor according to the law, has left the area [of the West Bank] before the specified date [June 7th, 1967] on the specified date or after the specified date and left the property in the area. But the property which is in the possession of someone other than the owner shall not be considered property of an absentee unless its owner or possessor were together absent from the area.

The tribunal which is authorized under the existing orders to hear appeals against decisions by the custodian of absentee property is the Objections Committee, constituted by order 172. It is composed of Israeli officers and is headed by a senior legal advisor of the Israeli Land Authority – who obviously is an interested party.[14]

The head office of the custodian of absentee property is in West Jerusalem. Its full title is the Office of the Administrator of Lands of Israel: Custodian of Abandoned and Government Property in the Area of Judea and Samaria. As the title implies, the custody of absentee lands in the West Bank is administered by the Israel Lands Administration (whose director ex-officio is the Israeli minister of agriculture). The Israel Lands Administration, which supervises the use of 93 percent of Israel's land area, has effective responsibility for the supervision of land acquisition and use in the West Bank.[15]

The Jerusalem head office acts through offices in each of the major West Bank towns. Those employed in these offices (Arabs and Jews) are constantly on the lookout for more lands to acquire under the pretext of abandoned property. They are aided in this effort by the legal and administrative changes that have rendered the approval of the custodian necessary for most transactions in land. This includes such operations as reregistration of land which has not been included in the settlement of disputes operations – an operation which does not involve any transfer of land. It also includes registration of land in the name of the heirs of deceased owners, the obvious objective here being to identify any share which a nonresident is acquiring to enable the custodian to lay his hands on it. The administrative network of the offices of the custodian also serves as a useful vehicle for identifying and arranging for the acquisition of land which is used by settlers, under the pretext that it is "state land" (as will be explained below).

It is clear from the working of Military Order 58 (and in particular the provision on transactions made in good faith), from the treatment by Israel in the past of the property of "absentees," and from the practice in the West Bank at present, that it is not the intention of Israel to hold the property of absentees in trust pending the solution of the conflict. The custodian is transferring property of absentees to third parties for use in a long-term, permanent manner.

14. Meron Benvenisti, *The West Bank and Gaza Data Base Project* (Jerusalem, 1982), p. 34.

15. Ian Lustick, "Israel and the West Bank after Elon Moreh: The Mechanics of de Facto Annexation," *The Middle East Journal* (Autumn 1981), 35(4):566.

ACQUISITION THROUGH ADMINISTRATIVE MEANS

Military Jurisdiction

The extent and position of lands to be acquired by the military authorities in the West Bank has varied with time. But the policy of the military authority to acquire maximum control over the West Bank and its population has been pursued since the early days of the occupation. The large degree of control acquired by the military government over the years has served well the policy of the succeeding governments, led by both Labor and Likud throughout the past twenty-two years, and whose declared aim is to acquire control over West Bank land and encourage extensive Jewish settlement there. Several changes in the West Bank administrative system have been effected in order to facilitate the legal acquisition of land for Jewish settlement.

Israel has held a consistent position towards what it regards as the legal status of the West Bank. It never accepted the position held by most of the countries of the world, namely that in 1967, as a result of belligerent action, the West Bank, which until then was part of the Hashemite Kingdom of Jordan, was occupied by force and that therefore the Hague and Geneva conventions applicable to occupied territories should determine the behavior of Israel – the occupying power – towards it. Israel has argued that the West Bank was not an internationally recognized part of Jordan, and that therefore in 1967 it did not occupy land over which another country had sovereignty.[16]

However, Israel's policies towards the inhabitants of its newly acquired territories were closely observed by the rest of the world. Israel could not afford to be indifferent to this international interest. The image it had projected was that of a small beleaguered state surrounded by a sea of antagonistic nations, from whom all it wanted was acceptance so it could live in peace with its neighbors. It also had the image of a country which respected human rights and observed and lived by the principles of the rule of law. With world opinion in mind, Israel devised a compromise: without giving in on the principle, namely that it was not an occupier of another people's lands, it made it known that despite the fact that legally speaking it did not consider itself bound to observe the Geneva Convention, it would

16. For the Israeli position on the status of the West Bank, see Yehuda Blum, "The Missing Reversioner: Reflections on the Status of Judea and Samaria," *Israel Law Review* (1968) 3:279. One response to the claims made there is by S. V. Mallison, "The Application of International Law in Occupied Territory," pp. 55-64 in I. Abu-Lughod, ed., *Palestinian Rights, Affirmation and Denial* (Wilmette, Ill.: Medina Press, 1982).

apply the humanitarian standards laid out in international conventions. A concerted public relations campaign was waged to show that this was in fact the case. Not only was Israel preserving the local laws and institutions that were in place before the occupation, as well as preserving public order, but it was also developing, modernizing, and economically benefiting the society over which it was now ruling.

Meanwhile, the military commander was carrying on many very significant changes in the local Jordanian law that was in force in the area, but the military orders were not made available to the general public and were not (until much later) brought to the attention of interested observers. The cases which came before the Israeli High Court challenging orders made by the military commander that changed Jordanian law were published and publicized. The arguments of the High Court seemed very convincing and discouraged further probes into the legislative activities of the military commander. In one such case, for example, *The Christian Society for the Holy Places* v. *The Minister of Defense,* the justices of the Israeli High Court were not in agreement. The dispute was whether – even if the change were to benefit the local population – the area commander could, under international law, carry it out. The dissenting judge, Justice Haim Cohn, argued that he couldn't. But the majority decided in favor of the change. Other similar changes that are customarily pointed out by apologists of Israeli actions on the West Bank when they are charged that in violation of international law Israel has changed the local law, are, for example, the change which allows women to vote in municipal elections, the change in the criminal law whereby flogging was one legal punishment of certain offenses, and the introduction of comprehensive and third party insurance.[17] Changes in traffic law, customs law, and tax law are also used to justify Israeli action – these, they claim, have become necessary because of the new situation whereby the West Bank and Israel have no borders and therefore standardization in these areas is inevitable.

For at least the first ten years of the occupation, these arguments convinced most outside observers, who unfortunately did not make a closer investigation of the legal situation in existence on the West Bank. In fact, as the Israeli apologists were pointing to these few and minor changes and were boasting that they were necessary if Israel were to succeed in its good work of modernization of Arab society in the West Bank, many hundreds of

17. These changes are pointed out in Meir Shamgar, *Military Government in the Territories Administered by Israel 1967- 1980,* vol. I, *The Legal Aspects* (Jerusalem: The Hebrew University, 1982), p. 54.

changes were being issued by the area commander, with very specific objectives in mind.[18]

Article 64 of the Geneva Convention, Relative to the Protection of Civilian Persons in Time of War, permits the occupying power to carry out (among others) those changes necessary for the occupier's security.[19] Consistent with Israel's announced policy towards the West Bank of observing the humanitarian provisions of the Geneva and Hague conventions, the attempt has all along been to justify (whenever possible) legislative (as well as other administrative) actions as being necessitated by security. This has necessitated an expansion of the interpretation of "security" to include what cannot normally be justifiable on security grounds. However the Ministry of Defense (which is ultimately responsible for the military government in the West Bank) is the undisputed arbiter of what is necessitated by security. The Israeli High Court, which has been hailed as an effective safeguard against arbitrary actions of the military because it hears appeals on such matters, refuses to consider whether an action is or is not justifiable on security grounds.[20] It is enough for the military authority to declare that its action is necessary for security and this would be the end of the matter.

Even so, it was no easy challenge that the military command had to face to bring about the situation which is now in existence in the West Bank. On the one hand, it had to keep the semblance of the local law continuing to be the law in force, and the local Arab courts the courts that rule according to that law – it could not impose an alternative system that would violate basic accepted principles of the rule of law, such as the right of an appeal from administrative decisions. On the other hand, it had to implement a government policy whereby in no case could a Palestinian state, or the infrastructure and institutions of such a future state, be allowed to arise. Nor could the whole of the area be returned to Jordan. The military also had to facilitate the settlement of large numbers of Jews in the area with all that such activity requires: the acquisition of lands, the establishment of infrastructure, and the stifling of any Arab protests, so that areas of conflict could be reduced, and future development of Jewish settlements made easier. This challenge was met in stages.

18. For a detailed survey of these military orders see R. Shehadeh and J. Kuttab, *The West Bank and the Rule of Law* (New York: International Commission of Jurists and Law in the Service of Man, 1980); see also R. Shehadeh, *Occupier's Law: Israel and the West Bank* (Washington: Institute for Palestine Studies, 1985).

19. See Pictet's *Commentary* (Geneva: International Com. of the Red Cross, 1958), pp. 334-35.

20. The only exception was the Elon Moreh case, which is discussed later.

In the first stage, the military issued orders which put all aspects of life in the West Bank under the military authorities' control (using as pretexts security and the necessity of preserving public order and ensuring the continuation of normal life, as required by section 64 of the Geneva Convention). All powers previously in the hands of the Jordanian government's officers and departments were acquired and concentrated in the hands of the military commander, or his delegates. Also, it was required that a permit be obtained from the military authority for carrying out any vital needs such as starting a business, importing, exporting, traveling, buying or selling lands, etc. Orders such as Proclamation No. 3 (later replaced by Military Order 378) were passed, which established military courts and enabled the soldiers to carry out various actions and issue a number of restrictive orders. Military Order 378 has been amended thirty-seven times, each of these amendments increasing the powers of the military and closing any loopholes which could possibly be used by lawyers defending so-called security offenders. The order also usurped control over many of those matters previously within the jurisdiction of the local courts, giving jurisdiction to the military court either exclusively or concurrently with the local civilian court.

In this first stage, changes in local law were effected whereby any decision which the military needed to take to carry out activities not justifiable under international law could not be appealed to the local court. Changes, for example, were made to the Land Expropriation Law, whereby the owner of expropriated land could not resort to the local court and whereby the necessity to publish the authority's intention to expropriate was done away with.[21] Similar changes were made to the Town Planning Law,[22] and others. The general right of courts to hear cases against administrative decisions of the executive branch of government, which Jordanian law preserved, was also restricted. According to Military Order 164, only if the military authority gave its permission could an aggrieved party take up a case to the local court against a decision of the military, or any of its branches or employees. Instead, appeal was allowed to the Israeli High Court, which, as explained above, restricted itself by refusing to question the security justification of an action if security was claimed by the respondent as the justification for the action appealed against.

The policy of the Labor party towards the West Bank during the first decade of the 1967 occupation was not as clearly defined as that of the Likud, which came to power in 1977. Labor agreed with the Likud that they

21. Military Orders 108 and 321; see *West Bank and the Rule of Law*, pp. 107-9.

22. *Ibid.*, pp. 117-18.

would not support the establishment of the Palestinian state. They also agreed that complete withdrawal from the West Bank was not possible. They supported and carried out Jewish settlement in the West Bank, but restricted these to certain areas (primarily around Jerusalem and in the Jordan valley) and avoided areas where there were large concentrations of Arabs. The Likud, however, have in fact carried out their declared intention to settle Jews anywhere in the West Bank. They seem to target areas with a large Arab population, in order to limit and stifle the growth of the Arab communities and perhaps to force them into a certain direction in times of hostility under the pretext of self-defense or the necessities of war.[23]

Given the Labor position it was sufficient to use security to justify its policies of acquisition, to acquire lands generally in remote areas. The first areas to be acquired were those military camps and positions which the Jordanian army had occupied. Military Order 59 gave the military authority the power to acquire any government property, exactly as Order 58 gave the custodian of absentee property the power to acquire property which he believed was "abandoned" property. In fact many of the first settlements began in military camps. The military camp was then removed and the settlement remained and grew.

Second were areas that were requisitioned for military purposes. The only justification given in orders acquiring lands in this way is simply that the land is needed for "vital and immediate military requirements." The military government offered payment for the use of the land. Many settlements also started in areas requisitioned initially for military purposes.

Third were areas which were closed by the military authority for use as training grounds, firing ranges, and as general "security" zones.

The fourth, and until 1980 the most extensively used method for acquiring lands for Jewish settlement, was expropriation for public purposes. One figure given for the areas acquired in this way is 1.5 million dunums.[24]

Reclassification and Registration of Lands

The second stage of the use of administrative methods to acquire possession of West Bank lands for Israeli settlements can be traced to 1979.

23. On the settlement policies in general, see W.W. Harris, *Taking Root: Israeli Settlement in the West Bank, the Golan and Gaza-Sinai, 1967-1980* (Chichester and New York: Wiley, 1980).

24. Benvenisti, *West Bank and Gaza Data Base*, p. 31. Benvenisti cautions that this figure seems outdated, but it is not possible to arrive at a better approximation in view of the restriction on inspecting land registers.

It was occasioned by a number of events, the most important of which was the case in the Israeli High Court concerning the settlement Elon Moreh. This decision, in which the High Court gave a favorable verdict to the Arab owners of the land who brought the action, did not have the effect of reducing Jewish acquisition of Arab lands, but only of bringing about a change in the tactics used by the military authorities to acquire those Arab lands.

Several events and legal changes and interpretations of the status of West Bank lands are facilitating the implementation of this new policy of land acquisition. First, a comprehensive survey of the ownership and registration status of all West Bank lands was begun in December 1979 by the Office of the Custodian of Absentee Property, under the direction of Mrs. Plia Albeck, who was seconded to the military government by the Justice Ministry.[25] Arab employees in the various land registries in the West Bank were put to work on this project. The survey was completed in the spring of 1981.

The survey discovered that approximately one-third of all West Bank land had become registered after all disputes over ownership were settled according to the Settlement of Land Disputes Law of 1952. The land settlement operations were begun by the British in the early 1920s, and were continued by the Jordanian government. In 1967 they were discontinued by Military Order 192, and requests by West Bankers to complete these operations, especially in the areas where all the stages except the final registration were completed (such as in the area near the Arab town of Betunia near Ramallah) were denied. Otherwise lands in the West Bank are registered mainly in the tax offices where surveys were carried out for the purpose of levying tax on the land. Owners generally understated the area of land which they owned to minimize the tax to be paid on their holdings.

Other landowners possess Turkish certificates of registration or have acquired their possession through devolution, purchase (which is not always registered), and use.

With the availability of opportunities for work in Israeli factories, many Palestinians who had previously cultivated their lands left to seek employment as laborers in Israel. Restrictions which the authorities have placed on drilling of artesian wells and the marketing and exportation of agricultural products have also fostered this trend.[26]

25. Lustick, "Israel and the West Bank after Elon Moreh," p. 568.

26. Very few permits for drilling artesian wells have been granted since 1967.

The law governing land holdings in the West Bank continues to be the Ottoman Land Code, with Jordanian and Israeli amendments and additions. The theoretical basis of the Land Code, however, continues to apply.[27]

According to the Land Code, all lands in the West Bank are classified into the following five categories. First, there are *wakf* lands, which are lands that are dedicated to a pious purpose. Then there is *mulk* land: lands initially given out by the Ottoman conqueror of the area (who considered himself the owner by conquest of all the lands he occupied) to the Muslim residents, and the *khuraj* lands handed over to non-Muslims. A Jordanian law of 1953 declared all *miri* lands falling within municipal areas as transferred to *mulk* lands.

Then there are the *miri, matruk,* and *mawat* lands, which the Israeli policy now in force considers to be "state lands." *Miri* lands are lands which the Ottoman Emir did not allow to be dedicated as *wakf,* nor did he distribute them as *mulk.* It is land whose *raqabeh* (or absolute ownership) continued to reside with him, but whose use he allowed for the public according to certain conditions. The theoretical basis of this conforms to the theoretical basis of other systems of land law, such as for example English land law. There also, all the land came to the ownership of the crown with the Norman invasion, when it was acquired by conquest. The crown gave out, in accordance with different rules, the land for the people to use. But "no land is without a lord," and the ultimate lord is the crown. However this only provides the theoretical basis. In practice the only lands which are in the actual ownership and possession of the crown in England are those areas which are classified as crownhold. The rest are in the actual ownership and possession of their registered owner or user, as the case may be.

The theoretical basis of the Palestinian land law was never altered, but the actual implications of this basis have been subjected to several amendments during the Turkish, British, and Jordanian regimes. Jordanian Law no. 49 of 1953, for example, removed all the restrictions previously existing on the extent of the use which the possessor of *miri* land could make of the land, thus removing any practical difference that used to exist between the powers of the owner of *mulk* land and *miri* land. Some differences, however, continue to exist in the way both types devolve upon the death of the owner. The present Israeli policy is to consider this category of land as "state land," confusing the theoretical with the actual.

---

27. For a more detailed discussion of this see R. Shehadeh, "The Land Law of Palestine," *Journal of Palestine Studies,* Winter 1982. See also Shehadeh, "Legal Status of the Occupied Land," (in Arabic), in *Political Quarterly,* vol. 2, editor Hamadi Essid, published in Paris.

Another category of land which is also considered as "state land" by the military authorities is *matruk* land. This category (as the name in Arabic implies) is land which has been left for public purposes such as the building of roads, cemeteries etc. The third is *mawat* – land considered as dead land because it lay further from the village "than the human voice could be heard" (in the words of the Ottoman Land Code).

The Ottoman system, and all later governments until 1967, acknowledged that the land surrounding the village was for the use of the villagers either as common pastures or for future development. The inhabitants of the village did not have any need to register their lands. They knew amongst themselves which of the village lands belonged to which families and which were owned in common (*mashaa*).

The Israeli policy has been to make the maximum use of the lack of specific legal documentation attesting to the villagers' ownership of their land – a fact for which the latter cannot be blamed, as the process by which registration is acquired has been stopped, as explained above.

The Elon Moreh Decision

This was the first instance when (because of the special circumstances of the case, such as the conflicting affidavits about the security necessity of the settlement and the Gush Emunim's statement that the settlement was for ideological grounds) the court did question the motives and professional judgments of those entrusted with the security of the state. The decision handed down was that security in this case did not justify the requisition of privately owned land for the purpose of building a Jewish settlement. The Court also decided that the Hague Convention of 1907 was binding on Israel's governance of the territories it occupied in 1967. The two limitations which the decision placed on future resort to the Court in cases of land requisition or possession by military authorities for Jewish settlements were the following: first, the High Court was not prepared to intervene in any disputations over the ownership status of land; second, only seizures of privately owned land could be prevented or reversed through recourse to the High Court.

Multiple Justice Systems

Some of the earlier changes to Jordanian laws which were carried out by the military authority to increase the powers of the military and abolish the right of appeal against military actions to the local courts have already been discussed. Specific changes have also been made to the laws and military orders in force in the West Bank which have been invoked to achieve the acquisition of large areas of lands for Jewish settlement.

The Israeli policy in this regard has been guided by three principles. The first is to centralize within the military establishment and tribunals administered by the military all matters relevant to the settlement of the West Bank by Jews. The second is to preserve the semblance of legality in all activities of acquiring lands for the purpose of Israeli settlements such that, for example, a right of appeal to the actions of the military is available although that appeal is to a military tribunal. The third is to organize the legal and administrative machinery by which land is acquired in such a way as not to allow objections by Arabs to hamper the quick and efficient execution of the settlement activities.

With these as the guiding principles, three systems of justice have been established in the West Bank.[28] The first is the system which is concerned primarily (with a few minor exceptions) with the Arab inhabitants of the West Bank. This system is what has been left after the numerous changes which have been made to the Jordanian system of courts throughout the twenty-two years of occupation. It applies the Jordanian law as amended and added to by the more than a thousand military orders which are now in force in the West Bank. It has been restricted to hearing cases which involve matters affecting only the members of the Arab community – cases that have no bearing on the Jews living in the area or on the policies of the military government as regards the area. Even within the confines in which it operates, this system has no independence, as its judges are appointed by the military.

The second system of justice is that of the Jewish settlements.[29] Municipal courts have been established and are empowered to hear cases on matters which arise within the area of the Jewish settlements, as laid out in the regulations made by the military authorities which are identical to the laws of local and regional councils that exist in Israel. Israeli courts also have acquired jurisdiction in some cases which involve Jewish settlers living outside the area of Israel and the military courts have jurisdiction over other matters. Rabbinical courts have been established in the West Bank to look into matters of personal status involving Jews. On the whole and with

28. See Raja Shehadeh, *Occupier's Law: Israel and the West Bank* 2nd ed. (Washington, D.C.: Institute for Palestine Studies, 1989).

29. See generally on this R. Shehadeh, "Legal System of Israeli Settlements," *Review of the International Commission of Jurists* (December 1981), 27; also by the same author, "An Analysis of the Legal Structure of Israeli Settlements in the West Bank," in I. Abu-Lughod, ed., *Palestinian Rights: Affirmation and Denial.*

very minor exceptions, Jewish settlers are subject to their own courts, to military courts, and to Israeli courts.

The third system, which concerns us most here, is the system which is established and administered by the military authority. Included in this system are the military courts which have jurisdiction over all the matters covered by the expanded definition of security applied by Israel. These are provided for under the Emergency (Defense) Regulations of 1945 and in the various military orders on "security matters," the most important of which is order 378. Other tribunals which are included in this system are the Objection Committees, established by virtue of Military Order 172, which now have jurisdiction over twenty-six different matters, as provided by Military Order 1019. These committees are what the Israelis claim to be the appeal committees. Their purpose is to preserve, on the face of it, the right of appeal for the party aggrieved, while placing the power to decide on that appeal in the hands of Israeli military officials. It is this board that hears appeals on expropriation orders, orders declaring land to be abandoned property, and orders declaring land to be "state land." Other bodies included in this system are the Compensation Board, which hears cases for compensation for damage caused by the activities of the Israeli army, and the special board which by an amendment to the Jordanian Town Planning Law of 1966 (by Military Order 604) hears appeals to decisions taken by the Higher Town Planning Authority, which is now composed entirely of Israeli officials.

Under these existing conditions, the military authority has carried out surveys of all lands in the West Bank and has prepared new town and regional plans. This has been done to determine the ownership and registration of land in the West Bank, and to plan the present and future position and development of Jewish settlement and Arab population centers there. These new plans demarcate the position of the Arab towns and villages and restrict their ability to grow – it also provides areas into which only Jewish settlements may develop. At present, when the right of the municipalities and village councils to grant building licenses has been restricted, and the only body authorized to give building permits in areas outside municipal areas is the Higher Town Planning Board, which is composed entirely of Israeli officials whose primary concern is with the Jewish settlements, it is clear that the control over the future spatial development of the Arabs and Jews in the West Bank is almost entirely in the hands of the Israeli authorities.

The main category of land now being usurped by the military authorities for the purpose of establishing and enlarging Jewish settlements in the West Bank is what is called state land. The reasons why the Israeli definition of state land is not justifiable according to the land law in force in the West

Bank has been explained above. It was also explained above that the High Court of Justice has ruled in the Elon Moreh case that it will not look into disputes over ownership of property. The present practice, which has been used extensively over the past ten years for occupying Arab lands in the West Bank, is for the military authority, or its branch, the Custodian of Absentee Property, to announce its claim over an area of land. The new rules provide that such a claim may be made orally. They also provide that whenever it is not possible to ascertain who may have claims over the land (the subject of the order) it suffices if the *mukhtar* of the village is informed of the claim. Whether the *mukhtar* (who is very often cooperating with the authorities) informs those who claim ownership of the land or not is not the concern of the authorities or of the objection committee. One month is allowed for the submission of an appeal against the order declaring the land state land. With the appeal must be submitted documents upon which the appellant bases his appeal as well as survey maps of the whole area guaranteed by a certified surveyor.

It is very often the case that thousands of dunums are affected by such orders. The expense and time involved in preparing the documents that must be appended to the appeal can be exorbitant. When the case comes before the objection committee, the burden of proof that the land is in the ownership of the appellant falls on him. This has become the case after Military Order 59 was amended in 1969 by order 364, which states as follows:

> If the person responsible [defined by the order as anyone whom the area commander appoints] signifies by a written certificate signed by him that any property is state property, that property shall be so considered as long as the opposite of this has not been proven.

To lift the burden of proof, the committee does not accept certificates of registration from the tax department nor any other documents attesting that the land was bought from a third party. The burden of proof in most categories of land can only be lifted if the appellant can prove actual continuous use of the land for the past ten consecutive years. To appreciate the difficulty of meeting this standard of proof it must be borne in mind that many lands are not arable, that permits to drill artesian wells are almost never granted, and that dependence on the unpredictable rainy season does not always render it economical to cultivate the land. Added to this is the inherent bias of the committee and the conception which its members hold as to what constitutes cultivation and who refuse to regard anything less than a programmed consistent cultivation of the land as constituting use of it. The result is that most of the cases brought before the objection committee end in the rejection of Arab claims. However, the Arab who loses his land does have an avenue for appeal open to him, but if he doesn't choose to use it, this can be held against him in the future as indicating that he did not believe he had a strong enough title – otherwise he would have used all the legal channels available to him. If he does resort to the committee, he may incur heavy financial losses, in addition to the possible loss of his land, and he will be providing the authorities with the opportunity to present the record as secure in favor of the Jewish acquisition of the property, as the matter was subject to appeal and the appeal tribunal did in fact make a decision in favor of Jewish aquisition after it heard all the evidence.

This method of acquiring Arab lands for Jewish settlement and the system in which it operates continue to be used to date. It has proved to be an efficient and effective method. The likelihood is that it will continue to be in use until enough lands have been acquired to carry out the proposed enlargement of the Jewish population in the West Bank.

When that stage is reached there are many pointers that the same tactics used in Israel after 1948 will also be used in the West Bank.[30] The property of absentees is already being leased for long terms by individual and corporate Israelis. The Jewish National Fund and the Israel Land Authority will assume control over what has been acquired as "state land" and will render these lands inalienable, as is the case with 93 percent of the lands in Israel. As to other lands, which are registered in the names of Palestinians with a clear and undisputable title in the land registers, if the Jewish settlements should have need of them and assuming the Palestinians have been allowed to continue to live in the West Bank, the claim could be made that whatever areas of them are needed for the Jewish settlements must be expropriated for public purpose. Whereas a substantial proportion of the West Bank public lands would then be Jewish (assuming the present government's settlement plans are successful) this claim would be justifiable in legal terms.

The Israeli methods and plans for acquisition of land holdings are understandable within the context of the solution which the present Israeli government is offering for the West Bank situation: namely to offer the Arab "inhabitants" there autonomy over their persons but not over land.

Should the time come, however, when Israel is held accountable before the international public according to the rules of international law, then the properties held, for example, by the custodian on the justification that their owners are not there to manage them would have to be returned. Similarly the land which, according to Israeli interpretation, is state land would have

---

30. For a general discussion of these tactics, see Lustick, *Arabs in the Jewish State*. chapter 2.

to be returned from these who have acquired ownership over it, because under the Hague rules an occupying state cannot make permanent use of them.

Clearly Israel is not leaving the door open to any such eventuality. All the lands that are being acquired are being given to private users who are encouraged to make permanent use of them, the obvious and declared aim being to create a *de facto* situation with which no future Israeli government will have the political power to interfere. The situation that Israel now is creating leaves both Arabs and Israelis few options for the future.

CHAPTER 8

Israeli Settlements and Palestinian Rights

Ibrahim Matar

At the turn of the century, Jews made up less than 10 percent of the population of Palestine, and owned less than 2 percent of the land. Year after year since then, these percentages have increased, so that by 1948 a Jewish state could be declared in an area from which much of the indigenous Arab population had been driven. The process continues in those territories occupied by Israel after the 1967 War. The goal of this process has remained the same: the establishment of an exclusive Jewish presence, with a greater or lesser degree of tolerance for those Arabs that may remain, in the land of Palestine. And the strategy for implementation of that goal has also remained the same: the creation of Jewish colonies, strategically located, and euphemistically called settlements.

HISTORICAL PERSPECTIVE

The early years of the Jewish colonization of Palestine were characterized by the gradual immigration of mostly European Jews, subsidized by the Jewish National Fund of the World Zionist Organization. The Balfour Declaration of 1917, in which the British government promised away land which was not theirs for the establishment of a "national home for the Jewish people," legitimatized and added impetus to the process, and by 1947 some 296 Jewish colonies had been established, mostly concentrated in the central coastal plains (see table 8.1). Some colonies were located so as to establish footholds in the various areas of Palestine. For example, during the Arab Revolt of 1936-1939, while the Palestinians were busy fighting the British, Jewish settlers established "watchtowers and stockades"

PALESTINE LAND OWNERSHIP 1945

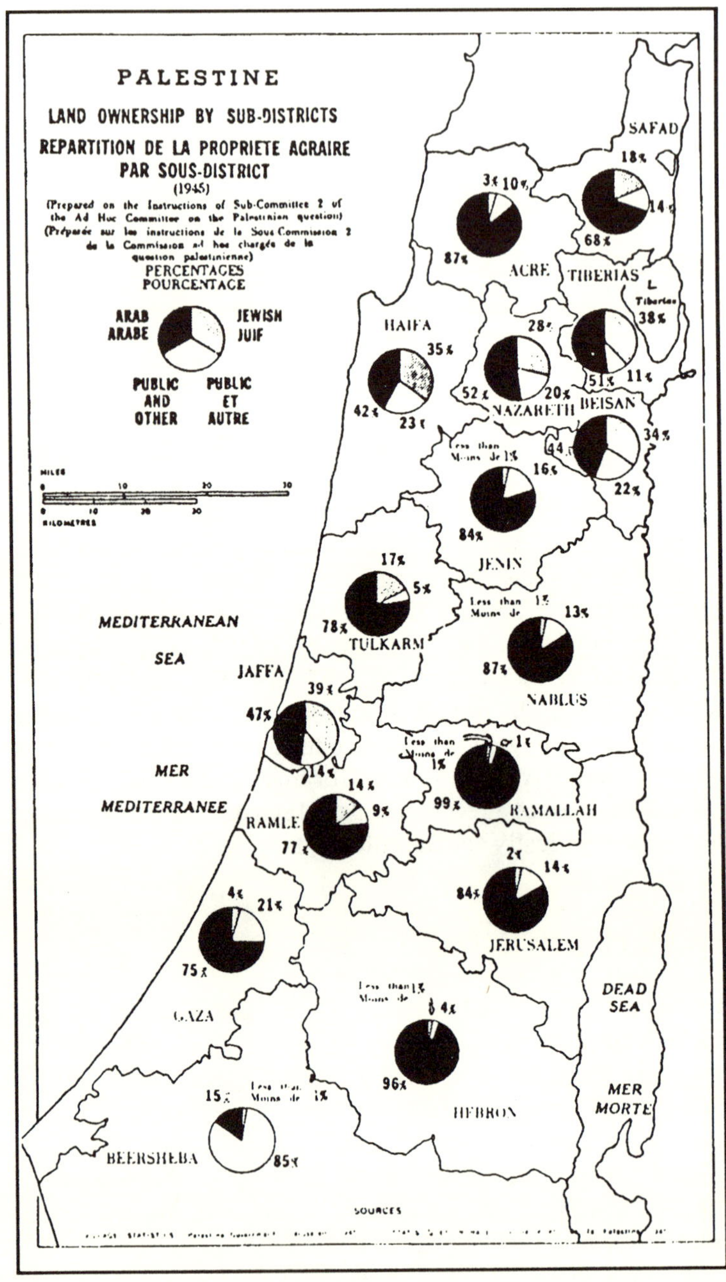

SOURCE: UN Subcommittee on Palestine Question, 1947; data from Rural Statistics prepared for British administration in Palestine, 1945.

TABLE 8.1

Jewish Colonies Established in Palestine, 1870-1982

Period	Total	Galilee Mountains	Northern Region	Central Region	Negev & Arava	Judea & Samaria	Jordan Valley	Golan Heights	Gaza Region
Before 1870	8	1	3	3	1	-	-	-	-
1870-1896	14	-	6	8					
1897-1900	-	-	-	-					
1901-1906	7	-	6	1	-	-	-	-	-
1907-1912	8	-	6	2	-	-	-	-	-
1913-1924	32	-	22	10	-	-	-	-	-
1925-1930	28	-	13	15	-	-	-	-	-
1931-1936	64	1	20	43	-	-	-	-	-
1937-1947	125	7	65	36	17	-	-	-	-
1948-1950	261	27	62	130	42	-	-	-	-
1951-1955	122	4	22	51	45	-	-	-	-
1956-1960	41	6	9	11	15	-	-	-	-
1961-1963	9	1	3	1	4	-	-	-	-
1964-1966	13	5	-	5	3	-	-	-	-
1967-1971	33	-	-	4	3	4	9	12	1
1972-1976	32	-	2	2	7	6	5	9	1
1977-1982	205	64	4	6	29	62	17	14	9
Grand Total:	1002	116	243	328	166	72	31	35	11

SOURCE: Pamphlet published by Settlement Department of Jewish Agency and Word Zionist organization, July, 1982.

between such areas of dense Palestinian population as the Galilee and Beisan valleys next to the Jordan River. And in October, 1946, under cover of night, eleven Jewish colonies were established in the northern Negev, in order to secure the south for the future of the Jewish state.

By 1947, Jewish footholds in Palestine had grown to the extent that the Zionists felt ready to take the offensive. From their secure positions, which had grown to such capability with the permission and sometimes encouragement of British Mandate governance, regular and terrorist Jewish groups were able to overpower the Palestinians. Between December 1947 and April 1948 some 800,000 Palestinians were driven from their homes, lands, and country, in preparation for the declaration of the Jewish state.

The years 1948 to 1959 witnessed the systematic destruction of over 350 so-called abandoned Palestinian villages and hamlets, on whose ruins 261 Jewish colonies were built. An additional 122 colonies were established on so-called empty lands – lands the Palestinians had been forced to leave behind and to which they were not permitted to return. In these years the new Jewish state tried to erase, as far as possible, all trace of Palestinian presence on the land – a presence that had been continuous since the days of the Canaanites and Jebusites, some three thousand years before the Christian era.

From 1955 to 1967 there was a slowdown in settlement construction. Only sixty-three new colonies were established, as Israeli concentration shifted to the consolidation of those colonies erected in previous years.

COLONIES IN THE OCCUPIED TERRITORIES

The June War of 1967 brought under Israeli occupation that part of historical Palestine not taken over in 1948: the Old City of Jerusalem, the West Bank, and the Gaza Strip. The same Zionist policies that had governed pre-1948 colonization strategy again came into play, with the same objective: the dispossession of the indigenous population and the incorporation of their lands into the Jewish state. This intention is clearly illustrated in a speech made by Mordechai Zippori, Israeli minister of energy, on October 10, 1982. The occasion was the opening ceremony of Inav, a new settlement, established on land seized from the villagers of Anabta, near Tulkarem.

> The continuation of settlement is the backbone of the Zionist movement in the West Bank and it is the only means to defeat any peace initiative which is intended to bring foreign rule to Judea and Samaria. . . . The presence of an Arab majority in the West Bank should not prevent the Israeli authorities from accelerating the settlement process in the occupied territories. . . . I was born in Petah Tikva [one of

the earliest Jewish colonies established in Palestine] which was surrounded by many Arab villages such as Kufr Anna, Abu Kisheh, and Khayriyeh – and no trace has been left of those villages today, but Petah Tikva remained.

Those closing words have clear and chilling implications for Palestinians in the occupied territories.

Since June 1967, the Israelis have established 125 colonies, or footholds, as they were called prior to 1948, in the occupied areas of the West Bank, including seven fortress residential colonies, consisting of over forty thousand apartments, encircling the Palestinians of east Jerusalem. In the Gaza Strip, which has the highest population density in the world, eleven Jewish colonies have been set up.

Colonization Strategy under Labor, 1967-1977

During Labor's ten-year period of power, settlement strategy was concentrated in two areas: Jerusalem and the cultivable lands of the Jordan Valley.

In Jerusalem, high-rise residential fortresses were constructed on confiscated or expropriated Palestinian land. These were strategically located so as to encircle the 135,000 Palestinians living in the eastern part of the city, thus preventing their expansion and ensuring permanent Israeli control of the entire city.

In the rest of the West Bank, Labor began the construction of two belts of settlements along the north-south length of the eastern border of the West Bank, one on the floor of the Jordan Valley and the other on the highlands overlooking the valley. A so-called Allon Plan road was constructed to connect the two belts. These settlements have an obvious economic importance – Israel is already in control of an estimated 50 percent of the cultivable land in the Jordan Valley and has developed an extensive network of electrical, irrigation, and other agricultural facilities to serve its colonies. They perform a strategic political function as well – they create a barrier between the populated areas of the west and east banks, cutting off the West Bank population from physical contact with east Jordan, and at the same time they encircle the Palestinian population of the West Bank highlands. This strategy is consistent with Labor's "Jordanian option," under which Israel would turn over administration of the populated areas of the highlands of the West Bank to Jordan, with a corridor through Jericho. Even in this "territorial compromise," however, Israel would retain the Jordan Rift (over one-third the land area of the West Bank), that part of Jerusalem occupied after the 1967 war, and several other clusters of colonies. Not much of an "option," from the Palestinian point of view.

Colonization Strategy under the Likud, 1977-1984

The victory of the Likud coalition in 1977 brought with it new policies for the colonization of the West Bank – not content with one-third of the area, Israel now wanted all of it. In general, the strategy for implementation of this goal was to isolate Palestinian population centers by the creation of barriers of Jewish colonies around and between them. The following maps show, first, existing or planned settlements; second, areas of greatest concentration of settlement blocs.

The government first adopted the Sharon Plan, named after Minister of Agriculture and Settlements General Ariel Sharon. This plan called for the construction of a third belt of settlements, extending from Jenin to the north and Bethlehem to the south. This would effectively bisect the western highlands, dividing them into two smaller areas. To connect the settlements (and divide the Palestinians), three lateral roads were planned: the first (in the south, already open) linking Israel with the Gush Etzion settlement bloc and on to the Dead Sea, the second (the Trans-Samaria Highway), cutting through the heart of the West Bank, and the third, in the north.

Even more ambitious settlement plans were to follow. In October, 1978, shortly after the signing of the Camp David accords, the World Zionist Organization came out with the first five-year comprehensive settlement plan for "Judea and Samaria." This plan was amended and updated in 1980 and 1981, and in 1982 a new five-year plan, extending to 1987, was prepared. However formulated, the objective is the same: to build Jewish colonies between and among the population areas of the "minorities" (that is, the one million Palestinian inhabitants). Settlement blocs are situated with two strategic considerations in mind: one, to surround the major Palestinian towns and prevent their expansion (for example, Nablus is surrounded by two blocs, Tirza and Elon Moreh; Ramallah is surrounded by Beit El, Givon, and Maale Adumim blocs); and two, to cut off the Arab towns from each other (for example, the Kedumim bloc would divide Nablus from Qalqilya; the Shavei Shomron bloc lies between Nablus and Jenin; the Kfar Etzion bloc would create a barrier between Bethlehem and Hebron). These plans would do away with the Jericho-Jordan corridor allowed by Labor under its "Jordanian option" strategy, by placing six settlements around the town of Jericho.

The general objective of the latest plan was to populate the West Bank with 120,000 Israelis by 1987 (not including the 100,000 Israelis already living in the annexed areas of Jerusalem).* This would ensure permanent

---

* This target was not achieved by the end of 1988. The number of colonial settlers was approximately 65,000 in the West Bank, in addition to the 100,000 in the occupied part of east Jerusalem. – Ed.

Israeli control of all the West Bank. The intent is clearly stated in the plan:

> The best and most effective way of removing every shadow of a doubt about our intentions to hold on to Judea and Samaria forever is by speeding up the settlement momentum in these territories. . . . The purpose of settling the areas between and around the centers occupied by the minorities [that is, the Arab majority in the West Bank] is to reduce to the minimum the danger of an additional Arab State being established in these territories. Being cut off, by Jewish settlements, the minority population will find it difficult to form a territorial and political continuity.

The Israeli government under the Likud strengthened and extended its juridical and administrative control over the occupied territories through the application of Israeli law to the Jewish colonies there. Through the arm of the military government, two military orders have been issued to this effect. The first, Military Order 783, established regional councils exclusively for the Jewish colonies, and divided the West Bank into six of these Jewish regional councils: Shomron, Binyamin, Etzion, Hor Hebron, Jordan Valley, and one for the Jericho area. The second, Military Order 892, established local town councils within these regional councils for nine urban settlements: Maale Efraim, Karnei Shomron, Elkana, Ariel, Givat Zeev, Maale Adumim, Gush Etzion, Efrat, and Kiryat Arba. The most strategically significant of these urban colonies are Givat Zeev, south of Ramallah, Maale Adumim, outside Bethany on the road to Jericho, and Efrat, to the south of Bethlehem. These three colonies will constitute the satellite towns, each consisting of more than seven thousand apartments, which will form an outer ring surrounding the annexed area of east Jerusalem, and which will be part of what the Israelis are now calling "metropolitan Jerusalem."

The policies of the Likud-Labor government of "national unity" aimed at continued colonization by increasing the number of Jews living in the existing Jewish colonies rather than by increasing the number of new colonies. Thus, this period can be characterized by an intensive effort to speed the construction of new apartments in existing colonies. This explains the rapid increase in the number of Jewish colonizers – from approximately 40,000 in 1985 to 65,000 in late 1987, that is prior to the Palestinian uprising. As of mid-1988, judging from the increasing number of completed but empty apartments in Jewish colonies, one can say that the Palestinian uprising has brought to a halt any further substantial increase in the number of settlers for the foreseeable future.

JEWISH SETTLEMENTS OF THE WEST BANK

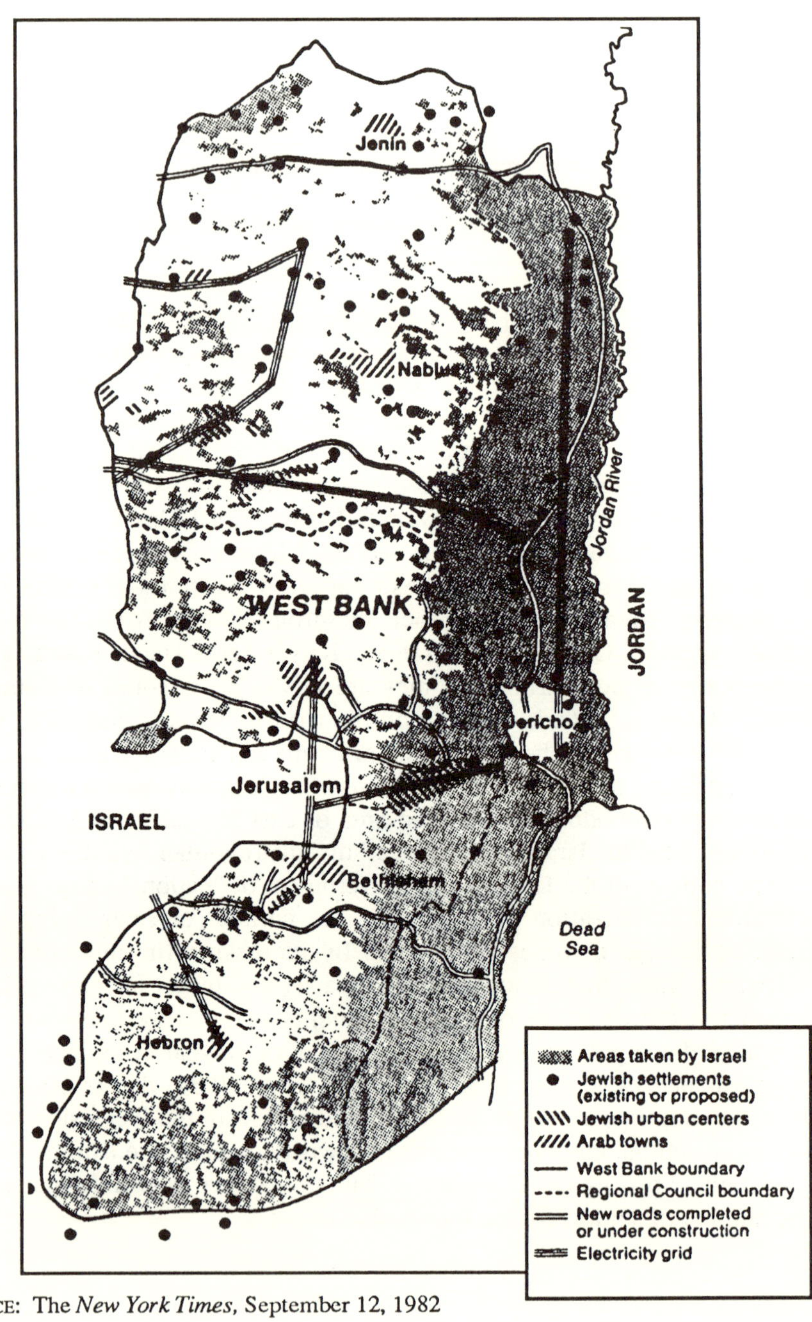

SOURCE: The *New York Times*, September 12, 1982

SETTLEMENTS OF THE WEST BANK
(Insert shows Areas of Concentration)

NOTE: Some settlements go through rapid name changes both for administrative and political reasons. The names listed on the map are not necessarily the final names of the settlements.

SOURCE: Master Plan for the Development of Settlements drawn up by Matityahu Drobles, Chairman of the Settlement Department of the World Zionist Federation.

PALESTINIAN RIGHTS AND JEWISH COLONIES

Israeli "divide and conquer" colonization strategy, like Prime Minister Menachem Begin's "autonomy for the people, but not the land" ideology, must have for its starting point the physical possession of the land. Yet at the turn of the century only 2 percent of the land of Palestine was owned by Jews. And although Israel claims that colonies are established only on state land, this is true only in a small percentage of cases, and in those cases where Israel has redefined longstanding traditional categories of land ownership to suit its own purposes (see chapter 7). A table at the end of this chapter lists Jewish colonies in the West Bank and indicates the previous status of the land on which they now stand – it can be seen at a glance that most of that land was indeed privately owned by Palestinians.

"Security reasons" are often cited for land seizures. Under Military Order 388 (Ghor Valley) the military governor is authorized to declare any area closed, and to prevent anyone from entering or leaving it without a permit. Villagers who previously owned or cultivated such land are simply denied access to it. Another ploy is the declaration or redefinition of lands as state lands – in the annexed area of Jerusalem, this objective is accomplished by land confiscation "for a public purpose" – public meaning, of course, only the Jewish public. If the closed areas have crops or fruit-bearing trees, these are defoliated, uprooted, or bulldozed.

It should be remembered that Israeli colonies, whether constructed on state *or* private land, are illegal under Article Four of the Geneva Convention, and under UN resolutions covering territories conquered by military force. Israel has consistently ignored such provisions, calling them inapplicable, but has claimed that only state land has been used for settlements. To test this claim, the author has carried out a survey of all the lands seized after 1967 and presently under direct control of Israeli civilian colonies. These land estimates *do not include* areas seized for military purposes as in the Ghor area, or those large areas closed off, again for undefined security purposes, in the eastern highlands of the West Bank overlooking the Jordan Valley. Categories of land ownership included under private are:

Mulk land – private land to which owners have clear title deed.

Miri land – land which has been actively cultivated for generations and has been registered at the Ministry of Finance for land tax purposes.

Jiftlik or *mudawwara* lands – lands actively cultivated by Palestinian farmers, which in the nineteenth century were nominally under the title

THE SHARON SETTLEMENT PLAN

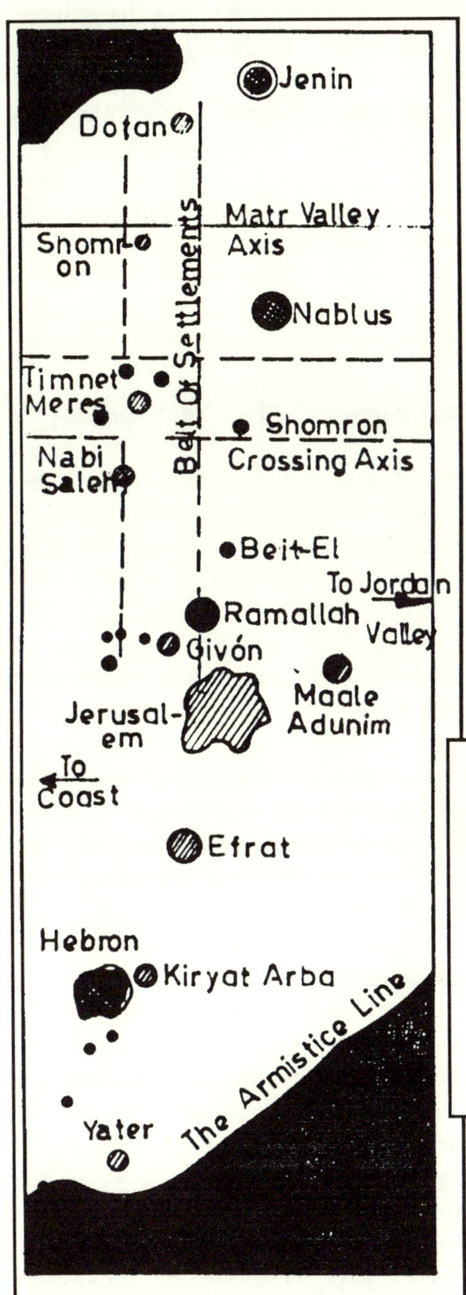

of the Ottoman sultan, and were subsequently recognized by the British and Jordanian governments as private lands. Prior to 1967 the Jordanian government was carrying out surveys in preparation for the issuance of title deeds to the farmers who were cultivating these lands.

Categories of land included under state ownership or "public domain" lands include the following:

Mawat land – waste land including deserts, forest, and rocky uncultivated mountaintops not owned by individuals.

Lands which were the sites of British Mandate Taggert forts and Jordanian police or army camps.

Lands designated for community purposes such as parks and hospitals.

Based on the above categories of land ownership, the aforementioned survey found that out of an estimated 198,000 dunums of cultivable land expropriated by the israelis for the exclusive use of civilian colonies (up to July 1982), 10,916 dunums were state lands and 186,304 dunums were private lands – that is, 5 percent state lands and 95 percent private.

These figures give the general picture. The following list, by no means comprehensive, gives some particulars of this systematic confiscation of Arab property for the use of Jewish colonies:

June 1967 – One hundred thirty-five homes of the Maghrabi quarter of the Old City of Jerusalem bulldozed to make way for the plaza next to the Wailing Wall. Since then five to six thousand Palestinians have been evicted from their homes, which were destroyed or remodeled to allow for the extension of the Jewish Quarter.

June-July 1967 – Twenty thousand dunums of cultivated land belonging to the three villages in the Latrun salient (Beit Nuba, Yalu, and Imwas) seized; over six thousand houses demolished; ten thousand Palestinians made homeless. Now the colonies of Mevo Horon and Canada Park stand on the ruins of these villages, and Israeli colonists are cultivating the lands that Palestinian farmers had tended for generations.

August 1967 – Three villages in the Jordan Valley, al-Ajajreh, Sattariyeh, and Makhruk, bulldozed. The colony of Massua rises on the ruins of al-Ajajreh; the colony of Argaman now uses the wells and cultivates the lands of the villagers of Makhruk.

1968 – Houses and vineyards of village of Artas (near Bethlehem) destroyed – now the site of Alon Shevut.

1970 – Houses and irrigated tomato plants of village of Beit Dajan destroyed – now the site of Hamra. Nabi Samuel, on the outskirts of Jerusalem, razed to the ground – residential fortress of Ramot built nearby.

1972 – Wheatfields at Akraba aerially defoliated – colonizers from Gitit now cultivate these lands.

1977 – Wheatfields of farmers from Tubas bulldozed – colonizers from Roi now cultivate these lands. Six hundred fifteen-year-old plum trees belonging to the farmers of Beit Omar cut down – colony of Migdal Oz now prepares this land for use.

1978 – Wheatfields of farmers from Beit Furik bulldozed – these lands now cultivated by colonizers from Mekhora.

1979 – Wheatfields of Akraba again destroyed, to allow for expansion of colony of Gitit.

1980 – Grapevines belonging to farmers of Beit Iskania uprooted to allow for expansion of the settlements of Rosh Tzurim and Alon Shevut.

1981 – Wheatfields, fig trees, and olives destroyed around village of Ain Yabrud, to make way for expansion of Ofra.

1982 – Two thousand olive trees belonging to the villagers of Jinsafout uprooted, to allow for expansion of colony of Emmanuel.

1984 – Grapevines belonging to the villagers from el-Khedder uprooted for expansion of Efrat in the Bethlehem area.

1988 – Grapevines belonging to el-Khedder again uprooted for expansion of Dariel.

As some of the above examples show, the threat to Palestinian property rights does not end with the initial establishment of a settlement.. As the colony grows and more colonizers are brought in, additional land is expropriated. Every colony is thus a continuing threat to the surrounding Palestinian villages.

Water Rights

The Israeli colonization process in the West Bank has not been restricted to land seizure. The scarce underground water resources have been exploited by the Israeli occupation authorities, who have drilled deep-bore wells and installed powerful pumps in all areas of the West Bank, but particularly in the Jordan Valley, where the Israeli agricultural colonies are completely dependent on this water for their domestic and irrigation purposes. To date, some forty deep-bore holes, or "Jewish wells," have been drilled in the West Bank pumping some forty-two million cubic meters of water per year. This water is for the exclusive use of the Jewish colonies, and already exceeds by 40 percent the quantity of water that Palestinians are allowed to pump from pre-1967 existing wells.

A number of these wells have been drilled in close proximity to local Arab springs, contrary to Jordanian laws regulating the drilling of new wells. These include two wells dug in the Jericho area above Ain Sultan spring, three wells drilled on the site of al-Auja spring, two on the site of the Fasail spring, five in the Wadi Fara basin, and two in the Bardala basin. The impact of these practices has already been felt in Jericho, where the salinity of the water being pumped from pre-1967 Arab wells has increased noticeably in recent years. The outflow of the al-Auja spring, which averaged eleven million cubic meters per year, dried up in the summer of 1979 and in 1987 – hydrologists link this to the three Israeli wells dug on the site of al-Auja. Farmers of the village lost all their crops in 1979 and 1987 – an estimated loss of $5 million – but when they asked the military government to stop pumping from their wells, or to supply them with water from the Israeli wells on their land,. or to allow them to drill a new village well to supplement the depleted supply from the spring, these requests were categorically denied.

Not only have the Israelis been diverting the scarce water supply for their own exclusive use, but they have also, since 1967, placed a ban, with a few exceptions, on the drilling of new Arab wells for irrigation purposes. They have also required that water meters be placed on wells existing prior to 1967, to control the quantities of water that Palestinians can pump from their pre-1967 wells. In this manner, not only do the indigenous Palestinians find that much of their water supply has been taken away from them, but they are also prohibited from the further development on their own of this most precious resource. Thus, as far as water development for the Palestinian community is concerned, one can say that time has stopped in 1967.

CONCLUSION

The impact of the colonization process on the Palestinian population has been devastating. Thousands of farmers have been displaced from their lands, their resources, and their livelihoods. The villages most hard-hit are those in the eastern highlands overlooking the Jordan Valley – Majdal Beni Fadil, Akraba, Beit Furik, Beit Dajan, Tamun, and Tubas. For example, the village of Beit Dajan has lost an estimated 80 percent of its prime land and as a result 90 percent of its population has lost its livelihood. In the nearby village of Beit Furik an estimated 60 percent of its land holdings were seized or closed off for the colony of Mekhora – 80 percent of the village population has become totally or partially landless. In the Jerusalem area, the village of Beit Hanina has lost thousands of dunums for the formation of three residential colonies. Such examples will multiply, as more colonies are planned and built, and as existing ones expand.

In the face of this continuing onslaught, Palestinians have no choice but to continue their struggle for survival. They must try to develop their resources, and the focus of this development should be the land. The land must be built upon and cultivated, and large-scale land reclamation projects should be initiated. Advantage should be taken of the new agricultural technologies, so that previously uncultivable land may be put to use

In addition, Palestinians whose land has been taken continue to fight in the courts. Court cases have been instrumental in regaining some lands, as in the Elon Moreh case, in which a settlement was dismantled after it had been established for some three months. In some other instances, such as those of the village of Surif in the Hebron area and Bartaa in the Jenin area, the occupation authorities withdrew their seizure orders when farmers challenged them in court. Even in cases in which landowners lost their lands, such as the famous Beit El and Tubas case, the Israeli Supreme Court established in its decision an important precedent – that although Jewish civilian settlements may be established on security grounds, they are temporary and by implication should be dismantled should the security reasons cease to apply in a state of peace.

Without any shadow of doubt, one of the underlying causes for the present on-going Palestinian uprising or *intifada* has been the continuing Israeli policy of the past twenty years of occupation, of violating Palestinian property and water rights, as described above. This policy has alienated all Palestinians and particularly the farmers in the rural areas. This explains the involvement in the uprising of almost all of the four hundred Palestinian villages in the West Bank, and the large number of casualties, in dead and wounded from these villages.

There are already growing indications that the *intifada* not only has stopped the growth of the Jewish population in the colonies, but could also be the beginning of the reversibility of Jewish colonization of the occupied territories, in preparation for the establishment of an independent Palestinian state.

APPENDIX: ESTIMATED LAND AREAS OF WEST BANK COLONIES ESTABLISHED UP TO MAY 1981[1]

Note: All areas are in dunums. 1 dunum = 0.247 acres. 1,000 dunums = 1 sq. kilometer = 0.386 sq. miles.

Settlement	Total Area (approx.)	Public Land (approx.)	Private Land (approx.)	Previous Status of Land and Village from which It Was Seized
THE JORDAN VALLEY SETTLEMENTS[2]				
1. Mehola	4,500		4,500	The entire area was previously cultivated and irritated by Bardala and Ain al-Baida farmers. The Israeli army used defoliants on Ain al-Baida lands in 1969. Wells and springs in area were depleted by two new deep-bore wells for settlements.
2. Argaman	8,600		8,600[3]	Previously cultivated and irrigated by six wells seized with land. Owned by residents of Zbeidat, Marj Naje, Nablus, and the village of Makhruk, which was destroyed in 1967.
3. Massua	4,300		4,300[3]	Located on the site of al-Ajajreh, destroyed in 1967. Previously cultivated and irritated by wells and Fara canal. The village of Sattariyeh was also destroyed in the area in 1967.

1 These estimates do not include all settlements listed on the map, for some of which information is inadequate. They include only those areas visibly in the control of West Bank settlements and should not be mistaken as being estimates of land areas under the control of the Israeli occupation authorities as a whole. Military reserves, state land not allocated for settlement, and absentee land not allocated for settlement are not included. The total land area controlled by Israeli authorities amounts to between 25 percent and 15 percent of the West Bank.

2 It appears that 40 percent of the lands under settlement in the Jordan Valley are absentee lands (which implicitly concedes that they are private property). On November 2, 1971 the *Jerusalem Post* reported that Yisrael Nedivi, of the Jordan Rift settlement committee, had said that 40 percent of the land in the Jordan Rift belongs to absentee landlords, who would claim their property once they were allowed to return following an agreement on West Bank autonomy.

3 These are so-called *jiftlik* or *mudawwara* lands, which in the nineteenth century were nominally under title of the sultan. The British and Jordanian Governments recognized the residents' rights of ownership to these lands, though registration in the name of individual owners has not been completed in some cases.

Settlement	Total Area	Public Land	Private Land	Previous Status
4. Yafit	500	500		Not previously cultivated.
Phatzael Bloc	24,000[3]		24,000[3]	Previously cultivated and partially irrigated by the Fasail spring. The owners came from Fasail, Akraba, and settled Bedouin.
5. Phatzael				
6. Tomar				
7. Netiv Hagedud				
8. Naaran				
9. Gilgal				
10. Yitav (old site of Naaran)	3,000		3,000	Previously cultivated and irrigated by former residents of al-Auja Fawqa and al-Auja Tahta. A high percentage of absentees (i.e., refugees from 1967), exists in this area. The homes of 10,000 refugees were destroyed in 1967. Banana and citrus groves dried up in 1979 as a result of the drying up of a village spring depleted by two Israeli deep-bore wells.
11. Mitzpe Jericho B	100	100		Not recently cultivated
12. Beit Haarava	100	100		Not recently cultivated.
13. Neima	50	50		Not previously cultivated.
14. Sheloh	50		50	Owned by residents of Tubas.
15. Almog	500	500		Site of pre-1967 horserace track. Irrigated by newly bored wells near Jericho.
16. Kalia	1,500	1,500		Not previously cultivated.
17. Mitzpe Shalem	100	100		Not previously cultivated

(The above settlements are located in the Jordan Valley floor.
Those below constitute the second chain in the foothills above the valley floor.)

18. Roi	2,000	2,000[4]	Owned by Tubas residents. Previously planted with field crops. Declared a closed military area in 1975. Continued under cultivation until 1977, when the Israeli army bulldozed wheat fields, The farmers lost their case in the High Court on security grounds.
19. Yabok	1,800	1,800	Also owned by Tubas farmers. Previously planted with field crops. Seized for security reasons in 1979.
20. Bekaot	3,000	3,000	Previously cultivated and owned by residents of Tamun village. Seized for security reasons in 1970.
21. Hamra	4,500	4,500[3]	Previously cultivated and partially irrigated, Several houses were destroyed in 1970. The owners are from Beit Dajan village. More land was seized in 1975. Tomato plants were destroyed.
Hamra	400	400	Absentee plot, previously cultivated.
Hamra	400	400	Absentee citrus grove.
Hamra	150	150	Absentee land, previously cultivated.
22. Mekhora	4,800[5]	4,800	Owned and previously cultivated by Beit Furik residents. The crops were uprooted in March 1978. The land was seized on security grounds in 1969.
23. Gitit	5,000	5,000	Owned and previously cultivated by Akraba residents. The Israeli army defoliated 1,800 dunums of wheatfields in 1972. More wheatfields were ploughed under in 1979. Another 1,200 dunums were seized in 1979.
24. Maale Efraim	6,300[6]	6,300	Previously owned and cultivated by Majdal Beni Fadil residents.

4 The exact area of the land in question here is known from High Court litigation, in which the villagers' claims of ownership were unchallenged by the government.

5 This excludes an area of 10,000 dunums that has reportedly been closed. Their location and intended use are uncertain.

6 Perhaps another 5,000 dunums has been closed, but their future use is uncertain.

Settlement	Total Area	Public Land	Private Land	Previous Status
				Defoliants were employed in 1978. Another 1,300 dunums were seized for security reasons in 1979. Wheatfields have been ploughed under for the Trans-Samaria Highway.
25. Mevo Shiloh	1,200		1,200	Previously owned and cultivated by Abu Falah, Mughayer, and Turmos Ayya residents. Land seized for security reasons.
26. Kochav Hashahar	800		800	Deir al-Jarir land. Seized initially for security reasons in 1976. More land was confiscated in 1980. A court case is pending in the High Court.
27. Ramonim	300		300	Previously cultivated and owned by Taibe residents, and seized in 1977 for security reasons.
28. Maale Adumim	5,000[7]	5,000[8]		Largely wasteland, except for valley floors cultivated previously by Issawiyya and al-Azzariyya residents.
29. Maale Adumim	7,000		7,000	Common grazing land owned by the village of Anata, seized in 1979. The owners lost their case in the High Court.
30. Mitzpe Jericho	50	50		A former Jordanian army camp. The settlement was constructed while negotiations at Camp David were in process, September 1978.

THE WEST BANK HIGHLANDS

Settlement	Total Area	Public Land	Private Land	Previous Status
31. Tekoah	2,000		2,000	Previously owned and cultivated by Rafida residents, and seized in 1975.

7 This does not include 70,000 dunums that have reportedly been closed, most of which would be public land. Their future use and exact location are uncertain.

8 This is land of the *mawat* or wasteland, a class generally held to be government property. However, isolated patches of cultivated land in the valleys might be claimed as private properly.

32. Kiryat Arba	1,200		1,200	Some 700 dunums were initially requisitioned, and an additional 500 later. Grape vines were uprooted and houses destroyed. The area was owned and cultivated by Hebron residents.
33. Dahariyya	20	20		Inside a former British and Jordanian police post.
34. Migdal Oz	300[9]		300	Owned and cultivated by Beit Omar residents. Plum trees and grape vineyards were uprooted in 1977. More land was seized in 1980.
Etzion Bloc 35. Alon Shevut	3,800	1,000	2,800	1,000 dunums are the site of pre-1948 Jewish settlement. An additional 2,000 dunums were seized from Artas and Nahalin villages. Several houses were destroyed and vineyards uprooted. More land was seized in 1980 and 1981. More grapevines were uprooted in 1980 by settlers.
36. Kfar Etzion				
37. Rosh Tzurim				
38. Elazar	350		350	Owned and cultivated by al-Khadr residents. Some grapevines were uprooted in 1973.
39. Efrat	2,000		2,000	Partially cultivated with grapevines and owned by farmers from al-Khadr. Seized in 1979 for security reasons.
40. Hargilo	600	400	200	Former Jordanian army base; area extended by requisition from Beit Jala owners.
41. Maale Adumim (permanent) (Ein Shemesh)	30,000		30,000	Owned by al-Azzariyya and Abu Dis residents, and partly subdivided for building lots. One house was destroyed on a site belonging to the Greek Orthodox Church in 1979. Parts of the fifth-century ruins of a Greek convent were destroyed in 1980.
42. Givon	100	100		A former Jordanian army camp. Settlers were threatening to seize private land around the camp.
43. Mitzpe Givon	130		130	Seized by settlers of Givon in 1980. The land belonged to farmers from Biddo.

9 Larger closures are reported in area. Their location and future use uncertain.

Settlement	Total Area	Public Land	Private Land	Previous Status
44. Mevo Horon and Canada Park	20,000		20,000	This area was largely owned by farmers expelled from three villages, Yalu, Beit Nuba, and Imwas, destroyed in 1967. Almond and olive tree orchards were seized with the land. Over 10,000 farmers were rendered homeless and dispossessed of their orchards and land.
45. Beit Horon	50	50		A former Jordanian army camp. Settlers are threatening to seize private land around camp.
46. Beit El	600		600	Owned by al-Bireh and Ramallah residents and subdivided for residential building sites. The area is adjacent to Bet El army camp on the site of a former Jordanian army base. The owners lost a case in the High Court in 1978 on security grounds.
47. Beit El B	300		300	This area consists of more land seized from al-Bireh and Dura El Qareh in 1979.
48. Ofra	400	50	350	Fig trees have been fenced in and other fruit trees uprooted. Wheatfields belonging to the villagers of Ain Yabrud were ploughed under and more fig trees uprooted by settlers in 1981.
49. Nevi Tsuf	110	40	70	40 dunums were the site of a British and Jordanian post. The private land was seized from Nabi Saleh.
50. Matityahu	500		500	The land was seized from the village of Niilin in 1979. The villagers lost a case in the High Court on security grounds.
51. Elkana	450	50	400	A former British and Jordanian police post. In 1976, an additional 100 dunums of olive orchards were fenced in which were owned by farmers from the village of Masha. In 1980, an additional 300 dunums of private land was seized by settlers from the same village.
52. Haris (Ariel)	6,500		6,500	Some cultivation was carried out. Thirty-six olive trees were uprooted at the site. The land belonged to Kufr Haris and Salfit villagers. An additional 6,000 dunums was seized in 1981 for the expansion of Ariel from the farmers of Salfit. The case is in the High Court.

53. Tapuah	150		150	The land was partially cultivated and was seized from Yasuf villagers in 1978.
54. Karnei Shomron	110	100	10	The original site was a forest. Pine trees were cut down. An additional 10 dunums was seized in 1979, and 30 olive trees were cut down.
55. Maale Karnei Shomron	50	50		The site of a forest. Pine trees were cut down, as were 30 olive and almond trees belonging to farmers in 1979, to make a road for the site.
56. Kedumim	300		300	Owned by Kaddum villagers. Some 30 olive trees were uprooted. The site is adjacent to an army camp.
57. Elon Moreh	100	100		This is a new site at Jebal Kalur. Forest pine trees were cut down in 1980.
58. Micmash	150		150	Grazing land of the village of Mikhmas seized in 1980.
59. Levona	250		250	Land seized in 1980 from the village of Abud.
60. Shilo "dig"	380		380	The land was owned and cultivated by Qaryut villagers. Fifteen almond trees were cut down by settlers in 1977. Olive trees were uprooted to make a new road to the settlement in 1979. Additional land was seized from the same village in 1980.
61. Salit	500		500	Communal grazing land of Kafr Sur.
62. Shomron	100	100		Former army camp.
63. Maale Nahal	300		300	Owned by Silat al-Dahr residents. Some 20 olive trees were uprooted and an uninhabited house was destroyed on the site in 1977.
64. Sanur	50	50		Former British police post.
65. Nahal Reihan	100	100		Uncultivated land.
66. Reihan	100	100		Uncultivated land.
67. Tel Dotan	100	100		Uncultivated land.

Settlement	Total Area	Public Land	Private Land	Previous Status
EAST JERUSALEM (enlarged municipal boundaries annexed to Israel, June 1967)				
68. Gilo (10,000 apartments)	4,000		4,000	Previously owned by Sharafat, Beit Jala, Jerusalem, and Beit Safafa residents. Vineyards and other fruit trees were uprooted, and some homes destroyed in 1976. More olive trees and vines were uprooted in 1978.
69. East Talpiot (4,000 apartments)	2,000	500	1,500	500 dunums were a former UN zone; the remaining land came from Sur Bahir and Sheikh Saed.
70. French Hill & Ramot Eshkol (6,000 apartments)	3,600		3,600	This area was confiscated from landowners from Lifta, Issawiyah, Anata, and Jerusalem. Attempts to destroy several houses in the area were resisted by landowners.
71. Neve Yaacov (4,000 apartments)	1,500		1,500	Owned by Jerusalem area residents. There was also a pre-1948 Jewish settlement site, now an Israeli army base.
72. Neve Yaacov South Planned 10,000 apartments	4,400		4,400	Confiscated from the residents of Bet Hanina and Hizma in 1980.
73. Kalandia (industrial park)	1,500		1,500	Owned by Jerusalem area residents.
74. Ramot (8,000 apartments)	4,000		4,000	Beit Iksa and Beit Hanina residents owned the land. The nearby village of Nabi Samuel, consisting of 50 homes, was destroyed in 1970. Three hundred and fifty villagers were forcibly evicted from their homes.
75. Jewish Quarter	20	6	14	Pre-1948, there was a Jewish population but two-thirds of the property was Arab-owned. After 1967, 6,500 Arab residents were evicted. The Maghrabi quarter consisting of 137 homes, was razed to the ground in June 1967 to create an open space next to the Wailing Wall.
Subtotal	183,710	10,816	171,354	

UPDATE: ESTIMATED LAND AREAS OF WEST BANK COLONIES ESTABLISHED BETWEEN MAY 1981 AND JULY 1982

Settlement	Total Area (approx.)	Public Land (approx.)	Private Land (approx.)	Previous Status of Land and Village from which It Was Seized
THE WEST BANK HIGHLANDS				
Hebron area				
1. Maon	2000		2000	Land seized from village of Yatta and surrounding hamlets.
2. Karmel	2000		2000	Land also seized from the village of Yatta.
3. Megohot	200		200	Land seized from the village of Freqis.
4. Adora	200		200	Land seized from the village of Dura.
5. Telem	200		200	Land seized from the village of Tarkumia.
Bethlehem area				
6. Maale Amos	300		300	Land seized from Rashayda Bedouin tribe; previously used as grazing land.
7. Meot Adumim	1000		1000	Land seized from the villagers of Ubeidiya.

Settlement	Total Area	Public Land	Private Land	Previous Status
Ramallah area				
8. Givat Zeev	1000		1000	Land seized from villagers of Beitunia and al-Jib. Orders of no-construction and no-entry into seized land were sent to municipality of Beitunia in 1979.
9. Pesagot	300		300	Land seized from al-Bireh residents. Closed for security reasons since 1977.
10. Ateret	150		150	Land seized from landowners from the village of Jibya.
11. Asael	500		500	Land seized from the villagers of Abud. This is the second colony established on the land of this village.
12. Nihi	500		500	Land seized from the village of Deir Qaadis.
Tulkarem area				
13. Yakkir	300		300	Land seized from the village of Deir Estya.
14. Emmanuel	800		800	Land seized from the villagers of Jimsafort. Over 2000 olive trees uprooted in May 1982 for expansion of colony.
15. Inav	1000		1000	Land seized from the village of Anabta.
16. Burkan	1000		1000	Land seized from the villagers of Sarta and Haris. Wheatfields also belonging to farmers from Haris bulldozed in May, 1981 for industrial purposes near settlement.
Jenin area				
17. Shekad	400		400	Land seized from the village of Tura.

THE JORDAN VALLEY SETTLEMENTS

18. Elisha	150		150	Land seized from landowners of Jericho.
19. Naama	3,100	100	3,000	Previously uncultivated land. Reportedly 3,000 dunums of private Palestinian lands, previously closed for security next to Jordan River, are now being prepared for use by this colony.
20. Rotem	200		200	Land seized from village of Tubas.
Subtotal	14,850	100	14,950	
Grand Total	198,020	10,916	186,304	
	100%	5%	95%	

CHAPTER 9

Israeli Settlement Policy Today

Peter Demant

Israeli settlements in the occupied territories have recently become much more central to the whole Israeli-Arab conflict. Massive loss of land by West Bank Palestinians, and an upsurge in Jewish settlements and in the number of settlers, have attracted international attention to Israeli colonization of Palestine – a phenomenon which dates back to the June 1967 war in the West Bank, the Gaza Strip, the Golan Heights and, before 1982, the Sinai. In Israel proper, this "Judaization" of the land has been a central tenet and practice of Zionism ever since the waves of Jewish immigration began in the late nineteenth century.

Since the beginning of this decade colonization across the "green line" (Israel's pre-1967 borders) has shown qualitative as well as quantitative changes. In an effort to assure Israeli-Jewish predominance over the West Bank, the government of Prime Minister Menachem Begin attempted to change its demographic balance by "transplanting" tens of thousands of Israeli Jews from the overpopulated coastal zone to "Judea and Samaria." Attracted by the subsidized housing, young Israeli families without strong ideological convictions are flooding the older, vanguard settlements formed by the pioneer zealots of Gush Emunim (Bloc of the Faithful). This chapter analyzes Israel's settlement policy as it has evolved in this latest period, with emphasis on the West Bank. A brief outline of the period of the first Begin government provides the necessary context for this discussion.

Reprinted with permission from MERIP Reports, July-August 1983.

THE FIRST BEGIN GOVERNMENT: 1977-1981

The "wild" settlement actions of the Gush squatters, a radicalized offshoot of the National Religious Party (NRP), contributed to the fall of the Labor government led by Prime Minister Yitzhak Rabin. The Gush stresses the need to keep the whole Land of Israel (Eretz Israel), including all occupied territories, and to resist all external pressure to relinquish them in return for peace with the Arab states. They took it upon themselves to stake out a Jewish presence precisely in heavily Arab-populated central regions of the West Bank. This was in contrast to the Allon Plan, the Labor Alignment's conception of the future of the territories: Israeli settlements in the arid and depopulated Jordan Rift to guard Israel's eastern frontier, but Palestinian concentrations in the Samarian hills would either be left to their own devices or be linked to Jordan through a corridor at Jericho.

When the Likud-NRP coalition led by Menachem Begin came to power in 1977, it inherited both the territorial intransigence of Begin's revisionist Herut (which had never accepted the 1947 partition of Palestine) and the messianic activism of Gush Emunim. Begin quickly legalized Elon Moreh (near Nablus), Ofra (near Ramallah) and Maale Adumim (on the road from Jerusalem to Jericho). These three illegal Gush Emunim settlements had challenged Rabin's authority, and in the process enjoyed the barely restrained support of his Labor rival, Defense Minister Shimon Peres. Begin promised to build "many more Elon Morehs."[1]

This was the honeymoon period between the Faithful and the Likud. General Ariel Sharon, Likud's new agriculture minister, set out to implement what was little more than a variation of the Gush's own plan, which proposed a second axis of Jewish population in Palestine, parallel to the coastal one, from the Golan through the West Bank and the Aravah Rift to the Red Sea.[2] The marked increase in the number of *garinim* (settlement nuclei) "going up to the soil," however, did not match the much more massive confiscation of private Arab lands. In other words, the "de-Arabization" of the land was not followed by a corresponding "Judaization."

1. Concerning the encouragement Begin gave to Gush Emunim during the "12 settlements" operation in the autumn of 1977, see Y. Litani in *Kol Hair*, 3 December 1982.

2. Gush Emunim, *Blueprint for settlement in Judea and Samaria*, (in Hebrew, n.d.); *Jerusalem Post*, 4 September 1977 (in *Israleft* 112). See Michel Korinman, "Israel, Jordanie, Palestine: trois scénarios israéliens," in *Hérodote, revue de géographie et de géopolitique* (1983), 29/30: 135-52. Sharon had been Rabin's advisor on settlement affairs during the 1975-1976 Sebastia crisis, the first and decisive government capitulation to Gush Emunim pressure.

An administrative order of September 1979 allowed Israeli citizens to buy West Bank lands privately from Arab owners, but few transactions occurred. Palestinians were unwilling to voluntarily part with their land, Jordanian law made its sale punishable by death, and speculators and middlemen escalated the prices.

Begin came to power at a time of growing international recognition of the PLO as the legitimate representative of the Palestinian people. International isolation was affecting Israel's morale. Zionism's crisis of legitimacy was, more than any other factor, responsible for the deep social and political metamorphosis which the Jewish state experienced under Begin. Israel succeeded in breaking the Arab encirclement by making peace with Egypt, but Sadat's price was the whole of Sinai, including the cluster of *moshavim* (cooperative settlements) in the Rafah Approaches around the new Israeli city of Yamit, which a few months before had been the object of ambitious planning.[3] Voluntarily giving up Jewish settlements was unprecedented in Zionist history. Begin was only persuaded to do it as a means of consolidating Israel's hold on the West Bank, with its heavier ideological weight.

The "autonomy" project for the West Bank and Gaza, adopted at Camp David in September 1978, threatened the prospect of Israel's indefinite and unrestricted *de facto* control over these territories. The various territorial compromises and settlement scenarios which the Zionist left had elaborated after the Six Day War, ridiculed at the time as "playing chess with oneself," as Golda Meir characterized them, suddenly became real again – this time under a regime which would not be content with less than peace *and* territories. This contradiction could only be masked by formulas that inevitably became the object of disputes the moment after they had been agreed on. Having accepted "autonomy" for the inhabitants, but simultaneously bent on annexing the soil, Israel set upon a course of transforming the reality in the West Bank by a speedy and large-scale Jewish influx.

Within Israel, one place this controversy emerged was in the World Zionist Organization (WZO) Settlement Division. Its heads were Matityahu Drobles, a Herut nominee appointed by Begin, and Raanan Weitz of Mapai. Drobles proposed to the government plans to neutralize the risks of autonomy: at the time, there was talk of settling 150,000 Jews in Judea, Samaria and the Gaza Strip in five years.[4] Labor-oriented settlement

3. *Haaretz*, 13 February 1978 (in *Israleft* 123).

4. *Al-Hamishmar*, 27 April 1979 (in *Israel & Palestine* Supplement no. 75, July 1979, p. 10).

professionals like Weitz considered the whole project a dangerous fantasy in view of Israel's limited financial and manpower resources. Weitz feared that neglect of the Galilee might lead to Arab "encroachment" on Jewish land in Israel proper.

Likud's grandiose programs yielded rather scarce results at first. Though the number of colonists continued to increase at a higher rate than under Alignment governments, the number of new Jewish settlements did not rise dramatically after Likud's first year. Growth took the form of consolidation.[5] In the autumn of 1979, the Supreme Court decided to uphold the claim of Arab villagers from Rujeib, near Nablus, that it was illegal for the government to seize their privately tilled lands for the (re-) establishment of the Elon Moreh *garin* on its original site (it had been displaced to the village of Kaddum in 1976 as part of the Rabin government's "compromise" with Gush Emunim). This important setback temporarily impeded further land seizures for civilian settlements.[6] American pressure on Israel at this time to "freeze" the establishment of new settlements also contributed to a certain slowdown in activity. In July 1980, the Israeli government announced it would erect only ten settlements more in the West Bank, and afterwards would concentrate on "thickening" existing ones.

The first Begin government's very narrow parliamentary margin was eventually eroded by a split in the Democratic Movement for Change (DMC) and by the "secession" of the Likud extreme right, Guela Cohen and Moshe Shamir, who joined the *Tehiya* (Renaissance) Party. Tehiya, established as the political arm of Gush Emunim to foil any Israeli retreat after the Camp David accords, was the political expression of a trend towards cooperation and even convergence of religious and secular Zionists, the latter often former Labor hawks from the *Ahdut Haavodah* faction. This trend was apparent in the establishment of a number of mixed religious/secular settlements in the West Bank: Maale Shomron, Tekoah, Beit Horon and Kfar Edumim. Gush Emunim hoped that their common devotion to the Land of Israel would catalyze a Jewish religious revival among the Israeli population at large. Yuval Neeman, an unemotive nuclear scientist, led this fervidly ultranationalist party which attracted a

5. Jewish population in the West Bank (not including the annexed "greater Jerusalem"): 1972-1,182; 1973-1,514; 1974-2,019; 1975-2,581; 1976-3,176; 1977-5,023; 1978-7,361; 1979-10,001; 1980-12,424; 1981-16,119. Central Bureau of Statistics, quoted in Meron Benvenisti, "The West Bank and Gaza Data Base Project: Pilot Study Report" (1982), p. 65.

6. See Rafik Halabi, *The West Bank Story* (New York, 1981), and Danny Rubenstein, *On the Lord's Side: Gush Emunim* (in Hebrew) (Tel Aviv, 1982).

considerable portion of Israeli youth, a generation for whom the "green line" was an antiquated concept.

While Tehiya clamored for more and faster settlement, a return to power of the Labor Alignment threatened from the other side to undo the "work" of the Likud in this field. Begin and Sharon feared electoral defeat in the June 1981 elections as a result of Likud's miserable economic performance. Polls showed close to 70 percent of Israelis in favor of colonizing the territories in one way or the other, so Begin and Sharon moved to capitalize on the popular issues of territory and settlement. Begin swore publicly that he would never give up "Judea and Samaria."[7] In Yamit, 80,000 came to demonstrate against withdrawal.[8] Likud's expected fall from power stimulated Sharon's eleventh-hour effort to augment the number of West Bank colonists to a degree that would impede any future attempt to repartition Eretz Israel.

Sharon's goal was to increase the number of West Bank colonists from around 17,000 to at least 20,000 before election day. To circumvent financial restrictions, the government negotiated with private building contractors to turn over land for a nominal fee (*e.g.*, in Karnei Shomron) in return for a promise to build large numbers of apartments. Sharon defended this "lands-for-flats" scheme by which city dwellers would be able to acquire a more or less free home in Samaria.[9] In Maale Adumim, the government offered land and infrastructure free to families who would build their own home. The Likud organized tours of the new West Bank settlements and building projects for tens of thousands of Israelis.

Gush Emunim and fellow colonists, meanwhile, were none too sure of victory, and "dug in" to weather a hostile Labor cabinet by soliciting support from sympathetic American and South African Zionists. The Council of Settlements in Judea, Samaria and Gaza tried to secure the support of the Labor-oriented Jordan Rift and Rafah Approaches settlements. The Jericho corridor was "filled" with Jewish settlements – Beit Haaravah was the first – to preclude Labor's "Jordanian option."

7. *Jerusalem Post International Edition (JPIE)*, 10 May 1981.

8. *JPIE*, 22 February, 5 April, and 10 May 1981. A similar percentage had favored annexation of the Golan (*ITIM* Agency, September 15, 1980).

9. *Yediot Ahronot*, 22 January 1981 (in *Israleft* 182); *JPIE*, 25 January and 1 February 1981.

THE SECOND BEGIN GOVERNMENT

Against all expectations, Likud's stunt politics on election eve – the bombing of the Iraqi nuclear plant, the sudden tax bonus for Israeli consumers – enabled it to retain power. But Yadin's Democratic Movement for Change, as well as Dayan's group and Weizman's influence, were eliminated. Begin thus formed a new and much more rightist coalition. The second Begin government had an even shakier political base, and much of this regime's actions can be understood in the light of its attempts to create a new "national consensus" around the Herut program of complete "Judaization" of the remaining occupied territories. For this, it needed a landslide victory that would smash Labor's remaining political strongholds and complete Israel's swing to the right.

In the early eighties, Herut exploited the Ashkenazi/veteran/elite image of the Alignment in the eyes of the Oriental Jews. The Alignment's greater openness to outside pressure, especially American, may have indicated its more realistic assessment of Israel's international entanglement. It reflects also the more "Westernizing" or "normalizing" character of left Zionism, in contrast to the more isolationist and anti-universalist bias of the right. This is precisely Labor's vulnerability *vis-à-vis* the Oriental majority. The Labor Alignment as a whole found itself in the unenviable position, occupied earlier by the then-Foreign Minister Abba Eban, of representing "gentile influence," whereas Begin took up Ben-Gurion's "It doesn't matter what the *goyim* are saying, it matters what the Jews are doing." Despite Israel's evident dependence on American support, the Likud was playing the anti-American card internally. This dovetailed with its resistance to further territorial concessions, and confirmed that it was the more "national" – *i.e.* unifying and Jewish – of the two main political blocs.

While Labor favored the return of the bulk of the West Bank to Jordan, its position on the existing Jewish settlement there was much less clearcut: it never declared that these should be removed for peace. This reflected, no doubt, the continuing strength of hawkish kibbutzim and moshavim federations in Labor's bosom, behind which there stood the historic tradition of initiating pioneer settlements as a living frontier of the Jewish state, along with the ideology of "normalizing" the Jewish diaspora's aberrant class structure through agricultural self-labor. For right Zionism, political power over a sovereign Jewish territory has always been what mattered. Its lack of colonizing ideology has been filled by Gush Emunim, with its different scheme for redemption. The right's attitude towards Jewish settlement was purely instrumental, unhampered by any residual guilt over the exploitation of Arab labor. For Herut, settlement was a means to achieve control over the whole of Eretz Israel; for Labor, control over the land was the precondition and the basis for settlement.

Likud faced the task of neutralizing the prestige of Labor's colonizing tradition while simultaneously using elements of it to reproduce its achievements in the occupied territories. This explains the accusations of Begin and Sharon, holding Dayan's and Peres' "soft" politics responsible for the prevalent pro-PLO feelings among Palestinians in the occupied territories. As defense minister, Sharon immediately set out to correct their "negligence."

The Begin government began to prepare the practical annexation of the West Bank and Gaza by a double strategy of uprooting all expressions of Palestinian national resistance to occupation and of simultaneously moving the maximum number of Jews across the "green line" in order to deprive the autonomy concept of any content. This policy was built on a hawkish trend in Israeli public opinion (only 19 percent of a September 1981 poll opposed continued colonization of the West Bank),[10] and was passively supported by Washington. In February 1981, President Reagan even declared that Israeli settlements were "not illegal."

The specter of recognition of the PLO obsessed Israel, especially after the partial recognition implicit in the July 1981 cease-fire with the guerrillas in southern Lebanon. Allowing the PLO noncriminal status would sustain Palestinian resistance in the territories and even risk a "spill-over" effect on the Israeli Arabs. Such a separate Palestinian Arab national identity fundamentally undermined Jewish "historical rights" to the whole of the Land of Israel. "Elimination of PLO influence" became the watchword under the new regime.

Sharon took a diversionary tack at first. He clashed with Major-General Dani Matt, Coordinator of Government Activities in the Administered Areas, under whom the "liberal" occupation regime had degenerated into the policy of the "strong arm." Sharon started with declarations suggesting a softer course.[11] Soon it became clear, however, that his pseudo-liberalization aimed only at stimulating an "alternative West Bank leadership" more willing to collaborate with Israel in developing docile "autonomous" institutions, based on the Village Leagues (see chapter 21). In November 1981, Sharon installed a civil administration in the West Bank, headed by Hebrew University orientalist Menachem Milson, to take over all but strictly security matters from the military government. West Bank cities greeted the new civilian governor with a massive boycott which triggered

10. *JPIE*, 13 September 1981.

11. *Haaretz*, 6 and 18 August 1981 (in *Israleft* 191 and 192); *JPIE*, 6 September 1981.

off an unprecedented wave of repression against all urban classes. Demonstrations in the first months of 1982 resulted in more Arab casualties than had fallen in all previous fifteen years of occupation. West Bank newspapers were closed, as was Bir Zeit University. Houses of relatives of convicted rioters were blown up. The National Guidance Committee was outlawed and most city councils dismissed. In what looked like an economic war, many shops, enterprises and farms of Palestinian notables suspected of nationalist sympathies were closed down. The rural classes were not spared, as the Village Leagues afforded their clients no protection against renewed massive land expropriations. Settler vigilantes became more freely involved in quelling demonstrations, and distinguished themselves from the Israeli Defense Forces (IDF) by their greater brutality. Their relationship to the military government or civil administration remained opaque. Israeli settlements in the occupied territories are integrated in a regional defense system, but there appears to be some latitude between their official tasks and their voluntary policing of the area by terrorizing the Arab population.[12] The vigilantes, insulated by a juridical vacuum, are doing the "dirty work" of the occupation, beating the Palestinians into submission or departure.

THE TRANSFORMATION OF GUSH EMUNIM

After Begin's reelection, Matityahu Drobles of the WZO reduced his earlier assessment and calculated that the West Bank's Jewish population would have to rise only from 20,000 to 100,000 in four years to secure the territory for Israel once and forever: this "Program of the 100,000" became Israel's operative guideline for actual settlement policy. Existing urban nuclei, such as Ariel and Elkana, would expand to 50,000 inhabitants; another 36,000 would dwell in satellite towns around Jerusalem and in West Samaria; the rest would go to smaller settlements.[13]

A program of these dimensions, however, could no longer count solely on the Land of Israel idealists. It was doubtful whether Gush Emunim could mobilize volunteers for the "ten last settlements." Over the years, Gush Emunim had exhausted its human reservoir. In addition, growing institu-

---

12. *Jerusalem Post*, 17 May 1981, 22 March and 12 May 1982; *Maariv*, 19 March 1982; *Haaretz*, 27 April I 982; and numerous other reports. See *In Their Own Words: Human Rights Violations in the West Bank*, affidavits collected by Law in the Service of Man (World Council of Churches, 1983). Several Israeli commentators have charged the Begin government with direct responsibility for the settlers' outrages.

13. *JPIE*, 4 October 1981.

tionalization and professionalization substituted for its original messianic impetus: today it employs professional activists, some of whom work for *Amanah,* the Gush settlement movement officially recognized and financed just like the older kibbutz and moshav movements. Many first-line cadres like Hanan Porat, now a Member of Knesset, decided to join Tehiya and left Gush organizationally weakened. Others, like Israel Harel, have devoted their energies to the Council of Settlements in Judea, Samaria, and Gaza. There they cooperate with non-Gush colonists, who are as numerous as the Gush settlers. Some Emunim express worries about the sectarian "in-crowd" ambience reigning in their settlements, which might discourage potential newcomers.

Gush Emunim's reaction to the intensification of West Bank settlement has generally been ambivalent. Increasingly they find themselves in the position of obsolete veterans. One reaction has been emphasis on "quality." Unhappy with private land transfers, they founded their own Land Redemption Fund (*Keren Lageulah Haqarqi*), under whose provisions Arab lands once bought may never be resold to gentiles. Jewish attachment to Eretz Israel is being fostered in Gush Emunim's "university" in Kedumim. While many Emunim wish to continue the colonization task, others want to concentrate on changing Israeli mentality to ignite a broader religious revival. This religious- nationalist vanguard has, in general, not yet succeeded in providing leadership to the recent wave of settlements.[14]

The Hebron Troubles

Though Gush Emunim continued to demand more settlements, the partisan "wild" settlement which had been its hallmark in the 1974-1977 era has largely given way to routinization and coordination with the settlement authorities. It survives only in Hebron with the followers of Rabbi Moshe Levinger, a precursor of Gush Emunim who settled there illegally as early as 1968 and forced Labor to establish, in 1970, the all-Jewish town of Kiryat Arba adjacent to it. Levinger's followers were untiring in their guerrilla campaign to extend Jewish religious rights at the Tomb of the Patriarchs and to reclaim property rights in what used to be the Jewish quarter of Hebron before its elimination in the 1929 troubles. In March 1981, they broke in weekly on Friday prayers in the Makhpelah Cave Mosque, the scene of many earlier religious incidents, demanding and eventually obtaining an extension of Jewish prayer rights.

14. *JPIE,* 1 and 15 February 1981 and 27 March 1983. Regional councils with responsibilities similar to their counterparts in Israel were also established. *Haaretz* (8 March 1981) specifies such councils for Elkana, Etzion, Kiryat Arba, Binyamin, Samaria and Gaza Coast (in *Israleft* 185).

A year later, yeshiva students from Kiryat Arba were involved in a violent pray-in on the Temple Mount in Jerusalem which caused serious rioting. This was one month before the outrage there perpetrated by Allan Goodman, an American immigrant connected with Rabbi Meir Kahane's Kach movement. Yeshiva students from the Jewish quarter of Jerusalem's Old City repeated the attempt in the summer of 1982. Eccentric *hassidim* from Reb Nahman of Bratslav's Yeshivat Birkat Avraham began to encroach on Arab rights in the Muslim quarter of the Old City of Jerusalem in 1983, behaving so unpredictably that inhabitants longed for the days of the Gush Emunim.[15]

Back in 1981, Kiryat Arba colonists began to encroach on Arab dwellings bordering the Hadassah House, a ruined Jewish edifice in downtown Hebron occupied illegally in 1979 by Miriam Levinger with a few score women and inhabited since as a yeshiva in defiance of the government's verbal objections. The continuous intimidation and acts of hooliganism at the hands of Kiryat Arba vigilantes against Hebronites, the connivance of IDF soldiers and the ambivalent reaction of Israeli authorities repeat on a smaller scale the "operations" carried out in Gush Emunim's pioneer days before 1977. Hebron's Arabs are so terrorized by Levinger's groups that they do not believe it worthwhile to lodge complaints at the Israeli military office. The settlers aptly exploit every Palestinian act of reprisal to wrest concessions in favor of "Lower Kiryat Arba."[16] Today, the reconstruction of Hebron's ancient Jewish quarter is underway, involving (as in the Old City of Jerusalem) the forced removal of a number of its Arab inhabitants.

Yamit and Beirut

Gush Emunim's severest setback after Elon Moreh was the final evacuation of the Sinai in the spring of 1982. Resistance to Israeli withdrawal was widespread in 1981, the opponents politically strengthened

15. *JPIE*, 10 April 1983.

16. Thus the murder of the yeshiva student Yehoshua Sloma in January 1980 led to government sanction of the reconstruction around the Avraham Avinu synagogue. Later, the murder of six others "yielded" the renovation of Hadassah House. The murder of a postman, Zvi Segal, resulted in the "Judaization" of 21 dwellings around Avraham Avinu. Zvi Bar'el, (*Haaretz*, 2 November 1982) captured the dynamics of this process: "Every time the answer was wrapped in the justification that '. . . these are the houses of Jews, and we come to take them back.' 'And what about our houses in Jaffa, Haifa and Akka?' the Arabs would ask. Instead of an answer, they got a smile with the expression of 'Now really! . . .' or something like 'Say thank you we didn't revenge ourselves on you for the massacre of 1929.' "

by the assassination of Sadat. The anti-withdrawal opposition enjoyed undercover aid from Jewish Agency sources,[17] while the Alignment's real position was less "dovish" than its official attitude. The government itself tolerated the Sinai activists' demonstrations. The new Egyptian president was able to assuage Israel's official fears, however. Internal disunity among the opponents of withdrawal and their threats of civil unrest gradually eroded support for them.

Some observers remarked that the "national trauma" was all too well orchestrated and staged,[18] but Yamit left an enduring mark on Gush Emunim and its national-religious periphery, which the impact of the Lebanon War would reinforce. Yamit signified, within the right Zionist camp, the defeat of the extremists of the lunatic fringe in favor of the "managers." The completion of the Sinai withdrawal opened the way for the participation of Tehiya in Begin's cabinet. Since Tehiya had no differences of principle with its coalition partners but only differences of degree and emphasis, it tended to become indistinguishable from Herut.

The military neutralization of Egypt, sealed by the return of the Sinai, opened the way for "Sharon's war" to liquidate the PLO's military and political infrastructure in Lebanon. The real target of the war was not Lebanon but the political identity of the West Bank and Gaza Palestinians: to demoralize them so much that they would accept their permanent subjugation and the incorporation of their territories into Israel under the guise of "autonomy," as an alternative to outright annexation and mass deportation to Jordan, the "Palestinian state" of Sharon's vision.[19] As far as the Labor Alignment was not itself drugged by the "collective adrenaline" of war, it remained confused and divided in the first crucial weeks. The invasion subsequently created a deep polarization in Israeli society, but the Begin government has held its own in the first year after Lebanon, and was able to continue its "Judaization" program in the West Bank.

The West Bank Palestinian population has maintained its near-unanimous identification with the PLO, but resistance to land deals reportedly

17. *Davar*, 9 October 1981 (in *Israleft* 194).

18. *Haaretz*, 30 April 1982 (in *Israleft* 205/206).

19. *Maariv and Yediot Ahronot*, 11 June 1982; *Haaretz*, 27 August 1982. See Chief of Staff Rafael Eitan in *Haaretz*, 4 July 1982: "There is a military solution to the terrorist problem in South Lebanon. . . . Only through a military blow shall we stop the situation in which the terrorists continue to play with Israel. *A crushing military blow will allow us afterwards to negotiate on our own conditions*" (emphasis added). Negotiate with whom? The hidden party, according to *Haaretz'* Binyamin Omri, was the moderate element in the West Bank.

weakened somewhat as the balance of power seemed to swing in Israel's favor.[20] While the recent period has witnessed a spectacular growth of West Bank settlement, Israel's occupation policy has been less successful in other aspects: the civil administration came under increasing fire, and Sharon had to appoint a commission to investigate the results of the division of powers. Milson, who had alienated both the mayors and the Village Leagues, resigned. The Village Leagues themselves were not immune to politicization, which affected their usefulness to Israel.

TAKING OVER WEST BANK LANDS

Sharon's transition from agriculture to defense diminished his direct supervision over the colonization process. In his place, the new Deputy Minister of Agriculture, Michael Dekel, assumed a less flamboyant but more efficient style. "How does the Government buy lands in Judea?" a reporter from *Haaretz* asked Dekel in September 1982. "There are various methods," he replied with a smile. "More than this I can't say."[21]

In order to implement the grandiose settlement scheme of which Drobles is the godfather, Dekel and the other settlement authorities needed a lot of land, a commodity which the Elon Moreh verdict of 1979 had threatened to render scarce. An estimated one-third of the surface of the West Bank had already come under *de facto* Israeli control by 1981. Only a small part was actually being settled. Most of this was seized on security grounds rather than purchased. Over the last few years, the Israeli authorities have made good use of a new system of land acquisition, that of declaring certain tracts to be state lands, paralleling a procedure used to "nationalize" lands of Israeli Arabs. According to Ottoman land law, most land belonged in

20. *Haaretz*, 11 June 1982. According to a public opinion poll by the political science department of Najah University (Nablus), 66 percent of the interviewees, who constituted a representative sample of the West Bank population. considered the PLO the only legitimate representative of the Palestinian people, 22 percent considered it a legitimate representative. 76 percent would like a PLO-led Palestinian state to take the place of Israel's occupation; 1 percent agreed with "autonomy." See Amnon Kapeliouk, *al-Hamishmar*, 30 April 1982 (in *Israleft*, 205/206). According to a report in *JPIE*, 16 January 1983, the supply of lands offered on sale by Palestinian landowners either despairing of their future or intent on making a fast *shekel* has since the Lebanese war outdistanced demand.

21. Interview with Michael Dekel in *Haaretz* Weekly Supplement, 7 January 1983.

principle to the sultan.[22] Continuous private cultivation enabled a person with certain restrictions to request registration in the *tabu* (land register): all remaining uncultivated nonprivate land was considered state land (*mawat*). Systematic recording of immobile property began only under the British Mandate, after 1928, and continued under Jordanian rule. One-third of the West Bank – the Jenin, Ramallah, and Jericho regions – had been registered when Israeli occupation interrupted the process in 1967. Of this cadastrated land, around 900 square kilometers is state land. The amount of state lands among the other two-thirds is unclear: depending on the definitions used, the total amount of West Bank state lands could amount to as much as 2700 square kilometers, or 47.5 percent of its total surface. This is still appreciably less than the 75 percent claimed by Sharon as the "indispensable minimum" for Israel's security.

Since the state of Israel considers itself heir to the Jordanian crown, itself successor to the Turks, it is now "reclaiming its properties." Israel's claims are painstakingly researched by Plia Albeck, an expert from the Ministry of Justice: she generally vetoes the seizure of cultivated lands, which in the past had caused much bad publicity. Enough remains, as about 55 percent of the West Bank is barren.[23] This circumstance limits the option to establish agricultural settlements, but agriculture had anyhow become a problematic sector of Israel's economy because of its small internal market. In Dekel's words:

> Zionism is a political movement, no boy scouts' movement for good citizenship. For some reason, we are still captive to old theories that settlement means agriculture. In Judea and Samaria, state lands are rocky lands. Every attempt to confiscate agricultural lands used to stamp us with the label of "expulsive Zionism." We don't do this any more, and the fact is there have been no Supreme Court cases in the last period. As far as agricultural lands in Judea and Samaria are in Jewish hands, they have been bought in cash by private entrepreneurs. In Gaza and in the Jordan rift, however, the state does possess agricultural lands, so settlements with an agricultural character are established there.[24]

By "reclaiming state lands," Israel has vastly extended its possibilities for settlement. Between 200,000 and 300,000 dunums (200-300 square kilometers) have been "recovered" in this way – about 10 percent of the

22. The description of land procedures is based on the interview with Plia Albeck in *Haaretz* Weekly Supplement, 11 February 1983.

23. Benvenisti, "West Bank and Gaza Data Base," p. 12.

24. Interview with Michael Dekel in *Haaretz* Weekly Supplement, 24 September 1982.

estimated maximum. Dekel imputes the slow pace to a lack of Israeli experts, and expects another five years to complete the process.[25] Palestinian owners informed of the impending loss of their land have three weeks to gather whatever documents they possess proving their claim and to prepare their case before a military court of appeal. This procedure was approved by the Supreme Court in a February 1982 verdict. Israeli settlements do not become owners of the soil, but obtain long-term tenancy rights (49 years renewable) as in Israel proper.

Other methods of land acquisition are quantitatively less significant. In Gush Etzion, property belonging to Jews before 1948 is being reclaimed. Private sales from Palestinians amounted to no more than 7,500 dunums by 1983: 1,500 were brought by Himnuta Company, the subsidiary of the Jewish National Fund across the "green line," and 4,000 by Gush Emunim and other private buyers. Of late there has been talk of more substantial transactions, but Israelis as well as Palestinians are inhibited in this activity, since registration in the *tabu* is impossible as long as Israel does not officially annex the West Bank. Property rights arising from such deals are afforded a measure of official protection by means of certificates of ownership under Jordanian law (*maliyah*), letters from neighboring property owners stating that the surveyor's data were correct, notarized affidavits from the *mukhtar* and from the seller stating that the latter was the legal owner of the land, as well as an official transaction approval form from the Israeli authorities in the West Bank (*heter isqah*).[26] According to official Israeli declarations, confiscation of private cultivated land occurs only when the construction of public utilities (such as roads to Jewish settlements) demands it. The owners have a formal right to indemnification. Land seizures for security purposes have been carried out by the Likud government only in the cases of Elon Moreh and Bracha, near Nablus.

The settlement authorities felt threatened by the Reagan Plan of September 1982 and began to work hard to foreclose this updated but more radical version of Labor's "Jordanian option." Immediately after the publication of the Reagan Plan, Israel announced the establishment of seven new settlements in the West Bank. Both Dekel and Deputy Prime Minister Ehrlich denied a direct link: the seven formed part of a group of eighteen whose planning antedated the Reagan Plan by two months. In 1982, Dekel boasted of a total of eighty-six existing settlements in the West Bank and Gaza Strip, of which the Likud had built fifty: twenty-three in the Jordan

25. *Ibid.*

26. *JPIE,* 24 April 1983, *Kol Hair,* 14 January 1983. See also Uri Davis and Walter Lehn, "And the Fund Still Lives: the Role of the Jewish National Fund in the Determination of Israel's Land Policies," *Journal of Palestine Studies* (1978), 7 (4): 3-33.

valley, thirty-six in Samaria, seventeen in Judea, and ten in the Gaza Strip. In addition, there are about thirty *nahals* (military agricultural settlements), some of which were founded as a means to circumvent the Supreme Court's 1979 Elon Moreh verdict. The West Bank's Jewish population had risen to 30,000,[27] living in 5,800 dwellings. Together with another 70,000 to be settled by 1986, these would form an irresistible pressure group of 100,000 – strong enough to block any significant territorial concession. Not even a dovish Labor cabinet would be able to overlook such a lobby. "Conquest through settlement" then would perpetuate, justify, and eventually supersede Israel's military reign over the West Bank. The 100,000 threshold would make evacuation unthinkable: such a mass uprooting would provoke a "non-ideological civil war," in the words of Gush Emunim's Benny Katzover.[28]

Nonideological Settlements

Expanding the West Bank's Jewish population by 70,000 to 80,000 people implies building an extra 20,500 dwellings at a rate of around 5,000 a year. Settling one family in the West Bank averages 3.5 million Israeli *shqalim* (IS) (around $100,000), 2.1 million of which comes from the government budget and 1.4 million to be paid by the families.[29] To combat the stunning

27. Interview with Michael Dekel in *Maariv*, 8 October 1982; 22,000 West Bank settlers according to Benvenisti's estimate, in "West Bank and Gaza Data Base," p. 65.

28. *Ibid.*

29. On paper, only the World Zionist Organization is responsible for financing the colonization across the "green line." A purely formal division exists between the Jewish Agency's Settlement Department (*Mahlaqah le-Hityashvut*), which retains responsibility for settlement within the "green line," and the WZO's Settlement Division (*Hativah le-Hityashvut*), which directs the settlements in the occupied territories. The Jewish Agency is largely financed by (tax-deductible) gifts from American Jewry; the *Hativah* is funded by the Israeli government and by Jewish contributions from countries which do not interfere with the use made of their monies, such as South Africa. Channeling settlement monies of the ministry of agriculture through the *Hativah* to its field workers in the occupied territories formally implies no direct Israeli government involvement in colonization across the "green line": legally the settlements are a venture of the WZO (Interview with Michael Dekel, *Haaretz* Weekly Supplement, 7 January 1983). WZO expenditure in the occupied territories' settlements amounted to IS 2 billion in 1982. The government is investing considerably higher sums in more devious ways, but this remains shrouded in secrecy (see Zvi Shuldiner in *Haaretz*, 25 July 1980). Benvenisti estimates total expenditure for the Jewish population of the West Bank at IS 5 billion in 1982 as against IS 650 million for the Arab population ("West Bank and Gaza Data Base," p. 18). A Peace Now pamphlet of January 1983 speaks of IS 6 billion ($200 million) in 1982 and a total Israeli investment in the West Bank settlements to date of IS 20 billion.

costs of this program, Dekel saw it as his task to slim down government financial participation from a current 60-68 percent to 45-50 percent. One of the considerations behind the new emphasis on building cities instead of the small, close-knit and perhaps more stable Gush Emunim-type villages is financial: settling one family in a rural settlement costs approximately IS 4.1 million, whereas providing them an apartment of 94 square meters in town, including infrastructure and basic amenities, comes to around IS 3 million.[30]

The government, in order to reduce its costs, offered private contractors profitable "development schemes." West Bank lands were being allocated to projected settlements through the Israeli Lands Authority (*Minhal Meqarqei Yisrael*), which had distributed an estimated 200,000 dunums (200 square kilometers) by the end of 1982. The new "cheapness" of West Bank land facilitated its transfer to contractors, bypassing the traditional system in which first the WZO Settlement Division (for temporary structures) and afterwards the housing ministry would lease the services of contractors. Herut's Housing Minister David Levy introduced the sale of lands to contractor consortiums who committed themselves to build, advertise, and sell the units to private citizens. Levy and Dekel pointed out that their respective ministries remained in effective control of the total colonization process. Subsidies to buyers are graded in function of a plot's distance from the densely populated coast. The most "popular" zones around Jerusalem and immediately to the east of Kfar Saba and Petah Tikvah enjoy least governmental aid; the barren region to the east of the Ramallah-Nablus divide and to the north of Jenin and south of Hebron receive the maximum. Contractors are reportedly building around 35 percent of the settlements now. In some cases they even took the initiative and began building villa projects that were approved after the fact.[31] In the Kafr Qasim-Qalqilya region in West Samaria, Jews already outnumber Arabs.[32]

30. *Maariv*, 8 October 1982; *Jerusalem Post*, 7 January 1983. IS 4.5 million per family according to Dekel in *JPIE*, 2 January 1983.

31. In late May, there were reports that some Knesset members had been involved in West Bank land transactions that represented conflicts of interest. According to a Jewish Telegraphic Agency account (31 May 1983): "The issue arose in the Cabinet after media reports that MKs of both Likud and the labor Alignment who happened to be lawyers were providing their firms' legal services to land entrepreneurs on the West Bank. The media questioned the validity of some of these sales after it was discovered that only a few entrepreneurs carefully verified the ownership of private land bought from local Arabs before they put it on the market for Israeli buyers."

32. *JPIE*. 16 January 1983; *Yediot Ahronot*, 14 January 1983.

The success of the new settlement drive can be simply explained. It enables Israelis who would otherwise never have the chance to exchange their cramped three-room apartment in Tel Aviv for a cottage in the West Bank. Unlike their predecessors, the Israeli families moving in today typically are not strong on Zionist convictions. Most are young urban dwellers attracted by a combination of "greed and need": relatively cheap housing and economic incentives such as tax deductions, combined with the crowded conditions, noise, and pollution of greater Tel Aviv. A home in the West Bank is, on average, two to three times cheaper than a comparable one inside Israel. Demand for Maale Adumim lots was so great that a distribution lottery had to be organized. Private enterprises like the one building beautifully situated Nofim in West Samaria – and incidentally spoiling a unique nature reserve – offered $100,000 villas for a down payment of $15,000, the remainder obtainable at easy loans which become permanent after five years of habitation: the success was so great that a second, similar project was immediately floated.

By the beginning of 1983, 1,300 temporary and 2,150 permanent dwelling units and 500 villas had been built in West Samaria, all due to receive their inhabitants by summer. The "100,000" are only a beginning: Herut settlement planners promise to increase the West Bank's Jewish population to 1.4 million within 30 years. Though Israeli buyers in the West Bank are warned that they will have no claim on compensation in case of Israeli withdrawal, thus being forced to shoulder the political risk together with the government, speculation is rife.

The architects of the new settlement drive emphasize suburblike "dormitory" settlements lacking a local economic base which would require higher expenditure and a slower tempo of "Judaization." A majority of "colonists" commute daily to their jobs in Jerusalem or the Tel Aviv metropolitan area and come home to spend their leisure time in the West Bank's Jewish enclaves. Small-scale high technology plants or artisan workshops have been opened in some places.

Often the new settlements cater to specific groups. Ariel, with its 200 families, is the "capital of Samaria"; most of its inhabitants are employed in the Israel Aircraft Industries and in other defense-related industries. They are veteran Israelis, including many ex-kibbutzniks. This town, which had been projected by Dayan in the early 1970s, is a stronghold of Labor hawks. Maale Adumim, originally a Gush Emunim site, is now inhabited by 650 mainly young families from Jerusalem. It is scheduled to become a spacious town of 50,000 by 1990. Planning of this settlement on the Jerusalem-Jericho road likewise goes back to the days of Labor hegemony. Alon Shevut, in the Etzion bloc, has a population of 800, all commuters. Kiryat Arba, with 600 families in 1981 the largest Jewish concentration in the West

Bank, is a special case because of its mixed make-up: 60 percent is religious, and the yeshiva element remains dominant; 55 percent is Oriental Jewish, but there are also many immigrants from the United States and the Soviet Union. Kedumim and Ofra remain typical industrial Gush Emunim settlements, whereas Emmanuel will be populated by *Agudat Yisrael* Orthodox from Bnei Braq, an overcrowded religious quarter of Tel Aviv: the originally anti-Zionist *Agudat Yisrael* has made a *volte-face*. Beit Aryeh is attracting Herut youth working in the aircraft industries. Other settlements will serve Liberal party families, Bank Leumi employees, or other identifiable groups. Elkana is a prosperous villa town, as will be Karnei Shomron and Alfei Menashe.[33] By offering them alternative housing, the Likud evidently hopes to bind part of the mainly Ashkenazi "middle classes" to its annexationist program.[34]

THE OPPOSITION

Opposition to the new settlement drive has not been very effective to date. The peace movement mobilizes only the left wing of the Alignment, while its right wing stands even to the right of Herut. Labor's ill-defined center criticizes the central West Bank colonization mainly on pragmatic grounds or in the light of electoral considerations: they must spare the sensitivities of the Jordan Valley colonists. In contrast to the current building boom in "Judea and Samaria," the older, Labor-affiliated Jordan Rift outposts are in trouble as a result of bad harvests and financial difficulties. Debts are high, morale is low because of internal problems and doubts about the future of Israel's presence. The colonists fear a "second Yamit." Gad Yaacobi opposes excessive West Bank colonization because it detracts from moving against "re-Arabization" of the Galilee.[35] The ambiguity of Labor's position is apparent in the approval of its political bureau to Histadrut participation in building the West Bank settlement infrastructure – something which, in any case, has been going on for some time.[36]

33. *JPIE*, 1 and 15 February, 1 March, and 3 May 1981; *Maariv*, 8 October 1982, *Yediot Ahronot*, 14 January 1983; and *JPIE*, 16 January 1983.

34. Another ingredient in the government's efforts to populate the settlement towns is the shift of ministries and other government offices from Tel Aviv to Jerusalem. The scarcity of affordable housing in Jerusalem or its Israeli suburbs leaves subsidized settlement housing as practically the only option for these thousands of employees and their families.

35. *Yediot Ahronot*, 18 December 1981 (in *Israleft* 198); *Haaretz*, 2 November 1982.

36. *JPIE*, 9 and 16 January, 1983.

More serious are the cracks within the religious front. Religious-secular cooperation and convergence have not materialized as Gush Emunim had hoped. "Mixed" settlements, like Maale Shomron, are running into difficulties. Participation in the Begin cabinet has blurred the identity of Tehiya, whose popularity has dropped. Like other ideological parties, it cannot escape the conflicts between purists and pragmatists.[37]

Under the impact of the Lebanon War, a dovish wing has crystallized within the National Religious Party. Heavy casualties among soldiers from military *yeshivot* have reportedly induced this soul searching. Rabbis from Mount Etzion in the West Bank have voiced veiled criticism of the government. Together with a number of disillusioned Emunim, they founded the religious pacifist group, *Netivot Shalom*. Even a former Gush Emunim stalwart such as Education Minister Zevulun Hammer has taken his distance from Israel's current occupation policy by intimating that the cause of "the unity of the Land" has been paid for by growing disunity of the Jewish people. The Gush Emunim group around Rabbi Haim Druckman, which remained part of the National Religious Party at the time when others opted for the religious-secular Tehiya, has broken away to form the separate party, *Matzad* (Rally for Religious Zionism).[38] The net result of all these shifts may yet be a reversion of the National Religious Party to its traditional centrism.

HERUT INTRANSIGENCE

With the Alignment in halfhearted opposition, the National Religious Party increasingly hesitant and Gush Emunim in crisis, the political burden of the new settlement drive devolves on Herut, whose apparatchiks also form its organizational backbone. Eschewing both the model of Jewish separatism and "Hebrew labor" underlying the classic left Zionist conception, and a future based on any minimally tolerable Jewish-Arab *modus vivendi,* they favor the Jabotinskian vision of an "iron wall" of Jewish military might to crush any gentile-Arab resistance to Jewish-Arab "coexistence" on their terms.

Certain provisions are taken to avoid direct Jewish-Arab contact in the field: thus, new roads to the settlements circumvent Arab villages so as not to deter prospective buyers. Politicians and functionaries such as Sharon,

37. *Kol Hair,* 5 November 1982; *Haaretz* Weekly Supplement, 28 January 1983.

38. *Jerusalem Post,* 1 October 1982 (in *Israleft* 212/213); *Haaretz,* 4 November 1982; *JPIE,* 2 and 30 January 1983.

Dekel, and Drobles are driving Israel inexorably to a major explosion which may very well involve the expulsion of all Palestinians living in "western Eretz Israel." Dekel has openly deplored their presence in the territories: he would gladly "exchange" them, if it were possible, since he is persuaded that "the aspiration to liquidate the people of Israel is part of the existential program of the Arab people."[39]

Dekel has also declared himself in favor of stimulating Palestinian education: the higher their schooling, the less chance they have to find employment. Upon realizing they have no future in Eretz Israel, they emigrate. In a renewed "demographic debate," directed primarily against Labor ideologues who warn of the "danger" of the higher Palestinian Arab birth rate, Dekel points out that Arab emigration from the West Bank has left their number stagnating since 1967. This makes "Judaization of Judea and Samaria" a sound proposition.[40] For Drobles, "the plan is a plan for Jews. I don't care if the Arabs accept it or not." For Dekel, the "Judaization" of the West Bank realizes an old dream of Ben-Gurion, the "population dispersal" of Jews all over their country. A more populist, "social-imperialist" note is struck by David Levy, who justifies West Bank settlement as a solution for Israel's housing problems.

POINT OF NO RETURN

Although the present massive settlement drive is running full steam, the champions of the "100,000 scheme" still have to surmount some obstacles before they reach the point where "nothing will be left to negotiate."[41] Until now, most colonists have clung to regions adjacent to the "green line." The dense urban clusters may bring in more Jews than do agricultural

39. Interview with Michael Dekel in *Haaretz* Weekly Supplement, 24 September 1982.

40. Interviews with Michael Dekel in *ibid.*, and *Maariv,* 8 October 1982. According to Dekel, the Arab population of the West Bank rose from 595,000 in 1967 to 699,000 in 1980, and is growing at the feeble rate of 0.6 percent yearly. According to another report, about 128,500 Palestinian Arabs emigrated from the West Bank in the same period (not counting refugees from the 1967 war), at an annual rate variously estimated at from 3,000 to 10,000 a year (*JPIE*, 4 October 1981). The natural growth rate of the Gaza Palestinians is 2.4 percent, that of Israeli Arabs 3.2 percent, that of Israeli Jews 2 percent. The WZO estimates a West Bank Arab population of 1.2 million within 30 years, to be counterbalanced by 1 million Jews. See also chapter 13.

41. Interview with Meron Benvenisti in *Jerusalem Post,* 10 September 1982 (in *Israleft* 211).

settlements, but in view of their greater mobility, it is doubtful whether this will produce an irreversible "Judaization" of the land. It is true, however, that each new settlement makes more hypothetical any political solution based on two states.

Is an enormous project such as the Drobles Plan at all realistic? In view of lagging immigration to Israel, and of the low Israeli Jewish birthrate, colonization will not increase but redistribute the Jewish population. Even at the present cut-rate prices, West Bank housing will remain too expensive for a broad stratum of the population. Disappointments may dampen the initial enthusiasm: basic amenities like telephones, post offices, and kindergartens often arrive long after the housing has been finished. Nor are the social conflicts characteristic of Israeli society at large absent from these new communities. Deficient coordination, red tape, and bureaucratic struggles are another problem, no less acute now than they were under Labor. Decentralized, often haphazard planning is fostered by the large number of committees and semi-official bodies whose interrelationships are much less harmonious than the hierarchies on paper suggest.

The main executive arm for settlement policy, the Jewish Agency/WZO, was internally divided, though Drobles and Weitz were theoretically held in check by a common director. Drobles' position was further weakened by competency fights with Agriculture's Michael Dekel: though Drobles was the author of the blueprint used as a guideline for the various government ministries, Dekel considered the Jewish Agency/WZO as an executive organ for the government's decisions. Drobles, on the contrary, stressed the autonomy of the Jewish Agency/WZO in settlement matters.[42] Dekel had enemies who resented his attempts to dominate the colonization apparatus. Housing Minister David Levy attacked him over the distribution of state lands to private entrepreneurs by the Israel Lands Administration, an organization subordinate to the agriculture ministry. Levy has also found fault with the concentration of Jewish settlements near the "green line" which enables easy commuting to the metropolitan area but leaves the "wilder" eastern West Bank relatively unaffected.[43]

Dekel has also been criticized for allowing contractors to misuse his words in advertisements. Cases of land fraud and cheated buyers have already led to pressure for stricter control over the private sector, which Dekel opposes. He had lukewarm support at best from his superior, Agriculture Minister and Deputy Prime Minister Simcha Ehrlich, who was,

42. Interview with Michael Dekel in *Haaretz* Weekly Supplement, 24 September 1982.

43. *Yediot Ahronot* and *Kol Hair,* 14 January 1983.

before his death in June 1983, *ex-officio* head of the Interministerial Committee on Settlements, formally the supreme body on colonization policy questions. Dekel has, however, been "covered" by Begin. Science and Technology Minister Yuval Neeman negotiated a separate budget for additional settlements as *quid pro quo* for Tehiya's participation in Begin's cabinet. This has not pleased Treasury Minister Yoram Aridor, who charged Neeman with planning settlements in a way inconsistent with that of other departments.[44] Other influences on settlement policy include the ministry of the interior, which finances the regional councils; Trade and Industry Minister Gidon Patt, who opposes industrially inefficient small-scale settlements; and Ariel Sharon, who has kept in touch with colonization through General Uri Bar-On. Even if these various counteracting forces could ever be brought together in one superministry of settlement, Israeli colonization would still be obstructed by its professional but inflexible and paternalistic planning tradition.

Such bureaucratic and political conflicts sometimes reproduce themselves on the microlevel of individual settlements: as in Israel proper, each settlement has to belong to one of several settlement federations affiliated to the political parties, thus sustaining divisive arrangements which pervade Israeli politics. An extreme example is the tug-of-war between the adherents of Rabbi Levinger and the Kach movement of Rabbi Kahane, which erected a "wild" settlement near Hebron called *El Naqam* (God Revenges), over monies from Kiryat Arba's council.[45]

Another factor that makes implementation of the Drobles Plan questionable is its financial dimension. At an estimated $100,000 per family dwelling, the 20,000 units needed to lodge 100,000 Jews in the West Bank require an outlay of US $2 billion. The World Zionist Organization will be hard put to muster this astronomical sum within three years.[46]

Lastly, current Palestinian "accommodation" to the metamorphosis of the West Bank is a product of coercion and intimidation rather than persuasion, and may be no more than a transient phenomenon. Even in the present adverse conjuncture, the Palestinians under Israeli occupation are displaying great resilience. Appeals of dispossessed land owners to the Supreme Court are frequent. Civil disobedience is raging on a wide scale during the past two years. Colonists and colonized are waging a relentless struggle over control over the land, in which not every weapon rests in the hands of the

44. *Jerusalem Post*, 1 September 1982 (in Israleft 211); *Haaretz*, 4 November 1982.

45. *JPIE*, 16 January 1983.

46. *JPIE*, 30 January 1983.

colonists. The permanent insecurity which Arab stones and grenades cause to the Israeli settlers induce psychological pressures. Already a number of settlers in Kiryat Arba talk of leaving.

In general, the immediate colonial relation between Israeli Jews and Palestinian Arabs which West Bank "Judaization" produces is likely to be a graver consequence than its being, in diplomatic parlance, an "obstacle to peace." The eventual willingness of Israeli society to forego the Sinai for what they assumed would be a real peace is a hopeful sign, but the problems with regard to the West Bank are much more complex. Future development will depend on the interaction of the Palestinians' steadfastness with the evolution of the opposition within the Israeli Jewish society. Of particular significance will be whether the peace movement will break through the ranks of Oriental Jewry, Israel's conservative "poor whites," and the mainstay of Herut ascendancy. Tehiya's Yuval Neeman may not be far off the mark when he sees the real cleavage in Israel not as one between religious and secular Jews, but as one between those who legitimize the Zionist presence in Palestine on the basis of historical continuity with the land, and the others who consider the existence of Jewish Israelis as sufficient legitimation in itself, for which exclusive claims on the land are immaterial.[47]

47. Interview with Yuval Neeman in *JPIE,* 7 June 1981.

PART III

CONSEQUENCES

OF THE

1967 OCCUPATION

CHAPTER 10

THE GAZA STRIP: CRITICAL EFFECTS OF THE OCCUPATION

Sara Roy

INTRODUCTION

In June of 1967, the Gaza Strip together with the Sinai, the Golan Heights and the West Bank fell under Israeli military occupation. Since then, a significant amount of attention has focused on the latter three territories to the virtual exclusion of Gaza. Sinai gained prominence as a result of the Egyptian-Israeli peace treaty of 1979. The Golan Heights has assumed strategic priority for Israeli security along the border with Syria. And the West Bank, given its geographic location with respect to Jerusalem and Amman, cannot be ignored or hidden. The Gaza Strip, however, has little geographical "clout." Often referred to as "the forgotten man of the Middle East," Gaza has no historical identity, and despite nearly two decades of Egyptian administration (1948-1967), Gaza has never been claimed by any Arab state.

The Gaza Strip is an artificial entity about forty-five kilometers (twenty-eight miles) long and eight kilometers (five miles) wide, encompassing an area that is 140 square miles or one-fifteenth the size of the West Bank (2,126 square miles). Close to 525,000 people inhabit the region, giving it a population density of 3,754 people per square mile, a density level equivalent to Hong Kong's and among the highest in the world. Nearly 50 per cent of the population are under fourteen years of age and approximately 386,964 are refugees, the majority of whom live in one of the eight refugee camps located inside the territory. At present rates of natural increase, Gazans will number close to one million people by the year 2000. The density of the area, furthermore, precludes expansion, particularly since the Gaza Strip is contained by the Mediterranean Sea on the west, the Sinai peninsula and Egyptian border on the south and Israel on the east and north.

Since its occupation of the territory, Israel has taken over one-third of the land (approximately 28,750 acres) through various methods ranging from declarations of state land to direct confiscation. Portions of this land have been used for the construction of eighteen Jewish settlements, inhabited by over two thousand settlers, whose presence inside Gaza creates and sustains the dualistic society which characterizes life there.

Officially, the Gaza Strip, like the West Bank, is considered an economically independent unit. However, the twenty-year occupation of the territory has created the basis for increased dependence on the Israeli economy. Israeli policies have introduced in the agricultural and industrial sectors of Gaza changes which are structural in character, thereby encouraging a process of integration within the dominant economic system. For example, measures imposed by the occupying authorities have continually threatened the traditional agricultural basis of Gaza's economy. Severe export restrictions on Gazan citrus production have transformed this once thriving business into a less than profitable activity. Vegetable production is largely limited to local markets, where it has difficulty competing with Israel's highly subsidized vegetables which daily flood Gaza's marketplaces.

Another traditional activity, fishing, has declined in recent years because of military restrictions on specific fishing areas. Fishermen must observe a dawn to dusk curfew and are limited to within twelve miles of the shoreline, an area that is one-quarter of its pre-1967 size. Between 1968 and 1984, the annual tonnage of fish hauled by Gazans dropped by 59 percent. In 1985, it was estimated that 3,900 fishermen were working legally and illegally to support 35,000 people.

The industrial sector, similarly, is in great measure restricted to small cottage industries which provide limited employment opportunities. The majority of firms (92 percent) employ ten persons or less. Gazan industries often rely on Israel for subcontracting work, which constitutes the main form of Israeli investment in Gaza's industrial sector. The development of new firms and factories is difficult due to various military restrictions on such activity. Trade union activity, furthermore, is restricted to six unions composed of seamstresses, weavers, carpenters, construction workers, agricultural workers, drivers, metalsmiths and mechanics. Founded in 1964 under Egyptian rule and banned by the Israeli government from 1967 to 1980, these unions have a total membership of about three hundred and are not allowed to recruit individuals who were not members before 1967. Furthermore, unions cannot hold elections, accept funds from abroad, register any workers without prior permission, hold educational and cultural lectures or hold any meeting without an Israeli officer in attendance.

Israeli policies encouraging Palestinians to work inside Israel have created significant changes in the composition and distribution of Gaza's labor force as well. Given the limited employment opportunities available inside the Strip and the higher wages offered inside Israel, large numbers of Gaza residents are employed in Israel as unskilled and semi-skilled labor. A certain percentage of this labor pool is comprised of the highly educated (doctors, engineers, and teachers) who are unable to find employment inside the Strip either in their chosen profession or elsewhere. As laborers working in Israel proper, Gazans receive comparatively low wages, (approximately 40 percent of the average Israeli wage) and enjoy few of the economic or political benefits given to Israeli workers. Furthermore, Palestinians who work inside Israel are excluded from membership in the Histadrut, Israel's General Federation of Labor. For 1985, it was estimated that 45 percent of Gaza's labor force were officially employed in Israel as compared with 10 percent in 1970.

The weakening of Gaza's economy is also reflected in the quality of health care and education inside the territory. Both sectors are, at present, unable to effectively meet the demands placed upon them by Gaza's rapidly growing population. Low levels of government expenditure (when compared with expenditure levels inside Israel) in both health and education have created clear constraints on the ability of either sector to expand beyond present levels. When viewed against the specter of Gaza's demography, continued restrictions on economic and social development inside the territory portend disaster.

Against this background of structural disequilibrium, the Gaza Strip is quickly becoming the Soweto of the state of Israel. Many transformations have taken place in Gaza's political, economic and social realities since the beginning of Israeli rule. These transformations not only reflect the impact of twenty years of occupation on Gaza's socioeconomic structure, but raise questions about the capacity of that structure to respond to future political realities.

Conducting Research on and in the Gaza Strip

There are many methodological difficulties in conducting research on the Gaza Strip, difficulties which are consistently encountered and which often interfere with effective and accurate data collection and analysis. Any study on Gaza should therefore acknowledge and, if possible, describe some of these problems in order to provide clearer insights into the strengths and weaknesses of the data being presented.

The first problem confronting the researcher is the existence of official government prohibitions on the disclosure of information that deals with the

Gaza Strip. Simply put, employees of Israeli administered offices, both governmental and nongovernmental, are unable to release information on the territory and numerous requests by the author to obtain such information were denied. Official procedures do exist for securing the release of information by obtaining permission from the appropriate government officials. But this permission can take months or years to acquire, with absolutely no guarantee of approval.

The problems created by the inability to access data from Israeli sources are exacerbated by the unreliability of much of the data that is available. The Central Bureau of Statistics in Jerusalem publishes what is probably the most comprehensive compendium of statistics on the West Bank and Gaza Strip. Most of the data is economic in nature, although information exists for other sectors as well. In his 1986 Report on the West Bank, Meron Benvenisti comments on some of the problems affecting the reliability of economic data published on the occupied territories:

> For statistical purposes the West Bank and Gaza Strip are considered by Israel's Central Bureau of Statistics, to be units independent of Israel. Economic activity there is investigated and reported as though they constitute a "national economy" united with Israel in a "common market." The official reporting of GDP, GNP, exports and imports and balance of payments of the territories is, however, inaccurate at best and misleading at worst. The daily, complex, economic interaction over the nonexistent "green line," lacking any effective monitoring and control, calls the reliability of the statistics into question. Moreover, the "national accounts" of the territories have no territorial basis. The economic activity of the Jewish settlers . . . as well as general government expenditure on Jewish residents [in the occupied territories] are all included in Israel's accounts, not the West Bank's [or Gaza's]. The accounting system borders on the absurd when economic interaction between two adjacent localities, such as Kiryat Arba and Hebron, is regarded as "international trade."[1]

Similarly, the reliability of official population statistics and demographic predictions is qualified by the fact that the last official census of the West Bank and Gaza Strip was conducted in 1967.[2]

1. Meron Benvenisti, *1986 Report: Demographic, Economic, Legal Social and Political Development in the West Bank* (Jerusalem: West Bank Data Base Project, 1986), p. 5. Sarah Graham-Brown also discusses the problems of conducting research in the occupied territories: see "The Economic Consequences of the Occupation," ch. 11 in this volume. Brian Van Arkadie similarly describes some of the difficulties confronting economic research on the West Bank and Gaza Strip in his preface to *Benefits and Burdens: A Report on the West Bank and Gaza Strip Economies since 1967* (New York/Washington: Carnegie Endowment for International Peace, 1977).

2. The last official census of the West Bank and Gaza Strip was conducted in 1967 by the Israeli military. See *Census of the Population 1967, 1,* State of Israel (Jerusalem:

A third problem encountered by the researcher is the dearth of information from Palestinian sources. Accurate and systematic Palestinian statistics are difficult and oftentimes impossible to acquire. Indeed, some official Arab government publications rely partially on Israeli statistics as the basis for their studies on the Gaza Strip. Many individuals interviewed described two reasons for the lack of an effective data base in Gaza. The first reason, endemic to the occupation, is a result of specific military restrictions placed on any form of research, survey, study or plan to be conducted by Palestinians in the Gaza Strip. Indigenous research is further constrained by a severe lack of academic facilities and financially supportive institutions inside the territory and elsewhere in the country. Moreover, given the constraints of the political environment on the exchange of information, those Palestinian statistics or studies that do exist on Gaza are often difficult to acquire. Individual interviews conducted inside the Strip provided an important source of data but again, a source which must be reviewed cautiously since information often varied from one person to another.

In conclusion, there appears to be no absolutely reliable set of statistics on the Gaza Strip. How does this affect any attempt, including the present one, to write about Gaza? It demands that, methodologically, the author seek information from as many different sources as possible, seek disconfirming information as a means of testing the validity of facts and assumptions, and triangulate as much data as possible. Data contained in this chapter was derived from a broad range of written and oral sources.

HISTORICAL AND POLITICAL TRENDS[3]

Gaza before 1948

In ancient times, Gaza occupied a strategic position on the important trade route between Egypt and Syria. In 1799, Napoleon Bonaparte occupied

---

Central Bureau of Statistics, 1968). In 1985, the CBS published a study entitled *Demographic Characteristics of the Population: National Data from the Complete Enumeration,* Special Series 7, 1983 in which all persons were accounted for except the Arab population in the occupied territories. Jewish localities in the West Bank and Gaza Strip were included.

3. (Historical and political trends). Several sources were consulted in preparing this section. Rather than annotate individual points, of which there are many, I list below the various studies used. Some notes have been used to highlight special points of interest or of extreme significance. In addition to interviews with individuals from a wide range of social, political and economic backgrounds inside the Gaza Strip, the sources used include:

Gaza on his way to Acre. A century later, Gaza fell under the successive occupations of the Ottoman and British armies.

When the British gained control over Palestine in 1923, Gaza was a small district of the entire territory. Located strategically between the Mediterranean Sea and the Negev Desert, the town of Gaza became the third largest port in Palestine after those of Jaffa and Haifa, serving the southern part of the country, which was the poorest in Palestine. Largely rural with no industrial activity, the Gaza district, together with the Beersheva district, produced various commodities including citrus, grapes, grain, livestock and poultry.

During the two decades of British control the Jewish population of Palestine nearly tripled; and by 1947 it comprised one-third of the population, in possession of 7 percent of the land. On November 22, 1947, the United Nations proposed a partition of Palestine into two states, one Jewish and one Arab. According to this plan, Gaza Province was to provide a central part of the Arab state in the Mandate Territory of Palestine and was to be comprised of the Gaza and Beersheva districts. As a result of the 1948 Arab-Israeli war, however, control over two-thirds of this province was lost (all of Beersheva district and most of Gaza district). Gaza City, together with one other town, eight farming villages and a few Bedouin encampments, was incorporated into an entity known as the Gaza Strip, which was less than one-third of the area intended under the Partition Plan.[4]

Graham-Brown, Sarah. "Impact on the Social Structure of Palestinian Society." In *Occupation: Israel over Palestine*, Naseer H. Aruri, ed., Belmont, Mass.: Association of Arab-American University Graduates, 1983, pp. 223-54.

Institute for Palestine Studies. *The Arabs under Israeli Occupation, 1979*. Beirut: IPS, 1980. (A chronology of events in the West Bank and Gaza Strip compiled from various domestic and foreign newspapers.)

Ann Lesch. "Gaza: Forgotten Corner of Palestine." *Journal of Palestine Studies,* (Autumn 1985) 15(1): 43-59.

________.*The Gaza Strip: Heading towards a Dead End.* Parts I and 2, nos. 10 and 11, Universities Field Staff International (UFSI) Reports, 1984.

________.*Perceptions of the Palestinians on the West Bank and Gaza Strip.* Special Study no. 3. Washington, D.C.: Middle East Institute, 1983.

Mandell, Joan. "Gaza: Israel's Soweto." *MERIP Reports* (October-December 1985), pp. 7-19.

Metzger, Jan, Martin Orth, and Christian Sterzling. *This Land Is Our Land: The West Bank under Israeli Occupation.* London: Zed Press, 1980.

Rubenberg, Cheryl. *The Palestine Liberation Organization: Its Institutional Infrastructure.* Belmont, Mass.: Institute of Arab Studies, 1983.

UNRWA for Palestine Refugees in the Near East. *UNRWA: A Brief History 1950-1982*. Vienna: Vienna International Center, 1983.

4. Van Arkadie, *Benefits and Burdens*, p. 29.

Separated from the agricultural area it once served as well as from the rest of Palestine, the Gaza Strip by 1948 found itself under Egyptian administration, with a population swelled by 160,000-180,000 refugees. Indeed, by the end of the war, the Gaza Strip and the remaining portion of Palestine, which had been annexed by Jordan and renamed the West Bank, were the only two areas of Mandatory Palestine (approximately 23 percent) that remained under Arab control. The Gaza Strip alone contained 26 percent of the total postwar Palestinian population who had remained within the borders of Mandatory Palestine.[5]

Egyptian Administration (1948-1967)

The immediate postwar situation in the Gaza Strip was extremely difficult. Due to the loss of much of its agriculture and grazing land and the closure of its port, Gaza's indigenous economy had all but collapsed. Furthermore, by 1949, Gaza's socioeconomic structure, being predominantly rural and based on small-scale agricultural activity, could not absorb the large numbers of refugees who had entered it. Indeed, unemployment had soared to 50 percent. In 1950, the United Nations Relief and Works Agency (UNRWA) began relief operations for the refugees, most of whom inhabited open encampments along the seashore and in citrus groves. By 1952, UNRWA had established eight camps and assumed total responsibility for the needs of the refugee community, two-thirds of whom were totally dependent upon UNRWA for food, housing, health care and education.

Egyptian policies during the early years of its military administration were structured to centralize authority and power in the military, and did little to improve the social and economic conditions of the refugee community or of the indigenous (pre-1948) population. Strict control was imposed over Gaza's civil and security affairs. All public offices, social services, legal and commercial activities were consequently in the hands of the Egyptian military governor. Egyptians were appointed to head all high level administrative positions including civil and military departments, and assumed control over appointments in other areas of public life including health, education and commerce. Refugees were excluded from mainstream

5. See Edward Said, Ibrahim Abu-Lughod, Janet Abu-Lughod, Mohammed Hallaj and Elia Zureik, *A Profile of the Palestinian People* (Chicago: Palestine Human Rights Campaign, 1983). According to this source, 1.4 million people lived in Mandatory Palestine. As a result of the 1948 war, 380,000 people left the country, leaving 1,020,000 behind. Of this number, 260,000 or 26 percent remained inside the Gaza Strip.

social and economic affairs, and indigenous Gazans were carefully monitored.

Within a framework of social and economic contraction, political activity inside Gaza was rigidly circumscribed. Political parties in particular were prohibited, as were most forms of political expression including publications and independent organizations. However, political activity was impossible to suppress completely. The Communist Party and the Muslim Brotherhood, both underground political movements at the time, provided the wells of political activism inside the Strip and were strongly supported by the refugee community. Their activity, particularly between 1953 and 1959, included attacks against Israel, which led to Israeli retaliation inside the Strip. Fears of continued attacks by Israel within Egyptian-controlled territory resulted in the imposition of harsher security measures on the residents of Gaza and in the imprisonment of large numbers of people belonging to the Communist Party and Muslim Brotherhood.

A turning point in Egyptian policy toward the Gaza Strip occurred after the Suez Canal crisis of 1956. During the Suez War, Israel occupied Gaza for four months, from November 1956 to March 1957, an event which in the eyes of the Egyptian government not only ended the delicate relationship that had existed between Egypt and Israel before Suez, but which also ended the need to prevent infiltration of Israel's borders by Palestinian commandos. Moreover, political conditions inside Egypt, under the leadership of Gamal Abdal Naser, encouraged a more lenient approach toward the administration of Gaza's economic, political and social affairs.

The ten years between 1957 and 1967 witnessed greater attention to the economic and political needs of Gaza's inhabitants. Economically, the port of Gaza was reopened and declared a free trade zone for the importation of consumer and industrial goods, many of which were banned inside Egypt itself. This encouraged growing levels of commercial corruption. New markets were also extended to Gaza's citrus producers, particularly in Eastern Europe, which quickly led to increases in the levels of citrus production and export and the enrichment of Gaza's merchant class. However, the refugee population and Gaza's lower classes still remained poor and continually dependent upon UNRWA and other sources of external aid. Vulnerable and dependent, the poorer residents of the Gaza Strip often found themselves exploited as cheap, abundant labor by the expanding class of citrus growers.

Politically, independent Palestinian action was still largely curtailed. However, four notable changes did occur inside Gaza after 1957 which provided the basis for enhanced political expression. The first change originated in Cairo with President Nasier's establishment of the Arab Socialist Union (ASU), the only political party in Egypt at the time. In the early 1960s, the ASU was allowed to establish branches in Gaza and local elections for these branches were held. The second change which occurred in 1962, concerned the leadership of Gaza's legislative council, a political organ established five years earlier. Formerly in the hands of an Egyptian official, the chairmanship of the council was given to a local Palestinian, while half of its representatives were elected by members of the ASU branches in Gaza. The other half were appointed by the Egyptian governor-general.

Third, with the easing of certain restrictions on political activity after 1960, certain kinds of organizations were also established. In 1963, the Palestine Student Organization, associated with underground political activism, was permitted to hold a conference in Gaza. Similarly, the Egyptians approved the formation of the General Federation of Trade Unions in Gaza in 1964 and the Palestinian Women's Society, two organizations which still continue to function today albeit under various constraints.

The fourth and perhaps most significant change in the political character of the Gaza Strip during this period focused on the establishment of the Palestine Liberation Organization (PLO). Sponsored by the Arab League and supported by President Naser, the PLO held its first conference in Jerusalem in 1964, with several residents of Gaza participating. This conference drafted a Palestinian declaration of independence, known as the National Covenant, and the General Principles of a Fundamental Law, which provided the PLO with a constitution. As a result of the Fundamental Law, the Palestine National Council (PNC) was formed to serve as the parliament of the PLO and its main policy-making body; its fifteen-member executive committee or cabinet included three residents of Gaza.

Soon thereafter, the military arm of the Palestine Liberation Organization, the Palestinian Liberation Army (PLA), was established as a conventional force of Palestinian recruits and stationed in three Arab countries, among them Egypt. Given the increasing tensions inside the Strip, Gazans received Egyptian sanction to open PLA military training camps for refugee youth where support for the organization was strongest. Despite continued prohibitions on the Communists, the Muslim Brotherhood, and other political movements such as the nascent Fatah, the Egyptians supplied the PLA with light arms and allowed it to base itself inside the Gaza Strip.

Between the birth of the PLO inside Gaza in 1964 and the Israeli occupation on June 6, 1967, little violence broke out across Gaza-Israeli lines. The United Nations Emergency Force (UNEF) patrolled the armistice line until it was replaced with Egyptian military personnel on May 21, 1967, an action which precipitated the 1967 war. Twenty-four hours later, Egypt announced a blockade of the Gulf of Aqaba, to which Israel responded in June of 1967.

Israeli Occupation

The occupation of the Gaza Strip by Israel is marked by specific events which are significant for their impact upon the political character of Gaza at different points in time. In this sense, the political history of the Gaza Strip can be divided into three distinct phases.

Phase I: 1967-1971. The Israeli occupation of the Gaza Strip in 1967 represented a significant departure from its first occupation of the area in 1956. Policy statements by Prime Minister Levi Eshkol and Defense Minister Moshe Dayan immediately after the 1967 War, indicated the government's desire to annex the Gaza Strip. Plans outlined to implement the annexation initially focused on the resettlement of Gaza's refugee population in northern Sinai and the West Bank. Indeed, between June and December 1967, 40,000 people, under the supervision of the Israeli government, left the Gaza Strip for Jordan, some of them in buses provided by the authorities.[6] Some 20,000-30,000 more emigrated during the following year. Plans also provided for the extension of Israeli citizenship to the indigenous residents of Gaza, who would thereby remain under Israeli rule. These terms were unacceptable to local Gazans, and a protracted period of armed struggle broke out between the Palestine Liberation Army and the Israeli military. A guerrilla movement developed whose targets included the Israeli army and Israeli establishments inside the Strip. The PLA operated from within the refugee camps and was largely sustained by the refugee community. In addition to the guerrilla fighting that permeated life in the Strip, civil disobedience became widespread. Student demonstrations, consumer boycotts of Israeli goods, and public demands by political officials for an end to the occupation, exacerbated an already volatile situation. In response to the severe unrest inside the territory, the Israeli government placed the Gaza Strip under direct military control. By January 1971, Gaza's municipal council had been removed and its mayor dismissed. Refugee camps were placed under twenty-four hour curfews and severe restrictions were imposed upon camp inhabitants.

By the end of 1971, the Israeli military had succeeded in destroying the Palestinian resistance movement which had developed inside Gaza. Systematic arrests of PLA fighters, public demonstrators and prominent political figures led to local imprisonment, expulsion to Sinai and deportation to Jordan. Large numbers of guerrilla fighters were killed inside the camps. King Hussein's offensive against the PLO in Jordan in September 1970 further weakened the foundations of the resistance

6. *New York Times,* 7 September 1967, p. 3, and 31 July 1968, p. 5.

movement. During this time, 12,000 relatives of suspected guerrillas were deported to detention camps in the Sinai desert. Shortly thereafter, in August 1971, 7,000 rooms in three camps were destroyed and close to 16,000 more refugees were displaced.[7] Their homes were destroyed as part of an Israeli program to build wider roads inside the camps which would facilitate access and ensure more effective control. Portions of the displaced population were relocated to El Arish in north Sinai and to the West Bank, while the remainder were left to find their own living arrangements inside the Strip.

Phase II: 1972-1977. Despite their defeat by the Israeli military, Palestinian forces continued to control the refugee camps through 1972. The activity of the guerrilla movement alienated more traditional social forces within Gaza which had, since the onset of Israeli rule, remained largely isolated from political life. These forces included Gaza's wealthy citrus merchants and landowning elite. Historically the source of Gaza's political leadership, these individuals sought to restore to the Strip some semblance of social and economic order, which they felt the guerrilla movement had effectively weakened. Consequently, a leading citrus merchant, Rashad al-Shawwa, agreed to become mayor in September 1971 at the request of the Israeli authorities. Mayor Shawwa then formed a municipal council composed of the upper classes of Gaza.

The appointment of the mayor and the municipal council generated intense controversy, since many nationalist forces viewed these events as a form of political compromise with the occupation forces and one which had little basis in popular support. The PLO, in particular, refused to endorse the municipal council and encouraged armed rather than political struggle inside the territory. Yet, with the reinstatement of a locally based municipal structure and the defeat of the resistance movement, political struggle began to challenge armed struggle as a tactical approach for dealing with the realities of the occupation.

In 1972 the mayor focused on the economic revitalization of Gaza's citrus industry, which had suffered greatly during the period of intense fighting as well as from various trade restrictions imposed by the Israeli government. Export markets were secured through newly established trade routes with Jordan. Several social and cultural organizations were either established or revived during this time, including the Red Crescent Society, a community-based health clinic founded by Dr. Abd al-Shafei; a Lawyer's Association, headed until recently by Fayez Abu Rahmeh; and a Women's Graduate Union. Other organizations, mainly charitable societies, were also given

7. UNRWA, p. 270.

permission by the Israeli authorities to form, but were often denied the right to accept external donations, a funding source upon which such societies often depend. This policy continues at present. Certain kinds of cultural activities were also prohibited, such as festivals, exhibits and public lectures, a policy which is also enforced inside Gaza today.

The positive effects of the mayor's activities were mitigated by the closure of the Bank of Palestine in 1967 and the imposition of new taxes by the military government. Moreover, the mayor alienated a majority of his constituency by backing a federation between Gaza, the West Bank and Jordan, proposed by King Hussein in 1972. Nationalist elements inside the Strip, outraged by Hussein's attack on PLO forces two years earlier, rejected any leadership emanating from Jordan.

Under intense criticism from both Gazans and Israelis, Mayor Shawwa resigned in October 1972. His resignation was followed immediately by the reinstatement of direct military rule in the Gaza Strip. The Israeli military governor assumed all the powers of his Egyptian predecessor and Israelis were similarly appointed to head all social service departments. Direct rule continued until October 1975, when Shawwa agreed to be reappointed as mayor of Gaza City, an act which again angered many Palestinian nationalists who insisted that Gazans reject the Israeli system of appointments and call for one based on elections. This sentiment was heightened by the April 1976 elections of municipal councils in the West Bank, where the victory of pro-PLO candidates eventually resulted in the termination of municipal elections in the West Bank as well.

Phase III: 1978-1985. President Sadat's visit to Israel in November 1977 touched off the third and perhaps most explosive phase of Gaza's political history. The explosion was fueled by the Camp David accords and their plan for Palestinian autonomy in the occupied territories. Most Gazans interpreted the accords as a renunciation by Egypt of all claims on the Gaza Strip. The autonomy plan, moreover, contained many clauses which Palestinians found unacceptable. Objections to the plan emphasized two key points: 1) Israel's continued control over land, water, settlements and security in the Gaza Strip and West Bank; and 2) continued prohibitions on the establishment of a Palestinian policy-making government. Furthermore, at the end of the process, Palestinians were to choose between Jordanian or Israeli citizenship, neither of which appealed to Gazans. Consequently, Sadat's initiative was totally rejected by the PLO and its constituency in the occupied territories.[8]

---

8. See *Jerusalem Post,* 21 January 1979, 29 May 1979 and 11 January 1980.

One month after the Camp David accords in September 1978, a rally was held in Gaza to denounce the accords and propose comprehensive negotiations for Palestinian self-determination which were to include the PLO. This rally, the only one ever allowed in Gaza since 1967, brought together individuals and groups from a wide range of political viewpoints, including members of the indigenous upper classes as well as representatives of the refugee community.[9]

Indeed, the differences between these two groups have, in large part, accounted for the lack of an organized, well led political movement inside the Gaza Strip. Unlike the population of the West Bank, which is more homogeneous and has strong middle-class leadership, the population of the Strip is comprised of two large groups: indigenous inhabitants, and displaced refugees, each of whom has its own set of goals, purposes and needs. The middle class in Gaza is very small and has been unable to challenge the traditional power base of Gaza's upper classes. This in turn has widened the cleavages between the very rich and the very poor and has limited the formation of group alliances which could have provided the foundation for more unified political activism inside the Strip.[10]

After the September rally, the Israeli authorities imposed a series of restrictions on political activity inside Gaza, particularly on the organization of future public assemblies and meetings. Specific individuals with known political preferences were confined to the Strip for long periods of time.[11] Over the next year tensions increased inside Gaza, and various municipalities and local councils issued a communiqúe openly proclaiming the PLO as the sole legitimate representative of the Palestinian people.

The fall of 1981 and the spring of 1982 witnessed a strong resurgence of civil disobedience in the Gaza Strip. A series of Israeli measures imposed upon Gaza's inhabitants catalyzed the upsurge in violence. The first of these measures concerned the government imposition of a special excise tax on professionals, which resulted in a strike on November 22, 1981 by doctors, dentists, pharmacists, veterinarians, lawyers and engineers. In response, the Israeli government welded shut the doors of 170 shops and 18 pharmacies, imposed heavy fines on doctors, and arrested protesters. The strike, which

9. In an interview with Mayor Shawwa, the significance of this event was discussed. See also Lesch *the Gaza Strip,* 1:8.

10. Metzger, Orth, and Sterling, *This Land Is Our Land,* p. 129.

11. For example, Dr. Haider Abd al-Shafei, an outspoken critic of the occupation and head of Gaza's Red Crescent Society, indicated that he was confined to the Gaza Strip for three years.

ended two weeks later, did not succeed in altering government measures, but merely delayed them for a brief period.

Soon thereafter, the Israeli government instituted a civil administration in the occupied territories, structurally parallel to that of the military administration. Implemented in the Gaza Strip on December 1, 1981, the civil administration was given responsibility over all nonmilitary sectors such as health, education and welfare. Interpreted as the first step toward the implementation of Begin's autonomy plan and the annexation of the territories, the imposition of the civil administration generated considerable frustration and fear inside Gaza.

On December 2, Mayor Shawwa announced a general strike protesting the excise tax and the civil administration. Shawwa, in conjunction with West Bank mayors, continued to boycott the civil administration by refusing to cooperate with its officials. In the spring of 1982, the West Bank mayors were removed and replaced by Israeli military officials; Shawwa was ordered to end the strike in Gaza. His refusal to do so culminated in his dismissal and the disbanding of Gaza's municipal council once again. By August of 1982, the Israeli Ministry of the Interior assumed control over Gaza's municipal structure and returned direct rule to the Strip.

In the spring of 1986, Mayor Shawwa approached Egyptian president Husni Mubarak with a proposal for returning Gaza to Egyptian administrative supervision, with Israeli approval, pending a final solution to the status of the territory. Shawwa's autonomy proposal called for setting up Egyptian consular services in east Jerusalem, reestablishing the Palestinian legislative council that existed under Egypt, and opening an Egyptian bank inside the territory. Reflecting an attempt to break through the political impasse confronting Gaza, the proposal failed due to a lack of support from President Mubarak himself, King Hussein and Prime Minister Peres.

Today, Gaza still has no elected Arab mayor, no election process, no daily newspaper and no right of public assembly. The Israeli Ministry of the Interior still controls Gaza's municipal structure. Channels for political expression have not been created and seem even more improbable in light of the reinstatement of preventive detentions and deportations. The number of Israeli settlements inside the Gaza Strip has grown significantly since 1982 and consequently, so have contestations over land, water and other economic resources. Indeed, it is Gaza's economic sector which has perhaps been most significantly affected by Israel's twenty-year occupation.

ECONOMIC PATTERNS

The impact of Israeli occupation upon the socioeconomic structure of the Gaza Strip has been the subject of considerable debate. The Israeli government in particular argues for the positive effect resulting from the interaction of its own economy with that of Gaza. Increases in per capita GNP achieved after 1967, for example, are seen as indicators of the greater prosperity generated under Israeli rule. Increased levels of income have, in turn, resulted in higher rates of consumption expenditure as found in the greater percentage of radios, TVs, ovens, refrigerators, private cars and homes inside the territory. The Government of Israel uses these indicators of economic well-being as evidence of improved standards of living. Advancements in education and health, including higher levels of school enrollment and the eradication of certain diseases, are similarly cited as additional indicators of enhanced living standards attained since 1967.

That specific economic and social benefits have accrued to the inhabitants of the Gaza Strip under Israeli rule is undeniable. However, these benefits must be viewed not in isolation, but within the wider economic context of the occupation itself, in order to determine the nature and extent of their impact.

Critics of the occupation argue that it has fostered the structural integration of the Gaza Strip into Israel proper, harming Gaza and benefiting Israel. This integration, illustrated most dramatically in the economic sector, has made the territory increasingly vulnerable to and dependent upon events inside the Jewish state. The critique further maintains that Gaza's dependence on Israel has been the result of, and itself is based upon, a severe lack of growth in the Strip's agricultural and industrial sectors. Consequently, it has been possible to achieve certain forms of economic prosperity without any form of economic development. Indeed, particularly since 1967, the distinguishing features of Gaza's economy have increasingly become the erosion of its own internal economic base and its resulting dependency on Israel. The remainder of this paper will therefore discuss those policies and measures which, over the past twenty years, have contributed to the steady decline of Gaza's economic sector.

Economy in the Gaza Strip before the Occupation (1948-1967)

The economy of the Gaza Strip just after 1948 was on the verge of collapse as a result of its isolation from the rest of Palestine and the influx of vast numbers of refugees. Having lost most of its cultivable land and many of its domestic trade links, the Strip could not absorb its massive population into the rural, agrarian sector. Indeed, only 14 percent of all households in the Gaza Strip had land as a source of income, compared with 42 percent in the West Bank, and a significant portion of this land (20-25 percent) was concentrated in the hands of a few wealthy families and was devoted to citrus production, Gaza's largest source of foreign exchange during this period.[12] Agriculture was clearly the primary economic activity, while industrial activity remained highly undeveloped. Prior to 1967, the Gaza Strip had no large-scale industrial enterprises; the industrial sector was characterized by small workshops engaged in the production of traditional crafts or the processing of food products. Moreover, unemployment was very high and labor force participation very low during the Egyptian administration because of Gaza's status as an economic unit separate from that of Egypt.

The service sector, however, developed rapidly as a result of the presence of Egyptian military forces, forces of the Palestine Liberation Army, United Nations Emergency Forces and UNRWA personnel.[13] Although it provided important sources of employment and contributed largely to the gross income of the Strip before 1967, the service sector introduced few structural changes into Gaza's economy, and those which did occur disappeared with the departure of the military and civilian forces. Trade and commerce, similarly, became important income producing sectors, focusing strongly on the development of an entrepôt and smuggling trade with Egypt, since custom duties inside Gaza were relatively lower than those in Egypt. Thus, on the eve of the Israeli occupation, the infrastructure of the Gaza Strip remained rudimentary and, in the absence of an integrated market and skilled manpower base, the economy as a whole had stagnated.

Economy under Occupation (1967-1985)

The occupation of the Gaza Strip brought its economy into direct contact with that of Israel. This was the second major dislocation of the economy since 1948. Small, unorganized and largely agricultural, the economy possessed few means to withstand the influence of a highly industrialized and technologically advanced economy such as Israel's. By 1967, the total GNP of the Gaza Strip and West Bank combined, equaled 2.6 percent of the Israeli GNP.[14]

12. Eliyahu Kanovsky, *The Economic Impact of the Six-Day War: Israel, the Occupied Territories, Egypt and Jordan* (New York: Praeger, 1970), pp. 174-75. See also E. Efrat, "Geographical Review: Settlement Pattern and Economic Changes in the Gaza Strip 1947-1977," *Middle East Journal*, 31(3):350; (Summer 1977) and Fawzi Gharaibeh, *The Economies of the West Bank and Gaza Strip* (Boulder, Colo.: Westview Press, 1985), p. 16.

13. Van Arkadie, *Benefits and Burdens*, p. 30-31.

14. Meron Benvenisti, *The West Bank Data Project: A Survey of Israel's Policies* (Washington, D.C.: American Enterprise Institute, 1984), p. 9.

During the years 1968-1982, however, the Gaza Strip experienced a substantial increase in GNP, averaging about 9.7 percent per annum. The economy attained a higher annual rate of growth in the first five years after the occupation (1968-1973) due to expanded income-generating opportunities inside Israel. After 1973, these rates decreased and fluctuated as Israel's economy moved into recession.

External payments, of which salaries earned in Israel are a large part, contributed directly to the increases in GNP after 1967. Contributing only 2 percent to GNP in 1968, this factor rose to 31 percent in 1973 and 44 percent in 1984.[15] This highlights the weakness of Gaza's internal economic base and its dependence on externally generated sources of income. Income derived from work outside Gaza (either in Israel or other Arab countries) grew by 9 percent in 1983 and 1984, a decrease from annual rises of 16 percent in 1982 and 1983.[16]

The importance of different sectors to total GDP has changed since the war. Percentages have fallen in the service sector's share of GDP from a high of 66 percent in 1968 to 23 percent in 1984. Industry, in contrast, has increased its share, although it still remains the smallest contributor to GDP at 11.6 percent in 1984. Agriculture accounted for only 13.4 percent in 1984, a decline of more than 50 percent from 28.4 percent in 1968. The construction sector, however, witnessed a large increase in its relative share of GDP from a 1968 level of 3.1 percent to a 1984 level of 22 percent.[17] Increased rates of residential construction have in large part accounted for this significant rise in the position of the construction sector. Indeed, capital formation in construction accounts for 90 percent of all private sector investments. Unlike typical patterns of economic development, where investment normally flows into nonresidential capital formation (i.e., industry), investment in residential construction accounts for 85 percent of total capital formation inside the Gaza Strip. Moreover, a report by the General Assembly of the United Nations states that there has been no public sector residential construction for the Arab population in the Gaza Strip

15. Calculated from the *Statistical Abstract of Israel,* no. 37 (Jerusalem: Central Bureau of Statistics, 1986).

16. *Judea, Samaria and Gaza Area Statistics,* vol. 15, no. 2 (Jerusalem: Central Bureau of Statistics, 1985).

17. *Statistical Abstract of Israel,* 1986.

since 1978, indicating that the burden of housing falls largely, if not entirely, on private individuals.[18]

Labor Force Composition

The labor force in the Gaza Strip constituted 19 percent of the total population prior to 1967, 15 percent in 1968, and by 1974 attained a level of 18 percent, where it has remained ever since. The low labor force participation rate is a function of several factors: a large percentage of people under fifteen years of age, a small number of males of working age, constant emigration of adults, high rate of school attendance and limited economic opportunities. As a proportion of the total population fourteen years and older (278,800), the labor force has fluctuated around one-third, and in 1985 was 33 percent or 92,000 people.

Employment

In 1960, it was estimated that 55,975 people of working age (fourteen and over) were employed inside the Gaza Strip, while 88,750 were unemployed. By 1966, employment was estimated at 71,000. Agriculture engaged one-third of the labor force and services and construction provided employment for over 60 percent; industry accounted for a very small share. After the 1967 War, the number of working Gazans declined to 45,000 in 1968. The number of unemployed increased by 20,000 above its highest prewar level, resulting in a 17 percent unemployment rate among Gaza's labor force in 1968.[19]

Access to the Israeli economy after 1969 led to a restructuring of Gaza's labor force. This is perhaps most clearly seen in the relative and absolute changes in numbers employed by sector between the years 1970 and 1985. Those employed in agriculture, for example, declined from 32 percent to 18 percent, while industry increased its share of total employed from 12 percent in 1970 to 17.5 percent in 1985. Construction engaged 23.9 percent of Gaza's labor force in 1985, a 100 percent increase from a 1970 level of 12

18. United Nations General Assembly, Economic and Social Council, 38th Session, *Living Conditions of the Palestinian People in the Occupied Palestinian Territories: Report of the Secretary General,* 22 June 1983, p. 10. See also Mona Younis, *Community Development versus Personal Property: Israel's Pacification Policy in the Occupied West Bank and Gaza Strip,* Yarmouk University, Center for Hebraic Studies, Information Series (February 1987), 2(1):46-48.

19. Gharaibeh, *Economies,* p. 38; Kanovsky, *Economic Impact,* p. 179.

percent. While services continued to provide a large percentage of paid employment, their 38 percent share in 1985 also represented a decline from prewar levels. Of the labor force employed within the Gaza Strip in 1985, agriculture accounted for 18 percent; industry, 16.2 percent; construction, 8.4 percent; services and other occupations, 57.4 percent.[20]

Clearly, since the Israeli occupation, there has been a noticeable shift away from jobs inside Gaza to those available inside Israel. This transfer of labor from the Gaza Strip to Israel has been accompanied by certain structural alterations in the composition of Gaza's labor force and by modifications in Gaza's economy.

Employment in Israel

Between 1970 and 1985, Gaza's labor force working inside Israel grew from 5,900 (10 percent) to 41,700 (45 percent), an increase of over 600 percent. In 1985, the number of Gazans employed in Israel was equivalent to 85 percent of the number employed inside Gaza itself.

However, these figures are based on the number of laborers registered with the Israeli Employment Service and do not reflect the large numbers of black market laborers who work inside Israel unofficially, among whom are children between the ages of eight and fifteen.[21] Israeli authorities estimate the number of illegal workers to be between 25 and 30 percent of those legally employed, and other estimates have been considerably higher.[22] Thus, in light of the high percentage of unregistered workers, not only is the number of Gazans working in Israel higher than official figures indicate, but the official unemployment rate of 1.1 percent is inaccurately low.

The composition of labor employed in Israel has, itself, experienced some significant changes during the postwar period. In 1970, for example, 40.7 percent of Gaza's labor force were employed in agriculture in Israel; 8.5 percent in industry; 47.4 percent in construction; and 3.4 percent in other branches, such as services. By 1985, the proportions were altered to 21.6

20. Calculated from *Statistical Abstract of Israel, 1986.* See also Civil Administration of Gaza, *18th Year of the Administration – April 1984-March 1985* (Gaza Strip: Civil Administration, 1985), p. 31.

21. Israel Zamir, "The Market of Children at Erez Junction," *al-Hamishmar,* 1 August 1978; and Amos Elon, "The Market of Children at Ashkelon," *Haaretz,* 2 August 1978.

22. Gharaibeh, *Economies,* p. 50; Ziad Abu-Amr, *The Gaza Economy since 1948* (Paper presented to the Welfare Association Symposium on "Economic Development under Prolonged Occupation," St. Catherine's College, Oxford, England, 3-5 January 1985).

percent employed in Israeli agriculture; 19 percent in industry; 42.3 percent in construction; and 17.1 percent in services. The construction sector has, since 1970, remained the largest employer of Gazan workers inside Israel.

The economy of Israel has benefited from the changes it has created within the economy of the Gaza Strip. The availability of a large pool of unskilled and semiskilled workers has provided Israel with a reserve of labor which it can utilize or marginalize without great risk to its own economy. In periods of economic prosperity, for example, the availability of large resources of labor has had a stabilizing effect on wages inside Israel; in periods of recession, it has acted as a repository for surplus labor. Given the state's control over the economy of the occupied territories, wages paid to workers from these areas do not drain Israel's economic reserves, since the consumption expenditure of Palestinian labor is directly tied into the Israeli economy itself.

The resulting state of dependency of the Palestinian labor market on the economy of Israel, renders the former vulnerable to the political, social and economic exigencies of the latter. This dependent condition and its potential consequences for the economy of the Gaza Strip are visible in the changes which have occurred within Gaza's main economic sectors.

Agriculture

Between 1948 and 1967, agriculture was the largest single economic activity in the Gaza Strip, constituting over one-third of the GDP, about 33-40 percent of employment, and 90 percent of all exports. During the postwar period agriculture's position in Gaza's economy weakened in relative terms. Between 1967 and 1970, the average annual rate of growth in agriculture was 8.8 percent. Between 1979 and 1981, it dropped sharply to 0.9 percent, as a result of the shift of the labor force into employment in Israel.[23]

Land use. There are approximately 360,500 dunums of land in the Gaza Strip. The percentage of land under cultivation by Arab farmers has declined since 1970. Competition with Israeli settlers for land and water rights and the reversion of approximately one-third of the Strip's total area to Israeli control (see table 10.1), has forced many Gazans out of agriculture, reducing the amount of cultivated land. Between 1968 and

23. Benvenisti, *West Bank Data Project*, p. 15.

1985, the number of dunums cultivated inside the Gaza Strip fell from 198,000 to 100,000, a decline of almost 50 percent.[24]

Table 10.1   Land Use Distribution in the Gaza Strip 1984

Category	Area in dunums
Construction and roads	41,000
Citrus	66,700*
Fruit	60,000
Vegetables and other crops	57,000
Private barren land	8,000
Sand dunes (mainly government land)	77,000
Government land (acacia scrub)	40,000
Other kinds of land	10,000
Total	359,700

SOURCE: Sharif Kana'na and Rashad al-Madani, *Settlement and Land Confiscation in the Gaza Strip 1967-1984* (Bir Zeit, West Bank: Center for Research and Documentation, Bir Zeit University, 1985), p. 9.

*Israel's Department of Agriculture quotes a similar figure of 66,000 dunums of citrus under cultivation in 1984. However, the 1985 Report of the Gaza Strip Citrus Producers Association places the figure at 58,000.

24. Gharaibeh, *Economies,* p. 62. See also (in English translation) Sharif Kana'na and Rashad al-Madani, *Al-Istitan wal-Musadarat al-Aradi fi Qita Ghazza 1967-1984* (Settlement and Land Confiscation in the Gaza Strip 1967-1984) (Bir Zeit, West Bank: Center for Research and Documentation, Bir Zeit University, 1985). Benvenisti, *West Bank Data Project,* p. 13, places the number of dunums under cultivation in 1967-68 at 204,000. The 1985 figure was quoted in State of Israel, *Report of the Military Government 1985-86* (1986). See also Hisham Awartani, "Agriculture," in Emile A. Nakhleh, ed., *A Palestinian Agenda for the West Bank and Gaza* (Washington, D.C.: American Enterprise Institute, 1980), p. 17; and M.K. Budeiri, "Changes in the Economic Structure of the West Bank and Gaza Strip under Israeli Occupation," *Labor Capital and Society* (April 1982), 15(1): 54.

Agricultural output. Agricultural output in the Gaza Strip is comprised of the following factors in order of economic contribution: citrus, fruits, livestock (which includes meat, milk, fish and eggs), vegetables, other fruits, melons and pumpkins, and field crops. In 1984, crops contributed a majority share of 74.1 percent to total output in agriculture; livestock comprised 25.5 percent; investment in forestry and new fruit plantations constituted the remaining 0.3 percent. Citrus, vegetables and other fruits have, in that order, proved the most productive within the crop category, followed by field crops and melons and pumpkins.

Crop output values, which reached a high of 78.3 percent in 1970-1971, have fluctuated between 72 and 77 percent ever since (see table 10.2). Within the crop category, citrus fruits enjoyed a 17 percent increase in their share of output in the first decade of the postwar period, reaching a high of 57.1 percent in 1976. However, citrus has subsequently experienced a sharp decline in its share of output, sinking to a level of 34.4 percent in 1984. Other fruits have also suffered reductions in their value share of agricultural output, declining from a high of 14.3 percent in 1967 to a low of 5.5 percent in 1983 but increasing to 11.7 percent one year later. Melons and pumpkins, in light of Israeli competition, were virtually eliminated as an agricultural product, dropping from just under 5 percent of output to 0.1 percent in 1984. Vegetables' share in output value declined somewhat in the mid-1970s but increased their share toward the end of the decade, averaging 18 percent of total value between 1979 and 1983 and 27.8 percent in 1984 alone. Measured in terms of tons, output of vegetables more than tripled between 1967 and 1984, as a result of increased use of irrigation methods and the introduction by Israel of drip irrigation technology inside the Gaza Strip. Livestock's percentage share in agricultural output has remained relatively stable through the 1967-1984 period, averaging around a 24 percent share in output value.[25]

Citrus fruits. Of all the sources of value of agricultural output, citrus has been the largest and most productive during the post-1967 period. Citrus production has accounted for 40-45 percent of the total area under cultivation in the Gaza Strip, and until 1980 provided an average of 50 per-cent of output value in the agricultural sector. Despite a decline in the value share of citrus to total agricultural output, it remains the largest single contributor.

25. Gharaibeh, *Economies,* p. 75; *Statistical Abstract of Israel,* various issues. See also David Kahan, *The Agricultural Development of the Administered Territories,* Part 1, "Palestinian Sector" (Jerusalem: The West Bank Data Base Project, April 1983).

Table 10.2 Agricultural output values in the Gaza Strip
1967-1984 (percentages)

Category	1967	1968	1969	1970	1971	1972	1973	1974	1975	1976	1977	1978	1979	1980	1981	1982	1983	1984
TOTAL OUTPUT	100.0	100.0	100.0	100.0	100.0	100.0	100.0	100.0	100.0	100.0	100.0	100.0	100.0	100.0	100.0	100.0	100.0	100.0
Total crops	77.5	77.6	76.6	78.3	76.1	73.3	75.5	73.8	77.0	77.7	72.4	75.3	74.8	72.4	72.0	72.8	73.3	74.1
Field crops	0.6	1.5	1.1	0.9	0.9	0.9	1.1	1.0	0.9	0.8	0.6	0.6	0.8	0.8	0.6	0.8	0.3	0.1
Vegetables	17.4	15.6	13.6	II.I	11.3	10.7	9.9	10.0	9.9	10.2	9.7	11.2	15.4	14.6	17.6	23.0	20.6	27.8
Melons & pumpkins	4.7	3.1	1.6	1.6	1.7	1.8	1.4	1.6	1.5	0.8	0.9	0.9	2.6	1.6	0.6	0.6	0.1	0.1
Citrus	40.5	43.5	48.9	53.3	50.6	47.9	51.6	50.3	55.5	57.1	49.6	50.3	39.1	43.1	45.5	40.2	46.8	34.4
Other fruits	14.3	13.9	11.4	11.3	11.7	12.1	11.5	10.9	9.1	8.8	11.6	11.8	16.9	12.3	7.7	8.2	5.5	11.7
Livestock	20.5	20.3	21.1	20.4	22.7	25.8	23.9	25.5	22.3	21.7	27.3	24.7	24.8	27.1	27.7	26.8	26.2	25.5
Meat	6.8	7.9	7.7	8.9	8.5	9.0	8.5	7.9	6.9	6.9	8.8	10.2	11.9	13.6	13.2	13.1	12.5	12.6
Milk	6.2	5.8	4.8	4.0	4.9	6.3	6.0	6.5	6.0	5.7	8.2	7.7	7.5	6.9	7.2	6.6	7.0	6.0
Fish	5.1	3.7	5.7	4.5	6.6	7.6	7.0	7.3	6.6	6.5	6.8	1.8	1.5	2.1	2.0	1.7	0.7	4.8
Eggs	2.1	2.6	2.9	2.9	2.5	2.5	2.1	3.0	2.3	2.2	3.1	4.4	3.8	4.0	4.7	4.9	5.1	0.8
Misc.	0.4	0.3	-	-	0.2	0.3	0.4	0.7	0.4	0.4	0.5	0.5	0.4	0.5	0.6	0.5	0.9	1.2

SOURCES. Fawzi Gharaibeh, *The Economies of the West Bank and Gaza Strip* (Boulder, Colo.: Westview press, 1985), 75 (for 1967-1981).
Statistical Abstract of Israel No. 36 1985 (for 1982- 1983).
Statistical Abstract of Israel No. 37 1986 (for 1984).

Agriculture in the Gaza Strip has always concentrated on the production of citrus, almost to the point of becoming a one-crop economy. Accounting for 70 percent of Gaza's exports, the citrus crop experienced a very high output between 1972 and 1976 which was solely attributable to the planting of 40,000 dunums of citrus trees prior to 1967. (Citrus trees require five to eight years to mature.) Beginning in 1977, citrus yields began to decline far below their pre-1977 levels to an output of 175,700 tons in 1984 from a high of 243,700 in 1975 (see table 10.3). The reasons for the decline in output are two: 1) Israeli policies directed against the development of citriculture in the Gaza Strip; and 2) dwindling water resources inside the territory. Measures have been enacted against the development of citriculture in the following areas:

Planting trees. The Israeli military government of the Gaza Strip has, over the past ten years, imposed various restrictions upon citrus producers and merchants which have greatly limited their ability to grow as well as market their product. Military orders make it illegal and therefore punishable to plant new trees or replace old, non-productive ones.[26] In 1984, a new order was issued by the military government making it illegal to plant fruit trees on a commercial scale without official permission. The restrictions on the planting of trees are, in large part, related to the shortage of water supplies in the Gaza Strip (see below). Permits for these activities must be secured from the military authorities and, when issued, have required five years or more to obtain. Permits, however, are rarely issued. As of the summer of 1985, only figs and dates could be planted without difficulty.

Taxes. Tax policies applied to the citrus industry further impede its ability to grow. Taxes include land taxes, value added taxes (VAT) and export taxes. Land taxes, perhaps the most severe, are levied according to the number of dunums owned. The tax rate used is based on yields per dunum achieved on Israeli citrus farms. Israeli producers and merchants receive government subsidies, tax breaks, and other financial supports Palestinian merchants and producers do not. Therefore, Israeli citriculture is far stronger, producing average yields that are substantially higher than those achieved in Gaza. Consequently, tax rates based on Israeli production amounts do not account for the different economic conditions confronting

---

26. Interview with several citrus producers who asked not to be identified. However, this is common knowledge among researchers working in the Gaza Strip. See Lesch, "Gaza: Forgotten Corner," p. 47. Also see Ikhlas Rayyes Nusseibeh, Gaza Orange Market Faces Difficult Time," *al-Fajr,* 29 March 1981, p. 6; Civil Administration of Gaza, p. 16; and State of Israel, Ministry of Labor and Social Affairs, Letter to the American Near East Refugee Aid (ANERA) outlining policies on planting of trees in the occupied territories, 1981.

Table 10.3 **Agricultural output in the Gaza Strip 1967-1984 (in thousand tons)**

Category	1967	1968	1969	1970	1971	1972	1973	1974	1975	1976	1977	1978	1979	1980	1981	1982	1983	1984
Field Crops	–	–	–	–	–	–	–	–	–	–	–	–	–	–	–	–	–	–
Vegetables	31.8	33.2	36.4	36.8	38.9	40.5	37.9	46.0	48.0	54.9	53.4	51.4	60.0	72.7	76.6	79.8	86.7	104.5
Melons & pumpkins	12.5	8.0	7.1	7.9	4.6	5.0	6.1	4.7	3.0	3.7	2.8	3.6	5.8	6.1	3.1	3.1	1.0	0.6
Citrus	91.0	106.2	142.0	175.0	178.0	205.2	207.0	201.4	243.7	232.3	180.6	192.2	171.5	179.3	199.9	166.5	159.5	175.7*
Other fruits	19.0	20.0	18.4	19.0	26.3	21.4	26.5	25.2	20.9	19.7	24.8	18.9	21.4	20.8	15.4	19.9	17.1	17.0
Livestock																		
Meat	1.7	1.9	2.4	2.6	3.0	3.5	3.4	3.7	4.4	4.3	4.8	4.8	5.6	6.2	6.3	6.0	5.9	6.1
Milk	6.8	6.9	7.4	7.2	9.7	10.2	11.7	12.9	12.8	11.7	14.8	15.5	4.7	13.9	12.4	11.4	11.2	10.0
Fish	3.7	3.8	3.4	3.2	4.7	4.6	3.5	4.8	4.7	5.1	4.5	1.5	1.2	1.4	1.3	1.1	1.0	0.6
Eggs (million)	10.0	-		-	24.0	30.0	30.0	32.0	32.4	35.0	40.0	47.5	42.8	45.6	45.8	46.0	44.5	49.5

SOURCES: Fawzi Gharaibeh, 71 (for 1977-1981).
Statistical Abstract of Israel No. 36 1985 (for 1982-1983).
Statistical Abstract of Israel No. 37 1986 (for 1984).
*The Gaza Strip Citrus Producers Association Annual Report (1985) estimated this figure to be 163.9 thousand tons.

Gaza's citrus producers and merchants nor do they allow for any form of compensation to those individuals in the event of financial loss.[27] The value added tax is also applied in a discriminatory manner inside Gaza, since Palestinian farmers are ineligible to receive the same VAT rebate to which Israeli farmers are legally entitled.[28] Citrus merchants consistently claim that they are subject to an export tax which they alone must pay before being given a permit to export their produce from the Gaza Strip.[29] Freddy Zach, deputy coordinator of government operations in the administered territories, has denied the existence of the export tax altogether.

Financial incentive. Inability to secure governmental subsidies and financial guarantees against loss, which are provided to Israeli producers, further hinders the capacity of Gaza's citrus producers to maintain, let alone expand, production. Similarly, low interest rate loans are unavailable to Gaza's citrus growers. In 1985, loans that were available carried prohibitive rates of interest: 36 percent per year for borrowing in U.S. dollars, 95 percent per year for borrowing in Israeli shekels. Consequently, many farmers have either discontinued production of citrus entirely or have decreased the area under cultivation. Others have been forced to uproot a portion of their citrus trees. By 1980 at least five hundred acres of trees had been uprooted, while the yield of those remaining had declined.[30] Attempts by the Citrus Producers Association in Gaza to negotiate with Israeli authorities on the issue of loans and taxes failed in 1985. The economic, political and legal relationships between Israel and the territories, furthermore, preclude commercial ventures between Israeli and Palestinian producers. Consequently, few if any economic or commercial links exist between the two groups.

Land reclamation. Legal prohibitions against the reclamation of land present great difficulties to citrus farmers. Land reclamation involves bulldozing a piece of land in order to remove rocks, boulders and any obstructive material in order to make the land cultivable. Gazan farmers are legally forbidden to reclaim their own land unless they obtain permission from the Israeli military authorities, which, if granted, involves considerable costs in the form of taxes.

27. Interview with an Israeli government official who asked not to be identified.

28. *Ibid.*

29. Interview with Abdel Latif Abu Middain, chairman, Agricultural Cooperative for Citrus Marketing, and other businessmen in the Gaza Strip, summer 1985 and winter 1986.

30. See *Report of the Gaza Strip Citrus Producers Association (GSCPA)* (Gaza Strip, 1985); and Lesch, "Gaza, Forgotten Corner," p. 47.

Export markets. The most severe problem confronting agriculture and citrus products in particular, lies in the area of exports.[31] Between 1967 and 1985, markets for Gazan citrus products have steadily been eliminated. Prior to 1967, Gaza traditionally marketed to parts of Western Europe, including England, Holland and Germany, through Port Said in Egypt. Having established these markets in the 1940s, Gaza expanded its trade in the late 1950s to the COMECON countries of Eastern Europe. Trade with Arab countries during this time was minimal. Trade with Egypt ended in the mid-1950s when Egypt became self-sufficient in citrus production.

Immediately after the June 1967 war all Western markets were banned to Gazan exporters, thus precluding competition with Israeli agricultural producers and then, as now, limiting Gaza's access to foreign economic and political circles. Between 1967 and 1974, Gazans were allowed to market their products to Europe indirectly through Israel's Citrus Marketing Board (CMB), but at less than competitive prices and under increasingly disadvantageous conditions. The COMECON market, however, continued, and markets to Arab countries, particularly the Gulf States, opened up through Jordan.

From 1974 to 1979, when Gazan citrus was at its maximum yield, all marketing to Europe through Israel's CMB was stopped. Seeking to reduce the share of Gaza's exports to Europe, the Israeli government encouraged Gazans to seek expanded markets in the Arab world, which Israel itself could not enter. A market with Iran opened up which proved extremely successful. During this five-year period the bulk of Gaza's citrus was exported to Iran, while the COMECON market, unable to compete with Iranian prices, stagnated. But with the overthrow of the Shah in 1979, Iran disappeared as a market for Gaza citrus.

By 1979 Gaza, having lost its major Iranian market and unable to access its traditional markets in Western Europe, turned again to the COMECON states. However, by 1979, these states had secured other sources, in particular Cuba, where they dealt in barter trade. Consequently, in order to enter the market, Gazans were forced to trade in barter, and since 1979 have not earned any hard currency in their East European markets. Examples of barter include sheep, wood and crystal products, on which Gazans are charged import taxes.

At present, Gaza's main export markets are Jordan and, through Jordan, other Arab states. In 1985, approximately 60 percent of Gaza's citrus was

---

31. The section on export markets is based on data collected through interviews with several members of Gaza's citrus community in the summer of 1985 and the winter of 1986. They include Mayor Shawwa, members of the Citrus Producers Association, members of the Arab Citrus Packing Company, and individual farmers and merchants.

exported through Jordan, and the remaining 20 percent was sent to Eastern Europe and Israel. However, Arab markets have imposed their own restrictions on Gazan merchants. According to the Arab boycott laws, no Arab country, including Jordan, will import Gazan citrus that may have used raw materials or processing facilities originating in Israel. Consequently these countries have, in the past, limited the quantities of citrus that they will import from Gaza. Between 1975 and 1984, the percentage of citrus exported to East Jordan declined from 26 percent to 10.2 percent.[32] In addition, markets in the Gulf States are steadily contracting because of the economic pressures resulting from the fall in oil prices. As a result, many producers have turned to the limited capacity of local markets inside Gaza and the West Bank as a temporary outlet.

Restrictions on export markets also include the Israeli market. Presently, Gaza's farmers are prohibited from marketing most fruits and vegetables inside Israel, a measure designed to avoid competition with Israeli products. Certain products. such as strawberries, eggplants and zucchini, which are not competitive with Israeli products are allowed to enter Israel's markets through the Vegetable Marketing Board. Second-class citrus products are also exported to Israel from Gaza for use in juice factories.

Israeli producers, on the other hand, have unlimited access to Gazan markets, exporting substantial quantities of fruits and vegetables at prices with which Gazan farmers cannot compete.[33] In 1984, Israel exported 60,908 tons of fruits and vegetables to the Gaza Strip; no figures exist indicating Gaza's exports to Israel for that same year.[34] This one-sided trade structure has effectively turned the Strip into a dumping ground for Israeli produce and has created a situation in which the Gaza Strip and West Bank are second only to the United States as importers of Israeli goods while Palestinian producers, unable to compete, continue to have the highest production costs and the fewest markets.

Water restrictions. In the Gaza Strip, water consumption averages 100-120 million cubic meters per annum.[35] Ninety percent of this total is used to irrigate 45 percent of the Strip's agriculture; the remaining 10 percent is

32. Report of the GSCPA.

33. Interviews with Israeli officials in the Department of Defense and with rural development consultants to the U.S.-funded private voluntary organizations working in the Gaza Strip.

34. *Agricultural Statistics Quarterly 1984-1985.*

35. Elias H. Tuma and Haim Darin-Darbkin, *The Economic Case for Palestine* (London: Croom-Helm, 1978), p. 74, and interviews with municipal authorities in the Gaza Strip.

utilized for domestic consumption.[36] Farmers depend in large part on water reservoirs located in the Strip and in the eastern Negev region, areas where the soil is porous and where arid weather conditions prevail. Consistent overpumping, in conjunction with adverse ecological conditions, has lowered the water table and caused seawater to seep in. Consequently, water used for irrigation is becoming more saline and damaging the quality of Gaza's agriculture, particularly citrus. In light of the critical water problems inside Gaza, the Israeli government, through its affiliated water company, Mekorot, has issued restrictions against the digging of new wells and has limited the amount of water utilized by Palestinian farmers. In Gaza, farmers are limited to 800 cubic meters per year for hard soil and 1,000 cubic meters per year for sandy soil. Indeed, water quotas for Palestinian farmers have been fixed for over a decade, and overuse can draw severe fines.[37]

These same restrictions on water consumption, however, do not apply to the Israeli settlements inside the Strip, which have installed thirty-five to forty new wells in recent years.[38] Gaza's main water reservoir is located in the northern part of the Strip, where several Israeli settlements are located. Indeed, water consumption by Israeli settlers far exceeds that of Gazans. According to the Israeli Water Commission, in 1985 alone Israelis living in the Gaza Strip consumed 2,326 cubic meters of water per capita, compared with an average consumption of 123 cubic meters for every Gazan.[39] The water policies implemented by the Israeli government inside the Strip are plainly discriminatory and pose clear threats to the future of Palestinian agriculture, especially to citrus production.

36. Joe Stork, "Water and Israel's Occupation Strategy," *MERIP Reports* (July-August 1983), 13(6): 23; and Lesch, "Gaza: Forgotten Corner," p. 47. For some studies on water, see Leslie C. Schmida, "Israel's Drive for Water," Link (November 1984), 17(4); Subhi Kahhaleh, *The Water Problem in Israel and Its Repercussions on the Arab-Israeli Conflict*, IPS Papers no. 9 (Institute for Palestine Studies, 1981); and Miriam Lowi, *The Politics of Water*, McGill Studies in International Development no. 35 (Montreal: McGill University). For an Israeli interpretation, see J. Schwarz, "Water Resources for Judea, Samaria and the Gaza Strip," in Daniel Elazar, ed., *Judea, Samaria and Gaza: Views on the Present and Future* (Washington, D.C.: American Enterprise Institute, 1982), pp. 81-102.

37. Interview with Abu Middain, winter 1986 (see n. 29).

38. Interviews with members of the local engineers association in the Gaza Strip. Data on water consumption is extremely difficult to acquire.

39. See David Krivine's critique of Sara Roy, *The Gaza Strip Survey* (Jerusalem: The West Bank Data Base Project and Jerusalem Post Press, 1986) in "The Brighter Side of the Gaza Picture," *Jerusalem Post,* 5 September 1986.

Continued restrictions on the agricultural sector inside the Gaza Strip will most likely accelerate the process of decline which has already begun. Lack of investment by the Israeli government in Gazan agriculture, continued restrictions on export markets, unequal access to financial resources, increasing costs of agricultural production (particularly recurrent expenditures), and limitations on water usage have eliminated incentives for economic investment and have forced growing numbers of producers out of agriculture into employment inside Israel. Consequently, these measures have undermined the potential for structural growth inside Gaza's economy and the possibility of promoting independent economic activity. The policies contributing to the steady destructuring of Gaza's agricultural sector have had a similar impact upon the territory's industrial sector.

Industry – General Features and Major Constraints

The composition of the industrial sector (manufacturing and mining) has remained largely unchanged since before 1967, when it was highly undeveloped and productively limited. Low levels of investment by the Egyptian administration in favor of agriculture's clearly dominant position precluded capital accumulation within the industrial sector, thereby ensuring the sector's stagnation. Contributing approximately 4.5 percent to GDP in 1966, industry continues to provide only a small percentage of Gaza's GDP (11.6 percent in 1984) despite early increases in the level of industrial output after 1967.

Expansion in the industrial sector has been horizontal, based on existing production processes, rather than vertical. Characterized by the absence of structural innovation, Gaza's industrial base continues to be dominated by small-scale workshops which are owner operated and household in nature, and primarily service local demand.[40] In 1985, the Gaza Strip contained fourteen factories for toilet paper, three for cookies, two for notebooks, five for packaging oranges for export, and two for soft drinks. In addition, there are small workshops and cottage industries engaged in a variety of areas. Industrial production, therefore, remains focused on the processing of primary food products, textiles, clothing, leather, wood and metal products. In 1985, 1,630 industrial firms were functioning in the Gaza Strip, an increase from 430 in 1978 (see table 10.4).[41] Seventy percent of these firms

40. UNECWA, *The Industrial and Economic Trends in the West Bank and Gaza Strip* (ECWA/UNIDO Industrial Division, December 1981), p. 2.

41. *Statistical Abstract of Israel 1986.* Another study, published by UNIDO in March 1984, reports 1,015 industrial firms in the Gaza Strip. See also Hisham Awartani, *A Survey of Industries in the West Bank and Gaza Strip* (Bir Zeit, West Bank: Bir Zeit University, September 1979), p. 24. See also Jelal Daoud, Industry in the Gaza Strip," *SAMED*, August 1980.

were established after 1967. Yet the industrial sector employed only 17.5 percent of Gaza's labor force in 1985. Thus, it is clear that in light of the large numbers of Gazans who work inside Israel, the manufacturing sector

Table 10.4   **Gazan Industry, 1985**

	Other indust. prod.	Basic met., metal prod., elect. & trans. equip.	Wood and its products	Textiles, clothing, leather & its products	Food, bev. & tobacco	Total
TOTAL ESTABLISHMENTS	296(295)	349	342	536	107	1,630(1,628)
Persons empl. in est.						
1	16	121	114	137	55	443
2-3	175	166	167	136	26	670(669)
4-7	84	47	48	162	17	358
8-10	8	7	6	54	4	79
11-20	12	2	4	42	3	63
21 +	1	6	3	5	2	17
Total persons empl.	1,111	1,137	1,038	2,537	403	6,226
Thereof: employees	658	614	519	1,651	220	3,662(3,661)
Revenue ($1,000)	444	923	330	527	358	2,582(2,852)
Employee's daily wage (dollars)	3.42	6.79	4.04	2.02	3.79	3.42
Establishments engaging employees-total	259	147	150	317	40	913(912)
Persons empl. in est.						
1-4	203	107	114	108(109)	21	553
5-10	43	32	29	162	16	282
11-19	11	2	3	42	1	59
20-49	2	3	1	3	–	9
50+	–	3	3	2	2	10
Total persons empl.	1,046	837	759	2,217	301	5,160
Revenue ($1,000)	425	863	252	478	342	2,360
Establishments not engaging employees-total	37	202	192	219	67	717(716)
Total persons empl.	65	300	279	320	102	1,066
Revenue ($1,000)	18	60	78	49	16	221

SOURCE: *Statistical Abstract of Israel No. 37, 1986.*
(Note: Some errors in the original have been corrected; original numbers are in parentheses.)

has been unable to absorb labor released from the agricultural sector or compete effectively with employment opportunities across the green line.

Subcontracting between Israeli industrial firms and Gazan businessmen constitutes Israel's major form of investment in Gaza's economy. As part of the arrangement, Israeli contractors provide individual firms inside the territory with semi-processed raw materials. Using labor-intensive methods, these firms will complete the processing and deliver the finished product to the Israeli firm at a contracted price. The utilization of cheap labor and low overhead costs make subcontracting a profitable venture for Israelis, particularly as men and women are employed near their homes by small firms inside Gaza. Women are paid at relatively lower rates than men and at considerably lower rates than women working inside Israel (of whom there are only a few). Subcontracted products include textiles, carpets, clothing, furniture and shoes.

Although subcontracting has increased the level of employment and output inside Gaza, it has failed to create any structural changes in Gazan industry. Industrial output, for example, has largely remained the same since 1967, concentrated in traditional sectors of production – textiles, clothing and leather – which are highly labor intensive and which continue to employ the majority of Gaza's industrial labor force. Furthermore, another characteristic feature of economic development, increases in the size of industrial enterprises, has not occurred to any significant degree inside the territory. In 1985, 90.2 percent of the establishments inside Gaza in all branches of industry employed seven persons or less. Only 4.9 percent of firms employed eleven or more employees.[42]

Investment in Gaza's industrial sector similarly continues to depend on private initiatives. In 1980, 76.5 percent of industrial firms surveyed in the Strip indicated that their initial investment was derived from private sources; consequently, many of those firms have failed. Because of this and other limitations such as taxation and political instability, many industrial firms have been unable to expand or utilize their full productive capacity. In 1980, 22.4 percent of ninety-four firms surveyed inside the Gaza Strip indicated use of 50 percent or less of their productive capacity; 40.4 percent were able to utilize half of their capacity; 31.9 percent achieved levels of utilization up to 75 percent; but only 5.2 percent were operating at 90 percent or more of their total utilization levels.[43] Limited marketing opportunities have had the greatest impact on utilization capacity. Markets are limited primarily to Israel, which determines demand and controls the

42. *Statistical Abstract of Israel*, 1986.

43. UNECWA, *Industrial and Economic Trends*, p. 36.

level of industrial exports from the Strip. This not only prevents firms from operating at full capacity, but in the process precludes the absorption of surplus labor into the manufacturing sector and the efficient use of capital resources.

Despite increases in its share of GDP under Israeli rule, Gaza's industrial sector has been unable to grow beyond its traditional structural parameters. Thus, although industry has expanded, it has not developed. There are several factors militating against the development of the industrial sector inside the Gaza Strip beyond its present level. They fall into two categories: marketing, and investment.

Marketing problems. With the exception of those subcontracted industries which enjoy a slight labor advantage, most industries in Gaza confront strong competition from Israeli firms. Israeli manufacturers enjoy distinct advantages over their Palestinian counterparts which effectively weaken the latter's bargaining capacity. These advantages include access to private and public sources of credit, government protection policies which serve to control imports into Israel, export subsidies, tax breaks and investments, greater economies of scale resulting from the larger capacity and technological sophistication of Israeli industry, and levels of training among industrial workers.

Furthermore, the government of Israel, through the Ministry of Trade and Industry, has established between 300 and 350 industrial centers in the Gaza Strip and West Bank where production costs are lower than they are across the green line. Israeli investors willing to locate their businesses inside the occupied territories are provided with various financial incentives including ministerial grants for up to 39 percent of their equipment costs.[44] Indeed, during the first seven months of 1986, the Ministry of Trade and Industries budgeted approximately $19.5 million for grants to Israeli industries in the Gaza Strip and West Bank.[45] The majority of these enterprises are export oriented factories which enjoy the same marketing privileges as their counterparts located inside Israel. This stands in stark contrast to the strict controls on Gazan exports into Israel and the outright prohibition of Gazan exports to a number of other countries.

In addition to the limitations imposed upon Gazan industrial exports by the Israeli government, industrial manufacturers in the Strip, like their agricultural counterparts, suffer from Arab-imposed export restrictions. The

44. "Business as Usual in the Occupied Territories," *News from Within* (Jerusalem), 26 January 1987, cited in "The Business of Occupation," *Palestine Perspectives* (May-June 1987), 29: 4.

45. *Ibid. Jerusalem Post,* 25 December 1986, published a report citing this figure.

Arab boycott of industrial products from Gaza has, since 1982, resulted in the total termination of any industrial export from the Strip.

The closure of certain markets to Gaza's manufacturers and the limited access to others, have forced Palestinians to focus inward on local markets and have, in the process, fostered a great deal of intra-market competition. Local competition inside Gaza is not regulated by policies to control competitive behavior. Hence, in the absence of these policies, the weaker and smaller firms are often defeated by their stronger and larger counterparts, further eroding any possibility for an industrial infrastructure to develop inside the territory.

Lack of investment. The lack of capital investment in Gaza's industrial sector by private and public sources has contributed greatly to the sector's stagnation. The political instabilities confronting the region make any form of investment by local Arab entrepreneurs extremely risky. Under present political arrangements, furthermore, Israelis have no reason to invest in the development of an industry that will compete with their own. Indeed, Israel's closure of all Arab banks and financial institutions after 1967 and the state's refusal to provide credit institutions inside the territories, have deprived the Strip of a critical source of funding. After 1967, credit facilities depended largely on a special government fund which was consistently reduced and finally eliminated altogether in 1981. Between 1969 and 1972, the Israeli government did grant Palestinian industry some loans, which amounted to $500,000, but since 1980 these loans have been unavailable.[46]

In 1981, the Bank of Palestine was allowed to reopen in Gaza, but it is prohibited from dealing in foreign currency, creating a major disincentive for borrowers. The Israeli banks presently operating in the Gaza Strip deal in foreign currency but are disinclined to make industrial loans. Moreover, the high interest rates charged and the onus of dealing with Israeli institutions effectively limit the number of Palestinian borrowers. In November 1986 a branch of the Cairo-Amman bank was opened in Nablus for use by Palestinians. The bank deals in Israeli shekels and Jordanian dinars. At present, however, only West Bankers can use the two currencies; Palestinians from Gaza wishing to use the bank are restricted to Israeli shekels.

Another form of investment inside local industry comes from the United States government as part of a program of direct assistance to the Palestinian people. However, U.S. foreign aid earmarked for industrial development projects inside the Gaza Strip and West Bank has been

46. *Al-Fajr,* 13 April 1984.

redirected by Israeli authorities. Between 1975 and 1983, only one-third of projects proposed for industrial development in the occupied territories were approved by the government of Israel.[47]

The lack of capital investment similarly affects the creation of other institutions designed to support the development of an industrial infrastructure. For example, the Strip does not have an indigenous municipal industrial zone, a critical component of industrial development generally. The Israelis have established an industrial zone at Erez, on Gaza's northern border with Israel. Local industry remains unaffected by this zone except for the limited employment opportunities it generates for Gaza's labor force, who produce assembly parts and completed products for Israeli industries.

The lack of growth in Gazan industry has resulted from policies which Meron Benvenisti has termed a form of "integration and exclusion": integration into the dominant economy when it benefits that economy and exclusion when it does not. This has created an industrial base inside the Gaza Strip of limited production, absorption and marketing capabilities. Consequently, the Strip has been unable to develop the infrastructure needed to accumulate capital on a level adequate to support and promote industrial growth. In effect, industry inside the Gaza Strip remains highly dependent upon Israel to generate activity within it.

Trade Patterns

The weakened potential for economic growth inside individual economic sectors is underlined dramatically by the foreign trade patterns which have evolved between the Gaza Strip and Israel since 1967. These patterns clearly reflect the structural alterations in the political relationship between the two actors.

Prior to 1967, agricultural exports and industrial imports characterized visible trade in the Gaza Strip. Imports exceeded exports, and between 1950 and 1966, the resulting trade deficit steadily increased, from 851,000 to 5.646 million Egyptian pounds.[48]

Exports from Gaza during this period consisted largely of agricultural products, while manufactured products constituted the bulk of Gaza's imports. Gaza's lenient import policies before 1967 also led to the

47. Meron Benvenisti, *U.S. Government Funded Projects in the West Bank and Gaza (1977-1983) (Palestinian Sector)* Working Paper no. 13 (Jerusalem: West Bank Data Base Project, 1984).

48. Abu-Amr *Gaza Economy.*

importation of goods which eventually were sold in Egyptian markets. Indeed, prior to 1967, Gaza traded primarily with Egypt, who supplied close to 50 percent of the Strip's imports. Gaza also traded with parts of Western and Eastern Europe, while no trade existed with Israel, Jordan or the West Bank.

The most dramatic change in Gaza's trading patterns after 1967 lies in the direction of her trade. Within one year of Israeli rule, trade with Egypt was terminated, and trade with Israel, Jordan and the West Bank began.

In 1968, exports to Israel accounted for 29 percent of Gaza's total exports, while exports to Jordan (and the West Bank) comprised 18 percent, and those sent overseas equaled 54 percent.[49] The very high percentage of overseas exports reflected fulfillment of citrus contracts arranged before 1967. Import ratios for 1968 dramatically reflected Gaza's changing foreign trade relationships. For example, goods received from overseas comprised only 27 percent of total imports to the Gaza Strip, those from Jordan 1.4 percent, and goods from Israel 71 percent.[50] The low imports from Jordan resulted from Israeli policies which allowed Gaza to export to but not import from that country. Since 1973, imports from Israel have, on the average, accounted for over 90 percent of Gaza's total imports. The remainder are imported from other countries, primarily Eastern Europe (see table 10.5). Imports from Eastern Europe, which accounted for 8.1 percent of total imports in 1985, consisted mainly of manufactured products received as barter for citrus exports. This relatively low percentage of imports from overseas markets has resulted, in large part, from Israeli-imposed tariffs which give Israel a comparative advantage over foreign competitors. Imports from Jordan continue to be prohibited.

Export patterns between 1973 and the present reveal increases in Gaza's exports to Israel through 1985. The level of goods sent to Jordan increased to a high of 30.4 percent in 1977 but has declined since then to a 1985 level of 13.8 percent of total exports, all of which were citrus products. However, of Gaza's total agricultural exports in 1984, 54.2 percent went to Jordan.[51] Exports to other countries have steadily fallen since 1973, dropping from 54 percent in 1968 to 4 percent in 1985, and similarly consist of agricultural products.

Since 1967 Israel has become Gaza's largest trading partner, followed by Jordan. In 1985, Israel received 82.2 percent of the Strip's exports and

49. Van Arkadie, *Benefits and Burdens,* p. 79.

50. *Ibid.*

51. *Judea, Samaria and Gaza Area Statistics, 1985.*

Table 10.5 **Imports and exports – Gaza Strip (selected years)**
(U.S. $ million)

	1978	%	1979	%	1980	%	1981	%	1982	%	1983	%	1984	%	1985	%
IMPORTS																
Total	**204.9**	*100.0*	**219.7**	*100.0*	**260.9**	*100.0*	**309.5**	*100.0*	**310.4**	*100.0*	**332.1**	*100.0*	**279.4**	*100.0*	**281.4**	*100.0*
From Israel	186.7	*91.1*	195.3	*88.9*	231.8	*88.9*	282.6	*91.3*	282.0	*90.8*	305.7	*92.1*	256.8	*91.9*	258.5	*91.9*
From Jordan	0.0	*0.0*	0.0	*0.0*	0.0	*0.0*	0.0	*0.0*	0.0	*0.0*	0.0	*0.0*	0.0	*0.0*	0.0	*0.0*
From other countries	18.2	*8.9*	24.4	*11.1*	29.0	*11.1*	26.9	*8.7*	28.4	*9.2*	26.4	*7.9*	22.6	*8.1*	22.9	*8.1*
EXPORTS																
Total	**122.3**	*100.0*	**123.5**	*100.0*	**154.2**	*100.0*	**197.8**	*100.0*	**190.0**	*100.0*	**180.6**	*100.0*	**114.9**	*100.0*	**116.9**	*100.0*
To Israel	79.9	*65.3*	80.0	*64.8*	113.1	*73.3*	159.1	*80.4*	149.4	*78.6*	151.1	*83.7*	95.8	*83.4*	96.1	*82.2*
To Jordan	33.7	*27.6*	34.2	*27.7*	31.3	*20.3*	31.2	*15.8*	34.5	*18.2*	22.5	*12.5*	14.9	*13.0*	16.1	*13.8*
To other countries	8.7	*7.1*	9.3	*7.5*	9.8	*6.4*	7.5	*3.8*	6.1	*3.2*	7.0	*3.8*	4.2	*3.6*	4.7	*4.0*

SOURCES: *Statistical Abstract of Israel No. 36, 1985* and *No. 37, 1986,* and calculations from the same sources.

supplied the Strip with 91.9 percent of its imports.[52] Gaza's exports to Israel are predominantly industrial products, the majority of which are subcontracted by Israeli merchants. In 1984, industrial and agricultural exports to Israel accounted for 100 and 31 percent of total industrial and agricultural exports respectively; however, the absolute level of exports has fallen since 1983 (see table 10.6).

Imports from Israel similarly comprise a substantial share of Gaza's trade. In 1984, industrial products imported from Israel comprised 93.1 percent of total industrial imports to the Gaza Strip. These goods consisted of durable and non-durable consumer items, construction materials and raw materials for domestic industry. Agricultural commodities originating in Israel accounted for 85 percent of the Strip's total imports in agriculture, and consisted largely of fruits, vegetables, poultry and eggs.[53]

In 1985, Gaza's trade deficit equalled $164.5 million, of which $162.4 million was accrued in trade with Israel. The trade balance with Jordan is positive since no imports from Jordan are allowed, giving the Strip a modest surplus. The deficit in Gaza's balance of trade has been financed by wages earned by Gazan workers inside Israel, external remittances, and the surplus accrued in trade with Jordan.

The trading patterns of the Gaza Strip have been dramatically restructured since 1967. It is quite apparent that in becoming Israel's major trading partner, the Gaza Strip has been placed in an increasingly dependent and vulnerable position. The structural reorientation in the territory's foreign trade has resulted from a series of Israeli measures which have created and sustained direct ties between the two economies.

The first measure, dubbed the "open bridges" policy, was enacted within a year of Israeli rule and resulted in the creation of trade with Jordan. Designed to prevent competition between Israeli and Palestinian products, the "open bridges" were open one way only, precluding the development of trade between Jordan and the territories beyond a specific level. Another measure enacted by the authorities imposed a system of tariffs and duties on the importation of goods through Israel. This measure places Israel in an advantageous trading position with Gaza and has limited the Strip's access to most foreign markets.

Perhaps the two most damaging measures affecting the trade structure of the Gaza Strip are directed towards the protection of the Israeli market. One measure imposes quotas on the type and amount of production that can be exported to Israel from the Gaza Strip, and the second removes all

52. *Statistical Abstract of Israel, 1986.*

53. Gharaibeh, *Economies,* p. 113.

Table 10.6   **Imports and Exports by Sector-Gaza Strip (selected years) (U.S. $ million)**

				1985	
	1982	1983	1984	I-III	IV-VI
IMPORTS-TOTAL	310.4	332.1	279.4	57.3	66.5
From Israel-total	282.0	305.7	256.8	52.3	60.6
Agricultural products	31.3	37.9	35.5	7.8	*na*
Industrial products	250.7	267.8	221.3	44.5	*na*
From Jordan-total	–	–	–	–	–
Agricultural products	–	–	–	–	–
Industrial products	–	–	–	–	–
From other countries-total	28.4	26.4	22.6	5.0	5.9
Agricultural products	5.5	7.0	6.3	1.5	2.1
Industrial products	22.9	19.4	16.3	3.5	3.8
EXPORTS-TOTAL	190.0	180.6	114.9	25.2	26.5
To Israel-total	149.4	151.1	95.8	16.9	19.1
Agricultural products	16.6	17.2	8.4	3.6	*na*
Industrial products	132.8	133.9	87.4	13.4	*na*
To Jordan-total	34.5	22.5	14.9	6.3	7.4
Agricultural products	34.5	22.5	14.9	6.3	7.4
Industrial products	0.0	0.0	–	0.0	0.0
To other countries-total	6.1	7.0	4.2	2.0	–
Agricultural products	6.1	7.0	4.2	2.0	–
Industrial products	0.0	0.0	0.0	0.0	–

SOURCE: Israel Central Bureau of Statistics, *Judea, Samaria and Gaza Area Statistics,* vol. 15, 2d quarter (Jerusalem, 1985).

restrictions on the flow of goods into the Strip from Israel. As a result, Gaza has become a repository for Israeli goods against which it cannot compete, ensuring Israeli producers against any future competition and providing the Israeli economy with an uncontested and captive market.

Public Finance

Another measure of government policy toward economic activity in the occupied territories is public finance, or the level of government services, expressed monetarily, which are provided to area inhabitants.

Since the beginning of Israeli rule, government expenditure inside the Gaza Strip has declined relative to GNP from 20 percent prior to 1967 to 9.8 percent in 1983.[54] A considerable portion of this expenditure was provided by UNRWA and the Egyptian administration, particularly in the areas of health and education. In 1986, the state of Israel reported a total budget for the Gaza Strip of $52.5 million (see tables 10.7a and 10.7b). Of this number, $45.2 million constituted the regular budget or expenditure, and $7.3 million comprised the development budget or investment.

In 1986, close to 53 million shekels or $35 million of revenue was collected inside the Gaza Strip. The contribution of internal revenues to the total budget that year was 67 percent – an increase from 58 percent the previous year. The Israeli government contributed the remaining third or approximately $17.5 million to cover the resulting deficit. These monies are taken from that portion of the Israeli budget known as the *Keren Hanikuyim,* the deduction fund, which constitutes the sums deducted at source from Gazan laborers employed in Israel. Current estimates indicate that Gazans who are employed inside Israel pay $2-3 million per month to the Israeli government in taxes and social security, producing an annual figure greater than the $17.5 million contributed by the government to Gaza's budget.[55] Consequently, the Gaza Strip does not appear to cost the Israeli taxpayer any money.

The Gaza Strip, furthermore, contributes substantial sums to Israeli public consumption through what is known as the occupation tax. Gaza's balance of payments (as published by the Central Bureau of Statistics and the Bank of Israel) focuses on what are termed government transfers, indicated in turn by "credits" and "debits." Transfers reveal that the deficit of the military government is paid by the Israeli government (credit) minus deductions collected from Gazans working in Israel (debit). Since the late 1970s, deductions collected from Gazans have exceeded Israeli payments, resulting in net transfers of money from Gaza into Israel that equaled 447 million (old) Israeli shekels in 1983 and 762 million old shekels in 1984. If we add the revenue accruing to the state in the form of indirect taxation (Israeli VAT, not Gazan VAT, which remains inside Gaza), which in 1984 amounted to approximately $20 million, it becomes apparent that if the Israeli treasury were to lose the Gaza market and Gaza laborers, it would lose direct and

54. *Ibid.,* pp. 100-102.

55. According to Meron Benvenisti of the West Bank Data Base Project, spring 1986. See also State of Israel, *State of Israel Budget 1986-1987* (Jerusalem, 1986).

indirect revenues amounting to $25-27.5 million per year.[56]

Table 10.7a   **Government Expenditure in the Gaza Strip**
                    Regular Budget (million shekels)

	1986	% of total	1985	% of total
Total budget	68,248	100.00	31,145	100.00
Education	22,411	33.00	10,325	33.00
Health	24,003	35.00	10,893	35.00
Welfare	5,518	0.80	2,548	0.80
Industry & commerce	206	0.03	98	0.03
Transport	517	0.07	224	0.07

Table 10.7b   **Government Investment in the Gaza Strip**
                    Development Budget (million shekels)

	1986	% of total	1985	% of total
Total budget	10,944	100.00	5,163	100.00
Loans to local gov't.	5,572	51.00	2,546	49.20
Agriculture	82	0.07	52	0.10
Planning & infrastructure	632	0.60	4	0.01
School construc.	2,029	18.50	1,248	24.20
Health	2,074	19.00	606	11.70
Welfare	101	0.09	40	0.08
Telephone	106	0.10	210	0.40
Reserve	348	0.30	258	0.50
Misc.	–	–	199	0.40

SOURCE: State of Israel, *Budget for 1986/87* (Jerusalem, 1986).
(Note: Not all items are included; percentages will not add up to 100 per cent.)

56. See Meron Benvenisti, "Gaza's Not So Bright Side," *Jerusalem Post*, 10
September 1986. This article was written in response to Krivine's critique (see n. 39).
Financial data was taken from the Bank of Israel Reports on the Administered
Territories.

The low level of government expenditure inside the Gaza Strip is further highlighted by the role of external sources of revenue in Gaza's economy. Loans advanced to local authorities from the Gulf States and from Jordan, for example, have consistently been used for municipal improvements, construction of public buildings and other development projects. Investment projects in the Gaza Strip have also been financed by the United States government through a program of development assistance to the occupied territories that contributed $42.2 million in direct aid between 1975 and 1984.[57] Usually implemented through Gaza's municipalities, projects financed under the U.S. program have focused on water conservation and sewage treatment. UNRWA is also responsible for a certain percentage of public investment expenditure through its construction of domiciles, schools and health clinics, staff salaries and relief aid.

The income and expenditure of towns in the Gaza Strip further reveal decreasing levels of government investment inside the local economy. For the most part, the budgets of towns in the Strip have been balanced since 1967. Table 10.8 indicates that between 1983 and 1985, towns have enjoyed a small surplus, revealing a revenue base that is small and largely dependent upon user charges in water and electricity for income. It is also clear that Gaza's municipalities rely, in part, on external funds for capital and development expenditure (extraordinary budget). Grants from Israel's civil administration to the extraordinary budget, however, have declined 44 percent between 1983 and 1985, dropping from 20.6 percent of total revenue in 1983 to 11.5 percent in 1985. Hence, low levels of government investment and high levels of government revenue stand out against the steady deterioration of living conditions and the poverty inside the Gaza Strip.

DEMOGRAPHY AND LAND

The pressures which currently foster the weakening of the economic sector inside Gaza are likely to worsen in relation to the demographic patterns of the territory. The age structure of the Gaza Strip is very young, with nearly half the population fourteen years of age and younger. Between 1977 and 1984 the two youngest age groups grew 9 percent (ages 0-4 years) and 34 percent (5-9). For that portion of the population composed of adults

---

57. U.S. Department of State, *Background on U.S. Government Funded Assistance Programs in the West Bank and Gaza* (unpublished document) (Tel Aviv: U.S. Embassy, 1982); and U.S. International Development Cooperation Agency, *AID-Supported Programs in the West Bank and Gaza as of September 30, 1984* (Washington, D.C.: Agency for International Development, 1984).

Table 10.8 **Income and Expenditure of Towns in the Gaza Strip**
(NIS at current prices)

	1985/86	1984/85	1983/84
Income-grand total	**37,692,266**	**8,386,388**	**1,596,269**
Ordinary budget-total	**31,072,259**	**6,284,130**	**1,127,570**
Ordinary income	7,021,288	1,505,107	286,063
Rates & fees	1,024,948	248,996	48,436
Municipal property	2,606,136	403,258	92,805
Other services	1,652,778	435,045	78,704
Miscellaneous	1,737,426	417,808	66,118
Establishments	24,050,971	4,779,023	841,507
Water	4,126,920	816,125	148,228
Electricity	19,660,896	3,892,592	679,655
Sewage	263,155	70,306	13,624
Extraordinary budget-total	**6,620,007**	**2,102,258**	**468,699**
Grants from civil adm.	4,338,930	1,477,887	329,432
Participation of owners & self-financing	1,529,323	290,112	64,600
Other [transfers from external factors]	751,754	334,259	74,667
Expenditure-grand total	**29,534,416**	**8,079,466**	**1,512,204**
Ordinary budget-total	**23,024,837**	**5,977,208**	**1,078,398**
Ordinary expenses	5,181,242	1,389,333	244,798
General administration	1,347,872	445,770	85,320
Sanitation	2,276,490	703,011	122,968
Public works	625,616	177,174	31,232
Miscellaneous	32,839	63,378	5,278
Establishments	17,843,595	4,458,359	783,081
Water	2,412,047	548,378	99,313
Electricity	15,154,659	3,808,941	668,582
Sewage	276,889	101,040	15,186
Transfers to extra ordinary budget	811,525	129,516	50,519
Extraordinary budget-total	**6,509,579**	**2,102,258**	**433,806**
Public property	1,809,796	645,393	133,134
Establishments	4,061,444	773,631	159,686
Other	638,339	683,234	140,986

SOURCES: *Statistical Abstract of Israel No. 36, 1985* (1983-1985).
Statistical Abstract of Israel No. 37, 1986 (1985-1986).

of prime working and reproductive age, rates of increase are similarly high: 10 percent for ages 20-24; 45 percent for ages 25-29; and 46 percent for ages 30-34.[58]

The demographic implications of these growth rates are indeed great. For as more people become available for marriage, the natality (birth rate) of the population can be expected to rise. Consequently, if mortality and fertility rates continue to decline slowly as they have in recent years, and the emigration balance and rate of natural increase remain constant at 1985 levels, Gazans could number close to one million people by the year 2000. From an economic perspective, therefore, larger numbers of young men and women will seek employment, probably inside Israel, exacerbating the level of economic dependency upon Israel and the attendant problems.

Moreover, the predicted population growth inside the Gaza Strip does not appear to be accompanied by increases in the land area available to accommodate such growth. To the contrary, Arab land inside the Strip has steadily declined since 1967, contributing further to the weakening of the economic structure. Through its land policies, the state of Israel has acquired one-third of the territory of the Gaza Strip, portions of which are used for the establishment of Israeli settlements. In so doing, Israel has deprived the Palestinian population of a significant part of its productive economic base and source of wealth, and has limited the ability of that population to expand physically. By 1986, there were eighteen Israeli settlements in the Gaza Strip, inhabited by approximately 2,150 people. The settlements occupy a known figure of 22,250 dunums (5,562 acres) of land, yielding an average of 10.4 dunums (2.6 acres) of land for each Israeli settler.[59]

This figure contrasts starkly with land ratios for the Arab population. According to the 1985-86 Report of the Military Government, Gaza's eight refugee camps presently occupy 5,500 dunums (1,375 acres) of state land, yielding .02 dunums (.006 acre) per Gazan refugee. During 1985, the government of Israel allotted an additional 3,500 dunums (875 acres) for the construction of refugee housing projects. Given a population density of 3,754 per square mile, it is clear that, legalities aside, land allocations between the Israeli and Arab populations in the Gaza Strip are highly discriminatory. Given the demographic trends among Arab residents of the territory, the inability to expand beyond present borders coupled with plans to increase the number of Israeli settlements inside Gaza, will clearly intensify the level of economic and political discord between the two populations living there.

58. *Statistical Abstract of Israel, 1986.*

59. Based on calculations from Kana'na and al-Madani, *Qita Ghazza 1967-1984,* p. 32. See also Lesch, *Gaza Strip,* Part 2, and *al-Fajr,* 18 October 1985, pp. 8-9.

SOCIAL CLASS STRUCTURE

Israel's occupation of the Gaza Strip has had a significant impact on the economic structure of the territory. Economic change has created social change. Perhaps the most dramatic development in the social structure of the Gaza Strip since 1967 has been the formation of certain, albeit loose, alliances across classes who before 1967 were totally isolated from each other. These alliances are based almost exclusively on nationalist politics. Although they have not breached the isolation of Gaza's social classes on an economic level, alliances have brought together members of Gaza's elite, farmer, petite bourgeoisie and working classes[60] in a common stand against the political consequences of the occupation. The occupation has affected these four groups in different ways and to varying degrees.

The *upper class* is relatively small, composed primarily of Gaza's landed elite, capitalist farmers and large merchants. This particular social class is distinguished by its lineage, the majority being direct descendants of the territory's original inhabitants. The occupation has produced little if any change in the size and composition of this class, which continues to depend on export trade for its income.

Unlike their upperclass counterparts, *farmers* as a group have been more severely affected by the economic dislocations resulting from the occupation. Primarily small and tenant farmers producing for profit and subsistence, many members of this class have become temporary laborers inside Israel. However, as indicated earlier, the number of individuals engaged in domestic farming activities has decreased since 1967, although many small farmers have returned to domestic agriculture in times of recession.

The *petite bourgeoisie* is composed of three categories. The largest consists of professionals, including academics, engineers, teachers, and administrative staff employed by UNRWA. Second in size are self-employed entrepreneurs in the commerce and service occupations. Few changes have occurred in the size and composition of both these groups since 1967 despite decreased job opportunities for professionals and fluctuating markets for merchants. Academics and engineers have either emigrated from the Strip or have become wage laborers inside Israel. Gazan merchants have in large part replaced their pre-1967 Egyptian customers with local ones.

The third group comprising the petite bourgeoisie consists of the self-employed in small industry and trade, whose numbers have been declining since 1970. Forced out of business by Israeli competition and lack of

60. Divisions taken from Metzger, Orth, and Sterzling, p. 127.

capital, many local craftsmen and contractors have been proletarianized, joining the ranks of wage labor inside Israel.

Employment opportunities inside Israel have directly affected the composition and size of the *working class* inside Gaza, contributing greatly to the formation of a proletariat inside the Strip. Drawn mainly from the marginalized refugee population and the groups mentioned above, Gaza's working class has increased significantly during the post-1967 period both in relative and absolute terms.

The economic consequences of occupation have varied across social class. The upper classes, for example, are better equipped than the working classes to withstand and compensate for the economic contractions produced by the occupation. The relative threat to the former is considerably less than to the latter, precluding alliances between classes based on common economic interests. However, it can be argued that although increasing economic integration with Israel has, on the one hand, reinforced many aspects of Gaza's pre-1967 class structure, it has on the other hand contributed to the development of a common political consciousness across classes, despite the clear political differences remaining between them.

CONCLUSION

In twenty years of Israeli rule, the Gaza Strip has undergone several changes. Perhaps the most dramatic of these changes have been economic. From one perspective, Israel's occupation has introduced limited economic prosperity into an economy that prior to 1967 was largely undeveloped and stagnant. This prosperity has resulted primarily from the creation of wage labor inside Israel and the comparatively high incomes earned by Palestinian workers within the Israeli economy, and remittances from Palestinian workers abroad. Domestically, the number of industrial establishments has grown since 1967, in part because of the availability of larger amounts of capital and subcontracting arrangements with Israeli business concerns. Capital derived from foreign Arab sources has contributed to the expansion of Gazan industry as well. Agriculture similarly enjoyed increasing levels of output through 1975 and the availability of Arab markets, in particular, led to relatively large increases in agriculture's share of GDP.

On the other hand, however, the Gazan economy has not developed. The higher incomes earned by Palestinian labor inside Israel, for example, have not stimulated economic growth, since these incomes are neither generated within the local economy nor invested within that economy. Low levels of investment in Gaza's economic sectors by the Israeli government have not only contributed directly to the stagnation of those sectors, but have discouraged similar forms of investment by other actors. Consequently, higher incomes obtained in Israel as well as remittances from abroad are used to purchase durable consumer goods, largely produced or acquired through Israel. This, in turn, has resulted in increased levels of consumerism within the Gaza Strip with little, if any, of the economic benefits derived from such consumerism accruing to the Strip. Indeed, in 1984, 66.8 percent of the National Disposable Income of the Gaza Strip went into private consumption.[61]

The economic benefits obtained by the Gaza Strip have clearly been achieved without any radical change in the resource base of the territory's economy. On the contrary, Gaza's limited prosperity has been attained within a framework of constraints, both natural and imposed, political as well as economic, which have, over two decades of occupation, accelerated Gaza's economic integration into Israel. As a result, not only is the local economy increasingly shaped by and adjusted to economic demand across the green line, but it has grown inappropriately dependent upon externally generated sources of revenue.

The lack of economic development inside the Gaza Strip has been the result of specific Israeli policies which have aimed to restrict and have, in effect, undermined the ability of the Gazan economy to create the necessary infrastructure required for sustained economic growth. Some of the policies contributing to Gaza's economic decline include: 1) restrictions on most forms of political activity which could support and complement economic growth; 2) low levels of governmental investment in social and economic infrastructure and development inside the Gaza Strip; 3) tax laws which discriminate against the Palestinian producer and weaken his economic bargaining position; 4) a lack of financial incentives, supports and guarantees for Palestinian producers, commonly available to their Israeli counterparts; 5) strict control over Gaza's terms of trade which has resulted in restricted access to foreign markets (other than Israel and specific countries in the Arab world and Eastern Europe where Israel cannot trade) and in little, if any, protection from the importation of Israeli goods; 6) restrictions on certain forms of economic activity such as the creation of industrial zones, union organizing, establishment of factories, cooperatives and other business enterprises, research and training; 7) prohibitions on the development of credit facilities and other financial institutions; 8) the growing dispossession of land from the Palestinian sector; and 9) the lack of political, economic and social linkages between Israeli and Palestinian groups, between Palestinian and other, foreign groups and, to a lesser degree, among Palestinians themselves (particularly along economic lines).

61. *Statistical Abstract of Israel, 1986.*

Furthermore, declining economic conditions inside the Arab world have resulted in fewer job opportunities for Palestinian labor, thereby reducing the level of foreign remittances flowing into the occupied territories.

Thus, when viewed against the lack of economic growth inside Gaza, the economic prosperity which has accrued to the inhabitants of the territory appears to have derived from a declining, rather than an increasing, set of economic options. The high percentage of Gazan labor in Israel, for example, is not a function of a society experiencing typical patterns associated with the process of industrialization (or modernization) in which labor gradually shifts from agricultural to nonagricultural activities, resulting in changes in labor's spatial location and occupational status. Rather, for Gaza's labor force, the decision to seek employment inside Israel is a function of the lack of comparable options inside Gaza's domestic economy. This contention is supported by the growing number of Gazan agriculturalists who are joining the ranks of wage labor inside Israel due to their financial inability to sustain domestic production. The highly educated among Gaza's labor force, similarly, are seeking gainful employment in semiskilled and unskilled professions inside the Israeli economy, not out of choice but of necessity.

Continued restrictions on economic activity by the Israeli military government threaten to dispossess the Palestinian producer of his means of production. As fewer jobs become available domestically and as land continues to diminish as a source of income, the local economy will become less viable in terms of its ability to absorb and utilize growing levels of Palestinian labor and to provide a functional, if not competitive alternative to wage labor inside Israel. Concomitantly, the labor force of the Gaza Strip will become increasingly proletarianized and dependent upon employment across the green line.

Without fundamental changes in the structural relationships within Gaza's economy and between the economy and Israel's, "prosperity" can be only ephemeral and short-lived. In the long term, this prosperity will be detrimental, for it not only intensifies existing dependencies, but in the process weakens and atrophies the ability of the economic structure to sustain itself, innovate and grow. As Gaza's economy becomes less and less able to function within existing (and future) constraints, the debilitation of that economy is likely to accelerate. In this sense, economic development inside the Gaza Strip should not be measured against pre-1967 conditions as is often the case, but against the standards of another alternative, that of structural transformation.[62]

62. Benvenisti, *West Bank Data Project* makes this point.

CHAPTER 11

The Economic Consequences
of the Occupation

Sarah Graham-Brown

INTRODUCTION

Few would dispute that the twenty-one year period of Israeli occupation since 1967 has brought major changes to the economies of the West Bank and Gaza Strip. These changes have occurred in part because of direct Israeli interventions on the economic level, reshaping patterns of trade and redirecting the labor force. But there have also been numerous and sometimes unexpected side effects in both the economic and social spheres.

However, in this author's view, whatever measures the Israelis may have taken to bend the territories' economies to suit their interests, and may be expected to continue to do while the occupation lasts, it is political considerations reaching far beyond the territories that will finally determine their economic and political future.

If, on the other hand, some settlement were reached whereby the territories, or at least the West Bank, became a Palestinian entity, a whole new set of circumstances would be created which would alter the economic realities of today. At present, these possibilities must remain matters of conjecture. What can be established is the degree to which Israeli policies and the pressures of its own economy have encroached upon the West Bank and Gaza economies and have changed or narrowed the options for economic maneuver. This in turn may indicate some of the ways these economies would respond to new political situations.

A Note on Statistics

A word should be said first of all about the quality of the socio-economic information which is available. The main source of statistics is the Israeli Central Bureau of Statistics, which produces annual abstracts and quarterly statistics on the occupied territories (described as the "Administered Areas" or "Judea Samaria and Gaza"). Where possible statistics from Palestinian or Jordanian sources or from international agencies have been used, but these are rarely available in a systematic form. There are now a few local sample surveys and studies on particular towns, villages or districts, and on subjects such as housing and education. These are quoted where they are relevant, but in the West Bank, where there are marked regional variations in economic and social conditions, generalizations cannot safely be made from them. Most of these studies are the work of staff and students at West Bank universities, particularly Bir Zeit and al-Najah, and of the Jerusalem-based Arab Thought Forum. Unfortunately no comparable body of work exists for Gaza – hence the quality and reliability of data on that area is generally lower.

In 1980, the Palestine National Fund in Damascus began producing a statistical yearbook of Palestine containing a section on the occupied territories, but ironically they were forced by the lack of alternative data to rely heavily on Israeli sources. In the same way, Meron Benvenisti's *West Bank Data Project* uses for the most part Israeli official statistics, although it treats them from a critical standpoint. Sara Roy's study of Gaza, published under the auspices of the Data Project, supplements official sources with empirical observations.

Given the role of Israel as an occupying power, these statistics certainly need to be used with considerable caution. Not only do the Israelis have a vested interest in making conditions in the territories look as favorable as possible, but the statistics are also distorted by the assumptions upon which they have been based. Benvenisti gives the following account of these assumptions:

> This system of accounting began immediately after the occupation and emanated from the assumption that the economy of the territories would remain separate and independent – an assumption resulting from fear that they might become a burden on the Israeli economy. The method persisted even though the assumption of economic separation was quickly invalidated by objective conditions and as a consequence of the economic integration policy pursued by all Israeli governments.
> . . .
> The daily, complex, economic interactions over the nonexistent green line, the movement of tens of thousands of workers, the transfer of goods and services worth hundreds of millions of dollars, lacking any effective monitoring and control – all these call the reliability of the statistics into question. At the end of the 1970's the

"national economy" model for the West Bank and Gaza Strip also lost its territorial basis. None of the activity in the Jewish settlements, nor the infrastructure investments of the Jewish Agency, were included in the national accounts of the territories. Israeli activity was included in Israel's account. . . .At the beginning of the 1980s the national accounts of the territories became merely instruments for reporting the economic activity of the Palestinian population, completely integrated into the Israeli system, but effectively isolated from it, in such a way as to serve Israel's own political and economic interests.[1]

The very high levels of inflation in recent years, which have affected the occupied territories as well as Israel, have had a particularly distorting effect on statistics based on monetary measures, for example those relating to wages, remittances and national income. In some cases, these figures are also given at constant prices, but as the base year has now been altered from 1976 to 1981 (when the New Shekel was introduced) figures for the 1970s are not always comparable with those for the 1980s. Population estimates were also revised as from 1982, based on new parameters for counting births and deaths, so that pre-1982 figures are not absolutely comparable with post-1982 figures.

Furthermore, the statistical indicators provided are not always consistent year by year, and particularly in sectors such as health and education there has been a marked reduction in the amount of statistical detail provided. Certain categories of data are known to be unreliable: for example, the figure for the number of workers from the occupied territories employed in Israel only includes those who are registered at labor exchanges and does not take into account the large numbers of "unofficial workers." There is also disagreement on, for example, such measures of the health of the population as the infant mortality rate. Palestinian sources argue that the Israeli figure represents a considerable underestimate, because many infant deaths are not reported to authorities. The Israelis now acknowledge that there is a problem of underreporting, but claim that they take this into account in their calculations. Most other observers still consider their figure too low.

If there are difficulties with statistical data on the West Bank and Gaza Strip, trying to extract information on economic and social conditions of Palestinians in annexed east Jerusalem and the Old City is equally problematic, as most such data are integrated into statistics on "greater Jerusalem," including both Israeli urban settlements within the city and west Jerusalem.

1. Meron Benvenisti, *The West Bank Handbook: a Political Lexicon* (Jerusalem: Jerusalem Post, 1986), pp. 158-59.

As far as data on population, housing, families, and other sociological aspects of the territories, most of the evidence is extrapolated from the 1967 census (which does include east Jerusalem), which was taken immediately after the war and occupation by the military government. Not only was the economy and social structure disrupted by the invasion and the creation of another wave of refugees, but for a census carried out under such conditions of coercion the last thing one could expect would be freely given or accurate information. Hence even where the presuppositions behind subsequent annual calculations or sample surveys – by Israelis or others – are not in themselves suspect, the use of the 1967 census as a basis either for calculation or comparison cannot be more than a rule of thumb. (See table 11.1)

Brian Van Arkadie points out another difficulty in using these figures from the first days of the occupation in the measurement of real growth:

> The major difficulty of measuring the growth trend achieved in the West Bank and the Gaza Strip is the uncertainty about the appropriate baseline for measurement. In 1968 when the Israeli statistical series on the product of the territories begins, the economic life of the West Bank and Gaza had not yet recovered from the immediate economic effects of disruption resulting from the 1967 war. Some of the subsequent growth was therefore simple recovery, rather than net expansion in the productive performance of the economies. [2]

But he also points out that it is very difficult to use pre-1967 Jordanian statistics to make comparisons, first because Jordanian national accounts did not treat the West Bank as a separate entity (and the same would apply to Egyptian statistics on the Gaza Strip), and second because the economies were affected by the major shifts of population which took place in the period from 1967 to 1968.

AGRICULTURE AND WATER

It is important not to oversimplify the effects of the occupation on the economies of the two areas. The impact has varied considerably from region to region, according to the kind of economic conditions that existed prior to 1967.

The West Bank is a region where, in the past, agriculture has provided the highest proportion of productive output and of employment. Some 70

2. Brian Van Arkadie, *Benefits and Burdens: A Report on the West Band and Gaza Strip Economies since 1967* (New York/ Washington: Carnegie Endowment for Internat'l Peace, 1977), p. 157.

TABLE 11.1

Consumer Price Index for Israel and for the Occupied Territories
(Base 1969 = 100   Jan. 1976 = 100)

Area	Annual Average						
	1973	1976	1977	1978	1979	1980	1981 (av. Jan.-Nov.)
Israel	160.9	—	134.6	202.7	361.4	834.9	—
West Bank[1]	179.9	1 14.9	156.3	235.1	395.3	946.2	1,961.9
Gaza[1]	190.3	1 13.2	151.5	216.4	373.0	954.7	2,564.8

SOURCES: Israel Central Bureau of Statistics: *Statistical Abstract of Israel 1981*, table XXVII/12: *Quarterly Statistics of the Administere d Territories*, vol. XI 2-3 (1981), tables D/1 and D/2.

1. Index for West Bank and Gaza/North Sinai does not include housing.

percent of the population still lives outside of the main towns, and yet agriculture employs fewer and fewer people. Hence it is in the rural areas that the changes are most evident in the economy and in class structure.

In Gaza, the artificial economy created after 1948 had a very small productive base. The most important element was the development in the 1950s and 1960s of plantation agriculture, mainly in growing citrus fruit for export. Since the early 1970s irrigated vegetable and soft fruit production has also been established. Otherwise, the Gaza Strip was little more than a large pool of unemployed labor, with a very few small industries and crafts and a very large service sector proportionate to total economic activity.

Thus up to 1967 agriculture was still the mainstay of the West Bank economy and an important export earner for the Gaza Strip. And it is in the sphere of agriculture and agricultural land that Israeli policies have had perhaps their most profound economic impact – on landholding, agricultural production, and employment in the West Bank. For Gaza the impact has been most serious at the level of marketing and new investment in agriculture.

The first and most devastating change has been the closing off and expropriation of large tracts of land either for military "security" purposes or for settlement. Meron Benvenisti's West Bank Data Base Project estimated that by April 1985 some 52 percent of West Bank land was under Israeli control. This includes lander the control of the army. By 1985 there were 104 Israeli settlements in the West Bank and 52,000 settlers, compared with 5,023 in 1977. In the Gaza Strip by 1985 Israel claimed control of just under one third of the land surface (100,000 dunums out of a total of 360,000 dunums). In the same year there were 2,150 settlers in 18 settlements, the majority of which are agriculturally based.[3]

In the West Bank, a region of hills terraced to grow mainly olives, fruit trees and grapes, interspersed with valleys in which field crops are grown, largely without irrigation, not all the land sealed off or expropriated is cultivated. But from the data compiled by those who monitor the expansion of settlements, the amount of cultivated land lost is substantially greater than the Israelis claim.[4]

---

3. Meron Benvenisti, *1986 Report: Demographic, Economic, Legal, Social and Political Developments in the West Bank*, American Enterprise Institute/West Bank Data Base Project (Jerusalem, 1986) chs. 3 and 5 passim; Sara M. Roy, *The Gaza Strip Survey*, West Bank Data Base Project/Harvard University (Jerusalem: Jerusalem Post 1986) p. 139.

4. For detailed lists of lands closed off up until 1979, see UN Security Council, *Report of the Security Council Commission Established under Resolution 446* (1979), vol. 2, annexes S/13450/ add. 1; see Chapter 8.

Furthermore, while the sealing off of so-called "rocky land" on the hills may not directly affect crop production, unless the land is planted with olive or fruit trees, livestock grazed on these rough pastures had always been an important part of the West Bank's smallholder agricultural economy. Sheep and goats particularly had been an integral part of the peasant farm. One of the effects of the expropriation of such land has been to reduce drastically the area available for grazing, and those areas still available for livestock may be in danger of overgrazing and erosion. The numbers of livestock have fallen dramatically since the occupation – for example, shortage of pasture combined with changing economic conditions produced a drop of 43 percent in the total number of sheep and goats between 1967 and 1970 and a further 10 percent drop between 1970 and 1979.[5]

The ambiguous legal status of agricultural land in the region has added to local people's problems in fighting expropriations. Under Ottoman law, which has been modified since the beginning of the twentieth century but never fully revised, agricultural land was in a form of tenure known as *miri*. This provided that ultimate ownership of the land rested with the state, but usufruct was given to individuals or families as long as the land was kept in cultivation.

In the 1920s and 1930s the British carried out a settlement and survey operation, but they concentrated first on the coastal plain and valley lands where land sales (mostly to the Jewish Agency and other Zionist organizations) were most frequent – in order to establish individual title to land and so facilitate these sales. By 1948 the survey of the hill areas which now make up the West Bank was still incomplete. By the end of Jordanian rule in 1967, according to a recent International Labor Organization report, still only 30 percent of land was listed in the land register (which entitles the person who works the land to a *tapu* or document which effectively establishes ownership.[6] Hence there are still cases of families who have farmed land for generations, but who do not have any proof of legal title which they could produce before a court.

The Israelis have used the confusion over individual title to land and over the concept of "state land" to their own advantage when owners of expropriated land have appealed to the courts (see chapter 7). Only a few appeals have been successful – for instance at Kaddum or Elon Moreh near Nablus when settlers were obliged to move the site of the settlement. But in test cases like Beit El/Tubas, arguments in court have usually centered on

5. *Al-Fajr Jerusalem Palestinian Weekly,* 28 June 1985, p. 8 (Hereinafter *al-Fajr*).

6. *Report of the Director General, 1982: Appendix.* "Report of the Situation of Workers of the Occupied Arab Territories" (Geneva: International Labor Organization, 1982), p. 113. Hereinafter *ILO Report.*

the question of "security" as conceived by the Israelis, rather than on the technicalities of land ownership. In most cases, little more than a stay of execution is achieved.

Expropriation of land has generally been carried out by the Israeli army, which in many cases simply closed off large areas for "security purposes." Some of these areas were subsequently converted into civilian settlements. On occasion, when farmers have refused to accept the closures and have continued to cultivate their land, strong-arm methods have been adopted. For example, in one instance in 1978, farmers from the village of Akraba in the central hills who persisted in cultivating land closed off by the military had their crops sprayed with defoliants.[7] In recent years settlers have also taken a hand in forcing Palestinians to abandon land, particularly in the vicinity of existing settlements. There have been numerous instances reported in the press of orchards and vineyards belonging to Palestinian farmers being uprooted by settlers. A further method of expropriation has been the building of numerous roads to link West Bank settlements. Land including cultivated areas adjacent to the path of the road is expropriated and trees and crops sometimes uprooted.

Some land has also been sold by Palestinian middlemen either to the Jewish Agency land-purchasing authority or to Israeli companies and individuals. It is often the case that such land is acquired fraudulently, with those who actually cultivate it not knowing what has happened until it is too late.[8] These sales, however, make up only a small proportion of the total area expropriated.

Contrary to a commonly held view, the settlement program was well underway in both the West Bank and the Gaza Strip before the Likud government came to power in 1977. Although the pace of expropriations and settlement has certainly speeded up since 1977, reaching a new intensity in 1981 and 1982, the local impact of expropriations, that is the loss of access to such key factors of production as land and water, was already well underway under successive Labor Alignment governments prior to 1977. Under Labor, eighteen legal and illegal settlements were established, and many of the land closures for "security" purposes – for instance in the Jordan Valley – were carried out in the first years of the occupation.

7. Interview with Ibrahim Matar, April 1979.

8. See, for example, Tawfiq Khouri, "How To Buy Land Beyond the Green Line," *Yediot Ahronot,* 1 November 1977. For allegations made by Israeli lawyer Felicia Langer for the League of Human and Civil Rights that the Israeli occupation authorities have assisted and covered up land frauds, and that a company owned by Gush Emunim is buying land in this way, see *Jerusalem Post,* 2 February 1982 (international edition). For more recent incidents, see Khaled Ayed, "Cisjordanie, colonization et scandales immobiliers," *Revue des Etudes Palestiniennes* (1986) 20:37ff.

But settlement strategies have certainly altered since 1977. Here is how the Labor government's concept of "strategic" settlement was outlined in a 1970 master plan drawn up by the Ministry of the Interior: the guidelines envisaged

> . . . the settlement of the unpopulated Jordan Valley and Dead Sea area and making it arable, the expansion of agriculture wherever possible, utilization of available groundwater resources, the clearance of slums and refugee camps, the development of the economic rural functions of the bigger villages. the improvement of inland and air communications, development of the tourist potential of the area for the benefit of the entire country, the development of the periphery of Samaria and Judea so that it may become integrated with the rest of the country.[9]

This policy led to the establishment of a chain of agricultural settlements in the Jordan Valley based on very costly irrigated agriculture and the establishment of Kiryat Arba, the large urban settlement on the edge of Hebron.

The intention stated here of integrating this " periphery" into the center – Israel – for the latter's benefit has remained under Likud, but by contrast the settlements established during the Likud period have often appeared to be based on ideological and strategic considerations first with economic concerns taking second place. The change of strategy can be divined from the following extract taken from the 1979-83 settlement master plan, drawn up by settlement "hawk" Matityahu Drobles, head of the settlement department of the World Zionist Organization. Note the ominous use of the term "minority" to describe the Palestinian majority of the West Bank population:

> The disposition of the settlements must be carried out not only *around* the settlements of the minorities, but also *in between* them, this in accordance with the settlement policy adopted in Galilee and in other parts of the country. Therefore the proposed settlement blocs are situated as a strip surrounding the [Judea and Samaria] ridge – starting from its western slopes from north to south and along its eastern slopes from south to north, both *between* the minorities population and *around* it.[10]

9. Quoted in J. Perera, "The West Bank, Up for Grabs," *The Middle East* (October 1977), no. 36.

10. Matityahu Drobles, *Master Plan for the Development of Settlement in Judea and Samaria 1979-83* (Jerusalem: World Zionist Organization, Department for Rural Settlement, 1978), p. 1. Emphasis in original. Revised in 1980 to include the "encirclement" of Jenin with settlements. This was updated in 1981 to include a target of 120,000 settlers in the West Bank by 1985, not including east Jerusalem. A further plan for 35 new urban settlements in the West Bank to accommodate some 70,000 Jews at a cost of £480 million ($768 million) was published in *Haaretz* on 8 December 1982.

In the period of Likud government from 1977 to the early 1980s militant settler groups such as Gush Emunim played an important role in the establishment of large numbers of new settlements whose character conformed in the main with Drobles' strategy. Most of these new settlements were small and did not have any agricultural base. In the early 1980s, there was also a rapid expansion of large "dormitory" housing settlements in the West Bank. The "settlers" who came to live in these apartment blocks were motivated less by ideology than by the attraction of subsidized housing not available to them within the 1948 borders. Both types of settlement led to a dramatic speeding up of expropriations of Palestinian land, whether agricultural or nonagricultural.

Since the advent of the Likud-Labor coalition government in 1984, the pace of settlement activity has noticeably slowed, partly because of political objections from some coalition members to the particular strategy of settlement advocated by Likud and groups of settlement activists such as Gush Emunim, and partly because of economic problems which have somewhat reduced the flow of funds to the settlement program.

The change of emphasis in settlement strategy is certainly of significance for the wider economic health of the occupied territories, but for the individual farmer whose livelihood is threatened by the loss of land these global considerations make little difference. Even for those who have not lost land but who live near settlements, there is the awareness of the glaring discrepancies which exist between the funds available for agriculture in the settlements and those existing in the villages.

A settler from a *moshav* (cooperative farming unit) in the Jiftlik – in the northern part of the Jordan Valley – described in an article published in an Israeli newspaper the kind of infrastructure and facilities available to the settler farmers. He calculated that every family in his moshav was costing the Jewish people IL 30 million to establish itself. He continued:

> All one needs to do in order to qualify for such a sum is to decide that one wants to join a settlement. Various institutions will then look after all one's needs: a truck is sent to help one move; one is given a place to live and a plot of land as well as other means of production worth many millions [of lira].
>
> All of this is usually paid for by a kind of credit card. The new settler does not pay for anything cash on delivery. Instead, everything from seeds to fertilizers is listed on what is called a "producer's card." The settler also receives a "consumer's card" which is another kind of credit card used to calculate his debt for electricity and water as well as his debt to the local food store.[11]

11. Danny Rubenstein in *Davar*, 29 June 1979.

The settler's situation is in stark contrast to that of the small Palestinian farmer in the next village, whose land and water may now be providing the settler with the comfortable living he enjoys on the account of the Israeli state. Take, for example, the story of a Palestinian village in the same area (Jiftlik). While it is not entirely typical in its social composition, being mostly inhabited by Bedouin refugees from the south given land to settle on in Jordanian times, its experience of Israeli land expropriations since 1967 is not dissimilar to that of longer standing agricultural communities in this area.

Zbeidat, now a village of about four hundred people, in 1968 lost half of the five hundred dunums of fertile land it had been allotted by the Jordanian government. (As luck would have it, the villagers were due to receive title in summer 1967, but the war put paid to that.)

Land confiscation, for the purpose of building Jewish settlements and for presumed security reasons, soon followed Israeli occupation. Suleiman al-Salih, the main landlord in the Marje Na'je region, whose land was sharecropped – in part – by Zbeidat and Marje Na'je peasants – lost 5,000 donums of his land to the Israelis (a substantial part of it was fenced off for " security reasons" along the river Jordan). In 1968 all the dwellings and institutions serving the farmers residing in the lands of Suleiman al-Salih were demolished by the Israeli armed forces. Those included 27 artesian water pumps, a school, a clinic, a post office and 600 farmers' dwellings. A 100 donums of orange groves were defoliated. The purpose apparently was to prevent the Ghor [Jordan Valley] farmers from resettling in their land and to create a land base for Israeli settlements along the Western Jordan valley, the scheme later known as the Allon plan. The incidents described here formed a pattern which recurred in al-Auja, Ghor al-Far'a, Diuk, Fasail, al-Hamra and within the vicinity of Jericho itself. To the east and south of Zbeidat, 2,000 donums were confiscated to build the settlement of Argamon [1968]. Of these, 600 donums belonged to one landlord, Muhammad Abdullah from Tubas. The remaining 14,000 donums belonged to a number of small farmers. The villagers of Zbeidat lost 268 donums about 200 of which were fenced off and declared a Security Zone by the river [Jordan]; the remaining 68 were considered absentee property [belonging to people who fled or were away when the Israelis came] and given to three absentee landowners as compensation for 550 donums of their land which had been seized for the use of Argamon settlers.[12]

Until 1980, Zbeidat villagers were not allowed to erect any new buildings because the military government defined their land as miri (and therefore not appropriate for domestic buildings which can only be built on another legal category of land known as *mulk*). Hence by 1980 when the

12. Salim Tamari and R. Giacaman, *Zbeidat: The Social Impact of Drip Irrigation on a Palestinian Peasant Community in the Jordan Valley* (Bir Zeit, 1980), pp. 4-5.

ruling was changed, the village was in a state of "indescribable squalor" because housing had not kept up with population increase.

One further point arises from this description. Although the West Bank (in contrast to the Gaza Strip) is mainly a land of small peasant holdings, in the Jordan Valley and in other valleys which intersect the region there is still a substantial amount of land, often in scattered blocks, owned by large absentee landowners. This is particularly true of the Jenin and Nablus areas, the latter which borders on the northern Jordan Valley.

Many of the peasants in these areas work either entirely as sharecroppers or supplement the insufficient income from their own plots by sharecropping on others' land. Hence, land expropriation does not just affect landowners, large or small, but restricts access to land for numbers of other peasants who have little or no land of their own.

The Israeli occupation and settlement policies have also had a serious impact on another crucial factor of production – water. At present, farming is dependent on relatively low and erratic rainfall levels. The village well provides water for domestic purposes and for irrigated vegetable and fruit growing where this exists. Only about 4 percent of total land under cultivation is irrigated (about 81,000 dunums).[13] Irrigated land is mostly found in the Jordan Valley and in pockets in the Jenin and Tulkarem areas.

Expanding irrigation would be an obvious way to raise productivity and improve agricultural income but Israeli water policies have generally blocked this development. In the first place, the Israelis have no interest in seeing a prosperous Palestinian agricultural sector on the West Bank which might compete too much with their own. Second, Israel itself has a very high rate of water use, particularly for its heavily irrigated agricultural sector which uses up some 75 percent of the total volume of water consumed each year. The coastal water table is now in danger of salinification from heavy use, and almost one-third of Israel's present water resources are derived from ground water in an aquifer lying under the western slopes of the West Bank.

This has given the Israelis a clear stake in maintaining control over this source of water. The Israeli proposals for "autonomy" in the territories from 1978 onwards have therefore always stressed that water as well as land would be excluded from its terms. In 1979, Israeli Water Commissioner Meir Ben Meir predicted that by 1985 on existing calculations Israel would have a considerable water deficit and could not do without the West Bank aquifer, which has been the case. This clearly makes control over West Bank resources crucial not just to prevent the Palestinians from developing

13. H. Awartani, *West Bank Agriculture: A New Outlook* (Nablus: al-Najah University Research Bulletin 1, 1978), p. 7.

the economy independently but also to fill Israeli water needs. The only long-term alternative, in Ben Meir's view, is costly desalination programs, which would make agricultural water expensive and thus make Israeli produce less competitive on the market. Thus, development of West Bank agriculture (settlements excepted) could only occur at the expense of Israeli agriculture.[14] Hence strict controls have been placed on water use, domestic and agricultural. The vast majority of villages in the West Bank and many towns suffer from water shortages in the dry summer months every year.[15] Wells are metered and those who pump over the stated limit are penalized. The authorities also generally forbid the drilling of new wells.[16]

Settlements, by contrast, are not restricted in their use of water and are permitted to drill deep wells. By the beginning of the 1980s, Israeli settlements in the West Bank had drilled at least seventeen new wells (Palestinian sources put that number at twenty-seven). These settlement wells, barely five percent of the total wells on the West Bank, drew more than 14 million cubic meters of water in 1978, about 40 percent as much as the 33 million cubic meters produced by all 314 Palestinian wells. In addition, Israeli settlements and military bases obtain large quantities of West Bank water from Palestinian wells and springs through pipes and tank trucks.[17] In the Jordan Valley region, where underground water is vital for agriculture, this appears to have led in several cases to the drying up or reduction in flow of shallower neighboring village wells. Among the best documented cases are those of al-Auja in the central part of the valley and Bardala in the northern sector.[18] A report from the military government's water department in 1978 gives the following picture of this unequal situation:

14. Meir Ben Meir interview with the author, May 1979. For an overview of Israeli water policies, see Subhi Kakhaleh, *The Water Problem in Israel and Its Repercussions in the Arab-Israeli Conflict* (Beirut: Institute for Palestine Studies, Study 9 (E),1981); Joe Stork, "Water and Israel's Occupation Strategy," *MERIP Reports* (July-August 1983), 116:19ff.

15. International Christian Committee for the Relief of Arab Refugees, West Bank Area Council, *Self-Help Village Development Programme 1978* (Jerusalem: Middle East Council of Churches, 1979).

16. Awartani, *West Bank Agriculture,* p. 7.

17. Stork, "Water and Israel," p. 22.

18. See Tim Coone, "Worries over West Bank Water," *Financial Times* (London), 22 November 1979; S. Graham-Brown, "Water: How Israeli Plans Hurt West Bank Arabs," *Arab Report* No. 9, 23 May 1979; Rami G. Khouri, Israel Drains West Bank Waters," *The Middle East* (September 1979), p. 38.

1. Total number of artesian wells in the West Bank is 331, of which 17 have been drilled by the Israeli water company (Mekorot) in the Jordan Valley to serve Israeli settlements in that area.

2. Arab wells have dried up after occupation. Many others in the Jordan Valley (mostly in the northern part) are suffering a declining water table and increased salinity.

3. Total volume of water discharged from 314 Arab wells amounted in 1977/78 to 33.0 million cubic meters (mcm). Whereas 17 Israeli wells in the Jordan Valley have discharged in the same season 14.1 mcm.[19]

Meanwhile, by the beginning of the 1980s the Jordanian government estimated that the water available to West Bankers from all sources amounted to 105 mcm a year, less than one-sixth of the area's total water resources.[20]

In the Gaza Strip the situation for agriculture is even more serious, since a greater proportion (45 percent) of agricultural land, mostly growing citrus, relies on irrigation. Heavy water use due to the overpopulation of the Strip, combined with the demands of agriculture and the growing number of Jewish settlements using irrigation, is straining the water table to its limits and there are fears that the aquifer will become saline if remedial measures are not taken soon. Aid officials in the area reportedly state that the Israeli outposts' profligate irrigation practices have greatly increased the pressure on resources.[21] As in the West Bank, water quotas for Palestinian farmers have been fixed for over a decade, whereas Israeli settlers have drilled some 35 to 40 new wells. According to Sara Roy's 1986 survey of Gaza, "In 1984 Israelis living in Gaza consumed, on average, 14,200 to 28,400 cubic meters of water compared to an average consumption of 200 cubic meters for every Gazan."[22]

Local plantations have their water use strictly controlled. Meters are placed "on the wells in orange groves of the Arab inhabitants in order to limit the water supply to them – for instance only 10 cubic meters per

19. Military Government, Department of Water, *Monthly Discharge of Underground Water in Tehuda and Shomron 1977/78,* quoted in Awartani, West Bank Agriculture, p. 8.

20. *ILO Report,* p. 113.

21. E. Pallis, "Stateless in Gaza" *Guardian* (London, 26 February 1982.

22. *Al-Fajr,* 20 June 1986, p. 7.

dunum. Any Arab who was entitled to only 10 cubic meters and took more was punished by having his water supply cut off."[23]

These constraints form the basic context within which agriculture now functions in the territories. In the Gaza Strip the agricultural sector has declined from its relative importance in the 1960s and 1970s. Its share in Gross Domestic Product fell from 31.2 percent in 1976 to 13.4 percent in 1984. (see table 11.2). Employment in agriculture also declined dramatically, from 31.6 of the work force employed in the Gaza Strip and North Sinai in 1970 to 18 percent in 1985 (see table 11.3).

In the West Bank the change in the position of agriculture has been less sharp, reflecting alterations in the patterns of agricultural production rather than a simple decline. Gross Domestic Product from agriculture was 34.4 percent in 1976, 37 percent in 1980, but 20 percent in 1984. The trends in agricultural output are less clear than those in the Gaza Strip because production in the rain-fed sector is erratic. However, in employment terms, there has been a marked trend away from agriculture, down from 42.5 percent of the locally employed work force in 1970 to 27.4 percent in 1985.

In neither case do these figures indicate a fundamental revolution in agriculture since the Israelis took over (for example, from smallholding to large-scale capitalist agriculture in the West Bank, or away from plantation production in Gaza). But – and this is particularly true in the West Bank – the trend is more complex than a mere decline in the traditional agricultural sector.

From the British Mandate period onwards, agriculture has been shifting from subsistence to market production but the area has not experienced either land reform or social development which would have matched relations of production on the farm to the changes which have taken place at the level of circulation and the market. In the Gaza Strip, the artificial nature of the economy meant that the capitalist agriculture of the 1950s and 1960s started virtually from scratch, with a wage labor force from the refugee camp population.

The restrictions on land and water use, combined with a number of other changes brought about by the occupation – especially in the composition of the labor force and in the market for agricultural goods – have brought to the West Bank rural economy decline punctuated with adaptations of existing agricultural and land tenure practices to fit the new situation.

The question of labor migration from the territories will be dealt with at length later, but it is relevant to point out here that in the West Bank the

---

23. UN Security Council *Report,* evidence of Abd Allah Mehana, p. 45.

TABLE 11.2

Gross Domestic Product (at Factor Cost) by Branch
(IS million at current prices unless otherwise stated)

Branch	Gaza Strip and N. Sinai			West Bank		
	1976	1978	1980	1976	1978	1980
Agriculture, forestry and fishing	48.5 (31.2)[1]	99.7 (28.4)	264.2 (19.2)	124.3 (34.4)	309.4 (34.5)	1518.7 (37.0)
Industry	15.9 (10.2)	39.7 (11.3)	141.3 (10.3)	23.8 (6.5)	63.9 (7.1)	275.9 (6.7)
Construction (building and public works)	31.5 (20.3)	73.3 (20.9)	291.2 (21.2)	51. 1 (14.2)	122.8 (13.6)	458.3 (11.2)
Public and community services (including water and electricity)	29.6 (19.1)	66.0 (18.8)	289.0 (20.9)	39.9 (11.1)	100.4 (11.2)	402.8 (9.8)
Transport, trade and other services, including ownership of dwellings	29.8 (19.2)	72.4 (20.6)	390.5 (28.4)	122.1 (33.8)	301.2 (33.6)	1,447.3 (35.3)

TABLE 11.2 (Continued)

Gross domestic product at factor cost and current prices	155.3	351.1	1,376.2	361.2	897.7	4,103.0
Gross domestic product at factor cost and 1976 prices[2]	155.3	162.2	144.2	361.2	381.8	433.6
Factor payments from abroad	63.9	158.5	781.2	1 12.3	263.3	1,110.3
Less: Factor payments to abroad	14	2.8	1 1.7	3.0	5.0	20.4
Gross domestic product – Total (at factor cost)	217.8	506.8	2,145.7	470.5	1,156.0	5,192.9

SOURCE: Israel Central Bureau of Statistics: *Quarterly Statistics of the Administered Territories*, vol. XI 2-3 (1981), table 7.

1. Parenthetical figures are percentages.
2. January 1976 IS = 100. This basis does not pretend to be an exact measure of value, but rather to give an order of magnitude.

TABLE 11.3
Sectoral Distribution of Employed Work Force
A = Percentage of total employed
B = Percentage of locally employed
C = Percentage of those employed in Israel

Sector	West Bank			Gaza Strip & N. Sinai		
	A	B	C	A	B	C
Agriculture						
1970	39.2	42.5	17.7	32.7	31.6	40.7
1975	27.4	34.6	10.9	24.0	26.3	18.5
1978	27.9	34.4	11.4	21.9	21.1	23.2
1980	26.3	33.3	9.4	18.3	18.5	18.1
Industry						
1970	14.4	14.5	12.9	11.8	12.1	8.5
1975	16.6	15.8	18.6	14.2	12.0	18.1
1978	17.5	15.2	23.6	17.4	15.4	20.4
1980	16.8	15.3	20.6	19.6	18.5	21.1
Construction						
1970	14.7	8.4	57.2	12.4	8.5	47.4
1975	22.7	8.4	55.0	22.2	5.1	53.3
1978	20.8	10.9	46.0	21.6	7.0	44.3
1980	22.4	10.5	51.3	23.0	7.6	44.2
Other branches						
1970	31.7	34.5	12.2	43.1	47.8	3.4
1975	33.3	41.2	15.5	39.6	56.6	10.1
1978	33.7	39.5	19.0	39.1	56.5	12.0
1980	34.4	40.9	18.7	39.1	55.4	16.6

SOURCE: Israel Central Bureau of Statistics: *Statistical Abstract of Israel 1977,* tables XXVII/23-24; 1981, table XXVII/19.

majority of those employed daily in Israel are classified as rural dwellers, most of whom would previously have worked in agriculture. In the early days of the occupation this new source of employment mainly soaked up the prevailing underemployment and unemployment in the agricultural sector. In Gaza it had the same effect, drawing on people in the camps who had previously had little or no work.

In Gaza's agricultural sector the main employment category is wage labor, either permanent or seasonal. In the West Bank, however, there is a whole range of permutations, from smallholders using family labor, possibly supplemented by seasonal wage workers at harvest time, through sharecroppers who own some land of their own, to landless sharecroppers, and finally to landless agricultural laborers, either permanent or seasonal. This last category had been growing slowly since the 1930s. The figures in table 11.4 give some idea of the situation in the West Bank districts in the early 1960s, although sharecroppers are not defined separately. Hillal also maintains that about 3,226 large and medium landholders, or about 5 percent of the total work for in agriculture at that time, employed the 20,000 agricultural wage laborers.[24] He also points to trends in land tenure apparently indicating further fragmentation of ownership, mainly through inheritance (all sons in a family can inherit land) and a trend towards landlessness or insufficient land for subsistence (see table 11.5). This may have increased the numbers of sharecroppers and laborers during the 1950s and 1960s. Another group of people who were very likely to become agricultural wage laborers or sharecroppers were the refugees from 1948 who lived close to agricultural areas – for instance around Jericho, where many refugees worked for large landowners. many of whom had bought up land in the valley in the 1950s when it was cheap.

Table 11.6, compiled by the Agriculture Department of the military government (and probably using different labor categories from those employed by Hillal) indicates that in 1968 the number of "laborers" in agriculture in the West Bank had reached 42,000, or 50 percent of total labor in agriculture. By 1976 the figure was down to 31,400 or 26.1 percent of the total agricultural work force. Even allowing for uncertainty as to how a "laborer" is defined (that is whether such a person could be a sharecropper or only a wage laborer, and whether it includes those who also own small amounts of land) this does indicate a trend away from employment in agriculture. This does not mean that there are fewer wage laborers – rather the contrary – but now most of them work in Israel, predominantly in construction and in agriculture. And it was those who were already wage laborers or landless sharecroppers who were among the first in any rural community to take this path.

Although wages in Israel for "commuters" from the territories have always been low by Israeli standards, they were initially higher than those obtainable at home, especially in agriculture. Thus over the years not only wage laborers with no land, but also farmers and their families were induced

24. Jamil Hillal. *The West Bank: Its Economic and Social Structure 1948-1974* (Beirut, 1975, in Arabic), p. 164.

TABLE 11.4

Agricultural Workers by Form of Employment, West Bank, 1961

Area	Total	Self-Employed		Working for Family, Relatives		Wage Laborers	
		N	%	N	%	N	%
Liwa of Jerusalem	20,901	10,345	49.5	1,988	9.5	8,373	40.1
Liwa of Nablus	30,486	17,978	59.0	3,126	10.3	9,348	30.7
Liwa of Hebron	13,418	6,545	48.8	4,528	33.7	2,329	17.4
Total for West Bank	64,805	34,868	53.8	9,642	14.9	20,050	30.9

SOURCE: Jamil Hillal, *The West Bank: Its Economic and Social Structure 1948-1974* (Beirut, 1975), p. 165.

to get on a bus and go to Tel Aviv daily. At the same time, working farmers had to pay more to hire and keep labor at home.

At first this had the effect of making farmers who had been working marginal land abandon it for better wages in Israel. Then it encouraged those farmers growing grains, olives, and other dry farming crops who needed more labor than their families could provide to give up rather than accept very low returns – in which the fast-rising cost of labor was an important component. According to West Bank economist A. R. Husseini,

> In the economic sense, the opportunity cost of labor has become so high that it no longer pays to attend to one's olive trees or rocky piece of land. The farmer chooses the more sensible course of action: to seek employment elsewhere. West Bank farmers have increasingly fallowed their land, and totally neglected the maintenance of their terraces [a vital defense against erosion and long-term damage to the soil in this dry, hilly region]. They rarely plough or care to control pests. Their neglect is approaching a point of no return. [25]

However, this story of decline is not the whole picture. A certain amount of mechanization has taken place since 1967. Before then it was minimal, and according to Hillal, such agricultural machinery as existed was concentrated in the Nablus area.[26] On the whole, the major landowners who had capital to invest tended to have a rentier mentality not conducive to major changes in the pattern of agricultural production. This contrasts with Gaza's landowners, who were obliged to invest in order to create a viable form of agriculture there.

Most smallholders, if not actually in debt to landowners, commission agents, or merchants, certainly had no reserves of capital to spend, and in any event small plots in hilly terrain are not suitable for large-scale mechanized farming. Nonetheless, since 1967, according to Awartani, mechanization has developed in equipment ranging from small tools to heavy-duty tractors and combines. The number of tractors rose from 147 in 1967 to 1,534 in 1977. There is also widespread use of Israeli seed stocks, which are certified and generally of higher quality than those available locally. Fertilizer use rose from 4,000 tons in 1968 to 15,100 tons in 1976.[27] It is to be noted that all this "technology" is imported either from or through Israel, both increasing Israeli trade and importing Israeli inflation into agricultural costs. Though details are sparse, it would seem that this

25. Interview with A.R. Husseini, *MERIP Reports* (September 1977) 60:21.

26. Hillal, *West Bank: Its Economic and Social Structure*, p. 164.

27. Awartani, *West Bank Agriculture*, pp. 17-18.

TABLE 11.5
Changes in Patterns of Landholding in the West Bank

Size in Dunums	1953		1965	
	No. of holdings	% of total	No. of holdings	% of total
Less than 10	16,816	25.2	27,406	49.8
10-49	25,497	38.3	18,932	34.4
50-199	20,852	31.3	7,930	14.4
200-499	2,801	4.2	575	1.0
500-999	459	0.7	105	0.2
1000-1999	117	0.2	26	0.05
2000-4999	59	0.09	4	0.007
5000 and above	39	0.06	—	—
Total	66,460	100.00	54,978	100.00

SOURCE: Jamil Hillal, *The West Bank: Its Economic and Social Structure 1948-1974* (Beirut, 1975), p. 156.

mechanization has not been so much a generalized trend as concentrated in areas where conditions for certain reasons favor it. The table of agricultural production shows that improved output is concentrated in specific crops – mostly fruit and vegetables – and not in the traditional field crops, or olives.

That overall output has not risen significantly, whereas the labor force has shrunk, indicates that although new technology may have substituted for labor-intensive work with good results in some areas, this is not a widespread phenomenon. But it is difficult to specify the weight of mechanization as a "push" factor towards work in Israel, when compared with the other factors mentioned earlier.

The shortage of water has meant that an area wide expansion of irrigation is impossible, but ironically this situation has led the more entrepreneurial owners, especially in the Jordan Valley and in Gaza, to invest in water-saving drip irrigation. This, combined often with use of plastic coverings, has been successful in increasing yields, especially of those vegetables that have proved profitable for export. Tamari sums up this selective trend towards new technology and intensive agriculture as follows:

TABLE 11.6
Employment in Agriculture in the West Bank, 1968-1976

Year	No. of Laborers	% of Total Labor
1968	42,000	50.0
1969	46,000	41.9
1970	42,400	37.0
1971	36,700	31.4
1972	34,300	27.5
1973	30,000	23.7
1974	36,000	26.2
1975	31,800	24.0
1976	31,400	26.1
Av. 1968 69	44,000	45.4
Av. 1975 76	31,000	34.1
Relative change	-28.2%	-47.0%

SOURCE: Moshe Levi, *Development of Agriculture in Yehoda and Shomron 1967-76*, mimeographed report published by the Dept. of Agriculture in the Military Government, p. 6, quoted in H. Awartani, *West Bank Agriculture: A New Outlook* (Nablus: Najah University, 1978), p. 6.

. . . agricultural productivity has not declined because large and middle landowners in the Jordan Valley and certain sections of the north, especially the Jenin, Tulkarem and Nablus areas, have introduced new agricultural technology — high-yielding varieties of seeds, hothouses, mechanization, labor-displacing machines. A number of wealthy peasants have substantially increased their income while a certain grouping of peasants have, without losing their land, lost agriculture as a main source of income and become workers in Israel.[28]

The other major aspect of the occupation's direct impact on agriculture has been in the sphere of circulation. From the earliest days of the occupation, Israel has been determined not to allow produce from the occupied territories to compete with or jeopardize markets for its own produce. Hence products which might compete with Israeli goods,

28. Interview with Salim Tamari. *MERIP Reports* (October-December 1981), 100:31.

particularly fruit and vegetables, have to be consumed locally or exported. Since the occupation, most agricultural exports, including those from the Gaza Strip, go via the Allenby and Damiya bridges across the Jordan to Amman, and thence to the Arab world. Even this export trade is wholly dependent on the maintenance by the Israelis of the so-called open bridges policy initiated soon after the occupation.[29] As a general rule the bridges have been kept open for goods, but every now and then for political reasons a particular district or town will be "punished" for some supposed misdemeanor or defiance by the closing of the bridges to its people and its product. The result for farmers and landowners is rotting fruit and vegetables and loss of income.

With the increase in West Bank production of tomatoes and other vegetables under irrigation, mainly sold via Jordan into the Arab world, new marketing problems have arisen. As more and more countries in the region begin to grow this same range of vegetables, prices, particularly of tomatoes, have plummeted, often leaving farmers both in the West and East Bank with an unsalable glut.

In the Gaza Strip, citrus, the main export, is even more dependent on the policies of Israel and of Jordan as well as on fluctuations in the international market. Joan Mandell gives the following account of the problem:

> Before 1967, Gaza citrus took up 20 percent of the land area and was the largest source of income. Until 1976, it employed 25 percent of the local work force in the fields, packing and subsidiary activities such as transportation. . . . . Before 1967, Gaza oranges brought about $150 a ton from Western European markets. Israel, which exports citrus to the same markets, passed a military order in 1968 banning independent Palestinian exports there. Gaza merchants were encouraged to search for markets in the Arab world, which were closed to Israeli goods. In 1975, Iran began to take the Gaza crop at a good price. After the Iranian revolution, the bottom dropped out of this part of Gaza's Gulf exports. Jordan's central marketing board formed a cartel to buy Gaza fruit at the lowest prices. The Gulf states have started to import more Turkish and Egyptian fruit at lower, government-subsidized prices, and Gaza citrus also faces competition from Australian and Californian fruit in the Saudi market.

According to the Gaza Strip Citrus Producers Association in 1985, the proportion of citrus exported to Jordan had sunk from 26 percent of the total in 1975/76 to 10.2 percent in 1984/85.

29. For a discussion of the formulation of this policy, see Van Arkadie, *Benefits and Burdens,* pp. 33 ff.

Mandell adds that Palestinian exporters in 1983 also had to pay some JD 50 (about $150) for export permits to cross the Jordan bridges, and a further fee for each driver's "security permit." The Israelis have also blocked applications by Gazan grove owners to build a canning factory to make use of undersized oranges. These difficulties, combined with restrictions on water use and on the replanting of orchards as well as on the planting of new trees, have resulted in a considerable decline in citrus production.[30]

Israel's concern with protection of its own highly subsidized agricultural produce has led to the imposition of restrictions on produce from the territories which might compete with Israeli agriculture. For example grapes, which are an important crop in the Hebron region, have been subject to restrictions imposed for the benefit of Israeli growers. In 1980 grapes were sold to Iraq and to the Israeli market under a special permit. But in 1981 the Iraqi market was closed due to the war with Iran, and according to *Maariv* on 22 September, the Israeli Fruit Council rescinded the Hebron growers' permit to send grapes to Israel. This was apparently done under pressure from Israeli grape growers anxious to maintain the price on the local market for their own produce. In 1984 another Israeli paper, *Z u Haderekh*, reported that the Israeli settlement of Kohav Hashahar had been allowed to plant one thousand dunums of vineyards, despite the ban on West Bank growers.[31]

In 1984 the Israelis also imposed restrictions on the new irrigated crops such as tomatoes and eggplants grown mainly in the Jordan Valley. The authorities imposed "integrated and comprehensive production planning for vegetable production in Israel, the West Bank and Gaza." This in fact entailed imposing a quota system on Palestinian farmers.[32]

In the Gaza strip recent problems with the marketing of citrus have led landowners to invest in drip-irrigated vegetables and soft fruit. Growing of some of the latter, such as strawberries, has been encouraged by the Israelis, but their hold over the market is such that if there should be a glut on the Israeli market, they have power to stop sales, leaving Gaza producers with a highly perishable product on their hands.

30. Joan Mandel, "Gaza: Israel's Soweto," *MERIP Reports* (October-December 1985), 136/137: 12-13; Roy, *Gaza Strip Survey,* pp. 44-50.

31. *Al-Fajr,* 11 October 1981; *Zu Haderekh,* 25 July 1984 (trans. *Israeli Mirror,* No. n97).

32. Benvenisti, *1986 Report,* pp. 9-10.

Vulnerability to competition for markets for agricultural produce is not confined to exports. Israeli agricultural goods, not to mention processed and canned food products, flow into the territories without restrictions. In the 1980-81 season, out of a total of 87,797 tons of vegetables which came onto the West Bank wholesale markets, 22,930 tons came from Israel, while for fruit, melons, and pumpkins, 32,095 tons out of a total 62,207 tons came from Israel. For the Gaza Strip the figure for vegetables was 16,036 tons out of a total 43,691 tons and for fruit, 22,800 from a total 33,476 tons.[33]

In the territories' markets Israeli farmers have the advantage of very high levels of subsidy. For example, according to A. R. Husseini, "On the eve of the occupation, we had a very flourishing poultry industry but now it is in bad shape. The problem seems mainly from unfair competition of Israeli products which enjoy a subsidy of 15-30 percent. Moreover, Israeli farmers enjoy a definite credit advantage which facilitates modernization and expansion. A similar situation exists in regard to dairy products, where our dependence on Israeli products is now almost total."[34]

Once-flourishing West Bank and Gazan melon and pumpkin cultivation collapsed dramatically after the occupation (see table 11.7). This, Awartani says, "has been due to the high cost of labor, low yields and inability to compete with Israeli producers. As a result of all this a great many farmers in the Jenin district suddenly abandoned what had been for a long time a specialty crop."[35]

On the other side of the coin, Israel has seldom offered incentives to grow new crops in the territories. The much-quoted exception was the distribution of onion seeds in the West Bank, which was promoted as not threatening Israeli farmers; the resulting product was exported via Israel. Over the years a few farmers in the territories have entered into arrangements for particular crops with Agrexco, the Israeli state agricultural exporting company, which buys the crop at a prearranged price. This has proved profitable for a few farmers but the practice has not become very widespread.

Smallholders and sharecroppers also suffer from lack of good indigenous marketing facilities. Here, larger scale farmers are at a considerable advantage in manipulating the prices they can get for the crops, making deals with, for instance, wholesalers in Amman or major West Bank

33. Israel Central Bureau of Statistics, *Quarterly Statistics of the Administere d Territories,* vol. XI, no. 2-3 (1981), table F/3.

34. Husseini interview, p. 22.

35. Awartani, *West Bank Agriculture,* pp. 13-14.

towns. Small farmers are often left in the hands of commission agents or merchants to whom they are sometimes also indebted for seasonal advances in money or seed. However, this problem of indebtedness and the resulting bondage to big landowners and merchants is somewhat less than it used to be, partly because of the advance of the commercial market in agriculture and partly because of the greater variety of outlets and because money can more easily be earned outside agriculture. Some smaller farmers also bypass middlemen by selling directly, peddling piles of fruit or vegetables by the roadside.[36]

A glance at table 11.7 covering agricultural output averaged over the years 1961-66 and selected years since the occupation shows that most of the traditional dry farming crops have been stagnant or declining. It is mainly in irrigated vegetables, fruit, and meat production that significant headway has been made.

The production of olives, one of the main West Bank crops from the end of the nineteenth century, is notoriously difficult to judge without very long time series because of the wide fluctuations in yield. This is primarily due to the two-year cycle of production of one good year, one poor year, the result of harvesting methods. With the attraction of wage labor, as we have seen, trees are not being well cared for, and there are numerous disincentives to planting new trees. They take some eight to ten years to come to full bearing; the Israelis do not encourage new tree planting; some of the land which might be used for new trees has been expropriated or is in danger of being taken; and finally the market has worsened with the free importation of cheaper Spanish oils.[37] In a few villages, aid organizations have been encouraging and assisting with terracing and planting of trees, particularly in the Hebron area, but this is only a small-scale development.[38]

Since 1984 the Agricultural Relief Committees, a new group comprising some fifty Palestinian engineers and agriculturalists, have taken a number of initiatives to try and improve conditions for smallholding farmers, in an effort to keep people on the land and to provide employment. Most of their work has so far centered on working with farmers to establish innovative techniques of cultivation and providing them with otherwise sparse extension services. However, tackling the more basic problems

36. For a detailed description of marketing practices in the Jordan Valley area. see Tamari, *Zbeidat*, pp. 43-44.

37. Awartani, *West Bank Agriculture*, p. 15.

38. International Christian Committee for the Relief of Arab Refugees, West Bank Area Council, *Annual Report 1978* (JErusalem: Middle East Council of Churches, 1979), p. 8.

TABLE 11.7

Output of Main Crops: West Bank and Gaza Strip
(In 1000 tons)

Crops	Average 1961-66	1967/8	1974/5	1975/6	1977/8	1978/9	1979/80
West Bank:							
Field Crops	65.9	23.5	38.3	34.9	46.0	41.2	51.9
Vegetables & potatoes	128.8	60.0	139.9	147.3	156.3	141.3	145.2
Melons & pumpkins	70.0	36.0	3.6	4.5	11.4	8.0	19.6
Olives	43.8	28.0	10.0	50.0	85.0	21.1	120.0
Citrus	23.5	30.0	63.8	74.1	80.0	79.1	75.4
Other fruits	76.4	47.9	78.1	76.6	95.4	87.0	89.3
Meat	—	10.3	21.4	22.4	19.8	23.5	23.1
Milk	—	30.3	46.0	41.5	39.9	39.4	36.7
Gaza Strip:							
Vegetables		31.8	46.0	48.0	53.4	51.4	61.3
Melons & pumpkins		12.5	4.7	3.0	2.8	3.6	4.3
Citrus		91.0	201.4	243.7	180.6	192.1	168.1
Other fruits (incl. olives)		19.0	25.2	20.9	24.8	19.5	21.7

SOURCES: 1961-66 figures: H. Awartani, *West Bank Agriculture: A New Outlook* (Nablus: Najah University, 1978), p. 1. 1967-80 figures from Israel Central Bureau of Statistics, Statistical yearbooks for relevant years.

caused by the occupation or dealing with the sensitive issue of ownership and control of land is at present beyond their scope.

The years of occupation have accentuated the trend in the West Bank away from agriculture as the sole source of rural family income – a process which first began on a very small scale as far back as the 1930s, but which since 1967 has become more or less the norm. In some cases agricultural income has been supplanted altogether. But this has not been accompanied, as it has in many other third-world countries, by either a drift of the rural population to the cities or by the development of fully capitalist commercial agriculture.

The first phenomenon has not occurred because of the Israeli refusal to allow resident migrant labor inside the borders of pre-1967 Israel. As a result there is instead the commuting migrant, who returns daily or weekly to his village and land – if he has any.

The second development has been hampered by the controls imposed by the military authorities on access to factors of production and by competition from Israeli agriculture; and also because of the lack of any thoroughgoing land reform by any of the succession of occupying powers in this region since the turn of the century: Ottomans, British, Jordanians, and Israelis. Change has occurred on the land because of the progressive commercialization of agriculture – of land and of labor – but none of these governments has seen it as in its interests to initiate a reform which would upset the existing socioeconomic power structure (see also chapter 12).

As it is, the existing patterns of land tenure have remained – a much adapted mixture of smallholding, share farming arrangements, and large holdings. However, neither large-scale capitalist farming nor independent smallholding – perhaps more appropriate to the West Bank's terrain – is possible without security of tenure and access to credit to raise the level of technology and intensify farming methods. In fact these requirements would apply whether a capitalist or a socialist approach to land policy were envisaged.

The Gaza Strip's position is rather different. Historically this was not an area of concentrated agriculture and there is no strong rural class structure as on the West Bank. Individual landowners are now rich and relatively powerful simply because there were not many other ways to make money in so circumscribed an economy. The present plantation agriculture is hampered but little changed by the constraints of occupation and ownership remains concentrated in the hands of relatively few families who mostly live in Gaza town and commonly have interests in commerce as well.

INDUSTRY

Industry was never a leading sector in the economies of either the West Bank or Gaza. As Van Arkadie put it, "industrial activity in the West Bank and the Gaza Strip was modest in 1968 and has remained modest." That judgment still holds. Furthermore, as he points out, the statistics for industry are somewhat misleading for several reasons:

> The fact that industry continues to account for a higher proportion of employment than output deserves comment, for it seems to conflict with the usual economic pattern, in which the manufacturing industry tends to be the highest productivity sector. In this case, part of the explanation is that a significant segment of gross domestic product is generated in the agricultural sector, where more of the work is done by family labour that does not enter the employment statistics. Also much of the so-called industrial activity in the West Bank and Gaza Strip is craftwork in low productivity, labour intensive activities.[39]

In the West Bank for example, there has been a long tradition of such small-scale craft industries in wood, glass, mother-of-pearl, pottery, and small agriculture-based industries such as soap (from olive oil, centered in Nablus), flour mills, tanneries, and cigarette and match factories. Some of these flourished in a modest way and certainly sustained a few local fortunes in the early part of the twentieth century. But since the end of the 1920s they were hampered – at first by the growth of larger scale, more heavily capitalized Jewish industry on the coast.[40]

Then under Jordanian rule industrial expansion was limited by the fact that the government as a matter of policy directed public investment in industry towards the east bank, and particularly toward Amman. Hillal gives a list of nineteen firms which received Jordanian Government capital in this period, only two of which were on the West Bank – a vegetable oil manufacturing company in Nablus an d a hotel in Jerusalem. Most of the other investment went to Amman.[41]

From 1967 onwards there has been little significant development of industry in the West Bank. Although Israeli figures at current prices show

39. Van Arkadie, *Benefits and Burdens*, pp. 123, 124.

40. For detailed descriptions of the growth of Jewish industry in the 1920s see B.J. Smith, "British Economic Policy in Palestine towards the Development of the Jewish National Home 1920-29," D. Phil. thesis, Oxford, 1978. For the effects on some of the small Palestinian industries, see S. Graham-Brown, "The Political Economy of Jebel Nablus, 1920-1948" in E. R. J. Owen, ed., *Studies in the Economic and Social History of Palestine in the Nineteenth and Twentieth Centuries* (London: Macmillan, 1982).

41. Hillal, *West Bank: Its Economic and Social Structure*, p. 139.

dramatic increases in the value of output, a table which appeared in the Ministry of Defense twelve-year study of the occupied territories covering the years up to 1979 indicated a decline in the West Bank's industrial output when calculated at 1969 prices (see table 11.8)

In their report for 1986, the West Bank Data Base Project noted that the contribution of industry to Gross Domestic Product remained below 7 percent.[42] As does Van Arkadie, the report stresses the small size of enterprises and points out that manufacturing industry forms a relatively small proportion of the total included in these figures. Employment figures for local industry remained constant (16,000 persons) but only 9,550 (9 percent of the total employed in the West Bank) were employed in industrial plants. The rest worked in quarries and olive presses. Ninety-two percent of industrial plants employed up to nine workers, the average, industry-wide, employees per plant is four.[43] According to Israeli figures for 1985, only 2 percent (55 out of a total of 2,494 industrial enterprises) employed more than 21 persons. Twenty-seven percent of establishments were one-person enterprises.[44] Such large-scale firms as have managed to survive and even flourish either have well-established local markets, or reasonably reliable access to the Jordanian market.[45]

An interesting but unusual example of local enterprise in the West Bank is the establishment of a small local pharmaceutical industry which now has about five firms, employing thirty to sixty people each. These ventures were initiated by local doctors and pharmacists, and are geared to the local market, using relatively few imported materials.[46] There is some question as to the efficacy of quality control for drugs, which some observers consider is lax due to problems in the health service.[47]

42. The higher 1984 figure (8.2 percent) in table 8.2 is probable explained by the exceptionally low contribution of agriculture in a drought year.

43. Benvenisti, *1986 Report,* p. 10.

44. Israel Central Bureau of Statistics: *Statistical Abstract of Israel 1986,* table XXVII/34.

45. For examples of such companies existing at the beginning of the 1980s, see N.W. Khouja and P.G. Sadler, *Review of the Economic Conditions of the Palestinian People in the Occupied Arab Territories* (UNCTAD August 1981), TD/B/870.

46. *Ibid.,* pp. 41-42.

47. Conversations between the author and a number of doctors and health care professionals in the West Bank, December 1980.

Given the importance of urban speculative building during the last ten years, and the rapid development of "villa suburbs," especially in the vicinity of Jerusalem, firms dealing in building materials, carpentry, and furniture have also flourished. Of those firms dependent on the Israeli market, the main sector has been textiles, relying mainly on subcontracts from Israeli companies. The subcontractors either employ cheap female labor in workshops or put out the work to women operating from their homes. This pattern is much the same in the West Bank and Gaza Strip and in the latter case, some observers have argued that it is only these very low labor costs that allow some of these enterprises to survive at all. According to a survey of Palestinian women workers in Gaza in the early 1980s, "factory owners [in the textile sectors] said they preferred hiring women to men since they had to pay men higher wages as an incentive not to work in Israel" (where wages are higher on average than in the occupied territories). "One sewing factory owner readily admitted that the [women] workers were actually paying him, since their daily wage of 500 shekels ($10) was covered by the first three hours of work, giving him five hours of free labour."[48] These textile factories have suffered in recent years from the sharp decline in the Israeli textile industry, which itself is based on cheap labor from the "development towns" and from the occupied territories.

Public utility companies have now largely fallen under Israeli control. It has already been noted that water distribution and use is strictly controlled by the Israelis, and in the case of electricity, local suppliers have increasingly succumbed to pressure to link up their towns and regions to the Israeli grid, transferring control of supplies to the Israel Electricity Company. The Gaza Strip's three main municipalities had independent supply companies which were connected to the Israeli grid soon after 1967, although refugee camps still depend on privately run generators. In the West Bank, Qalqilya in the northwest was the first to be connected to the Israeli grid in 1971. This was followed by the connection of Hebron to the grid in 1973, and by the mid-1980s most of the major West Bank electricity companies had been put out of business, in some cases − for example, Nablus − despite strong resistance from the municipality and the company concerned.[49] Generally speaking the Israelis used the pretext that local utilities were outdated and inefficient, and at the same time put obstacles in the way of attempts by some of these companies to modernize their operations.

48. Susan Rockwell, "Palestinian Women Workers in the Israeli-occupied Gaza Strip," *Journal of Palestine Studies* (Winter 1985), 14(2):114.

49. Sami Aboudi, "Jenin Electricity Falls under Israeli Control," *al-Fajr*, 15 February 1985, p. 7 ff.

TABLE 11.8

Industrial Product and GDP in the Occupied Territories, 1974-77 (at factor cost) (£I 1000, in current prices)

Year	West Bank			Gaza Strip & North Sinai			Total		
	Industrial output	GDP	Industry as % of GDP	Industrial output	GDP	Industry as % of GDP	Industrial output	GDP	Industry as % of GDP
1974	144	2,257	6.4	52	967	5.4	196	3,204	6.1
1975	197	3,269	6.0	94	1,468	6.4	291	4,737	6.1
1976	238	4,727	5.0	148	2,117	7.0	386	6,844	5.6
1977	297	6,250	4.7	225	2,992	7.5	522	9,242	5.6

Industrial Output in the Occupied Territories, 1974-1977 (~ million, in 1969 prices)

Year	West Bank	Gaza Strip & North Sinai	Total
1974	60	22	82
1975	58	28	86
1976	54	34	88
1977	50	40	90

SOURCE: Israel Ministry of Defense, *A Twelve- Year Study 1967-1979,* by the Coordinator of Government Operations in Judea and Samaria, Gaza District, Sinai and Golan Heights.

The longest and most bitter struggle has been over the Palestinian-owned Jerusalem Electric Company (JEC) which supplies sections of the West Bank surrounding greater Jerusalem and which employs a substantial number of workers from the West Bank as well as from Jerusalem. The JEC, whose franchise covered east Jerusalem, including the Jewish settlements within the boundaries of greater Jerusalem, and some contiguous areas of the West Bank, is finally being forced to surrender a substantial part of its concession to the Israel Electricity Company (IEC). The dramatic increase in population and power consumption in Jerusalem since 1967 put an impossible strain on the JEC plant. The Israelis, however, would not permit the installation of new generators by the JEC and hence there were increasing complaints of breakdowns and power failures, especially from the Jewish settlements and from Israeli army installations in the area served by the company.

Since the beginning of the 1980s the Israelis have interfered increasingly in the affairs of the company, which was obliged to purchase increasing quantities of electricity from the IEC in order to maintain its supplies. This increased its debts, which over the recent period have mainly been paid by Jordan. The JEC's difficulties were compounded by internal political disagreements and periodic conflicts between management and workers. The Israelis have meanwhile moved closer to their desired goal of controlling electric power supplies for the whole of Jerusalem.

In the Gaza Strip, industrial development in the pre-1967 Egyptian period was even more limited than in the West Bank, with only a 4.4 percent share of GDP in 1966. Since the occupation industrial production has risen somewhat, with industry making up 11.6 percent of Gross Domestic Product in 1984 and 16.2 percent of local employment in 1985, down from 18.5 percent in 1980. Several large-scale factories have been established, although some of these are Israeli-owned, but on the whole industry has remained small scale – in 1985 only 17 out of a total of 1,628 enterprises in the Strip employed more than 20 workers.[50] Apart from these, local production has mostly been along the same lines as in the West Bank – food processing, manufacture of building materials, and subcontracting in textiles.

One local industry which has suffered a sharp decline has been fisheries. Prior to the occupation, fishing had been an important source of income and employment in the Gaza Strip. Since 1967, Israeli restrictions, combined with some changes in natural conditions, have made fishing a

50. Israel Central Bureau of Statistics: *Statistical Abstract of Israel 1986*, table XXVII/34; for the development of Israeli industry see also Sheila Ryan, "Israeli Economic Policy in the Occupied Areas," *MERIP Reports* (January 1974), 24:20.

less and less attractive occupation. A fisherman from Beach Camp, interviewed by researchers in the early 1980s, explained the problems:

> My family were fishermen in Jaffa. We made a pretty good living out of it and I remember as a child that we were well-off. In 1948, we were driven south and came to Beach Camp. My father had left everything behind – the boats, nets, crates – everything. He bought a boat in the early fifties and started again from scratch. Times were hard in the Egyptian period – there wasn't much money about and we had to struggle to make ends meet. By 1967, we had two boats, each with a crew of seven. For six months after the war, there was no fishing at all. We weren't allowed onto the sea. Then we were issued with licenses and we got going again. We could fish from Erez [northernmost point of the Gaza Strip] to Port Said, but not beyond that. And we were curfewed as we still are now. No one is allowed to launch or land a boat between 8 P.M. and 4 A.M. Since Camp David,we are only allowed to fish from Erez to Rafah and there just aren't enough fish in this little area for the seven hundred boats in the Strip. Another thing too – since the Aswan Dam was built, the Nile no longer floods. It used to bring lots of things down with it that the fish loved, but that's all stopped too. A lot of people are going out of business, or already have done.[51]

Restrictions based on Israeli "security" considerations are combined with a wish to limit competition for the Israeli fishing industry and Israeli plans to develop tourism along this coast. Furthermore, since most outlets for the sale of fish are now in Israel, Gaza's fishermen have little control over the prices they obtain for their catches. As a consequence the number of license-holding fishermen declined from 1,400 in 1978 to 1,000 in 1982.[52]

In industry in general, Israeli policies have had their effect on access to markets, perhaps to an even greater extent than for agricultural products.

> The tariff walls set up by Israel for the protection of its own industries were applied to the newly occupied zones but the latter were denied the opportunities made available to Israelis to exploit that protection. Thus the Israeli industrialist has received favoured treatment over his Arab counterpart, in that although the economies of the occupied territories are being absorbed into that of Israel, the Arab entrepreneur is denied the grants and loans and other incentives available to the Israelis.[53]

51. Paul Cossali and Clive Robson, *Stateless in Gaza* (London: Zed Press, 1986), p. 81.

52. Mandel, "Gaza: Israel's Soweto," pp. 13-14.

53 Khouja and Sadler, *Review of the Economic Conditions of the Palestinian People,* p. 38.

In 1986 the Israeli Defense Minister Itzhak Rabin gave permission for the establishment of an Arab Chamber of Industry in the West Bank. Clearly members of this chamber will lobby the Israelis for greater access to markets and also for an easing of restrictions on import of raw materials and export of finished goods. But under the conditions of occupation, their influence is unlikely to be great. Furthermore, the 1961 Jordanian law under which the chamber was established limits membership to factories which have had least JD 2,500 worth of equipment and employ at least twenty workers all year round. Thus the chamber will be representative of only a few large companies, not of the majority which fall below these limits.[54]

Investment in Industry

The economic and political climate in the territories over the past twenty years has not generally encouraged investment in industry. Private Israeli capital has invested directly only to a very limited extent (as in the Eretz estate in the Gaza Strip), preferring to take advantage of the cheaper labor by subcontracting without committing funds to enterprises in the territories.

The only exception has been the establishment of small industries linked to settlements, but almost all of these are financed or supported by public funds. Some of the smaller workshops, for example those making metal products, received contracts farmed out by Ministry of Defense industries. In a few cases, there are larger industrial estates, as at Kiryat Arba near Hebron (which unlike most of the settlement industries has a history of employing Arab workers for tasks other than construction); the estate at Maale Adumim on the Jerusalem-Jericho road; and, until 1982, Yamit in the Rafah salient.

Historically, the Palestinian landowning mercantile class – the only group with capital to invest – has preferred to invest in land, commerce, and urban real estate rather than in industry, which entails longer term risks. This phenomenon is not unique to either the West Bank or to Palestine. In fact the economic history of the Middle East in this century shows it to be the rule rather than the exception. In the present circumstances of occupation, rational economic calculation as well as predisposition dictate that it is more profitable and safer not to put one's money into a long-term investment such as an industrial enterprise.

54. *Al-Fajr*, 20 June 1986, p. 16.

All banks in the occupied territories were closed after the occupation in 1967, and in the West Bank, none was given permission to open until 1986. In the Gaza Strip, the main branch of the Bank of Palestine in Gaza town was permitted to reopen in 1981, under the supervisory regulations of the Bank of Israel (central bank), but it is only allowed to deal in Israeli shekels, not in foreign currency. In 1986 the Bank of Palestine branch in Khan Younis was also reopened.

In the West Bank, the Israeli refusal to sanction the reopening of banks seems to have been part of a wider strategy to prevent the development of any independent economic structures in the territories. However, in the altered political climate of the mid-1980s, this policy was finally reversed. Pressure from the United States for an improvement in the "quality of life" in the occupied territories, combined with the efforts of the Jordanians to establish a five-year "development plan" for the territories which would increase Jordan's economic influence, particularly in the West Bank, seem to have been the key factors. In 1986, after applications from a group of leading businessmen in Nablus, Israeli and Jordanian officials, through an American mediator, negotiated the reopening of the Cairo-Amman Bank branch in Nablus. This particular bank was chosen because it is backed by the Jordanian central bank. Under the agreement, the Central Bank of Jordan supervises dealing in Jordanian dinars and the Bank of Israel oversees dealings in shekels. Residents of annexed east Jerusalem cannot use the bank's services.

This rapprochement between Israel and Jordan appears mainly to stem from political motives: for the Jordanians to increase their political and economic influence in the territories, since the Cairo-Amman bank in Nablus can handle development funds coming from Jordan; and for the Israelis to strengthen the economic and political position of individuals, and groups in the territories who are not connected with the Palestine Liberation Organization, including influential businessmen and merchants who have close ties with Jordan.[55]

Until recently, the only sources of credit available in the West Bank were Israeli banks, which usually had high rates of interest and dealt only in Israeli shekels, or the "banking" facilities provided by money changers. However in the last few years, the economic recession and heavy Israeli demands for value-added tax (VAT) payments have driven a large number of moneylenders out of business. According to *al-Fajr* in November 1986, only 120 moneylenders remained out of some 600 who had been active in

55. *Jerusalem Post,* 14 June 1986, 15 November 1986; *Daily Telegraph,* 14 October 1986.

the 1970s.[56] Thus in the occupied territories, what investment there has been in industry has, until very recently, been effected almost exclusively outside the banking system. According to a study by Abu Kishk, about 90 percent of industrial firms in the West Bank stated that their investment came from their private funds or from a partnership.[57]

The West Bank, however, has one economic advantage not available to the Gaza Strip: the Jordanian dinar, a reasonably stable currency over the last ten years, has been allowed to continue operating alongside the Israeli lira/shekel, whose decline in value, particularly since 1977, has been nothing short of phenomenal. This decline, influenced by and coupled with the high levels of inflation imported from the Israeli economy, make the Israeli currency most undesirable for anything other than the most rapid of transactions. As Mansour puts it, in the West Bank today, the shekel may be the "medium of exchange," but the dinar fulfills the other two roles of a currency – to be a "unit of account" and "a store of value."[58] A further defense against inflation in the West Bank is that the dinar is the medium for paying rents and the salaries of all former Jordanian civil servants, and also of employees in larger firms, and in scholastic and public institutions.

In the Gaza Strip no such hedge against inflation exists, and this should be taken into account when examining any statistics on wages, prices, or remittances.

The net result of this situation is that for those with capital to invest, the most attractive options are real estate and urban land at home or, increasingly, the investment opportunities offered by the more prosperous Jordanian economy where many leading merchants and landowners have long had connections, through business and family ties. The pull of this latter option was increased in the late 1970s, according to Mansour, by the relative stability and prosperity of that economy, by the fear that the Israelis might make the dinar illegal in the West Bank, and by hyperinflation locally, caused by problems in the Israeli economy. The establishment of the Amman Financial Market or stock exchange in 1979 may have attracted some investment from those with Jordanian citizenship but the downturn in the Jordanian economy in the mid-1980s has diminished this and other investment opportunities.

56. *Al-Fajr,* 14 November 1986.

57. Bakr Abu Kishk, *Report on the Industrial and Economic Trends in the West Bank and Gaza Strip* (ECWA/UNIDO, August 1981), p. 37.

58. A.S. Mansour, "Monetary Dualism: The Case of the West Bank under Occupation," *Journal of Palestine Studies* (Spring 1982), 11(3).

Another result of the peculiar financial situation in the territories is that their economies are highly liquid. Hoarding is commonplace, as there are no interest-bearing methods of saving locally. Hoarding is usually of dinars, foreign currencies, gold, and jewelry.

On savings, Mansour reports that they

> . . . consist principally of the remittances of Palestinian emigrants in the Arab countries of the Gulf. However, these savings probably account for only a modest part of these remittances. Emigrants do not generally send all their funds to the West Bank: a considerable part is transferred directly from the Gulf countries to their accounts in Amman banks.[59]

Mansour's point was borne out by the observations of the governor of Jordan's central bank:

> Almost half of the remittances we receive [that is remittances from Jordanians as well as Palestinians] are originally destined for the West Bank, but those who remit these funds send them to Amman through the banking system and deposit them there. The beneficiaries often convert it [the remittance] from foreign to Jordanian currency and keep it in the banking system in Amman. The beneficiaries in the West Bank do not take funds into the West Bank except as much as they need for consumption. They rarely carry funds for investment in the West Bank. Some of them spend it on investment in the East Bank or even outside the country [Jordan] altogether.[60]

Remittances, public and private, made up one-third of the Gross Domestic Product of the Gaza Strip and just under one-quarter of the GDP in the West Bank in 1980. Since that time, however, there has been some falling off in remittances as declining oil prices have brought about a recession in the Gulf, and many non-national workers have been laid off. In addition, since the Israeli invasion of Lebanon in 1982, it has become harder for Palestinians to obtain permits to enter or work in the Gulf states. A recession in the Jordanian economy and increased restrictions by both Jordanians and Israelis on the movement of Palestinians across the Jordan bridges have further diminished the flow of remittances to the territories.

In the case of private funds, most of the money which is brought into the country is either hoarded, spent on children (especially on their education), on building a house, or on consumer durables. For the better off, other options are speculation in urban real estate or possibly the purchase of capital equipment for agriculture or business (for instance a

59. *Ibid.*, p. 111.

60. Interview with Mohammed Said Nabulsi, March 1981.

tractor, agricultural machinery, a taxi or a truck). In Gaza, building houses and apartments seems at the moment to be the most common use of remittances.

In contrast, money coming from daily or weekly paid work in Israel (in shekels, of course) is more likely to be spent on day-to-day needs and on consumer goods. Workers also spend some proportion of their earnings inside Israel – on food, transport, and so on.

COMMERCE AND TRADE

Ibrahim Dakkak has pointed out that after the occupation in 1967 "the West Bank and the Gaza Strip added almost one million consumers to the Israeli market."[61]

Perhaps the most striking aspect of the way in which increased consumption has increased dependence on Israel is the fact that most of the cars, trucks, air conditioners, heaters, televisions, radios, stereos, refrigerators, and other durable goods to be found in homes in the territories either come via Israel and Israeli wholesalers or from Israeli factories. Either way they leave some or most of their value in the Israeli economy. In addition, as was mentioned earlier, substantial quantities of agricultural products come from Israel, and now much of the canned food, dairy products, powdered milk, and many grocery, hardware, and pharmaceutical goods originate in Israel. Hence there has been a dramatic reversal of the direction of trade in Israel's favor. Even when shekels are converted into dollars, this deficit for both the West Bank and Gaza is steadily growing (see table 11.9)

The only country with which the territories have a positive balance of visible trade is Jordan, though even this has declined since the high point reached at the beginning of the 1980s. But even in 1980, 88 percent of imports into the West Bank came from Israel and 59 percent of exports went to Israel. For Gaza and North Sinai the respective percentages were 91 percent and 76 percent. *Le Monde* has quoted Ministry of Defense statistics showing that in 1968 the picture was the reverse: 60 percent of exports from the occupied territories went to Jordan and only 40 percent to Israel. Imports from Israel, even that early on, were already 75 percent of the total.[62] In these circumstances, the local economy sees little benefit from

61. Ibrahim Dakkak, "Development and Control in the West Bank, " *Arab Studies Quarterly* (Spring/Summer 1985),7(2-3): 75

62. Francis Corn, *Le Monde,* 2 April 1982.

TABLE 11.9
Occupied Territories: Balance of Trade

Year	Trade with Israel		Trade with Jordan		Trade with others	
	IS million	US $ million	IS million	US $ million	IS million	US $ million
West Bank						
1978	-248.6	-142.3	99.8	57.1	-48.2	-27.6
1979	-548.0	-215.4	128.3	50.4	-105.1	-41.3
1980	-1255.9	-245.1	342.2	66.8	-195.6	-38.2
1981 (3 quarters)	-2082.9	-182.2	400.2	35.0	-280.7	-24.6
Gaza Strip and N. Sinai						
1978	-174.3	-99.8	57.5	32.9	-17.0	-9.7
1979	-280.1	-110.1	77.5	30.5	-25.1	-9.9
1980	-613.6	-119.8	138.2	27.0	-68.8	-13.4
1981 (3 quarters)	-961.6	-84.1	271.5	23.8	-46.2	4.0

SOURCE: Israel Central Bureau of Statistics: *Quarterly Statistics of the Administered Territories*, vol. XI 2-3 1981, table C1.

NOTES: Minus signs indicate trade deficits.
Dollar conversions at the average rate for each year – from International Monetary Fund, *International Financial Statistics*, June 1982.

the increase in local purchasing power and many merchants are now little more than channels for Israeli goods to reach these markets. Hillal argues that the trading bourgeoisie as a group in the West Bank has benefited from the occupation. But it seems more likely that this would apply more to the larger scale import-export merchants and those who have acquired franchises for selling Israeli goods than to small traders. For small businesses (the majority), soaring inflation and the imposition of a 15 percent value added tax on all but the smallest operations (a source of much bitterness in the merchant community, which vehemently opposed its imposition) may well have eroded the gains of increased trade.

In 1986, the European Economic Community (EEC), as part of a large aid package, agreed in principle to extend preferential access to its markets to the occupied territories, as an entity separate from Israel. However, the plan has run into difficulties because of Israeli objections, and so far this move has not substantially altered the trading situation of the territories.

Jerusalem

Jerusalem is still the center of commercial activity. During the Jordanian period it was the leading commercial center in the region, despite the challenge to its position by the government-sponsored growth of Amman. It provided the largest market on the West Bank, had the best developed services, and in addition, was the natural connection for transport between the northern and southern parts of the West Bank.

Annexation in 1967 meant that in legal and fiscal terms the city was integrated into Israel, but infrastructure and economic links with the occupied West Bank remain strong. The importance of these economic links alone, in the sphere of commerce and services, quite apart from religious and political claims, would be argument enough against separating the city from its West Bank hinterland.

Jerusalem may not now be physically divided in two, but in economic terms there is still a gulf between the Israeli-dominated western sector and the Old City and east Jerusalem, where trade is still largely in Palestinian hands. But economic life in the east has become dominated by the western sector in a number of ways that go beyond the subjugation to Israeli law and payment of Israeli taxes.

First, the city is being swamped by an influx of Israelis, particularly to the barracklike tower-block settlements which now cover the surrounding hills in every direction. This physical encirclement seems symbolic of the Israeli desire to cut the city off from the occupied West Bank economically and politically.

Commercial life and the provision of services are the key elements in Jerusalem's economy, in the absence of significant economic growth either before or after 1967. But although the central commercial districts in the Old City and the eastern sector continue to function, and in individual cases even to flourish, they have become more and more dependent on Israeli custom. Except in periods of severe tension, the Old City and even the commercial streets outside the Damascus Gate are nowadays patronized by Israeli almost as much as by Palestinian shoppers.

Jerusalem's other lifeline has, for most of the last century, been tourism and pilgrim traffic, primarily to the Christian holy places. Until 1982 much of the tourist trade catered to by east Jerusalem hotels and services came via Amman. Under the open bridges policy, tourists based in Amman could get permission to visit Jerusalem and then return to Amman. Since the end of 1981, the Israelis have refused to allow tourists from Amman to return there via the Allenby Bridge. They now have to leave from Israel, and the only way they can get back to Amman is via Cairo. This may not have had a drastic effect on shops catering to tourists, but has had a more serious effect on east Jerusalem hotels and services, as these depended heavily on tourists from Amman. Those who come to Jerusalem via Israel usually stay in Israeli-owned hotels in west Jerusalem. A 1985 Israeli survey of the city's economy stated that the number of hotel bookings in west Jerusalem has doubled since 1975 (from 0.9 million to 1.7 million in 1983), whereas there has been virtually no change in bookings in hotels in east Jerusalem, which have remained at around one-half million in 1975 and 1984. The increase in incidents of violence and clashes between Palestinians and the Israeli religious right in the Old City during 1986 and 1987 has further discouraged tourists from staying in the Arab sector of the city.

Another consequence of the limited opportunities in the Arab sector of the Jerusalem economy is that large numbers of Palestinian residents have become dependent on working, usually in menial capacities, in Israeli enterprises and services: in hotels, restaurants and cafes, on buildings sites and on roadworks.

For the rest of the West Bank, with the exception of Bethlehem, tourism is now all but defunct. Towns such as Jericho and Ramallah, which during the Jordanian period attracted tourists from the Arab world, saw few tourists who were not passing through in Israeli coaches during more than two decades of occupation. Since the *intifada,* tourism came to a complete halt.

PATTERNS OF WORK

Patterns of work have changed substantially since 1967 as a result of the shifts in the economy. In the first place, many more people, mostly men, have been drawn into the wage labor force whether on a permanent or temporary basis.

When the Israeli economy began its boom period of the early 1970s, there was a reservoir of unemployed or underemployed labor in both areas, but particularly in Gaza's overcrowded camps. Conditions of life made people willing to take unskilled jobs which were very poorly paid by Israeli standards, but better paid than the relatively few jobs available at home.

From the Israeli point of view, these workers formed a convenient and controllable force of unskilled and semiskilled labor to do jobs which Israelis, even the least privileged, were less and less willing to do. The territories workers were, and still are, largely unorganized – unions in the territories are not recognized in Israel. Hence they will take wages that are unacceptably low for Israeli unionized labor. In recent years the Israeli trade union federation, the Histadrut, has theoretically extended "protection" to legally employed workers from the territories – although they are not admitted as members – but in practice this protection amounts to very little, despite the fact that these workers are obliged to pay 1 percent of their wages for this "service".[63] In fact, in the early days of the occupation, the Histadrut raised objections to this flow of cheap labor, but dropped this opposition when it became clear that these workers were mostly doing jobs Histadrut members would rather not do. The only possible clash of interests might be with Palestinian workers who lived in pre-1967 Israel, for whose interests the Histadrut had never shown undue concern.

The majority of jobs in question – unskilled building labor, agricultural work, and service jobs such as cleaning, working in restaurants, garbage disposal, and so on – do not present any real threat to the wage structure of organized labor. In the Israeli economic and social pecking order, the workers from the territories are in all respects at the bottom of the heap. Furthermore, any Histadrut concern over "competition" has to be counterposed against the fact that Histadrut's corporate industries (particularly the construction giant Solel Boneh) are some of the largest employers of this form of cheap labor.

Because of the overall stagnation in most sectors of the territories' economies, the numbers working in Israel grew steadily through the boom period, faltered somewhat as the Israeli economy went into recession from 1976 onwards, but despite continuing economic problems rose again from 1979 onwards.

63. See for example J.R. Hilterman, "The Emerging Trade Union Movement in the West Bank," *MERIP Reports* (October-December 1985), 136/137:28; Michael Shalev, "Winking an Eye at Cheap Arab Labour," *Jerusalem Post*, 18 January 1986.

The change in the balance of employment is most marked in Gaza, where the official percentage of the total number of employed persons who work in Israel has risen from around 10 percent in 1970 to around 43 percent in 1980. In the West Bank the increase was from 12.8 percent in 1970 to about 30 percent in 1980 (see table 11.10).

However these figures do not tell the whole story. They only record the workers who pass through the official labor exchanges and there are many who do not. According to Meron Benvenisti, "An estimated 90,000 workers from the West Bank and Gaza cross the Green Line daily to work in Israel. Less than half this number are workers legally registered through the government Employment Service."[64] These people who work "unofficially" are thought to total twenty thousand or more, but no estimate of their numbers has any claim to reliability. For statistical purposes, this part of the work force, like family labor in agriculture, is to all intents and purposes invisible.

The formal characteristics and conditions of work in Israel are quite clearly defined. Workers are forbidden to remain in Israel overnight without a special pass for night or shift work. But in order to save time and money on travel (which is not cheap unless transport is provided by the employer), workers do quite frequently stay overnight during the week, sleeping rough, sometimes with the connivance of their employers.

In doing this they run the risk of being arrested – or worse. In 1976, four Palestinian workers from the territories died in Tel Aviv one night when the shed into which their employer locked them every night for their illegal stay caught fire and they were trapped inside. In 1981, a building worker from the Gaza Strip suffocated from a fire in an airraid shelter in Ness Ziona where he and two others were spending the night – with the knowledge of the building contractor who employed them.[65]

Wages rose, even in real terms, until hyperinflation began to bite in the late 1970s. Since then they have slipped back substantially. But even at their highest point these wages were well below those paid to Israelis, even where the jobs were comparable (see table 11.11). Workers from the territories also on average tend to work longer hours. According to the Bank of Israel annual report of 1980, between 1977 and 1980 the average number of hours put in by workers in the main economic sectors came to roughly 36-37 hours a week for Israeli workers; workers from the territories worked an average 39-41 hours per week. This figure would only cover "official" workers; those employed illegally are likely to work longer.

64. Benvenisti, *1986 Report,* p. 11.

65. *Yediot Ahronot,* 16 March 1976, 13 January 1981.

TABLE 11.10

Occupied Territories: Balance of Trade

Year	Trade with Israel		Trade with Jordan		Trade with others	
	IS million	US $ million	IS million	US $ million	IS million	US $ million
West Bank						
1978	-248.6	-142.3	99.8	57.1	-48.2	-27.6
1979	-548.0	-215.4	128.3	50.4	-105.1	-41.3
1980	-1255.9	-245.1	342.2	66.8	-195.6	-38.2
1981 (3 quarters)	-2082.9	-182.2	400.2	35.0	-280.7	-24.6
Gaza Strip and N. Sinai						
1978	-174.3	-99.8	57.5	32.9	-17.0	-9.7
1979	-280.1	-110.1	77.5	30.5	-25.1	-9.9
1980	-613.6	-119.8	138.2	27.0	-68.8	-13.4
1981 (3 quarters)	-961.6	-84.1	271.5	23.8	-46.2	4.0

SOURCE: Israel Central Bureau of Statistics: *Quarterly Statistics of the Administered Territories*, vol. XI 2-3 1981, table C1.

NOTES: Minus signs indicate trade deficits.
Dollar conversions at the average rate for each year – from International Monetary Fund, *International Financial Statistics*, June 1982.

TABLE 11.11

Average Daily Wages for All Employees from the Occupied Territories and for Employees from the Territories in Israel

Year	Agriculture		Industry		Construction	
	IS	at 1976 prices	IS	at 1976 prices	IS	at 1976 prices
West Bank						
1977 Total	5.6	3.6	6.0	3.8	7.9	5.1
Israel	5.5	3.5	7.0	4.5	8.0	5.1
1978 Total	8.6	3.6	9.4	3.9	12.0	5.1
Israel	8.5	3.6	11.0	4.6	12.1	5.1
1979 Total	14.4	3.6	16.6	4.2	21.6	5.5
Israel	14.2	3.6	19.1	4.8	22.0	5.6
1980 Total	29.0	3.1	32.8	3.5	42.7	4.5
Israel	29.0	3.1	37.7	4.0	43.2	4.6
Gaza Strip & N. Sinai						
1977 Total	5.4	3.5	6.1	4.0	7.3	4.8
Israel	5.8	3.8	6.9	4.5	7.5	5.0
1978 Total	8.2	3.8	9.7	4.4	11.8	5.4
Israel	8.8	4.0	11.0	5.0	12.0	5.5
1979 Total	16.0	4.2	19.5	5.2	24.2	6.5
Israel	16.9	4.5	21.8	5.8	24.7	6.6
1980 Total	32.1	3.4	35.4	3.7	46.2	4.8
Israel	33.6	3.5	39.9	4.2	46.8	4.9

SOURCE: Israel Central Bureau of Statistics, *Statistical Abstract of Israel, 1980,* table XXVII/20 and 22.

NOTE. The deflator used here is the consumer price index for each territory for each year (see table 11.1). It is not intended to reflect exactly the value of wages but simply to establish trends. The total figures include higher Israeli wages soft should be expected that in most cases wages in each territory would be lower than the total. It should also be noted that wages for workers in Israel only apply to "official" workers.

For a similar exercise on 1973-76 wages, see S. Graham-Brown: "Structural Impact of Israeli Colonization." *MERIP Reports* 74:13

The most conspicuous feature of this commuter-migrant work force is the large number of workers engaged in construction. Since the early 1970s construction has absorbed almost half the workers from both areas, with the proportion only declining slightly in the last few years.

There have been apparent changes in the structure of employment in Israel over the last decade, most noticeably a percentage shift from agriculture to industry and services. Industry now makes up about 20 percent of employment among workers from both the West Bank and the Gaza Strip, although these figures may be deceptive: more of the unofficial workers are probably in agriculture and construction than in industry, which may lower the real proportion of workers in the latter sector.

However one cannot view the workers in Israel from the West Bank and Gaza as an undifferentiated whole. Several groups may be distinguished, first by the terms and length of employment, and second by their origins and motives for working in Israel.

A first group consists of those who are employed officially and have reasonably steady jobs. One-fifth of all workers (in the "legal" category) – most typically those in semi-skilled work, especially in industry – have worked for the same employer for more than four years. However, while these workers may receive higher wages than the "illegals," they are obliged to pay at least 30 percent of their wages in taxes and social security payments. Despite these payments, workers from the territories are not entitled to a variety of benefits available to Israeli workers, including old age and survivor's benefits, disability benefits, unemployment benefits, and children's allowances. Only in the construction industry has there been a move, since 1985, to pay some disability pensions. Even in areas where workers from the territories are deemed eligible for benefit, these benefits are often restricted – for example, childbirth grants, available to women workers and the wives of male workers, which pay hospital expenses and paid maternity leave, are only available to women who give birth in Israel, rather than in the territories. Furthermore, the deductions made from the pay of territories' workers do not, as in the case of Israeli workers, go to the National Insurance Institute, but are transferred directly to the Treasury, so that in effect the workers are helping to finance the cost of the occupation.

It has also been pointed out that even for "legal" workers, there is little to prevent their employers paying them illegally low wages, particularly when special payments, for example overtime or bonuses, are involved. Michael Shalev, in a *Jerusalem Post* article in January 1986, gives the following example:

In October 1985, Yussuf, who lives in a refugee camp a short distance from Jerusalem's Gilo neighborhood [one of the Israeli urban settlements] and works night shifts at one of the city's big bakeries, earned a net monthly salary of NIS

136.6 (just over $90). His pay slip, prepared by the State Employment Service, shows that on the first eight hours of each shift, Yussuf grossed just above the legal minimum for industrial workers. But he was paid 20 percent *below* this minimum for overtime hours! Had Yussuf earned what was due to him under the legally binding collective agreement for the bakery industry, the cost to his employer would have risen at least threefold.

The Employment Service, which administers the salaries of the 40,000 West Bankers and Gazans who legally commute to work in Israel, had not made a clerical or computational error. Except for construction workers, it simply does not check employers' calculations, except to ensure that the general minimum wage is honoured for the standard workday. Insofar as a worker is entitled to specific branch or company wage supplements, seniority increments, or bonuses for shift or overtime work, it is up to his boss to make the necessary adjustments. The result is illegal labour on a large scale, aided and abetted by the government itself.

Those who work in Israel illegally are subject to much more arbitrary levels of pay, and are often forced to pay Histadrut dues and social security payments even though they are ineligible for any benefits. In this respect, workers from the territories, whether legal or illegal, lose out on the social wage, measured by the efficacy and availability of services that improve the quality of life for the worker and his or her family, rather than simply by monetary payments.

A second category of workers is made up of those who come in groups from particular villages or districts and who work through a local labor contractor who deals with the Israeli employers. These people more often than not work unofficially, usually in building or agricultural work. They may have work on a regular basis but move from job to job and site to site as organized by the labor contractor. Compared to the first group, they generally have less contact with Israelis and often work with members of their own family or village. Some may have low-level skills in building or other trades.

Tamari, in his study of workers from the village of Ras al-Tin in the West Bank, describes in detail how workers in this category function.[66] In these circumstances, working unofficially is considered preferable: more cash in hand and less chance of trouble with the authorities. Despite occasional Israeli police statements of intent to root out illegal workers, little is done: it is in too many people's interest to keep the system as it is.

At the bottom of the labor scale in terms of bargaining power and security are those men who seek work on a daily basis by going to what are commonly known as the "slave markets" – the gathering points for casual labor, to be found in or near most big cities, for instance near the Damascus

66. Salim Tamari, "Building Other People's Homes: The Palestinian Peasant's Household and Work in Israel." *Journal of Palestine Studies* (Autumn 1981), 10(1):31ff.

Gate in Jerusalem and at the Ashkelon junction outside the Gaza Strip. There at dawn every day contractors, Israeli bosses, and even individuals wanting an unskilled worker for a day or two, pick out workers from the crowd gathered there, which often includes children under legal working age.[67] Supply usually exceeds demand so the daily battle for a job can sometimes be lost.

Women workers are employed in certain sorts of unskilled factory work, particularly in the garment industry, but the main area of work for women and children is in Israeli agriculture, both in settlements in the territories and inside Israel. Pay in this sector is the lowest of all. In 1978 a scandal erupted in Israel when Rafiq Halabi of Israel Television and Amos Elon of *Haaretz* discovered that large numbers of underage children from the Gaza Strip were being employed on kibbutzim and moshavim in the south of Israel. However, despite the furor at the time child labor (employed by both Israelis and Palestinians in the territories and Jerusalem) continues to be a feature of employment.[68]

Motivation to work in Israel also varies, as does opportunity. The distribution of longer term workers seems to suggest that in the West Bank, those who still have land are more likely to work in agriculture or on building sites, both of which allow for seasonal breaks to return to the farm at harvest time and other periods in the year when agricultural work is at its heaviest. It is among those who do not have land that more of the long stayers are to be found, perhaps suggesting a larger proportion from refugee camps and from the towns.[69] It should also be noted that in the West Bank not all areas are uniform in the proportion of workers who go to Israel or in the sectors to which they go. In Gaza the variations are smaller.

There are relatively high proportions of workers in Israel from the Tulkarem, Ramallah, Hebron, and Bethlehem-Jericho areas – nearest to transport and to the major Israeli centers of employment in Jerusalem and on the coast. For these areas the percentage of total employees working in

67. For a description of children from Gaza hired in this way, see an article by Zeev Mefet in *Haaretz*, 10 September 1981; on the Jerusalem "slave market" see Michael Meron, "The Arab Slave Market: Waiting on Line for Work," excerpted from *Yediot Ahronot* in *al-Fajr*, 29 January 1982; and Colin Smith. "Long Wait in Line for West Bank Slave Market," *Observer* (London), 21 February 1982.

68. See, for example, Yaron Ahituv, "Would You Like Your 10-Year-Old Brother To Work in a Bakery 9 Hours a Day? Report on Palestinian Child Labor in Israeli Enterprises," *Kol Hair*, 26 February 1982, translated in *al-Fajr*, 12 March 1982. On child labor employed by Israelis and Palestinians, see Awad Abdel Fattah, "Child Labor under Occupation," *al-Fajr*, 4 October 1981.

69. Tamari, "Building Other People's Homes," pp. 20-21.

Israel is 34-35 percent in 1980 (as usual not counting illegal workers), whereas for more isolated districts, Jenin and Nablus, the figures are 21.8 percent and 13.8 percent respectively.

In Gaza the proportion of employees in Israel is very much higher – highest of all for Khan Yunis, 45.6 percent in 1980; then Rafah, 43.6 percent; and 40.1 percent for Gaza town. Another striking feature of the Gaza figures is the very high proportion of "other" occupations, that is service employment in the local economy: an average of 56.6 percent for 1980 of all local employment.

The proportions of workers in Israel from each area depend first on the number of unskilled and semiskilled people of working age there are in any given town or village. People with skills are seldom able to find appropriate work in Israel and would usually only go there if no other employment could be found. For example, the Israeli *Monthly Bulletin of Statistics* in March 1982 showed that of the requests for workers through Israeli labor exchanges in the territories during 1978-81, only one professional position and eleven clerical positions had been filled in that whole period. In December 1981, out of a total of 3,873 positions filled, 3,299 were for unskilled workers.[70] Official statistics also show that 20 percent of those working in Israel lack any formal education and about 50 percent have only one to eight years of primary school.

Another factor is proximity to major Israeli centers of employment, and what transport is available. Distances are not very great, but in the West Bank some villages have very poor communications. Further considerations are the amount of land available to the village and its overall level of affluence, including the size of remittance flows from abroad. In towns, this latter, along with local employment conditions, would be the determining factors.

Although the Israeli economy was beginning to show signs of recession from the mid-1970s, it was not until 1980 that, for the first time in many years, unemployment among Israelis, rising to 5 percent, became more than a fringe phenomenon. In the territories, it was not until 1984 that unemployment began to show a significant rise. According to a Bank of Israel report, unemployment in the West Bank rose from 1.2 percent in the early 1980s to 3.7 percent in 1984 and to 5.3 percent in early 1985. Most of the unemployed, the report noted, were young, 60 percent below the age of twenty-four, with the more highly educated (over nine years of schooling), making up two-thirds of those out of work.[71]

70. Israel Central Bureau of Statistics, *Monthly Bulletin* (March 1982), table K-7.

71. Dan Zakai, "Economic Developments in Judea-Samaria and the Gaza District 1983-4" (Jerusalem: Bank of Israel Research Department, July 1986), p. 43.

Even while unemployment in Israel rose, the numbers of workers going to Israel from the territories continued to rise until 1984, but showed a slight downturn in 1985. Thus the impact of the overall employment situation on employment of workers from the territories in Israel is not entirely clear. It was argued at the beginning of the recession in the Israeli economy that it would result in the laying off of workers from the territories, since they were the least secure and least organized workers. It was predicted that this would precipitate an unemployment crisis in the territories, as it was quite clear that their economies had not changed in ways that would make them any more capable of absorbing these workers than they had been before 1967 – probably quite the reverse.

This dramatic downturn in the employment of territories' workers did not occur, and this can mainly be explained by the sectors in which Palestinian workers are concentrated, and the types of work they do. The recession did hit the sectors in which territories' workers are most often employed – agriculture, construction, and personal services. Labor Minister Benzion Rubin said in February 1982 that employment in these sectors had shrunk by 3.1 percent, 2 percent and 4.1 percent respectively.[72] It may well be that in these sectors, bosses opted to get rid of more expensive Israeli workers rather than those from the territories. However, Palestinians from the territories are also afforded an ironic kind of security by doing very low status jobs: not only are they the cheapest form of labor, but they do work which Israeli employers openly admit they could not find an Israeli willing to do. Nonetheless, it is particularly difficult to assess employment trends among the "unofficial" workers who sell their labor on a daily basis. It seems that, especially since 1985, such workers may be getting less regular work and tend to be working fewer days each month. However, what is quite clear is that for territories' workers in Israel, even those employed legally, there has been a sharp fall in real wages (see table 11.8). Between 1982 and 1985, wages at 1981 prices for workers in Israel had fallen even more sharply than the average wage for all workers. For example, workers from the village of Yabad in the West Bank who commute to Israel report that in the five years since 1980 their real wages have been halved by inflation. "If they used to earn the shekel equivalent of 5 (Jordanian) dinars in 1980, today they receive the shekel equivalent of 2.5 dinars a day."[73]

Most of the conditions of territories workers in Israel also obtain among those who are employed by Israeli concerns in the occupied territories, particularly those engaged in construction of settlements and in wage labor on agricultural settlements. Companies building settlements during the

72. *Jerusalem Post*, 7 February 1982.

73. Hilterman, "Emerging Trade Union Movement," p. 28.

boom period in new settlement construction in the early 1980s, including Histadrut-owned subsidiaries, usually employed local Palestinians as unskilled and semiskilled labor. The kibbutz bulletin *Amudim* in 1983 quoted a settler from the Kativ bloc of settlements in the Gaza Strip as openly admitting that the reason agriculture was profitable for him was the low gages he paid to Palestinian workers. " 'No problems here, ' he told me, 'I employ Arab workers, and each of them brings in four times the amount I pay him in wages. That's what I live on.' "[74]

The question of whether labor migration to Israel will continue in its present form will be determined not just by the needs of the Israeli economy, but by the future Israeli policies towards the West Bank and Gaza as well as by regional and international developments relating to the overall future of the Palestinians. If those Israeli leaders who pursue the goal of "Judaization" of the occupied territories (with the corollary of pushing out a large proportion of the Palestinian population) were to succeed, the logical conclusion, like that of "pure" apartheid in South Africa, would be to deprive the Israeli economy of most of its cheap labor force. However, the chances are that, just as in South Africa, such policies will not be pushed to this logical conclusion, and that the state will endeavor to protect its economic interests whatever ideological turn it takes.

Nonetheless, as far as the West Bank and Gaza Strip themselves are concerned, the problem of a labor force far larger than current economic capacity remains. Even if the territories were to form the basis of a Palestinian state the problem of absorbing this labor force, plus a large number of Palestinians from elsewhere – probably mainly the poorer, less skilled section of the diaspora – would remain a very serious one. Massive investment would be needed in all sectors if the new entity were to avoid heavy dependence on one or more of its neighbors – Jordan and/or Israel – to take up its surplus labor. This would be a dangerous situation – economically, if not politically, little different from the present one.

EMPLOYMENT AND EDUCATION

By the late 1970s, emigration from the occupied territories, particularly from the West Bank, had reached crisis proportions. Not that emigration was a new phenomenon: people had been emigrating in small numbers since the beginning of the century (see chapter 12), but during the 1970s this steady flow turned into a flood. It is difficult to be exact about the numbers who left, or to distinguish between those who left to study or work for short periods and those who were long-term emigrants. However, during the late

74. *Davar*, 15 May 1983 (trans. *Israeli Mirror*, No. 656).

1970s, net population loss from the West Bank was in the region of fifteen thousand a year or more, and from Gaza net loss was four to five thousand a year (see table 11.10).

It is noticeable that the population loss was proportionally much greater from the West Bank than from Gaza. One of the main reasons was that although many of the same pressures to emigrate exist for Gazans, it is more difficult for them to do so. Most West Bankers, unless they are *persona non grata* with the Jordanian authorities, have, or can obtain, a Jordanian passport, which helps them both to travel and to get permission to work, especially in the Arab world. Most Gazans do not have this possibility, as only a small proportion have Egyptian citizenship. However, emigration from the West Bank has dropped sharply since the early 1980s due to a combination of factors: the recession in the Gulf and the consequences of the 1982 Israeli invasion of Lebanon made it much more difficult for Palestinians to gain admission to the Gulf states, or to find work; and both the Israelis and the Jordanians began to impose new restrictions on Palestinians leaving and returning to the territories.

During the exodus of the 1970s emigration was not spread evenly across the class spectrum. Most of the poorer people went to work in Israel, although some went to Jordan or the Gulf states as laborers in the 1970s during the construction boom in those countries. But it was the educated middle class, in the West Bank particularly, that emigration offered chances of employment and prosperity not available at home. The middle class on the West Bank is made up mainly of the educated sons (and sometimes daughters) of landowners and businessmen, and more recently from among the refugees and villagers who have gained access to education. In Jordanian times this group had a good chance of employment in the Jordanian civil service or army. But since the occupation professional work has been hard to find. The occupation authorities employ a limited number of Palestinians, but in any case working for the occupying power does not have great attraction for most people. Public expenditure is meager and as Husseini points out, "the civil service [as a form of employment] has declined sharply in importance . . . recruitment of new personnel is kept to a minimum.[75] For a university graduate, or a person with other professional qualifications, opportunities are very slim. An Israeli count showed that in the West Bank in 1979 there were a total of 66 civil engineers, 40 architects, 17 electrical engineers, 21 mechanical engineers, 6 chemical engineers, 128 agronomists and 26 veterinary surgeons.[76]

75. Husseini interview, p. 22.

76. Israel Central Bureau of Statistics, quoted in *Statistical Yearbook of Palestine 1980* (Damascus: Palestine National Fund, 1981.

The 1986 Bank of Israel report on the occupied territories noted a marked correlation between education and unemployment: "The figures for unemployment at age 18-24 suggest that it is positively correlated with the level of education: some two-thirds of the unemployed had over 9 years of schooling, and this schooling group had a considerably higher unemployment rate than the less educated."[77] The rapid increase in the numbers of Palestinians going to the four universities in the West Bank as well as to the Islamic University in Gaza has certainly contributed to the numbers of unemployed whose qualifications cannot be utilized within the largely stagnant economies of the territories.

The health care field offers some possibilities, but compared to working abroad, even in Jordan, neither pay nor conditions are attractive. Some nursing schools are insisting on local employment for their graduates for one to two years to try and stem the flight of nursing personnel to the Gulf and other Arab countries.

Teachers are still in demand, and those who were employed before 1967 still get their Jordanian salaries as well as salaries from the Israelis. Employees of the Jordanian Ministry of Education make up 72.9 percent of the civil servants still paid by Jordan.[78]

But teachers hired after 1967, now the majority of younger staff, do not get this privilege. Pay has now fallen behind so badly that teachers are sometimes worse off than unskilled workers in Israel. Some take on second jobs to make ends meet. The Israeli journalist Yehuda Litani interviewed several West Bank teachers on their conditions in 1981. One, who was among the 15 percent who get the Jordanian salary, said he earned IS 2,200 from the Israeli administration and the equivalent of IS 1,500 from the Jordanians, after having taught English in a high school for many years. Other teachers said they got much less than this. One teacher of religious studies in a high school said, "Most of us teachers have much lower salaries, which makes us wonder whether the Israeli government means to starve the West Bank teachers until they agree to emigrate to the oil countries where they can earn an average IS 10,000 a month."[79] The gains in pay made by a two-month "government" teachers' strike in the school year 1980/81 were rapidly eroded by hyperinflation. For example, in March 1983 a teacher with five years' service in a government school in the West Bank received

77. Zakai, "Economic Developments," p. 43.

78. Mansour, "Monetary Dualism," p. 114.

79. Yehuda Litani, *Haaretz,* 6 February 1981.

IS 12,800 (JD 109). By 1984 this had become IS 48,340 (JD 80).[80] The universities in the territories do offer some employment opportunities, as do Hebron Polytechnic and other small institutes of higher education. But, in the universities at least, the period of rapid expansion of the late 1970s and early 1980s is now over, and Bir Zeit University in particular is suffering a severe financial crisis. In all the universities too, frequent disruptions and closures make for very difficult working conditions.

As is true in most Arab countries, the number of people with middle-level technical qualifications is small, partly for the same reasons as apply elsewhere – that these skills are not much sought after and are accorded low prestige in comparison with even the worst sort of university degree. But in the occupied territories there are further complications. The lack of industry means there is little demand for technical skills, except perhaps those of a metal worker or garage mechanic. The Israelis do offer some technical and vocational courses but they have been criticized on a number of occasions by the International Labor Organization for being too short and for offering training in only the low-level skills demanded of Palestinians from the territories in the Israeli labor market.

The United Nations Relief and Works Agency (UNRWA) has several vocational schools in the territories that provide much longer and more solid training, but a survey in the late 1970s by the American Near East Refugee Agency (ANERA) showed that of 215 graduates of seven vocational training institutions in the West Bank, 45 percent found work in Israel, 30 percent in the West Bank, and 25 percent emigrated.[81]

PUBLIC FINANCING

Apart from the structural dependence on Israel which has been built up in the labor market and in trade, the occupying power – whether it calls its administration civil or military – has a key role in determining what public finance is available in the territories, and how it will be spent.

As we have seen, private capital is not used to any great extent for productive investment. Therefore, the role of public funds – either from domestic sources or from aid – would, on the pattern of other Arab states, be important in promoting development projects. But in the territories the

---

80. S. Graham-Brown, *Education, Repression, Liberation: Palestinians* (London: World University Service, 1984), p. 77.

81. *U.S. Economic Aid for the West Bank and Gaza – A Positive Contribution* (Washington: U.S. General Accounting Office, 1978), p. 9.

occupation prevents this, for a number of reasons.

First, the Israelis do not wish to allow any Palestinian centers of power to operate freely. Hence there is no overall local authority to ensure that what funds are available are channeled into planned development. The National Guidance Council, an informal coalition of Palestinian mayors and other leading nationalist political figures which was formed in the mid-1970s, did attempt to perform this role for sectors such as health and education. But by the early 1980s, the Israelis, by means of arrests, house arrest orders, and bans on travel had effectively prevented the council from operating. Most of its leading members, representing municipal and professional bodies, are now either in jail, in exile, debarred from public office, or otherwise silenced.

The municipalities, which in the late 1970s could play a somewhat active role in local development as well as politics, have since had their activities severely curtailed by the Israelis. In the 1980s the elected mayors of almost all the main towns were dismissed and replaced first by Israeli military officers and then in a number of cases (Nablus, Hebron, Ramallah, and al-Bireh in 1986) by Israeli-appointed Palestinian mayors. No new elections are envisaged. Annexed Jerusalem has an Israeli mayor, and there is no form of authority there independent from the Israelis.

The economic effectiveness of the municipalities in the territories is also curbed by lack of money. According to Mansour, investments by the public sector (including the municipalities) came to only 10-15 percent of total investments between 1973 and 1979, whereas the rate was as high as 30-40 percent from 1968 to 1973.[82]

The budget provided by the Israeli Ministry of Defense for the territories is scarcely generous, particularly when compared with the funds available to Israeli settlers in the territories. Those involved in health and education services particularly report declines since 1980 in their budgets in real terms, mainly because of hyperinflation. For health, the ILO report said that in 1981 Arab sources reported "deteriorating health conditions" in the territories, as a result in particular of the freezing of budgetary appropriations for government hospitals.[83] In education, classroom space has not kept up with demand in what is a very young population. According to Israeli figures, 1,490 rented rooms were being used for teaching in 1980 in the territories.[84] Indeed, it seems that the territories today largely finance

82. Mansour, "Monetary Dualism," p. 12.

83. *ILO Report,* p. 122. The author formed the same impression from interviews conducted with West Bank health care workers in 1980.

84. "The Occupation Generation," *The Middle East* (June 1982), p. 13.

the Israeli occupation, rather than vice versa. The annual report of the civil administration for the fiscal year 1984/85 notes that taxes collected from the population under occupation (including 15% VAT) amounted to IS 7.4 million, an increase in real terms of 39 percent. The report suggests that the occupation (excluding military expenses) now "hardly costs the Israelis anything." The same conclusion emerges from calculations made by Meron Benvenisti on the hidden gains made by the Israeli treasury from the occupation. He remarks that this "refutes Israeli claims that the low level of public expenditure and investment derives from budgetary limitations. If net fiscal transfers had been invested in the area, rather than added to Israeli public expenditure, it would have been possible to improve local services significantly, and in particular, to develop local economic infrastructure."[85]

The Israelis are reported by the ILO to have complied with their suggestion that income tax paid by occupied territories workers in Israeli employment should go into the territories' budget fund, but this was only implemented at the beginning of the 1980s. Thus, until that time, taxes paid by workers from the territories were apparently going to Israel's own budget income.[86]

Most of the funds for development projects come neither from local sources nor from the Israeli government, but from external sources. The main source of aid since 1978 has been from the allocations made at the Arab summit conference of Baghdad (1978) for the front-line states. Other major sources are American Near East Refugee Agency (ANERA) (which is mainly funded by USAID), UNRWA, and various smaller international charities, several connected with Christian churches.

Much of UNRWA's current funding, transferred via Jordan, is not spent on development but on salaries for their teaching, health, and administrative staff and on food and relief payments for the poorest refugees – although this program now seems to be running down. Hence, given the structure of the economy, much of this money is spent on consumer goods and therefore finds its way into the Israeli economy via payments for Israeli goods and services.

The Israelis are generally hostile to any development projects which appear to them to be designed to make the economies of the territories more independent. The case of water use in agriculture has already been mentioned, and the municipalities have also faced problems with Israeli restrictions on the expansion of domestic water facilities. Another very sensitive area of infrastructure is electricity. Nablus mayor Bassam Shaka

85. *Al-Fajr,* 21 June 1985, p. 1; Benvenisti, *1986 Report,* p. 19.

86. ILO Report, p. 112.

was refused permission to install a new local electricity generator in the town and was pressured, as have been other municipalities, to allow Nablus to be connected to the Israeli central electricity grid. Another such case, mentioned above, is that of the East Jerusalem Electric Company, which symbolizes both the political and economic dimensions of Israeli attempts to subordinate the territories.

This interference with the development of local infrastructure is in addition to the establishment of infrastructure by the Israelis for their own use. This includes a number of roads, water pipelines, and wells to serve settlement and military requirements.

When outside agencies provide funds, the projects for which they are given are scrutinized by the occupation authorities. The U.S. General Accounting Office report on aid – giving in the territories sums up the situation of U.S. organizations as follows:

> Because the U.S. government does not recognize Israeli sovereignty over the occupied territories it does not officially acknowledge the Israeli government's authority to direct U.S. funded activity. However, the reality of the occupation requires coordination between the voluntary agencies and the military government, since the latter has overall responsibility for the welfare of the residents.
>
> A problem arises when drawing the line between cooperation and obtaining approval. The Israeli Ministry of Social Welfare is responsible for voluntary agency activity and at times attempts to direct that activity. It justifies these actions on the basis of coordinating its own and other organizations' assistance to avoid duplication and monitoring all activities for security purposes. The voluntary agencies resist these attempts because of U.S. policy regarding the segregation of U.S. and Israeli activities and because of their own policies of self-direction.[87]

Despite its coy approach to the subject, this document does outline the constraints upon aid agencies. What is questionable is the giving of equal weight in Israeli motives to the need for "welfare" coordination and the needs of "security." Taking security in the wide sense usually ascribed to it by the Israelis, it is arguable that this consideration plays a much more important part in their decisions than "coordination." The cautious tone of this document may be viewed in light of the vast discrepancy between the sums of aid given to the occupied territories ($6 million in 1982, $10 million for 1984-85 and $18 million for 1985-86) and the sum approaching $3 billion which goes in economic and military aid each year to the occupying power, Israel. The steep rise in U.S. aid since 1984 was the result of the policy of "improving the quality of life" in the occupied territories promoted by U.S. Secretary of State George Shultz, evidently

87. G.A.O., *U.S. Economic Aid for the West Bank and Gaza.*

with the aim of lessening discontent with the occupation and drawing people away from allegiance to the Palestinian Liberation Organization (PLO).

Prior to this initiative, USAID money channeled through ANERA, like other funds for projects subject to Israeli official approval, was often never disbursed. In general, projects which would be likely to increase economic independence are not passed or are severely delayed. For instance, ANERA, whose relations with the occupation authorities are generally not considered as difficult as those of some of the smaller voluntary agencies, had had a number of categorical rejections of proposed projects as well as long bureaucratic delays and evasions – another commonly used weapon of the administration. For instance, in mid-1979, of nineteen projects submitted for the financial year 1979, five had already been rejected out of hand. Three of these were electrification projects – for Nablus, Hebron, and Dura. One was an agricultural cooperative services project for Halhul. Some other projects of this kind were approved, so it seems likely that Halhul (which also was refused a new fruit and vegetable market for a couple of years) was being politically penalized – particularly for the views and actions of its mayor Mohammed Milhem. The fifth was a private hospital project in Hebron.

In 1983-84 only half of the $8 million budget was actually disbursed. In the case of ANERA, at least, the proportion rose after the Shultz initiative as the Israelis somewhat eased the criteria for approval. Yet as Benvenisti has observed, projects involving land reclamation or the development of enterprises which might conflict with Israeli interests or settlement plans were not approved, whereas those which might save the occupation authorities money tended to be regarded with more favor.

Henry Selz, Middle East representative of ANERA for nine years up to 1985, explains the Israeli use of the "quality of life" concept as a means of increasing individual wealth and political quiescence:

> There are two radically opposed interpretations of the phrase "quality of life." It can either mean trying to give the Palestinians a little greater control over their day-to-day existence, such as small-scale development programs of the type we have been trying to do, or it can mean projects which increase personal wealth without strengthening institutions or strengthening communities, in a way which the Israeli government is perfectly happy about.[88]

Refusal to allow aid agencies to fund particular projects had also been used by the Israelis as a form of political manipulation – as a collective

88. Interview with Henry Selz, *MERIP Reports* (October-December 1985), 136/37:25.

punishment of towns or villages whose leadership does not cooperate with the authorities or where there is particularly strong resistance to the occupation; or as a carrot of easy access to funds and services for those who have proved cooperative.

However, it does not appear that the Israelis have been alone in attempting to manipulate the economic development of the territories for political ends, though clearly they are in the best position to do this. Tamari analyzes the way the funds from the Arab states channeled through Jordan and the PLO were disbursed before funding was cut off.

> This money is channeled through Jordan, which uses it politically to buttress pro-Jordanian forces in the West Bank. The appropriations usually go for to municipal and village councils, often reaching their destination through traditional pro-Jordanian *mukhtars* and village elders. Professional associations, housing organizations, women's and social societies also receive funds. Funds have been withdrawn quite often to penalize individuals, groups and sometimes whole cities who choose not to cooperate with Jordan in such schemes, especially during periods when Jordan and the PLO are at odds.
>
> Part of this dispute has been resolved for the moment by the creation of the Joint Palestinian-Jordanian committee, in charge of receiving and screening applications for aid and channeling the funds to prevent misappropriation and political use. However, this committee is overwhelmingly, or unduly, under Jordanian influence. The Jordanian state is adjacent to Israel and Israel implicitly cooperates with Jordan by approving funds to favored individuals and societies and municipal councils, and punishing those who are seen by the Israeli authorities as fomenting resistance. This tacit cooperation with Jordan may change in the wake of an Israeli order in July 1981 forbidding the transfer of funds from the . . . committee, and Israel's own program of funding unrepresentative village councils in the West Bank in an attempt to create an alternative political leadership.[89]

It is clear that the PLO also viewed the "steadfastness" funds primarily as a way of achieving political influence as well as keeping people "on the land." Certainly the record of the disbursement of "steadfastness" funds does no indicate a commitment to economic development or self-sufficiency as a priority. Of the $435 million transferred by the joint committee between 1979 and 1984, only 13 percent went to agriculture, water, industry, and transport, 25 percent as direct subsidy to the "individual sector," 18 percent to education, and 9 percent to "social development."[90]

89. Salim Tamari, "West Bank Politics and Social Forces," *MERIP Report s* (October-December 1981), 100/101:33. The point about the strong Jordanian influence on the decisions of the committee was also confirmed to the author in an interview with Haidar Abu Shafi, head of the Palestine Red Crescent Society, in Gaza, January 1981.

90. Benvenisti, *1986 Report,* p. 20.

over four years to the development of the territories seemed equally to be motivated by a wish to buy political influence, this time without the PLO. However, with the current recession in the Jordanian economy, these funds could only come from outside donors, whether the United States or the Arab world, and in the present political and economic climate there is no certainty that the money will be forthcoming.

STANDARD OF LIVING

It is one of the constant boasts of the Israeli authorities that people in the territories have "never had it so good" in material terms. If the ability to purchase goods is taken to be the sole measure of prosperity and economic well-being, individual or collective, then there might be some truth in this assertion.[91] This type of argument has been used in the white settler states of southern Africa to justify their economic policies, but in any other context, few would admit the validity of this point of view.

First, the immediate gains in living standards came mainly from employment in Israel or abroad, not from an increase in productive capacity at home. Migrant labor, even if it is more profitable to individuals than work at home, is always vulnerable to the closing off of the labor markets which employ them. In Europe over the past few years, for instance, Turkish and north African workers have found to their cost the basic insecurity of their positions, as the recession made them unwelcome "guests." In the Israeli case, political as well as economic factors will play a crucial role in determining where people from the territories can sell their labor power – and on what terms.

Second, the undoubted gains in material living standards up to the mid-1970s have lessened in the 1980s as Israel has headed into recession. This is not so much because of a reduction in work opportunities, but because of the enormous rate of inflation imported into the territories by the increasing domination of the ailing Israeli economy, which has eroded the earning power of those initially higher Israeli wages. It is also clear that real wages for territories workers, whether at home or in Israel, have not kept pace with inflation (see table 11.11 for general trends).

91. Early analysts of the economic effects of the occupation emphasized this aspect – see A. Bregman, *The Economy of the Administered Territories 1974-75* (Jerusalem: Bank of Israel, 1976) and V.A. Bull, *The West Bank: Is it Viable?* (Lexington, Mass.: Lexington Books, 1975), The first to look in detail at the structural effects of Israeli domination was Brian Van Arkadie, in *Benefits and Burdens: A Report on the West Bank and Gaza Strip Economies since 1967.*

In these respects, it is clear that in order to obtain the refrigerator or television set which so many more people now have, those people must pay the price of the ever increasing structural dependence of the economy on external forces, most of which emanate from Israel. This naturally does not preclude Israeli statisticians and analysts from finding enough examples of individual short-term gain to paint a rosy picture of an economic situation that is unhealthy. Thus after twenty years of occupation it is the needs and policies of the Israeli economy which predominate at a number of levels in determining the direction and the prosperity of the economies of the occupied territories.

Of the two, the gaza Strip has less room to maneuver because the local economic base is so small and artificial. For the West Bank, however, there is a second, though less crucial dependence on Jordan, which exists parallel to the dominant dependence on Israel. Jordan has to be relied upon for trade with the Arab world, for banking facilities, and for stable currency. At various times it has also been the channel for aid and a source of employment. These trends have been sharpened by the recession in the Israeli economy and the boom in Jordan since the mid-1970s.

The impact of the Palestinian uprising against the occupation, which began in December 1987 has yet to be assessed. But it is clear at the time of writing that it has already had a significant effect on the Israeli economy. long-running commercial strikes in the territories have reduced the consumption of Israeli imports, and there have been moves by some Palestinians to implement a systematic boycott campaign against certain Israeli products.

Workers in Israel from the territories have generally observed calls to general strikes put out by the underground national leadership, At other times, many of these workers are driven to continue commuting daily to Israel by economic hardship. However, although no hard figures are yet available, it appears that many of these workers are crossing the green line no more than half the working days in the month. Although the withdrawal of labour is far from complete, it has already had a significant impact on those sectors of the Israeli economy which depend heavily on cheap Palestinian labour – construction, agriculture, textiles and services – and this has led to discussion in the Israeli press of possible alternative sources of cheap labour.

Nonetheless, whatever the outcome of the uprising, the economic and social changes brought about by those various forms of dependency will have to be taken into consideration by any future Palestinian administration. Although certain of the economic patterns that have developed can be reversed if a greater degree of economic independence can be achieved – self-sufficiency could never really be in the cards – many of the changes in the social formation which have been wrought by the Israeli economic domination are not so easily reversed, and would have to be accommodated in the new state.

CHAPTER 12

Impact on the Social Structure of Palestinian Society

Sarah Graham-Brown

The economic changes since the occupation in 1967 have inevitably left their mark on the social structure of the West Bank and the Gaza Strip. But the shifts in power, class, and status which have occurred should not be considered as simple cause-and-effect relationships. They also need to be understood in the context of the differing histories of the two regions.

SOCIAL BACKGROUND BEFORE 1967

West Bank

Until the war of 1967, the West Bank could be characterized as a rural economy where the dominant class was composed of medium-and large-scale landowners, some absentees who had lived in the city for several generations, others still living in villages and small towns close to their land. To these were added merchants dealing primarily in trade in agricultural commodities and imported manufactured goods. Small industrial enterprises were mostly based on agricultural raw materials – for instance the Nablus olive oil soap industry – and owned by members of one or another of the above two groups. These interests in trade, agriculture, and industry were often consolidated by family ties.

Much of the rest of the population in this predominantly rural area made a living from agriculture, and most had some access to land, either as smallholders or as sharefarmers or sharecroppers. Agricultural wage labor was the exception rather than the rule. Landowners were often powerful local figures who played an influential part in the economic and social life of villages where they controlled all or part of the land. Within the village, the extended family remained the dominant social and economic unit. To this day many villages in the West Bank remain divided into factions based on extended families vying for influence.

In 1948, life in the West Bank was not disrupted to the same degree as it was in the areas which fell inside the borders declared by the state of Israel. The immediate effect was a large influx of refugees, mostly from the central region of the country including the towns of Jaffa, Ramle, and Lydda, though the majority came from rural areas. Some of the refugees were housed in the camps established by the United Nations Relief and Works Agency (UNRWA), scattered over the West Bank and in the Jordan valley near Jericho. Others gradually settled into established village communities, although not without social tensions. As the new inhabitants had no access to land, their status tended to be a lowly one in communities where until recently land was the main indicator of wealth and prestige. Certainly in some cases, this influx of people increased social differentiation in village communities and put pressure on existing land and resources. For the West Bank as a whole, the flow of trade as well as economic, social, and cultural contacts suddenly switched direction: towards Jordan and away from the Mediterranean coast which had been its previous focus. Furthermore, the burden of the extra population put a strain on the economy. Many of the refugees could not find work, as the West Bank's economy did not have a high absorptive capacity to cope with large numbers of landless people. The local population was also cut off from opportunities for wage labor, which coastal agriculture and public works had previously provided, and most literature on the period of Jordanian rule in the West Bank reports substantial underemployment, especially in the rural areas.

Emigration offered one way out of this situation, and both refugees and local people took this option in increasing numbers from the 1950s onwards. The main destinations were Jordan and the Gulf and other Arab countries and though some areas, especially Ramallah, Bethlehem, and Jerusalem, had a long tradition, mainly among the Christian communities, of emigration to the United States and Latin America. However, as J.S. Migdal points out, this phenomenon was not evenly spread through all the towns and villages of the West Bank, nor were its social effects the same in all communities.[1] For instance, in the early 1960s, the Hebron area, the

1. J.S. Migdal, ed., *Palestinian Society and Politics* (Princeton, N.J.: Princeton University Press, 1980), pp. 57 ff.

least agriculturally well endowed in the West Bank, apparently had the highest level of emigration; far fewer people left from the Nablus region, traditionally more prosperous. Migdal further argues that the previous economic status of the migrants made a difference in the effects their departure (and the remittances they sent back) had on the community. Many of those who went to the United States from the Ramallah and Jerusalem areas came from well-to-do families, some of whom already had relatives in the host country or at any rate could afford to send their children and relatives abroad in some style. On the whole these emigrants, mainly through their remittances, simply reinforced existing patterns of stratification in the home town or village, making those who were already well off more affluent. On the other hand, in areas such as Hebron, where many of the emigrants came from poorer families, their remittances had a more significant impact on local social and economic patterns.

Towns and cities in the West Bank developed increasingly strong ties with Jordan and its capital city, Amman. The business and professional community began to look to Amman for contacts both locally and in the wider Arab world, and these ties have in many cases persisted since the occupation.

The Jordanians looked on the West Bank as an agricultural hinterland for the East Bank, and were in no hurry to make changes that would shift the socio economic structure away from that role. However the promotion of Amman as the country's capital city had a detrimental impact on the status of an already divided Jerusalem, and affected the distinctive position of the major families of that city. Their importance and prestige had rested not so much on land ownership as on their relations with the Muslim religious establishment, their claims on the Ottomans (and to a lesser extent the British) for access to the positions of power in the city administration, and their consequent primacy in the nationalist movement until the 1940s.

Among the landowning class as a whole, the Jordanian period saw a further drift of the younger members of the major families to the cities and larger towns. In some cases, it seems, large landowners were shedding some if not all of their holdings – probably for more profitable investments across the River Jordan. If Hillal's figures are accurate, the number of holdings above two thousand dunums declined from ninety-eight in 1953 to four in 1964 (see table 11.5 in previous chapter). However, in a countervailing movement during the 1950s, landowners from both sides of the Jordan cashed in on the cheap tracts of land available in the Jordan valley with the hope that in the future a comprehensive irrigation scheme would make farming profitable. It was on these lands that numbers of refugees from the camps around Jericho worked as sharecroppers or wage laborers.

Another trend, which began to bear fruit in the 1950s and 1960s, was the expansion of state education to a wider section of the community. Poorer sections of the rural community remained mostly untouched by this development – illiteracy is still high today, especially among women and older people, in the more isolated villages. But in the urban areas, among the landowning or merchant classes wherever they lived, and among some well-to-do villagers, education of sons, if not daughters, was increasingly seen as a means of social mobility. The rich invested in their children's education, usually at private schools in Jerusalem or abroad, and in university education for their sons.

During the mandate period this trend had already created the beginnings of a small middle class of lawyers, doctors, and teachers, although they were concentrated mainly in Jerusalem and the coastal cities of Haifa and Jaffa. In the Jordanian period, according to the 1961 census, Jerusalem had the highest proportion of both men and women with a high-school education or more. By contrast, the Hebron district had the worst record in this respect.[2]

Until 1948, secondary schools were mostly private, usually run by Christian or Muslim religious institutions. Some of these have remained the most prestigious private schools, still favored by the elite. They were concentrated in the Jerusalem-Ramallah area and to a lesser extent in Nablus. It is in these areas that the West Bank's four main universities are now situated (Bethlehem University, al-Najah University in Nablus, Hebron University, and Bir Zeit University near Ramallah. In the villages, the British had established little more than a skeletal school system and even in later times, the level of education as well as attitudes towards it were often dictated by the presence or absence of mission schools.[3] Among refugees, education was often the only way for families to climb out of their landless and often jobless situation and to regain some kind of independent status – by helping their children to do so. Schools established by UNRWA provided some opportunity for escape from the limitations of camp life. In fact UNRWA is still a major provider of schooling up to the preparatory level (12-15 years), both in the West Bank and in Gaza. By the early 1980s, the agency served 37,931 pupils in the West Bank and 73,874 pupils in the Gaza Strip at the elementary and preparatory levels.[4] The employment

2. *Ibid.* p. 57.

3. K. Mahshi and R. Rihan, "Education: Elementary and Secondary," in E.A. Nakhleh, ed., *A Palestinian Agenda for the West Bank and Gaza* (Washington: American Enterprise Institute for Public Policy Research, 1980), p. 53.

situation in the West Bank during the Jordanian period encouraged this trend towards more education, as professional and service jobs requiring some education were comparatively plentiful. The bureaucracy in the West Bank, though not very large, was locally recruited and there was a demand for doctors, teachers, nurses, clerical staff, and other salaried employees. UNRWA also employed teachers, doctors, social workers, and clerical staff. An important additional source of employment was the Jordanian army. And in the 1960s, parts of the Arab world, particularly the Gulf, had a growing need for professional and white-collar workers.

Hence by 1967 there was a group of people in white-collar employment who, although they could not be said to constitute a definable class, had emerged as an important new status group. Moreover, a whole generation of children was being educated with this destination in mind.

Gaza

Whereas the history of the West Bank up to the occupation was one of relatively slow class reorientation, without very dramatic upheavals (by Palestinian standards), that of the Gaza Strip can reasonably be described as traumatic. In 1948 Gaza town was swamped by a vast wave of refugees uprooted from their homes. During the mandate period it was a large town by contemporary standards – 34,170 in 1944 – serving the agricultural hinterland of southern Palestine. After 1948 an area consisting of Gaza, three other small towns, and eight villages was cut off from that hinterland and from the rest of the country and attached to Egypt, whose main centers of population and economic activity were hundreds of miles away across the Sinai Desert.

The refugees numbered some one hundred fifty thousand, three times the population of Gaza town. Not only was there no land for these refugees, most of whom were peasants, but there was the problem of housing and sustaining them in this semiarid area, an artificial economic and political entity cut out of its former economic and social fabric. Furthermore, the people who had fled there seem by and large to have been the poorest, least skilled, and least privileged of all the groups forced to flee Palestine in 1948.

4. United Nations Relief and Works Agency for Palestinian Refugees, *Report of the Commissioner General, 1 July 1980-30 June 1981* (New York: UNRWA, 1981), p. 25. Hereinafter UNRWA *Report.*

During the period of Egyptian rule stagnation was the prevailing characteristic: little industry existed and the public sector was small compared with that of the West Bank. One of the few flourishing occupations was smuggling, conducted via the local Bedouin population. The only major development was the establishment by local merchants and landowners of capitalist plantation agriculture, growing citrus fruit for export. Thus the richer stratum of the town's previous inhabitants succeeded in maintaining if not improving its economic and social position. Otherwise the very high levels of unemployment among the refugees prevented the emergence of new social forces. Rather it reinforced what has been clumsily but accurately called the "declassing" of this dispossessed population. The only ways out were through education – less available beyond UNRWA provision than in the West Bank – and through emigration, a path which considerable numbers of Gazans took in the 1950s and 1960s.

SOCIAL CHANGE SINCE THE OCCUPATION

In the West Bank the most marked changes in social structure that have occurred since the Israeli occupation have been in the rural sector, where some 70 percent of the population still lives. It is a measure of the change to contrast this figure with one from an earlier period. In the 1930s and 1940s, 70 percent of the population gained a livelihood from agriculture, but today, despite the fact that the same proportion of the total population lives in the countryside, only just over 30 percent earn a living from local agriculture. In many ways the key to understanding the changes in the rural areas lies in grasping the changes in people's relationship to the land, and through it, to each other. However, this cannot be seen as a straightforward, linear process of change. The forces at work for change and for stasis are numerous and their interactions are not always easily predictable. Sometimes the pace of economic change is not exactly matched by its social impact.

First of all, the effects of direct interventions by the occupying power on the social structure cannot be discounted. The Israeli authorities have certain perceptions of the nature of Palestinian society and sometimes attempt to act on these views in order to manipulate the situation politically to their own advantage. But their policies in the economic sphere – tying the territories firmly to Israel's economic apronstrings and using them as a reservoir of cheap labor – have themselves brought about social changes which were not always anticipated, and do not necessarily fit with Israeli sociological theories.

One line of analysis emanating from left-labor Zionist circles going back to the 1920s and 1930s was that Palestinian society was backward and feudal, and that until the landowning class had been overturned no real social change could occur. But the view that has become more prevalent in the academic establishment and among those Israeli "Arabists" who advise the occupying administration is that Palestinian society is still firmly based at the village level on the *hamula* structure of extended families, with relations of patronage the dominant characteristic both within families and between "notables" and peasantry. In this view, these relationships should not be destroyed but rather maintained and used as a means of leverage. In the 1950s and 1960s these methods were used in the villages inside the 1948 borders of Israel. The Israelis tried to establish relations of patronage with those whom they saw as having this kind of kinship-based power within each village.[5] It was thought that in the West Bank after the occupation, such policies would be even more relevant, because the social structure had undergone less disruption and family ties were still very strong. However, in neither case did this take sufficient account of the fact that the swinging economic changes brought in by the new regime, although they did not overturn the social order in the countryside, did modify it considerably. These changes have, in fact, eroded (although not destroyed) the economic and political position of this class of "notables" through the effects they have had on social relations of production on the land.

Israeli attempts to manipulate this group politically have had very mixed results. During the rule of the Labor Alignment prior to 1977, attention was concentrated with varying degrees of success on the landowners and merchants who were considered pro-Jordanian (that is, those who had strong connections, social and economic as well as political, with the Hashemite Kingdom and were influenced by these ties), while Moshe Dayan's overall strategy for the occupation was to keep a relatively low profile while attempting to co-opt these groups.

One of the problems with this strategy was that the Israelis had relatively little to offer this class in the way of rewards, except to channel public funds their way. But as chapter 11 showed, agriculture, from which many of this group derive at least a portion of their income, either through farming or trade, has not generally prospered. Even those willing to introduce new technology, especially irrigation, have found themselves from time to time up against Israeli restrictions. The settlement program and closures of land by the Israeli military have also alienated the landowners.

5. S. Jiryis, *The Arabs in Israel 1948-1966* (New York: Monthly Review Press, 1976).

Supporting the Israelis led to neither credibility nor power, and in recent years, the political hegemony of the "notables" has been sharply challenged by other groups, mainly urban based, including professionals and some merchants as well as the rising generation of school and university students. Despite Israeli interference with some of the candidates, evidence of this shift was to be found in the 1976 municipal elections. No further elections have been permitted and those elected in 1976 have now been dismissed from office by the Israelis.

After Jordan's rejection of the Camp David agreements, the Israelis have found the field of potential allies even further narrowed. Even those who would previously have gone along with the Israelis, if only tacitly, see little hope of power or influence from the discredited "autonomy" plans, and follow Jordan's lead in rejecting them.

Wealth and influence can still be derived from economic and political relations with Jordan, and some Israeli politicians may hope that any future rapprochement with Jordan will increase "cooperation" with this class, but there is no immediate prospect of this. During the period of Likud governments from 1977 to 1983, however, Israeli civil administrators, particularly Menachem Milson, attempted to implement a more active policy to encourage collaboration.

The policy sought to counteract the increasing influence of the urban-based middle class, both by curtailing opportunities for political activity and by creating conditions in which substantial numbers of this class left the country. In this, as we have seen, they were assisted by the economic situation and the lack of professional jobs in the territories. At the same time the Israeli administration created the Village Leagues, rural-based groups beholden to the Israelis which were intended to counterpose the "conservative" village population against "radical" townspeople. Milson, who was instrumental in the establishment of the leagues, also believed in the importance of manipulating family ties and building on relations of patronage. For example, the leader of the Hebron Village Leagues, Mustafa Dudin, was a long-time collaborator and a local landowner who could mobilize clients from his rural district.

Nonetheless, the numbers of people whom the Israelis were able to co-opt on this basis was small, and they began to weight the scales in the leagues' favor, by giving them physical power – issuing arms to members, and permitting them to use force against anyone with whom they had accounts to settle; and by using the leagues as channels for the whole array of permits, travel documents, and services required for Palestinians under occupation. By the mid-1980s, however, the leagues had faded into insignificance, stymied by their own contradictions: first, their open links with the Israelis earned them contempt in the community; and second, the

Israelis' determination to keep tight control over them led to splits with some groups wishing to distance themselves from this close association with the occupying power.

Israeli techniques for dealing with Gaza have been rather different. They were initially directed against the violent opposition the occupation encountered in its first three years – Ariel Sharon presided over the brutal suppression of this resistance. By the end of 1970 this uprising was effectively crushed. Since that time, the Israeli authorities have continued to exercise much tighter control in the Gaza Strip than in the West Bank. Curfews, searches, arrests, punitive demolitions of houses, and other collective punishments have been, particularly in the camps, even more regular features of life than they have been in the West Bank. During the recent uprising which began in December 1987, intensified repression by the Israeli army initially focused on the refugee camps of the Gaza Strip but subsequently affected all the refugee camps and most of the towns and villages in the territories.

As there was in Gaza only a miniscule class of the kind the Israelis sought to co-opt in the West Bank, they turned their attention to the vast refugee population whom they hoped to wean away from their sense of identity as Palestinian refugees – the only identity that gave them any sense of community or purpose. By drawing them into wage labor in Israel and by gradually moving them out of the camps, it was apparently expected that resistance to the occupation and desire for change would be muted. But as Sheila Ryan pointed out a few years back,

> In the course of trying to "solve" the old problem in their relations with the people of Gaza – their refugee standing and the destitution of unemployment – by offering a solution very much in the interests of Israeli employers, the Israeli government is in fact creating new contradictions. A man from Gaza working in Israel knows he is treated much worse than an Israeli worker, that he does not earn enough to support his family on [*sic*] a reasonable standard and the conditions in which he must work are inhuman.[6]

Ryan's views are supported by the following story, which appeared in the Israeli magazine *Monitin* in 1981 and illustrates a Gazan worker's frustration and feelings about his Israeli employers. The dead relatives referred to in the story were a brother and an uncle who also worked in Israel, and were killed along with eighteen other workers in an accident while traveling to work from the Gaza Strip.

6. S. Ryan, "Israeli Economic Policy in the Occupied Areas," *MERIP Reports* (January 1974), 24:17.

I arranged to meet Ahmed in a cafe in the center of Rishon Lezion. He arrived wearing his stained work overalls. He had just finished his quota which consisted of emptying 1,200 dustbins. He is 33 years old, has 7 children, is a high-school graduate and has been working for the town council for 12 years. He earns 2,500 shekels a month. . . . Speaking in good Hebrew, Ahmed tells me the story of his life. . . . "I was born on the day of independence" he says. "Your independence, that is. The past is gone. I was a month old when my parents fled from Majdal, which you now call Ashkelon. But let's cut out the politics," he checks himself. I try to understand how a high-school graduate who reads the newspapers (*al-Quds* and *al-Fajr*) and knows many books (his favorite author is Victor Hugo) as well as knowing much about modern filmmaking is still emptying dustbins at the age of 33 for IS 2,500 a month.

He does not share my astonishment. "It's no disgrace," he says several times. "Anyway, that's my life. That's how things turned out. I can't start doing something new today." A few minutes later he says: "Sometimes I feel ashamed . . . but what can I do? I can't get transferred to another department. The Israeli bosses say anyone who has a job in a certain department must stay there." "I am not complaining," he keeps saying, but from what he says many accusations emerge, although they are formulated with great moderation. His salary is very low and there is no chance of promotion. "An Arab can't even become the man in charge of the dust car. How can we advance without a union? The workers union of the Jews won't let us join."

He is also disappointed by the way his employers treated the families of his dead relatives. He thought the employers could have shown some consideration for the victims of the accident. And then he says angrily: "Why do we only have 7 days off a year, while the Jews have 14? I won't be able to go abroad even once in my life, to Europe or America, even once. It is in my character to travel, why shouldn't I be able to? Am I not a human being?"[7]

The policy of removing people from refugee camps to place them in alternative accommodations has continued, though slowly, and UNRWA too has made efforts in this direction. Although the goal of providing alternative housing – given the poor conditions in the camps – may be legitimate enough, the Israelis apparently have a further motive in pursuing this policy. It is again linked to attempts to separate camp people from their community and their refugee status.

The Israeli Defense Ministry coordinator for the occupied territories in 1985, Shmu'el Goren, associated this policy of moving camp inhabitants to new homes outside the camps with the improvement of the "quality of life" (see chapter 11). But another motive was political: to disperse people from camps which have been centers of resistance. The two camps Goren singled out as priorities for resettlement – Jabaliya in the Gaza Strip, and Dheisheh camp in the West Bank – both have records as strong centers of opposition

7. D. Halevi, "Jobs for Arabs," *Monitin,* December 1981.

to the occupation. According to Goren, the resettlement so far carried out in the Gaza strip is regarded as a success by the authorities because "not one family resettled has been engaged in hostile activities."[8]

UNRWA regularly reports tussles with the authorities in Gaza over the demolition of existing shelters before people are moved to new houses – this apart from the demolition of housing used as collective punishment for alleged offenses by a family member. UNRWA's 1981 annual report described the situation as follows:

> To reduce the overcrowding in the Gaza Strip it is essential that the total complement of housing should increase very substantially. There has been an improvement in the standard of living of refugees who have been able to pay for and move into housing projects developed by the Israeli authorities or who have built their own homes on land they have purchased in these developments. However the overall situation has not been helped by the insistence of the military authorities that refugees moving from the camps into projects should demolish their shelters before doing so. . . . In the year under review 272 rooms were demolished for this reason and were therefore not available to alleviate overcrowded conditions in the camps.[9]

The agency also reported resistance to its own scheme to move 381 families living in very poor, crowded, barrack-block accommodations to new houses. This perhaps indicates the people's suspicion as to the motives behind all attempts by the authorities to make changes that affect community and social patterns. And despite these new housing schemes, almost half the population of the Gaza Strip – 244,416 people in 1987 – still live in refugee camps, while 445,397 are registered refugees.

REMITTANCES AND WAGE LABOR

Whatever the consciously manipulative aims of the Israeli authorities in the occupied territories, the social changes that were the direct result of their policies are minor compared with those that have resulted from economic factors, especially by migrant labor and remittances, coming both from workers inside Israel and from emigrants abroad.

Information on this whole question is fragmentary both in terms of overall statistics and specific examples. The changes have been emerging slowly and have only begun to take a clear shape over the last few years.

8. *Jerusalem Post,* 13 May 1985, quoted in *Journal of Palestine Studies* (Summer 1985), 14(4):181-82.

9. UNRWA *Report,* pp. 21, 37.

Hence it is only possible to piece together what detailed research has been done with the overall figures (which themselves are not very trustworthy – see note on statistics at beginning of chapter 11) and conclusions can be no more than tentative.

What does emerge from the data on the West Bank is that the impact on the rural areas (from which some 70 percent of the migrants to Israel come) has been the most striking. There is rather more information on change in the villages than there is for the towns or the refugee camps, where the impact of remittances from abroad is probably a key factor.

Even at the village level it is clear that there is no simple formula for the way change occurs. Among the factors determining the impact of remittances on village society are the viability of agriculture in the village and access to land per capita, the patterns of internal and external migration in the community, the power structure in the village, and the proximity to major towns.

The following examples, taken from research done over the last fifteen years, may illustrate some of the different permutations that may occur. The first, described by M. Escribano and N. el-Joubeh, is from Deir Dibwan, a village in the Ramallah district which now has a population of about four thousand.[10] It is a particularly striking instance of the effect of migration abroad which, as in many villages of this area, began as long ago as the turn of the century and has continued sporadically ever since. The first waves went to Latin America, chiefly to Brazil, Colombia, and Venezuela. In the 1950s the focus shifted to the United States, where the majority of the migrants, thought to number about three thousand, are now – most of them in California.

This longstanding migration has had quite dramatic effects on the demographic structure of the village, and on its sources of income and patterns of work. "Of the 4,000 inhabitants, over 70 percent are either younger than 16 years of age or over 60 years of age. The others constitute the population which could be considered in the "productive age" bracket, the – majority of whom are females or males waiting for a visa and an opportunity to emigrate."[11] The economy of the village depends largely on money that the migrants send to their families, and up to 80 percent of families in the village depend on this income for their livelihood (it must be borne in mind that many "families" have their male head of household abroad).

10. M. Escribano and N. el-Joubeh, "Migration and Change in a West Bank Village," *Journal of Palestine Studies* (Autumn 1981), 11(1).

11. *Ibid.,* p. 151.

The village is not only prosperous, but has a substantial amount of land, much of which is fertile – 70,740 dunums in all. Yet in 1981 out of 411 households, only 50 male heads of household were engaged in agriculture. Labor and trade accounted for 87, the civil service, including teaching, for 22, and 252 were migrants. Contrast this with the situation in the 1950s when, out of 364 households, 285 male heads of household were involved in raising sheep and goats and in agriculture, 39 in labor and trade, 17 were civil servants, and 23 were migrants. Prior to 1967 the village sold agricultural goods on the Ramallah and Jerusalem markets, whereas today the area under cultivation has shrunk and production is insufficient for local needs. The only local industries apart from carpentry workshops and blacksmith shops are two small clothing factories, locally owned but supplying the Tel Aviv and Jerusalem markets, exclusively employing unmarried Deir Dibwani women (some twenty in each factory).

Migration has produced a dramatic swing in the village away from agriculture, and socioeconomic differentiation is based on migrant, not on locally generated income. In this case work in Israel is scarcely necessary and relatively few people work outside the village.

One of the most conspicuous signs of wealth from outside remittances – and this is a very common way to use the money – is the appearance of numbers of larger new houses on the edge of the village, with the old central core inhabited mainly by those who do not have migrant family and are now considered "poor." The relative affluence of Deir Dibwan means that its housebuilding boom has attracted labor from other villages to build the new houses. The newly rich tend to go in for ostentatious display, and the architectural style and contents of houses often ape American middle-class fashions.

Escribano and el-Joubeh observed that the dependency on remittances had other effects, social and psychological:

> On one hand it establishes new values of social prestige. The more financially successful migrants, presumably influenced by the values of the societies in which they work, superimpose some of the material manifestations of these values on the traditional values of the village. . . .On the other hand, for the Deir Dibwanis who stay behind, this dependency has brought about tendency to passivity, as a result of the lack of hope and opportunities.[12]

They also observed that the attitude to land had changed:

12. *Ibid.,* p. 153.

The older generations consider their land both a symbol of their country – which has been abandoned in the case of migrants – and also a link with the village. The land has acquired a symbolic value, since it no longer provides a major source of livelihood. Together with the new built houses it represents the migrants' sense of identification with the village though, unlike the new houses, it does not represent a source of social prestige nor a measure of success in the life of the migrants.[13]

Another village where there has been a major shift away from agriculture as a source of income, but for different reasons, is Ballata near Nablus, studied in the early 1970s by Linda Ammons. She found that only 6 percent of Ballata's work force was employed in agriculture in 1974. This could be ascribed, as Tamari summarizes it, to "the village integration into the periphery of Nablus (city) and its attachment to the Ballata refugee camp built on nearby village land." Here it is not, as in Deir Dibwan, that land has ceased to occupy more than a symbolic role in the village, but rather that it has shifted from being a source of income through agricultural production to being a source of value as real estate. This provides an example of the full commercialization of land – its conversion from a use value to an exchange value. It has also led "to the emergence of a new stratum of land speculators and *rentiers* (who lease land to refugee farmers) a phenomenon which applies only to the rural hinterland of the big towns." This sort of situation, where the socioeconomic life of the village shifts to a pattern closer to that prevailing in urban than in rural areas, applies, Tamari estimates, in less than 30 percent of West Bank villages which are close to the main towns.[14]

Yabad, a community of fifteen thousand in the Jenin area, seems to fall halfway between the patterns of a small village and those of an urban area. According to a recent study by Joost Hilterman, employment opportunities in Yabad are limited.

The local Taher family owns about 70 percent of the village lands, which are very fertile. Consequently, most Yabad villagers either work for Taher or must find a job outside. Some have worked in the local tobacco industry, but the Israeli military government has recently prohibited tobacco production to protect its own industry. About 3,000 villagers are employed in the Gulf or Jordan. Others have little choice but to cross over into Israel daily in search of a job.

One common method of finding work is by showing up at the "black" (labor) market in the nearby Israeli Arab town of Baqa al-Gharbiya. There, workers are picked up by an Israeli-Arab contractor, or directly by an Israeli employer, who brings them to the Israeli worksite, usually in a city like Hadera or Karkur. Women

13. *Ibid.,* p. 159.

14. S. Tamari, "Building Other People's Homes: The Palestinian Peasant's Household and Work in Israel," *Journal of Palestine Studies* (Autumn 1981), 11(1).

working seasonally in Israeli agriculture, like the walnut harvest, are picked up by Arab contractors at their homes in Yabad. Some workers will stay with the same contractor for several years (and thus do not have to go to the labor market), but rarely longer than five years.

Yabad now has a trade union with a small membership, mostly of workers in Israel, which tries to improve workers' conditions both locally and in Israel and to help people find jobs. However, like all unions in the occupied territories it suffers from difficulties with the occupying authorities, lack of formal rights in regard to workers in Israel, and opposition from the local property-owning class.[15]

Tamari has examined in considerable detail another example – the village of Ras al-Tin, a village in the central hills.[16] Ras al-Tin "is typical of those hilly West Bank villages where the majority of peasants are owner-cultivators and where land is increasingly marginalized. The village . . . shares several features both social and ecological with villages of Nablus, Hebron, Ramallah, and Bethlehem mountains and with the Judean hills in particular." Thus in many respects this seems a more representative example than either of the previous two. Ras al-Tin would be considered a "poor" village in comparison with Deir Dibwan. Among its 1,400 inhabitants are both emigrants abroad and workers in Israel. Emigrants abroad number 300 (mostly men without their families), in the Gulf, Latin America, and West Germany. A further 120 to 140 men work in Israel.

Early patterns of emigration seem to substantiate the point that in this region the first wave of emigrants came mainly from richer families, and therefore did not effect much change in stratification in the village. Early emigrants from Ras al-Tin came mostly from the wealthy and influential family in the village, the Barghutis, part of a large landowning clan in the region, who had economically and politically dominated the other faction in the village known as the *fellahin*. But in the 1960s and 1970s both factions sent emigrants abroad and this "created a new source of wealth in the village which radically changed the importance of landownership as a source of social differentiation – given the meager yields of the reduced plot holdings by the middle of this century."

The village controls 5,000 dunums of land: 4,500 dunums are planted with olive trees and the remaining land with fruit trees and field crops. None of it is irrigated. Farmers who before 1967 worked as sharecroppers

15. J.R. Hilterman, "The Emerging Trade Union Movement in the West Bank," *MERIP Reports* (October-December 1985), 136/137:26ff

16. Description of Ras al-Tin from Tamari, "Building Other Peoples Homes."

in neighboring villages to supplement earnings from their land now work in Israel for the same purpose but for better money. Almost all the Ras al-Tin workers in Israel are "illegal" (see chapter 11) and most work in construction through family connections. Many of these workers are semiskilled. As we have seen, construction work offers a seasonal flexibility which allows farmers to continue in agriculture, taking time off for the harvest, planting, and other necessities. Where, as in Ras al-Tin, the main crop is olives, which only yield well every two years under the prevailing system of cultivation, release of most family members from construction to agricultural work may only be necessary every second year.

Most families still own some land but few have it as a sole source of income, and most families have at least one member working in Israel. Maintaining agricultural production under these conditions depends very much on the individual peasant's "proper utilisation of his household members' labour (including the labour of women and children throughout the year) so that he can derive optimum benefits from the opportunities for wage labour, without, at the same time, neglecting his farm totally." Success in this enterprise obviously depends on the labor available in the family and the ability of the head of the household to control his grown sons, who may not want to work in agriculture.

It seems that this pattern of seasonal work outside the village is common elsewhere. In a survey of villages involved in an International Christian Committee self-help project in 1978, it was noted in a number of cases that the main occupation of the villagers was agriculture, but in the off-season some of the men worked outside the villages. (The villages mentioned were Dahriyya, Surif, Tarkumia, Seir, and Beir Kahel in the Hebron area and Kurf Malek and Saffa in the Ramallah district.)[17]

There are indications (see table 12.1) that in some villages these conditions have not been satisfied and people have stopped cultivating their land altogether. But in Ras al-Tin, according to Tamari, "money sent from abroad often becomes the most crucial variable in alienating family members from their agricultural land, since the sums sent allow the remaining members to become village entrepreneurs."

Whether or not land is actually abandoned, as a source of wealth it has become less important. On this theme, Tamari makes the following points:

17. International Christian Committee for the Relief of Arab Refugees, West Bank Area Council, *Self-Help Village Development Programme 1978* (Jerusalem: Middle East Council of Churches, 1979).

TABLE 12.1

**West Bank Workers in Israel Who Are Heads of Households,
according to Cultivation of Land and Seniority of Work in Israel, 1977**

	Cultivation of Land			Total (000s)	Percentages		
	Total	Land cultivated (000s)	Land not cultivated		Total	Land cultivated	Land not cultivated
Total (000s)	20.7	6.2	14.5	20.7	X	X	X
Present Economic Branch:		(percentages)					
Total	100.0	100.0	100.0	X	100.0	30.0	70.0
Agriculture	(9.2)	(14.3)	(7.0)	(1.9)	100.0	(46.8)	(53.2)
Industry	22.7	(19.1)	24.4	4.7	100.0	(25.1)	74.9
Construction	48.0	50.6	46.7	9.9	100.0	31.7	68.3
Other	20.1	16.0	21.9	4.1	100.0	(23.9)	76.1
Seniority in Work:							
Total	100.0	100.0	100.0	20.7	100.0	30.0	70.0
0-2 years	(3.9)	(4.9)	(3.5)	(0.8)	100.0	(37.6)	(62.4)
2-4 years	22.5	(25.4)	21.3	4.6	100.0	33.6	66.2
4+years	73.6	69.7	75.2	15.1	100.0	28.4	71.6

SOURCE: Israel Central Bureau of Statistics: *Quarterly Statistics of the Administered Territories*, vol VIII no 2, p. 113

One of the most important changes in village stratification has been the decline in the value of unirrigated land as a source of village wealth. This decline has been accompanied by the emergence of new sources of income: wage labour income from migrant relatives abroad; salaries of educated sons; investment in village enterprises (oil presses, shops, electric generators); investment in building equipment (compressors, cement, mixers etc.) and – in some regions – investment for leasing purposes in agricultural machinery (tractors, harvesters, sprayers).

But the village economy. in terms of local investment, has remained as stagnant as ever and the conditions of the rural population are even more integrated with and dependent on an urban sector which has ceased to develop meaningfully after 1948. Today in Ras Tin as in most West Bank villages, one of the highest ambitions for the better-off peasants is to own a block of flats or commercial space in the regional town and to lease it out, living off the returns for the rest of his life.

Land is no longer the criterion of wealth . . . indeed there does not seem to be a correlation in dry farming areas today between a peasant's wealth and the cultivable area he owns.

It seems that the only parts of the rural community where villages have not witnessed this kind of alienation from the land to some degree are those where agriculture is irrigated. Irrigation systems have mostly been installed by large landowners in the Jenin and Tulkarem areas and in the Jiftlik – the valley leading down from Nablus to the Jordan Valley. Although the villagers there are not all owner-operators some, being sharecroppers on the land of absentee owners, the existence of irrigation has made farming profitable enough to keep most of the population on the land and consequently out of the Israeli labor market. A case in point is the village of Zbeidat in the Ghor al-Faraa area of the Jordan Valley. It is unusual in several ways. First it is a relatively recently settled community – most of the inhabitants were refugees in the Jordan Valley, having been displaced in 1948 from the Beersheba area where they had been living a seminomadic existence. Like so many of the refugees who ended up in the valley they became sharecroppers for absentee landlords from Tubas and Nablus (who were among the landowners who bought up land in the Jordan Valley during the 1950s).[18]

In the 1950s the Jordanian government offered to settle this still tribally cohesive group – known collectively as the Zbeidat – and their new village was named after them. Under the government scheme they were supposed to receive title to their land in summer 1967 – thus they lost it to the Israeli invasion. By 1980 they had also lost 49 per cent of their total of five hundred dunums to confiscation and Israeli military closures, although this loss was unevenly distributed among the four subclans in the village.

18. S. Tamari and R. Giacaman. *Zbeidat: The Social Impact of Drip Irrigation on a Palestinian Peasant Community in the Jordan Valley* (Bir Zeit, 1980).

As a result, although they were much better off than they had been prior to receiving the land, some members of the village again had to resort to sharecropping for local landowners to supplement income from their own land. There were six main landlords in Zbeidat in 1980, two resident and four absentee.

Water was a major problem, as several sources had been confiscated and strict controls had been placed on remaining sources. Drip irrigation was first introduced in 1967, with the backing of an aid agency which has continued to support the project into the 1980s, and gradually more land has been brought under irrigation. Productivity has soared, and "many people have disposable income for the first time in their lives." This in a village which, in Tamari's view, was on the verge of disintegration before drip irrigation was installed – from demographic pressures and deprivation of water and social services.

"Thus the Zbeidat community, perhaps one of the most underdeveloped in the Middle East – lacking health services, electricity, running water, schools – acquired one of the most developed systems of agricultural technology in the world."[19] Initially, the visible changes were signs of differentiation – in consumer goods and so on – but unlike the other villages mentioned earlier, this change came from agriculture, not from outside work. There are only four full-time wage workers in Zbeidat and some men who do off-season wage work, plus some women and children who do off-season work in the settlement of Argamon and the village of Marj Naje. Of the thirty-two farming households, twenty-three own some land: eleven of these are owner-operators and a further ten supplement their own land by sharecropping, another two by tenancy. Only eight are purely sharecroppers.

Tamari also points out that the funding of the irrigation network by an aid agency means the villagers take more of the profits than they would if, as in other villages in the area, the drip irrigation had been installed by the local landowners. In the latter case, the "uneven and exploitative relationship between absentee owner and sharecropper would have been further accentuated, at least for the short run."

A question that arises on the future of Zbeidat is how the new-found wealth will affect what was previously quite a tight-knit community. As Tamari puts it,

> The important question here lies not in the potential differentiation between wealthy and poorer peasants but in whether Zbeidatis are going to invest their newly accumulated surplus in infrastructural projects for the development of the whole

19. *Ibid.,* p. 20.

village or in the further fostering of peasant individualism. While the seeds of wealth differences among households can be seen in the contrasting indices of consumption items (ownership of refrigerators, TVs, electric generators etc.) the majority of Zbeidat farmers realise that communal projects (such as piped water) may be a prerequisite for their own individual welfare.

Subsequent research suggests that this trend towards greater differentiation and individualist consumerism has continued and that efforts to develop community-based projects have met with difficulties.

It is hard to know how far the situations in the villages in these examples reflect general trends and how far they are the result of particular combinations of circumstances in each village. But what is clear is that the nature of village society is gradually being transformed so that it no longer represents a hierarchy of power and influence resting primarily on ownership of land, and access to it.

Some would argue that the Israeli occupation is producing a new proletariat through the creation of a migrant labor force in the territories. The empirical evidence on which this or any other opinion can be based is patchy so that it is difficult to argue any case with complete conviction. However, if proletarianization is taken to mean the divorce of the worker from the means of production so that he or she becomes entirely dependent for subsistence on the wages provided by an employer, this has clearly not happened in the villages of the West Bank. But it could be argued that proletarianization in this "pure" sense has not occurred in many third-world countries where migrant workers maintain roots – land and family ties – in the villages while working in the cities. This kind of halfway house situation, it has been argued, is one that can continue for decades because it suits employers who, because of their workers' rural ties, do not have to pay the higher wages their workers would need if they had to live in the city.

But in the case of the occupied territories, there are further factors preventing full proletarianization in the above sense. The Israelis have forcibly prevented the migration of this wage work force to the cities where they work. Instead, in this relatively small country, the migrants are commuters from their villages, and this, for the time being at least, reinforces family, social, and economic ties in the village.

Also, if the example of Ras al-Tin is anything to go by, the way in which much of the work force in Israel is recruited serves to reinforce connections with the village. This is in many cases not done through impersonal bureaucratic or market channels, but through family or village connections. Tamari points out that particularly in the construction industry the "hierarchical forms of organisation" keep Palestinian workers separated from their Israeli employers through the existence of Palestinian labor contractors and foremen. "These hierarchies create not only a sense of 'false consciousness' among rural workers, but an efficient system of labour management in the absence of workers' organisations and work tenure stability."[20]

Further factors which strengthen attachment to the village are the relative instability, for both economic and political reasons, of work in Israel, which does not encourage most people to rely on it completely in the longer term, and also an emotional if not an economic attachment to the land. This has been heightened by the landgrabbing of the Israeli settlers and the army. Hence there seems to be a tension between two sets of feelings and ideas – the first that in the present circumstances the land cannot provide a living and therefore it is better to give it up and look elsewhere to different ideals of affluence and status; the second, often held in parallel with the first, that for Palestinians there has been a hard-learned historical lesson that if you lose your land you lose your future.

Nonetheless, the situation in the West Bank has not yet reached the point where, as in the villages of the Galilee and the Triangle within the borders of pre-1967 Israel, villages are little more than workers' dormitories.[21] The workers who come from the camps of the West Bank and the Gaza Strip have been separated from their means of production by dispossession rather than by economic and market forces. They only make up about 10 percent of workers in Israel from the West Bank but 60 or 70 percent of those who come every day from the Gaza Strip. Here the impact of wage labor has been different – the camps do not have a productive basis that would be altered by the new work patterns. The refugees, particularly in Gaza, are not really faced with a choice as to whether they should continue trying to work locally or go to a building site in Tel Aviv or in an Israeli settlement. The choice is usually between working and not working. Under Israeli rule the refugees have come to fit the definition of a proletariat in the sense that they are wholly dependent on wage labor for their livelihoods. However, according to one Gazan intellectual, this has not led to a proletarian class consciousness. He argues that during the latter half of the period of Egyptian rule, from 1957 to 1967, many refugees as well as townspeople became involved to some degree in petty trading, smuggling,

20. Tamari, "Building Other People's Homes," p. 46.

21. For a discussion of the proletarianization of the Palestinian peasantry in Israel, see E. Zureik, "Transformation of Class Structure among the Arabs in Israel: From Peasantry to Proletariat," *Journal of Palestine Studies* (1976), 6(1); and S. Carmi and H. Rosenfeld, "The Origins of the Process of Proletarianization and Urbanization of Arab Peasants in Palestine," *Annals of the New York Academy of Sciences* (March 1974), 220(6).

and handling money coming from migrants in the Gulf. After the Israeli invasion and the severing of these opportunities for trade, legal or illegal, most of this small trading class, as well as those who had been unemployed, were drawn into the Israeli work force:

> "As Israel has consolidated its monopoly capitalist system in Gaza by undercutting indigenous Gazan manufacturing industries and refusing permission for the establishment of new industries, this proletarian class has became totally dependent on Israeli enterprises. There is no alternative work in Gaza which could strengthen the bargaining power of these workers by providing competition to attract labour. . . . But this class does not yet have a sense of the power of the proletariat – they have no roots in Gaza and they could perhaps better be described as fallen petit bourgeoisie.[22]

Social networks in the camps may vary from place to place, but they are not, as in the villages, clearly based on relations of production. However, in the absence of other structures, family connections have remained very strong and work, including work in Israel, is often obtained as in the villages, through these connections. Earnings from Israel or abroad go into many of the same kinds of expenditure as those in the villages, but most especially into education of children and into building houses and apartments. In Gaza particularly extended families sometimes build small apartment blocks in which several nuclear families can live, so reinforcing these ties.

In the West Bank, the situation of camp populations is less homogeneous than it is in the tiny Gaza Strip. Israeli statistics tend to lump all West Bank camp dwellers (94,824 people, approximately 11 percent of the total population) into the "rural" category, but in fact many of the larger camps like Qalandiya (between al-Bireh and Jerusalem) or Ballata near Nablus are much more akin to poor urban quarters (as are the Gaza camps) than to a village environment. The social tensions and alienation caused by overcrowding and poor physical conditions are also more like those in city slums. Added to this, camp populations in both areas tend to suffer a high degree of harassment from the Israeli authorities such as the imposition of curfews and a wide variety of collective punishments, from the demolition of houses to making inhabitants stand outside their houses all night. All these techniques are used in towns and villages as well, but the camps are the most frequent targets.

22. Paul Cossali and Clive Robson, *Stateless in Gaza* (London: Zed Press, 1986), p. 57.

The towns of the West Bank have not been greatly changed by the countrywide trend towards wage labor because that trend has not been accompanied by a significant movement of population into the urban areas. Jerusalem is the only exception. Up to the 1960s, some of these towns were attracting richer village families from the countryside, but most of this movement took place before the Israeli occupation. Since the occupation, the towns have generally stagnated economically, apart from the activities of the service sector – transport and travel agencies, money changers, real estate dealers and the like.

The other mainstay of many towns, like some of the villages, is remittances from abroad. In the towns where emigration has been substantial, it has made the social structure more fluid than in those where the traditional forms of wealth still have importance.

The towns where migrant remittances have had most impact on the economy and social structure are Ramallah, Bethlehem, and al-Bireh. Ramallah and al-Bireh were small villages at the beginning of the century, and have now grown into sizable towns where most wealth and prestige is derived from commerce and migrant remittances. Ramallah particularly has a very large subsidiary community in the United States and this is being added to year by year. Apparently between 1975 and 1977 some five thousand Ramallah residents left for the United States and Latin America.[23] The effects of this migration are not merely economic: contacts are maintained with the migrants and many return from time to time, influencing both social and cultural attitudes in these towns. The migrants' desire not to lose contact with their families at home is sometimes expressed by sending home teenage daughters to complete their educations and get married in their home town.

Bethlehem combines this migrant pattern with a commercial life based on tourism. As in Ramallah, the population is predominantly Christian, with the Greek Orthodox forming the largest section of the community. Al-Bireh, which shares many social and economic characteristics with adjoining Ramallah, is predominantly Muslim.

The main towns of the northern part of the West Bank, Nablus, Jenin, and Tulkarem, have a rather different character. Unlike the communities around Jerusalem, there has not been a long tradition of migration and the social structure has changed less. It is only in recent years that numbers of people from these towns have begun to work abroad and they tend to go to the Arab world more often than to the United States.

23. *Maariv,* 16 May 1978.

Nablus, the largest of these towns, has historical importance as a center of small industries (especially soap manufacturing) and, sporadically since the 1930s, its inhabitants have played an important role in nationalist politics. This role was resumed between 1976 and 1981 with the election of Bassam Shaka as mayor. However, like Jenin, Nablus is still dominated socially by a group of well-established landowning and merchant families who set a generally conservative social tone. Despite the wealth of individuals and families, it is not a prosperous or outward looking town.

Hebron has probably been more directly affected by Israeli settlement in the occupied territories. Since early in the occupation it has had the settlement of Kiryat Arba rising on the hills next to the town. The social and religious tensions caused over the years by this implantation have been considerable. Particularly since the mid-1970s, there have been a number of clashes over the mosque and tomb of Abraham, which is a holy place for both Muslims and Jews. In 1979 members of Gush Emunim (which has numerous followers in Kiryat Arba) occupied an old hospital building in the center of Hebron; they have since pursued a campaign to take over property in the town which they claim belonged to Jews who fled or were killed in attacks on the community in 1929. Israeli authorities made no attempt to remove these squatters, and since that time the settlers interference with and physical violence against Hebron's inhabitants has escalated, provoking violent attacks in retaliation.

Jerusalem has also been severely affected by the Israeli settlement drive. Apartment blocks sprout on every hillside around the city, creating a ring of Jewish population on the east and north in addition to the earlier expansion of the Israeli city to the west and south. These fortresslike housing complexes are inhabited predominantly by new immigrants and young couples who could not find other accommodation because of the housing shortage in Israel. But there is also a housing shortage for Jerusalem's Palestinian inhabitants – Jerusalem is one of the few occupied towns to which there has been a substantial influx of population over the last few years. For those without the money to build their own villas, accommodation is scarce. There has been a slow but steady succession of demolitions of houses to make way for Israeli building programs, both inside and outside the Old City. Only one medium-sized housing estate has been put up, to the north of the city near Beit Hanina.

The annexed city is still dominated by merchants and small traders who are now obliged to deal much more closely with the Israelis since the latter have become customers in the Old City and the east Jerusalem commercial areas (see chapter 11). Likewise, proximity to the Israeli-dominated areas to the west has led to more Israeli influence on lifestyles among young people than would be the case in most West Bank towns.

The city's old aristocracy, which derived its authority from the religious institutions of the city, as well as from political office, has lost influence under the Israelis as principal offices for the "united" city are under the control of an Israeli mayor. But despite the decline in its social and political role, Jerusalem remains both an economic and social entrepot and a powerful national and religious symbol.

The socioeconomic impact of the large inflows of aid money, particularly from the joint PLO-Jordanian committee administering the "steadfastness" funds from Arab states, has become very evident in some urban centers. As was noted in the last chapter, quite a substantial proportion of this money has been used not for development projects, but to bolster the position of individuals and small groups. The recipients of these funds tend to have been influential individuals whose support was regarded as important either by the Jordanians or by the PLO leadership abroad. Since the early 1980s, this has accentuated the development, both in the West Bank and Gaza Strip, of a small but affluent stratum with a conspicuously consumerist lifestyle not previously evident even in the wealthy sectors of society. This in turn has generated opportunities for another small group able to act as middlemen in the import of desirable Western consumer goods.

Under Israeli occupation political and social structures tend naturally to be organized along the lines of national identity rather than of class. This blurs class boundaries by muting conflict between employers and employees, factory owners and workers, landowners and peasants, men and women, though all these forms of conflict certainly exist. Many workers in Israel deal with their Israeli bosses through Palestinian intermediaries – labor contractors or foremen, who are often people they already know. This is particularly true in construction and agriculture. Equally, Israeli employers are regarded first and foremost as occupiers rather than as exploiters of labor, although people are evidently aware of both roles.

In many respects, there are more signs of proletarianization to be found in the camps and villages in the occupied territories than in the towns, which are now centers of service rather than of production. But partly because the new stratum of wage workers is scattered across the country, rather than concentrated in a large city (as for example in Casablanca in Morocco) or in a major industrial area (for instance, in the industrial areas like Chubra al-Kheima and Mahalla al-Kubra near Cairo), there is little "class consciousness" as the term is understood in the West. At the present stage changes in social status, wealth, and stratification are often perceived primarily as forms of competition within a community. The new economic circumstances have also led to gaps between individuals' or families' economic status and their social standing in the community. Unskilled workers may earn more than schoolteachers who would normally be considered as privileged members of the community. This may also make those who have improved their economic position without earning social recognition resentful of the traditionally powerful individuals or families who still expect deference. Certainly the increase in wage labor has decreased the dependence of the majority of villagers on the good will of local landowners. As yet these new forms of social mobility have not fundamentally changed the patterns of social relations in villages or towns but the process of erosion is well under way. In the camps there is also a trend towards greater differentiation, but this does not upset well-established hierarchies of power and status as it does in the villages and towns.

EDUCATION AND SOCIAL CHANGE

Education has been one of the main avenues to social mobility, of individuals and families, in Palestinian society both inside and outside the borders of Palestine. In the West Bank and Gaza, the status attached to educational qualifications has grown since the occupation, despite the shortages of funds in both the "government" school sector and in UNRWA schools. The development of university education within the territories, already projected in the mid-1960s and implemented in the 1970s, has increased this trend.

This does not imply that everyone who completes secondary or even university education necessarily moves from one class or status group to a higher one. As we have seen, under occupation education is frequently wasted through lack of job opportunities and the highest levels of unemployment are to be found among the most highly educated groups. Nonetheless, most families continue to regard education as an investment, offering their children opportunities which they did not have and enhancing the status, and possibly the earning powers, of the family.

Education as a form of investment used to be confined mostly to the elite who wanted to see their sons in prestigious professions. But after 1948 and again after 1967 the range of people who wanted education for their children increased in proportion to the feelings of insecurity that their stateless condition evoked. The social effects of education are most marked in the towns where there is a longer tradition of schooling and where education is easily available. In the camps the experience of landlessness, poverty, and impotence has been a powerful incentive to use education as a means of escape. Hence families will sometimes go to extraordinary lengths to send their children, especially their sons, through school and university or professional training. The remittance economy has played a very important part in making this possible. It is not unusual, for instance, to hear of eldest sons working in the Gulf to put a younger brother through college or medical school.

In the villages, especially those far from schools, the incentives are not as great, but there has still been a considerable increase in the numbers of children in school. In the West Bank, the overall growth in enrollment was above the rate of natural increase for the ten years from 1967 to 1977, and enrollments in the preparatory and secondary cycles more than doubled over the same period.

The dropout rate for girls, however, especially after the primary cycle, is still very high. Many rural families still do not want their daughters to continue their schooling beyond the first six years, and this is reinforced by the fact that many village schools only cover the first six years – the primary cycle. After that, the children have to go to school in the nearest town for the preparatory and secondary cycles. Parents are reluctant to allow girls to travel to school every day and few would allow them to stay the week in town, several sharing a room, as the older boys sometimes do. The fact that older village children do go to the towns to school has the effect of changing their outlook as they mix with urban children.

At times of tension in the West Bank, in which high schools are inevitably involved, the Israelis have sometimes tried to reverse this integration by refusing to allow village children to come to school in the towns, making teachers go to the overcrowded village schools to teach them, regardless of the lack of proper facilities.

The economic changes in the villages already discussed have affected rural attitudes to schooling in various ways, but the net outcome of these pressures is not yet clear. The fact that in many villages a large number of able-bodied men are employed outside the village can mean that the labor of women and children becomes more important in agriculture, and girls are therefore pulled out of school to help in the fields or with domestic work.

In villages such as Zbeidat, where agriculture is still the main source of income, Tamari found that the installation of drip irrigation seems, surprisingly, to have increased proportionally the workload of women and children. "This dependency on female farm labour lends a positive incentive for Zbeidatis to keep their daughters illiterate, a tendency which is reinforced by the traditional low status females hold in a semi-nomadic community."[24]

In the early 1980s, it became evident that some young girls were being taken out of school after only two or three years. For women generally,

24. Tamari and Giacaman, "Zbeidat," p. 34.

access to education depends on a number of factors including proximity to a school, attitude of the local community towards education (some villages, towns, and even regions have much higher illiteracy rates than others), and the views of immediate family members, particularly the males, on whether women should be educated, as well as the affluence of the family and the number of boys to be educated.

Illiteracy is now highest among older rural women, but it has been pointed out that the illiteracy rates for younger women in the villages tend to be inflated by the fact that women who have received education tend to marry outside the village. It has been suggested that migrant labor in Israel may also have had an unexpected effect on education: that while insensitivity to education as a means of advancement is most common among older males employed in agriculture and trades, "young males from the West Bank [now] tend to seek employment as unskilled or semiskilled labourers in Israel, undoubtedly contributing to the renewed significance of this factor."[25] Since according to Israeli statistics 40 percent of the work force in Israel from the territories is in the age group between fourteen and twenty-four years, the longer term effects of this tendency cannot be discounted.[26]

Absenteeism and dropping out among the older children are common enough, particularly in camp schools, and this is not just a matter of truancy. Far more often it is because teenagers are drawn into the labor force, either on their own initiative or because of family pressures. One West Bank social worker was quoted as saying: "They [the Israelis] don't care for our children, they're happy to have another source of cheap labour and the lack of economic and social planning will always be there to force children onto the labour market." A Jenin schoolteacher alleged in the same report that a contractor's van waits outside his school recruiting children for work in the fields. "Many take his offers," the teacher said. "Sooner or later most of them join the ranks of the school dropouts."[27]

Despite both institutional and economic impediments the proportion of the population in higher education has grown in recent years. Generally speaking, university students tend to come from fairly well-off families, but remittances have enabled more people to afford a university education.

25. Mahshi and Rihan, "Education: Elementary and Secondary," p. 53.

26. *Report of the Director General, 1982;* appendix; "Report of the Situation of Workers of the Occupied Arab Territories" (Geneva: International Labor Organization, 1982), p. 123.

27."The Occupation Generation," *The Middle East* (June 1982), p. 14.

Also, for refugee students some scholarships are available from UNRWA and other sources. (Most of the UNRWA scholarships go to male candidates. It is not clear whether this is the result of selection procedures or the small number of women who apply.)[28] The development of local universities – Bir Zeit, al-Najah, Bethlehem, Hebron, University Colleges in Jerusalem, and the Islamic University of Gaza – has provided more opportunities for students who cannot afford to go abroad and also for women who would not be permitted by their families to study abroad. However, the existence of a relatively large university student population has not led to the expansion of the middle class of professionals in the West Bank and Gaza in quite the way one would expect in a society under less abnormal conditions.

A large proportion of those who come out of institutions of higher education, whether in the territories or elsewhere, do not return to their home towns to work, but either immediately or after a few years leave the country. The main reasons are lack of job opportunities and the frustrations – especially for people with relatively high expectations – of living under the numerous constraints of occupation.

There is little systematic evidence on exactly what happens to graduates either from West Bank universities or from abroad. An early study done in the mid 1970s with a very small sample of graduates from Bir Zeit between 1962 and 1974 provides some insights, although the small sample and the period of study mean that the results should be treated with some caution.[29] The study showed that out of a sample of 112 graduates, only 36 percent lived in the West Bank, whereas 64 percent were employed "outside," mainly in Jordan (15%) and the Gulf (15%). What is most interesting is that the survey shows decisively the difference in post-university life patterns between men and women. Of the women graduates, 51 percent, compared with 22 percent of the men, still lived in the West Bank, and the majority of these women were married. Twenty percent of the total said they were unemployed, and all of these were women. Today the situation has worsened as the universities, which expanded their intake rapidly in the late 1970s, are producing large numbers of graduates, male and female, who cannot find jobs locally, and who in recent years have had more difficulty in finding jobs abroad. (see chapter 11). By 1984 it was estimated that there were already twenty thousand unemployed graduates in the territories.[30]

28. UNRWA *Report,* p. 74.

29. P.E. Davies, "The Educated West Bank Palestinians," *Journal of Palestine Studies* (Spring 1979), 8(3).

30. *Al-Fajr,* 15 June 1984, p. 8.

Apart from the more general social restraints, it seems likely that this situation reinforces the difficulties for women graduates who wish to pursue a career. Family pressure might not prevent a woman from receiving higher education, and in some cases might even encourage it. But after it is completed, the family view is often that enough is enough and the woman ought to settle down and get married – and not necessarily work after marriage. By contrast a man is free to pursue a career with or without a family.

Pressures for women to marry are still very strong, even in more easygoing urban communities. There are now some urban middleclass women who remain single, at least in their twenties, and pursue a professional career – in part because many men of this age group are abroad studying or working – but this is still not generally socially acceptable.

The graduates in the Bir Zeit study came mainly from the urban middle class, and many of them had studied at private schools (76%). The class range has broadened since that time, with a higher proportion of students from villages and camps and from Gaza. This also applies to nursing and teacher training institutions in the main towns.

Even at the time of the survey some social mobility was evidenced by the range of fathers' occupations listed by the graduate sample:

> The graduates fall solidly in the white collar categories of employment whereas in some instances what they listed as their fathers' employment is of a blue collar nature or in the service or agricultural sector. For example while no graduates listed the following as occupations, they were reported by graduates under "father's occupation": worker, driver, carpenter, florist, farmer. And while few graduates indicated that they were self-employed or involved in commercial or business affairs, it appears that their father's generation was.
>
> Thus graduates' fathers' employment includes ownership of restaurants, coffee-houses, bookshops, and local companies in addition to work as building contractors, goldsmiths, or traders. The fact that only two graduates listed their current employment as being the same as their fathers' is perhaps another indicator of the intergenerational economic and occupational mobility referred to.[31]

SOCIETY IN TRANSITION

Family relationships continue to play an important part in the lives of most Palestinians. It has often been argued that the more insecure people's lives are, the more they will cling to family bonds. On this criterion, one would expect that the ties of family would remain strong in occupied

31. Davies, "Educated West Bank Palestinians," p. 78.

Palestine and that uncertainties would also serve to strengthen the patriarchal role of the head of the family.

Although there is certainly some truth in this assertion there are several factors that complicate the picture. Many families no longer reflect the classic three-generational pattern, and even the nuclear family – husband, wife, and children – is frequently disrupted by the absence, sometimes for prolonged periods, of male heads of household and older sons. Depending on the reason for absence and the nature of the family, this can have a number of different effects.

The fact that men are away may cause much of the day-to-day responsibility for the family to devolve onto the wife or mother, perhaps in consultation with brothers or uncles. Tamari found that in households where the husband was away – at work, in exile, or in prison – it was the women who acted as the bearers of tradition in the family. This tended to have a conservative influence, based primarily on holding the family together.

For sons who go abroad to work, there is the possibility of distancing themselves from family ties and certainly of acquiring a different set of cultural and social attitudes, but many are bound to their families at least insofar as they are obliged to provide money for the family's support.

In some respects remittances and wage labor in Israel might be expected to encourage the development of nuclear rather than extended families. A son with an independent wage is more likely to be able to live independently of his father and uncles than if he depends on them for access to land or to a family business. Those who earn more or have remittances from abroad may be able to build new houses where they are physically separate from parents and in-laws. However, this does not always happen. It is just as likely that the family will build a house with several apartments in which different parts of the family live. This is apparently a common use of remittance income in Gaza, and serves to reinforce family bonds by physical proximity. In addition, even for those who would like to move away from the family orbit, in both villages and camps it is common to find work through family or neighborhood connections and to work alongside relatives – thus strengthening family ties.

In families where the men work in Israel the changes are of a different sort. If the family has land, women's status may be altered by the need to do more agricultural work. In the West Bank the once strict division of labor has broken down so that jobs previously reserved for men, such as plowing and climbing olive trees to beat down the fruit during the harvest, are now also performed by women.

Apart from agriculture (and women's labor there has never been counted in the statistics), women still form a small part of the labor force.

According to Israeli statistics, women working for wages outside their own villages represent less than 5 percent of the work force (although this is likely to be an understatement).[32] Women, whether they are employed in Israel (in agriculture and textiles mainly) or by local employers in much the same types of work, are, along with children, the worst-paid section of the work force. Therefore even when a woman does bring a wage into the household it is subsidiary to that of the man and does not permit the woman anything like independence. Of Palestinian women in villages in Israel, Yvonne Haddad comments: "The exploitation of Arab women as cheap labour has not freed them: rather, it has led to their enslavement as they assume two jobs, one in the labour market and one at home, since the low wages they receive and the high taxes they pay do not provide for labour-saving devices in the home."[33] Although most working women from the territories do not pay taxes, their wages are even lower and their overall situation is much the same as described here.

Many men are reluctant, for social or religious reasons, to allow wives and daughters to work outside the village, and this is reinforced by the need to use women's labor in agriculture. It is noteworthy that proportionally more women from the camps than from the villages work away from home.

In urban middle-class families, it is possible for women to take professional jobs and have some element of independence, but as shown in the section on education, this is a small group. Some of these women have begun to take a lead in establishing women's organizations in the territories which, while they operate parallel to existing women's charitable organizations, are more radical in their approach both to politics and to women's issues. They have also made efforts to reach women outside the main towns. In this they are joined by some of the the charitable associations such as Inash al-Usra in Ramallah.[34]

32. Figures from Israeli Ministry of Labor, quoted in Tamari, "Building Other People's Homes," p. 14.

33. Yvonne Haddad, "Palestinian Women," in K. Nakhleh and E. Zureik, eds., *The Sociology of the Palestinians* (London: Croom Helm, 1980), p. 155 (also New York: St. Martin's Press); Susan Rockwell, "Palestinian Women Workers in the Israeli-occupied Gaza Strip," *Journal of Palestine Studies* (Winter 1985), 14(2):114ff.

34. For details, see Rita Giacaman, "Palestinian Women and Development in the Occupied West Bank," paper presented at the 7th UN seminar on the question of Palestine (Dakar, Senegal, August 1982); Haddad, "Palestinian Women"; and Rosemary Sayigh, "Encounters with Palestinian Women under Occupation," *Journal of Palestine Studies* (Summer 1981), 10(4).

Since the early 1980s, these women's committees, along with the Union of Medical Relief Committees, have taken important initiatives in establishing new ways of addressing the numerous social problems created by the occupation, and others which are endemic in the present structure of Palestinian society. Through community-based work in primary health care and preschool education, both previously neglected areas, these and other groups have begun to change the terms of the debate on social issues. In particular, they have attempted to direct attention away from the prestigious aspects of health care and education towards the needs and concerns of the poorest sectors of society – for example, the poorer and more isolated villages of the West Bank and the camp dwellers in the Gaza Strip. They also attempt to work within these communities and to establish self-help projects, training members of the community to run them, rather than relying on handouts and control by urban-based organizations.

Their work has stirred awareness and controversy over issues such as the position of women in family and society, the nature of health care, and the disparities between the relatively privileged urban middle classes and poor peasants and migrant workers. The Medical Relief Committees (MRC) have also, in cooperation with other organizations, succeeded in collecting systematic health data at a village level, particularly in crucial areas such as the health of women and children. Such data and statistics had not previously been collected during the occupation, either by the Israeli authorities or by Palestinian organizations. As well as challenging some traditional assumptions, the work of these new organizations also clearly challenges the occupation authorities who regard all forms of organization and self-help by Palestinians as subversive. Many of the leaders of the committee movements and their allies have consequently been subjected to various forms of harassment, including house arrest, refusal of travel permits, and on one occasion in Gaza, refusal to allow MRC doctors and health workers to operate a free clinic.[35] During the current uprising the various committee movements are playing important roles in community self-organization in the face of Israeli army violence, curfews, and detentions.

The generation born under occupation or just before it has perhaps been most affected by changing circumstances. Clearly this applies most to children in highly politicized families and those who live in the camps, where the impact of military rule is inescapable. Least affected are children brought up in more isolated villages and in very sheltered middle-class homes.

35. S. Graham-Brown "Gaza, Where Health Care Is a Crime," *The Middle East* (October 1986), p. 30.

But the experience of school for many children in the territories is not the usual one of study, friendships, quarrels, and tussles with teachers but is punctuated with demonstrations, soldiers breaking into classrooms, arrests and so on. This has made many teenagers militant if not politically sophisticated.

Even for the more timid and those who try to stay out of trouble, the mere business of getting to and from school during periods of unrest means exposure to possible violence and even danger to life and limb. In an uprising early in 1982 sixteen Palestinians under the age of twenty-one were shot dead by Israeli soldiers and settlers – the youngest victim was seven years old.[36] Girls as well as boys become caught up in these violent incidents. In the uprising which began in December 1987, hundreds of Palestinians, many of them school-age children, have been shot and killed by the Israeli army or by Jewish settlers.

In this respect alone, this generation has a view of the world and expectations that are different from those of their parents – this can put a strain on family relationships. It also means children are subject to considerable psychological stress. A recent study compared the psychological and emotional attitudes of 128 Palestinian children from the West Bank, mainly eleven-year-olds, with a group of Israeli children and another group of Palestinian children from Nazareth. An indication of the disruptions in West Bank children's family lives was that two-thirds of the sample had lost a family member to an Israeli prison during their lives. Many of these children's fears centered around disruption of their families by the actions of the authorities – "Father will be imprisoned," or "Our house would be destroyed." A typical answer to the question, "What happened at school today?" (to which most Israeli children give "normal" accounts of regular happenings at school) was, for West Bankers, "Soldiers broke into our classroom and teargassed us" or "Israeli soldiers had beaten us and the teacher."[37]

Another factor that shapes the attitudes and expectations of numbers of teenage boys from both the West Bank and Gaza is that of work in Israel, which children do from a young age (see chapter 11). The effects of this experience are complex. Workers from the territories are generally treated as "invisible" by most Israelis, and despised when they are noticed, which undoubtedly makes for bitterness and resentment, particularly among the

36. "Occupation Generation," p. 13.

37. Extracts from a study by Raija-Leena Punamaki, "Children of Conflict: Attitudes and Emotional Life of Israeli and Palestinian Children in the Shadow of War," *al-Fajr Palestinian Weekly,* 29 January 1982, pp. 8-9.

young. But at the same time, those who work in the big cities may also pick up some of the external norms of Israeli consumer society – the desire for fashionable clothes, stereo equipment, and possibly a different lifestyle from the one they are used to at home.

The occupation has certainly had a disturbing and radicalizing effect on young people, but this expresses itself in different ways. Since the late 1970s the Muslim Brotherhood and other Islamic fundamentalist groups have gained influence, particularly in schools and universities – this at the expense of the secular ideology which has generally been the hallmark of Palestinian nationalism. At the moment, fundamentalist politics do not seem set to dominate the political scene in the territories, but they have certainly emerged as a significant component, which has been reinforced both by the Iranian revolution – which at a broader level also offered an example of how a mass movement could overthrow an authoritarian regime – and by the more recent activities of militant Shiite movements against the Israelis in southern Lebanon.

For the young, the sense of repression, helplessness, and isolation could lead them to turn to religious politics. As one Gazan nationalist explains it:

> The absence of the *fedayin* created a vacuum for young guys with nationalist feelings against the occupation. There were no political organisations or currents doing significant work here. We are not a secular society; everyone comes from a religious background, so their [the fundamentalists'] ideas were easy to assimilate. The success of the *ikhwan* [Muslim Brotherhood] in Gaza lies in the loss of hope in the possible success of our issue and in a feeling of separation from other nations – no one supports us. People here feel a kind of depression, and have given up and turned to God.[38]

But social as well as political factors can account for these attitudes. Munir Fasheh, who has taught in West Bank schools and universities for twenty years, gives the following description of the trend towards an Islamic emphasis in politics:

> . . . for the Palestinians, what is left from the 1967-70 period? Just some words and slogans. Many who were born in the 60s and went to high school, say, in the 70s were exposed concretely to two things: Israeli occupation and their traditional upbringing. They cannot accept the Israeli point of view so they're left with their traditional way of looking at and dealing with the world, which is primarily religious. The secular perspective is also strong among the youth. It is. But we are talking about why religious sentiments are now penetrating the hearts and minds of people. For me it is not difficult to comprehend. The Palestinians were crushed in

38. Joan Mandell, "Gaza, Israel's Soweto," *MERIP Reports* (October-December 1985), 136/137: 16.

Amman, beleaguered in Lebanon, they were denied the right to anything and everything. So naturally they started looking for solutions to change their conditions. Some choose to look backwards for a model from the past, others chose to look forward and outward for new models.[39]

The Israelis do not discourage fundamentalist groups unless they are a direct threat to Israeli authority: as Fasheh comments, "their interests often converge to combat new ideas and radical change." Sometimes they are willing to use such groups to smash the influence of the left. There was a particularly clear case of this in Gaza in 1980. "It is interesting that the only Palestinian demonstration which the Israeli army did not try to stop was one in early 1980 by Islamic extremists from the university in Gaza who burned a library and a clinic and a restaurant."[40]

It is also true that for many people, whether or not they subscribe to fundamentalist beliefs, there is a desire to look backwards – to a culture and society that existed before the disruptions of occupation. This is expressed in any number of ways – in nostalgia; in the interest, during the 1970s, among some of the urban intelligentsia in village life and the survival of rural crafts; in evocation of folkloric themes in art and in drama,[41] and in revival of interest among young women in traditional dress embroidery which is now often used to express nationalist symbols. Even those who do not look to the past for models often want to look to the past for their identity. But for others, clinging to tradition and religion is a way of coping with the erosion of familiar ways of life. As we have seen, in the villages of the West Bank changing patterns of work and consumption and new attitudes to wealth, which the occupation has brought in its wake, have altered these ways. Religion is seen as a defense against Israeli attempts to undermine their society, and this view is certainly encouraged by conservative Arab regimes, especially by Saudi Arabia.

Both economic and social change and the proximity and domination of Israel often create tension and confused attitudes, especially among young people. One Gazan who works in Israel remarks on this:

39. Munir Fasheh, "Political Islam in the West Bank," *MERIP Reports* (February 1982), 103:15-16.

40. *Ibid.*

41. See, for example, "Palestinian Theater," in *The Middle East* (December 1981), pp. 44-45.

I think it is the same in any occupation – a small group of the occupied people try to copy the occupiers. It is only an expression of their helplessness really. Having this Israeli society next to ours strengthens the conservatism within our own society. It breeds a kind of hypocrisy among us. Some Gazans, especially those who consider themselves modern, go to the beaches in Israel because women can't swim in Gaza. It's not forbidden in law, but you can always expect some criticism from the people in general. But the problem is that Israel is used as a place to release tension – to do things which you can't do at home.[42]

For those women, especially among the young and educated, who feel oppressed both by the occupation and by attitudes in their own families and society, the importance of religion and the preservation of social traditions pose some difficult problems. A nineteen-year-old trainee nurse from Gaza expresses the position of those women who see the need to challenge some of these social norms, even under occupation:

For sure women suffer from the occupation; the conditions they work in in Israel are terrible, there's lots of exploitation, and like men they're denied the basic human rights of freedom to speak and organize, but if you ask me if I suffer more from occupation or Gazan society, I have to say from society. Of course the occupation reinforces everything that is reactionary in Gaza. I don't think Palestine will be liberated without the women being liberated first. I mean how can our society be called progressive enough to defeat Zionism if half of that society is enslaved inside the home?[43]

For the majority of people, men and women, however, social contradictions are largely submerged beneath the realities of occupation and the difficulties of day-to-day existence. During the recent uprising, too, many of these ideological differences have, at least temporarily, been set aside in an unprecedented show of united resistance against Israeli rule. Nonetheless, those who oppose the use of religious politics as a means of combating the occupation and feel that appeals to conservative traditional values will not solve the society's problems would argue that, like it or not, major social changes have occurred during twenty years of occupation. These changes will not be reversed simply by appeals to the past or to religious rules. Any strategy for the future must take into account the new social forces, and the contradictions which the occupation has created.

42. Cossali and Robson, *Stateless in Gaza,* p. 48.

43. *Ibid.,* p.44.

CHAPTER 13

The Demographic Consequences
of the Occupation

Janet L. Abu-Lughod

The residual areas of Palestine occupied by Israel in June 1967 contained a population of between 1.3 million and 1.35 million Palestinians. At that time, this population represented over half of all the estimated 2.65 million Palestinians in the world. At present, the number of Palestinians who remain in these zones does not exceed 13 million or approximately the same as lived there fifteen years ago. Had the population of 1967 remained in place, natural increase would have yielded a present population in post-1967 occupied Palestine in excess of 2 million. Therefore, we estimate that the June 1967 war was responsible for the dispersion from their homeland of over 700,000 additional Palestinians. Given the fact that there are now an estimated 4.5 million persons of Palestinian birth or origin in the world, those who remain in eastern Palestine (the West Bank and Jerusalem) and Gaza now constitute only 29 percent of the total. This dramatic drop (from 50 to 29 percent of the total) is the major demographic consequence of the June 1967 war. It is, however, not the only one.

We might summarize the demographic consequences of the occupation as follows:

1) a massive expulsion of residents sufficient to stabilize numbers, despite a natural increase rate that has averaged 3.5 percent per year;
2) a distortion in the normal population characteristics of the residual population, due to the selectivity of expulsions and emigrations; and
3) a transformation of the remaining population from a diversified independent society of peasants, businessmen, and professionals to a proletarianized and dependent reserve labor army at the mercy of Israeli political and economic interests.

These changes in the demographic characteristics of the territories occupied by Israel in 1967 have been the outcome of concerted policies adopted by the occupier. These policies have been intentionally designed both to contain the size of the population over whom dominance would have to be exercised and to "reduce" its capacity to resist domination.

EXPULSIONS AND THE STABILIZATION OF POPULATION SIZE

At the outbreak of the June 1967 war, there were approximately 900,000 Palestinians living in what was then called the "West Bank," including perhaps 80,000 in the walled city of east Jerusalem and in the villages and towns in the vicinity. This population not only included Palestinians originally from the zone that had been annexed to Jordan in 1949 but also several hundred thousand "refugees" from the 1948 war who had resettled there from the portions of Palestine preempted by Israel. Some of these "refugees" were still living in camps, concentrated largely in the Jordan Valley just west of the river. Most, however, lived outside camps, and the region, although relatively neglected in Jordanian development plans, managed to sustain a normal economy based upon agriculture, tourism, commerce and services, and to a much lesser degree, industry. During the early 1960s a modest amount of emigration occurred, as Palestinians filtered toward Amman or left the country entirely in search of better economic opportunities. But such emigration amounted to under 15,000 persons per year (many the sons and daughters of families that remained at home) and was viewed as temporary. Movement to the east bank of the Jordan was simply internal migration without long-term significance. Movement abroad in search of employment was facilitated by the fact that the population enjoyed Jordanian citizenship and therefore carried acceptable travel documents.

In the Egyptian-administered Gaza Strip the situation was quite different. Within that extremely small area were concentrated between 400,000 and 450,000 Palestinians, about half of whom were refugees from the 1948 war together with their descendants. Almost half of the population lived in the densely settled villages that had evolved from refugee camps, and many residents were still being assisted by the United Nations Relief and Works Agency (UNRWA), as citrus growing, the chief economic base of the zone, was insufficient to provide a living to all. Because the residents lacked an internationally recognized passport (they carried Palestinian travel documents), emigration from Gaza was more difficult. However, there was relatively free movement to Egypt for specific purposes notably – to attend institutions of higher learning (Gaza had none) or to serve in the Egyptian armed forces – and from there many individuals moved on to Kuwait or other parts of the Gulf. At the time of the June 1967 war, there were probably some 400,000 Palestinians actually residing in the Gaza Strip; the rest were temporarily outside.

Had there been no war or conquest, these 1.3 million Palestinians living in eastern Palestine and in the Gaza Strip in June 1967 would have increased, through an excess of births over deaths, to about 2.3 million by June 1982.[1] Even assuming some gradual outmigration for employment and/or education, the districts would have contained some 2 million persons by 1982, of whom two-thirds would have been residing on the so-called West Bank, while the remaining third would have been in Gaza.

Today, however, there are fewer than 1.3 million Palestinians still left in the two districts Israel occupied as a result of the 1967 war – more than one-third in the Gaza Strip, somewhat less than two-thirds on the West Bank, including east Jerusalem and environs.[2] The brunt of the expulsions and emigration has been borne by the West Bank areas outside Jerusalem. The population of the Gaza Strip has grown only slightly, despite a natural increase rate that approaches 4 percent per year. This means that net outmigration has come close to natural increase. In the area of east Jerusalem and environs, population has increased by 80 percent in the past fifteen years, which indicates that natural increase has been occurring without heavy pressures to leave. In contrast, however, the remaining portions of eastern Palestine have been subject to systematic decimation. There have been numerous forced expulsions and deportations; there has been systematic economic strangulation through land confiscations and water deprivation; and there has been a systematic undermining of local institutions. The net result is that, despite fifteen years of natural increase at

1. A natural increase rate of 3.5 percent per year is a reasonable minimum. The Israeli Palestinian population, until fairly recently, has been increasing at close to 4 percent per year. Crude birth rates in Gaza have remained remarkably constant at about 50/1000, while those in the West Bank have fluctuated between 44 and 47/1000. Death rates are presumed to be between 10/1000 on the West Bank and 15/1000 in the Gaza Strip.

2. Soon after the 1967 war, Israel unilaterally (and illegally) expanded the boundary of Jerusalem to absorb not only the walled Arab city of east Jerusalem, with its 24,000 inhabitants, but a very wide peripheral area including heavily populated towns and villages. In all Israeli-released statistics, the population inhabiting this "annexed" zone has been reclassified and recorded as part of the "non-Jewish" population of Israel, even though they remain Jordanian citizens and an integral part of the occupied West Bank. In our analysis we have transferred this population back into the occupied territories.

the rate of some 3.5 percent per year, the population now stands at 110,000 *less* than it had been in June of 1967.

Table 13.1 shows our estimates of change in the size of the Palestinian population under occupation since 1967. Three phases of demographic decline are evident, but their impact has varied in the three regions: Gaza, Jerusalem, and the remaining West Bank. This precipitous drop reveals the number of persons who became "refugees" (some for the second time in their lives) as a direct result of the war. As best as we can determine, some 250,000 West Bank residents, plus at least 75,000 residents of Gaza, were driven from their homes between June 1967 and December 1968.[3] As, during that year and a half, these 325,000 persons would normally have increased through an excess of births over deaths by some 17,000, we conclude that the number of Palestinians directly displaced as a result of the hostilities was close to 350,000. (This figure does not include the estimated 25,000 to 50,000 Gaza residents who were temporarily outside at the time of the Israeli invasion and who were subsequently prevented from returning.)

The second phase, from the beginning of 1969 to the latter part of 1974, was marked by a much slower rate of depopulation. On the Palestinian side there was great resistance to leaving. Many assumed that the occupation was a temporary inconvenience rather than a permanent change of jurisdiction, and furthermore, there was a strong conviction that future rights in Palestine might be compromised by emigration. There was also some hope that the United Nations' resolutions might bring about an Israeli withdrawal or that, lacking this, the Arab states might succeed in liberating the lost territories through renewed hostilities. On the Israeli side there was, after the first flush of victory (coupled perhaps with some trepidations about having to control so large a number of "captive" Palestinians), a growing appreciation of the economic value of the captured lands and even of their inhabitants. The considerable economic expansion that occurred in Israel between 1969 and 1974 can be attributed in large part to 1) the incorporation of West Bank and Gaza Strip workers as low-cost day laborers in Israeli agriculture and construction, and 2) the opening up of the occupied territories as marketing outlets for Israeli manufactured goods.

Given this congruence of interests, it is not surprising that between 1969 and 1974 the population of the Gaza Strip expanded by about 3 percent per year; that of the West Bank (excluding Jerusalem and environs) grew by an average of some 2.2 percent annually. Clearly, this growth rate

---

3. This estimate is quite consistent with those reached by different methods, notably figures released by the Jordanian government based upon bridge traffic and those estimated by J. Abu-Lughod (1980), based upon school transfer records, and presented in the Educational Statistics Yearbook for Jordan for 1968.

was considerably below that of the natural increase rate (4 and 3.5 percent annually for Gaza and the West Bank, respectively), so that expulsions and emigrations were taking their toll. But a general *modus vivendi* seemed to have been worked out that was not radically altering the demographic picture.

This state of affairs, however, began to change after the October 1973 war, which introduced the third phase. By the beginning of 1975, it was clear that depopulation of the West Bank had become a central goal of Israeli policy. Particularly after the Likud came to power in 1979, pressure mounted to clear much of the West Bank of its indigenous population, especially since the cheap labor required by the Israeli economy could be provided by Gaza which, with the signing of the final agreements with Egypt, was quietly "absorbed" into the Jewish state. The 1973 war contributed considerably to these changing circumstances.

First, the Israeli economy, after its first windfall from occupation, went into a deep recession, accompanied by overheated inflation. This was in part related to local conditions, in part related to the worldwide economic recession that followed the oil embargo, higher oil prices, etc. The Israeli economy no longer needed as many Palestinian workers on its farms and in its industrial plants. The number of Palestinians working in Israel peaked in 1974; since then their numbers have declined annually.[4] Preference was shown toward workers from Gaza who could more easily be controlled. Male workers from the West Bank were less sought after, although women continued to be drawn into domestic service.

Second, after the collapse of the "Arab military option" in 1973, the Palestinians, particularly on the West Bank, began to realize that the occupation was long-term and that quick liberation from outside was unlikely. They were faced with a number of possible alternatives, none of them attractive. They could remain and resist. By doing so, they risked imprisonment, death and, increasingly, deportation. Much of the decline in population since 1975 can be attributed to this "war of attrition."[5] Another option was to emigrate. Many families living on the West Bank had sons or husbands working abroad; their remittances helped to support those who

4. The number of West Bank residents employed in Israel rose from about 12,000 in 1969 to 42,400 in 1974. It has subsequently stabilized at about 35,000. West Bank workers have increasingly been employed on the West Bank itself but this does not indicate any regained autonomy as they are employed in Jewish enterprises – road building, settlements, agriculture. Unfortunately, it is impossible to determine the size of this dependent labor force, as no statistics are released.

5. Thousands of names have been recorded (some of which appear in Ann Lesch's article in *The Journal of Palestine Studies*). However, this appears to be only the tip of an iceberg.

TABLE 13.1

Movement of Population in Eastern Palestine and Gaza (Estimated)

Time		Eastern Palestine West Bank	Jerusalem	Total	Gaza	Total	
1967	June 1	820,000	80,000	900,000[1]	450,000[2]	1,350,000	
	Sept. 1	599,377[2]	66,000	665,377	356,260	1,022,000	
	Dec. 31	585,700	66,000[3]	651,700	350,700	1,002,400	
1968	Dec. 31	581,700	69,000[3]	650,700	325,900	976,600	
1969	Dec. 31	595,200	72,500[3]	667,700	330,000	997,700	
1970	Dec. 31	603,900	76,134	680,000	337,700	1,017,700	
1971	Dec. 31	617,300	81,000[3]	698,300	344,500	1,043,000	
1972	Dec. 31	629,000	86,300	715,300	353,500[3]	1,068,500	
1973	Dec. 31	646,200	91,000[3]	737,200	365,000[3]	1,102,200	
1974	Dec. 31	661,600	95,000[3]	756,600	378,500	1,135,100	
1975	Dec. 31	665,100	97,500[3]	762,600	388,500	1,151,100	
1976	Dec. 31	670,900	99,500[3]	770,400	399,000	1,169,400	
1977	Dec. 31	681,200	103,776	784,976	41 1,300	1,196,300	
1978	Dec. 31	690,400	108,000[3]	798,400	420,000	1,218,400	
1979	Dec. 31	699,600	114,200	813,800	431,500	1,245,300	
1980	Dec. 31	704,000	1 18,400	822,400	441,900	1,264,300	
1981	Dec. 31[4]	707,100	122,000	829,000	450,000	1,279,000	
1982	Dec. 31[4]	710,000	125,000	835,000	460,000	1,295,000	

NOTES:

1. According to Jordanian projections, there was a resident population on the West Bank (including Jerusalem) of about one million. However, this did not take into account net outmigration from the zone between 1961 (census date) and 1967, which amounted to about 100,000, according to Sakhnini. I have therefore adjusted this figure downward to take account of net outmigration in the years just prior to the war.

2. During the period during which the Egyptians administered the Gaza Strip, they kept a register of *de jure* residents. However, at the time the war broke out there was no way to determine how many of the 455,000 *de jure* occupants were actually within the Gaza Strip. We know that some were working abroad, others were studying in Egypt, and still others were serving with the Egyptian army. There may also have been over registration due to a failure to remove individuals who had died. My best estimate is that the population of the Gaza Strip just before the outbreak of the war was no more than 400,000.

The figures for September and end of I 967 are taken from Israeli sources. The first was from the census undertaken by the occupying army; it was a *de facto* census taken during a curfew and is presumed to be relatively complete. The December figure is given in official Israeli sources (various issues of *Statistical Abstracts*). The September figure specifically excludes the 33,000 Egyptian residents of northern Sinai (the town of Al-Arish and other parts of northern Sinai occupied as a result of the June war). All figures for Gaza after 1978-79 also specifically exclude the 30,000 residents of northern Sinai after that region was ceded back to Egypt. The intervening figures have been adjusted to exclude approximately 30,000 Egyptians, as Israeli totals presented successive issues of *Statistical Abstract* do not distinguish between Palestinian Gaza and Egyptian Sinai.

3. It has been difficult for me to obtain annual totals for the area of east Jerusalem and its surrounding hinterlands which was illegally "annexed" from the West Bank to the Israeli state. The figure of close to 66,000 in September 1967 is taken from the census conducted by the Israeli armed forces after the war. Where a figure appears for Jerusalem, it has been taken from published Israeli sources. Where a [3] appears next to a figure, this represents my rough interpolation between data points and is only provisional.

4. The most recent "official" figures are those for the end of I 980. Beginning with the advent of Likud to power in I 979, a stepped up expulsion of Palestinians began to show its effect on growth rates of the population in the occupied areas. I have projected these new lower rates to the end of 1982.

SOURCES:

For the period just prior to the 1967 war we have used data (adjusted) from the 1961 census of Jordan and the Egyptian registered population of Gaza. For subsequent figures we have depended upon Israeli-released data for the "Administered Territories" with adjustments to include east Jerusalem with the "West Bank" and to exclude Egyptian Sinai from Gaza.

remained under occupation. Initially, such moves for employment had been viewed as temporary and families were willing to endure the separation to keep their foothold at home. However, as Israeli land confiscations increased, as the military governor denied access to irrigation water, and most recently, as barriers were placed in the way of remitting funds from abroad, many dependent subfamilies were forced to leave and join their breadwinners abroad. Israeli policy has been to facilitate such moves and to make them irreversible. A final option was to become dependent upon Israeli employers to eke out a living. Such dependence has had the effect of "co-opting" a small portion of Palestinians; members of the Israeli-created Village Leagues have been given lucrative rights over licensing and preferential access to jobs in return for their "services" to the occupying power. In turn, they have been helping to put pressure on their compatriots and to assist the Israelis in their unconcealed policy of driving out recalcitrant Palestinians.

Thus, after 1974, both Israeli and Palestinian actions contributed to heightened depopulation. Average annual growth rates in Gaza since 1974 have hovered around 2.5 percent, and rates of population growth in eastern Palestine outside Jerusalem have recently been averaging only 1 percent per year. There was a noticeable drop in the increase rates after 1979, when Likud programs of stepped-up Jewish settlements on the West Bank were introduced. And although the data are not yet available, it is likely that a fourth phase of depopulation of a severe kind will follow the exodus of the Palestine Liberation Organization from Lebanon. Recent literature out of Israel has begun to take a sanguine attitude toward Palestinian increase in the occupied territories; some already believe that the "demographic nightmare" of a Palestinian majority has been averted.[6]

Selectivity of Expulsions and Emigrations

The structure of the population remaining in eastern Palestine has been increasingly distorted by the selective expulsion or emigration (or incarceration, for which data are not available) of young adult males. Although the overall sex ratio appears balanced, in fact, in the middle years of life, the absence of males is particularly noticeable.[7] Recent increases in the crude

---

6. See Merlon Benvenisti et al., *The West Bank and Gaza Data Base Project: Pilot Study Report* (mimeo., 1980) for information on what appears to be a new relaxation of concern.

7. By 1978, the sex ratio in the middle years (ages 25- 60) on the West Bank stood at 80 males for every 100 females; in the Gaza Strip there were only 75 males for every 100 females in these productive years of life. The sex ratio in the productive years is the single most sensitive indicator of selective outmigration for employment.

birth rates on the West Bank (from 44 to 47 per 1000) may be attributable to the "feminization" of the population, although they may also be due to its proletarianization.

Whereas adult males are most likely to be engaged in resistance and are therefore more likely to be expelled, families in which at least some workers have skills that are demanded in the oil-boom countries are more likely to emigrate as economic pressures mount. Professional workers and upper middle-class businessmen have been particularly hard-hit by the "merging" of the Israeli and West Bank economies. Unable to practice their professions or unable to survive in an unfair competition with Jewish businesses that are subsidized by the state, the members of the urban middle and upper classes have gradually been leaving.

Emigration from Gaza has been far less selective economically, but it must be remembered that the population of Gaza was never as occupationally diversified as that of the West Bank. Proletarian to begin with, it had little bourgeoisie to lose. Incarceration rather than expulsion has been the fate of young males who resist the occupation. Furthermore, we have no records of the number of persons who lost their lives in the resistance in Gaza, although there are almost daily incidents.

PROLETARIANIZATION OF THE POPULATION UNDER OCCUPATION

The final demographic trend that can be noted is the reduction of a diversified society to the status of a reserve labor army dependent upon the Israeli economy. This trend has been most marked in eastern Palestine, as Gaza was unviable from the start. As can be seen from data shown in table 13.2, the labor force characteristics of the West Bank (excluding Jerusalem) have begun to approximate those for Israeli Palestinians who earlier underwent the process of transformation from a peasantry to a proletariat.[8] There has been a radical reduction in the proportion of the population that makes a living through farming.[9] To some extent this is due to the confiscation of land and the deprivation of water to irrigate it. But to some extent it represents the marginalization of agriculture. Given the imported

8. See Elia Zureik, *The Palestinians in Israel: A Study in Internal Colonialism* (London: Routledge and Kegan Paul, 1979) for a description of this precursor to West Bank changes since 1967.

9. At the time of the 1967 war, fully one-half of the West Bank labor force was engaged in agriculture. It is currently under 20 percent.

TABLE 13.2

Occupational Distribution of Palestinian Males in Selected Countries and Regions

Country or Region of Residence	Percentage in Occupational Categories by Descending Status (rough order)						
	Profes sional, Technical	Admin./ Manager	Clerical	Sales and Commerce	Industrial, Transport, Utilities	Services (personal)	Agriculture, Fishing, Mining
SAUDI ARABIA[1]							
(1974)	5.51	2.9	6.0	3.2	28.9	3.3	4.3
of which:							
Jordanians	63.0	3.1	6.1	3.1	20.1	1.9	2.1
Palestinians	36.9	2.6	5.7	3.3	39.3	5.0	7.1
KUWAIT[2]							
(1975 Census)	20.8	1.3	17.8	8.6	41.1	8.4	2.1
JORDAN EAST BANK[3]							
(1975 Amman)	9.7		7.0	11.8	45.4	11.2	14.5
SYRIA[4]							
(970 Census)	10.8	0.7	8.2	8.9	57.0	6.6	7.9
ISRAEL[5]							
(1972 Census)	6.6	3.9		8.2	51.4	10.0	19.9
(1976 Census)	6.2	0.4	3.9	7.3	57.3	9.7	15.2
WEST BANK[6]							
(1977)	6.2	0.9	3.0	12.5	50.1	7.8	19.5
GAZA[6]							
(1977)	5.1	0.6	3.1	11.9	47.4	8.7	23.2
LEBANON CAMPS[7]							
(1971)	3.7		1.4	15.3	46.1	8.9	24.7

SOURCE NOTES:

1. Compiled by the author from the information by muhafazat in the Saudi Census of 1974.

2. Compiled by the author from the information on Palestinians and Jordanians in the Kuwait Census of 1975. See *Census of Kuwait 1975* (1977), table 47, p. 232.

3. *Caveat lector.* There is, of course, no breakdown by national origin in the Jordanian *Labour Force Census,* 1975. I have taken, instead, the labor force breakdown for Amman alone. Unfortunately males and females have not been separated and the categories of occupations have been arranged in a manner somewhat different from that employed in other censuses. I have therefore regrouped the various occupations in order to replicate, as closely as possible, the categories generally employed in other countries. While it is impossible to estimate, from the figures presented, the distribution of occupations of male Palestinians alone, it is possible to specify in which directions the figures might change, if we were able to separate males from females and Palestinians from Jordanians of Jordanian origin. First, removing females would decrease slightly the proportion of labor force engaged in farming and would increase, commensurately, the proportion in industrial, transport and construction occupations. Second, removing those of Jordanian origin would also decrease the proportion in agriculture and probably also the proportion in services, although the latter is less certain. Removal of Jordanians would undoubtedly increase the proportion in technical, professional and managerial positions.

4. These figures have been computed from the 1970 census of the Syrian Arab Republic. It is interesting to note that the occupational distribution of Palestinians in Syria is almost identical to the occupational distribution of Syrians, once the agricultural sector is removed.

5. These figures from 1972 have been adapted from table 5.8b in Elia Zureik, *The Palestinians in Israel: A Study in Internal Colonialism* (London: Routledge and Kegan Paul, 1979), p. 123. These figures include the population of east Jerusalem and have been taken from the Israeli Census of 1972. The 1976 figures come from Israel, Central Bureau of Statistics, *Labour Force Surveys* 1976, special series no. 564 (Jerusalem, 1978). p. 234.

6. The *Statistical Abstract of Israel 1978* (no. 29, published 1979) includes figures from a labor force survey undertaken in the occupied areas see table XXCII/ 24, pp. 790-91. These figures refer to employed persons and are therefore not exactly comparable to labor force studies that give "usual occupation" of unemployed persons as well.

7. Males and females combined. Source is Lebanese Ministry of Planning, *Sample Survey in Camps,* 1971.

inflation that has caused prices to rise in the West Bank at rates that exceed even the recent Israeli rate of 130 percent per year, farms that were adequate to support their owners before are sufficient now to offer only an income supplement. Many family members are thrown into the wage-labor market, grateful for day labor jobs in construction and road building-- even if these actually advance the Jewish settlement expansion into the West Bank.

In more than two decades of occupation, then, economic self-sufficiency has been severely eroded. As selective emigration and the deportation of leaders continue, the upper ranks of the social class pyramid are thinned. As land confiscations and economic strangulation of agriculture (through water deprivation and Israeli control over marketing) proceed, relatively autonomous peasants are increasingly reduced to dependence upon daily wage labor and upon the Israeli employers who provide it. Although wages in Israeli enterprises have been slightly higher than those in the West Bank economy, Palestinians are paid only half of what Jewish citizens receive. Their costs of living have risen sharply, however, due to the equalization of prices. This has created a serious economic squeeze for those Palestinians who remain. Thus far, remittances from abroad have masked the precarious position into which Palestinians in the occupied areas have been pushed. However, the levers that control their dependency are now in Israeli hands. Access to jobs is a major lever; the right to receive foreign remittances is another. Both of these can be cut off at will.

CONCLUSION

Over the past two decades there has been a real net decline in the population of eastern Palestine and Gaza. Present Israeli policy is committed to intensifying the pressures upon Palestinian residents in order to further depopulate the areas intended for Jewish expansion. The "absorption" of east Jerusalem has been concealed by Israeli demographic practices which exclude the residents from any totals for "the administered areas." The Israeli economy has increasingly drawn upon the Gaza Strip as its source of cheap labor, and the military governor has used control over jobs as the carrot, in combination with force as the stick, to "pacify" the population. In West Bank areas outside Jerusalem a very different policy is being followed – one aimed at reducing the number of inhabitants but also at reducing the capacity of the remainder to resist occupation. The selective "ridding" of the region of its males in the productive years of life, of its professionals, and of its leaders is one part of this process. The second part is the systematic proletarianization of the remaining population and its reduction to dependence upon Jewish employers.

The final act in this drama remains unplayed. Just as the 1967 war initiated the process and the 1973 war marked its turning point, so the invasion of Lebanon in 1982 is likely to set in motion a new phase in the struggle for Palestine – a struggle which has been demographic from the very beginning and which continues to be.

A NOTE ON DEMOGRAPHIC SOURCES:

Close to one hundred demographic sources were consulted in connection with the preparation of Janet Abu-Lughod, "Demographic Characteristics of the Palestinian Population," Annex I to *Palestine Open University Feasibility Study,* Part II (UNESCO: Paris, 1980), c. 125 pp. The report includes a complete listing of these sources and detailed tables based on them. Critical evaluations of their relative accuracy and explanations for how and why various published figures were adjusted are also included.

Since the time of that analysis, additional issues of the *Israeli Statistical Abstract* have appeared, and these have been consulted in connection with this chapter. Also available for consultation were three issues of a new publication, *Palestinian Statistical Abstract* (Damascus: P.L.O. Central Bureau of Statistics, 1979, 1980 and 1981).

PALESTINE: DISTRIBUTION OF POPULATION BY SUB-DISTRICTS

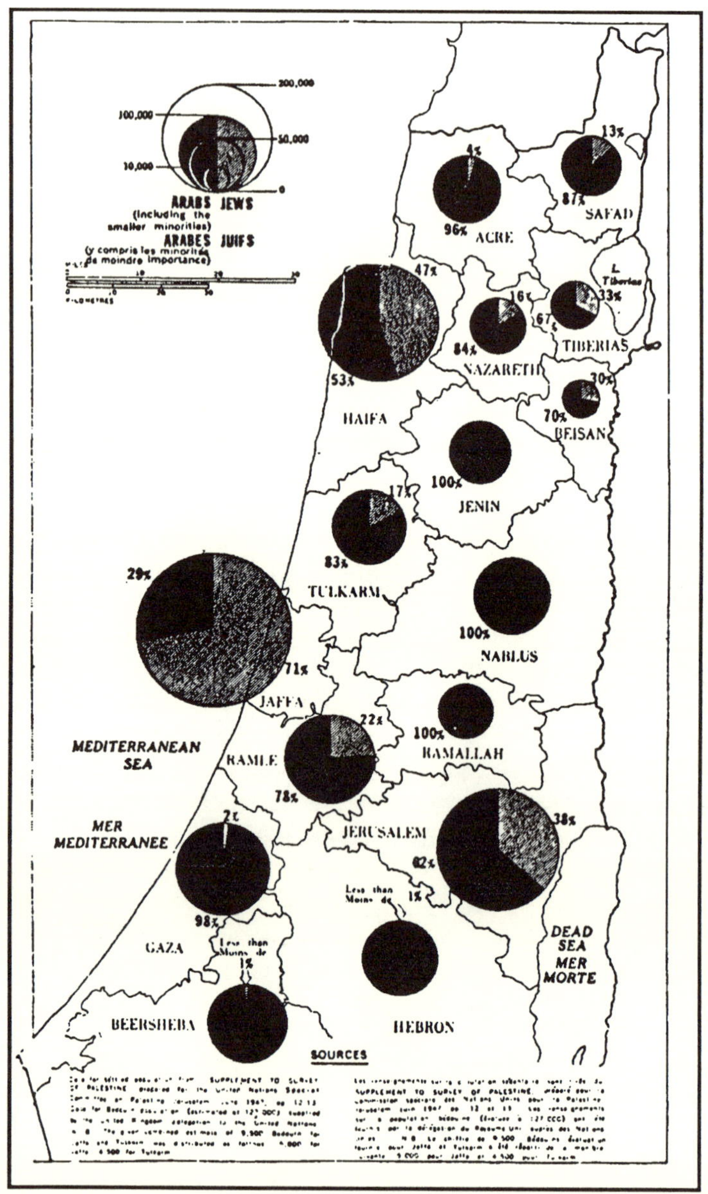

Distribution of population Palestine, as prepared for the United Nations sub-Committee on the Palestinian Question in 1947. Data obtained from the Supplement to the survey of Palestine, United Nations Special committee on Palestine, June 1947.

CHAPTER 14

HEALTH AND HEALTH SERVICES

Union of Palestinian Medical Relief Committees, West Bank and Gaza Strip

What is the present status of health and health care services in the West Bank and Gaza Strip? Israeli authorities claim that there has been steady improvement in the health of the population in the occupied territories, and that the structure is in place for continued progress. But there is evidence that Israeli claims are exaggerated; that the health care structure is unsound and fragmented, and does not address the real needs of the people it is supposed to serve.

Refutation of Israeli claims is made difficult by the fact that we must rely heavily on Israeli statistics. Independent evaluations have of necessity been on a small scale, and generally have not been able to deal with such broad but vital areas as water quality, housing, sanitary conditions and the like. Still, even the official figures seem to contradict themselves, and several small studies have indicated that the situation is not good and getting better, but rather the opposite.

We will first examine the present health status of the Palestinian population of the West Bank and Gaza Strip, using such recognized

This chapter is adapted from a paper presented on September 1987 at a meeting of the U.N. Non-Governmental Organizations in Geneva by the Union of Palestinian Medical Relief Committees, on behalf of Dr. Moustafa Barghouthi. Dr. Barghouthi had intended to read the paper, but was, without explanation, denied an exit permit by the Israeli military authorities. This fact in itself is perhaps indicative of the difficulties faced in the health sector, as indeed in all aspects of life under military occupation.

indicators as infant mortality rates and medical services-to-population ratios. Then, we will look at the health services structure under occupation, including the role of outside agencies. Finally, we present some priorities for future development, based in large part on our own experiences in trying to serve the diverse and unique health care needs of this population.

PRESENT HEALTH STATUS

Infant Mortality

Infant mortality is defined as the ratio of children that are born alive and die before they reach the age of one year to each one thousand children born alive that year. It is considered one of the best indicators of the health of a population, in that it reflects the health of the mother, the availability of pre- and postnatal care, and in a more general way, the overall standard of living – sanitary conditions, housing, and the like.

The Israeli military government claims that infant mortality in the West Bank and Gaza Strip is 24-30 deaths per 1,000 live births. It also claims that the rate has dropped to 30/1,000 in the Gaza Strip.[1] These figures are based on official records of births and deaths, which, especially in the case of infant mortality, are often inaccurate.

Even the Israeli Central Bureau of Statistics disagrees with this rather optimistic picture (optimistic, that is, unless one compares it to the 14/1,000 rate for Israel – see table 14.1). The Ministry of Health figure is 70/1,000 for the West Bank for 1985. Other studies corroborate these higher rates. A study conducted in 1986 in the village of Biddo near Jerusalem (where living conditions are relatively good compared to other localities in the area) placed infant mortality there at 49 / 1,000.[2] In three villages in the Ramallah district in 1983 the rate was 91 / 1,000[3] and an initial assessment of recent data indicates that the infant mortality rates in the Hebron districts and the Jordan Valley are higher than those of the Jerusalem and Ramallah villages, perhaps reaching 80 to 100 deaths per 1,000 live births. In general, then, the overall infant mortality rate is most certainly not less than the 70/1,000 figure reported by the Israeli Central Bureau of Statistics, and might even approach 10 percent in some regions.

1. T.H. Tulchinsky, "Medical Services in Gaza," *Lancet* (21 February 1987).

2. Union of Palestinian Medical Relief Committees and the Community Health Unit, Bir Zeit University, "Profile of Life and Health in Biddo" (interim report, unpublished data), 1987. (Hereinafter Union Profile).

3. R. Giacaman, *Life and Health in Three Palestinian Villages* (Bir Zeit, 1986), p. 144.

TABLE 14.1

Infant Mortality Rates (1985)

Israel	14/1000
Syria	60/1000
Jordan	55/1000
West Bank/Gaza Strip	70/1000

SOURCE: Israel Ministry of Health: *Report to the World Health Organization, 1986,* p. 8.

Although it appears certain that infant mortality rates have declined since 1967, the point to raise is whether this decline might have been even more pronounced had there been no Israeli military rule. It should be emphasized that a pattern of improvement in infant mortality rates was quite evident in the area in general, including Jordan and other Arab countries, prior to the advent of the occupation. Military rule, with its damaging effects on the cohesiveness of families and its deliberate policy of undermining any coherent infrastructure, in health as in other areas, would not appear to foster conditions leading to any real reduction in infant mortality.

Child Health

It is becoming clear from field studies conducted in the area that a high rate of malnutrition is found among the children of the occupied territories. One such study, done in a rural area near Jerusalem, indicated that 34 percent of children under the age of three suffered from malnutrition; the same study showed a 20 percent incidence of low birth weight among babies born in the area.[4] Another study of the Diuk area of the Jordan Valley revealed a malnutrition rate of 55 percent for girls and 34 percent for boys.[5] Initial analysis of data from an all-country nutritional study of

4. Union Profile, p.23

5. Union of Palestinian Medical Relief Committees and the Community Health Unit, Bir Zeit University, "A Survey of Health Conditions in Kin Diuk" (unpublished data), 1987. (Hereinafter Union Survey.)

children being conducted by the Union of Palestinian Medical Relief
Committees shows a rate of malnutrition of 40 percent among children in
the Hebron area.

Most of these cases of malnutrition are mild to moderate. One does not
see dying children with swollen bellies and sticklike limbs – those images of
starvation that pricked the consciences of television viewers in more
fortunate countries. Because these cases are less extreme, they are
neglected even by local health care providers and by their own families.
But these children are especially vulnerable to infectious diseases, and to the
insidious long-term effects of malnutrition on physical, mental, and
psychological development.

Parasite infestation remains a major public health problem today in the
occupied areas. A study by the Israeli military government in Gaza
revealed a 50 percent rate of parasite infestation among schoolchildren.[6]
Other studies have shown rates ranging between 40 and 60 percent in
various localities of the West Bank and Gaza.[7] Also indicative of the poor
living conditions are the periodic outbreaks of infectious diseases such as
hepatitis, Maltese fever, typhoid, and meningitis, among others. At present,
the public health apparatus in the area is not equipped with concrete plans
for the containment and control of such epidemics. These outbreaks are, in
any case, nonexistent to anyone who looks only at official statistics – most
are never documented through appropriate public health notification
procedures.

Eye Diseases

A study of 9,548 cases from the West Bank and Gaza, conducted by a
team of physicians from St. John's Ophthalmic Hospital in Jerusalem,
found a rate of binocular blindness of 1.74 percent, or eight times the rate
for Great Britain. Single eye impairment reached a rate of 6.8 percent of the
sample studied,[8] and the rate of infection with trachoma reached 28.4
percent. This study documents a high rate of eye infection, leading to
serious complications including blindness, related to the absence of early
diagnosis and appropriate treatment.

6. Israel Ministry of Health, *Report to the World Health Organization, 1986*, p.
137.

7. Union Profile; Union Survey.

8. I.M. Thompson and L.C. Chumbly, "Eye Disease in the West Bank and Gaza
Strip," *British Journal of Ophthalmology* 68(8) 598-602.

Medical Services per 10,000 Population

Data for the year 1986 indicate that the physician/population ratio for the West Bank and Gaza Strip is 8/10,000,[9] compared with 28/10,000 for Israel[10] and 22/10,000 for Jordan. Even this figure must be viewed in light of the fact that about 200 physicians in the West Bank and 80 in Gaza were either partially or completely unemployed during the past few years. The ratio also includes more than 120 physicians employed by the Union of Physicians Absorption Program for the West Bank, under which they receive a monthly salary that does not exceed US $300 (if indeed they are paid at all – they have not received any salary for the past six months).

Thus, the actual working physician/population ratio in the West Bank does not exceed 6/10,000. In the Gaza Strip, the figure for physicians working in the governmental sector is 4/10,000,[11] at a time when the Israeli government claims that 85 percent of the population carries government health insurance. It is quite clear, then, that the West Bank and Gaza Strip have a pressing need for physicians, especially in the public sector, where their number is especially low. This deficiency is further illustrated by the fact that 248 of a total of 489 population localities (villages, towns, and refugee camps) lack any form of modern health care.[12]

This situation translates into an overwhelming doctor-patient load, especially in clinics. In the Gaza Strip, where the military government operates twenty-five clinics, each physician must see an average of 110 patients daily.[13] In clinics run by the United Nations Relief and Works Agency (UNRWA), a physician must examine 70 to 120 patients in a four-to-six-hour period – an average of about three minutes per patient.[14] The situation is not much better even at the Kapal Holim clinics operated by the

9. Information from the Union of Physicians in the West Bank and the Arab Medical Association in Gaza.

10. Calculated using data from Israel Central Bureau of Statistics, *Statistical Abstract of Israel, 1986,* no. 37, pp. 26 and 63.

11. Sara Roy, "The Gaza Strip," *West Bank Data Base Project* (Jerusalem, 1986), p. 17.

12. Union of Physicians in the West Bank, "Primary Health Care in the West Bank, 1986," p. 4.

13. United Nations Relief and Works Agency, *Report to the Director of Health* (Vienna, 1986), p.28.

14. Information obtained from physicians working in the UNRWA system.

Israeli Ministry of Health that attend to the health needs of Palestinian Arabs in east Jerusalem; there a physician must examine an average of fifty patients daily.

Today in the occupied territories a curious situation exists: there are people who need doctors and doctors who need work, but no bridge between them. The existing health apparatus is incapable of absorbing physicians and other health professionals; this leads many to emigrate in search of work opportunities. The Israeli military government tries to employ as few professionals as possible in the governmental health sector, and UNRWA, a major part of the health care delivery system, is incapable of employing the number of trained personnel that the situation demands.

Deficiencies are also apparent when we look at the hospital bed/population ratio. Even official Israeli statistics indicate that this ratio is 1.6/1,000 in the occupied territories, compared to 6.1/1,000 in Israel. What makes the observation more interesting is the relationship between the change in the number of hospital beds over the years of occupation and natural population growth. As table 14.2 shows, the population of the West Bank increased by 21 percent between 1974 and 1985, whereas the number of hospital beds actually fell 6 percent. In the Gaza Strip in the same period, the population grew by 26 percent; the number of hospital beds declined 13 percent.[15]

It is obvious that, in hospital beds per person as in other indicators of public health, the facts refute Israeli claims of progress. Even more telling than the large disparity between the figures for Israel and those for the occupied territories in this respect is the fact that under occupation, the number of beds has actually fallen from 2.2 to 1.6 per thousand.

Health Problems Unique to the Occupied Territories

Any discussion of present-day health conditions in the occupied territories must consider some factors particular to the area in question. Many assume that the health profile in the West Bank and Gaza Strip is identical to that in undeveloped and developing countries, characterized by infectious disease, malnutrition, a high infant mortality rate and the like. Although, as we have seen, it is true that these conditions occur in the occupied territories, it is also true that there has been a sharp increase in those health problems more characteristic of modern industrialized society, such as hypertension, heart disease, cancer, diabetes, and psychiatric disorders. For example, three-quarters of all clinic patients in the areas

15. *Statistical Abstract*, pp. 683, 688.

TABLE 14.1

Hospital Beds to Population

Year	Population	Hospital Beds
West Bank		
1974	669,700	1,393
1985	813,300	1,308
Gaza Strip		
1974	414,000	1,004
1985	525,000	872

SOURCE: Israel Central Bureau of statistics, *Statistical Abstract of Israel, 1986*, no. 37, pp. 16, 641,683, and 733.

suffer from infectious diseases, and 74 percent of all childhood deaths are due to infectious disease.[16] Yet the number one killer of adults is heart disease. One study found that 47 percent of all families in the area under study had at least one family member suffering from a chronic disease such as hypertension (15% of families), diabetes (10%), asthma (7%), and psychiatric illness (7%).[17]

Several factors could account for this duality in the health picture. The occupied territories have undergone dramatic changes in their economic and social infrastructures as a result of Israeli military rule; such drastic changes must have an effect on health. Economic dependence on Israel and contact with a developed capitalist system have led to pervasive changes in lifestyle. Food is now more likely to be processed in Israel rather than home-grown. There is an increasing reliance on agricultural chemicals and pesticides. To such factors must be added the psychological stresses of living under military occupation. For example, some 250,000 Palestinians have spent time in Israeli prisons in the past twenty years. Surely such experience must have had some effect on health.

16. J.H. Puyet, *Infant Mortality Studies Carried Out among Selected Refugee Camp Communities in the Near East* (Vienna: UNRWA, 1979).

17. Union Profile.

This duality – the development of new patterns and types of diseases in the area superimposed on an existing situation where basic problems such as proper sewage disposal and provision of an adequate water supply are still not solved – creates a complicated setting calling for a high level of creativity in devising solutions for health problems. Neither solutions based on third-world medicine, nor those that seem to have worked in industrialized societies, can be imposed without modification on this unique situation.

NATIONAL HEALTH SERVICE APPARATUS

In most countries of the world, the state takes major responsibility for the health care of its citizens. Particulars vary, but in most cases a centralized apparatus oversees funding and control of health insurance, coordination among the existing health sectors, infectious disease containment, occupational and environmental safety, public health and sanitation, and long-term health care planning.

On June 5, 1967, the occupied territories lost this health apparatus. The occupying power has not been able to replace it, and will not be able to do so in the future. The most obvious reason for this is that Israel does not want to supply the funds necessary for such a task. But more fundamentally, building a local national health infrastructure contradicts in a radical way the Israeli strategy of weakening the structure of Palestinian society and fostering dependence on the occupying power.

Neglect of the Primary Health Care Sector

At present, most health care facilities are located in towns, although no less than 70 percent of the population lives in rural areas and in refugee camps. We have noted that no form of modern health services whatsoever exists in 248 of 489 population localities of the West Bank. In general, maternal and child health facilities are lacking; there is little regularity and follow-up in immunization campaigns. One study showed that basic maternal and child health services were found in only 29.4 percent of the inhabited localities in the West Bank, and that in 69 percent of the localities where the population was under 3,000, no modern services whatsoever existed.[18] In addition, coordination between private and public health centers, clinics, and hospitals is nonexistent. There is no apparatus in place for the control of communicable disease and no structure for dealing with environmental problems – a large proportion of the population still drinks

18. Union of Physicians, "Primary Health Care," p. 7.

nonpotable water.[19] This neglect of the basic elements of health care, of course, sets the stage for mortality and morbidity that might easily be prevented.

Failure of Governmental Health Insurance Programs

In the West Bank and Gaza, the governmental health sector represents the greater proportion of the entire health services infrastructure of the country. It should be noted here that the Israeli military government is in charge of levying taxation on the occupied population. In addition, it deducts a substantial amount from the paychecks of those who work in Israel proper. A minimal amount of what is collected is spent on health education and other basic services. It has been estimated that in 1986 the average military government expenditure for health services in the West Bank and Gaza Strip did not exceed US $30 per capita, compared to US $350 per capita for Israelis.[20] In 1985, the budget for governmental hospitals of the West Bank was 8 million dollars, including 3 million dollars spent on the treatment of Palestinian Arab transfer patients in Israeli hospitals. In the same year, the budget for one Israeli hospital (Akhilot) was four times the amount assigned to all nine government hospitals in the West Bank.

Up until 1977, it was possible for any ordinary person to obtain health services in the government sector at relatively little cost. In that year, however, the Israeli military elected to introduce a governmental health insurance scheme. Under this program, those who wish to be insured must pay a monthly fee of about US $18.

Official Israeli statistics indicate that 38 percent of the population is insured under this program, but we feel this figure is inflated. A study by the Israeli military government found, for example, that only 55 percent of those registered as insured and regularly paying their premiums actually made use of the health service.[21] The Biddo study revealed that only 22 percent of the villagers were insured; a meager 4 percent of the population regularly used the government health services.[22] Another study gave the

19. Chris Smith, "A Survey of Drinking Water in Eight Jordan Valley Villages" (Bir Zeit University, 1985).

20. M. Benvenisti, *The West Bank Data Base Project, 1986 Report* (Jerusalem, 1986), p. 17.

21. Joint Committee on Health Services in Judea and Samaria, *Report to the Ministry of Health* (Jerusalem, 1985), Appendix, p.30.

22. Union Profile.

following percentages of population covered by government insurance: 12.6 percent in the Hebron district, 19.5 percent in Ramallah, 29.9 percent in Jerusalem, and 13.9 percent in Jericho.[23]

Military authorities themselves admit that there has been a decline in the proportion of insured persons in the Gaza Strip during the past years, from 83 percent in 1981 to 56 percent in 1985.[24] Most agree that this decline and the general lack of enthusiasm for the government health insurance program are due to its high cost, coupled with the deteriorating quality of the services provided.

Lack of Balance in Distribution of Health Services

This problem has three dimensions. First, there is an imbalance in expenditure between primary health care and hospital services. We have already seen how the primary care sector is neglected – what funding there is tends to go to curative hospital care rather than to preventive services. The distribution of services also suffers from a geographical imbalance, and imbalance based on social inequities.

The emphasis on hospital rather than preventive care necessarily leads to a concentration of services in more urban areas. Another type of regional inequity exists, especially in the West Bank. There, health services are concentrated in the central part of the country, most notably in Jerusalem, Ramallah, and Bethlehem and Nablus. In both the northern (especially the regions of Tulkarem, Qalqilya, and Jenin) and southern (Hebron and further south) regions, there is a disproportionately low share of available facilities. Whereas in the central regions the hospital bed/population ratio is 2.3/1,000, in the north it does not exceed 0.5/1,000. In Hebron, only one hospital (Alia), with a meager one hundred beds, serves the needs of a population of some 300,000.

Planners for the future of health care in the region must address these problems of structural and geographical imbalance, and they must deal with the difficult problem of social inequities. Those who suffer most under the present system are the very poor, and especially poor women and girls. A review of Caritas Baby Hospital records, for example, revealed that 79 percent of children admitted for cold injury were the offspring of workers.[25] The Biddo study showed clearcut inequalities between the sexes – infant

23. Union of Palestinian Medical Relief Committees, "Lights on Health Problems in the West Bank" (February 1984), p. 16.

24. Roy, "Gaza Strip," p. 107.

25. Information obtained from records of Caritas Baby Hospital, Bethlehem.

mortality rates were 58/1,000 for girls, compared to 41/1,000 for boys.[26] The Ramallah three villages study showed a 52 percent rate of malnutrition among girls, as opposed to 32 percent for boys.[27] In Kin Diuk, 55 percent of the girls and 34 percent of the boys were malnourished.[28] Clearly, such class and gender inequalities must be taken into account in any future plans for development of a comprehensive health care system for the region.

Lack of Coordination among Health Institutions

Structural, geographical, and social imbalances in the distribution of health services are a reflection of the fragmented nature of the entire system in the occupied territories. There are five major sectors in that system: the governmental, controlled by the Israeli military government; UNRWA, specializing in services to Palestinian refugees, and other United Nations agencies; the private sector; charitable institutions such as Maqassed Hospital and various women's societies; and, of recent development, the popular sector.

Under normal circumstances, some national apparatus assumes the responsibility for coordination among the various sectors. No such system exists for the occupied territories. The military government has as its main priority the control of the population under its rule; despite the good intentions of Palestinian Arab physicians and others who work within this system questions of efficient health care delivery must be subordinate to those of containment and control. The "state of siege" recently faced by the Palestine Red Crescent Society in Gaza is one of many examples that highlight this problem.

For the past twenty years, the aim of the Israeli government has been the dismantling of the Palestinian native infrastructure, with the concomitant effect of creating dependency on Israeli institutions and structures. In the health sphere, this has entailed such actions as limiting budgets, closing hospitals, and stifling any attempts to develop efficient distribution systems. Recently, there has been an important shift in Israeli policy for health services, compatible with a general shift in policy toward the occupied territories. The earlier agenda, aimed at the breakdown of local institutions, entailed the frequent transfer of Palestinian Arab patients to Israeli medical facilities. In the past few years, there has been a change in this policy – a change based on Israeli perceptions that first, the creation of a state of

26. Union Profile.

27. Giacaman, *Life and Health*, p. 79.

28. Union Survey.

dependency has indeed been successful, and second, that the West Bank and Gaza Strip are likely to remain under Israeli occupation for a long time, if not permanently. The emphasis is now on creating services – albeit second-rate services – especially for Arabs.

One sees signs of this new emphasis throughout the area, even in Jerusalem, where it appears that the Hadassah Hospital in Mount Scopus specializes in Arab patients, whereas the more developed Hadassah Hospital Ein Karem caters to the needs of Israeli Jews. Recently, support was provided for the creation of an open heart surgery department at Ramallah Hospital, and the establishment of a cancer wing at Beit Jala Hospital. It must be remembered that such developments are implemented without adequate planning and without provision of the infrastructure that might ensure their successful operation. It is hard to imagine how an open heart surgery ward is to succeed in providing quality services in a hospital that remains inadequately staffed with physicians and nurses, and where even sanitary conditions could stand improvement. It is hard to grasp the rationale behind the establishment of such highly technical facilities, when the training of Palestinian physicians to staff them is inadequate and incomplete. From the Israeli point of view, the logic seems to be that the creation of a second-rate system for Arabs will not only reserve the first-rate Israeli system for the exclusive use of the Israelis, but also gain credit for the Israelis for improving health conditions in the occupied territories.

Outside agencies such as UNRWA play a major role in the provision of health services, but here again a lack of coordination with other sectors is evident. Major policy and funding decisions are made outside the county – in Vienna, in the case of UNRWA with little or no input from Palestinians. But the major problem with such endeavors is that they must operate under the aegis of the Israeli military government, which makes every effort to bend the aid provided by these agencies to its own policies and interests.

Examples abound. The World Health Organization (WHO) center in Ramallah initiated a study of infant mortality rates in selected villages in the Hebron district. Local Palestinian employees collected data, initial analysis of which led to derivation of a death-to-live birth ratio of 60/1,000. When these figures appeared in the yearly report that was to be presented to WHO, the military government protested and attempted to change the figures to fit the data they had (about 24 deaths per 1,000). When this act was met by resistance from local employees, on professional grounds, the Israelis in charge elected to omit completely the section on infant mortality from the report.

The United Nations Development Program (UNDP) suffers from similar problems. Its manpower development program recently paid for specialization training in Israeli hospitals for twenty-one Palestinian Arab physicians. This program, although inadequate and incomplete, has been the subject of official Israeli boasting about its specialization training of Palestinian physicians. Such boasting completely omits mention of the fact that UNDP has paid large amounts of money to Israeli hospitals for the program – US $51,000 just for Hebrew language training for example. Many questions can be raised about such well-intentioned projects. Why does training take place in Israeli hospitals at all? Why in Hebrew? Why are these Palestinian physicians not completely trained? It is as if the program were designed to cement a relationship of dependence on Israeli hospitals – surely this is not what the United Nations had in mind.

A United Nations Children's Fund (UNICEF) project is no less problematic. It was originally intended to establish health centers in the Hebron district and to train village health workers to take charge of these centers. The entire program was placed under the supervision of the governmental health sector in Hebron, which suffered from grave professional inadequacies including the unavailability of properly trained manpower. An observer of one of these centers today senses little or no benefit from this considerable outlay of UNICEF funds.

It is time to raise fundamental questions about the role of these agencies in the provision of health care. Is any United Nations agency capable of working independently, without interference from the military? Should UNRWA services continue to take the form of classical clinic-based medicine in the Gaza Strip, for example, when clearly the need there is first and foremost for improvement in environmental sanitation? Should not UNRWA seriously consider cooperation with local institutions in these and similar situations? Although few can doubt the good intentions behind such efforts, under the present circumstance of dependence upon the good will of the military authorities it may be impossible to realize those intentions.

As for the remaining sectors of the present health care structure, attempts to coordinate Palestinian efforts have met with little success, despite some admirable endeavors. Of course the main problem is the overriding one of operation under military authority, but in some cases competition among institutions and disagreement on priorities have stood in the way of development of comprehensive plans. Imported ideas have sometimes been applied, without regard to the unique realities of the situation in the occupied territories. For example, attempts were made to apply the principles enunciated in David Werner's book, *Where There Is No Doctor*.[29] This book, based on apparently very successful experiences in Latin America, called for the establishment of a network of trained village

29. David Werner, *Where There Is No Doctor – a Village Health Care Handbook*, 6th rev. ed. (Palo Alto, Cal.: Hesperian Foundation, 1977).

health workers as the primary health care providers. The results of efforts to impose this system, in total isolation from the existing apparatus and without consideration of local conditions and needs, soon became apparent. For example, male workers were trained to deliver maternal health care; often local norms and customs forbade this. Workers were trained to perform curative functions and prescribe drugs, in a country where access to physicians is not the major problem. The workers were left on their own in isolated villages without any form of support, which might have been supplied through the existing health apparatus. They were trained to deliver preventive services, such as improvement in sanitary conditions, but the local population did not always appreciate the need for changes in the ways they had always done things. No wonder some of these workers became the laughingstock of their villages. The point to be made is not that there is no need for village health workers. They can perform a vital function, but only if they have received training based on the realities of the situation, and if they can draw on the support of the existing health structure. There are other instances of inappropriate manpower development; for example, several institutions provide nursing training at the bachelor's level, but there is not enough local employment opportunity for such highly trained nurses. This leads to outmigration of these nurses, in a situation where there is a clear need for nurses and health workers.

Thus, the lack of comprehensive, sensitive planning cuts across all sectors of the present system.

CONCLUSIONS AND PRIORITIES FOR FUTURE DEVELOPMENT

The Israeli military government claims that it has been responsible for improvement in health conditions in the West Bank and Gaza over the past years – in effect, that military rule is good for your health. This claim is based on selective health indices, on inappropriate comparisons, and on neglect of the indications that the situation may well have seen even greater improvement had there been no military occupation.

Some progress has indeed been made. The Palestinians themselves, working under the difficult conditions of occupation, have made some strides in attempting to fill the health needs of the population. Examples include the contributions made by Maqassed Hospital in Jerusalem, the primary health care centers of the Union of Palestinian Medical Relief Committees, and the numerous health care delivery programs operated by charitable societies, women's groups, and other Palestinian institutions.

There have also been instances of successful cooperative efforts, involving such groups as the Near/Middle East Council of Churches, the Palestine Red Crescent Society, the Arab Medical Association, and others. Such efforts have addressed themselves to the solution of local problems, and to such matters as the production of health education materials in Arabic.

But there is much to be done. Based on our own experiences in the field, we present the following priorities for the future direction of health services development in the occupied territories.

1. Emphasis must be placed on the development of primary health care in general and preventive and social medicine in particular. At present, most aid goes to hospital and curative care. We must question the value of high-technology developments such as the open heart surgery ward at Ramallah Hospital, when thousands of children lack basic primary care and are, for example, at high risk of contracting rheumatic fever because simple and early treatment of respiratory infections is unavailable to them.

2. Underprivileged and deprived groups must have top priority in future planning. Health projects must be designed with a focus on the needs of the poor and of women and children.

3. Underserved geographical areas must also be given priority. There seems little point in spending exorbitant amounts of money on high-technology services for the central part of the country when the villages and refugee camps in the north and south often lack the most basic facilities.

4. Quality must be emphasized as well as quantity. This must encompass training of primary health care workers, because primary health care centers should become places where other social needs of the community may be fulfilled. Health is not only the absence of disease; a healthy human being is one with the opportunity to lead a happy, active life.

5. Priorities must be locally generated. The interests and needs of local people must be placed before those of external aid agencies. Unfortunately, this has not always been the case and has even led to situations in which local institutions have changed their policies in order to better fit the agency's ideas on development – in order to "land another grant." The real interests of the people are not well served by this process. The principle of priority for local interests is not

impossible to apply. Agencies such as OXFAM, NOVIB, and others operate in this manner today, and supply a model for cooperative relations between nongovernmental aid agencies and the local community.

6. Support should be given to public health projects rather than to individually operated, private enterprises. Arab "steadfastness" funds have been used to buttress the position of the private medical sector – such efforts have had limited success. The private sector is already in retreat from the highly technological and competitive Israeli system. And by their very nature, private profit-making institutions have little interest in serving the broad health needs of the population at large.

7. There must be coordination and cooperation among local institutions. In the past, much local initiative was characterized by lack of coordination with existing and planned services, and by an unhealthy competition clearly not in the best interests of those who need health care the most. Factionalism, petty personal interests, and duplication of services must be overcome in the interests of the greater good of the society.

A difficult prospectus, made even more difficult in light of present emergency conditions in the occupied territories. It would require another chapter to deal with such issues as the medical treatment of those wounded by Israeli bullets, the disruption resulting from seigelike conditions, the psychological effects, especially on children, and all the other effects of war on health and health services. But whatever the future may hold for the occupied territories, a viable health system must be part of that society, and the priorities we have suggested will enable that system to truly meet the needs of the people it serves.

PART IV

THE INFRASTRUCTURE

OF RESISTANCE

CHAPTER 15

Mass Organizations in The West Bank

Lisa Taraki

The popular insurrection that broke out in the West Bank and Gaza in December 1987 has renewed the debate on the revolutionary potential of the Palestinian national movement in the occupied territories, and has generated interest in understanding the structures and processes that have sustained this unprecedented uprising. Palestinian activists, political observers, and social scientists are all agreed that the success of the popular insurrection is in large part due to the existence of an infrastructure of mass organizations which predate it and which facilitated the mobilization of different sectors of society to take part in the struggle.[1] It is indeed difficult to imagine how a vigorous campaign of mass mobilization could have been carried out without the politicized cadres of seasoned young men and women who received their training in the numerous mass organizations operating in the occupied territories for almost a decade. The integration of these organizations within the framework of the uprising, and the creation of new organizations such as the popular committees to meet new "field conditions" are both developments that deserve the attention of social scientists and political activists alike.

---

1. See, for instance, Jamil Hilal, "The Uprising and Desired Changes," *Al-Fikr al-Dimuqrati* (Spring 1988), 2:4-7 (in Arabic); Penny Johnson, et al., "The West Bank Rises Up," *Middle East Report* (May-June 1988), 152:10; Joost Hiltermann, *Before the Uprising: The Organization and Mobilization of Palestinian Workers and Women in the Israeli- Occupied West Bank and Gaza Strip* (Ph.D. dissertation, University of California at Santa Cruz, June 1988), p. 590.

We shall deal here with the emergence and proliferation of mass organizations in the West Bank that began in the mid-1970s until the eve of the December 1987 uprising. This period can be considered one in which the West Bank and Gaza "came into their own" and began to assert a distinctive identity within the world Palestinian community. This identity was shaped both by the special circumstances of life under Israeli military occupation and by the local initiatives taken to respond to these circumstances. Among the most notable of these initiatives was the founding of the mass organizations which have asserted themselves with great force into the national life of the Palestinians living under occupation.

The emergence of the mass organizations was directly linked to the course being charted by the Palestinian national movement both inside and outside the occupied territories. They emerged at an historical juncture when the national movement as a whole began to incorporate political struggle into the strategy for national liberation and turn its attention to mobilizing the population in the occupied territories in the service of this strategy. This period was also one in which political forces in the West Bank and Gaza began to see the limitations of restricting political and community work to existing organizational structures, especially in the face of mounting Israeli assaults upon both clandestine and public bodies. The formation of open frameworks for mass organizing started as an initiative of certain forces on the left, but was quickly adopted by the national movement as a whole once its potential had been demonstrated.

The discussion will be restricted to the history of Palestinian mass organizations of the West Bank. Primary material was obtained from two main sources: interviews with founders and current members of the main categories of mass organizations indicated below[2]; and published material produced by mass organizations. This includes statements of purpose and platforms; magazines and newsletters; and newspapers and leaflets distributed on university campuses and schools and at public rallies and meetings.[3]

2. Interviewees were selected upon recommendation of activists within specific mass organizations and according to the length of their involvement in those organizations.

3. Much of this literature is "underground," in the sense that it is produced without license. One indicator of the proliferation of the mass organizations is the fact that the military authorities are largely unable to control the printing and distribution of this literature, which is widely available.

MASS ORGANIZATIONS: DEFINITION AND TYPES

Mass organizations in the West Bank are open, semilegal[4] structures designed to mobilize and work among specific sectors within the population such as women, students, youth, and workers. They actively seek to recruit new members, and engage in a sustained effort to widen the social base of their membership and constituency. Most importantly, the mass organizations view themselves as part of the national movement, and take open political stands reflecting this identification. While the mass organizations do not share a consistent political and social outlook, they clearly view themselves as progressive forces performing functions very different from those of more traditional structures.

This definition excludes a wide range of professional, charitable, cultural, and educational organizations active in the West Bank. They differ from the mass organizations in their membership, recruitment policies, decision-making structures, extent of community involvement, and scope of work. And while many of these latter organizations, especially those termed "nationalist institutions" by Palestinians, adopt clear political stands and view themselves as part of the national effort, they cannot be designated as mass organizations because they serve limited constituencies and have not adopted the strategy of mass mobilization and participation to further their aims.

The mass organizations in the West Bank can be subsumed under the following broad categories: women's organizations, student and youth organizations, labor blocs and unions, and voluntary work organizations.

SOCIAL AND POLITICAL CONTEXT

Because we consider the mass organizations an organic component of the national movement in the occupied territories, it is important to locate their emergence and development within the course that movement took in the roughly twenty years following the occupation of the West Bank and Gaza in 1967. Special emphasis will be placed here on the period preceding the early 1980s, by which time most of the mass organizations existing today had been established. Of particular interest is the crystallization of three political and social trends of which the mass organizations became the most developed expression: the evolution of increasingly open frameworks

---

4. One, the Student Youth Movement (Shabiba) recently has been declared illegal by the military authorities.

for political expression and action; the continuous widening of the extent of public participation in political activities; and the gradual but steady incorporation of segments of the underprivileged strata into institutions and organizations created during this period. The following periodization of the national movement in the West Bank will help us trace the emergence of these trends.

The First Stage: 1967-1971

The occupation of the West Bank and Gaza in 1967 set in motion a political and social process through which the occupied territories emerged as a crucial arena for the Palestinian national movement. The first years of the occupation, however, did not witness the emergence of any substantial or mass-based local initiative in response to the occupation. These years constituted a period in which armed struggle was the major component of the national liberation strategy. But the conditions of occupation did not allow the national movement in the occupied territories to mobilize the population for armed action, and to strike roots within society. The national movement, despite its general legitimacy, was therefore relatively isolated from society and lacked a mass base.

The process of formulating a local initiative and taking the national movement to the masses was initiated in this period, however. The formation of the Higher Islamic Council and the National Guidance Committee immediately following the annexation of east Jerusalem in June 1967 was the first step in this process. The Higher Islamic Council was established to safeguard the interests of Muslims and their institutions in the West Bank; the National Guidance Committee was a semiclandestine political coordinating committee with branches in the major West Bank towns. It included representatives from different political groups as well as from the Higher Islamic Council.[5] According to an activist who was deported later,

> [We] faced a reality . . . where the population was not trained in arms, and where party or mass organizations did not exist in the occupied territories. Therefore we saw it as our duty in the West Bank to build the nucleus of a national political movement based on rejecting the occupation and resisting it by political means. . . . The aim of the establishment of the [National Guidance]Committees was to bring together the widest possible sectors of our people who reject the occupation and

5. Ibrahim Dakkak, "Back to Square One: A Study in the Reemergence of the Palestinian Identity in the West Bank, 1967-1980," in Alexander Scholch, ed., *Palestinians over the Green Line* (London: Ithaca Press, 1983), pp. 70-71.

who have no interest in its continuation. And we began to initiate passive resistance to the occupation through protests, demonstrations, strikes, and . . . sit-ins. Statements issued urged people to obstruct the work of the occupation authorities in Jerusalem and the occupied territories.[6]

The National Guidance Committee structure represents the first attempt to give the national movement social depth. But Israeli measures against the nascent leadership in the occupied territories dealt a severe blow to their attempts at mobilizing the population against the occupation. In the words of Abdul Muhsin Abu-Maizar, "we cannot deny the effect of these punitive measures in weakening the development of the mass awakening, especially in the absence of nationally supported popular political organizations capable of meeting the requirements of the struggle our people was waging against occupation.æ[7]

Deportation from the occupied territories was the most damaging of these measures. During 1967 and 1968, when public protests against the annexation of east Jerusalem and the occupation of the West Bank and Gaza were being organized, seventy-four individuals, including pro-Jordanian figures, unionists, teachers, and other professionals and activists, were exiled from the West Bank and Gaza. The deportations in September and December 1967 of several key figures in the National Guidance Committee were only the prelude to a wave of banishments in the first years of the occupation; the largest was in 1970, when over four hundred persons (64 percent of them from the West Bank) were deported.[8]

The Israeli measures, which also included wide-scale arrests and the demolition of homes, were aimed not only at preventing the emergence of a local leadership, but also at retarding the crystallization of a mass-based resistance to the occupation. By 1969, the National Guidance Committee structure was effectively defunct.[9]

6. Abdul Muhsin Abu-Maizar, in "The West Bank: Occupation, Resistance, and a View of the Future" (roundtable discussion with Abu-Maizar, Abdul Jawad Saleh, and Arabi Awwad), *Shuun Filastiniya* (April 1974), 32:45 (in Arabic).

7. *Ibid.,* p. 46.

8. Information concerning deportations was obtained from Ann M. Lesch, "Israeli Deportation of Palestinians from the West Bank and the Gaza Strip, 1967-1978," *Journal of Palestine Studies* (Part I, Winter 1979), 8(2):101-31; and (Part II, Spring 1979), 8(3):81-112.

9. Isa Shuaibi, *Palestinian Statism: Self-Consciousness and Institutional Development, 1947-1977* (Beirut: PLO Research Center, 1979), p. 192 (in Arabic).

After the demise of the National Guidance Committee, there came a short period when the Popular Resistance Front, which was composed of Communists and their supporters, tried to fill the political vacuum created by the disbanding of the Guidance Committees. This experience cannot be considered a success in popular terms, however, since the organizations active in the Palestinian resistance did not participate in the front's activities.[10]

The Second Stage: 1972-1975

This stage in the development of the Palestinian national movement in the occupied territories was characterized by a political and cultural renaissance born, paradoxically, out of the realization that the occupation was not of a short duration.

Politically, the most significant development was the process initiated in 1972 to establish the Palestine National Front. On the cultural level, the period witnessed the flourishing of "committed" art, especially theater, and a vigorous literary movement.[11] The voluntary work movement, which was later to become a framework for mobilizing Palestinian youth, was born in 1972 and grew during this period. In terms of infrastructure, this period witnessed the initiation of the "institution-building" phase, when Palestinians began to focus on building an organizational infrastructure to accommodate changes brought about by the occupation, to allow for the development of potentials unleashed by these changes, and above all, to lay the groundwork for the future Palestinian state.

The formation of the National Front came against the backdrop of the defeat of the Palestinian resistance in Jordan in 1970-71 and mounting differences between the Arab states and the Palestinian national movement. The movement found itself increasingly isolated in the Arab arena, and was forced to reexamine not only its strategy for conducting the struggle but the goal of the struggle itself.

As regards the first point, the Palestine Liberation Organization (PLO) began to realize the importance of giving direction and organizational coherence to the beginnings of mass stirring in the occupied territories. At the eleventh session of the Palestine National Council (PNC) held in January 1973, the PNC, while stressing the centrality of armed struggle,

10. *Ibid.*

11. Between 1970 and 1975, at least ten theater groups were formed in the West Bank, most of them in the Jerusalem-Ramallah area. For details, see series of articles in *al-Katib* (December 1978-July 1988), nos. 92-99 (in Arabic).

committed itself to a program designed to "mobilize the masses in the West Bank, the Gaza Strip and the entire occupied Palestinian land, . . . and to direct attention to the organization of our masses in the occupied territory and help mass organizations oppose the Histadrut efforts at drawing Arab workers into its membership, [to] reinforce and support the Palestinian and Jordanian labor unions' endeavors in realizing the above aim."[12]

The Palestine National Council also called for the founding of a Jordanian-Palestinian national front, which, in order to be realized, required that

> all forms of day to day mass struggle must be immediately activated, so that the agitation of the masses for both their daily and general demands leads to the rise of an organized leadership and organizations expressive of the interests of the various segments of the masses, i.e. the kind of leadership and organizations that have been *absent from the day-to-day fights of the masses over the past years.*[13]

Perhaps because the formation of such a Jordanian-Palestinian effort was not seriously contemplated but rather represented a political message to the Jordanians, the PNC adopted an apparently secret decision at the same session to establish a national front in the occupied territories to coordinate resistance activities there.[14] The idea of forming a national front in the occupied territories had actually been formulated by the political forces there in the preceding year and proposed to the PLO.[15] In this sense the front represented the first organized joint venture between the PLO leadership outside and the people of the occupied territories.

The Palestine National Front, which publicized its program in August 1973, declared itself an "integral part of the Palestinian national movement as represented by the Palestine Liberation Organization," and announced its intention of supporting "mass organizations, such as trade unions, students' and women's federations, religious and social clubs and associations, in their efforts to defend the interests of the groups they represent, and [mobilizing] their energies for the struggle against the occupation."[16]

12. *International Documents on Palestine 1973* (Beirut: Institute of Palestine Studies, 1976), p. 407.

13. *Ibid.,* p. 408; emphasis added.

14. Helena Cobban, *The Palestine Liberation Organisation: People, Power and Politics* (Cambridge: Cambridge University Press, 1984), p. 172.

15. Dakkak, "Back to Square One," p. 75.

16. *International Documents on Palestine 1973*, pp. 459-60.

The front brought together some of the elements of the by-then defunct National Guidance Committees, most of the resistance organizations, along with new political and social forces. Among the latter were representatives of professional, labor, students' and women's organizations.[17] The front was successful in organizing public protests on a scale not witnessed before. Its most effective campaign was organizing a workers' boycott of elections for the Israeli Federation of Labor (the Histadrut) in Jerusalem in September 1973. It also managed to bring together five hundred public figures in a rally in 1974 to call for Palestinian self-determination. The growing influence of the front was met with swift action on the part of the military authorities: eight leading figures were deported in December 1973, and over four hundred and fifty activists were arrested during spring and summer of 1974.[18] Four more activists were deported after the Rabat Summit in 1974. They were accused of organizing a petition sent to the summit signed by nearly 180 residents supporting the PLO as their representative.[19]

The arrests and deportations, along with the fact that the front as a clandestine body was prevented from building open links with the community, meant that the scope of public action remained relatively circumscribed. But the significance of the Front was that for the first time, a wider based organizational structure had been created to sustain public action and protest. The front continued to be active through the turbulent period surrounding the municipal elections in 1976, but was disbanded in 1977.[20]

The recognition on the part of the PLO of the importance of political mobilization inside the occupied territories was accompanied by other important changes in PLO thinking in this period. The most relevant in this regard was the decision taken at the twelfth session of the Palestine National Council in June 1974, which stated that "the PLO will struggle by every means, the foremost of which is armed struggle, to liberate Palestinian land

17. Shuaibi, *Palestinian Statism,* p. 192.

18. Ann Lesch, *Political Perceptions of the Palestinians on the West Bank and the Gaza Strip* (Washington, D.C.: Middle East Institute, 1980), pp. 54-58.

19. Lesch, "Israeli Deportation of Palestinians" (Part I), p. 111.

20. For some views on the reasons for the weakening and demise of the National Front, see Ibrahim Dakkak, "Back to Square One," pp. 77-80; and Jamil Hilal, "Indicators of the Regenerated Uprising," *Al-Fikr al-Dimuqrati* (Winter 1988), 1:15 (in Arabic).

and establish the people's national, independent and fighting sovereignty on every part of Palestinian land to be liberated."[21]

This momentous decision, which in effect committed the PLO to accepting a state in part of Palestine, was taken in the context of the increasing alienation between the PLO and the Arab states, and had important consequences for the national movement in the occupied territories. It meant that since the West Bank and Gaza were the site of the future Palestinian state, the quality of the struggle of the people there to build its infrastructure was of crucial importance.

These developments were unfolding during a period in which the prolonged nature of the occupation was becoming apparent, as mentioned earlier. The rapid progress of the policy of de facto annexation and the integration of the economy of the West Bank into that of the state of Israel had important consequences on the social and political level. Since a number of contributions to this volume document and analyze the various aspects of this process, only brief mention of some of the salient ones will be made here.

Perhaps the most important structural transformation brought about by the occupation was the emergence of a significant sector of mostly unskilled or semiskilled wage laborers working in Israeli construction, industry, and the service sector. In the West Bank, the number of workers employed in Israel was steadily rising in the early 1970s: in 1970 just under 13 percent of the labor force was employed in Israel, but by 1975 that ratio had jumped to 30.5 percent.[22] Furthermore, the vast majority of West Bank laborers employed in Israel were from villages rather than towns.[23]

The most dramatic effects of this reorganization of the labor force can be found in agriculture: whereas in 1970 almost 40 percent of the West Bank labor force was engaged in agriculture, by 1975 only 27.4 percent was so employed.[24] This decline reflected itself in the increased marginalization

21. *International Documents on Palestine 1974* (Beirut: Institute of Palestine Studies, 1977), p. 449.

22. Israel Central Bureau of Statistics, *Statistical Abstract of Israel, 1978,* tables XXVII/22-23. These figures do not include the significant number of workers not registered with the labor exchanges and therefore declared illegal workers.

23. *Ibid.,* table XXVII/21. In 1975, 84.5 percent of West Bank laborers employed in Israel came from villages.

24. *Ibid.,* table XXVII/23.

of the family farm. Although wage labor was not the only determinant in the decline, it was a major factor.[25]

No comprehensive picture has emerged of the consequences of these changes for village life and social structure. Researchers have studied aspects of the problem in disparate West Bank communities, but the definitive study of the impact of wage labor in Israel, remittances from abroad, land confiscation, restrictions on water use and marketing of produce, emigration, demographic pressures, and a host of other factors has yet to be written.[26] Furthermore, the impact of wage labor, emigration, and impediments to the growth of trade and industry on the refugee and urban population has not been subjected to systematic scrutiny. But it is possible to say that the integration of the West Bank, and the rural sector in particular, into the Israeli economy set in motion a process that began to modify social relationships in both rural and urban communities, especially the social division of labor, the prevailing power structure, and authority relationships within the family.

The realization that the *status quo ante* was being irrevocably destroyed developed gradually over the first years of the occupation. By the mid-1970s, the Palestinian national movement had developed the rudiments of a national reconstruction and "steadfastness" program to complement the political strategy embodied in the establishment of the National Front. It was ironic, however, that this program of building an infrastructure of national institutions ignored almost completely the sector most affected by the occupation, namely agriculture. Instead, considerable energy and funds were expended over the next five years in strengthening municipalities and charitable organizations; establishing or expanding universities and colleges; founding newspapers and journals; and sponsoring housing projects, research centers, and a host of other cultural, social, and charitable organizations.[27]

The enterprise, however, did have potentials built into it that would alter the social character of some of these new national (or recently "nationalized") institutions. The fact that these institutions were supported by Palestinian public resources meant that individuals from peasant, refugee

---

25. Salim Tamari, "Building Other People's Homes: The Palestinian Peasant's Household and Work in Israel," *Journal of Palestine Studies* (Autumn 1981), 11(1):34.

26. The two essays by Sarah Graham-Brown in this volume are admirable attempts to provide an overall view given the paucity of available date.

27. For example, between the years 1972 and 1980, at least seven newspapers and magazines, nine universities and colleges, and two research centers were established in the West Bank.

camp, and lower-middle-class urban backgrounds had to be accommodated and given a voice within them. The role of the universities – particularly Bir Zeit, which until then had catered to the sons and daughters of the middle and upper-middle classes – in spearheading the drive for the empowerment of the underprivileged cannot be underestimated. Interestingly, this process mirrors the one which occurred in the Palestinian resistance a decade earlier, when the resistance organizations provided the framework for the rise of the poor and underprivileged cadres to positions of responsibility in the movement.

The Third Stage: 1976-1981

This stage witnessed the emergence of open frameworks for political and social action, the increase in the magnitude and extent of public mobilization around national issues, and the formal entry of segments of the poor and underprivileged strata into Palestinian institutional life. The latter was accomplished by the assertion of these social forces into institutions such as universities, research centers, newspapers, professional associations, and a host of other cultural and social organizations. The formation of alternative institutions in the form of the mass organizations was the most significant development in this respect.

These developments occurred within the context of important political events, notably the municipal elections of 1976, the "autonomy" plan publicized in 1977, the Camp David accords signed in 1978, and the emergence and demise of the second National Guidance Committee. The nationalist municipal councils elected in 1976 and the National Guidance Committee formed in 1978 were the first open, nonclandestine frameworks for political action. The emergence of a public leadership in the West Bank began with the municipal elections in April 1976, in which a National Bloc composed of nationalist figures and some Palestine National Front members won the overwhelming majority of municipal seats in twenty-two councils in the West Bank. The municipalities quickly assumed political significance, and became platforms for the discussion of issues normally not within the scope of municipal affairs. This was particularly notable in view of the administrative impotence of the municipalities due to the severe legal and administrative limitations imposed on them by the occupation authorities.[28]

28. For a discussion of these limitations, see Khalil Nakhleh, *The West Bank and Gaza: Toward the Making of a Palestinian State* (Washington, D.C.: American Enterprise Institute for Public Policy Research, 1979), pp. 9-24.

The nationalist majors were also a leading element in the National Guidance Committee, which was formed to confront the diplomatic and political initiatives launched by the Likud government after it came to power. The severity of the threats to national independence embodied in the autonomy plan and the Camp David accords necessitated an all-out campaign of resistance, and the Guidance Committee was designed to serve that purpose. The committee was composed of prominent mayors and professionals, as well as representatives of chambers of commerce, unions, the student movement, charitable societies, and women's organizations.[29]

As mentioned earlier, this period witnessed an increase in the extent and magnitude of public mobilization against what amounted to the Israeli response to the PLO decision to establish a national authority in the occupied territories. Demonstrations, strikes, sit-ins, and the issuing of public proclamations constituted the main forms of political action in this period. Students played an especially prominent part in organizing and mobilizing for these activities; university campuses were sites of mass rallies convened to fight the autonomy scheme and the Camp David accords.[30]

The formation of the mass organizations came at this juncture in the struggle being waged in the occupied territories. It came against the backdrop of increased repression of public protests and the imposition of harsh measures such as town arrest, imprisonment, and deportation against members of the municipalities, the National Guidance Committee, and members of the political organizations. The years 1981-82 saw the final collapse of the Guidance Committee and the paralysis of the municipalities.[31]

Several factors explain the emergence of the mass organizations at this time. The campaign of repression carried out by the Israeli military authorities against both the clandestine and the public leadership in the West Bank necessitated certain adjustments in the strategy of the national movement. As the occupation encroached on the "national institutions" and targeted the political leadership, the national movement had two options:

29. Dakkak, "Back to Square One," pp. 84-86.

30. The events of this period are very well documented; for a brief survey, see *Middle East Report* (May-June 1988), 152:36-37.

31. In 1982, the National Guidance Committee was banned, and the mayors of Nablus, Ramallah, al-Bireh and Gaza were dismissed from their posts. For a detailed account of the crippling of the municipalities, see Abdul-Jawad Saleh, *Israel's Policy of Deinstitutionalization: A Case Study of Palestinian Local Governments* (London: Jerusalem Center for Development Studies, 1987).

either to confine itself to clandestine work but sacrifice a growing mass base; or to evolve alternative, open, structures that would be more difficult to destroy. Furthermore, the movement realized that as long as popular mobilization was restricted to purely political action, the mass base of any structure created would remain circumscribed; efforts had to be directed to addressing the concrete needs of different sectors of society within the framework of mass organizations. This option was pursued vigorously by all political forces during this period, albeit at different stages and with varying conceptions of the meaning and aims of work at the mass level.

> This new strategy was of course not unknown to the Palestinian national movement, especially to the forces on the left. For by the time the mass organizations were established in the West Bank, the Palestinian resistance in Lebanon and Syria had accumulated over ten years of experience in organizing camp residents and other Palestinians into mass organizations as part of the overall strategy of a people's war. This strategy, fashioned after the Vietnamese experience, was based on the principle that the revolution needs the mass organizations to understand the problems of the masses in order that it may . . . be capable of analyzing social and economic problems and formulating a clear conception of the reconstruction effort after liberation. Political organizations need mass organizations to mobilize and develop the energies of the masses; they rely in this on the efforts of unions and mass organizations such as the workers', peasants', and women's federations.[32]

Although the political forces in the occupied territories did not view themselves as being engaged in a classic people's war, they held up the successful experience of the National Liberation Front in Vietnam as a model worth emulating.[33]

Equally important was the shift in the balance of power within the national movement in favor of Fatah, and the growing rift between it and the other organizations within the movement. The ascendancy of Fatah within the PLO had been taking place since 1974, but was further strengthened in 1977 when the PLO, at Yasir Arafat's initiative, entered a dialogue with the Jordanian regime which would essentially make it a partner in seeking a political solution and in the development of the infrastructure in the occupied territories. This partnership was embodied in the Palestinian-

---

32. Nabil Badran and Adnan Abdul-Rahim, "The Reality and Prospects of the Activities of Palestinian Mass Organizations," *Shuun Filastiniya* (January-February 1975), 41-42:451-67 (in Arabic).

33. The title of an article in a local leftist journal discussing different forms of mass organization during the Vietnamese war of liberation reflects this: Naim al-Ashhab, "Some Lessons from the Vietnamese Revolution," *al-Katib* (September 1985), 65:10-28 (in Arabic).

Jordanian Joint Committee, which after its establishment at the Baghdad Summit in 1978 was a major source of funding for municipalities and other national institutions and organizations in the West Bank.[34]

Concern over the rapprochement with Jordan and the regional and international consequences of this new relationship began to be increasingly voiced by forces on the left, both inside and outside the occupied territories. They were particularly concerned that the PLO, under pressure from Jordan and other Arab regimes, could be forced to make concessions compromising its newly recognized status as the sole representative of the Palestinians. They also began to express dissatisfaction at the inability – or unwillingness – of the Palestinian side represented by Fatah to withstand Jordanian dictates regarding who received Joint Committee funds.[35] This sentiment was heightened by what they saw as a discriminatory policy carried out by the committee and by Jordan against municipalities and other institutions critical of the Jordanian-Palestinian alliance, and in favor of those showing a more conciliatory stance.

The relative alienation of the left from what they viewed as the increasingly conservative institutions supported by "steadfastness" funds paved the way for an initiative which would both restore some of the influence they had previously wielded during the National Front period *and* create a new, more progressive framework for political and community work. The latter point is worth emphasizing here, since it would be incorrect to assume that the impulse for the founding of the mass organizations was generated primarily by a struggle for power and influence within the national movement.

A related factor in the founding of the mass organizations was the dissatisfaction in progressive circles at the inability and unwillingness of existing organizations such as charitable societies and women's organizations to deal with the real problems of life under occupation, such as the exploitation of Palestinian workers in Israel, the condition of women, the neglect of agriculture, poor health conditions in the countryside, and other social issues. They viewed these organizations as either being dominated by conservative and bureaucratic elements unconcerned about

34. The committee was to distribute an annual amount of $150 million for ten years. See interview with PLO official in *MERIP Reports* (December 1979), no. 8, pp. 12-14.

35. This issue was the subject of a great deal of public discussion throughout this period. Some of these concerns are voiced in the roundtable discussion, "Issues of National Struggle in the West Bank and Gaza Strip," *Shuun Filastiniya* (May 1981) (in Arabic).

these issues or as being unsuited by their nature to tackle the social problems in Palestinian society. The social insularity of these institutions was also seen as limiting their effectiveness in facing the challenges of the occupation.[36]

The decision to establish mass organizations was of course based on the availability of a large enough core of unionists, students, and other activists to initiate and lead them. The potential constituencies of these organizations were also in the process of formation; this process had started in the early 1970s, after which we witness the continuous widening of the circle of public protest and the acquisition of organizing skills by increasing numbers of youth, women, and other activists.

In summary, we can say that a configuration of factors led to the founding of the mass organizations: the prevailing conditions limiting political expression within existing frameworks; the estrangement of the left from the national institutions; the limitations of charitable and professional organizations and their restricted social outlook; and the availability of youthful politicized elements capable of leading and giving weight to the mass organizations.

The Fourth Stage: 1982-1987

The expulsion of the Palestinian resistance from Lebanon in 1982 ushered in a new stage in the history of the national movement, and had important consequences for the occupied territories. The disbanding of the National Guidance Committee structure in 1982 and the blows dealt the PLO in Lebanon both generated a state of disarray within the ranks of the national movement in the West Bank and Gaza. This was reflected in the increasing fragmentation of the movement, and the deepening of factional conflicts among its components. This period also witnessed the increasing ascendancy of Fatah within the PLO and within a wide range of institutions and organizations in the occupied territories.

It should be noted that the fragmentation of the national movement did not lead to a paralysis of public action; indeed, the widespread protests and demonstrations during 1981-82 and 1985-87 could not have been carried out without a modicum of coordination between the major political forces in the area. Having said this, it is also important to point out that the national unity displayed in the early years of the occupation had largely dissipated by this time, and had been replaced by often bitter struggles and the exchange of recriminations among the main political forces.

36. These views were often expressed in interviews with founders of the different mass organizations.

The fragmentation of the national movement had a direct impact on the rate of proliferation of the mass organizations, however. This seemingly paradoxical situation reflected the factional conflicts existing on the level of the national movement, and can be considered their natural outcome. Competition between the different political forces led to a rapid expansion and inevitable duplication of effort on the mass level. Thus rival and parallel women's, workers', students', and other mass organizations intensified their recruitment drives, and stepped up the establishment of regional centers for their activities.

In general, the 1980s may be considered a period when a great deal of energy and effort was expended in incorporating different sectors of society within a wide variety of organizational frameworks. We witness the establishment or strengthening of associations of writers, artists, performers, journalists, academics, professionals, and even university graduates. The main functions of these organizations were to give political and professional identity to previously unorganized or partially organized elements, and to serve as forums for political and cultural expression. Among the organizations formed during this period were what may be called the voluntary professional organizations. These organizations, which became active after 1980, are composed of volunteer professionals providing basic services in health and agriculture to underprivileged communities in the West Bank and Gaza. Their mode of work, social outlook, and conception of development priorities make them a unique experiment in organized work at the community level.

THE MASS ORGANIZATIONS IN THE WEST BANK: AN OVERVIEW

We shall now turn to a survey of the major mass organizations in the West Bank in the order of their emergence as public frameworks. In general, these can be categorized as organizations of workers, voluntary work organizations, student organizations, and women's organizations.[37]

Labor Unions and Union Blocs

Largely due to the influence of Palestinian communists dating back to the 1920s, the labor movement supplied one of the few frameworks for

37. For a detailed discussion of the workers' and women's organizations, see Hiltermann, *Before the Uprising*.

some degree of mass participation in the first years of the occupation.[38] Union membership remained insignificant until the mid-1970s, however, when the different forces within the national movement turned their attention to organizing workers employed in the West Bank and in Israel.

On the eve of the occupation in 1967, the official organization within which the unions in the West Bank operated was the General Federation of Jordanian Trade Unions. The main political forces active within this framework at the time were the Jordanian Communist Party and the Ba'ath Party.[39] Despite the fact that the number of unionized workers was very small, the first two years of this occupation witnessed an increase in union membership. So although on the eve of the occupation only 444 workers were registered in West Bank unions, the number had increased to 2,453 by the end of 1968,[40] and to 4,872 by 1969.[41]

Palestinian unionists and the Israeli authorities were both quick to perceive the role unions could play in the struggle against the occupation. By 1969, the arrests of unionists and the closure of union headquarters had virtually paralyzed union activity; in Jerusalem, which had been the second most important center of unions after Amman, only three unions out of an original thirteen survived.[42] In the same year, however, unionists took the initiative to revive the General Federation framework by renewing the license of the Nablus branch, thus moving the center of union activity to Nablus.[43] In 1972, after several unions from different parts of the West

38. Information on union blocs was obtained from active unionists and from publications issued by the various blocs.

39. George Hazboun and Bassam al-Salihi, "The Workers' and Trade Union Movement in the Occupied Territories, 1967-1983" (Part II), *al-Katib* (June 1984), 50:38 (in Arabic).

40. Ghassan Harb, "Labor Unions in the West Bank and their Role in the Development of Steadfastness," *Proceedings of the Conference on Development for Steadfastness* (Jerusalem: Arab Thought Forum, 1982), pp. 12-14 (in Arabic).

41. George Hazboun and Bassam al-Salihi, "The Workers' and Trade Union Movement in the Occupied Territories, 1967-1983" (Part IV), *al-Katib* (August 1984), 52:11 (in Arabic).

42. George Hazboun and Bassam al-Salihi, "The Workers' and Trade Union Movement in the Occupied Territories, 1967-1983" (Part III), *al-Katib* (June 1984), 51:40 (in Arabic).

43. *Ibid.,* p. 41.

Bank had joined this new framework, it was renamed the General Federation of Trade Unions Based in Nablus.[44]

This renewed union activity was seen by some activists as the victory of the "revolutionary" trend within the trade union movement, in contrast to those union elements which in the early years of the occupation had bowed to Israeli pressures and voluntarily closed down their unions.[45] The Communists in particular were active in reviving dormant unions and establishing new ones throughout the early 1970s [46]; they were the major political force actively engaged in union work until the late 1970s, when other organizations within the national movement began to take an interest in organizing workers.

From its inception, the federation saw itself as an integral part of the national movement, and did not hesitate to issue pubic statements on political issues being debated within the movement. Unions were also represented in the national coalitions in this period, the National Front and the National Guidance Committee. In 1976, three unionists ran for and were elected to posts in municipal councils.

The mobilization of workers through unions proceeded during the 1970s; one source estimates that by the end of 1980, union membership had increased by almost 427 percent since 1968, bringing the total number of unionized workers to 12, 926.[47]

The real flowering of the labor unions as mass organizations occurred, however, after the late 1970s, when the major political forces in the West Bank began to turn their attention to unions as frameworks for mass organizing. Thus began a new chapter in the history of the trade union movement in the West Bank, one characterized by great vitality as well as intense conflict between the contending parties.

The differences between the various political forces centered on the issue of representation in individual unions as well as in the federation (which had been renamed the General Federation of Trade Unions in the West Bank). The irreconcilability of these differences led, in the end, to the formation of three parallel general federations and a myriad of parallel

44. *Ibid.,* p. 42.

45. *Ibid.,* pp. 40, 42.

46. Muhammad Abu-Shama, "The Condition of the Working Class and the Palestinian Trade Union Movement in the West Bank and Gaza Strip," *al-Nahj* (1987), 14:107 (in Arabic).

47. Harb, "Labor Unions in the West Bank," p. 14.

unions bearing identical names.[48] This situation is decried by all the major contending parties, but a solution, despite initiatives by some, does not seem to be close at hand.

A direct result of the conflict over representation in the union framework was the creation of union blocs. These blocs were the organizational expression of the different political forces within the trade union movement, and became the main vehicles for mobilizing for union work. At first the blocs worked within labor unions and competed with each other over representation on union councils, but very soon they became almost totally synonymous with the unions themselves, as they began to found new unions or to revive dormant ones. At the present time, there are almost no unions with representation of more than two blocs in the union council.

The first union bloc was established in 1978 by unionists reflecting the political outlook of one of the leftist factions within the PLO. The Workers' Unity Bloc quickly established a strong presence on the union scene, and pursued its strategy of reviving and establishing unions with great enthusiasm. The major split within the trade union movement, however, came in 1981, when the Workers' Youth Movement, a newly formed union bloc identified with the Fatah movement, set up an alternative General Federation of Trade Unions. This federation was subsequently recognized as the legitimate one by the Jordanian-Palestinian Joint Committee, which meant in effect that the original federation (which still included in the rest of the factions within the trade union movement) was denied financial assistance earmarked for unions in the occupied territories. The consequences of this development for the unity of the trade union movement should be obvious.

The period after 1981 saw the formal emergence of other union blocs, each reflecting the political outlook of a major political force within the national movement. This period also witnessed the proliferation of unions organized around specific trades, and the formation of union and bloc branches in towns, villages, and refugee camps all over the West Bank. A great number of what have been called "cardboard" unions were formed during this period, namely organizations with no membership other than the initial twenty-one personnel required for their registration as unions.[49]

Despite the concerted membership effort undertaken by the union blocs during the 1980s, union sources estimate that not more than 15 to 20 percent of the West Bank labor force is unionized. The difficulty of enlisting

48. For details, see Hiltermann, *Before the Uprising*, pp. 291-327.

49. *Ibid.,* p. 308.

workers in unions is emphasized by all major blocs, and the reasons given include the dispersal of workers in small-sized workplaces; the difficulty facing unions in providing effective protection to workers employed in Israel; fear of punitive action from employers (this also applies to workers employed in the Palestinian sector); the limited resources of unions which makes it difficult for them to provide adequate services to members; harassment of unionists by the military authorities; and the prevailing skepticism among workers about the efficacy of union work.[50]

The issue of striking the correct balance between class interests and the national interest has been one that has been debated a great deal within the trade union movement. The blocs identified with the left have developed almost identical positions on this question, despite some minor differences. They view the labor movement as an integral part of the movement for national liberation, but also stress the necessity of protecting the rights of workers against exploitation, even if this means coming in conflict with Palestinian employers. At the same time, they stress the necessity of protecting the "national economy," which means defending the interests of wealthy Palestinian industrialists, merchants, and growers against Israeli designs to block the growth of the Palestinian economy.[51] The tensions inherent in this position are obvious, and enough experience has accumulated to indicate that at best an uneasy relationship prevails between Palestinian employers and workers. Not surprisingly, some of the most bitter labor disputes have in fact erupted in "national institutions." According to one unionist interviewed, these institutions are no better than private entrepreneurs; they take advantage of their standing in the community to deprive their employees of their basic rights.

The unions, despite the fact that they were the first mass organizations to appear in the West Bank, did not have a significant mass base until the late 1970s. The subsequent period, which coincided with the general drive for mass mobilization launched by the national movement, witnessed the emergence of union blocs, the revival of many dormant unions, and the creation of new ones. On the organizational level, the most important development was that the different streams within the trade union movement had become institutionalized through blocs and increasingly

50. Interviews with union activists. For some views on the subject, see Mahmud al-Shaykh, "Workers across the Green Line," *al-Katib* (August 1986), 76:31-33 (in Arabic); and Harb, "Labor Unions in the West Bank," pp. 19-20.

51. Interviews with unionists. Also see Mahmud Abdul-Fattah, "The Trade Union Movement in the Midst of the National and Class Struggle" (interviews with leading unionists), *al-Katib* (May-June 1982), 27:3-30 (in Arabic).

utilized blocs rather than unions to carry out their work. This fragmentation of the trade union movement is viewed as a negative factor by all blocs, and calls for the unification of the movement are issued regularly in their publications. But it is important to note that this fragmentation was probably the single most important factor in the dramatic increase in unionized workers in the West Bank.

This last point has a bearing on the question of the "quality" of the working masses organized in union blocs and unions. Although all blocs conduct educational seminars and distribute educational material to their members, clearly not all are equally dedicated to the promotion of union consciousness or successful in doing so. Consequently, the spread of union consciousness is very uneven, and depends to a great extent on the nature of the leadership in a given locality; the social and political backgrounds of the workers; the extent of political activism in the workers' communities; and the nature and location of employment, among other factors.

In conclusion, it can be said that although the trade union movement may not have succeeded in creating genuine workers' organizations, it has gone a long way in creating vehicles for the politicization of workers. And it has certainly succeeded in bringing into the framework of national struggle a sector of society which had traditionally remained outside.

Voluntary Work Organizations

The history of the voluntary work organizations illustrates best the way in which mass organizing took hold in the West Bank. From an enterprise initiated by a small group of middle-class young professionals and teenagers, it blossomed into a mass-based structure which today is guided by a leadership mainly of peasant origins and resting upon a membership drawn from youth in villages, refugee camps, colleges, universities, and schools all over the West Bank.[52]

The first voluntary work group emerged from a social-literary club in Jerusalem in 1972. The founders of this group included college and school teachers, young professionals, and a number of teenagers living in Ramallah and Jerusalem. Most considered themselves progressive in their outlook, but, with a few exceptions, were not active in any political organizations. They found a home for their new group in the Ramallah and al-Bireh

---

52. information on the voluntary work committees was obtained from interviews with two generations of participants in these committees, and also from the following: Walid al-Rammuni, "The March of Voluntary Work in the West Bank and Gaza," *al-Katib* (December 1981), 23-24:18-25; and Muharram al-Barghuthi, "Creativity of a People under Occupation: Voluntary Work as the Nucleus for a Mass Movement," *al-Katib* (June 1987), 86:209-14 (both in Arabic).

municipality libraries, and began by tutoring secondary school students preparing for their matriculation exams. They soon expanded their activities to cleaning the local vegetable market, building a playground in al-Amari refugee camp, erecting a wall for the local high school, and tackling the municipal garbage dump. At the same time they held weekly meetings, where they would organize their work plans and hold discussions of literary and political works by international and Arab authors. Young participants were encouraged to lead discussions, and to make presentations on their readings. According to one informant, who was then a high school student, the general aims of the group were to break the barrier between manual and physical labor; to combat selfishness and inculcate a collective consciousness; to promote women's rights; and to help the community. Another informant, now a university professor in his forties, put it simply: "we wanted to do something to serve our country."

In 1973, the group began to expand its work to the surrounding villages, and in the process drew increasing numbers of volunteers to build roads, clean cemeteries, and help farmers during the harvest. By the end of 1973, committees began to form in Nablus, Hebron, and Jericho. One memorable event from this period was the two-week work camp held in the remote village of Udaysa in the Hebron area, where students from Bir Zeit and the Jerusalem area built the first road linking the village with the outside world.

The quantitative leap in voluntary work occurred after the municipal elections in 1976. "Nationalist" municipalities became the focus of voluntary work efforts, and the first centralized work camp drawing participants from different areas in the West Bank was held in Ramallah under the sponsorship of the municipality. Similar camps were held under the aegis of the municipalities of Hebron, Nablus, and Jericho. Regular work camps in villages, refugee camps, and towns became forums for political and cultural expression, and came increasingly under the scrutiny of the local military authorities who tried on many occasions to stop the work by arresting activists or turning back busloads of volunteers.

The dramatic spread in the number of voluntary work committees necessitated an organizational framework. In 1980, the formation of the Higher Committee for Voluntary Work in the West Bank and Gaza Strip was announced at a conference at Bir Zeit University attended by representatives of thirty-seven regional committees. Five days later, the committee organized twelve hundred volunteers to participate in the fifth Annual Voluntary Work Camp in Nazareth. One year later, close to three thousand West Bank volunteers participated in the Nazareth event. This linkage of the committees with the work camp in Nazareth (which is sponsored by the Communist-run municipality there) is one indicator of the leftist outlook of the leadership of the Higher Committee.

As the movement gained momentum, differences began to emerge within the ranks of the Higher Committee. By 1982, many groups were formed outside the framework of the committee, and organizations similar to union blocs began to appear; at the present time, three federations in addition to the Higher Committee organize voluntary work in schools, universities, unions, villages, refugee camps, and urban neighborhoods. Like the union blocs, each formation reflects the political outlook of one of the major components of the national movement.

From the inchoate but portentous "doing something to serve the country," the voluntary work movement went on to articulate more clearly its aims and objectives. It began to view itself as part of the national reconstruction effort, and a vanguard in the drive to protect Palestinian land from confiscation for settlements. The activities undertaken in the 1980s reflect this focus: land reclamation, afforestation, road building, and laying sewage systems in villages and refugee camps. Land Day has become an occasion where voluntary work committees organize collective tree-planting efforts and hold rallies carrying the nationalist message of voluntary work.

The contribution of the voluntary work committees to the emergence of a politicized and activist sector of youth cannot be underestimated. Especially in its early stages when the student movement had not yet gained momentum, the committees provided the only alternative to youth and sports clubs, and the only framework within which the energy and enthusiasm of the youth could be absorbed and given political direction. Many "graduates" of the voluntary work committees went on to become activists in the student, trade union, and women's movements. One woman affiliated with a mass organization today credits the voluntary work committee in Ramallah for her political awakening; several student activists from the early 1980s period also claimed that they were politicized through their voluntary work experience in the 1970s.

Student Organizations

By far the most visible mass organizations are the student federations and blocs found today in almost all secondary schools and colleges and in all the universities in the West Bank and Gaza.[53] Although the student organizations underwent more or less the same stages of development as the other mass organizations, they differ from the latter in some important respects. The preponderant weight of the student movement within the national struggle, especially during the late 1970s and early 1980s, is one

---

53. Information on student organizations was obtained from interviews with past and current activists, and from publications issued by student blocs.

major factor setting apart the student organizations from the others. Other distinctive features have to do with the peculiarities of the student body and the nature of the institutions within which it was brought together as an entity.

In the period immediately following the occupation in 1967, the Palestinian Federation of Students was the only student organization in the West Bank. Because it functioned as a clandestine organization, it was limited in its membership and activities, which included issuing leaflets and organizing demonstrations. The federation continued to exist until about 1980, when it was overtaken by the open student blocs which began to appear in schools and universities all over the West Bank.

The beginning of the 1980s witnessed a dramatic increase in the size of the student body as a result of the expansion of some and the establishment of other universities and colleges beginning in the early 1970s. Enrollment figures show that while in 1977-78 only 2,601 students were enrolled in colleges and universities supervised by the Council for Higher Education, the number had increased to almost 8,000 by 1981-82.[54]

Harnessing the energies of this critical sector of society became a vital necessity for the national movement. Although students had already, since the early 1970s, begun to play a leading role in public protests and demonstrations, they had done so largely as an unorganized body lacking discipline and political direction. Since the limitations of clandestine work were well known, the alternative of public frameworks was adopted by all the major political forces.

The period between 1980 and 1983 saw the formation of such frameworks both on the secondary and postsecondary levels. The secondary school students' organizations became active during the teachers' strike in 1980-81, and attracted large numbers of students at events in solidarity with the teachers and in antioccupation activities. The scope of the school organizations, however, remained limited; by the start of the 1980s, the weight of student activities had shifted to the universities and colleges.

The first student bloc to appear at the universities was the Progressive Student Action Front, which announced its formation at Bethlehem University in 1980. This bloc was followed by the Student Unity Bloc in

---

54. In 1985-86 the number had reached 11,544. These figures do not include students enrolled in vocational and teacher training institutions operated by the United Nations Relief and Works Agency and the few private colleges founded in the mid-1980s. The figures quoted above were compiled from the following: Samir Katbeh, *O n Higher Education in the West Bank and Gaza Strip* (Jerusalem: Council for Higher Education, April 1983); and *Statistical Guide to Palestinian Universities* (Jerusalem: Council for Higher Education, n.d.) (both in Arabic).

1981, and the Progressive Student Union Bloc and the Student Youth Movement in 1982-83. The student blocs quickly took control of student politics, and also began to overshadow official university frameworks which until then had organized student activities. The blocs developed their own voluntary work committees, sports teams, folkdance troupes, and theater groups. They also organized book fairs, picnics and excursions, lectures, rallies, and study circles. Newspapers published by blocs began to make their appearance in 1984.

The leadership and to some extent the membership of the student blocs were drawn from the "graduates" of three institutions which were the primary agents of political education at the time: the student organizations in the secondary schools; voluntary work committees; and the prisons. The ex-prisoners were most prominent in the Student Youth Movement, and played an important role in consolidating the mass following that group increasingly began to attract. These charismatic and hardened young militants were the backbone of the Youth Movement during the critical first period; several of them were subsequently deported by the Israeli authorities.

As expected, the major focus of the student blocs was on national politics. During the turbulent years following their establishment, they spearheaded the antioccupation drive and organized the successive waves of demonstrations and protests that were gripping the West Bank. These heady events led some circles within the student movement to view it as the vanguard of the national struggle, and as the force that would bring about unity within the national movement.

Unity, however, was one element which was lacking in the student movement after 1981. The rivalry between student blocs was best reflected in the student council elections, which became major events in the academic calendar and which were followed with great interest on the part of political activists and observers alike. Coalitions of different blocs won elections in the early 1980s, but by the mid-80s the Student Youth Movement, which reflected the political outlook of the dominant force in the national movement, began to be elected to student councils largely on its own.

Student blocs have played an important role in the political and social education of individual students, particularly at the universities and colleges. Some student blocs have been more interested than others in giving their members a wide political education; these blocs hold regular study circles where classical Marxist works and works on imperialism, national liberation struggles, and issues of development are discussed and debated. Student blocs also perform functions which in other countries university counseling services and student governments are meant to perform: initiating the student to university life (which in this case is sometimes radically different from life at home), providing the first social contact with members of the opposite sex, and helping new students fight their way through the hurdles of registering for classes, buying books, applying for financial aid, and finding housing.

The ascendancy of the student movement in the national struggle during the late 1970s and early 1980s gave weight to student struggles aimed at changing the character of their universities and colleges. The issues over which students came into often bitter conflict with administrations included recognition of student councils as official representatives of students; student participation in determining admissions and financial aid policies; the operation of student facilities; the grading system; the right to hold cultural and political events on campuses; and above all, the issue of tuition fees.[55]

The question of fees brought into focus student concern over the social character of their institutions. And although the students at the universities and colleges were in fact drawn mainly from villages, refugee camps, and the middle and lower strata in the towns, student organizations throughout the 1980s warned against the "elitification" of the universities as a result of the steady rise in tuition fees. A leaflet issued by all four student blocs at Bir Zeit University in September 1984 is entitled, "The Administrative Decision To Increase Fees is a Massacre against the Students." Similar sentiments were voiced in student newspapers and publications, often embellished by sociological analyses of the proper role of universities in Palestinian society.

In contrast to unions and women's organizations which had to grapple with the national and social questions at the same time, the student movement as a whole did not view its struggle for student participation in university policy making and for the "democratization of education"[56] as being in contradiction with its purely political role in the national struggle. Indeed, from the point of view of student leaders, the universities and colleges were national institutions supported by national funds, and thus did not have the option of ignoring the demands of the constituency to whom they owed their existence.

This last point emerged as the focus of much discussion with university administrations throughout the 1980s. Particularly after the assault on the nationalist municipalities and other national institutions, students saw it as

55. Discussion of these issues has taken up a great deal of space in student newspapers and leaflets issued by student councils and blocs over the last ten years.

56. "Democratization of education" is the main slogan of the blocs associated with the left.

their duty to ensure that the administrations of their institutions not only adhered to a generally nationalist line, but also took open political positions when required.[57] This has presented problems to some administrations, who often have been wary of what they view as the excessive politicization of the universities.

This rather brief portrait of the student movement would not be complete without referring to some critical self-reflection now taking place in student circles. Informants have noted that the student movement, despite its still considerable weight within the national movement, has suffered a setback at the university and national levels. This is attributed to the increased factional conflicts between student blocs; the increasing dissatisfaction of segments of the student movement with the student bloc structure; and the feeling that the student movement is neglecting its aim of safeguarding the rights of students as students.

The popular uprising of 1987-88 has further changed the position of the student organizations in the national struggle. Since the focus of protests has shifted from places of learning to places of residence, the student bloc structure has been overtaken, at least temporarily, by other structures at the regional level as frameworks for mobilization and action.

Women's Organizations

The women's movement in Palestine dates back to the early decades of this century, when it developed within and was shaped by the national struggle.[58] During the war in 1948, women's organizations played a support role, mostly in charitable and relief activities. These kinds of activities remained the dominant mode of women's public activities over the next three decades, until in the late 1970s a new generation of women activists appeared and began to challenge the prevailing definition of women's public

57 A former president of the Bir Zeit University Student Council puts it this way: "[T]he students did not play their role as an isolated movement within the universities; rather, they succeeded in [making] the university as an institution . . . take a collective and open stand regarding a number of political issues. Administrators with vacillating positions were never able to speak in the name of their institutions." Bassam al-Salihi, "Discussion concerning the Nature and Role of the Student Movement," *al-Katib* (September 1983), 41:16 (in Arabic).

58. Information on the women's committees was obtained from founders and current members of all four organizations, and from the considerable amount of literature produced by the committees.

work.[59] The more established women's organizations continued to be active and even to proliferate after the formation of the new mass-based organizations; in some ways, however, their priorities and activities were shaped by the successes being registered by the mass women's organizations.

The "new" women's movement was launched at a meeting in the Ramallah public library on International Women's Day in 1978. A group of about fifty young professional women and university students announced the formation of the Women's Work Committee, which was to be the nucleus of a unified women's movement addressing the national and social oppression of Palestinian women. The announcement of the committee, however, was preceded by a series of meetings held in 1977, where, according to a participant, "middle-class and petit-bourgeois women hotly debated the idea of creating a new kind of charitable organization; many of the women held liberal views, and wanted to do something, but it was not clear what."

Although the question of whether the new women's organization which was founded subsequently was a new kind of charitable society has been debated, it is clear that the "liberal" elements quickly stepped aside to make room for a more politicized and committed cadre of women to carry the movement forward. These women, like so many activists of this period, had received their political education in the voluntary work committees during the early 1970s, when during weekly study circles young women (and many men) discussed works on women's emancipation and debated the condition of the Palestinian woman.

The need for creating a new kind of women's organization was dictated by several factors. According to women active during this period, the existing women's charitable organizations did not welcome the entry of young women who might challenge their agendas; some young women who did try to join these organizations were quickly disappointed by the unwillingness of the influential elements to identify their organizations with an openly political and feminist position. Furthermore, the activist women viewed the leadership of these organizations as

---

59. For a discussion of women's activities during the early period, see Matiel Mogannam, *The Arab Woman and the Palestine Problem* (London: Herbert Joseph, 1937). For brief descriptions of the "traditional" women's organizations, see Rita Giacaman and Mona Odeh, "Reflections on the Palestinian Women's Movement in the Israeli Occupied Territories," in Nawal Sadawi, ed., *The Challenges Facing Arab Women in the Twentieth Century* (London: Zed Press, 1988); and Union of Palestinian Women's Work Committees, *The Development of the Palestinian Women's Movement.* (n.d., in Arabic).

resting on a restricted social stratum, and characterized by an elitist outlook concerning working in society. The organizations also lacked the structures to enable them to draw on the energies of the masses of women. Most of their activities were centered in the cities; this further deepened the gulf separating the city from the countryside, and neglected the needs of a large sector of women. They were unable to introduce any qualitative changes in the condition of women. . . . It was [thus] necessary to put forward new forms for incorporating women from different classes, and to organize them in mass organizations capable of absorbing the thousands of women willing to fight for their rights, and ready to link the national political struggle with the improvement of the economic, social and cultural condition of Palestinian women.[60]

Armed with this outlook conditioned by the progressive movement for mass mobilization under way at that time, the Women's Work Committee quickly established branches in other parts of the West Bank. In 1980, the main committee began to form committees in villages, beginning with the Ramallah area. Within three years of its founding, another women's organization, the Union of Palestinian Working Women's Committees, was formed in Nablus, this time emanating from a local trade union. In the same year, two other organizations were formed: the Palestinian Women's Committees, and the Women's Committees for Social Work. The Women's Work Committee was renamed the Palestinian Union of Women's Work Committees, and continues to be the largest of these organizations. This fragmentation of the women's movement into organizations identifying with different political tendencies coincided with similar schisms observed in the trade union, student, and voluntary work movements. However, in contrast to these other movements, the split within the women's movement has never been as problematic, and a good measure of cooperation between the different women's organizations has characterized their work.

The agendas of the various women's organizations are strikingly similar. They all view the women's movement as inseparable from the national struggle, and try to reconcile, with varying degrees of seriousness and success, the conflicting requirements of national liberation and social emancipation. The groups identified with the left (the first three mentioned above) are perhaps more keen to highlight the social oppression of women, but in fact cannot escape the pressing demands of mobilization around national issues and have great difficulty implementing a feminist program of action.

60. Zahira Kamal, "The Development of the Palestinian Women's Movement in the Lands Occupied in 1967 Twenty Years after the Israeli Occupation," *Darb al-Mara* (one-time publication, June 1987), p. 7 (in Arabic).

One area which has been almost completely avoided by the women's organizations is the status of women in the domestic sphere as wives, sisters, and daughters. No women's organization has been willing to challenge prevailing legislation governing the personal status of women, especially in matters concerning inheritance rights and divorce. Disputes within families over such issues, when they do come to the attention of the committees, are generally dealt with on an individual level, and rarely are conflicts in the domestic sphere made public. According to one woman activist, "the women's movement is not prepared to take on the religious and legal establishment on this issue, and therefore must reconcile itself to forfeiting some of the social rights of women at this stage in the national struggle." Not all agree with this, however; as a founding member of one leftist women's committee put it, "there are no pressing feminist issues at this time. Problems such as divorce are not feminist issues; they are social problems, which will have to be solved after national liberation. But at the same time, we must agitate for the adoption of a unified feminist program by the national movement, so that women's rights will be protected after independence."

It would not be correct, however, to claim that the "new" women's organizations have avoided playing an advocatory public role altogether. The most prominent example is the role some of the women's committees have played in fighting for the rights of working women. Although the number of women in the labor force still remains small,[61] some of the committees, notably the three committees identified with the left, have gone some way towards enlisting women in trade unions, establishing women's committees within trade unions, and providing counseling services to women workers. In fact, one of the first projects undertaken by the Women's Work Committees was a survey of women employed in factories and workshops in the Ramallah district conducted in the summer of 1978; an important component of the survey effort was unionizing women, and the survey report indicates that the committee was able to enlist one hundred women in a Ramallah union in the course of conducting the survey.[62]

Another role some of the women's committees have played in the public domain is in pressing for better working conditions for women in both private and public institutions. While they have not been able to register too many successes in improving regulations concerning maternity leave and

61. Israeli statistics for 1986 put the total number of employed females at 23,200, or 14 percent of total employed persons in the West Bank. See Israel Central Bureau of Statistics, *Statistical Abstract of Israel 1987*, table XXVII/18.

62. Women's Work Committee, *On The Condition of Palestinian Women in the Occupied Territories: A Field Study* (Ramallah-al-Bireh, 1980) (in Arabic).

working hours and conditions, they have had one victory in a largely symbolic area: the recognition of International Women's Day as a paid holiday for working women. This victory, however, has been restricted mainly to "nationalist" institutions and has not extended to the private sector.

The activities and projects sponsored by the women's committees fall within three broad categories: the provision of basic services, vocational training and productive work, and education and mobilization.

The services, vocational training, and most forms of productive work are largely aimed at either helping women cope better in the domestic sphere, or at increasing their room for maneuver within it. Disengagement from the domestic sphere is not on the public agenda of any of the committees at the present time. The activities which fall under the first two categories indicated above are shared by all the women's committees, although some emphasize certain areas more than others. These include day-care centers for children of working mothers; summer camps for children; primary health care; instruction in first aid; literacy classes; seminars on childcare, nutrition, and pre- and post natal care; workshops in sewing and knitting; and production and marketing of products produced at home. Some committees have set up productive workshops for women, where a range of products from pickles and toys to biscuits and decorative wall-hangings is produced for the market. One exemplary effort is a productive cooperative operated by the Palestinian Women's Committee in two villages in the West Bank. The cooperative is run by village women, who produce and market their pickles, lemonade, and other preserves virtually on their own.

The mobilization of women for political work is a central task for the women's committees. They organize solidarity visits to families of prisoners, launch voluntary work campaigns carried out by young women, and hold demonstrations and sit-ins on national occasions or during the recurrent waves of arrests and deportations. The publications of the committees are also vehicles for political education, and regularly incorporate political analysis into discussions of women's issues. The main occasion of the year is International Women's Day, when the women's committees hold centralized rallies and organize meetings in local chapters. The military authorities have also appreciated the political significance of these events, and have tried almost every year to ban them.

While some women in the committees recognize that the struggle for the social emancipation of women must take second place on the national agenda, they insist that the participation of women in the political process, through women's committees and other organizations, makes it more difficult for the national movement to ignore the social question both during the struggle for liberation and after independence. They invariably point to marginalization of the women's movement in Algeria after independence, and are concerned that this not be duplicated in the future Palestinian state.

The question of whether national liberation movements can accommodate women's demands has been discussed by Julie Peteet in relation to the women's organizations within the Palestinian resistance in Lebanon prior to 1982; some of her observations are relevant to the women's movement in the occupied territories. Peteet views women's political activism as grounded in domesticity on two levels: the mobilization of domestic duties for political action, thus politicizing their meaning; and the fact that women's political tasks are frequently an extension of traditional domestic duties and visiting patterns. She argues that although women's participation in militant national politics may initiate the process of challenging structures and ideologies that assign women to the domestic sector, it does not ensure any permanent transformation. In her view, community mobilization devoid of ideologies and prospects for gender equality may further institutionalize women's association with the domestic sphere by infusing it now with national, patriotic meanings.[63]

Women's activism in the occupied territories is also grounded in the domestic sphere to a large extent, in the sense that many of the activities of the women's organizations accommodate and are meant to enhance women's domestic functions, as mentioned earlier. The mobilization of domestic duties for political action, such as infusing the reproductive function with political meaning, providing support and sustenance for fighters, and carrying out mass work in the traditional visiting mode also characterizes women's political activism to some extent, especially in villages and refugee camps. Despite this, however, there is a definite tendency within the women's organizations, especially those identified with the left, to de-emphasize the domestic function. This is done primarily through mobilizing women for political activism and creating contexts very removed, both physically and socially, from the traditional meeting places of women. And although this kind of activity is largely restricted to younger, more educated, and mainly urban women, constant efforts are made to bring women out of the village, the camp, and the home to participate in public events.

What long-term consequences this de-domestication of women will have will be determined by many factors, not least the vitality of the progressive forces within the national movement and their ability and willingness to challenge dominant structures and ideologies.

63. Julie Peteet, "Women and the Palestinian Movement: No Going Back?" *Middle East Report* (January-February 1986), 138:21, 24.

CONCLUSION

The mass organizations which were in part initially conceived as alternatives to the existing Palestinian organizations and institutions can today be considered an integral part of the national organizational infrastructure in the West Bank. Their singular success has been their ability to mobilize tens of thousands of youth, workers, women, and students under the slogans of national independence and social progress. They have also provided their constituency with the opportunity to participate in national life in a way which was unimaginable two decades ago at the onset of the occupation. Despite their integration into the national organizational infrastructure, most mass organizations continue to view themselves as the vanguard of the national institutions, primarily in terms of their social character and outlook.

The successful implantation of the mass organizations into the Palestinian body politic represents a watershed in the social and political history of the West Bank in two main senses: first, it represents the crystallization of a large and organized social base for the national movement represented by the PLO; and second, it marks the social and political enfranchisement of those sectors that had been traditionally excluded from Palestinian political and institutional life. The consequences of this development are obvious; it is expected that the mass organizations will establish a strong presence in the process of constituting a Palestinian state, and will, especially if the present balance of forces within the national movement is maintained, constitute organized instruments of pressure agitating for progressive social, economic, and political legislation.[64]

65. A similar process can be observed in postrevolutionary Nicaragua, where the mass organizations have demonstrated the capacity to determine national objectives and to criticize and express dissent. See Carlos M. Vilas, *The Sandanista Revolution: National Liberation and Social Transformation in Central America* (New York: Monthly Review Press, 1986), pp. 230-62.

CHAPTER 16

Encounters with Palestinian Women under Occupation

Rosemary Sayigh

INTRODUCTION: THE NEED FOR A POLICY

At the beginning, anyone setting out to examine the situation of Palestinian women confronts a dilemma, both practical and ideological: the need to decide whether or not there is a problem of woman independent of the collective national problem, and what is the correct relation between the two. Any attempt to escape this dilemma leads either to a feminism that ignores the effects of Ottoman/British/Israeli oppression on Palestinian social/family structures; or to a sterile nationalism without social content.

Current interest in the situation of third world women has naturally had its effects in the Palestinian arena. After decades of media-starvation, Palestinians are suddenly being bombarded by journalists, filmmakers, researchers, novelists, conference-conveners, all interested in one topic: Palestinian women. Torn between their need for international exposure, and their distrust of singling out any particular category (especially women) for the spotlight, Palestinians have responded with confusion.

Invited to attend the Copenhagen Conference of July 1980 (the second in the UN Decade for Women), with discussion of the situation of Palestinian women tabled on the official agenda, the General Union of Palestinian Women (GUPW) sent a delegation armed with data on the "Case," but little on women. Whether this way out of the dilemma was due to a principled stand, or to insufficient preparation, it missed a rare

Reprinted with permission from *Journal of Palestine Studies* (Summer 1981), 10(4). 3-26.

opportunity to present a world audience with researched information about Palestinian women: their conditions, educational levels, employment, health problems, participation in national struggle, social, political, and cultural activities. One must admit that the GUPW's implicit stand (the priority of national struggle over women's "rights") represents a broad national consensus, well expressed by Samih Khalil Salameh in a letter to the Palestinian Human Rights Campaign, when she answered an invitation to speak on Palestinian women by commenting that women suffer the occupation like all other Palestinians, and do not demand to be singled out for special attention. This argument is cogent and clear, and has the advantage of satisfying a nationalist need to challenge Western frameworks in general (including feminism, seen by most as a "foreign ideology"). The problem with it is *not* that it fails to meet a public relations opportunity, but that it does not try to grasp what is happening at the level of reality. Equally it fails to meet the need to imagine concretely a future Palestinian society.

The feminist/nationalist debate in Palestinian circles has proved rather sterile so far, unable to move beyond statements of principle, reactionary or progressive. The weakness of the feminist statements is that they have all, except for that of the Popular Front for the Liberation of Palestine (PFLP), been the product of individual women,[1] without organizational roots, easily discounted by the mainstream as Western-oriented and bourgeois. On the other side, the topic is of such low priority that the only considered statement is that of Munir Shafiq[2] which expresses in quasi-Marxist terms the Fatah preference for avoiding the "woman question." PFLP leader George Habash's two pamphlets[3] put women's liberation on the same footing as national and class liberation, but his arguments remain abstract, not closely articulated to mass conditions or culture, and informed sources

1. For feminist statements see: 1) May Sayegh, *The Arab Palestinian Woman: Reality and Impediments* (Beirut: GUPW, 1980), in Arabic and English (May is a Fatah member but without strong following on this issue); 2) Raymonda Hawa-Tawil, *Mon Pays, Ma Prison* (Paris: Seuil, 1979); 3) Nuha Abu Daleb, "Palestinian Women and Their Role in the Revolution," *Peuples Méditerranéens* (Oct.-Dec., 1978), 5:35-46.

2. Munir Shafiq, "Mawdu'at hawla Nidal al-Mara" (Themes on the Struggle of Women), *Shuun Filastiniya* (January 1977), 62:200-227.

3. George Habash, *Hawla Tabarrur al-Mara* (On the Liberation of Women), (Beirut: Information Centre of the Rejection Front, n.d.). The PFLP also published a pamphlet in 1970 on "The Revolution and the Liberation of Women Issue" (K. Abu Ali, *Muqaddimat hawla Waqi al-Mara wa Tajrubatiba fi al-Thawra al-Filastiniya* (Beirut: GUPW, 1975). For an individual PFLP statement, see Rasmiyeh Odeh in S. Antonius, "Prisoners for Palestine: A List of Women Political Prisoners," *Journal of Palestine Studies* (Spring 1980), 9 (35): 29-80.

say that PFLP praxis is not markedly different from other groups. As long as progressive positions continue to sound like translation of Marxism-Leninism into Arabic, while reactionary positions continue to idealize the Arab past and the *jihad,* the debate is bound to remain out of touch with reality.

Restricted and infertile as the debate has been, however, things look very different on the ground. There has been an extraordinary development since 1965 in what women undertake, particularly in areas like Lebanon and occupied Palestine where crisis has been continuous. This is not to say that women's activism is in itself a sufficient guarantee of irreversible change in gender relations; definitely this cannot happen without a policy of radical social change at the leadership level. But if properly used by the women's movement and the progressive forces, it does provide a campaign basis for change "at the top."

Part of the interest of women's situation in occupied Palestine, apart from their increased involvement in resistance, is the emergence of new groups with a more radical stand on class and gender relations than those of the national movement outside. These will be described briefly in the following paper, along with a selection from meetings with women in occupied Palestine made during a brief visit in 1980.

ESCALATING RESISTANCE

Since Camp David the tempo of resistance has accelerated, involving all strata of the population of the West Bank; students, school children, and women have been particularly visible, almost as if a new division of labor has emerged, with men's obligations as family providers moving them out of political roles.[4] Every day brings fresh evidence of women's activism. A typical incident is the arrest of eight women in Nablus (including Mayor Shaka's wife) on charges of illegal demonstrations and throwing stones at the vehicles sent to break them up. Women I was advised to meet were hard to disengage from a maelstrom of sit-ins, demonstrations, press conferences, and other national/social work. Of those I managed to meet, most had been interrogated and / or imprisoned.

---

4. Of course, men still comprise the bulk of militants, political prisoners, and deportees. But women have joined men in the most dangerous kinds of resistance, while they play a predominant part in civil resistance (which can also be quite dangerous).

Visual images remain longest: a TV newscast shows a women's demonstration in Ramallah dispersing as a helicopter drops tear-gas bombs, and an elderly woman limps slowly out of the square. . . . On the same day, in Tel Aviv, three young women, primary school teachers, wearing Palestinian colors, defy the Israeli court's right to try them for sabotage. My last sight of Palestine, on the road to the Bridge, is of three white-scarfed, long-robed women shouting angrily at an Israeli roadblock. . . .

Between 1967 and 1979, according to a recent researcher,[5] 1,229 named women have been arrested or detained, but this is definitely an undercount since it omits: 1) over 150 names for which no other details were obtainable; 2) mass detentions such as those in Gaza in the early 1970s; 3) cases not reported in the press. Cases of administrative detention are generally not reported though detention may last for periods longer than a year. This is an impressive record that totally explodes the "silent, passive" Arab woman image, as well as the idea – sometimes encountered – that Palestinian women are less involved in the national struggle than were their Algerian sisters. The difference is that they have had less media exposure.[6]

A lawyer who defends many Palestinians on political charges says that women resist interrogation better than most men, attributing this to women's lesser daily-life contact with Israelis. Another explanation is that men's involvement in politics is "natural," part of their male role, so that many who get drawn in are not particularly heroic. Women, on the other hand, usually have to defy the "government" of the family before they defy the occupation; hence, those who cross the line between sentimental and active resistance are a courageous minority with a minority's capacity for stubbornness and secrecy.

The inevitability of interrogation is taken for granted by all the women I meet – indeed it has become an initiation rite marking their graduation to an (adult) national role, the abandonment of the (child / woman) domestic one. R.E. tells me unemotionally of her two weeks in the Moscobiya, when they tried to force her to sign a "confession" that she belonged to the PLO. Apart from interrupted sleep and continuous discomfort, interrogation was accompanied by forced stripping, name calling ("prostitute"), and threats of rape.

5. S. Antonius, "Prisoners for Palestine."

6. Special committees were set up in France, involving eminent intellectuals such as Picasso, Mauriac, de Beauvoir, Tillion, to mobilize public opinion against the torture and imprisonment of Algerian women militants – see D.C. Gordon, *Women of Algeria* (Cambridge, Mass.: Harvard University Press, 1968), pp. 54-55. Later French disillusion with women's situation in independent Algeria may have been partly a reaction to this support.

Schoolchildren have increasingly been subjected to violence: I meet Intisar al-Sheikh Qasim, the 15-year-old schoolgirl from Jalazun camp who was severely beaten on both thighs with rods early this year in an attempt to force her to give the names of others in her school who had participated in demonstrations. Press photos showed Intisar's swollen, blackened thighs (her head covered). I find a smiling, neatly dressed, attractive girl, apparently completely recovered from a terrifying ordeal. She is doing so well in secondary school that her father intends to give her teacher or nursing training; the Israeli occupation is evidently concerned to repress leadership qualities even at this early stage. It's no longer rare for schoolgirls to be arrested, or harassed in class by occupying forces who break in, using tear-gas bombs and their rich assortment of riot-control equipment.[7] The effect is repercussive: teachers in Jerusalem comment on the ever-earlier politicization of girls.

The meeting in Jalazun with Intisar's family makes very clear what all the testimonies of political prisoners show, that the occupation deliberately uses family relationships for control and collective punishment. The life of the al-Sheikh Qasim family was completely disrupted for the three weeks of Intisar's interrogation (first in Ramallah, then in Moscobiya). Each day her mother or father accompanied her for day-long sessions; it was her mother who was there the day of the beating, sitting in the corridor, unable to do anything while her daughter screamed. Her father (a building laborer whose father owned olive-growing land near Lydd) lost two weeks' pay and faced a lawyer's fee of IL 20,000. The family has also suffered from Intisar's press exposure – her father told me he would not forbid his daughter taking part in demonstrations but did not like her photo in the newspapers. Knowing that the authorities could easily disrupt his daughter's education (as they have done in many other cases, especially in Jalazun), he had signed a statement denying allegations of his daughter's beating.

Everyone engaged in resistance, from the most active to the mildest form, knows that their families will suffer if they are caught. Parents are often jailed along with children accused of resistance, or for refusing to tell of their whereabouts. The homes of militants are blown up or sealed off, sometimes even houses where they have lodged (as in the case of one of the teachers currently on trial). To the stubborn resistance of children, for instance in stoning or petrol-bombing Israeli vehicles, the occupation invariably responds with curfews and punishment of the whole community.

7. Occupation troops seen in Ramallah and Hebron bristled with arms. Besides machine guns and cudgels, several carried quivers filled with rods.

Where girls and women are concerned they are vulnerable *as females,* not just as Palestinians, because the Israeli reading of Arab psychology leads to sexual aggression or threat being used against them as a means of intimidating the population as a whole. Apart from what women have suffered on their own account as activists, perhaps three times as many have been tortured or threatened to put pressure on husbands, brothers, or sons. Many men who had otherwise resisted interrogation have broken down when threats were made against their sisters. Rasmiyeh Odeh's father was forcibly involved in his daughter's sexual violation in a complex attempt to shame both of them.[8] All possible combinations of family-bound male/female feelings – love, fear, shame, protectiveness – are employed to shock and break down resistance. Up to now, this form of pressure has not been successful: the politicization of women appears to be increasing rather than lessening. But the fear is that the occupation will not draw the lesson that its family punishment policy is a failure, but will rather conclude that it has not been pushed far enough. Gush Emunim violence is particularly likely to choose this form of punishment/provocation,[9] and only a more alert world public opinion can prevent this violation of human and women's rights from reaching new levels.

LOCAL WOMEN LEADERS (*Shakhsiyat*)

Quite apart from their involvement in national resistance, Palestinian women under occupation are highly visible in social work that takes on a national significance under present conditions. With the growth of their access to education, they are also becoming an important element in intellectual and productive work. In what follows I shall consider the *shakhsiyat*[10] and the "women intellectuals" separately, with a final brief section on "ordinary" women (that is, those without any apparent public role).

8. See Antonius, "Prisoners for Palestine."

9. In Ramallah last year a girl was kidnapped by settlers for a few hours in what appeared like an attempt to provoke mass disturbances.

10. *Shakhsiyat* is used colloquially in the West Bank/Jerusalem area, though perhaps not elsewhere, to indicate prominent women involved in social/national work. It implies both a forceful personality and a leading social/family status.

Assia Djebar, speaking of Algerian women under French colonialism, remarks that:

> The woman, traditionally the guardian of the past, became (increasingly) passive in her role. The Algerian man was only colonized at that time in the street, in his work. Obliged to speak a language that was not his own, he found his real life at home, in his house, with his wife. The house was still a sacred place, which the foreign power never entered.[11]

Djebar puts her finger here on the repercussive effect of foreign domination on family relations (an effect ignored by orientalists who portray colonialism as "modernizing"), and it is useful to apply her perceptions to the Palestinian case. One feels their truth very much in Israel, where male Palestinians have greater access than women to the dominant system, speak Hebrew, work in Israeli institutions, occasionally marry Jewish women, while women remain much more confined to the indigenous sector. But in those parts of Palestine occupied in 1967, their validity is challenged by the visibility of women, not only in resistance, but in community organization and the cultural renaissance that has been such an important accompaniment of political struggle.

The difference between these two population segments, one occupied twenty years longer than the other, is striking, attributable to the cultural as well as political suppression of the Palestinians in Israel, their isolation from the Arab world, and their starvation of funds for community development. Women here have a much harder struggle against the combined effects of national and family oppression, and it is one more evidence of the power of Israeli propaganda that even a rather enlightened book like Lesley Hazelton's on Israeli women[12] should remark of Arab women in Israel: "Their status is higher than most women in Arab countries, yet lower than that of Jewish women," for, whatever criteria one takes – education, employment, family/ legal status, or participation in public life – there is no objective evidence to prove this statement.

Historically, the *shakhsiyat* (like their male counterparts) emerged in a situation of intermittent mobilization against a powerful foreign occupation, in a society composed of deeply-rooted local lineages, where social structure remains relatively stable and repression prevents nation-wide

11. Assia Djebar, interview with Sylvie Marion, *France Observateur*, 24 May 1964, quoted by Gordon, *Women of Algeria*, p. 47.

12. L. Hazelton, *Israeli Women: The Reality behind the Myths* (New York: Simon and Schuster, 1977).

organization. The local leader role is evidently class-bound, yet within its class limits there remains a significant difference between the Jerusalem leader-families, those of the more important provincial towns (like Gaza, Jaffa, and Acre), and those of small townships and large villages. One finds a growing radicalism as one moves outwards (in space) and downwards (in wealth). The same transformation of the role is also evident over time, with the *shakhsiyat* of today much more overtly political than those of the mandate period.

The *shakhsiya* has never been by any means purely an ascribed role, even though incumbents come from "known" families; it involves hard work, commitment, and efficiency. Perhaps some of the great ladies elected to the Executive Committee of the first Arab Women's Union in 1929 were brought in because of their family connections, but the escalation of violence through the course of the mandate would certainly have weeded out all but the most committed. After 1948, with the national movement apparently annihilated, there was even less scope for tokenism: those who continued to be active were only the most dedicated. This is the period when many of the best known *shakhsiyat* showed their mettle: Miss Andalib al-Amad set up an orphanage and hospital in Nablus; Zulaykha Shihabi, secretary-general of the first Arab Women's Congress, started projects for the refugees near Jerusalem; Widad Khartabil kept the Union going in Lebanon, also setting up women's projects and an orphanage; and the Halabi sisters rescued Palestinian peasants' designs in their Jerusalem workshop. Similar projects, and similar women, were to be activated by the June 1967 war.

As a group, the local women leaders have certain things in common besides the fact of coming from "known" (property-owning) families: their activities, though intense, fall within the boundaries of the socially acceptable, for example, social work; they are broadly nationalist but do not join political parties or groups; they are strong culture loyalists, careful not to disturb existing structures of class and gender relations.

Each town, each village has its local women leaders. In Gaza, the lady everyone counsels me to meet is Sitt Yusra Berberi (whereas in Lebanon and Israel women leaders are called *ukht* – sister in the occupied territories a touch of feudalism is retained in the widely used *sitt* – lady).

Member of a well-known nationalist family, Sitt Yusra refused to continue her work as inspector of girls' schools under the Israelis, and now devotes herself full time, but on a volunteer basis, to the Women's Union,[13]

13. Several branches of the pre-1948 Arab Women's Union survive in occupied Palestine where the GUPW (founded in 1965) is prohibited.

whose center is the neatest I have ever seen. It contains a large day-care center (one of four) where working mothers can leave children from four months to five years old. Kitchen and bathroom are immaculate. In another room are laid out superb specimens of crochet work and handknitting. Gay colors and orderliness make the Union a little oasis in the greyness of the Strip.

The person behind the order, Sitt Yusra, is a straight-backed lady with iron-grey hair, flat shoes, a simple black suit. She has an almost Germanic reputation for neatness and hard work-perhaps because, as a girl, she attended the Schiller College in Jerusalem. But it is more for her defiant stand towards the occupation than for her efficiency that other Palestinians admire her. As headmistress from 1950 to 1958 of Gaza's only girls' high school, she brought up a nationalist generation, among them Um Jihad, said to be Fatah's first woman member. I feel Sitt Yusra embodies the pride of Gaza, once Palestine's second city. The black bandeau she wears in her hair seems a sign of mourning for it, now the saddest.

She emphasizes the national importance of social work of the kind the Women's Union does. "We help prisoners' and needy families, educate children and bring them up with a nationalist consciousness. We help working women, and the wives and daughters of martyrs and prisoners." Gaza has a population upwards of 411,300 (1977), most of whom are refugees; there's little employment, whether for unskilled workers or university graduates. An unusual number of women are without male support (owing to the ruthless repression of the early 1970s), and several thousand are bussed daily to work in Israeli factories. The means the Women's Union has to confront the problems of the mass of women are minute, and it is with anger – well controlled – that Sitt Yusra says, "The Union of Palestinian Women has money. We don't. We work."

Closer to Jordan and to funds, the West Bank situation is less stagnant. Most of the occupied territories' one hundred fifty charitable associations are located here, and women's role in them is crucial: every township and large village has its association and its active women leaders. Dr. Amin al-Khatib, president of the Federation of Charitable Associations, admits their preponderance in work that has taken on a national importance under occupation: "Women are more active than men – it's a fact and I can't deny it." But he notes another significant fact: that before 1967 women *headed* the voluntary societies as well as forming the bulk of active membership; now, they still do most of the work but men have tended to take over the leadership. Men leave social work to women unless they are blocked from normal political activity; when social work becomes national work, men move into leadership.[14]

With so many prominent women to meet, and so little time, choice becomes arbitrary. I am touched to find Sitt Zulaykha in her office in the Jerusalem Women's Union by 8 A.M. Her life spans the history of the national movement, and I gather from her some precious details about their work in the mandate period. A visit to friends in Ramallah makes it easy to see Um Khalil, whose *Inash al Usra* (Family Resurgence Society) is widely admired for its growth and success. Other outstanding women I regretfully leave to another time.

The *Inash* started out in 1965 with JD 100 – just enough to rent two rooms, hire a sewing teacher, and recruit ten girl students. Now there is a three-story building with thirty-two rooms, sixty-seven employees, and a monthly payroll of JD 2,500. There is also a day-care center for the children of working women; thirteen literary centers in nearby villages (run in conjunction with Bir Zeit University); help for 130 needy families; a sponsorship scheme for war victims and the children of martyrs and prisoners. The *Inash* also markets the product of about two thousand women who work at home. Local doctors and dentists have been enlisted to give treatment to ten cases each a month. There is also a food-processing factory.

Successful in its mixture of social work and profit-making, the *Inash* has moved into the cultural field. It has a folklore museum and a magazine, *Culture and Society,* that is widely read by Palestinians outside for its contribution to the post-1967 renaissance of Palestinian culture and identity. A study of a West Bank village – Turmusayya – a collection of proverbs, research into women's traditional handicrafts, are further enterprises in this line.

Um Khalil is very much the center of this spreading network of projects, obviously a woman of energy and drive. Perhaps sixty, with black hair combed straight back into a bun, she has the noble profile and stance of an Indian chieftain. It's 8:30 A.M. when we meet in her modest home on the outskirts of Ramallah, and already she has a pan of stuffed squash on the stove – no domestic help and a long day ahead. Her friend Rima Terazi tells me that Um Khalil brought up her four children and kept house almost unaided throughout the growth of the *Inash.*

14. The charitable associations were originally a response to Jordanian oppression. Women's role in them varies depending on generation and overall conditions; in Lebanon, where women can join political parties, their membership in voluntary social organizations has declined, whereas in Jordan and the occupied territories it remains high.

Now she lives alone with her husband – all of her children are outside [the country], and only one can return to visit her. Two sons were deported, one was imprisoned.

Like Yusra Berberi, Um Khalil is loved because she symbolizes defiance to the occupation. Her social work has spilled over into demonstrations and sit-ins; she has been imprisoned six times. The occupation has tried to interfere with the *Inash's* activities, closing down most of its village centers, but the maintenance of Jordanian law in the West Bank has given the charitable societies their small basis for action.

I ask Um Khalil if she thinks women's earning power is improving their position in the family – "Yes, it is. In the past men wouldn't let women go to meetings; now they *ask* them to go. Village people used not to let their daughters have education. Now many are in university." But she is no feminist: "When a girl begins to earn money she may begin to impose conditions on her family. We don't encourage such a spirit in our girls. To open the door too wide would cause a bad reaction."

She responds enthusiastically when I ask how she views women's position in the future Palestinian society: "1 will work to make women the majority!" She finds women better to work with, more hardworking, more loyal, less egoistic. For her, social concern and nationalism are inseparable: "This is the way to liberate our land."

Before 1967, the charity-running middle and upper class used to draw a hard line between social work and politics,[15] viewing the first as respectable, the second as suspect; but the occupation has had the effect of obliterating the line, and legitimizing the expansion of women's social role into a national/ political one. The difficulty will be to sustain this expansion once the national problem is solved; but if there is any good to be found in the long-drawn-out nature of the Palestinian struggle it is that mass and women's participation may have irreversibly changed sex and class relations.

Where an earlier generation of local women leaders turned belatedly to mass work, without real knowledge of mass conditions or culture, those who have assumed this role after 1948, though not *from* the masses, have

15. See R. Hawa-Tawil, *Mon Pays, Ma Prison*, p. 77, for a description of her struggle with Miss Andalib al-Amad to broaden the activities of the Women's Union of Nablus. (Her sobriquet, "the Florence Nightingale of Nablus," gives an idea of her life's work; Raymonda's proposal to start jazz concerts and mixed discussions must have shocked her culturally *and* politically). Andalib was posthumously awarded a shield by the Union of Charitable Societies in Jerusalem last year.

been much closer to them than the great ladies who founded the AWU in 1929.[16] They are not separated from the women of villages and camps by high status, great wealth, foreign education, or different lifestyle: they talk the same language, cook the same food, perform the same domestic duties. Reflections of this role can be found in any camp or village, and from its pervasiveness one can guess that it meets both the subjective needs of women for a public sphere of action, the cultural/social restraints of the local community, and the overall oppression which maintains fragmentation by blocking nation-wide organization.

Um Khalil well illustrates the way the *shakhsiya* role has changed in response to growing national mobilization: 1) she comes from a small land-owning family in a small township (al-Bireh); 2) she is not highly educated, sat for the *tawjihi* with her son Saji;[17] 3) her organizational methods are personal and charismatic; 4) her own involvement is nearly total, leaving the irreducible minimum for domestic/social obligations. The directing nucleus remains essentially uni-class – a group of friends who trust each other – and is not expanded to incorporate other classes.[18]

ISRAELI VARIATIONS

In Israel, political and economic oppression have blocked the emergence of a Palestinian leadership, male or female, and women's domestic role has been deepened by land confiscation, the spread of capitalist relations of production, and by the cultural conservatism that has been one reaction to alien domination. Surveillance and lack of public funds have prevented the emergence of local development projects on the scale of the West Bank, and women's absence from the few that exist is as marked as their presence the other side of the "green line." Palestinian women who work outside the home (14.2 percent of all women aged 14 and

16. See M. Mogannam, *The Arab Woman and the Palestine Problem* (London: Herbert Joseph, 1937), pp. 70-73, for details. Among Executive Committee members were Mrs. Jamal Husseini, Mrs. Mousa Alami, and Mrs. Ouni Abdul Hadi.

17. *Shakhsiyat* of Yusra Berberi's generation were the first, almost, to be university-educated (Matiel Mogannam had a law degree); Palestine lacked a university. Today, the enrollment of Palestinian girls in tertiary level education is probably one of the Arab world's highest.

18. See K. Abu Ali, "Revolution and Liberation of Women," for a critique by younger politicized women of older women's domination of the PLO's social institutions.

over in 1978) tend to be absorbed into the dominant Israeli institutions, and have little time for extra community work. Women's public role is thus more limited here than elsewhere; yet the shadow of the *shakhsiya* is still visible. I hear of several active women in the villages of Galilee, and there is a Women's League in Acre, running a kindergarten and a teacher-training workshop. In Nazareth there are several groups including the Democratic Women's Movement (affiliated to the Israeli communist party Rakah and to the International Federation of Democratic Women), whose president is Samira Khoury.

In spite of her membership in the Communist party,[19] Ukht Samira bears a strong resemblance to the *shakhsiyat:* the same energy, the same simple life-style (very different from that of most bourgeois women), the same mingling of domestic and public roles. Like them, she began to work in response to national crisis, when, in 1948, her training to be a teacher interrupted, she joined with a few friends to help the refugees who poured into Nazareth from the surrounding villages. In that period, the Jewish forces would surround refugee quarters, round up the men and threaten to deport them in an attempt to get families to leave. Samira's group distributed food and clothing (there was no international relief organization inside Israel), and led demonstrations against deportation threats. "We felt the pressure to organize, saw people helpless, without consciousness, ignorant, felt we must teach them, lead them."

From this early social/national work grew a first women's group, the Union of Democratic Women, later to become the Democratic Women's Movement (DWM). Samira joined Rakah (losing her teaching job), and the same year married a fellow teacher and fellow party member, Fuad Khoury.

Contacts with Palestinian women's groups were only made after 1967, and have remained restrained by the presence of Jewish members in the DWM. All but seven of the DWM branches are in Arab areas. Peak activities are the three big annual celebrations, Woman's Day, Children's Day, and Worker's Day. Recently instituted summer work-camps bring up to two thousand volunteers to Nazareth each year.

It is hard to tell in a short visit whether Rakah/DWM social policy is as conservative as younger critics say, but its progressive political platform does not seem to have differentiated its social praxis from the West Bank charitable associations. The cultural residues of a class society remain,[20]

19. Concerning the attitude of Arab communist parties to the "woman issue," K. Abu Ali remarks that before 1948 Rakah had a "European approach" because of its Jewish members, but that this was later modified to take into consideration prevalent social customs and values.

and family values have changed less here than elsewhere, at least in the villages. Rakah has a strong following in the villages, but women's liberation is not part of its aim there. There continues to exist a *de facto* gender separation, both in villages and towns, with women members meeting separately, and engaged mainly in social activities on the old, pre-1948 pattern. "Starting from reality" has the problem that, without a clear policy of change, one tends to get stuck there.

If, to some of the younger generation (increasingly drawn to the *Abna al-Balad* movement), Rakah seems insufficiently radical on the "woman question," their criticisms are parallel to those that can be heard in the West Bank or Lebanon. Younger women find the *shakhsiya* generation anachronistic. In Jerusalem a young professional woman told me: "The problem with that generation is that they need to be constantly worshiped. But we have to work from a sense of obligation, not for praise. Besides, their methods are outdated." What divides the local women leaders from the category I am calling the "women intellectuals" is primarily a generation gap, sharpened by crisis-accelerated change.

THE WOMEN INTELLECTUALS

The category of women intellectuals came to maturity after the 1948 disaster; this fact has marked them deeply. Their movement into universities and professions must not be viewed as a response simply to economic pressures or to "modernization"; it is also a reaction to national crisis, part of the collective quest for revival. As a group, they are educated to a more advanced level than the *shakhsiyat* (for whom universities were not available in Palestine), and are more specialized. They are also more likely to be employed, and the organizations they join are more likely to be professional or political, not charitable. Their nationalism has a different, more ideological, more book-learned flavor. Where, in the past, nationalist women competed with each other from family and local power bases, younger women are divided along party and ideological lines. Another important difference is the much broader class spectrum from which the women intellectuals come; though still overloaded at the upper end (because of maldistribution of education), they include women from the small bourgeoisie, villages, and camps.

20. In spite of what people often say, the elimination of the local and national leadership in and after 1948 did not turn remaining Palestinians into a classless society. See Sherif Kenaana, *Socio-Cultural and Psychological Adjustments of the Arab Minority in Israel* (California: Rand Corp., 1976).

In using the term "woman intellectual," I am keeping in mind the distinction that Nakhleh makes between an intellectual and someone who is university educated.[21] While entrance to university remains restricted by class, oppression and crisis are creating, along with growing literacy and mass communication, the conditions for a new "mass intellectualism" that does not overlap with the official education system, particularly not with its upper levels. Because of continuing pressures towards early and universal marriage, because of their relative exclusion from tertiary education and the professions, Palestinian women are a large part of this phenomenon. For this reason, I include within the category not just the prominent women whom every journalist hears of, but also the thousands of anonymous primary school teachers, laboratory assistants, nurses, students, and literate housewives.

L. is a social worker from a small village near Jerusalem, her family belonging to the medium land-owning peasant class that provided fighters and local leaders to the 1936 Revolution. Her father, of whom she speaks with great warmth,[22] is one of that tough breed; jailed together a few years back, L. discovered that this was his twenty-third time in prison (under the British, the Jordanians, and now the Israelis). As *mukhtar* he still refuses to use an Israeli stamp. One of her brothers is in prison, another deported. Her admiration for the male members of her family makes her cool towards women's liberation.

Some of the women intellectuals, for example Raymonda Tawil and Sahar Khalifa, attack the family subordination of women from a straight feminist standpoint. Others, like Hanan Ashrawi, have a theory linking women's oppression to collective weaknesses that impede liberation. I suspect the majority would agree with L. who says: "I would feel guilty if I asked for more rights as a woman at a time like this."

When I ask her what she thinks of certain Palestinian feminists, she makes a gesture: "They're only interested in liberation from here down." Unmarried, she teases a male colleague who has just gotten engaged to a family-picked girl from his village; I sense she has no sympathy for girls who don't fight their way out of the domestic trap as she has. Employed ever since leaving school, she financed her own university training abroad to demonstrate her independence. With men around the office she employs

21. K. Nakhleh, *Palestinian Dilemma: Nationalist Consciousness and University Education in Israel* (Shrewsbury, Mass.: Association of Arab-American University Graduates, 1979).

22. In contrast S., a university student, remarks that an Arab girl's most difficult first step in growing up is confrontation with her father.

a kind of tough flirtatiousness that reminds me of the Italian film star Anna Magnani, once famous for her "daughter-of-the-people" roles.

L. has been under Moscobiya interrogation and imprisoned twice, but the experience seems to have left her unsubdued: "I would have been happy to have had another year there. I learned a lot. There were two Bedouin girls with us, older women; it was a cross-section of Palestinian life. We taught each other English, French, Hebrew, and Arabic to those who were illiterate." She shrugs her shoulders, smiles. Prison is something Palestinians have to face, like the occupation:

> Even if you try to forget the occupation and lead a normal life. the Israelis won't let you. A woman taking a sick child to the doctor is stopped at a barricade, people are beaten for doing nothing. People who won't resist, we should walk over them.

R., as a teacher of sciences, represents the largest occupation sector within the female labor force. Her profession is one that attracts the great majority of qualified women: it's approved by society and easy to combine with marriage. Often teachers come from a stratum less well off than the old middle class: small shopkeepers, civil servants, medium or small farmers. R.'s father was a teacher in the public system.

She is from Jerusalem where education for girls has the oldest roots. Home was full of books, visitors, political talk. Her father wanted all his seven children to go to university, but the year R. finished school the Jordanian government retired him without a pension. Somehow she found the means to get to Ain Shams University, where she studied physics and chemistry, graduating the year after the annexation of Jerusalem.

Unmarried, R. still lives with her family in Jerusalem, commutes some twenty kilometers to work every day.

She tells me of the Graduates Club and the Civil Servants Club, foci of national/cultural activities in which she takes part. In July 1979, she directed an exhibition for the first Palestinian Social Conference which brought together all the charitable associations. The occupation had tolerated their activities as *local* groups; but meeting *together* gave them a dangerously national character. There were arrests, and R. was one of those taken in for interrogation.

It took place in the Moscobiya and lasted more than a month:

> They try to give you the idea that they know everything about you. They kept accusing me of belonging to the DFLP [Democratic Front for the Liberation of Palestine]. I stuck to my position that I have no links with any organization, that I have a political *stand,* but my activities are social. They told me, "You talk against Camp David." I said, "Of course I'm against it, because it's against the interests of the Palestinian people."

Because a Jerusalem detainee should be charged within twenty-four hours of arrest, they moved her to Ramleh where she was brought before a military court and forced, under a new law, to choose from a list of authorized lawyers. Her subsequent imprisonment was for her, as for L., a "learning experience."

The Women's Action Committee

I had first met R. on a one-day bus trip to Gaza with members of WAC, a new group launched from the Ramallah area. Unlike the charitable associations whose structure reproduces class boundaries (the middle class directs *for* a needy clientele), WAC members include professional, clerical, and factory workers. Other signs of difference: it is moving fast to outgrow its local origins; it is trying to avoid the paraphernalia of institutionalism (offices, elections, etc.); it is an all-woman group, combining in its manifesto the goals of women's class and national liberation.

R. says:

> We formed the Committee because the older societies did not encourage working women. They only give money and services, don't have development projects, don't try to change consciousness. We go to women, try to involve them in social and political activities. At first the older societies resented us as newcomers. This has been a big problem. But now some of them help us.

Classical income-generating projects for women are geared to women working at home – practical but limited, without any effect on the social and cultural conditions in which low-income women live. WAC is focusing on literacy classes and social centers in camps and villages. To find out more about the problems of working women and housewives they recently conducted a field study in the Ramallah area, where there is a concentration of industrial projects employing women.[23] As far as I know, this is the first research study to be done by any Palestinian women's group.

Women in Science

The proportion of Arab women now entering the "hard" fields of science, medicine, and engineering is probably higher than in the United States. Though there are many accomplished Palestinian women writers

---

23. *Hawla Awla al-Mara al-Filastiniya fi al-Manatiq al-Muhtalla: Dirasa May-daniya* (The Situation of Palestinian Women in the Occupied Territories: A Field Study), (Ramallah, 1980).

and artists,[24] I give up the chance to meet them in favor of meeting a woman scientist.

M. teaches biology at Bir Zeit University, and is deeply concerned about the deteriorating public health situation in the West Bank. The military authorities closed two hospitals and froze health facilities when they occupied the West Bank, and there is an ever-increasing pressure of population on inadequate resources. Medical personnel are too few, demoralized by poor equipment, lack of funds, and the heavy workload. The authorities' annual health reports are naturally unrevealing. There is a pressing need for systematic monitoring, but no indigenous institution has the funds, and no foreign institution is (so far) interested. M. began collecting public health data two years ago, and is now trying to involve her students.

There are indications that infant mortality rates are rising (a reversal of the overall Palestinian trend), but the only studies so far have been based on samples too small for conclusive evidence. Still unanalyzed data from the Zbeidat village study undertaken by Bir Zeit for the Mennonites indicate a level of more than one hundred deaths per thousand.*

Malnutrition and frequent pregnancy are certain causes, but probably gastroenteritis is the biggest killer. Conditions in Zbeidat as M. describes them (she undertook the health side of the study) sound like those in Iraqi villages I saw before the 1958 Revolution. Lying in the Jordan Valley about forty kilometers north of Jericho, far from the municipalities, Zbeidat was almost starving when the Mennonites decided to experiment there with drip irrigation.

The inhabitants are originally Bedouin from Bir Saba, refugees from the 1948 war, who now pay rent to the Israeli government for land they were promised by the Jordanians. Nutrition is low on proteins, with meat eaten on average once a month. They grow grains and legumes for the market, live mainly on bread and *khubbayzeh.* There is no doctor, nurse, or clinic in the village, nor even near it, and women generally resort to herbal and magical cures, often giving birth in the fields. Many of their rituals surrounding childbirth are those that Hilma Granqvist described almost half a century ago.[25] What more convincing evidence could there be of the "de-development" of Palestinian society by colonialism?

24. Among writers, outstanding names are Fadwa Tuqan, Sahar Khalifa, Hanan Mikhail-Ashrawi; among artists, a young ceramist whose work I liked (in Notre Dame, Jerusalem) is Vera Tamari.

* See chapter 14.

25. H. Granqvist, *Birth and Childhood among the Arabs* (Helsinki: Söderstrom, 1947); and *Child Problems among the Arabs* (Helsinki: Söderstrom, 1950).

Women Intellectuals in Israel

Some of the special difficulties faced by women intellectuals in Israel emerge in an evening's discussion with girl students at the Hebrew University. Out of a total Arab population of 570,000, only 2,000 (about 0.35 percent) are in Israeli universities, and of these only a handful are female. The difficult *bagrut* exam (in Hebrew) and special college entrance tests form the first barrier (apart from inadequate access to secondary schools). Then there is the difficulty of gaining access to the field of their choice: all I meet have had to switch: it is almost impossible to enter pharmacology, medicine, or engineering. University fees are high and there are no public scholarships for Arab students. This and the difficulty of finding jobs after graduation make many families draw back from investing in university for their daughters.

A girl from Deir Hanna thinks that parents' readiness to educate their daughters is directly related to their own level of education. Her mother and father are both teachers; her father is also a member of the *Abna al-Balad* movement. They are even ready to send her abroad to do a Ph.D.; but the problem is what she will do when she returns, an over-qualified pharmacologist, to a village which has no hospital and not even a secondary school.

A girl from another village says her father has only elementary schooling, while her mother is illiterate, but they too are ready to send her abroad. Only one other girl from Meshed has gone to university. But she plans to return – all of them do – and maybe she will be able to find a teaching job in Nazareth. Life in the villages sounds dismal: a club for women was opened by the Meshed Local Council a few years back but closed after only a week. Even Rakah holds separate meetings for men and women.

N. from Tarshiha is studying sociology and speaks of the backward situation in her home town (whose sons in the Dispersion are famous for their high educational level). She estimates that though about 80 percent of girls go through high school (a much higher figure than in the villages), only about thirty out of two hundred university students are girls.[26] Most families don't allow their daughters to work; training courses provided locally are the usual sex-stereotyped ones: secretarial, accountancy, sewing, home management. She herself plans to do social work but expects no encouragement from her family.

A problem that all the girls face in the university is isolation: Jewish and foreign students avoid them, and so do young Arab men. There are few

---

26. In Bir Zeit about 40 percent of students are female; in the other West Bank universities the figure is slightly lower.

social or cultural activities on campus, so they end up spending their free time studying, not much more liberated than back home.

Two out of the seventeen-member Arab Student's Council are female, but the boys don't encourage the girls to take part in politics except just before elections ("After the elections they don't even say *marhaba*," one of the girls tells me). Male students have been known to accuse political girls of behaving like Israelis, and recent moves to start a women's consciousness-raising group have been strongly opposed by the male students, almost as if they wish to keep the girls in a prepolitical state.

The narrowness of chances for Palestinian girls to get higher education in Israel does not mean that the "woman intellectual" phenomenon does not exist there, but means its wider diffusion, particularly among younger women. The "de-development" of the Palestinian minority has produced a mood of acute rebellion against class and family structures that transmit Israeli oppression. Both in Nazareth and in a village near Haifa I encounter small women's study circles – none university-educated – eagerly reading Nawal el Saadawi, the Egyptian radical feminist.[27] Z., a young newly married woman from Qariya,[28] tells me that she only found confidence to speak on politics in the presence of men after reading el Saadawi.

Z. belongs to the *Abna al-Balad* movement, the first Arab political movement to arise in the villages, not the cities.[29] Her father, though educated, took her out of school in ninth grade, saying, "The girl is for the house. What does she want with education?" and since then Z. has carried on a sustained struggle with her family, to attend political meetings, to marry a man from the movement, to let her younger sister stay on in school. Her politics have been sharpened by this struggle; in a village almost totally without independent cultural facilities – its schools being part of the Israeli control system – this girl reads, thinks, observes women's lives, draws clear and hard conclusions.

In Z.'s generation (or a minority of it), rebellion against Israeli oppression and the patriarchal family are fused. I hear of more than one teenager running away to join the Resistance movement in Lebanon. It is not hard to imagine their passionate hope, at this age, of belonging to a

27. One of Dr. el Saadawi's books is now available in English: *The Hidden Face of Eve* (London: Zed Press, 1980).

28. An invented name.

29. The majority of Israeli Palestinians are rural in origin and place of residence. The coastal cities lost their preeminence in 1948 with the elimination of their national élites and administrative functions.

collectivity more inspiring than clan or village. For them, the idea of Palestine has become the symbol of this larger belonging. Z. expresses something of this when she says:

> When I was small we didn't even know the word "Palestine," we used to think Jenin was in Jordan. On Independence Day we used to carry the Israeli flag. But now children know; they sing *Biladi*[30] even though it's forbidden. This year some of them refused to take part in Independence Day.

To this new Palestinianism (which is the driving force of *Abna al-Balad*) is linked Z.'s drive for autonomy as a woman, and a part in the struggle. She supports birth control, seeing clearly the way large families pin women down in the home, and not only women but men too, drawing them out of politics through heavy economic obligations. She intends to have only two children, whether or not they are boys, and to bring up daughters in the same way as sons. She thinks all women should be able to provide for their families in case their husbands are imprisoned.

Later, in an *Abna al-Balad* meeting (mixed), I meet other girls like Z., mostly unmarried, though there is also an older woman with two small children who has been a candidate for the local council. The rapporteur is a competent girl in a Muslim headscarf (a reminder that it is possible to be both pious and progressive). Because of the difficulty of desegregating the sexes after so long, the women also meet separately to discuss their problems: for example, family restrictions on attending meetings.

The group discussion leader – a young man who steadily encourages the girls to participate – makes a statement on the movement's stand towards women's liberation:

> The main stand of *Abna al-Balad* towards the issue of women is that we must destroy all traditional values and all obstacles to the participation of women in struggle. Our main goal now is to form women cadres who will reach the stage of taking part in all levels of organization, so that they will be able to work side by side with men.

Z. assures me later that "All the group is committed to the struggle for the liberation of women. This is one of our fundamental principles, not a minor point." What she says is confirmed by the young men at the meeting. One makes a speech opposing the subordination of women, and looks forward to the day when men and women workers will make decisions together, when more girls will go to university, when children will see their mother and

30. "My country," best known of Resistance songs, and unrecognized national anthem.

father involved in the same struggle. He and other speakers stress the links between capitalism, Zionism, and the domestication of women.

THE THIRD CATEGORY

It is very clear to me, in constructing a three-category framework through which to view Palestinian women, that the third category is no more than a rag-bag. There are no "ordinary" women. I try other labels: "uneducated"? "illiterate"? "housewives"? "traditional women"? All of them are unsatisfactory, loaded with elitism; but they do point to the way schooling has increasingly become a discriminating factor between women, shattering the older unity of a similar domestic/social role and a shared "protection" by (= subordination to) the family.

There are still regions, classes, and a whole generation hardly touched by the spread of schooling: outside the cities and the middle class, few women over thirty-five are schooled, and though not numerically preponderant in this young population (50 percent under 18), they undoubtedly account for most of what remains of female illiteracy (recently estimated at 40 percent for the West Bank).[31] In peripheral areas (small outlying villages like Zbeidat, or the Negev), there are still no girls' schools at all. Bedouin as a class still have highly inadequate public schooling, though richer families are sending daughters to private schools. Girls in the poorest areas – refugee camps, villages, city slums – may have elementary schools, but not the secondary levels that open the door to skilled employment.

Wherever girls are excluded from secondary education they remain subject to pressures towards early marriage (as a form of economic security), large families,[32] and exclusion from acceptable employment. Current conditions of internal colonialism, brought about mainly by land confiscation, are increasingly forcing unqualified women into the labor market, to work in Israeli factories or on plantations at discriminatory wage rates. This trend is, of course, much more advanced in Israel, but it can be seen too in the occupied territories in spite of their greater scope for national industry and public services.

31. Based on data from the literacy survey undertaken recently by Bir Zeit University.

32. There are growing signs of female opposition to large families. I ask girls in an UNRWA sewing class in Gaza how many children they want. Answers range between none and eight, with an average of three, and two as the most often chosen number.

In Qariya we visit one of the new village factories employing girls. It is financed by Jewish capital from Haifa but there is a local "partner" who also supervises production. About twenty-five unmarried girls and two slightly older married women "foremen" work from 7:30 A.M. to 3:30 P.M., with two quarter-hour breaks, machine-sewing women's dresses. For this they are paid three and a half dollars a day.

This wage is lower than they could get in larger factories outside the village, but their families prefer to give Israeli capital a higher surplus-value because of their fear of Muslim Brotherhood violence: two buses that carried women to work were burnt last year. In Nazareth, there is the same pay difference between the large, Histadrut-organized factories and the small, backstreet workshops where women's participation remains socially invisible.

In spite of the low pay and the strict control (they must not talk between breaks), the girls seem happy to be away from home. Their political consciousness is awakened: they have already carried out two strikes, one to get paid regardless of electricity cuts, the other for a 10 percent pay increase. This year they refused to work on *Yawm al-Ard* (Land Day), and when we ask why their pay is so low and taxes so high, they answer, "Because the government wants to build settlements and hit the Palestinians."

It is true that in certain areas, particularly Gaza now, even secondary education does not necessarily lead to skilled employment. The ratio of girls in secondary school in Gaza is higher than most other parts of the Dispersion[33] but there is heavy unemployment. I remember Amneh in Beach Camp, whose marks in the *tawjihi* were good enough for her to have gone to university if her refugee family could have afforded it, but, even with secretarial and sewing courses, she hasn't been able to find a job. Unmarried – there's a big male/female imbalance in Gaza from Israel's iron repression in the early 1970's – she sits at home with nothing to do except help the neighbors' children with their lessons. She would gladly go to Saudi Arabia to work but lacks a male guardian.[34] Like Intisar's family in Jalazun, her family considers work in Israel shameful, only excused by dire need.

33. See *Statistical Yearbook 1977-78* (Vienna: UNRWA-UNESCO Department of Education, 1979), p. 19.

34. A husband or male relative within the degree prohibited for marriage.

Whatever the importance of schooling in determining women's status, it has no clear relationship to participation in national struggle. Everyone who has been in prison confirms the wide age and class range of women prisoners.[35] I hear of a Bedouin girl jailed for throwing a bomb to avenge her husband, and of old women imprisoned for refusing to tell the whereabouts of *fedayiin* sons, or for feeding them. I hear of women who resist eviction from their homes for extraordinary lengths of time, and am shown photos of one old widow, the last of her village, who hangs on to her home despite the daily growing encroachment of a vast Israeli housing project. I think also of the victims: the wives of prisoners, the mothers whose children are all in prison, or dead, or deported, and the women of the Bedouin settlements in the south, isolated from the world, subjected to mass uprootings and depredation. Reflection on our extreme ignorance of the lives of "ordinary" Palestinian women leads to the conclusion that funds for a nation-wide survey must somehow be found. What organization is likely to fund such a project?

Another important form of "ordinary" women's resistance – not remarked because taken for granted – is the capacity for staying put. If the Palestinian emigration rate out of the occupied area is much lower than Israelis would wish, this is not a little due to women who make no special pleas for an easier life. Several men I meet pay tribute to their wives' steadfastness, and a politicized girl in Bir Zeit tells how she blocked her father's plan to move the entire family to the Gulf. Women, one sometimes feels, have even deeper roots in this soil than men, with their wider circle of mobility. They have domesticated and "Palestinianized" many an alien terrain, from barracks in the Biqa to Kuwaiti suburbs, but they remain attached to the native landscape at deeper, prepolitical levels of consciousness. Laila S. says the only time she ever weeps is when she hears the word "Haifa."

If "ordinary" women cannot be distinguished from the other two categories in their Palestinianism, I think they can in the degree to which they suffer from the occupation. Indeed, one of the reasons why it is so necessary to bring them into view, even while knowing so little about their conditions and feelings, is that if one considers *only* the *shakhsiyat* and the intellectuals, one leaves room for a false link between their "advancement" and Zionist intervention. That Israel has nothing to do with women's increased education or wider public participation is clear from a comparison

---

35. Wider than for the women deportees, who seem to belong mainly to the *shakhsiya* or intellectual categories.

of Israel and the West Bank,[36] or occupied Palestine and Lebanon. But it becomes even more obvious if we consider the broad effects of the occupation on the third category in particular, that is, on women who have no chance to "compensate" through interesting work or a leader role.

It is not easy to measure the psychological strain on "ordinary" women of threats to the families with which they are so completely identified, but one can get some idea by reading accounts of the curfew in Hebron after the deportation of Mayor Qawasmeh. The mayor's wife suffered a breakdown, when, soon after her husband was deported, troops threatened to shoot one of her children seen playing in the garden. There is no Palestinian wife/mother in the occupied territories who has not gone through similar traumas, larger or smaller.

A different set of problems arises from Israeli "de-development" policies which starve Palestinian communities on both sides of the "green line" of funds needed for social infrastructures. As unpaid family/social labor, women's workload automatically expands to fill in deficiencies in public facilities. Inadequate public hygiene means more time spent cleaning. Poor transport and health facilities mean more time spent carrying sick children to clinics, more time spent waiting for care. Inadequate water and fuel supplies mean more time spent on housework.

Samira Khoury, president of the DWM, in an interview given in Nazareth showed understanding of both types of effect. Although she began by saying the "women are part of the whole population and face the same general problems," her presentation implicitly recognized the double burden. She began by speaking of:

> . . . the neglect of Arab towns and villages, and discrimination between Arab and Jewish localities. The Ministry of the Interior gives three times more to Jewish than to Arab municipalities. For example, Affuleh with a population of 14,000 gets a budget of IL 250 million while Nazareth with 45,000 has just had a budget of IL 180 million refused. . . .
>
> In the so-called "mixed" cities (Acre, Haifa, Jaffa and Lydd) the situation is even worse because the Arabs live in separate quarters which are starved of municipal funds. They can't develop, can't build schools and kindergartens, or sports centres. It's the same in the villages. Children are learning under the trees, without equipment, without even lavatories.
>
> It's the same story with the Ministry of Health: medical facilities for Arab areas lag far behind. The Histadrut gives health insurance to all its members, but their

---

36. See F. S. Nasru, *Education in the West Bank: Government Schools 1968-1976/77* (Bir Zeit: Bir Zeit University Documentation and Research Office, 1977), for evidence that girls' enrollment in school has suffered in the West Bank as a consequence of parents' fear of Israeli army violence.

clinics only exist in Jewish centers, and Arabs, especially from the villages, can't always reach them. In a recent measles epidemic, many children died because their mothers couldn't reach the clinics.

Of course, such conditions affect women psychologically. They are always under the strain of problems and anxiety. The bad economic situation affects them, inflation, unemployment. Their men often have far to go to work, there are many checkpoints, and if they are a few minutes late they are sent back, and lose a whole day's pay.

In the conditions of internal colonialism which characterize the situation of Palestinians under occupation, women can only be seen as "advancing" if we focus exclusively on political consciousness, and eliminate from view the deterioration in women's situation caused by forced proletarianization, and the transformation of the indigenous household from a center of multiple activities – social, cultural, economic into – a dormitory for workers and schoolchildren.

Beyond this, there is the problem of woman's centrality as a symbol of social order. With Palestinians increasingly polarized between progressive and reactionary currents, women are likely to pay a heavy price for "over-visibility." Here again, Israeli hegemony, seen as "modern" and "Western," has strengthened ideological countercurrents that place false emphasis on "our" women remaining "traditional." The fear of loss of control over the female sector, of a sexual revolution, of emancipation on the Israeli model (with miniskirts and premarital sexuality falsely equated with "emancipation"), have added new dimensions to the "woman problem." I hear of an increase (more in Israel and Gaza than the West Bank) of "honor" crimes, and daughter- and wife-beating; and though such things are not publicized, they point to the need for a national policy not based on an idealization of the Arab past, or the Arab family, but on understanding of the new, complex realities which are coming into existence.

CHAPTER 17

Universities under Occupation: Another Front in the War against Palestine

Naseer H. Aruri

McCARTHYISM REVISITED

Professor/Colonel Menachem Milson, who resigned his post as the "civilian administrator" of the West Bank and Gaza in September 1982, once wrote in *Commentary* that freedom of expression was guaranteed in the occupied territory:

> The Israeli authorities proclaimed that they did not care what the Arabs in the territories said or what political views they espoused and that nobody would be punished for expressing his views. This was Israeli policy, and also Israeli practice – and it was a practice for which Israelis took great moral credit having brought the blessings of freedom of expression to the West Bank.[1]

Not long before that assertion of a "civilizing mission" was made by the man who was to become governor, the Western and Israeli press had carried headlines that revealed that Palestinian students and faculty were not only excluded from the "blessings of freedom of expression," but had also been

1. Milson, "How to Make Peace with the Palestinians," *Commentary* (May 1981), p. 31.

the target of a systematic campaign of repression.[2] An escalation of attacks on Palestinian universities during the academic year 1981-82 was the direct result of Milson's policies. The Israeli army and settlers killed students in the streets and in the classroom during the uprisings of the spring of 1982.

Bir Zeit University was closed three times for a total of seven months during Milson's one-year tenure as civilian administrator. Milson, a professor of Arabic literature at Hebrew University, began in August 1982 to require "nonresident" faculty members, mainly Palestinians, who applied for work permits to teach at the three major universities, to sign an anti-PLO pledge. When nearly all of them refused, the governor decided not to issue them work permits, and ordered the deportation of Jordanian passport holders who refused to sign. The contentious paragraph in the required statement read:

> I hereby declare that I am committed not to do any kind of work and not to give any services directly or indirectly which will help or support the so-called PLO organization [*sic*] or any other hostile organization.

Twenty-two faculty members, all but two of them Palestinian holders of Jordanian passports, were deported, mostly from al-Najah University in Nablus. They included the president, Dr. Munther Salah; the vice president, Dr. Abdul-Rahman Shahin; the dean of the College of Education, Dr. Taysir Kilani; the dean of the College of Engineering, Dr. Suleiman Samadi; and the chairman of the Economics Department, Dr. Yusif Abd al-Haq.[3]

When these measures met with strong resistance, the occupation authorities announced on 21 November 1982 that a revised work permit would replace the anti-PLO pledge. But what in fact happened was that the pledge was incorporated into the new work-permit application. The final paragraph read:

2. For example: "Israeli Troops Open Fire on Palestinian Students," headlined a news article by the *Times* (London) 19 November 1980; "Israeli Troops Shoot at Arab Students' Legs," *Times* (19 November 1980); "Fifty West Bank Pupils Held without Charge," *Times* (28 November 1980); "Israeli Soldiers Wound 2 at West Bank Demonstration," *Washington Post* (26 November 1980); "Israeli Troops Wound 9 in West Bank Protest," *Washington Post* (19 November 1980); "Bir Zeit University Ordered Shut for Week," *Jerusalem Post* (16 November 1980); "Israeli Soldiers Shoot Palestinian Students in West Bank Melee," *New York Times* (1 November 1981); "Israel Shuts West Bank University after Palestinian Demonstration," *New York Times* (5 November 1981); "Israel Again Shuts West Bank School," *New York Times* (17 February 1982) . . . and so on.

3. *New York Times*, 21 October 1982; *al-Talia*, 16 September 1982 and 7 October 1982.

During the time of the permit the receiver of the permit will avoid any action which can damage or hurt security and public order and abide with all judicial and security laws that prohibit any activity and services which help or support the so-called PLO or any other hostile organization.[4]

The regulation applied to any faculty member not a certified West Bank resident. About one hundred one-fifth of the total academic community — were affected by these measures. They reacted by organizing themselves as the Ad Hoc Committee of Foreign Passport Holders and argued that the signature requirement was an unwarranted addition to their contracts with their employer, constituting an undue form of political pressure. Hugh Harcourt, an American professor of cultural studies at Bir Zeit who taught in the Arab world for twenty-two years, drew a parallel with the McCarthy era in the United States:

No Arab government or organization has ever requested that I sign a pro-PLO statement. I would have refused. I lived through the McCarthy era and I knew what a loyalty oath means.[5]

In fact U.S. Secretary of State George Shultz, a former professor, criticized the measures as imposing a "loyalty oath," which he said had no place "in a setting where we expect to have freedom of thought and encourage freedom of thought."[6]

The West Bank faculty members stood united in their refusal to sign, but stated that they had no objection to committing themselves to obeying the law of the land, including the security regulations established by the occupation regime. Their statement of 13 September 1982 reads:

. . . Indeed we already do so, both in our application for work permits and in signing the receipt of the work permit. We have no objection to declaring (again) that we will abide by the Act for the Prevention of Acts of Belligerence and Enemy Propaganda (Amendment Number 1) (Judea and Samaria No. 938 for the Year 5742-1982) although such separate signatures would appear to be redundant.[7]

4. *Middle East International* (London), 26 November 1982; see also *Washington Post,* 23 November 1982.

5. Michael Precker, "West Bank Oath Stirs Controversy," *Boston Globe,* 21 November 1982.

6. *Ibid.*

7. Text of statement appears in Isam Aruri, "Hal al-Maksund lghlaq al-Jamiat?" (Is the objective closing the universities?) *al-Katib* (Jerusalem, October 1982), 30:28-29. See also Bob Lange, "An Untold Story: Israel and the Palestinian Educator," *The Justice* (Brandeis University), 19 October 1982.

ISRAEL'S PERCEPTION OF HIGHER EDUCATION IN THE OCCUPIED TERRITORIES

Such actions on the part of Israeli officials raise the question of how the occupying power perceives the status and mission of higher education in the occupied territories. Universities and even high schools are generally viewed by the occupation regime as "hotbeds of radicalism" and "schools of terrorism."[8] A "center of political incitement and activity" was the way the military government described Bir Zeit University to the Israeli High Court after the university was closed in November 1981. Israel's deputy attorney general summed up this prevailing attitude in testimony before the Israeli High Court of Justice on 14 July 1980: "Where there are schools, there will be demonstrations, stone-throwing, raising of flags, and therefore a threat to security."[9] Raising the Palestinian flag is considered a threat to security in Israel; it is prohibited by law. Indeed, a student does not have to express his or her Palestinian identity by raising the flag to be punished; it is enough that he or she wears a shirt with the white, red, black, and green.[10] Bir Zeit dean of students put it this way:

> We have committed the crime that some of the students, with coloring pens, colored small pieces of paper with the colors of the Palestinian flag and had this flag on their chest.[11]

An economics professor at Bir Zeit adds:

> It is absurd to pretend that you can have Palestinians who have no national feeling. . . . [They] will have to close kindergartens too; it will have to go down right to the bottom of the educational ladder.[12]

8. William Clairborne, "Israeli Troops Wound 9 in West Bank Protest," *Washington Post*, 19 November 1980; see also Raja Shehadeh and Jonathan Kuttab, *The West Bank and the Rule of Law* (Geneva: International Commission of Jurists and Its West Bank Affiliate Law in the Service of Man, 1980), p. 89.

9. *Washington Post*, 19 November 1980.

10. See Israel Shahak, "Banning the `Terrible' White, Black, Green and Red," *Christian Science Monitor*, 3 March 1981.

11. David Shipler, "West Bank Students Assail Israeli Measures on Schools," *New York Times*, 20 November 1980.

12. *Ibid.*

But Army Major General Danny Matt, former coordinator of the occupied territories, insisted that the display of Palestinian national feeling, such as in the Palestine Week activities which led to the closure of Bir Zeit University in 1980, was seditious. He pinned the blame on "agitators" at Bir Zeit University, "the center of all violence," acting upon orders from abroad, i.e. Beirut.[13]

Professor Menachem Milson's first major act upon assuming the top position of civilian administrator was the closure of Bir Zeit University for two months beginning on 2 November 1981. The crime was a student demonstration commemorating the sixty-fourth anniversary of the hated Balfour Declaration. Milson, however, in conformity with his ongoing attempts to restructure Palestinian leadership in the area, tried to co-opt the board of trustees of al-Najah University. During a visit with the board on 16 December 1981, while Bir Zeit was still closed under his orders, he gave his approval to the long-sought request for an engineering college.[14] Shortly after that, he placed the eight members of the Bir Zeit student council under town arrest, warned the Bir Zeit administration not to have contacts with the deported university president Hanna Nasser,[15] and banned a Haifa mathematics professor, Dr. Carmella Armonies, from the West Bank for one year, thus forcing her to give up her teaching position.[16] February 1982, he closed Bir Zeit University for the second time in less than three months, after the university refused to meet with some of his aides.

"Divide and rule" and the use of the "carrot and stick" was the approach of the orientalist governor to his subjects. His hope was to promote Village League types in Palestinian academia – people who would repay favors granted by the occupying power with their unquestioning loyalty to it. The arrest of faculty and students, the town arrest of student councils, the physical evacuation of university campuses, and the frequent closure of universities, are all examples of collective punishment. The university is punished for assuming its proper position among many other Palestinian institutions and groups that assert Palestinian identity and reject all attempts to eradicate it. It is punished for rejecting a military occupation dressed in civilian clothing and bent on a *de facto* application of the "autonomy" plan, i.e. annexation of eastern Palestine and Gaza.

13. *Washington Post*, 19 November 1980.

14. *Al-Fajr Weekly*, 26 December 1981-7 January 1982, p. 16.

15. *Ibid.*, 5-21 January 1982.

16. *Ibid.*, 5-11 February 1982, p. 4.

The Israeli foreclosure on the option of statehood for the Palestinians is the real context for the campaign against academia. The issue involved is not only academic freedom; it also relates to how Israel perceives its relationship with the Palestinian people. That Israel and Zionist doctrine deny the very existence and the peoplehood of Palestinians is well known; that Israel is intent on creating another Galilee in the West Bank is also well known;[17] that Israel has embarked on a process of interrupting the geographic and demographic unity of Palestine is also well known.[18] Our study will focus on the methods by which Israel manipulates the rules governing military occupation in order to achieve its long-range goals. Israeli policy towards the institutions of higher learning exemplifies Israeli perceptions of the relationship between the occupant and the occupied in Palestine.

LEGAL AUTHORITY IN THE OCCUPIED TERRITORY

The relationship between the occupying power and the civilian inhabitants of the occupied territory is regulated by international law. Numerous charters, international conventions, and declarations define the rights and obligations of the occupant and the occupied.[19] Israel, however, denies the applicability of the Fourth Geneva Convention of 1949 governing belligerent occupation. Israel's ambassador to the United Nations, Yehuda Blum, reiterated his government's position in a speech to the Security Council on 19 March 1979, in which he argued that the 1950 annexation of eastern Palestine to Transjordan was in violation of international law, that the loss of that area to Israel in June 1967 resulted from "renewed aggression" by Jordan, and that the rights of Jordan as an "illegal occupant"

17. See Khalil Nakhleh, *The Two Galilees: Zionist Practices in the Context of Military Occupation in Palestine* (Belmont, Mass.: Association of Arab-American University Graduates, Occasional Paper #7), 1982.

18. See Meron Benvenisti, "Four Plans To Swallow the West Bank," *al-Fajr* (Jerusalem) 20 June - 4 July, 1981; William Clairborne and Edward Cody, "Israel Shapes Immutable Future for West Bank," *Washington Post,* 7 September 1980; Helena Cobban, "West Bank Hostages," *Christian Science Monitor,* 5 April 1982; Ellen Cantarow, "The West Bank: A Journal of Occupation and Resistance," *Village Voice,* 30 September 1980.

19. For example: the Hague *Regulations Respecting the Laws and Customs of War on Land,* annexed to the Hague Convention IV of 1907; the *London Charter* of 1945, Article 6; the *Geneva Convention Relative to the Protection of Civilian Persons in Time of War,* 1949 (IV), Articles 27-28; the *Convention on the Prevention and Punishment of the Crime of Genocide,* December 1948.

were terminated with its ouster in June 1967.[20] Blum inferred selectively from the writings of experts in international law, including Rostow, Lauterpacht, Stone, and Schwebel, that Israel had a better title to any Palestinian area than did Jordan or any other state.

It will be concluded from Blum's argument that Jordan retained no jurisdiction in the area after 1967, as Jordan did not constitute a legitimate sovereign. Hence, Israel, as the administrator responsible for law and order pending a sovereignty decision, is under no obligation to apply the Fourth Geneva Convention! Yet Israel has chosen to "amend" Jordanian laws instead of enacting direct decrees to supercede these laws. The double bind in which Israel finds itself is not accidental; it is calculated. Although Israel is not ready for the measures of legal annexation, it has, in fact, taken giant operational steps toward effective annexation. In the meantime, selective application of Jordanian legislation provides Israel with a justification to repress, subdue and control within the "framework of the law." Jordan may not claim any rights in the West Bank and Gaza, but the Israeli occupation regime may invoke Jordanian legislation to promote its own ends. Israel, therefore, has the best of two worlds. It reserves the right to act in the manner of an occupant, but denies, at the same time, that it is an "occupying power" within the meaning of international law.

MILITARY ORDER NUMBER 854

The West Bank military governor decreed on 6 July 1980 two amendments to the Jordanian Education Law Number 16 of 1964 and the Regulation of Teaching Licenses Number 23 of 1965, and decreed other military orders relevant to education in the West Bank. The entire package represented a new code for higher education in the area, which in effect transferred control of the universities from their respective boards of trustees to a "responsible officer" in the military government. Specifically, the first amendment, known also as Military Order Number 854, extends to institutions of higher learning a whole series of regulations previously applied under the Jordanian Law Number 16 to elementary and secondary schools.[21]

20. Excerpts from Blum's speech in *Judea, Samaria and Gaza — The Israeli Record* (Israeli Ministry of Foreign Affairs, n.d.).

21. Text of Military Order No. 854 was made available to a member of an American academic delegation, which visited Palestinian universities 24 November - 1 December 1980, by Dr. Emanuel Lottem, Israeli Consul for Academic Affairs in New York; other "amendments" to Jordan's law of education appear as appendices to a memorandum issued by Bir Zeit University shortly after 6 July 1980, hereinafter referred to as Bir Zeit Memorandum.

The academic regulations package of 6 July 1980 illustrates the duality in the Israeli posture. Order 854 is technically an amendment to the Jordanian Law Number 16, but the amendment is in effect a law in itself. On the one hand, it removed the distinction between academic and preacademic institutions in the West Bank, despite the fact that both Jordan and Israel observe that distinction in their own spheres.[22] On the other hand, it introduced new elements, new restrictions, and new intrusions into the academic process.[23] Israel, therefore, attempts to maximize its control by relying upon Jordanian law and by going beyond it, depending on which course best suits its interest. Not only did Order 854 change the concept of existing law, but it also went beyond the intended scope of its application. It intrudes on the autonomy of the university in recruitment, choice of educational materials, admission of students, design of curriculae, promotion of faculty and staff, and pursuit of research interests. In a report released in October 1981, a Hebrew University faculty committee reacted to this aspect of Order 854 in the following statement:

> Licensing academic staff, licensing institutions of academic education, supervision of curriculae and teaching material are alien to the idea of academic freedom. Restrictions on party activity, beyond those existing in the population at large, may be acceptable with regards to teachers in the government school system, who may be regarded as public servants or state employees, but it is clearly out of place with regards to academic staff or private universities, which are supposed to preserve their independence.[24]

Another report, by Bir Zeit University, referred to the same aspect of 854 as attempting

---

22. See "amendments" to Sections 2, 8(c), 20 of Jordan's Law of Education #16 (1964).

23. See "amendments" to Sections 59, also Amendment to Regulation of Teaching License No. 23, 1965; Decree Regarding Closed Areas No. 34; General Entry Permit No. 5, all of which decreed by the military government on 6 July 1980.

24. "Report on the Condition of Universities in the Occupied Territories," prepared by a committee of five Hebrew University professors (Ruth Gavisow, Law; Yahoshua Kolodny, Geology; David Kretchmer, Law; Eliezar Rabinovitch, Physics; Menahem Yaari, Economics) for an ad hoc faculty meeting to discuss the issue. Mimeographed, October 1981. For a summary, see Benny Morris, "Report by the Hebrew University Teachers: Army Policy on West Bank Colleges Scored," *Jerusalem Post*, 21 October 1981, p. 3.

. . . to impose on universities considerations that conflict with the concept of a university . . . [and which] will turn them into "schools of a higher level" and invalidate their status as universities. [A] university cannot fulfill its mission in a serious and healthy manner if it is attached to an officer within a military command.[25]

The official justification of 854 and the entire package, prompted by criticism in Israel, Europe, and the United States, posited that a "legal and administrative framework for the functioning of universities, similar to those existing with respect to universities throughout the world" was needed "in order to avoid a legal vacuum."[26] A spokesman for the military government was quoted by the Washington Post as saying: "Only in the West Bank was there no law for the universities. We decided that Arab universities must stand up to the criteria of universities elsewhere."[27]

The following is an item-by-item analysis of the principal features of Order 854:[28]

25. See Bir Zeit Memorandum, p. 3.

26. Documents and oral presentation by Dr. Emanuel Lottem in Columbus, Ohio, December 1980. Lottem's argument follows:

a) There is a need for a law on universities to enforce standards so that a few people cannot get together and say they have established a university.

b) Amendments to Jordan Law No. 16 impose less control than the statute for the University of Amman. Order 854 effects a removal of Jordanian barriers to establishment of universities.

c) Legal restrictions on teachers coming from abroad are necessitated by security. German teachers were not allowed to teach at American universities during WW II. As for administration detention disqualifying teachers, the U.S. itself did not bat an eyelash at throwing hundreds of thousands of its citizens into detention camps during WW II.

d) Academic freedom refers only to intramural activities.

e) There is no accreditation board in West Bank. Israel will be criticized for further interference if it creates one.

Lottem presented a document which quotes extensively from the British Manual of Military Law Part III (HMSO, 1962) p. 148; M. Greenspan, *The Modern Law of Land Warfare* (1959), p. 234; G. VonGlahn, *The Occupation of Enemy Territory* (1957), p. 63; and the U.S. *Judge Advocate General Service* No. 11, p. 66. All such quotations are open to interpretations regarding security considerations in regulating education.

27. William Clairborne, "Israel Restricts Arab Colleges in West Bank," *Washington Post,* 1 August 1980.

28. See other studies on this subject such as Michael Griffin, "A Human Rights Odyssey: In Search of Academic Freedom," *The Link* (New York, April-May 1981), 14(2); Muhammad Hallaj, "Palestine: The Suppression of an Idea," *The Link* (January-

Accreditation

The accreditation of academic institutions is normally granted by a special academic association according to well-defined criteria. In the West Bank and Gaza, no such association or council was allowed to discharge that function, despite the existence of the Council on Higher Education, and the fact that accreditation is defined as a proper function of that council. Not unlike other institutions, the Council on Higher Education has been subjected to severe restrictions by the occupation authorities, so that it has been unable to effectively discharge its functions. Such restrictions included bans on meetings of its general assembly and the imposition of town arrest orders on members of its executive committee. Hence, while the occupation authorities claim that Order 854 was promulgated to "enforce standards" (see note 26), the fact is that it has prevented the structure that the universities created to fulfill that function from discharging its obligations. Instead, Order 854 conferred the right to license institutions of higher learning on the educational officer in the "civilian" military government. These licenses must be issued annually and can be revoked at any time. The power to issue and revoke licenses places the university at the mercy of the education officer and his military superiors who have shown no hesitation to close universities whenever they wanted. The validity of the Israeli claim that 854 aims to protect the local residents from the inequities of substandard education is certainly to be questioned. In fact, the occupation regime, through the power of licensing, can hold the universities hostage and blackmail them into compliance with the policies of the regime.

Moreover, the so-called amendments to Jordan's Education Law Number 16 went beyond the scope of that law by conferring consultative powers in the issuance of licenses on the police commander and the "civilian" governor of the district, who must ensure that "public order" will not suffer by licensing a university. The influence of the police over academia is thus consolidated.

March 1982), 15(1); Naseer Aruri, "Repression in Academia: Palestinian Universities versus the Israeli Military" *Arab Perspectives* (April 1981), 2: 14-19; Penny Johnson, "The Next Day in Nablus," A.A.U.G. *Newsletter* (January-February 1981), 14(1); Milton Viorst, "Bir Zeit: The Search for National Identity," *Science* (5 December 1980), 210: 1101-2. For a legal study of Military Order 854 see Jonathan Kuttab, *Analysis of Military Order No. 854 and Related Orders concerning Educational Institutions in the Occupied West Bank* (Geneva: Law in the Service of Man, May 1981); see also Shehadeh and Kuttab, *The West Bank and the Rule of Law.* See also Munir Fasheh, former dean of students at Bir Zeit, "Why Israel Closed Palestinian University," *New York Times,* 28 December 1981.

The Work Permit

Faculty recruitment is normally regarded as the function of academic departments and administrative staff at the university. Under Order 854, the "civilian" military government enjoys a virtual veto over all appointments through the power to issue a mandatory work permit and grant and revoke licenses to teach. The so-called amendment to the Regulation of Teaching Licenses (Nov. 23, 1965) empowers the authorities to declare ineligible any teacher "who has been convicted under security regulation or who has been placed under administrative detention."

In previous years, the normal procedure was for the universities to apply for educational permits several months before the beginning of the academic year. Authorities generally gave their approval during the academic year with written approval obtained later, sometimes even by the end of the academic year, but teachers were allowed to work in the meantime.

The duration of faculty permits was reduced from one year to six months, then to three months, then one month, fifteen days. These restrictions clearly disrupt the educational process and depress the quality of education. Instructors can hardly engage in rational planning, let alone assure their own presence to conduct their classes. Nor could the institutes of higher learning engage in even short-term planning, since faculty work permits could be revoked at the whims of army officers without explanation or proper notice. Thus, at Bir Zeit University, Jawad Brogouthi, professor of cultural studies, who was on leave from North Carolina State University at Raleigh to teach in the West Bank, was suddenly denied a permit in November 1980 after he had begun to teach. This incident took place while a U.S. academic delegation was visiting Palestinian universities in the occupied territories. (This delegation consisted of professors Mary Gray of American University, Harold McDougal of Rutgers, Robert Lange of Brandeis, Masao Miyoshi of Berkeley and the author.) At al-Najah University, the delegation met with an American professor who had to leave his passport at the Israeli Ministry of Interior for six weeks and wait to obtain his work permit.

Shortly after the enactment of Order Number 854, the Israeli occupation authorities tried to force the universities into compliance with that order by withholding the work and residence permits of nonresident faculty, including many Palestinians. The U.S. academic delegation, which visited the area in November 1980, was told by a Bir Zeit University official that forty faculty members – twenty of whom were Palestinian – had no permission to work. He said: "Last week, I asked the military governor about the work permits for these forty teachers. He said, 'They are here on my desk, but I wouldn't give them to you.' In addition to the forty at Bir Zeit, there were thirty at al-Najah and twenty at Bethlehem University who had not yet received their work permits at that time. The report of the Hebrew University faculty committee commented on the question of permits thus:

> If the Government allows someone to enter and move about more freely, one would infer that the Government regards that person as no danger to security. Preventing such a person from joining the university staff can't be based on security considerations and it involves unwarranted interference by the military government in the personnel policies of the academic institutions.[29]

Teaching Licenses

The power to grant and revoke teaching licenses is still more ominous than the manipulation of the permit requirement by the authorities. Under Jordanian law, the minister of education was empowered to "withdraw the license of a teacher who committed a moral offense punishable by law"; the Israeli "amendment" substitutes "conviction under security regulations" or "administrative detention." This unusual legislation allows the authorities to declare instructors ineligible and to bar them from practicing their profession by issuing an order of administrative detention against them in accordance with the 1945 Defense Regulations, where the requirement of show-cause does not exist.

Implementation of these procedures has three results. First, they impede the development and retention of an intelligentsia and community leadership. Local Palestinian intellectuals under constant harassment will be induced to emigrate to the Arab world or to the West.

In fact, officials of the military government who met with the Hebrew University faculty committee were rather candid on this point, as may be seen in the following:

> In the Committee's deliberations, a further charge was raised concerning the involvement of West Bank universities in politics rather than academic matters. According to this charge, the true purpose of the West Bank universities is to develop cadres of leaders and to build an intelligentsia that will, when the time comes, serve the needs of a Palestinian State. . . . The Committee rejects such a charge, and declares that the development of educated leaders who will serve the community to which the universities belong is an academic objective of the first importance.[30]

29. "Report on the Condition of Universities," p. 6.

30. *Ibid.,* p. 4.

The second consequence of these regulations is to impede the development of the universities beyond the level of community colleges or "schools at a higher level," in that foreign faculties, Palestinians living abroad, or even Israeli faculty wishing to teach at these institutions, are effectively hampered by the arbitrary withdrawal of permits and licenses.

Third, these rules contribute to the ongoing process of segmentation and atomization of Palestinian society so as to further foreclose on the option of Palestinian statehood. The Decree Regarding Closed Areas Number 34 further "amends" Jordanian law by making it a requirement for any "inhabitant of any administered territory" or "an Israeli or foreigner" who wants to enter the area and work as a teacher to obtain "a personal permit" issued in writing by a military governor. The restriction applies also to students and administrators with the cumulative effect of undermining and disrupting Palestinian national unity and demographic continuity. As has already been observed, a Gazan student or a Palestinian faculty member with an Israeli citizenship is regarded a "foreigner" in the West Bank.

Moreover, Order 854 and the other "amendments" apply to the West Bank only. No analogous regulations pertaining to Gaza are in existence, despite the endeavor of the military government to fill the "legal vacuum" in higher education.

The Academic Curricula

The curriculum is normally considered a responsibility of academic departments and councils. Dr. Gabi Baramki, acting president of Bir Zeit University, told the *Washington Post* (1 August 1980), "until now they have interfered in our operations . . . [but] with the new amendments . . . they are responsible for our operations." The permit system enables the "civilian" military government to control the creation of additional departments, programs, colleges, buildings. Full use of this power was employed by the authorities to delay or prohibit the institution of new programs. Examples abound:

- At al-Najah University, the request for permission to inaugurate a college of agriculture was denied in 1980 without explanation. Agriculture is of course a particularly sensitive field of study in an area where the government's settlement policy is aimed at preempting or confiscating Palestinian farmland and water resources. The university also encountered a series of delays involving building permits for the new campus near Nablus.

- At Bethlehem University, a Vatican-supported institution, our delegation was told that a request for a new program in the hotel management field designed to train and qualify students as tourist guides was denied by the military authorities. "The emphasis in guided tours in the occupied areas now is on Hebrew sites. Coverage of Muslim and Christian monuments is slipshod," according to the president of Bethlehem University. Order 854 has also affected the nursing and social work programs at Bethlehem. The students required to do practical training at the Hussein Hospital at nearby Beit Jala were stopped and turned back at military checkpoints in October 1980 for having failed to produce entry permits.

- At Bir Zeit University, a letter was received from the education officer of the military government on 9 January 1979, denying approval for continued practice teaching, giving no explanation for the sudden decision.[31] It should be noted that practice teaching is a requirement for teacher certification in the West Bank. Inquiries about the arbitrary decision went unanswered.

  Other programs of Bir Zeit University were placed in jeopardy, such as the community work program which requires 120 hours of such practical work in the community as picking olives, cleaning streets, or improving playgrounds.

  The university helped create a primary health care project, which caters to the health needs of sixteen villages with a total population of approximately 20,000. This program, which faces harassment frequently, becomes totally inoperable during forced closures of the university. Equally unpopular with the Israeli authorities is the university's program to combat illiteracy, which operates on the national level.

In the absence of a national government in the occupied territory, the universities have attempted to fill the void at least in the areas of community work and preservation of the national culture. Hence they are constantly targeted for reprisal. The occupation regime seems unhappy with the infrastructure which has enabled Bir Zeit and the other universities to promote and preserve Palestinian culture and folklore, and to interact with the larger community through public service programs.[32]

31. Bir Zeit Memorandum, Appendix 3/A, p. 1.

32. When BZU was ordered closed on 13 November 1980 for one week, the military regime charged that the university administration delayed the cancellation of

By controlling the curriculum and extracurricular activities, the Israeli authorities again hope to maintain the development of Palestinian universities at a politically tolerable level and to inhibit the emergence of an infrastructure for a future state. Moreover, they anticipate the rise of a docile intelligentsia to reinforce the discredited Village Leagues. A restructured leadership would be more amenable to negotiations on the basis of the Begin plan, which vests sovereignty over all of Palestine in Israel.

Academic Libraries

Library and laboratory acquisitions are subject to extensive restrictions. Books and educational materials entering the country must all be censored. Books on nuclear physics, certain scientific equipment, even discs with less radioactive material than a television set, are strictly prohibited. The president of Bethlehem University told us: "You have to prepare three years ahead for equipment and books . . . we bring them across the bridge [Allenby Bridge] and give them to the censor who will go through them book by book. It takes several months to determine what goes and what does not." At Bir Zeit, the visiting American delegation was told about a list of 1,187 books which had been banned since 1977. They deal with a wide range of subjects, from Palestinian folklore to Islamic thought, and include such books as *The Islamic Dictionary; Arab Society and the Palestine Question; With Kamal Junblatt; The Arab Awakening,* etc. Bir Zeit classified these books under the following subjects:

- Folklore, games, tales, children's books – 33 percent of those banned.

- Religion, Islamic thought and philosophy, Islamic revolutions against foreign domination – 25 percent.

- Palestinian history and politics constitute the rest.

The list of banned books has been growing larger. The Hebrew University faculty committee estimated the number at 3,000, whereas the military government, which refuses to provide a list or explain the criteria of

---

Palestine Week, a cultural event sponsored by the students and obviously regarded as subversive by the authorities, who claimed that the plans included "meetings with a political character." This allegation was made in documents presented by Emanuel Lottem.

censorship, insists that the list consists of 648 books.[33] In fact, all books entering the occupied territory must first receive permits from the army censor. "They are automatically forbidden unless formally approved by the censors."[34] Books that are rejected by the censor are returned at border posts to the seller. The Hebrew University report stated that "there have been cases where the disapproved books have disappeared and the addressee has been unable to retrieve the purchase price, let alone the VAT tax which has already been paid."[35]

The book ban is policed by frequent army searches of schools and university libraries. Periodicals published by the Arab "East" Jerusalem press are almost impossible to obtain at the universities, as most of them are banned throughout the West Bank. Professional periodicals published in the Arab world are much more likely to be available at Israeli university libraries than at the universities of the West Bank. Since 1980, no Arabic books or periodicals have been allowed to enter the area, and the universities have been forced to rely upon Western literature. The occupation regime hopes to effect a cultural reorientation, which might ultimately lead to the creation of a benign intelligentsia detached from Arab nationalism. The history of French and Portuguese colonialism in Africa may offer valuable lessons to the occupant and the occupied in that regard.

As for laboratory equipment, the authorities not only scrutinize it closely to guard against military potential, but they also levy exorbitant taxes reaching in some cases 100 percent of the value of the article. Customs duties are charged on approved educational equipment, office machines, and construction materials, which are normally tax exempt. Bir Zeit University, the only institution of higher learning that existed under Jordanian rule, was exempt from customs duty. Under the Israeli occupation, Bir Zeit was denied similar treatment in conformity with existing law, on 8 October 1970. A statement released by the university on 16 March 1979 revealed that more than $46,000 was paid in duty for

33. See "Report on the Condition of Universities," p. 7; also Benny Morris, "Controversy over Books Banned in Territories," *Jerusalem Post*, 8 March 1981.

34. *Jerusalem Post*, 8 March 1981; for an account of censorship in the occupied territories, see David Shipler, "Israel Tightens Control over Arab Newspapers," *New York Times*, 20 March 1982; also "Begin vs. the Press," *Newsweek*, 19 April 1982, p. 50.

35. "Report on the Condition of Universities," p. 7; Bir Zeit Memorandum Appendix 3/A reveals that although Bir Zeit University is not subject to custom duties on books, it does pay VAT of 12 percent which is not refunded, unlike the situation of Israeli universities (p. 2). Also see Shehadeh and Kuttab, *The West Bank and the Rule of Law*, p. 93.

laboratory and cafeteria equipment since 1967, "sufficient to build a new building or equip a laboratory." The duty on the steel alone for the library building amounted to $20,000.[36]

In the words of the Hebrew University report, "it is axiomatic that academic activity can't take place without free access to books, journals, and documents";[37] the occupation authorities who know this fact too well are only happy to oblige. Academic activities seem to be utterly incompatible with the aims of the occupation regime. For the occupant, these activities are "at best a guise for political activity and at the worst a guise for subversive activities."[38] He can do well without them, and indeed, this may be the long-range goal of the military government, which has kept the universities and schools closed throughout 1988 and up until now.

Bir Zeit University is in a different position from Bethlehem, al-Najah and the other specialized institutes in that it was the only chartered university prior to 1967. Other universities had to obtain permits in order to exist, but Bir Zeit is faced with having to relinquish its autonomy and submit to a foreign army.[39] Neither in Israel nor even in Jordan does the government exercise such authority and control over the universities. They are academically independent of the ministries of education, let alone the army. Hence, it was at Bir Zeit where violence first erupted over Order Number 854 in November 1980.

POSTSCRIPT

The crippling restrictions imposed on Palestinian universities by Israel are part of a systematic effort to hamper the development of Palestinian community organizations. They are an integral part of the more general repressive atmosphere of daily life under military occupation. Yet more specifically, they destabilize higher education, which is one of the key

36. Bir Zeit Memorandum, Appendix 3/A, p. 2.

37. "Report on the Condition of Universities," p. 7.

38. *Ibid.*, p. 3.

39. For example, in a raid that took place on 11 May 1982, soldiers broke into a Bir Zeit student dormitory in Ramallah (Rabah Hotel) at about 2 A.M. They conducted an I.D. check and took thirty students to the military headquarters. On the same night, soldiers broke into the girls dormitory and conducted a search. Earlier a similar raid took place at Bethlehem University, in which two members of the student council were arrested. *Al-Fajr* (14-20 May 1982), p. 1.

resources of the Palestinian people. The Israeli strategy is calculated to induce an exodus of intellectuals and to disrupt the educational process, if not to close the universities altogether. Just as mayors were retired and some deported, just as municipal councils were restructured, the universities are being harassed in order to demoralize the Palestinian community and render its institutional infrastructure meaningless and ineffective.

Since this chapter was originally written in 1982, the Israeli campaign against the universities was intensified and also extended to all educational institutions at all levels. The *New York Times* headlined a front-page story on May 8, 1989: "For West Bank Arabs, Education Has Been Deemed a Criminal Act." The Israeli occupation authorities have kept schools and universities closed since January 1988, thus depriving 18,000 university students and 20,000 elementary and secondary pupils of education, a right guaranteed under Jordanian law and upheld by the Geneva Convention of 1949, the Universal Declaration of Human Rights, and the International Covenant on Economic, Social and Cultural Rights.

The prolonged closure has forced Palestinian educators to seek alternative education by holding clandestine classes at teachers homes, churches and mosques. These "basement schools" have been deemed illegal since August 18, 1988, when all "popular committees" that had been organizing this type of education, distributing seed, and supervising other projects aimed toward self-sufficiency were outlawed by the authorities. It is not uncommon now to read announcements that the army or the police have "uncovered a network of illegal classes."[40] Previously, such announcements dealt mainly with the uncovering of armed cells or what Israel likes to designate as terrorist organizations. But even these clandestine classes have proven to be of value only to students in their junior and senior academic years; the younger students lack the necessary experience needed for this type of free university education.

Needless to say, the effect of such drastic measures on Palestinian society has been disastrous. There are now thousands of eight–year–old illiterates in the occupied territories. The repeated and extended closure of schools and educational institutions has denied students and faculty the continuity which is so vital to the academic process. Also a large number of students and teachers have been compelled to seek jobs inside the educational field as a means of survival. The occupation authorities have consistently maintained that the closure was needed in order to prevent disturbance to the public order which threatens security. Palestinians, however, argue that the closure policy is a form of collective punishment

40. *New York Times,* 8 May 1989.

against the students, who constitute 35 percent of the population. Al-Haq, the Palestinian affiliate of the International Commission of Jurists, concludes in its 1988 report that:

> The security rationale put forth by the government to justify school closing is neither supported by facts or by law. The Israeli government's actions force the conclusion that it is education itself that is targeted and that it is intended as another means . . . [of] collective punishment in the hope that the will of the local population fighting for Its legitimate rights will be broken.[41]

The United Nations Relief and Work Agency (UNRWA) rejected the Israeli rationale of security in a statement issued In Vienna in October 1988:

> Security considerations have been invoked to justify the closure of educational institutions, but the major consequence is that a generation of Palestinian children are unable to exercise their basic right to education.[42]

In fact, the outlawing of "basement schools" is in itself an indication that reasons other than security have impelled the authorities to close all schools and universities. The consensus among Palestinians is that the closure is part of an Israeli policy of enforced ignorance. One seven–year–old Palestinian student explained the policy by saying;

> They [the Israelis] want to make us stupid. They are afraid to allow us to be educated . . . they know that education is our most powerful weapon.[43]

Some Israelis have also rejected the security explanation offered by their Defense Ministry. Four hundred Israeli professors petitioned the Defense Ministry to reopen the schools on May 1, 1989, charging that the real reason for the closure was collective punishment.[44] Otherwise, they asked, "why did the army refuse even to allow school librarians to go to work so they could keep up their collections?" The statement which was released by Hebrew University professors in Jerusalem on May 1, 1989 questioned the motives of the military government;

41. *Punishing a Nation: Human Rights Violations during the Palestinian Uprising December 1987-December 1988* (Ramallah: Al-Haq/Law in the Service of Man, 1988), p. 305.

42. *Jerusalem Post,* 12 October 1988.

43. *Palestinian Education: A Threat to Israel's Security* (Jerusalem: The Jerusalem Media and Communications Center, 1989), p. 17.

44. *New York Times,* 8 May 1989.

> We, Israeli academics, continue our academic activities while a few kilometers from our university the Palestinian institutions of higher education have been closed for 15 months by order of the military government . . . We know that the authorities claim that the universities serve as a center for demonstrations and violent confrontations with the army. However, even if we assume this to be the case, there is no justification for the general closing of all the universities without distinction, for an unlimited period. Furthermore, the attempts of the army to prevent alternative off-campus academic activities by the universities raise doubts whether the closing rests only on public order considerations.[45]

The signers then challenged their government to live up to declared Jewish values:

> Denying higher education to an entire community is particularly distressive in the light of the historical experience of the Jewish people and its cultural values.[46]

At the time of this writing, neither the prospect for a short-term solution for schools and universities, nor that for a long-term solution for the conflict between Israel and Palestine is in sight. According to one Palestinian educator, the closure policy is "creating a whole generation of students who are not going to have a proper education . . . we are going to suffer for 10, 15 years."[47] According to another educator, "It's an attempt to destroy vengefully the Palestinian infrastructure. It's our schools, our agriculture, our businesses."[48]

45. From text of press conference dispatched by Professor Shalom Baer to Dr. Joseph Atick on 1 May 1989.

46. *Ibid.*

47. *New York Times,* 8 May 1989.

48. *Christian Science Monitor,* 12 June 1989.

CHAPTER 18

Impact on Education

Munir Fasheh

INTRODUCTION

Education has played two principal but opposing roles in the Palestinian experience. On one hand, education has been used by Israel as a tool to control the Palestinians under its domination. But on the other hand, education, both formal and informal, has been used by the Palestinians as a means to survive, to develop, and to express their identity and their rights. We will come across these two roles in various places in this chapter.

With respect to education, there are four main segments of the Palestinian people who came under Israeli domination. First, the Palestinians who remained in the part of Palestine that was occupied by Zionist forces in 1948 – the part that is now known as Israel. Second, the Palestinians who live in the part of Palestine known as the West Bank. Third, the Palestinians who live in what is now known as the Gaza Strip. And fourth, the Palestinians who live in east Jerusalem. These last three regions came under Israeli domination in 1967.

There are of course characteristics and aspects pertaining to education that are peculiar to each of the four regions, but there are also certain characteristics common to all four. Later in the chapter, I will point out some of these common characteristics.

The following table gives a general idea of the distribution of Palestinian students in the different regions. No separate statistics for east Jerusalem have been published since its annexation by Israel in 1967. However, the Palestinian population of east Jerusalem was estimated at about 82,000 in 1973 and at over 110,000 in 1981.

TABLE 18.1

	1973/74		1977/78	
	Total Population	**Number of Students**	**Total Population**	**Number of Students**
West Bank (excluding eat Jerusalem)	646,200	207,729	681,200	240,009
Gaza Strip	406,300	123,556	441,300	141,401
Palestinians in Israel/ east Jerusalem	497,200	131,000	—	—

SOURCE: Based on information from Khalil Mahshi, *Some Aspects of the Educational Conditions in the Palestinian areas Occupied in 1967* (Bir Zeit University, 1981, in Arabic), pp. 14-18; and Sami Mari, *Arab Education in Israel* (Syracuse N.Y.: Syracuse University Press, 1978), pp. 20,22.

Thus almost one third of the Palestinian population are students. It is also worth noting that Palestinians under twenty years of age represented 58 percent of the total Palestinian population in 1978.

Mainly, in this chapter I will discuss the impact of Israeli occupation on education in the West Bank. The situation in the other three regions will be discussed briefly. There are several reasons for this. First, the space allotted does not permit for an in-depth and detailed discussion of all the regions. Second, discussing the situation in one region will shed light on the overall situation. Third, the West Bank has been more "active" educationally. And fourth, securing statistical data and conducting studies in any of the four regions, especially in the public schools, is extremely difficult, almost impossible. So in many instances I have had to depend on personal experience and first-hand knowledge in describing and analyzing the impact of occupation on education and on the people directly involved with education. In this regard I am much more familiar with the West Bank than with any of the other regions. I have lived there almost all my life: I passed all my school years there, and later worked there in education for many years in various positions and settings (including fifteen years of teaching at all levels – elementary, secondary, teachers' institutes and universities; five years as head supervisor of math instruction and director of in-service training courses in the West Bank region, which includes over 800 schools; two years as dean of students at Bir Zeit University in the West Bank; and work in informal settings related to education such as summer programs for children, community programs, and adult education).

The schools in the West Bank and Gaza are of three types: public, UNRWA, and private. Public schools comprise 77 percent of the schools in the West Bank and 40 percent in the Gaza Strip; UNRWA schools comprise 9 percent of the schools in the West Bank and 47 percent in the Gaza Strip; and private schools comprise the remaining 14 percent in the West Bank and 13 percent in the Gaza Strip.[1]

EDUCATION IN THE ARAB SECTOR IN ISRAEL

Historically, the first Palestinians to come under Israeli control were those who stayed in that part of Palestine occupied by Zionist forces in 1948. They "became overnight a minority in their own land. . . . Forced

---

1. Khalil Mahshi, *Some Aspects of the Educational Conditions in the Palestinian Areas Occupied in 1967* (Bir Zeit: Bir Zeit University, 1981, in Arabic), p. 2.

rcsidential segregation was carried out until 1967 as part of state policy, restricting the geographic areas where Arabs could live as well as the hours during which they could circulate."[2] Education for this segment of the Palestinian people has been controlled by the Department of Arab Education (a department within the Ministry of Education and Culture in Israel), which has always been run by Israeli Jews. Khalil Nakhleh, an Israeli Palestinian Arab who studied in Arab schools in Israel, asserts in his book *Palestinian Dilemma,* written while he was a visiting lecturer at the University of Haifa, Israel, that "the politization of the Israeli Department of Arab Education is so abrasive that it permeates every level from the elementary grades to the teachers' college. Blatantly and openly, it is a means of political pressure, control and reward. In most cases, political rather than pedagogic criteria are considered paramount in hiring and firing. Furthermore, extension or withdrawal of recognition of certain Arab schools by this Department is judged by political considerations."[3]

There is no declared Israeli policy for Arab education.[4] There are no declared general goals of education for the Arabs in Israel. The Law of State Education of 1953 and later the Israeli Knesset specified the goals of education in Israel, but the goals of Arab education were not referred to at all. The Yadlin Document of 1972 was the first publication to address this issue. That was followed in 1975 with a report by a panel on Arab education which examined the situation, but failed to address the main issues and basic assumptions.

A look at the curriculum for the Arabs in Israel, especially in history, language and literature, is extremely revealing. Consider the following examples:[5]

In grades 7, 8, and 9, only 10 out of 216 class hours in history are devoted to Arab history.

In grades 9, 10, 11, and 12, the total number of hours in Arabic language is 366, Hebrew language 224, Arabic literature 366, and Hebrew literature 544. Not only must Arab students take more Hebrew literature than Arabic literature; they are required to take more Hebrew literature than

2. Arpi Hamalian, "Educating Immigrant Children in the Middle East," in Joti Bhatnagar, ed., *Educating Immigrants* (New York: St. Martin's Press, 1981), p. 166.

3. Khalil Nakhleh, *Palestinian Dilemma* (Detroit: Association of Arab-American University Graduates, 1979), p. 14.

4. See, for example, Sami Mari, *Arab Education in Israel* (Syracuse, NY: Syracuse University Press, 1978), p. 50.

5. *Ibid.,* pp. 80-85.

the Jewish students, who have to take only 512 hours during the four years. In addition, over two-thirds of the Hebrew given to Arab students is devoted to literature, almost half of which consists of Jewish religious texts (Bible, *Mishna,* and *Agada*). Yet Arab public schools in Israel offer no religion classes using Christian or Muslim religious texts for the Christian and Muslim Arab students. Further, Palestinian poets and writers are not even mentioned in the courses on Arabic literature, despite the fact that much of modern Arabic poetry has been written by Palestinians.

It is important to remember that literature, any literature, is heavily value-laden. It is also important to mention that this emphasis on Hebrew literature in Arab schools has been increasing with time.[6]

Concerning the standards and nature of the textbooks in Arab schools in Israel, Dr. Haveh Lystros-Yafeh, professor of Oriental Studies at the Hebrew University of Jerusalem, has warned of "academic, moral, and political gaps, resulting from the publication of studies about the Arabs and textbooks for Arabs compiled by writers who do not have a thorough knowledge of Arabic and have not studied the history of the Arabs or Islamic culture."[7]

EDUCATION IN THE WEST BANK AND GAZA STRIP

General Education (Preschool through High School)

The West Bank and the Gaza Strip are divided into several educational districts, each of which is headed by an Arab director of education. However, in each of the two regions there is in the military compound an officer of education, assisted by a number of people, all of whom are Israeli Jews, who is in charge of all important matters relative to education in the West Bank and the Gaza Strip. Thus, hiring, firing, books, activities, new programs, in-service courses, new school construction, etc., have all to be approved by the Israeli officer of education in the corresponding region. Only minor technical or personal issues can be handled by the local Arab directors of education.

6. *Ibid.,* p. 84.

7. *Haaretz,* 11 March 1971, as cited in Sabri Jiryis, *The Arabs in Israel* (New York and London: Monthly Review Press, 1976), p. 279.

While it had taken Israel several years to figure out how to deal with education for the Arabs in Israel, that was not the case with regard to the West Bank and Gaza.[8] When these areas were occupied in 1967, Israel had the experience of nineteen years behind her. Immediately Israel annexed east Jerusalem and imposed its own syllabus on the schools there (although later it had to back down and allow schools to use the syllabus they saw fit). The next step was the banning of textbooks in the West Bank and the Gaza Strip.[9] On August 9, 1967, a military order was issued banning 78 out of 121 textbooks that had been officially approved by the Ministry of Education in Jordan for use in all the schools in Jordan, including those in the West Bank and east Jerusalem. As a result of this and as an expression of opposition to the Israeli occupation, teachers and students declared a general strike. A bitter struggle followed in which many administrators, teachers, and students (including the director of education in Jerusalem and his assistant and the director of education in Ramallah) were jailed, mistreated, threatened, or deported. However, in early November, 1967, under various kinds of pressures, a compromise was reached: 59 of the 78 banned textbooks were reprinted with some modifications; teachers and students who had been arrested were released; and the schools were reopened. By mid-November 1967, more than five months after Israel occupied the West Bank, the schools were again functioning.

The justification Israel offered for the changes and omissions in textbooks was the "anti-Semitic content"[10] of the material in question. But a look at the actual changes and deletions makes it clear that, in most cases, "anti-Semitic material" meant anything that linked the Arabs and Muslims to Palestine and expressed Palestinian feelings, identity, experience, and history. Some examples will help clarify this. Statements referring to Arab unity were omitted, as were statements expressing cooperation between Muslim and Christian Arabs (in the textbooks entitled *Al Watan Al Arabi* for

8. The number of students who were evacuated, along with their families, from the West Bank, and who were absorbed by the schools in the east bank (Jordan), was 48,343, according to the *Year Book of Educational Statistics in Jordan for the Year 1967/68*. More than 150,000 persons, including all the inhabitants of the two refugee camps Ain al-Sultan and Aqbat Jaber in Jericho, were expelled to the east bank by the Israeli Army in June 1967.

9. For more details see Najla Bashur, "Changes in School Curricula in the West Bank since 1967" (in Arabic), *Shuun Filastiniya* (July 1971), p. 229.

10. See, for example, "Coordinator of Government Operations In Judea-Samaria (i.e., the West Bank], Gaza District, Sinai – A Fourteen-Year Survey (1967-81)" published by Israel's Ministry of Defense (April 1982), p. 20.

the eleventh and twelfth grades, for instance). The Arab resistance to the Crusaders and the defense of Palestine by Saladin in the Middle Ages were omitted (pages 69 and 83 in the history textbook for the fifth grade). The steadfastness of Port Said against the 1956 attack on Egypt by Britain, France, and Israel was omitted from page 22 in the history textbook for the sixth grade. Many sentences, sections, and poems, especially in history and religious textbooks, were either omitted or replaced. The question, "Where is Saladin's tomb?" for example, was replaced by "Where is the Mediterranean?" The sentence in the grammar book for the seventh grade, "Our unity will frighten the enemy," was replaced by "Our success will please our parents." The poem entitled "Beautiful Jaffa"; the visit of the Prophet Muhammad to Jerusalem; and even the fact that the tomb of Hussein Ben Ali (King Hussein's great-grandfather) is in Jerusalem, were omitted. And as was mentioned earlier, anything that referred to Palestine or the Palestinians as well as any reference to what happened in 1948 or before 1948 was omitted. Apparently the Israelis hoped that by erasing such events from the history books, they could also erase them from human memory.

In fact, much information that needed revision was kept unchanged. In the sixth-grade geography textbook that was still in use in West Bank schools as recently as 1977 – the last time I had a look at the book – Libya still figured as a kingdom dependent on cattle-rearing as its main source of livelihood!

With respect to this issue I would like to mention a comment by one of the assistants to the Israeli officer of education, who tried to convince me, in 1976, that the hostility towards Israel on the part of Palestinian students in the West Bank and Gaza was a result of the "propaganda" they had been exposed to in the textbooks used in those regions. It was amazing how completely he failed – and probably still fails – to perceive what was happening under occupation and to see that, since the Israelis had taken control of the curriculum, opposition among Palestinian students to Israeli policies and practices had increased. For example, the number of students who were killed, wounded, arrested, or tortured in the spring of 1982 exceeded the corresponding number for the preceding ten years.

In addition to these problems with textbooks, facilities in West Bank and Gaza schools are in generally poor condition. The last academic year that saw a full-time librarian or a full-time or part-time lab technician in any of the schools in the West Bank was 1975-76. That year, there was only one full-time librarian, at a girls' school in Bethlehem, and one lab technician, at a boys' school in Hebron. Moreover, the vast majority of school libraries and laboratories, where they exist, are in such pitiful condition as to be useless. As a simple example, one rarely finds lists of books recommended for purchase by schools; instead one finds lists of books that are banned. Forbidden books – over two thousand titles in 1981 – are mostly works on the religion and history of the Arabs and the Muslims, such as the Islamic dictionary; but many books by foreign writers and poets, such as Pablo Neruda, are also banned. Books written by Palestinians, whether from inside or outside the occupied territories, are of course forbidden.

While the educational system was deficient in many ways prior to 1967, most of these deficiencies have been aggravated, rather than improved, under occupation. Three issues in particular stand out: salaries, the *tawjihi* or general exam, and the bias in favor of the purely academic track as opposed to vocational and technical training.

The salaries of people working in public education in the West Bank and Gaza have ranged between the equivalent of $95 and $220 per month. (During the five years that I worked in public schools, 1973-1978, my salary fluctuated between $150 and $190 per month.) On December 13, 1980, the teachers of the West Bank declared a general strike demanding an increase in their salaries. (Teachers' unions are not allowed in the West Bank and Gaza.) The strike lasted several months. Neither Israel nor Jordan wanted the strike to succeed, each for its own reasons; but one reason in common was the fear that if the strike did succeed it would encourage teachers in both Israel and Jordan to demand higher salaries, and would, in addition, give power to the teachers. Different ways were used to exert pressure on teachers to break the strike and to discourage them from striking again. One peculiar line of attack was the use of grades on the general exam, the *tawjihi*, which affects the students' admission to universities, as part of a psychological war on the teachers. The scores on the exam that year, 1981, were very low compared with other years. After the results were published, the general military governor of the West Bank went on television to blame the teachers' strike for the low scores. Now, it may or may not be true that the strike affected what and how much the students knew, but it is a well-known fact that grades on general exams such as the *tawjihi* are never meant or claimed to be a measure of what students know, but rather a measure of the relative standing of students in comparison with each other. In addition, it is also known that the published grades of the students in the West Bank are worked out and agreed upon between the examination committee in the West Bank and the examination committee in Jordan, and that in many cases averages are raised or lowered arbitrarily, for various reasons. Clearly, the strike was fingered as the cause of the low scores for political, rather than educational, reasons.

Another incident that will further clarify the way students and their families are manipulated through the grading system on the general exam occurred in 1975. I and two other persons wrote the questions in math for the general exam in the West Bank for that year. One question was not in precisely the same form that the students were familiar with, but was within the knowledge they had. There was an angry uproar by students. This was understandable, because of the importance of grades to be accepted in universities. That anger was used, however, by different individuals and groups to attack those who put the questions. The attacks were vicious and unrealistic. I felt it necessary to write an article in a local newspaper to explain, among other things, that such a question does not affect the relative standing of the students and thus does not affect the grades they finally receive on their transcripts. I was then accused of revealing secret information about the educational system. As a result, a hearing was scheduled, and a three-person committee chosen by the officer of education questioned me. I received a warning and an order forbidding me from writing in any newspaper. That order remained in effect until I left the Department of Education in 1978.

One additional point concerning the *tawjihi* should be mentioned. Starting in 1978, general questions on every subject were distributed by the departments of education at least four months before the exam, both in Jordan and in the West Bank. The writers of the questions on the exams were instructed to choose half of the questions exactly as they had appeared in these general questions, and in the other half to make only minor changes. At most one question could be different from the set of questions distributed to students. Rote and meaningless learning has never been treated better anywhere in the world!

The third problem area that I mentioned earlier is the bias towards the pure academic track in the high schools of the West Bank and the Gaza Strip, which has been slightly increasing rather than decreasing since 1967. The following table compares the number and percentages of students who took the *tawjihi* in 1969 and 1977:

TABLE 18.2

	1969		1977	
	No.	%	No.	%
Literary	3,021	60.4	5,398	65.0
Scientific	1,780	35.6	2,655	32.0
Vocational	137	2.7	171	2.1
Commercial	37	.7	57	.7
Agricultural	24	.5	19	.2
TOTAL	4,999	100.0	8,300	100.0

SOURCE: Rihan and Mahshi in Emile Nakhleh (1980).

It is both significant and revealing to compare the above figures with what has happened in Jordan since 1967. The percentage of students in the vocational stream in Jordan rose from less than 3 percent in 1967 to over 15 percent in 1980. Vocational schools in Jordan have been equipped with adequate workshops. In contrast, the only public vocational school in the West Bank with acceptable workshops is the one that was established in Nablus under Jordanian administration. A community college has been established in almost every district in Jordan since 1967, while not a single one has been established in the West Bank or Gaza. What is more, in 1977 Khalil Abu Rayya, a Palestinian Arab from Ramallah, donated a large building to the Ramallah municipality. The municipality decided to start a technological institute (polytechnic) beyond the high school level. The plan, the money, and the necessary technical assistance were ready. The Israeli military government objected and suggested instead that the building be used as an academic-track high school. The municipality refused on the grounds that there were already about eight such high schools in Ramallah – a town with a population of less than 20,000 people. Today, not only is the building not in use; not only is there no technological institute in Ramallah – there is no longer a municipality in Ramallah. (At least seven major municipalities were dismantled in the West Bank and Gaza Strip during the early months of 1982.)

Among the Palestinian Arabs in Israel, fewer than 10 percent of the middle and high school students are enrolled in vocational-technological educational programs, compared with about 50 percent of Jewish students in middle and high schools enrolled in such programs.[11]

The steadily declining interest in the agricultural track among youngsters in the West Bank and Gaza Strip is mainly due to the facts that most of the cultivable land in these two regions has been confiscated by Israel since 1967, and that water in these regions is under Israeli control, making an agricultural career futile.

Worse yet, the academic tracks, which thus absorb the vast majority of youngsters, are of very poor quality. Both the literary and the scientific tracks are useful only in helping students get accepted in universities. Students in these tracks do not learn any skills or acquire any important knowledge to help them in their careers and their lives. Since only a small percentage of these students finally enroll in universities, the majority of students in the West Bank and Gaza receive nothing useful, to themselves or to their communities, from the educational systems in their regions.

From 1967 through this writing (October 1982), the department of education has not sent a single teacher or educator from the public education

---

11. Mari, *Arab Education in Israel*, p. 22.

sector in the West Bank or Gaza to study abroad on scholarship. Educational reforms that took place in the 1960s in other parts of the world, including the Arab countries, have found no parallel in the occupied territories, and the department of education has offered no training courses for the teachers in these areas. The first attempt to introduce some change in the curriculum was a two-year course organized by Bir Zeit University for all high school math teachers in the West Bank and east Jerusalem (a total of 215 teachers). A similar course organized by Bir Zeit University in 1976 for high-school math teachers in Gaza was ordered canceled by the Israeli authorities four days prior to the opening date. The reason given was that "Bir Zeit has nothing to do with Gaza." (In fact, prior to that, early in 1974, Bir Zeit had been told to stop offering courses for teachers in the West Bank.) That same year (1976), a request to use Bir Zeit University's laboratories for an in-service course for high school physics teachers was rejected by the Israeli officer of education because, he claimed, Bir Zeit is a "political institution." When I told him that the facilities of a university were needed and that I didn't care whether it was Bir Zeit or the Hebrew University or the University of Jordan, he said, "Write me a letter proposing the University of Jordan, and I'll look into it."

In September 1973 a new office – the Technical Education Office – was established by the Israelis in Ramallah to take charge of all in-service courses for the West Bank. No equivalent office was established in Gaza. I worked in that office for five years in charge of math instruction and in-service courses; for a few months I was acting director of the office. Through my work there, I had a chance to come into close contact with some of the realities of education in the West Bank. In addition to the points I have mentioned earlier, I learned that occupation is not the only authority opposing change and development in the West Bank. When, for example, a course for first-grade math teachers was proposed in 1974, both the Israeli officer and the Arab directors opposed it. The Israelis opposed it mainly for financial reasons, because it implied the printing of the new textbook (in color) that had been adopted in Jordan and Syria. (In fact, when the new syllabus was finally adopted two years later, the Israeli officer asked to have the books printed in black and white.) The Arab directors, on the other hand, initially opposed the course out of a conviction that first-grade math does not require training.

In my capacity as acting director of the Technical Educational Office, in 1976 I proposed a conference to discuss education in the West Bank – a very legitimate concern for any person in that position, I thought. I earned a warning from the Israeli officer and scorn from the president of one teachers' training center; but the other Arab directors agreed. The conference, however, never took place.

A suggestion to create a few positions for school counselors in the various districts was encouraged by the Israeli officer but opposed by the majority of Arab directors. Again no such positions were created.

My years at the Technical Educational Office also taught me that it is extremely hard to effect real changes – changes in attitudes, values, and relationships – through the formal curriculum and the formal structure. Gradually I became strongly convinced of the importance of informal forms, structures, and activities in education. One informal activity that attracted the interest of many students and teachers was setting up math and science clubs in schools. The main objective of such clubs was to provide a free atmosphere and an opportunity and encouragement for interested students to perform experiments and gather information and data about topics they were interested in. The strong positive reaction of many students (most of whom were between 15 and 17 years of age) was surprising to everybody. Their enthusiasm, questions, and ability to organize, work together, and follow up and conduct discussions on different topics and issues were extremely exciting and interest-generating. However, when the idea was first discussed in schools, most principals and teachers thought it would not succeed without incentives for both teachers (such as reduced loads or more pay) and students (such as grades). In addition, while male students were very enthusiastic, female students were initially more cautious and critical, though also very interested.

What actually happened was very revealing. The clubs ceased to exist in boys' schools a few months after they were established – exactly as predicted by the principals and most teachers. But, contrary to all expectations, they continued to flourish in some girls' schools for almost two years, and in the end, external pressure was needed to stop them. The Israeli authorities started to interrogate and harass the students and teachers who were involved in the clubs; and some fanatic conservatives in the Arab population started to verbally attack the clubs and people working in them. The Israelis claimed that the clubs were used as a cover for illegal gatherings and subversive activities and thus caused a "security" problem – the usual reason that Israel gives to justify its action. The fanatic conservatives, on the other hand, claimed that the clubs were corrupting the youth and spreading "foreign" ideas and "radical" attitudes. I was puzzled for a while, because I knew exactly what was going on in these clubs; none of the accusations was true. But then I realized that encouraging youngsters to think freely and critically and to question things honestly is very dangerous to any authority. For the first time, I faced in action the fact that teaching is basically a political activity: it either helps "unveil reality," as Freire puts it, and creates new attitudes, values, and intellectual models that will help students understand and be critical about what is going on around them and confident that they can go beyond existing structures; or it produces students who are passive, rigid, timid, alienated, and lacking in self-esteem.

Teachers who helped in the clubs were not paid extra and their loads were not reduced; but they had a strong urge to "do things for others." This positive attitude – to volunteer to do things for and with others – occurred again and again among people from different walks of life in the West Bank in that period. It seems that the sense of isolation created by life under occupation increased the urge for cooperation, responsibility, and solidarity. These qualities found more room for expression in "informal" settings and forms than in formal ones. In addition to the math and science clubs, other types of "informal" education flourished in the West Bank, especially in the period between 1972 and 1977; they included community-oriented voluntary work groups, theatrical and folkloric groups, children's programs, publication of books and magazines,[12] women's groups and organizations, health care projects, and adult education (eradication of illiteracy). Here I am using the expression "informal education" in a wider and more comprehensive sense than is usual in Western societies, where it usually refers to acquiring new skills or new technical knowledge, primarily for the purpose of getting a better job.[13] The informal forms of education that flourished in the West Bank between 1972 and 1977 came mainly as a reaction to two things: first, against the useless and detached knowledge given in the formal educational settings; and second, as a result of the motivating force generated by the rise of the Palestinian national consciousness, which started to develop strongly and rapidly after 1967 in Palestinian communities everywhere.

These informal forms of education were fascinating and very moving.[14] They attracted many people (especially youngsters) strongly, and as I

12. In the period between 1973 and 1978, six magazines on teaching mathematics and four on teaching science were published in the West Bank on a voluntary and self-sustaining basis. Expenses were covered by selling copies to interested teachers and students. On the average, about 4,000 copies of each issue were printed and sold.

13. See, for example, E. Owens and R. Shaw, *Development Reconsidered* (Lexington, Mass.: Lexington Books, 1973), p. 126.

14. Television, however, is one type of informal education that has had a generally bad effect upon youngsters, interfering with evening social gatherings among neighbors and relatives, which had been the main source of horizontal communication. In a study that started in 1978 and was never finished, a group of eight people tried to examine the thoughts of children aged six to twelve. In response to one of many questions, "Who are your heroes?", the children usually began with TV figures. In areas where televisions were not common, however, Palestinian personalities were given as heroes.

mentioned earlier, generated feelings of cooperation and solidarity among individuals and among groups in different places. The Israeli authorities are very sensitive about any feelings of cooperation among the Palestinians, and especially among different regions. In January 1976, for example, the officer of education sent a memo to all the schools in the West Bank forbidding them to cooperate with any voluntary group. Many clubs and groups were dismantled and many projects were ordered canceled by the military governor. In 1980 alone, four work projects – in Gaza, Hebron, Jericho, and Jenin – that had been organized by the Community Work Committee in Bir Zeit University in collaboration with the municipalities, were canceled by the military governor.

I have not yet mentioned pre-elementary education, which is little developed in the West Bank and Gaza. There are some private organizations and individuals, both local and foreign, that run special programs for this age group, but they cover only a very small percentage of the preschool children in the West Bank and Gaza. In 1980/81, UNICEF allocated money to establish pre-elementary centers throughout the West Bank. This gave rise to an argument between Israel and UNICEF over who should get the money: Israel, or local organizations and institutions. Exactly how that issue was resolved I don't know. An Arab woman was appointed director of the project but found herself working for the military officer for social welfare; she never received any money, was able to accomplish nothing, and eventually resigned.

INSTITUTES OF HIGHER EDUCATION

The situation in postsecondary education is no better than in the earlier grades. (See also chapter 17.) The first attempt to establish a Palestinian university came from a Palestinian family in Jerusalem in the 1940s. But this proposal, submitted to the British Mandate authorities who were occupying Palestine at the time, was rejected. The events of 1948, which resulted in the dispersal of the Palestinian people, postponed the fulfillment of this need until 1951, when Bir Zeit, then a high school, decided to add classes beyond the secondary level. It started the first such class that year, but was unable to add the second until 1961. In 1962, Bir Zeit College was recognized by many universities, including the American University of Beirut, and its students were able to transfer directly to these universities without any difficulty. That was satisfactory at the time. In addition to Bir Zeit College, seven other institutions of education beyond high school (mainly teachers' training colleges) were in existence in the West Bank and Gaza prior to 1967.

The 1967 War created new conditions. For example, it became more difficult for students from the West Bank and Gaza to study abroad, mainly because of financial considerations and travel restrictions (one such restriction forbids any male between the ages of sixteen and twenty-six who leaves the West Bank for Jordan, to return for at least six months.) In addition, the demand for higher education among the Palestinians in general (both inside and outside Palestine) increased tremendously after 1967. Because of the loss of most of their land, which was the means of livelihood of the majority of Palestinians, they increasingly turned to the only thing that was left for them to invest in – their minds. It is not uncommon to find many members of a Palestinian family working to support a brother or sister studying in a university. This also explains why the number of university graduates among the Palestinians relative to their population is one of the highest in the world, possibly the third highest.[15] Unfortunately, however, in the absence of a Palestinian state, Palestinian higher education is not geared to the needs and interests of the Palestinians as much as to the needs of individuals and other countries.

Given the importance of education to the Palestinian community, the Israeli administration's disruptive tactics aimed at education – tactics that would pose a threat to any community – are of particularly grave concern.

These conditions (financial difficulties, travel restrictions, loss of land, etc.) put tremendous pressures on different groups and organizations to establish universities in the occupied areas. In 1972 Bir Zeit decided to expand. Bethlehem University was established in 1973, followed by Najah University in 1975. Later, al-Quds (Jerusalem) University was formed as an "umbrella" university comprising three existing colleges: the Nursing College in al-Bireh, the Scientific Institute in Abu-Dis, and the College of Religious and Islamic Studies in Beit Hanina. In addition, a technical college and a religious college were established in Hebron, and the Islamic University was founded in Gaza. In general, the Israeli authorities did not initially oppose the establishment of such institutions, possibly hoping that students with university degrees would leave the West Bank and Gaza to seek jobs outside.

In order to coordinate the work among these universities and institutions of higher learning in the West Bank and Gaza, the Council for Higher Education was established in the late 1970s. Its members included administrators in the different universities, professionals, and religious and

15. See, for example, M. Hallaj in Emile Nakhleh, ed., *A Palestinian Agenda for the West Bank and Gaza* (Washington, D.C.: American Enterprise Institute for Public Policy Research, 1980), and Mari, *Arab Education in Israel,* p. 109.

national figures. The council, however, is still struggling to establish itself as a viable body for higher learning in the West Bank and Gaza.

In addition to other positive effects of the universities in the West Bank and Gaza, one very important effect was to open the doors of university education to students from poor families and to women, mainly because of the relatively low expense and easy accessibility.

But, while it is true that higher education has advanced in the West Bank, it has advanced much more in the east bank (Jordan) in terms of student enrollment and diversity of fields offered. In addition to community colleges and liberal arts colleges, schools in almost all professional fields (medicine, engineering, agriculture, etc.) have been established in Jordan, while only two professional schools, engineering and nursing, have been established in the West Bank. Requests to send student-teachers for training in public schools have been turned down by Israeli authorities (Bir Zeit was permitted to send its students for two years, then was ordered to stop). Students "in the Nursing and Social Work program at Bethlehem University were not allowed to do practical training at the Hussein Hospital in nearby Beit Jala."[16] Requests from universities to conduct research and studies concerning education in the public sector have also been denied.[17] Universities of the West Bank and Gaza cannot get periodicals and find it extremely hard to obtain books from Arab countries. Laboratory and other educational equipment and materials are taxed (up to 100 percent of their value), although both Jordanian and Israeli law exempt educational institutions from taxes; Bir Zeit, for example, was exempted from paying Jordanian taxes before 1967.

Such harassment did not take place only under the Begin government and after Camp David, although it intensified under the conditions created by them. In 1974, Bir Zeit University was closed and its president, Dr. Hanna Nasser (a physicist educated at Indiana's Purdue University), together with four other persons from the West Bank, were blindfolded and deported in the middle of the night to Lebanon.

Running an educational institution under such conditions is, to say the least, not easy. No plan or schedule can hope to survive for more than a month at the most. Extending the semester or teaching during holidays is common and that, of course, disrupts everyone's plans, both personal and professional.

16. Naseer Aruri, "Repression In Academia: Palestinian Universities versus the Israeli Military," *Arab Perspectives* (April 1981), 2: 14-19.

17. K. Mahshi of the department of education at Bir Zeit University, for instance, had to conduct his study on cognitive development in private rather than public schools — thus his sample was unfortunately not truly representative of West Bank youngsters.

It is extremely difficult for someone who has never left the West Bank or Gaza to imagine academic life devoid of jails, demonstrations, beatings, closures, and harassment. Being an educator in the West Bank or Gaza (or a mayor or in any other responsible position) is a very difficult and painful job. Again an example (although it hurts me to describe it) may help illustrate the point. On one occasion of national significance, the Palestinian flag was raised on top of the cafeteria building at Bir Zeit University. The army surrounded the village, and the military governor called the acting president and demanded "immediate removal of the flag if the university wants to avoid the consequences." The acting president asked me in my capacity as dean of students to try to do something. For some reason I felt that it would save the university and everybody in it a "storming" by the army if the flag were removed. I climbed to the top of the building and pulled the flag down. I will never forget the looks in the eyes of the students who were standing around the building. I had never felt so shattered inside. I went to my office and looked at the flag more closely: the pole was made of a dry olive branch and the flag itself of ragged pieces of cloth in the four colors, sewn together loosely. I wondered, "Is it possible that these ragged pieces of cloth provoked the strongest and most sophisticated army in the region?!"

I don't know exactly why I took the action I did, although certainly I was influenced by what had taken place almost a year earlier when, on a similar occasion, several students had been shot, one in his lower jaw. When this student's condition worsened we contacted some French academicians in Paris. They were very concerned and arranged through the French government to cover all the student's expenses for travel, surgery, and a stay in France. The student, however, decided to postpone the trip for a few months until he graduated. Meanwhile he was arrested again, and I have no idea what has happened to him since.

The Situation in Jerusalem

Israel annexed east Jerusalem immediately after the 1967 War, and imposed on its schools the syllabus for Arab schools in Israel (the one referred to in the section on Arab education in Israel in this chapter). The Arab inhabitants and students in east Jerusalem opposed the change. Many students in public schools transferred to east Jerusalem's private schools, which were later allowed to choose their own syllabus. Some students enrolled in schools in the nearby towns of Ramallah and Bethlehem, but this became impossible after 1976, when a new military order was issued forbidding this practice. The Israeli syllabus was finally abandoned in the junior- and high-school levels in east Jerusalem in the mid-seventies. Despite this shift back to the Jordanian syllabus, the trend towards private schools in east Jerusalem has continued, mainly because services and conditions are much better than in public schools. Qualified teachers, for example, are much more scarce in east Jerusalem public schools than in the West Bank. There is no doubt that, in this and other respects, since 1967 the private schools in east Jerusalem have played and continue to play a vital role for the Arab inhabitants of the city.

This discussion of Arab education in Jerusalem will of necessity be brief and inadequate, because, unfortunately, very little information has been gathered and very few studies conducted about the effects of Israeli occupation on the Palestinian children in east Jerusalem. The special status of east Jerusalem – annexation by Israel; daily contact with Israelis; the dual "official" belonging of the inhabitants to both Israel and Jordan; the feeling of the inhabitants that they are part of the Palestinian people – has made the impact of occupation much deeper in east Jerusalem, and has left its special marks on the minds and hearts of its inhabitants.

One of the rare articles I have seen on this subject was an unpublished account by an American teacher who taught art in one of the private schools in east Jerusalem during 1980/81. "With nearly 600 students aged 6- 12 on my hands," that teacher wrote, "I had endless drawings appear before my eyes every day. . . . When I asked a child one day to draw a zoo, and he drew a small monkey cage with an elaborate Palestinian flag with a Star of David in its center, I had my first encounter with the issues which preoccupied my students' minds. . . . These issues were not easily articulated in words. . . . In drawing . . . the boys discovered a magical means of uninhibited self-expression."[18] Drawing and symbols provided a means for them to express concretely their Palestinian feelings.

When young children, both Christian and Muslim, were asked to draw their country, the dominant themes that appeared were the Palestinian flag and the Dome of the Rock – one of the holiest Muslim shrines in the world.

In many instances, the children would draw a Palestinian flag with a Star of David inside or outside it and the word *Filastin* (Palestine) in Arabic script on top of or inside it. These "six-year-old students' drawings innocently proved that their sense of nationality had been injected with a heavy dose of the Israeli occupation." We have to remember that these children were born after Israel occupied east Jerusalem in 1967. They have never seen a Palestinian flag raised on a real pole – a serious crime under

18. Suzan Kerr, "The Socialization of Palestinian Children in East Jerusalem under Israeli Occupation: Case Study of an East Jerusalem School" (unpublished paper, February, 1982).

Israeli occupation – while they see the Israeli flag and symbols displayed everywhere. In fact, the only Palestinian flags publicly displayed in all of Palestine today are two flags that were engraved in 1931 on the western wall of the compound enclosing the Dome of the Rock and Haram al-Sharif Mosque in Jerusalem.

Other themes expressed in the childrens' drawings were "expressions of imprisonment, abandonment, immobility, and resignation. ... Again and again, a drawing will show the sun in the sky and it looks down over the scene below; the sun is either frowning, crying, or turning its face away. The sun is used by the 'artist' as a judge over the events taking place in the picture."

One drawing showed the Damascus Gate in the Old City of Jerusalem immersed in blue water. Drawings of the cross, the crescent, and two Palestinian flags on top of the gate were sinking with the gate. The head of Begin and the Israeli flag were drawn above the water. The words, "Help us! Jerusalem is sinking," were written on the drawing.

The situation of the Palestinian Arabs in Israel with regard to higher education is even worse: they have never been allowed to establish an independent institution of higher learning, although there has been a constant need for such an institution. In 1981 Israel rejected a request to establish a university in Nazareth; a community college is now in formation in the same town. Arab students make up about 3.5 percent of the student population of Israeli universities, although Arabs comprise about 15 percent of the total population of Israel.[19] In addition, Arabs in Israel seeking to enroll in West Bank universities encounter many difficulties from the Israeli authorities.

CONCLUSION

The Palestinians have always been an obstacle to the Zionist dream of establishing a "pure" Jewish state in Palestine. The Zionists, and later Israel and its supporters, have tried to make the Palestinians invisible, or at best insignificant.[20] They have tried to convince themselves and the world that

19. Mari, *Arab Education in Israel,* p. 106.

20. The British Balfour Declaration of 1917, for example, was in harmony with this policy when it referred to the Palestinians as "non-Jewish communities," despite the fact that at the time they made up 93% of the population of Palestine. This is like referring to the majority of the inhabitants of New York City as "non-Puerto-Rican communities." And as late as 1969, Israeli Prime Minister Golda Meir told the London *Sunday Times* (15 July 1969) that there was "no such thing as a Palestinian."

Palestine was empty. "Give the land without people to the people without land," was one of the Zionists' slogans. "Making the desert green" was another. The ignorant actually believed the slogans; those more knowledgeable wished that the Palestinians did not exist and actively sought to make that wish come true.

But the Palestinians existed, and still do. They were there, constituting a people with developed towns and villages, with cultivated lands, and with a heritage and culture they were proud of and happy with. Instead of accepting that fact and working within that reality, the Zionists, Israel, and its supporters went along with their plans to try to eliminate everything Palestinian. The attempt to transform that wish into reality has thus been the central theme of Israel's policies towards the Palestinians. It is impossible to understand the past and future prospects of Palestinian-Israeli relations without keeping this fact in mind. Israel's educational policies toward the Palestinians, at all times and in all regions, have been consistent with this overall policy. The attempt at what Noam Chomsky calls a "cultural genocide"[21] lies at the core of Israel's educational policies.

Although Israel's policy in action is clear and consistent, its *official* policy has been consistently and deliberately ambiguous. This ambiguity "has helped the system of control serve the ideological ends of Zionism while reaping propaganda benefits for Israel among liberal circles abroad."[22] The invisibility of the Palestinian Arabs in Israel is an aim in action. "Writing in 1975 in *Davar,* the official organ of the Labor Party-controlled Histadrut (General Federation of Israeli Workers), one Israeli journalist observed that 'during the last decade there has been no discussion in the Cabinet on the subject of the Israeli Arabs.' A major text concerning the Arab-Israeli conflict published in 1972 included a lengthy section in which Israel's domestic political structure and problems were discussed. The piece, written by one of the foremost scholars in the field, contained no mention whatsoever of Israel's Arab minority."[23]

21. This threat of "cultural genocide" was one of the main reasons behind the PLO's decision to establish the Palestine Open University in Beirut, which was destroyed by the Israelis when they invaded the city in 1982 in violation of the cease-fire agreement. At the same time they looted the Palestine Research Center there.

22. Ian Lustick, *Arabs in the Jewish State: Israel's Control of a National Minority* (Austin and London: University of Texas Press, 1980), p. 268.

23. *Ibid., pp.* 4-5.

In the eighty pages of a report on education for the Arabs in Israel,[24] the word "Palestinian" appears only once. When some Arab members of the committee who wrote that report suggested "love of the homeland" as a goal of education for the Arabs, the Jewish members of the committee refused. Finally, a compromise was reached: "love of the common homeland."

The situation is no different in the West Bank and Gaza. In 1976, while I was acting director of the Technical Education Office in Ramallah, I sent the officer of education a copy of a book about school libraries to be recommended to school libraries in the West Bank.[25] The book was rejected. Asked for the reason, the officer's assistant mentioned two words as being objectionable. The words appeared in the titles of two books suggested, among hundreds of other books, for school libraries: *Tales from Palestine* and *A Lover from Palestine*. When I asked if blocking out the word "Palestine" in the two titles would solve the problem, the assistant replied in the affirmative. But early next morning he called and said, "You can recommend the book without covering the words." No doubt the authorities had realized that covering the two words would only draw more attention to them.

While visiting a school in Tulkarem in 1978, the officer of education noticed a small map of Palestine hanging on the wall with the word "Palestine" on it. The principal of the school was immediately summoned before the military governor of Tulkarem. Defending himself, the principal said, "I swear by the Great God that I didn't make it; it was made in Great Britain in 1942."

This is not unlike what has happened at other places and at other times throughout history, most notably to the American Indians.

But the policy to destroy Palestinian national consciousness, culture, heritage, and history, and to create a helpless people, has not succeeded. In fact, it has backfired. Palestinian national consciousness is now probably one of the most developed, best articulated, and most strongly felt in the world. The works of Palestinian poets and writers, eliminated from the school curriculum, are read and recited all the more often everywhere else. The Palestinian flag, outlawed in the West Bank and Gaza, has been raised in Tel Aviv (as was the case in April 1982 in a demonstration against Israel's policies in the West Bank, and in more than one demonstration against the

24. Israel Ministry of Education and Culture, Department of Education, Panel on Planning Arab Education, "Project for the Planning of Education for the 'Eighties," (in Arabic and Hebrew; Jerusalem, 1975).

25. Mary Fasheh, *A Guide for the Teacher-Librarian* (in Arabic; Jerusalem: Salah Ed-Din Publishing House, 1976).

war in Lebanon). The attempt to blot out Palestine with Israel has merely imprinted Palestine more deeply in the hearts and minds of the Palestinians. In fact, as Perez, Ehrlich, and Yuval-Davis, in referring to the Arabs in Israel, assert in "National Education for Arab Youth in Israel": "The disregard of Arab nationalist desires in the schools of Israel will not kill such desires. The Arab students who find no solution for their difficulties in school look for, and find political leadership elsewhere."[26]

These contradictions[27] in the conditions of the Palestinians are reflected in Palestinian education, especially higher education: in the conflict between satisfying individual, non-Palestinian needs, and fulfilling national needs; between attempts to suppress Palestinian feelings and identity, and the assertion of these feelings and identity; between the heavy pressures on students to leave school as early as possible, and their need to continue their educations as long as possible; between the need to assert one's own culture, and an openness to new ideas and other cultures; between a growing conservative and religious tendency, and more secular and democratic attitudes;[28] between increasing dependence on international organizations and Arab states, and the need for more independence, autonomy, and self-reliance; between the extreme difficulty of formulating an educational policy, and the urgent need for such a policy; between the destruction of social structures necessary for nation building, and the need to weaken social taboos that hinder national development; between a loss of access to many means of survival and the need to gain access to new means of survival; and between the need to integrate higher education with national development and planning, and the need for greater autonomy of institutes of higher learning. Obviously, higher education in particular should reflect an awareness of such contradictions, and seek ways to deal with them.

Almost every Palestinian has been deeply affected by the Palestinian tragedy. Palestinian students who have grown up in the shadow of the occupation do not live in an abstract world. Their lives are filled with

26. Y. Perez, A. Ehrlich and N. Yuval-Davis, "National Education for Arab Youth in Israel: A Comparative Analysis of Curricula," *The Jewish Journal of Sociology* (1970), 12(2): 147-63.

27. The strong contradictions in the Palestinian experience have led a Palestinian writer, Emile Habibi, to coin a word in Arabic, *Mutasha'el*, which is a combination of the words for pessimist and optimist. In fact, that was the title of a very successful book by Habibi.

28. The polarization of these two tendencies (the religious and the secular) has been intensified by the rise of Khomeini in Iran. My hope is that a genuine and dynamic synthesis of the two tendencies will develop in the future among students.

events that profoundly affect their families, themselves, and their future. The impact of occupation on students is sometimes good and sometimes bad; sometimes intended, sometimes unintended. Some of the negative, intentional effects have been mentioned earlier. On the opposite side of the ledger, the raising of Palestinian consciousness and the growth of cooperation, solidarity, and participation are a few of the positive, unintentional effects. The feeling of the students that their existence has meaning and purpose and that their deeds make a difference is another such good, unplanned effect. I have watched students try to take control of their lives and of events. Their efforts, though not always successful, constitute an irreversible breakthrough in the thick military, political, and cultural walls that surround them, walls that inhibit the energies, potential, and creative forces of youth.

Yes, there have been bad moments and negative experiences. But there have also been hopeful, powerful, challenging, and exciting moments and experiences. It was such a moment when, in a matter of minutes, almost all of Bir Zeit University – administrators, faculty, staff, and students decided to march from Bir Zeit to the prison in Ramallah, where twenty-four students had been detained for over a month under the worst conditions with no charges and no trial. A few days later, the students were released.

Both types of experiences are needed by a people trying to transform their aspirations into new visions, new structures, and eventually a state.

I have watched the students in the West Bank and Gaza trying to make sense of the world and of the complex events around them. Whenever they make a real attempt to understand the world and to act on that understanding, they find themselves imprisoned: sometimes within real walls with guards wearing the Star of David on their chests who hate and fear their very existence; at other times, within the social, intellectual, and cultural structures they have grown up with. I have watched them struggle against a cruel, merciless, and indifferent world with their bare hands, sometimes with stones, sometimes with words and ideas; some with tears, others with laughter, some with prayer, others by dancing the *Dabkeh* and singing. When the occupiers' actions, official Arab inaction, and daily problems weigh too heavily on them, they turn for solace to the songs of Marcel Khalifeh and Mustafa Kurd, the lyrics of Rajeh Salfiti, the poems of Tawfiq Zayyad[29]-- songs and poems with the power to dispel some of the

---

29. Kurd is a Palestinian singer from Jerusalem who was forced to leave because of harassment. Salfiti is probably the most popular Palestinian folklore singer, or *zajjal,* who uses the traditional form for Palestinian songs but draws his content from current Palestinian issues and aspirations. Now about 65 and ailing, he has spent much of his life in prison. Khalifeh is a Lebanese singer whose songs have captured the imagination

overwhelming misery that at times afflicts the students. I have seen these students in their courageous moments and in their frightened moments. I have seen schoolgirls with rosy cheeks, not from the latest in cosmetics, but from their struggle to assert their rights. I have watched the students under occupation feeling the weight of the Arab regimes pressing on their people, while the same regimes are helpless to deal with anything threatening the Arab world. They have come to see clearly the simple truth that there really are "two Arab nations, not one."

At the same time, blind hatred has not found its way into their hearts or minds. They are constantly seeking and responding to voices that are ready for dialogue, whether these voices are Israeli, Jewish, French, American, Iranian, or Soviet. They are always sharing their hope to humanize and revolutionize their environment and they are always actively trying to realize that hope.

Immersed in fighting the ills confronting them, the students under occupation are probably not fully aware of the long-range effects of their actions and the hopeful and humanizing seeds they are helping to sow. However, their daily struggle against all types of oppression is not motivated by indoctrination or by a desire for victory; rather, it is a natural human reaction against what they perceive to be inhuman and wrong. Their guiding principle is faith: faith that the world one day will be, must be, better, more peaceful, and more just. I have watched these students reacting to the conditions, realities, and needs created by occupation.[30] I have seen them in olive oil factories distributing hundreds of empty tins to be filled by contributors and sold to raise money for needy students. I have seen them meet from four o'clock in the afternoon until eight the next morning to discuss an issue or how best to deal with a problem. I have watched them sweeping streets,[31] building playgrounds for children, gathering olives with farmers, cleaning hospitals, and building roads. I have watched them go to jail and emerge more hopeful and more determined.

------

of Arab youth despite an official blockade against them both by Israeli and Arab authorities. Another non-Palestinian singer who is popular among students in the West Bank is the Egyptian singer Sheikh Imam. Tawfiq Zayyad is a Palestinian poet from Galilee, as are Samih Qasem, Mahmoud Darwish, and Rashid Hussain, among others.

30. When Bir Zeit University was closed during academic year 1981/82 (the university was closed three times that year for a total of seven months), the students and teachers decided to hold classes in private schools in Jerusalem. The Israeli army surrounded the schools, arrested some of the students, and warned the schools. But later classes were held in mosques, churches, private homes, and most of the courses were salvaged.

There are some qualities that cannot be learned at even the best universities, but that seem to spring naturally from certain experiences. These are qualities of character, like courage, faith, commitment, and intuitive understanding. I have watched these students struggling to orient themselves to a new vision, despite the hard and rigid conditions surrounding them, always ready to share in the long, arduous task of keeping that vision alive. Such readiness obviously comes not through intellectual commitment alone, but through commitment of the spirit.

The purpose of this chapter is not to glorify the Palestinian students under occupation and their actions; its purpose is to learn from their experience. If that experience, and the tension between present reality and the dream of a better world, does not help move us along the path of truth and liberation not only for Palestinians and Arabs, but for Jews and for humanity at large, then we will have missed another opportunity to transform self, society, and the world.

CHAPTER 19

AL-INTIFADA AND A NEW EDUCATION

Munir Fasheh

The preceding chapter was written in 1981 and 1982. In this addendum, I pursue four issues raised above which are particularly accentuated by the Palestinian uprising – *al-intifada*: the escalation of attempts by Israel to destroy or disrupt Palestinian life and Palestinian society in general and Palestinian education in particular; the irrelevance of the knowledge given in Palestinian formal educational settings to Palestinian needs and realities and the marginal role, if any, of academics and academic institutions in current events; the necessity of developing an education that is more relevant to Palestinian needs, realities, and survival; and the response of people in general and students in particular to the new conditions created by *al-intifada.*

In terms of the Israeli attack on Palestinian life and society, there is nothing new. Practices such as closing schools and universities, jailing, deporting, and killing people (including teachers and students), harassing and torturing students, confiscating land and stealing water, dismantling institutions and public bodies (such as municipal councils) have never ceased since 1967. More than three hundred twenty-five thousand Palestinians were expelled immediately after the war; more than fifteen hundred were deported, over 55 percent of the total land of the West Bank and almost one-third of the total land of the Gaza Strip were confiscated. No water wells (with two exceptions) were allowed to be dug by Palestinians in the West Bank (instead, Israeli settlers were allowed to dig wells so deep that water springs which traditionally Palestinians had used dried up); settlements were established, and humiliation was a common practice. What has been new during *al-intifada* is the scale and intensity of Israeli oppression and attacks. As of this writing (September 1988), almost three hundred Palestinians have been killed since December 9, 1987 in the

West Bank and the Gaza Strip; thousands have been injured permanently (more than fifty were paralyzed, thousands with arms or legs broken, many blinded); tens of thousands have been beaten severely and tortured; tens of thousands jailed or put in detention centers; hundreds of homes completely destroyed; thousands of trees uprooted or bulldozed; scores of people have been expelled; several have been buried or burnt alive or electrocuted; and at least five have been killed in jails. Moreover, 20 percent of those killed are children (under 16 years old), most of whom were killed at home. Thousands of children have been jailed, and about fifty schools have been converted to army centers, many of which serve also as detention centers. Curfews have been imposed under the worst conditions: with an average of 6.5 people per room in Gaza Strip refugee camps and with hot and damp weather reaching over 100 degrees and with the cutting off of electricity and water, a curfew of ten, twenty, and sometimes forty consecutive days can be unbearably stressful. This, accompanied by the common Israeli practice of breaking into homes and beating people during curfews, creates a climate of unprecedented terror and anger. In fear of soldier's raids or settler's attacks, thousands of people (especially the young) have not slept in their homes since the early days of *al-intifada*. In fact, the terror that prevails almost everywhere in the West Bank and Gaza and the criminalization of grass-roots committees (more on this later) are the most serious brutal disruptions of Palestinian society. This climate of terror is much worse than closings of schools. Closing of schools is visible, measurable, limited, and whatever technical knowledge was lost can be regained later. Terrorizing children is much more serious: it is less visible and its impact and effects are much deeper and much more lasting and much more unpredictable.

The most serious effect of this terrorization is in the absence of a solution: the internalization by the youth of the logic embedded in the Zionist ideology and Israeli practices: the logic of either-or, the logic of full control and total suppression, the belief that advanced technology and military force are the only way to win, and the logic of justifying claims and actions through God. In spite of this possibility in the future, the current level of hope and understanding felt by Palestinian youth and their readiness to give and to act are also unprecedented. Within the larger picture of current events, the fight between Israeli soldier and Palestinian youth is really a fight between two types of power: a power that depends on military and technological superiority and a power that depends on internal human strength of people, on their ability to say no to oppression and be ready to pay a high price for it, including death. The hope embodied in *al-intifada* is, thus, a hope that transcends the Palestinians to reach humanity at large. There is no power and no control system that can suppress people indefinitely. No matter how little external power people have and no matter how little material resources they may have, they can do a lot to shake existing oppressive structures, including mental ones. Humanity cannot be suppressed indefinitely. Like the wildflower seeds in the Palestinian landscape, humanity may dry up for awhile, but with the first rainfall it will all bloom again. The history of the Jews themselves confirms this power in humanity.

The following words by M. Scott Peck fit, in my opinion, the climate of terror and misery imposed currently by the Israeli occupation on the Palestinians and the corresponding courage, actions, and hope exercised by the Palestinians. Peck says: "Courage is not the absence of fear: it is the making of action in spite of fear." He goes on:

> Evil is the exercise of political power – that is the imposition of one's will upon others by overt or covert coercion (in order to avoid confronting the real issues one faces including the moral issue). . . . There really are people, and institutions made up of people, who respond with hatred in the presence of goodness and would destroy the good insofar as it is in their power to do so. They do this not (necessarily) with conscious malice but blindly, lacking awareness of their own evil – indeed seeking to avoid any such awareness. . . . They will destroy the light in their own children and all other beings subject to their power in order to avoid the pain of self-awareness. . . . Evil is laziness carried to [an] extreme. . . . If necessary, they will even kill to escape the pain of their spiritual growth. I have come to conclude [however] that while entropy is an enormous force, in its extreme from of human evil it is strongly ineffective as a social force. . . . Evil backfires in the big picture of human evolution. For every soul it destroys . . . it is also instrumental in the salvation of others.[1]

These words gain new dimensions in conflicts such as the Israeli-Palestinian conflict where a racist-colonialist ideology prevails.[2] Current

---

1. M. Scott Peck, *The Road less Travelled* (London: Century, 1978), pp. 131, 278-79.

2. According to Maxime Rodinson, the effort to deny the existence of and/or the dehumanization of the Palestinians "was a product of the prevailing philosophy of the European world . . . which held that 'every territory situated outside that world was considered empty . . . constituting a kind of cultural vacuum, and therefore suitable for colonization' " (*Israel and the Arabs* [New York: Random House, 1968], p. 14). Ghandi "steadfastly resisted Zionist attempts to secure his endorsement by saying 'you want to convert the Arab majority into a minority.' . . . As Nehru once put it, the Zionist scheme neglected 'one not unimportant fact, . . . Palestine was not a wilderness or an empty, uninhabited place. It was already somebody else's home.' " M. Hallaj, "Palestine: The Suppression of an Idea," *The Link* (1982), 15(1):1,3. The Zionist colonialist trend was by no means true of all Zionists or all Jews. Ahad Ha-Am, for example, who represented the other main trend within Zionism, wrote in 1920: "There is a Jewish proverb which says: 'A mistake which succeeds is none the less a mistake.' . . . The Arab people . . .

Israeli practices seem to be in harmony with what Theodor Herzl, the founder of political Zionism, wrote ninety years ago in his book *A Jewish State:* that the Jews in Palestine would "form a portion of the rampart of Europe against Asia, an outpost of civilization as opposed to barbarism."[3] Herzl's recommendation "to spirit the penniless population across the border"[4] was as far as the founder of Zionism went in recognizing the Palestinians. Herzl's recommendation predates, by ninety years, the "transfer" idea which some are trying to make us believe is new and advocated only by extremists such as Meir Kahane and Rehavim Zeevi. Actually, Israel's practices always have been in agreement with Herzl's recommendation to transfer the indigenous population, sometimes on a large scale (as in 1948 and 1967), and at other times on a small scale (as in deportations and moving people out of their villages, then destroying them).[5]

Dehumanization is a necessary ingredient in racism. Sometimes dehumanization works by making the suppressed invisible (in 1970 Israeli Prime Minister Golda Meir asked "Who are the Palestinians? They don't exist"). At other times, it takes the form of name-calling (in 1982, Israeli Prime Minister Menachem Begin called Palestinians "two-legged animals," and his chief of staff Raphael Eitan referred to them as "cockroaches"). At still other times it takes strange forms as in September 1985, when people randomly stopped by Israeli soldiers were forced to, for example, kiss donkeys' behinds, spit in their parents' or children's faces, or dance

---

which we have always ignored from the very beginning of the colonization movement, listened and believed that the Jews were coming to expropriate its land" (*Ten Essays on Zionism and Judaism,* [London: George Routledge and Sons, 1922], pp. xv, xviii, xx). Hannah Arendt mentions, as another example, "Martin Buber's denunciation of the Zionist Biltmore program as admitting the aim of the minority to 'conquer' the country by means of international maneauvers" (in R. Feldman, *The Jew as Paraiah* [New York: Grove Press, 1978], p. 211). Similarly, Judah Magnes, cofounder and president of the Hebrew University, was opposed to the expulsion of Arabs (Feldman, *Jew as Paraiah,* p. 212).

3. Theodor Herzl, *A Jewish State,* (New York: Maccabean Publishing Company, 1904), p. 29.

4. Theodor Herzl, *Complete Diaries,* ed. Raphael Patai, trans. Harry Zohr (New York: Herzl Press and T. Yoseloff, 1960), 1:88.

5. Transfer on a small scale is illustrated by what happened to Igrit and Birim in 1948 and to Emmaus, Yalu, and Beit Nuba in 1967.

sometimes partially disrobed in the streets.[6] During that month also over ten people were shot arbitrarily while walking or riding in cars or buses. More recently, comments made by Israelis after three Palestinian workers were burnt in Or Yehuda (near Tel Aviv) on August 16, 1988 (by locking them in the shack while they slept, pouring benzine and igniting it), included "What does it matter if an Arab burns? What does an Arab matter at all? It's not a human being."[7]

Among liberals, academicians, experts, and scholars, racism takes the form of hypocrisy and double standards: the Palestinians, for example, are asked to recognize the right of Israel to exist but the reverse is rarely mentioned; some people can choose their representatives but the Palestinians are denied the right to hold elections to choose their own; building a state based on religion is hailed as a progressive step in the case of Israel but condemned as backward and fanatic if thought of by Muslims. At times, this hypocrisy breaks down into outright lies. I wish only to cite one example. Webster's *New Universal Unabridged Dictionary* (deluxe second edition, New York: Simon & Schuster, 1979) defines Palestine as follows: "1. a territory on E. coast of Mediterranean, the country of the Jews in Biblical times. 2. Part of the territory under a British mandate after World War I: divided into Israel and Jordan by action of U.N. in 1947." The lies embedded in the statement are amazing. The United Nations resolution did not divide parts of Palestine into Israel and Jordan but into independent Arab and Jewish states in addition to Jordan, which existed on the east bank of the Jordan River. The United Nations action is not a secret: it did not happen in distant time or distant lands, and it was not stated in controversial or vague terms or documents. It was stated clearly: it took place in 1947 in New York (where the dictionary was published), and it is described in United Nations documents that are open to everyone.

LEARNING GOES ON

Attempts by some universities to hold classes for graduating students outside the campuses (a practice followed in previous closings) were forbidden recently. The building, for example, that was used for such a purpose by al-Najah University was closed indefinitely. Teachers from al-Najah University and from Abu Dis College were arrested for being

6. See, for example, David Hirst's article in the *Manchester Guardian,* 17 September 1985.

7. Yediot Ahronot, 17 August 1988.

involved in teaching such classes. Similarly, attempts by schoolteachers and others to teach kids in their neighborhoods (at homes, in mosques, or other public places) were attacked. The attack, at the beginning, took such forms as threatening government schoolteachers with losing their jobs if they taught in their neighborhoods, beating a few teachers, and beating and arresting kids caught carrying textbooks. Later, however, the attack took a much more brutal form. On August 18, 1988, a military order banned all activities of what the order referred to as "popular committees." According to that law, people involved in activities such as teaching or guarding at the neighborhood or community level are liable to penalties of up to ten years imprisonment.[8]

Mutual help at the neighborhood level is part of the Palestinian tradition and culture. The development of committees to respond to basic needs at the local level is, thus, a "natural response" by Palestinians. Some forms, however, have been an extension of tradition. Moreover, many committees that were formed in order to deal with basic needs (ignored by existing institutions), such as medical, agricultural, and women's needs, have existed since the late 1970s and early 1980s. But judging from the behavior of the United States in Grenada and Nicaragua or Israel's in the West Bank and Gaza, it is obvious that the development of a more self-reliant society is the most threatening development to any exploitative economic or political dominating system or power. Just as in the 1970s, the current brutal attack on the development of the more self-reliant Palestinian society has been augmented by the sudden increase of U.S. "assistance" to the West Bank and Gaza Strip. Just as it disrupted the healthy development that was taking place in the West Bank in the 1970s, current pressures by the U.S. government and by Israel on U.S. private voluntary organizations have one goal in mind: to disrupt the Palestinian society and force it into a dependent position once again.[9] In comparison, the current policy and behavior of European Economic Community countries towards the development of the Palestinian society has been much more healthy. Their insistence, for example, on direct deals between their countries and Palestinian producers will improve both the quality of the Palestinian products and the development of healthy and lasting economic activities, and consequently will improve the chances of developing a lasting peace in the region.

8. What happened in Beit Sahur is one example of such penalties. Several people, including Dr. Jad Isahaq, the former dean of the faculty of science in Bethlehem University, were jailed for their involvement in agricultural activities in their town.

9. One man likened the U.S. aid program to the disease of AIDS: when it enters a country, the internal immune system breaks down.

In spite of the total attack on education, teaching, and educational institutions, learning goes on. Just as closing restaurants would not stop people from eating and closing mosques or churches would not stop people from praying, closing schools would not stop people from learning. Such activities are, essentially, not functions of institutions: they are not even human rights, but rather they are part of life itself, they are signs of life: people continue to eat, learn, pray,[10] breathe, and fight oppression as long as they live. In fact, closing institutions such as schools, mosques and churches, or restaurants often improves the quality of the activities associated with them. Deinstitutionalized, these activities become less rigid, less ritualistic, less abstract, less ideological, and more meaningful, more profound and more authentic. In addition, people tend to be more self-reliant, more independent, more supportive of each other, more creative and more in control of their needs and how to satisfy them.

I repeat: in spite of all attacks on education, learning goes on. The relevant question here is: what kind of learning goes on and what is actually missing in this type of learning? In order to answer this question, we have to distinguish between firsthand knowledge, which is forged out of our own experience of reality through confronting fundamental problems and having to solve them one way or another, and secondhand knowledge, which includes technical information and skills as well as knowledge outside of our immediate experience (such as knowing whether a certain water is polluted or not, how much concrete is needed to build a safe and lasting ceiling in a certain house, and so on). There is not meaningful knowledge unless it starts and ends with personal experience, personal awareness, and personal growth, and with questions of ends and purposes.

The kind of learning that is taking place today in the West Bank and Gaza Strip is the one referred to above as firsthand knowledge. Under the conditions of *al-intifada*, the problems faced by people are concrete, profound, and urgent. When problems reach the level of survival, people are capable of reaching new peaks of their capacity to learn and new peaks of creativity and innovativeness. That enables them to understand and deal with problems. They discover new attitudes, relationships, values, and structures. Now, people are learning about the importance of organizing themselves in order to effectively solve problems: they are learning how to outwit the Israeli army, they are learning firsthand about history, the various roles of religion in society, the central and crucial role of women within the Palestinian society and struggle, and they are learning that change does not

10. Here, a distinction is made between eating and consuming food, between learning and schooling, and between praying and belonging to a certain religion.

come as a gift or through wishes but out of people's sense of responsibility and their actions: that people's actions make a difference. Moreover, the kind of learning that is taking place among the youth in the West Bank and Gaza Strip is potentially crucial in moving the stress only on individual success, which characterizes formal education, to a stress also on increasing the viability of a community in the future.

They are also learning firsthand about Zionism. What the Palestinian youth have learned during the past few months about Zionism, about its ideology (including its language and logic), practices, tactics, and strategies is much more concrete, and probably far more accurate, that what most people in our generation have learned during decades. The different shades of Zionism the new generation experiences are not the same as the ones my generation learned (mainly from books and conversations). The shades we learned were more verbal and more abstract. The shades they experience are more concrete and real. The differences they see are related to differences and *action* among Israelis. Asked by an American friend of mine about what he would do if he found himself alone with an Israeli soldier standing next to him, a fourteen-year-old boy from Jabalia refugee camp in Gaza said, "If I can, I'll try first to find out what group he sees as most reasonable in Israel. If he feels sympathetic to Yesh Gvul (There Is a Limit, organization of Israeli soldiers who refuse military service in the occupied territories), for example, I'll try to make friends with him." In another incident, a soldier monitoring a demonstration in Ramallah by about fifty Israelis protecting the closure of universities told the protesters that if he were not in his uniform he would be on their side. He was ordered to take his position and be ready with his club and his gun; as a result, he threw his hat on the ground and handed his gun to his superior. He was taken away immediately in a military car. Another example on the concrete dimension of the learning that is taking place is the response of a seventeen-year-old girl when she heard that during autopsies, Israeli doctors steal body parts of Palestinians killed by soldiers. She said "I think Palestinian doctors should try to get to these bodies before the Israeli doctors and try to get to the parts first to use them for needy Palestinian patients." My generation would have stopped, at best, at the level of saying "let us call the ABC or NYT or BBC correspondent and report this." Another example still is that of a perceptive young Palestinian girl who, reflecting on what has been happening during *al-intifada*, said, "We have a society that is building a state: the Israelis have a state that is destroying their society." My main worry, as I mentioned earlier, is that in the absence of a solution the new generation of Palestinians will eventually internalize and practice the logic practiced on them by Israel, the logic of either-or.

If we are going to survive, make sense, and change things we cannot survive on secondhand knowledge. There has to be understanding, commitment, action, and expression at the personal level. Learning, at best, is freeing the imagination from ready solutions in the face of serious real problems. A crucial element in learning is students' interests – these are crucial in the building up of the theoretical attitude (in the sense of theory as critique) that will be in tune with their experience of reality and that will help them choose an appropriate course of action. In this sense, personal experience and firsthand knowledge are not enough: they cannot encompass the totality of a situation or phenomenon. Knowing about others' experience and ideas is crucial. Learning to be skeptical about one's own experiences and conclusions and comparing them with others' is absolutely necessary. The experiences of the young people, their awareness, and their actions are far ahead of their cognitive level. They also need what was referred to earlier as secondhand knowledge. Moreover, one has to search for a way to "transform one's personal experience of the microcosm into a personal experience of the macrocosm.[11]

People with technical knowledge and technical skills, however, are rarely helpful to people going through rich experiences of reality. One significant fact about Palestinian education today is the painful discovery that the youth no longer need us (I am referring to people working in educational institutions, and to other similar hegemonic intellectuals) to acquire knowledge: neither do they need us to understand and to act. Their experiences, awarenesses, commitments, and actions are different from, and often are far ahead of, those of traditional intellectuals. In addition, their expressions and articulations are more dynamic and relevant: they express ceaseless activities. Our expression, in comparison, is for the most part a dead product: a piece in a final and rigid form. They are speaking a language of their own. It is completely our choice as to whether we immerse ourselves in their reality and learn to speak their language or stick to our ways and structures, and lose the ability to make sense to them, to be relevant to their experiences, and to be responsive to their worries and to the possible pitfalls in their course. I am not talking about intentions and conscious policies, but rather about a certain training, certain structures, certain interests, and a certain philosophy and practice that has characterized the dominant formal education among Palestinians today.

11. Peck *Road.* p. 195.

EDUCATION AS PRAXIS

By April 1988, popular education started spreading at the neighborhood level in several places in the West Bank and the Gaza Strip. Generally, it followed school textbooks and school format. The prevailing circumstances, however, produced diversions, such as having children from different grades in the same class or group, having to cover material in less time, and having few texts, and no grades, and no principals. These things forced people to think of priorities in knowledge and made them more flexible and more creative. As was mentioned earlier, these attempts to teach at the neighborhood level were harassed but people's enthusiasm kept spreading – this was probably a significant factor in the Israeli reopening of the schools (which are easier to control) in late May 1988. By July 1988, however, schools were ordered closed again, and since August 18, popular committees including those for teaching have been criminalized, making anyone involved in such activity liable to penalties which include deportation or imprisonment for up to ten years.

The closure of schools affects younger children (the first four or five grades) more than older ones because they lack the basic skills needed in order to be able to acquire knowledge on their own. For older students, current conditions *could* be more conductive to learning than formal education. If a student has acquired the habit of reading (in the large sense of the word, i.e. reading that includes reading critically within context, and having the ability to express one's ideas, actions, and feelings clearly), and if he or she has learned where, and how to get to, and use resources (such as books or other written materials, and certain people or other oral materials), and if he or she is involved in some action related to a real problem or to producing something, then that student has the means to acquire the necessary knowledge, and to expand it. For such a student, formal institutionalized education, which depends mainly on ready packaged materials and rigid forms, usually unrelated to each other or to the students' environment, is an obstacle to learning. Self-discipline, self-reliance, and creativity, which are desperately needed in education, are usually missing in our schools and universities. Creativity requires both freedom and action at the individual level. The interaction between the individual and reality must be free, and "spontaneous, resulting from individual experiences, motivations, and highly sensual, which embodies the sensitive, and emotive." Out of this interaction, knowledge is acquired. The interaction between the individual and action "depends on imparted knowledge, skills, and motivation." On the other hand, the knowledge that an individual acquires through interaction with reality "will play into action only when it has taken a theoretical attitude in the sense of theory as critique . . . when an interior process begins to operate, guided by consciousness."[12]

The building up of the critical-theoretical attitude through the interaction between the individual and action "is the decisive step for expanding, and even transgressing limits, which characterizes creativity."[13] In other words, "we are led to a process of getting immersed in a reality, reflecting upon this reality, and choosing a course of action, which will be imprinted in the reality itself, modifying it to the extent the process was creative."[14] Teaching and schooling (which usually reflect certain interests) do interfere with the interaction between the individual and his or her reality and actions.

The freedom and action required for the individual to speak his or her language and create meaningful and relevant knowledge are being blocked by a system of power which "blocks, prohibits, and invalidates this discourse and this knowledge, a power not only found in the manifest authority of censorship, but one that profoundly and subtly penetrates an entire social network. Intellectuals are themselves agents of this system of power – the idea of this responsibility for 'consciousness' and discourse forms part of the system. This refers basically to legitimation procedures which are exerted through validation schemes in the educational systems, such as examinations, degrees, and diplomas, peer recognition, publications, and others."[15]

This brings us to the fact that the most crucial issue in education, which was raised seriously for the first time after the 1967 War, and again after the 1982 invasion of Lebanon, and which *al-intifada* raises even more seriously and more urgently, is the relation of education to the world of which it is a part. These major events in 1967, 1982, and 1987 shook the foundations of the world created by formal education and Western hegemony;[16] they revealed the gap between what we – the formally educated – had learned and taught in schools and universities (in terms of conceptions, convictions, explanations, expectations, analyses, skills, and so forth), and the events and

12. U. D'Amborsio, *Socio-Cultural Bases for Mathematics Education* (Campinas: UNICAMP, 1985), p. 32.

13. *Ibid.,* p. 34.

14. *Ibid.,* p. 31.

15. *Ibid.,* p. 30.

16. This is true, in general, of peoples in the third world: education and Western hegemony have created a world that replaced the real world for them.

needs of the real world.[17] They revealed how little we knew, and how irrelevant and rigid that little knowledge was – and still is.

What we started to see in 1967, which was magnified and brought into focus in 1982 and 1987, was the practical limits of the education we had been given. The 1967 War started a process that made the real environment, power relations, and the role of education in generating hegemony more visible. It was difficult to see this role of formal education before 1967 due mainly to two reasons: first, during the 1950s and 1960s peoples around the world had high expectations of education, and second, formal education actually provided a means towards a secure livelihood and decent living for many Palestinians after the 1948 disaster (which resulted in the loss of our lands and in our dispersion) at the same time as it kept our hope and sense of worth alive. By the early 1970s, for example, the percentage of the Palestinian population in universities was among the highest in the world, and high-level manpower among the Palestinians accounted for some 10 percent of the total Arab pool of trained personnel, although at that time Palestinians formed less than 3 percent of the total Arab population.[18] Moreover, "whatever was . . . achieved was the product of intense personal commitment,"[19] not only on the part of those of us who were students but of our families. Given the inability to provide security in shelter and stability, our parents' traditional Palestinian concern for children expressed itself in providing security through education. The shelter my generation inhabited between 1948, and 1967 was one carefully and lovingly constructed within the educational system by the generation of Palestinians displaced in 1948.

The 1967 War shattered the security of what had been built since 1948. The defeat exposed both the narrowness and frailty of the shelter provided, and the fact that our education neglected long-term communal needs in favor of individual and personal success. With our growing national awareness came an increased sense of the importance of questions concerning the relevance of education, and an increased understanding that the purpose of education was to enable us to make sense of the environment we actually inhabited and to be more productive in it, not only materially but also culturally and spiritually.

17. For more detail see my dissertation, "Education as Praxis for Liberation: Bir Zeit University and the Community Work Program," Harvard University, Graduate School of Education, March 1988.

18. See A. and R. Zahlan, "The Palestinian Future: Education and Manpower," *Journal of Palestine Studies,* 6(4).

19. *Ibid.*

The failure of formal Palestinian education to live up to its larger promises was not only due to Israeli occupation but also to the fact that it, like formal education in other third world countries, was mainly shaped by Western hegemony, which, in the case of the Palestinians, was mainly British, and, later, American. Hegemony is to be understood here as a form of domination. It often precedes political, and military conquests, and continues after them. But unlike the situation in military conquest, hegemonic conquest permeates almost all spheres, and in it the dominated facilitate their own domination. Hegemony is always linked to an ideology that reflects the manners, and interests of the invaders, and their culture. This ideology embodies certain conceptions, values, language, relations, and interests, which are translated into daily practices. Crucial to the hegemonic relationship is the belief that there is a universal and neutral path for progress, which is the path followed by Western nations. Thus, although Palestinians, for example, struggled against British armies and policies, including their educational policies in Palestine, we have hardly been critical of the British educational system or academic institutions. In fact, we ideologized them. During most of my experience as an educator our goal in education has been to build institutions and adopt curricula as "good" as the British (and later American) ones.

Because ideology is a world view that embodies conceptions, values, relations, and interests that are translated into daily practices and that produce a certain consciousness, the role of intellectuals and institutions is of primary importance; the reproduction of a hegemonic ideology is achieved mainly through them.

Intellectual development in a colonial hegemonic context is designed to provide ideology without a basis in power. It allows intellectuals to participate vicariously in the moral, intellectual, humanitarian, and technical aspects of Western culture as well as in educational, scholarly, and research activities. Individuals are sometimes acknowledged and rewarded for their participation and contribution. The training of colonial intellectuals directs them to derive their sense of worth and status from this vicarious participation, alienating them from their own culture, history, and people. The indigenous population often supports this tendency by giving status to such intellectuals. Hegemonic education produces, generally speaking, intellectuals who have lost their power base in their own culture and society, and who have been provided with a foreign culture and ideology, but without a power base in the hegemonic society. (Compare the situation of a Palestinian intellectual at Bir Zeit University, for example, with that of an American intellectual at Berkeley, MIT, or Harvard, who may actually participate in decision making concerning weapons production and in weapons production itself; or be involved in the policy decisions of multinational corporations; or with U.S. government policy concerning other countries.) Lacking a power base at both ends, third world intellectuals tend to overvalue symbolic power and tokens such as titles, degrees, access to prestigious institutions, and awards.

As with individuals, the institutional hegemonic connection does give an illusion of power. Moreover, in some third world countries, these institutions do produce people who govern the country, compete in international business, and build bombs. In that sense the institutions have become part of the community of the oppressors rather than of the oppressed; they have moved from the third to the first or second world. It is precisely this possibility that directs third world institutions to ally themselves with hegemony, and with the dominant trend in education.

The education we had been given fitted us to live in a world created by education and hegemony, the world referred to here as the ideological environment. This environment serves to (borrowing an expression from T. Jackson Lears in his analysis of language) "mark the boundaries of permissible discourse, discourage the clarification of social alterations, and make it difficult for the dispossessed to locate the source of their unease, let alone remedy it."[20] It "functions to 'position' people in the world, to shape the range of possible meanings surrounding an issue, and to actively construct reality."[21] There is a big difference between building an ideological world that replaces the real one and building theoretical models that help us understand, act, and transform the real world which we inhabit.

Our education left us blind to its ideological dimension: to the relationship between the knowledge transmitted to us, and power. This blindness, characteristic of hegemonically educated third world people, left us unfit to live in the real environment. The term "real environment" as used here represents what the ideological environment omits and excludes. It extends from the immediacies of the historical process as experienced to the social institutions (material, spiritual, and intellectual), productive activities, and cultural traditions that shape people's responses. Hegemony, in short, is not only characterized by what it includes but also by what it excludes: by what it renders marginal, deems inferior, and makes invisible.

The way language (and the choice of language) is used in schools and in public discussion and the choice of words, and their meanings is all very crucial to the hegemonic process. Language acts as a means of control by

20. T. Jackson Lears, "The Concept of Cultural Hegemony and Problems and Possibilities," *American Historical Review,* 90:569-70.

21. H. Giroux and P. McLaren, "Teacher Education and the Politics of Engagement," *Harvard Education Review* (1986), 56(3):231.

"using concepts whose meaning is defined, and controlled by the actor, and whose validity is also defined by [him/her]."[22] The silence of the oppressed is not the silence of those with nothing to say; rather it is the result of structural relationships between the dominated and the dominators which have developed over a long period of time.

In summary, the shortcomings of education were rooted in the character of the educational endeavor itself, which responded to the ideological environment and to the wants created by it, rather than to the real environment and its needs. The education was an investment in foreign cultural capital, and was, in many ways, like an investment in foreign money capital. There was an immediate, short, deceptive boom, which gave the illusion that things were improving. Then there was a collapse which revealed that the investment was counterproductive. It revealed that the investment had substituted short-term for long-term goals, wants for needs, theory and application for praxis, dependent for self-reliant development, and individual for societal interests. It substituted money and techniques for individual, and societal transformation.

The hegemonic culture and the ideological environment are not the only forces acting on or shaping third world educational institutions, however. The indigenous culture and the real environment also act on such institutions. The fundamental challenge to hegemonic institutions comes from events and crises in the real environment. The impact of the real environment on an educational institution such as Bir Zeit University, for example, is of a nature that is not easy to communicate to a first world person. How many people in the first world, for example, have lived under four completely different regimes, none of which represented the aspirations of the local population, within the past sixty years? How many institutions have had the borders within which they could operate change drastically and repeatedly within that same period? How many have experienced frequent disruptions and closings, official and unofficial, for two, three, seven, or even more months of a single academic year? How many have had their president and two members of the board of trustees expelled from their country, another member of the board lose a leg from a car bomb, and yet others placed under town arrest? How many faculty and administrators have had tear gas dropped into their classrooms and offices.? How many students have experienced continuous harassment, including town arrest, imprisonment, torture, wounding, expulsion, and killing? How many institutions have had faculty prohibited from entering the university or

22. C. Argyris, *Inner Contradictions of Rigorous Research* (Orlando, Fla.: Academic Press, 1980), p.12; and *Reasoning, Learning, and Action* (San Francisco: Jossey-Bass, 1982), p. 86

expelled from the country? How many have taken on primary responsibility for functions normally belonging to government agencies: testing and control of pharmaceutical products; adult literacy programs; health care and health education programs? The problems posed by a third world environment are unprecedented in first world settings.

There were several attempts within Palestinian universities to respond to the real environment, and to try to integrate it into the educational process. The Community Work, the Community Health, and the Environmental Health programs at Bir Zeit University; the Center for Rural Development and Research at al-Najah University; the Nursing, Hotel Management and Tourist Guides programs at Bethlehem University;, and the building of an education based on Islamic principles at Gaza University are examples of such attempts. But despite the impact of the real environment, and although there were attempts to build a more relevant education, Palestinian education (mainly due to the massive financial "assistance" from outside in the late 1970s) continued to move mainly in the direction of traditional colonialist education. Like 1948-67, 1973-82 was a period of dramatic expansion in Palestinian higher education. But unlike the earlier period, the new expansion did not rest on local resources and internal commitment. It depended almost entirely on external finances, and was characterized by expensive building projects, a sharp increase in the number of advanced degrees, especially Ph.Ds, and expanded bureaucratic structures. In other words, in the new period the money generated the expansion whereas in the earlier period the needs and commitment of people generated the expansion. Despite the setback within Palestinian education, authentic, grass-roots level development flourished in the 1980s within the larger Palestinian community: women's committees, medical and agricultural relief committees, and organizations for self-reliant economic development.[23] The relevance of such committees under the conditions created by *al-intifada* will be discussed below.

In the final analysis, the power of Western hegemony rests on the claims of superiority, universality, and ethical neutrality of Western (positivist) science, technology, research, and education, leading to belief in Western superiority in the social, cultural, moral, political, and intellectual spheres. But this linear concept of progress has to be abandoned: the belief

23. The 1982 Israeli invasion of Lebanon and its aftermath produced conflicting trends among the Palestinians. On the one hand, there was a sense of despair, yet on the other hand, a strong sense of responsibility and determination to act in order to deal with pressing problems. Factionalism and escalation of oppression by Israel and the Arab governments accompanied the first trend. The flourishing of grass-roots committees and other forms of self-reliant actions and structures were manifestations of the second trend.

in a best and universal path is detrimental to the richness that is manifest in life and in communities as well as to the production of conceptions, practices, and attitudes (including those in education, science, and research) that are meaningful and relevant to the majority of people. The strongest case against hegemonic formal education is, in my opinion, that it is useless and meaningless to the majority of the students.

Education perceived as praxis is the opposite of hegemonic education. Praxis is the combination of concrete conditions (social, cultural, and material), reflection, and action in constant interplay. Education perceived as praxis, according to Paolo Freire, "implies the existence of two interrelated concepts . . . the context of authentic dialogue . . . [and] the real, concrete context of facts, the social reality in which [people] exist."[24] Freire also says, "As beings of praxis, in accepting our concrete situation as a challenging condition . . . we are able to change its meaning by our action." Education as praxis is "an instrument of transforming action, a political praxis at the service of permanent human liberation. This . . . does not happen only in the consciousness of people, but presupposes a radical change of structure, in which process consciousness will itself be transformed."[25] According to Roland Barthes, "There is . . . one language which is not mythical, . . . it is the language of [the human being] as a producer: Wherever man speaks in order to transform reality, and no longer to preserve it as an image, wherever he links his language to the making of things."[26]

The primacy of the learner's experience and of production (not only in the national sense but also in such areas as literature and art) in this type of pedagogy is obvious. Within this perception of education, the essential functions of third world intellectuals and institutions are to make sense of the world, of our experience, and of our culture[27]; to respond to the challenges posed by the real environment; to empower people; to overcome the culture of silence; to remove obstacles to learning; and to release the human capacity to understand and act in order to help transform consciousness and society. Crucial to achieving these aims are: gaining a

24. Paolo Freire, *Cultural Action for Freedom* (Harvard Education Review, 1970), p. 14.

25. Paolo Freire, *The Politics of Education,* trans. Donaldo Macedo (S. Hadley, Mass.: Bergin & Garvey,), pp. 155, 140.

26. R. Barthes *Mythologies* (Magnolia, Mass.: Peter Smith, 1983), p. 146.

27. Following Giroux, culture here refers to "the particular ways in which a social group lives out and makes sense of its 'given' circumstances and conditional life."

power base in one's own culture and society; starting with the perspective and experience of the indigenous population; and creating an education relevant to the community's needs and geared towards production. The purpose of both structure and teachers is to facilitate that praxis and that empowerment. Empowerment as used here includes also acquiring "the means to critically appropriate knowledge existing outside of [our] immediate experience in order to broaden [our] understanding of [ourselves], the world, and the possibilities for transforming the taken-for-granted assumptions about the way we live."[28]

Because the choice of words and their meanings is effective in establishing control, "re-naming the world" is one powerful way to break down that control. "To exist, humanly," says Freire, "is to name the world, to change it. . . . The essence of dialogue [is] *the word.* But the word is more than just an instrument which makes dialogue possible. . . . Within [it] we find two dimensions, reflection, and action, in such radical interaction that if one is sacrificed the other immediately suffers."[29] In other words, developing accurate ways of thinking about reality and a critical view of it means actually thinking about what we do while we actually do it.

Al-intifada, more than any other event, has challenged hegemony – in fact, it is the first real challenge to hegemony. It has opened the way to develop alternatives in many aspects, and has embodied and exemplified many of the above-mentioned ideas concerning the conceptualization and the practice of an education which is more relevant to the Palestinian situation. Before I elaborate on this, however, I would like to stress the fact that things were not calm before *al-intifada,* neither in terms of escalation of Israel's oppression,[30] nor in terms of people's response to that oppression. *Al-intifada* basically magnified both. Some examples – again from Bir Zeit University – will help illustrate. Concerning Israeli oppression, the following are some of the events that took place within the Bir Zeit scene during the year before *al-intifada*: three students were shot dead (two on December 4, 1986, and one on April 13, 1987); many students were wounded; hundreds were arrested and tortured; the head of the student council was deported;[31] the university was ordered closed for four months;

28. Giroux and McLaren, "Teacher Education," p. 229

29. Freire, *Pedagogy of the Oppressed* (New York: Continuum, 1970), pp. 75, 76.

30. The escalation took place in almost all aspects of life: stealing of land and water, harassment, taxes, killings, destruction of homes, etc.

31. After Marwan Barghouti was deported, the student who replaced him was jailed and the one who replaced *him* was put under town arrest.

and on one occasion, the army entered the university at night and searched papers and books in the faculty and administrative offices. On the other hand, concerning student's reaction to Israeli oppression, the students managed to steal (from the hospital) the bodies of the two students killed in December but failed to get them to their families; in April, however, they managed to take the body of the killed student to his family. (The usual Israeli practice in incidents in which they kill people is to keep the body with them, and call in a few members of the family, to bury the body at night.) At another level of student action, during the student election campaign at Bir Zeit University in January 1987, the various groups running for office (nationalists, leftists, and fundamentalists) participated in a debate. Over two thousand of the twenty-three hundred students at the university, along with many members of the faculty and staff, attended. The representatives of the various groups on the platform expressed their views (including criticisms of other groups and points of view) freely, and with no interruptions. The event was so moving that I, as moderator (in my capacity of dean of students), told the audience that that type of event – almost the whole university student body participating in an activity concerning students,[32] and views from the far right to the far left being expressed freely on the same platform – is very rare in the world. I also mentioned that the new generation of Palestinians has lived a life that even we, the older Palestinians, find difficulty in comprehending, and that this new generation will one day surprise us all. Still another student response to occupation was the Palestine Week of September 1987, which the students managed to hold (though over an extended and interrupted period) in spite of some success of Israeli attempts to disrupt it. The students also managed to earn a sizable revenue from the activities of the week, which was added to the student aid fund at the university.

BEYOND *AL-INTIFADA*

As I mentioned earlier, *al-intifada* embodies and exemplifies much of the discussion mentioned in this addendum. It makes the real environment more visible, and puts us again face to face with the fundamental issues, problems, and needs within that environment, and challenges us to respond to them at the level at which they exist. Such response tends towards the long-term interests of the majority of people, and towards their empowerment to take charge of their lives and their future. Creating strong

32. About 85 percent of the students voted in that election.

forms of empowerment has probably been the most significant characteristic and contribution of *al-intifada*.[33] *Al-intifada* helped free people's minds and imaginations from ready answers and packaged solutions. This was accompanied by the questioning of certain established convictions and ways of doing things and by gaining concreteness and new meanings of words and ideas through action and dialogue in real-life situations. New solutions are being thought of and practiced concerning economic, social, educational, and personal problems. The monopoly of schools and universities over education and learning and the grip of textbooks and exams on the educational process, for example, are being questioned. Such words as dependency, solidarity, development, self-determination, self-reliance, waste, and planning are gaining new and concrete meanings.

Another form of empowerment which *al-intifada* helped produce is the reclaiming by people of their abilities as human beings: abilities such as creativity, innovativeness, the ability to organize and deal with fundamental problems and basic needs, and the ability to understand, act, and transform the reality around them.

Al-intifada also creates an atmosphere more conducive to the development of new attitudes and values which have accompanied these forms of empowerment: the readiness to be receptive to new ideas and to alternative ways of doing things, the readiness to give and to share, the readiness to take initiatives, feelings and acts of solidarity and responsibility, the new awareness of self, and values of self-reliance, courage, and sacrifice.

Perhaps the most important form of empowerment to which *al-intifada* contributed is a recognition of the crucial role of grass-roots groups in the survival of communities. *Al-intifada* helped strengthen and give credibility to existing groups working at the grass-roots level: groups such as medical and agricultural relief committees, women's committees, and groups working to develop new forms of education and self-reliant forms of economic development. In addition to giving viability to existing groups, *al-intifada* also helped create new structures at the grass-roots level. The neighborhood committees that sprang up all over the West Bank and the

---

33. In contrast to the characteristics of empowerment, fostered by *al-intifada*, formal education does the opposite: it disempowers people. It hinders the creation of alternatives by limiting the imagination to ready solutions and technical issues only; it hinders the questioning of crucial fundamental issues in one's society and the world; it ignores context and personal experiences and feelings; in general, it separates both learners and teachers for many years from being involved in producing anything; and it values consumerism and individualism over production and communal interests.

Gaza Strip as a result of *al-intifada* have been very effective in dealing with basic problems and needs of the population. Their activities include storage and distribution of food; responding to health needs; taking care of the needy, the wounded, and the elderly; planting and taking care of vegetable gardens; teaching kids; guarding and alerting the community against army raids and settlers' attacks, and so on.[34] *Al-intifada* also helped revitalize some aspects of the indigenous society and culture (which is another form of empowerment): aspects such as traditions of mutual help and self-reliance, and the social functions of mosques, and churches. Such institutions help in the delivery of such services as the distribution of food, medical services, and teaching, at the same time as they facilitate communication among people in the community.

As a result of the circumstances and conditions that accompanied *al-intifada,* new forms of community leadership have developed. The new structure depended in several localities on changing individuals in leadership positions (which is very appropriate for protection, continuity, and training purposes). Flexible goals and ways of doing things have been adopted, in order to respond to the fast-changing conditions, needs, and problems. The new forms of leadership also depend on participation by all groups in the community, and on staying in touch with the realities of the situation, with people's moods, and with what is possible. The relationship of these new forms of leadership to the Palestine Liberation Organization is clear and simple: the community leadership takes on the responsibility of responding to basic needs and problems at the level of the community, of coordinating and initiating activities within it, of articulating feelings and ideas of the community members, and of helping the joint leadership of *al-intifada* to formulate general guidelines and direction, whereas the PLO takes on the responsibility of responding to and dealing with problems of national character such as negotiating the future of the Palestinian people and the issue of self-determination.

In other words, the form of leadership that has evolved in the West Bank and Gaza Strip is conceptualized as praxis: thinking while actually doing. In order to be effective and successful, the leadership (any leadership) could not separate itself from its context, from actual

---

34. Of course, all these attempts and forms of self-empowerment elicited a strong Israeli response. In fact, the attack by Israeli authorities on these acts of Palestinian survival and attempts to meet basic needs has been much more serious, harsh, systematic, and more subtle and much less publicized than the attack on other activities of *al-intifada*. Most Palestinians who have been jailed since *al-intifada* began are those who were active and involved in activities aiming towards self-reliance and meeting basic needs of the population.

participation of the people, from action, and from coordination with other groups. Moreover, structural changes and empowerment of people are probably the most important characteristics of any sincere and honest leadership. In fact, the form of leadership that has evolved in the West Bank and the Gaza Strip makes the concept of having a Gandhi or a Martin Luther King unneeded, and, in a certain sense, even harmful: a charismatic and powerful leader usually, although most probably unintentionally, robs people of their initiative and sense of responsibility, and downplays the importance of internal convictions and commitments in relation to one's actions and beliefs. Although charismatic leaders may empower people at the beginning, they eventually produce people who are dependent, hypnotized, moved by external directives, and who adopt symbolic and often false forms of empowerment. People working with or under a charismatic leader adopt the belief that they cannot do things as fast and effectively as he can. They may eventually become lazy and apologetic, and adopt short-cut ways and short-term interests as a substitute for the time, tedious work, self-discipline, organization, and feelings of solidarity, that are needed for the transformation of self, and society, of consciousness of the structure. In this sense, the main contribution of *al-intifada* to the world is, I believe, the accentuation of the fact that there is no substitute to the empowerment of people, for their feelings of compassion (even with people on the "other" side), and for the change of structures, both social and mental. *Al-intifada* also accentuates the fact that people, no matter how small their number, and no matter how little power and few resources they seem to have, can do much to shake existing oppressive structures, both material, and ideological.

An extremely crucial way of breaking up oppressive structures, and the myths surrounding them (another form of empowerment), which *al-intifada* exemplifies, has been the embodiment of a logic and language different from the dominant ones. In several places, for example, Palestinian youth collected the arms provided by the Israeli military authorities to local collaborators, and sent the arms back to the military governors, telling them that they (the youth) had no use for them. When Abu Jihad was assasinated by Israeli marauders in Tunis, over twenty Palestinians were shot dead, and hundreds were wounded by Israeli soldiers and officers during the protests that took place in the West Bank and the Gaza Strip that day; not a single Israeli was killed as a form of that protest. *Al-intifada* does not depend on superior technology or big money or military operations. It depends, rather, on human power, on the internal struggle of human beings: on their ability to say no to oppression and be ready to pay a high price, including death for that resistance. In fact, one major problem in the current confrontation between Israeli soldiers and Palestinian youth is the gap between the internal human power of the youth and the power of the Israeli soldiers, which stems mainly from external strength, from military and technological superiority. Moreover, and at another level, *al-intifada* shows that resisting oppression is not only a right and not only a responsibility but also, and probably more importantly, a sign of life and a matter of survival.

In this sense, *al-intifada* produces hope (another form of empowerment) not only to Palestinian and Arab youth but also to Jews, and to humanity at large: humanity cannot be crushed completely, it cannot be controlled permanently. At a time when things seemed to be completely hopeless, when people seemed to be adapting to deteriorating conditions, when occupation seemed to be in full control, when Arab governments (in addition to the Israeli and American governments) were actively involved in a concerted and seemingly successful effort to suppress the Palestinian voice and Palestinian rights and to destroy the Palestinian leadership both inside and outside Palestine, *al-intifada* sprang up with a powerful presence. In fact, its full impact is yet to come; it can hardly be guessed at or imagined at this point. Certain forms and manifestations of *al-intifada* can, obviously, be crushed; other aspects, however, work at a much deeper and more profound level. Just like plants in the Palestinian landscape, individuals and societies seem to dry up and die during certain periods, but with the first drops of rain the seeds flourish again, and come to full life. My personal guess at this point is that *al-intifada* will prove to be the most significant, and inspiring event the Arabs have experienced in recent history. Just like the Israeli occupation, the Palestinian uprising has affected a whole population down to the level of every individual, and every detail in every life: it has affected the foundations of a whole society.

The significance of all this to Palestinian education is tremendous. *Al-intifada* reminds us that the most crucial issue in education is the relation of education to the world it inhabits. It also reminds us of the big difference between building an ideological environment that replaces the real one, and building theoretical models in order to understand, act, and transform the real environment which we inhabit. An education designed to be relevant and meaningful to Palestinians would start at the base, with the concrete conditions in which people find themselves, and would facilitate the transformation of these conditions through understanding and action; that is, through praxis. As was mentioned earlier, the purpose of such education is to enable us to make sense of our environment, and to be more productive in it, not only materially but also culturally and spiritually. The purpose of both structure and teachers is to facilitate that praxis and that empowerment. The primacy of the learner's experience of context and of production in this type of pedagogy is obvious.

Al-intifada produced irreparable cracks in the old facade of myths and convictions covering almost all aspects of life. In education, for example, those myths include: the myth that education can take place only in special places (usually called schools and universities); the myth that the educational process consists mainly of rigid syllabi, fixed textbooks, and courses, and tests, and grades; the myth that learning is equivalent to formal education, and that schools and universities have the right to monopolize the definition of what constitutes learning;[35] the myth that learning can be measured through tests; and the myth that the best form of education is a full-time course of study that cuts students off from producing anything for many years.

Although education has been of persistent importance for Palestinians for many years, both the character of the education and the meaning of that importance have varied greatly. Since 1948, the importance of education has largely been its connection with economic, cultural, and even physical survival. This connection has been variously defined during the past forty years, and will inevitably continue to change. My strong conviction is that change in the direction of community-based response to the real environment, and education perceived as praxis, and as empowerment of people, offer the best chance for that education's goal of Palestinian survival to be realized.

---

35. In contrast to formal education that takes place in certain institutions, learning takes place in many settings in streets, in jails, in the field; in fact everywhere people exist and live and try to make sense of their surroundings.

PART V

SUBJUGATION

VERSUS

LIBERATION

CHAPTER 20

Plans to Regularize the Occupation

Sheila Ryan

INTRODUCTION

As the Israeli occupation of the Palestinian territories conquered in 1967[1] reached the midpoint of its second decade the military government has taken on a character at once semipermanent and anomalous. Israel shows no sign of readiness to leave these occupied areas: in fact, the government has made a matter of principle out of refusal to withdraw. Ordinarily, in international law and human history, however, military occupation is a transitory matter.

This tension between formal status on the one hand and present policy and future ambition on the other has encouraged the formulation of various plans to regularize the occupation. Israel has left the door wide open for such change by refusing to categorize itself as a "belligerent occupier," for indeed those ruling Israel now believe they are in the West Bank (or, in their parlance, "Judea and Samaria") and Gaza Strip by historical right. Instead, Israel officially identifies its rule over the West Bank and Gaza Strip as "administration," a terminologically innovative category in international law, rather than as a military occupation.

1. This study deals only with Israeli proposals regarding the Palestinian West Bank and Gaza Strip. Because various Israeli views of appropriate futures for these territories are linked so closely to viewpoints on the the Palestinian national issue as a whole, these plans require treatment distinct from discussion of Israeli views on the occupation of the Egyptian Sinai, from which Israeli troops have withdrawn, or on the Syrian Golan Heights, which the entire Israeli mainstream seems determined to retain and annex.

In the years since the June War, no Israeli government has ever been willing to withdraw from the entire West Bank and Gaza Strip; moreover, no individual in power or close to power in Israel has proposed a resolution entailing such a withdrawal in favor either of a Palestinian state or of a return to the *status quo ante*. At least three proposals have been offered, however, that seek to "regularize" the occupation and to normalize Israeli rule in part or all of these occupied areas.

The first of these was the Allon Plan: Yigal Allon advocated Israeli annexation of about one-third of the West Bank in a wide swath along the Jordan River and Dead Sea, and a large portion of the Gaza Strip, with the more densely populated parts of the occupied areas to become a demilitarized part of a single Jordanian-Palestinian entity. Prime Minister Menachem Begin proffered an "autonomy plan" under which residents of the occupied areas would have a limited range of functional authority over their own affairs, though not over the territory itself, while Israel would continue to colonize the regions with their own settlers and to retain the option of declaring the area under Israeli sovereignty. The Sharon Plan, espoused by cabinet minister without portfolio Ariel Sharon is not inconsistent with the Begin Plan, but it goes far beyond it. Sharon advocates the establishment of a Palestinian state on the east bank of the Jordan, premised on the resettlement of Palestinians from the diaspora and possibly from the occupied areas in the new state, and on Israeli sovereignty in the occupied areas and dominance over the Palestinian state in Jordan.

Neither the Allon Plan nor the Sharon Plan was ever formally adopted by an Israeli government. None of these plans has yet been implemented. Yet all of them have had enormous practical effect on life in the occupied areas. The Allon Plan prescribed the geographical parameters of settlement under the Labor governments, and served the political function of providing a middle road down which both "minimalists" and "maximalists" could proceed to the tangible tasks of creating a land base and population base for retention of parts of the conquered lands.

The Begin Plan of autonomy for the West Bank and Gaza, while not yet imposed on a population which has strenuously rejected it, did receive the partial sanction of the Camp David agreement and has served as an ideological and political framework for steps to move from military government of the occupied areas, with its connotation of an abnormal and temporary situation, toward a "civilian administration," with its implication of a normal and quite possibly permanent arrangement. This transition has been accompanied by extreme official pressure on all of the indigenous political institutions, particularly the municipalities.

The Sharon Plan widens the geographical area within which the "normalization" of the occupation is to be accomplished; although its goals for the east bank have not been achieved, the expanded vision it embodies appears to have played a role in gaining support within the government for plans for the invasion of Lebanon, and may continue to provide an impetus for Israeli government action to rearrange the demography of the Palestinians, whether by resettling them from Lebanon to the east bank or even by expelling large numbers from the West Bank.

The three plans were all formulated in a double matrix of internal Israeli political factors and external relations, particularly those with the United States. The willingness of the United States to subsidize Israel's continuing occupation of the West Bank and Gaza speaks louder than any official pronouncements against settlements as "an obstacle to peace" or pious invocations of United Nations Security Council Resolution 242 with its call for Israeli withdrawal. The U.S. military aid to Israel has not merely remained constant during the occupation, but has in fact skyrocketed. For example, from 1950 to 1971, foreign military sales credits extended to Israel by the United States totalled $820 million; the amount equivalent to this two decades of military assistance was given in six months of 1983, when the annual military aid level had risen to $1.7 billion. Even this astronomical level, however, was dwarfed by the bonanza year of 1979, when Israel received $1.3 billion in military aid as recompense for agreement to the Camp David treaty.

The role that this assistance (and the underlying political support that it manifested) played will be examined in this essay, as will the effect that fluctuations in the attitude of the United States have had in changing the context in which successive plans have been proposed.

THE ALLON PLAN: ITS PROVISIONS

Yigan Allon, while deputy prime minister of the predominantly Labor government after the June War, shared a common premise with two men who were his ideological foes and who would later frame their own plans for regularization of the occupation: Menachem Begin and Ariel Sharon. All three believed that Jews had a sacred historical right to the conquered West Bank: indeed, even in a piece written for foreign consumption Allon wrote that

> According to the compromise formula I personally advocate, – Israel within the context of a peace settlement – would give up the large majority of the areas which fell into its hands in the 1967 war. Israel would not do so because of any lack of historical affinity between the Jewish people and many of these areas. With regard

to Judea and Samaria, for example, historical Jewish affinity is as great as that for the coastal plain or Galilee.[2]

The "compromise" the Allon Plan promoted was a matter of pragmatism. The plan was an attempt to maximize Israel's military security and minimize its Arab population in order to retain Israel's "Jewish character." It called essentially for annexing security belts along the 1967 armistice line with Jordan and south of Gaza City in the Gaza Strip, and the establishment of some form of demilitarized Arab entity in the Palestinian population centers of the West Bank and Gaza.

Allon insisted that his plan was in accord with UN Resolution 242, twisting the resolution's clauses to the interpretation that in calling for Israeli withdrawal from territories taken in 1967, the resolution meant merely from some territories, not from all, and that further the resolution acknowledged "the need to provide Israel with secure and recognized boundaries – in other words that changes must be introduced in the old lines of the armistice agreements."[3] Israel's security, Allon argued, cannot rest upon international guarantee: it required defensible borders. The pre-1967 borders, and especially the border with Jordan, were unacceptable because the lines themselves lacked "topographical security value," and even more seriously, denied Israel "the essential minimum of strategic depth":

> The gravest problem is on the eastern boundary, where the entire width of the coastal plain varies between 10 and 15 miles, where the main centers of Israel's population, including Tel Aviv and its suburbs, are situated, and where the situation of Jerusalem is especially perilous. Within these lines a single successful first strike by the Arab armies would be sufficient to dissect Israel at more than one point, to sever its essential living arteries, and to confront it with dangers that no other state would be prepared to face. The purpose of defensible borders is thus to correct this weakness, to provide Israel with the requisite minimal strategic depth, as well as lines which have topographical strategic significance.[4]

Allon proposed therefore that Israel annex a security area along the eastern ceasefire line of 1967. In the first version of the Allon Plan, articulated in

2. Yigal Allon, "Israel: The Case for Defensible Borders," *Foreign Affairs* (October 1976), 55(1): 44.

3. *Ibid.*, pp. 40-41.

4. *Ibid.*, pp. 41-42.

the month after the occupation, Allon called for annexation of a strip twelve to fifteen kilometers wide along the Jordan River south to the Dead Sea. About the southern area of the West Bank, Judea, as he called it, Allon was undecided: either the region as a whole would be annexed, or it would be split, with the densely populated part of Hebron joining the Arab entity and the area to its east being annexed to Israel.[5] A few weeks after he first proffered the plan, Allon told the cabinet that he believed that the area of concentrated Palestinian population in "Judea" should be allotted to the Arab entity. Allon's view on the future of the area was shaped to some extent by the effort in April 1968 by a group of Israeli zealots led by Rabbi Moshe Levinger to settle in Hebron, an effort which began by their checking into the Park Hotel in Hebron and refusing to leave. William Harris, who interviewed Allon on the issue and who studied the settlements in detail, wrote that:

> The Hebron settlement bid exposed the fundamental conflict in the Allon Plan between belief in the right of Jews to the whole historic land and arguments that this could not be implemented because of demographic dangers to the Jewish state. Hebron, the city of Abraham, ranked second to Jerusalem as a Jewish holy site, and Allon, with the majority of Ministers (only Sapir, Eban and the Mapam representatives were opposed) tended to sympathize with the settlers. Yet how could a Jewish presence be established without absorbing 40,000 Arab Hebronites into Israel? Allon resolved the dilemma, in late 1968, with the concept of a dual city, similar to Nazareth, involving the building of a separate Jewish quarter on the hills immediately to the east of the existing Arab city. This quarter would form an integral part of the Jordan Rift security strip with the Arab city excluded, the line of separation between the two sections marking the western border of the strip.[6]

This new Jewish quarter took the form of Kiryat Arba.

While Allon moved in the direction of reserving part of "Judea" for an Arab entity, in practice the parameter of his proposed annexed area of "Samaria" swung to the west over the years, leaving a smaller area for the proposed entity. By 1975, rather than the twelve- to fifteen-kilometer strip that Allon had originally proposed, a belt which would have essentially been limited to the valley floor, the authorities had decided that a fifteen- to twenty-kilometer strip was required, extending up the slopes rising from the

5. See text in W. W. Harris,"War and Settlement Change: The Golan Heights and the Jordan Rift, 1967-1977," *Transactions of the Institute of British Geographers* (New Series, 1978), 3(3).

6. W. W. Harris, *Taking Root: Israeli Settlement in the West Bank, the Golan and Gaza-Sinai, 1967-1980* (Chichester and New York: Wiley, 1980), p. 108.

valley to the highlands.[7] Although Allon called the area a strip, it actually comprises at least one-third of the West Bank.[8] (Allon estimates the area to be annexed at about seven hundred square miles, which is almost exactly one-third of the West Bank including the already annexed territory of east Jerusalem.)[9]

Allon disparaged the regions he wanted to annex as "the arid zone" and "the Judean desert,"[10] but in fact, the Jordan Valley is probably the West Bank's potentially most lucrative and productive agricultural area: it functions as a vast natural hothouse, an ideal setting for the production of winter crops for export. Israeli settlements are producing vegetables, berries, tomatoes, and cut flowers for export now in lushly irrigated acreage, some of it under glasshouses or plastic. Palestinian farmers in the area have, meanwhile, seen their fruit trees and other crops wither and die when new deep-bore wells for the Israeli settlements lowered the water table and dried up the springs upon which the Palestinians relied for irrigation.

Allon also describes the area as "almost devoid of [Arab] population";[11] this argument is disingenuous, however. The reason that the valley is as sparsely populated by Palestinians as it is today is that so many were forced to flee in the 1967 War. While an estimated 30 percent of the West Bank inhabitants fled between June and December 1967, the population loss was not evenly distributed: an estimated 23 percent of the residents of the highlands left, but 88 percent of the people of the Jordan Valley were forced out.[12] Some of this disproportion may be attributed to the fact that the line of escape was shorter for valley residents, and that those seeking immediate refuge nearby in the valley would have crossed the Jordan River, whereas people in the highlands with the same objective might have traveled to fields or caves not far from their towns and villages, areas which later came

7. This was reflected in the August 1975 Jordan Rift Development Plan of the Settlement Department of the Jewish Agency; see Harris, *Taking Root*, pp. 106-9.

8. Abraham Becker suggests that the area earmarked by Allon for annexation is about a quarter of Samaria (the northern sector of the West Bank) but perhaps as much as half or more of Judea (the southern sector). Abraham S. Becker, *Israel and the Palestinian Occupied Territories: Military-Political Issues in the Debate* (Santa Monica: Rand, December 1971), p. 28.

9. Allon, "Case for Defensible Borders," p. 47.

10. *Ibid.*

11. *Ibid.*

12. Harris, *Taking Root*, p. 16.

under Israeli occupation. But it seems also that Israeli tactics, such as the aerial strafing of population centers in the Jordan Valley, seemed particularly calculated to empty the area of its existing population. Israel has, moreover, consistently refused to allow refugees from the Jordan Valley to return to their homes; three sprawling refugee camps in the valley, where many of the region's agricultural laborers lived, remain empty despite the requests of the United Nations that these people be allowed to return. Furthermore, the Israeli authorities have been particularly careful not to permit the return to the Jordan Valley of indigenous property holders: they maintain special lists of their names at the bridges.

The Allon Plan of the summer of 1967 also projected annexation of land extending from Jericho to the Latrun salient north of Jerusalem, and curving south of Jerusalem to embrace the Etzion bloc of settlements, Jewish settlements lost in the 1948 war and reestablished after 1967.[13] Quite soon after the original proposal, however, Allon decided that it would be a mistake to sever the connection between the east and west banks: the political and economic importance of Dayan's "open bridges" policy was becoming rapidly apparent. Consequently, in later versions, the Allon Plan included a corridor linking the two banks, running along the Ramallah-Jericho road.[14]

Allon also proposed to annex the sector of Gaza south of Gaza City and its environs: indeed, he advocated at this point retaining part of Sinai as well, arguing that "Israel must continue to control fully the strategic desert zone from the southern part of the Gaza Strip to the dunes on the eastern approaches of the town of El-Arish, which itself would be returned to Egypt."[15] Allon's projection of the division of Gaza appears to allot only a very small portion of its densely populated urban center of the city itself and surrounding refugee camps to the Arab entity, reserving the remainder of the strip, including its smaller towns and most of its citrus growing area, for Israeli annexation.[16]

These annexed areas would serve as Israeli "security zones" in which Israeli military units would be stationed. The densely populated parts of the West Bank and Gaza would be demilitarized zones, perhaps "under joint Arab- Israeli control." Allon declared that

13. *Ibid.,* pp. 38-39.

14. *Ibid.,* p. 106.

15. Allon, "Case for Defensible Borders," p. 48.

16. See map, *ibid.,* p. 45.

. . . if Israel were to forfeit the densely populated heartland of Judea and Samaria, it would not be able to forego – under any circumstances – the effective demilitarization of these areas. Apart from civilian police to guarantee internal order, these areas would have to be devoid of offensive forces and heavy arms. In the same way as any other country, Israel would be unable to abandon areas so close to its heartland if they were liable to again become staging areas for full-scale, limited or guerrilla attacks upon its most vital areas.[17]

What political arrangement did Allon favor for the areas to be left for an Arab entity? Initially he appears to have envisioned a kind of Palestinian statelet, closely linked to Israel: a "sovereign political state with close economic and security ties to Israel."[18] Allon was not the only Israeli politician to think, in the first months of occupation, that a "Palestinian entity" might be established in the West Bank and/or Gaza under Israeli hegemony, but this vision shriveled in the mainstream of Israeli politics as Palestinian nationalism itself became more organized through the Palestine Liberation Organization, and created more serious a problem for the Israeli government, both locally and in international diplomacy. By the time the occupation was a year and a half old, Allon was proposing several options: the entity could become a Palestinian state, forever forbidden to ally itself to any force hostile to Israel. Or it could be returned to Hussein – if the King of Jordan agreed to the permanent demilitarization of the part of the West Bank he would receive, to recognize Israel's right to military intervention in the West Bank to repress "terrorist bases" or any breach of demilitarization, to acknowledge Israeli sovereignty in Jerusalem and the annexed area along the Jordan River and Dead Sea, and to resettle the Gaza refugees on the east bank.[19] By 1976, near the end of the tenure of the Labor government, Allon had eliminated all but one option for the future of the areas he was willing to cede in the West Bank: it should provide the basis to help "resolve the problem of Palestinian identity that could then find its expression in a single Jordanian-Palestinian state."

The Allon Plan also provided for use of a land route (in distinction to sovereignty over a land corridor) between the West Bank and Gaza sections

17. *Ibid.*, p. 50.

18. *Ibid.*

19. *New York Times,* 16 August 1967.

of the entity, particularly significant in Allon's view as it would afford the eastern portion of the Arab entity access to the Mediterranean. Israel, of course, was to have access for its exports to the markets of Amman, and to the Jordan bridges.[20]

THE ALLON PLAN: ITS CONTEXT

In the first few years of the occupation, the Israeli government made no formal offer whatever and no significant informal offer as to the eventual disposition of the areas it conquered in June 1967, nor did it advance any plan for the regularization of the occupation it was conducting under a military government. Three salient reasons account for this vacuum.

Political and Public Support

There was, first of all, enormous political support within the Israeli government and within the society as a whole for making major border changes and retaining at least parts of the newly seized territories; concurrently, there was no powerful movement for withdrawal in the immediate aftermath of the war. Part of the enthusiasm for the new parameters of Israeli control was phrased in terms of military advantage of the "natural barriers" which the June victory had provided. Some four months after the war, for example, Major-General Itzhak Rabin, then the Israeli chief of staff, said to an interviewer with evident satisfaction:

> The present borders run along natural barriers: Egypt – the Canal; Jordan – the Jordan River, a less impressive barrier than the Suez Canal, but nevertheless a barrier, and with Syria there will no longer be a need to climb up mountains.[21]

20. *Jerusalem Post*, 12 December 1968; Becker, *Military-Political Issues*, p. 29.

21. Yitzhak Rabin, "How We Won the War," *Jerusalem Post Weekly*, 4 October 1967.

Mystical justification for the Israeli occupation was invoked not only by the politicians of the extreme right, whose allegiance to the claims of biblical borders as Israel's sacred right had long been their ideological hallmark. Prime Minister Levi Eshkol of the Labor Alignment resorted to biblical allusions of return in his victory speech to the Knesset on June 12:

> The prophesy has been fulfilled. 'There is recompense for thy work, the sons have returned to their borders.' [Jeremiah 36:16-17] . . . To the nations of the world I say: Be under no illusion that the State of Israel is prepared to return to the situation that prevailed up to a week ago.[22]

Moshe Dayan, then the defense minister, resonated with the sentiments of a Begin at a reinterment ceremony in the summer of 1967 for Israeli soldiers who had been killed in Jerusalem in 1948:

> Our brothers who fell in the War of Independence: We have not abandoned your dream nor forgotten the lesson you taught us. We have returned to the Mount, to the cradle of our nation's history, to the land of our forefathers, to the land of the Judges, and to the fortress of David's dynasty. We have returned to Hebron, to Shechem [Nablus], to Bethlehem and Anatoth, to Jericho and the fords over the Jordan. . . . We know that to give life to Jerusalem we must station the soldiers and armor of Zahal in the Shechem mountains and on the bridges over the Jordan.[23]

These religious justifications of the mainstream political leadership were underwritten by the declaration of the Chief Rabbi of the Sephardic community, Yitzhak Nissim, in October 1967, that no religious or secular Jewish authority, including the government of Israel, had the right to renounce any of the Land of Israel, the "heritage of every Jew."[24]

It should be noted in passing, moreover, that even government figures associated with Labor, including relative "doves" like Yigal Allon, had expressed a penchant for expansion of Israel's borders long before the war. In a book published in 1959, Allon argued that Israel had committed a major error in not seizing the West Bank in 1948. He averred:

22. Becker, *Military-Political Issues*, p. 6.

23. Shabtai Teveth, *Moshe Dayan: The Soldier, the Man, the Legend* (Boston: Houghton Mifflin, 1972), p. 342.

24. Becker, *Military-Political Issues*.

> If indeed the Arab rulers once again force upon Israel a total war, the existing borders will no longer bind the Israel Defense Forces. ... If Zahal should cross the borders of the divided land, it is forbidden to retreat again, but we must aspire from then on to stabilize the borders, which from the historical, economic and security aspect are the most natural.[25]

There was in addition a massive popular opposition in the years immediately after the conquest to withdrawal from the newly taken Arab territories. Public opinion polls disclosed virtual unanimity with regard to remaining in east Jerusalem, and a strong majority for staying in the West Bank, Gaza, Golan, and Sharm el Sheikh.[26]

Domestic Political Factors

A second factor tended to discourage official planning, even on a contingency basis, for any alternative to continued military government of the occupied areas. This was the nature of the National Unity Government then in power. The National Unity Government was formed on the eve of the June War in order to mobilize the strength of Israel's usually fractious parties. It spanned the political gamut from Mapam on the relative left to the Gahal on the right. The Gahal, represented in the government by three cabinet ministers (of a total of twenty-four) would not remain in government if that government offered to withdraw from any of what the right regarded as historically Eretz Israel.

The inclusion of the Gahal in the National Unity Government was quite a significant step in the legitimation of right-wing politics in Israel. The Gahal bloc had been formed prior to the 1965 elections by the Herut and Liberal parties. The Herut, led by Menachem Begin, who headed the terrorist Irgun gang before Israel's establishment, was the ideological heir to Vladimir Jabotinsky's Revisionist Zionism, and had been effectively isolated from power during nearly two decades of Labor party rule. During that time, while Labor sought international affirmation for the armistice

25. Yigal Allon, *Masch shel chol: Yisrael vearav ben michama veshalom* (A Curtain of Sand: Israel and the Arabs between War and Peace (Tel Aviv, 1959), pp. 81-82; quoted in Rael Jean Isaac, *Party and Politics in Israel* (New York: Longman, 1981), p. 126.

26. Mordechai Nisan, *Israel and the Territories: A Study in Control* (Ramat Gan: Turtledove Publishing, 1978), p. 6.

lines of 1949, Herut continued to claim that Israel's sovereignty should extend over all of mandatory Palestine – including the territory of the Hashemite Kingdom of Jordan. When Gahal was formed, Herut dropped specific references to Transjordan, but retained vague advocacy of "the wholeness of the land."[27] The position of Gahal in the government was that not one inch of Judea and Samaria, as they persisted in calling the West Bank, should be relinquished.

The positions of other political elements in the National Unity Government varied, though no grouping favored withdrawal from all the territories seized in the war: indeed, there had been no dissent within the ruling coalition from the cabinet decision on June 18 to annex east Jerusalem.[28] The least intransigent element in the National Unity Government was Mapam: even that party, however, wanted to annex not only east Jerusalem but also the Gaza Strip, and furthermore, according to the position which its Political Committee formalized in the summer of 1967, insisted upon retaining Israeli defense positions on the ridges of the Golan Heights, to be otherwise demilitarized. Mapam did, however, ask that the West Bank be returned to Jordan.[29] Levi Eshkol, then prime minister, floated the possibility of an autonomous Palestinian entity in the urban concentrations of the West Bank,[30] while insisting on an Israeli "security border" along the Jordan River[31] and the annexation of the Gaza Strip.[32] Shortly after the war, Yigal Allon, then minister of immigrant absorption, had presented a plan for an Arab enclave in the population centers of the West Bank, the germ of what would later be known as the Allon Plan. Moshe Dayan, minister of defense and therefore in direct charge of the occupied areas, did not specify a plan, but did call for "economic integration" of the West Bank and Gaza Strip.[33]

27. Isaac, *Party and Politics*, pp. 138-55.

28. Michael Brecher, *Decisions in Israel's Foreign Policy* (New Haven: Yale University Press, 1975), pp. 37-47.

29. Becker, *Military-Political Issues*, p. 7.

30. *Le Monde*, 9 July 1967.

31. *Los Angeles Times*, 14 September 1967.

32. Becker, *Military-Political Issues*, p. 7.

33. *Ibid.*, p. 109.

In this initial period, the Israeli government confined itself to ambiguous formulas – "no withdrawal without peace," "territories for peace," and "secure and recognized borders." It carefully evaded the naming of what territories might be relinquished. All elements of the governing coalition were willing to consider yielding some territory – even the Gahal was at this point not wedded to retention of the Sinai, and indeed, it was partially in response to the perceived "softness" of Gahal that the "Land of Israel" movement of Israel Eldad arose, with its slogans of "not one inch" and Arab emigration. But because all of the elements in the government wanted to retain part of the territorial war booty, and because a strong Israeli government was perceived as an important ingredient in holding on to the occupied areas, the "consensus of immobility" endured. In order to safeguard the consensus the government avoided endorsing Security Council Resolution 242, though the Israeli ambassador at the UN voted for it.[34]

Role of the United States

A third, extremely important, factor militating against any Israeli withdrawal, was that the Israeli government had the effective backing of the United States for an aggressive and intransigent position both in launching the war and in retaining the benefits of that aggression. Many of the government officials belonging to the Labor Alignment were particularly concerned – even obsessed – with the viewpoint of the United States. There was, moreover, the growing importance of U.S. aid to Israel, including overt military aid, initiated only with the war.

Jon Kimche, a man with close contacts in the Israeli ruling elite and particularly within its intelligence apparatus, writes of "two American policies operating on two distinct levels." Underlying any *pro forma* U.S. statements of caution to Israel, he declares, was a clear message that Israel should stand firm. Immediately before the war, he reports,

> In secret talks which they had with Yariv and Amit, Israel's Military and Secret Intelligence Chiefs, the Pentagon and the CIA were satisfied that Israel could well take care of the situation as long as the Great Powers did not intervene. . . . [CIA Director] Helms told his Israeli colleagues that Israel would have to conjure up all her inner strength to withstand pressures from the outside. Even the Americans might find it necessary to join in these pressures for they had to protect themselves at all costs against the suspicion of collusion – and they could do so only by

34. Brecher, *Decisions in Israel's Foreign Policy*, pp. 442, 487.

ensuring that there was no collusion. But — and this was conveyed to Yariv rather than spelled out in so many words — if Israel wanted to have tangible results this time, she would have to be as solid as a rock and not weaken before, during or after the actual military encounter.[35]

The reason for the favorable U.S. attitude toward the Israeli position becomes clear when the global context is examined. In the late 1960s, the United States was deeply embroiled in a losing battle in Indochina. The administration of President Lyndon B. Johnson, although eager to extend U.S. influence abroad, was acutely aware of the difficulties of mustering support for the human and economic sacrifices foreign military adventures required of the population in the United States — indeed, political difficulties over the Indochina war ultimately caused Johnson to decide to forego a contest for reelection.

Israel suddenly presented itself to the Johnson administration as an attractive Middle Eastern alternative to the Indochina model: a means by which the United States could rebuff what Washington strategists perceived as Soviet clients in a vital region, without incurring the military, political and economic expenses entailed in the dispatch of U.S. troops. The Johnson administration had been particularly bedeviled by the Middle East: since 1956, with a brief respite early in the Kennedy years, official Washington viewed Gamal Abdal Nasser as an enemy of U.S. interests in the region, and tended to depict him as a "Soviet client." The regional influence of the radical nationalism that Nasser represented was expanding during the early Johnson administration years, with the rise of the neo-Ba'ath in Syria seen in Washington and Tel Aviv as an especially distressing development. Nadav Safran writes of the manner in which the Johnson administration would have viewed an Arab victory in June 1967:

> A military victory for Nasser would not only have crippled or destroyed Israel, but would also have put him in a position to establish his hegemony in the Middle East and sweep it clean of any remaining American positions, including the oil-rich Arab countries with the principal of which he was still engaged in war in Yemen. Even just a political victory would have placed Nasser in a strong position to venture a new confrontation with Israel later on and in the meantime would have put him in a perilously powerful position in the entire Arab world, to the detriment of the United States and the benefit of the Soviet Union. The United States would then have faced

35. Jon Kimche, *There Could Have Been Peace* (New York: Dial Press, 1973), p. 258.

the dilemma of taking drastic action to check and reverse these outcomes at a time when the Vietnam War was sapping its national unity and will and absorbing a vast portion of its military resources, or resigning itself to them with incalcuable consequences for its global position.[36]

Instead, the Johnson administration was presented with the advantages of an ally that could succeed in regional battles unaided by dispatch of U.S. troops. Safran's words reflect the satisfaction of Washington policymakers at this turn of events:

> It was the United States that was now in a position to use its client's victory to check and roll back the Soviet position in the Middle East, to promote a new order in the area that protected and advanced its own interests, and to use its Middle East position as leverage to influence the Soviets' behavior in the global arena.[37]

After Israel's victory in the June War, its relationship with the United States became much closer than it had ever been previously. Military aid to Israel began in earnest: no longer did Washington cast the thin cloak of the Kennedy era – when a U.S. initiative to arm Israel was disguised as a German weapons transfer – over the escalating supply of arms assistance. During the final years of the Johnson administration, despite the formal adherence of the United States to UN Resolution 242 calling for Israeli withdrawal, most U.S. strategists believed that no U.S. interest was to be served by pressing at that point for Israeli withdrawal from the conquered territories.

Israeli Policy: Domestic Disagreements

Within Israel, however, a debate about the disposition of the occupied areas began nonetheless. The terms of the discussion and the basic positions within it were set to a considerable extent in the first two years or so after the June War, though the arguments were of course considerably elaborated over the years.

We have already mentioned in passing the position of Herut and its Gahal bloc, which opposed withdrawal from any territory which they considered part of historic Eretz Israel. The Land of Israel movement, led by Israel Shaib-Eldad, gathered together activists not only from the far

---

36. Nadav Safran, *Israel: The Embattled Ally* (Cambridge, Mass.: Harvard University Press, 1978), p. 582.

37. *Ibid.*, p. 583.

right-wing parties but also from Labor to put pressure on officials who might consider withdrawal from any of the "historic territory." There were broad hints from this movement that a massive departure of Arabs from the occupied areas would be most desirable.[38]

Within the mainstream of the Labor party itself, moreover, there was considerable divergence in attitude about the benefits and burdens of retaining various parts of the occupied areas. For the electoral campaign of 1969, the Labor party used the device of formulating an "Oral Law": the cohesion of the National Unity Government was salvaged by not having the Oral Law formally adopted by the government. The Oral Law specified those territories that Israel must keep in any settlement: Jerusalem, united under Israeli sovereignty; the Golan Heights, the Gaza Strip and Sharm el Sheikh with a corridor linking it to Israel; and the Jordan River as a "security frontier," with no Arab army to be allowed on the West Bank.[39] Within these parameters, party members could espouse what positions they chose.

Two special concerns dominated the thinking of those who objected to the annexation or wholesale integration of the occupied areas. One anxiety was demographic in character: Pinhas Sapir, for example, was preoccupied with the effect that absorption of so many Arabs would have on the "Jewish" character of Israel. The state would, in the foreseeable future, he maintained, become Jewish in name only. There seemed to be significant statistical basis for his distress: because of the relatively high birth rate of the Palestinians under Israeli rule, whether within the Green Line or under the military government in the West Bank and Gaza, they would eventually come to outnumber the Jewish population, with its relatively low birth rate and unimpressive growth through immigration.

Concern for demography led Sapir to be a minimalist in regard to views on how much occupied territory should be retained, but not all Israeli politicians bothered by the prospects of population imbalance adopted the same position. David Ben-Gurion's favored approach was not withdrawal from occupied territory but campaigns to alter the balance of birth rate. Observing that if the Palestinian natural rate of increase continued as it had, in twenty years "the complete Land of Israel, including Transjordan, will contain 3.5 million Arabs," Ben-Gurion concluded that if the Jewish birth rate continued to decline as it had in previous years, the outcome for the

38. Becker, *Military-Political Issues,* p. 56.

39. *Ibid.,* pp. 56-57; Harris, *Taking Root,* pp. 45-46.

state of Israel is not hard to imagine.[40] Therefore he urged that "every Jewish woman capable of understanding the unique needs of a nation such as Israel [be told that] their prime obligation is to have at least four children, and, as far as possible, within eight to ten years after being married."[41] To reinforce such an explanation of national duty he proposed that "incentives" be offered in the form of special economic assistance to large families. Because the state would presumably be obliged to aid both Jews and Arabs, Ben-Gurion advocated that the incentives be handled through the Jewish Agency or a similar parastate institution.[42]

In general, the ambivalent attitude of many in the Labor party toward the occupied areas can be summarized in an ugly metaphor of Levi Eskol's: "The dowry is gorgeous, but the bride is so homely." This group was attracted toward retention of the occupied areas for many reasons, including some very like those of the historical mysticism of the Herut, but they were simultaneously repelled by the prospect of integrating the Palestinian population of the occupied areas into Israel's political, social, and economic life.

The question of economic integration was a particularly sensitive one for the Labor Zionists of the alignment. As Defense Minister Moshe Dayan's policy of "economic integration" was implemented, thousands of workers from the West Bank and Gaza Strip were hired by employers in Israel to work in unskilled and semiskilled positions. The fact that such workers could be hired for about half the average wage, coupled with the fact that they had no union protection or right to collective bargaining, helped to build a constituency of employers for retention of economic access to the West Bank and Gaza. On the other hand, it was deeply troubling to Labor Zionists, whose political ideology was dominated by the concept of "Hebrew labor." This idea, formulated during the British Mandate period, exalted the boycott of Arab labor and exclusive employment of Jewish, even if higher wages made that a less profitable course of action. Yitzhak Ben Aharon, the secretary-general of the Histadrut, was perhaps the most outspoken critic with this point of view. He told a meeting of the Labor party secretariat:

40. David Ben-Gurion, *Israel: A Personal History* (New York: Funk & Wagnalls, 1971), pp. 837-8.

41. *Ibid.,* p. 839.

42. *Ibid.,* p. 837.

I do not know whether the territories that we hold are bargaining cards or perhaps embers burning away at our foundations. . . . I am not at all sure that one of these days we will conclude that a certain portion of the population and certain sections of the country should not be under our control even without receiving a counter signature [on a peace treaty]. Without being an extreme Marxist, I must say that it's very sweet building Zionism with Arab labor, to build cities of the economy and enjoy it. We shall soon hear that anyone who says he does not want to get rich on the work of the Arabs from the territories questions the realization of Zionism and holds back redemption and development.[43]

The debate within Israeli society did not develop in a "natural" and independent way, however. The willingness of the United States to provide increasing amounts of military and economic assistance had the effect of reinforcing those in Israeli political life who wanted to maintain the *status quo* of occupation.

United States Policy: Underlying Support

The attitude of the United States toward a resolution of the Arab-Israeli crisis in 1969-1970, and particularly its stance toward the occupation of the West Bank and Gaza Strip, had an important influence on the internal debate these questions generated within Israel. It might fairly be stated that although overt American moves toward peace and Israeli withdrawal occasioned significant vicissitudes in the public political discussion in Israel – and indeed helped to create the situation in which the National Unity Government collapsed – an understanding of the underlying U.S. support encouraged the Israeli government not to waver in its refusal to promise to yield territory at that time.

The Middle East diplomacy of the early years of the presidency of Richard M. Nixon came out of a divided bureaucracy and lacked presidential pressure to achieve its aims. The essence of the divergence within the administration was that State Department officials, headed by Secretary of State William Rogers, believed that the post-June War situation was not healthy for U.S. interests in the region. The Soviets, these officials feared, benefited from growing regional polarization and Arab radicalization which seemed from this U.S. perspective to be the inevitable consequence of continued Israeli retention of so much newly conquered Arab territory.

43. *Maariv,* 2 February 1973, translated in *Israleft News Service,* 15 February 1973.

When Nixon came into office, there were some indications that he subscribed to the view that U.S. policy should turn away from the marked bias toward Israel that characterized the Johnson years. Shortly after his election, he sent former governor William Scranton on a "fact-finding" mission to the Middle East, during which the governor inflated hopes in a number of Arab capitals by announcing that the incoming administration would be "evenhanded" in its dealings with the Middle East, with the tacit premise that such an attitude would be a departure from the previous U.S. stance. Shortly after assuming office, Nixon agreed to open "Big Two" talks with the Soviets, and to begin the "Big Four" talks at the United Nations which the French government had been proposing for some time.

There are strong indications, however, that Nixon was not wholeheartedly convinced of the wisdom of a conciliatory path; indeed, that even during his first year or so of office he was strongly influenced by the contrary approach which later became the operative principle of his administration, and that this bifurcation caused Nixon to stop short of serious pursuit of a settlement.

Henry Kissinger, Nixon's national security advisor, was opposed to moves toward a rapid settlement; as he wrote later,

> . . . the resulting strategic disagreement was never really settled. The bureaucracy wanted to embark on substantive talks as rapidly as possible because it feared that a deteriorating situation would increase Soviet influence, I thought delay was on the whole in our interest because it enabled us to demonstrate even to radical Arabs that we were indispensable to any progress and that it could not be extorted from us by Soviet pressure. The State Department wanted to fuel the process of negotiations by accepting at least some Soviet ideas, to facilitate compromise. I wanted to frustrate the radicals – who were in any event hostile to us – by demonstrating that in the Middle East friendship with the United States was the precondition to diplomatic progress.[44]

Kissinger did not win out immediately in the administration's infighting, but by the end of 1971 his position had risen to dominance. Nixon himself seemed to vacillate during this earlier period between wanting and not wanting a resolution of the crisis. Kissinger recalled in his memoirs:

> On one of my memoranda in late 1969, informing him of King Hussein's pessimism about peace prospects in the face of Israel's tough stand, Nixon wrote in longhand: "I am beginning to think we have to consider taking strong steps unilaterally to save

44. Henry Kissinger, *The White House Years* (Boston: Little, Brown, 1979), p. 354.

Israel from her own destruction." But on further consideration he always stopped short, because in 1969 the beneficiaries of such a course would have been the Soviet Union and Soviet clients vociferously hostile to us.[45]

It was under such ambiguous circumstances that the State Department produced the Rogers Plan (or Rogers Plan "A" as it became known later). The secretary of state, in a speech in New York, called essentially for Israeli withdrawal from the territories taken in the June War in exchange for Arab recognition. Rogers declared:

We believe that while recognized boundaries must be established and agreed upon by the parties, any changes in the pre-existing lines should not reflect the weight of conquest and should be confined to insubstantial alterations required for mutual security.[46]

He spoke vaguely of the need for settlement of the refugee problem and called for Jordanian-Israeli negotiations to resolve the issue of Jerusalem, which he said should remain a unified city, but should permit both Israel and Jordan roles. For Israel and Egypt – an issue which does not concern us here directly – he laid out a plan for direct negotiations to result in Israeli withdrawal and creation of demilitarized zones in the Sinai.

The Rogers initiative was immediately rebuffed by the Israeli cabinet meeting in emergency session, which rejected his plan as an attempt to impose a resolution on the parties.[47] The thrust of the Rogers initiative was followed up shortly afterwards when U.S. Ambassador to the United Nations Charles Yost presented a document at the Four Powers Talks on the Middle East that underlined the view that Israel should withdraw from the West Bank and Gaza within the context of a peace agreement. The Knesset rejoined with a sweeping rejection of both the Rogers initiative and the Yost document, rejecting them by a vote of 57 to 3 with 2 abstentions.[48]

During the winter the U.S. administration did not act to press Israel to look more favorably towards withdrawal. A glint of the reasoning behind the absence of such pressure can be gleaned from a marginal note which Kissinger reports Nixon scrawled on a memorandum from the national

45. *Ibid.*, p. 373.

46. *New York Times*, 10 December 1969.

47. *Jerusalem Post*, 12 December 1969.

48. Brecher, *Decisions in Israel's Foreign Policy*, pp. 483-85.

security advisor: " 'Even Handedness' is the right policy – but above all our interest is what gives the Soviets the most trouble – Don't let the Arab-Israeli conflict obscure that interest."[49]

Moreover Kissinger also described – albeit from the viewpoint of interested combatant in the intra-administration battle – the offhand manner in which Nixon dealt with the initial Rogers initiatives: "Nixon indicated to me that he shared my skepticism about what could come of it, but said it would give State something to do while we handled Vietnam, SALT, Europe and China in the White House."[50]

Events themselves intervened to create new terms of discussion. In March 1969, Nasser declared the ceasefire of 1967 terminated, and launched a "war of aggression" along the Suez Canal with artillery barrages that inflicted heavy casualties on Israeli forces. Egyptian casualties were still heavier, but Egypt appeared willing to make heavy sacrifices and take advantage of its relative strength in population and number of men under arms. In July Israel adopted a strategy of using its air force as a "flying artillery" against Egyptian positions along the canal, and in January 1970 escalated to "deep penetration" raids, sending its air force far into Egypt, not only hitting military targets but also inflicting significant civilian casualties, even in the environs of Cairo. Egypt responded by seeking aid from the Soviets: the Soviets not only sent large amounts of equipment, but by early spring, Israeli and American policy makers were convinced, dispatched Soviet pilots to defend Egyptian air space. By the summer, Israeli jet fighters and Egyptian planes (believed to have Soviet pilots) were involved in heated air battles.[51] Nixon weighed in with alarming statements about his intention to "expel the Soviets" from the Middle East.

It was in such a tense context that the United States won acceptance for its Rogers Plan "B". The plan was far less detailed than the secretary of state's original proposal: it called simply for a ceasefire between Israel and Egypt, and for talks between Israel and Egypt and Israel and Jordan, under the auspices of Ambassador Gunnar Jarring, on the basis of mutual acknowledgment of sovereignty and Israeli withdrawal from territories occupied in 1967, on the basis of Resolution 242. (In fact, the Israeli government had for a long time evaded statements using the word "withdrawal," and indeed statements affirming 242 – although its ambassador at the United Nations

49. Kissinger, *White House Years,* p. 563.

50. *Ibid.,* p. 357.

51. Safran, *Israel: The Embattled Ally,* pp. 264-65.

had done so. It was only at the end of May that Prime Minister Golda Meir formally announced that Israel was ready to reach a settlement based on 242. The National Unity Government was saved from collapse only by permitting Gahal to abstain on the matter.[52])

Golda Meir conveyed privately to the United States that Israel was not willing to accept Rogers' new formulation; the United States responded by asking that Israel allow the Arabs to be the first to reject it. Then, in a stunning surprise, at the end of July the Egyptian government accepted the Rogers Plan. The United States pressed Israel to reciprocate averring that it understood that Israel should not return to borders the same as those of June 1967, and promising continued military and economic aid on a large scale.[53] After receiving specific assurances that more Phantom jets and Shrike missiles could be expected, the Israeli government embodied the substance of the Rogers Plan B in its own letter, and sent it to Nixon to signify assent. This roundabout method was chosen to obviate the embarrassment of accepting a proposal that had been rejected six weeks earlier. Gahal, with Begin at its head, left the National Unity Government in protest.[54]

A ceasefire between Israel and Egypt was put in place in short order, though Israel quickly began to complain about Egyptian violations thereof. No immediate steps were taken under Rogers Plan B in regard to Jordan, but it was in Jordan that the plan had its most profound impact. The Palestinian *fedayiin* were the ascendant force in Jordan: after the ignominious defeat in 1967, and the massive social dislocation of the influx of refugees from the West Bank, the political and social conditions were favorable to the growth of an authentically Palestinian liberation movement. The Palestine Liberation Organization did not concur in Nasser's ceasefire arrangement, and in fact was deeply worried about its implications. This divergence between Nasser and the PLO gave Hussein an opening to attack the Palestinian organizations, which had grown to the point of exercising a kind of sovereignty in Jordan, particularly in the sprawling refugee camps and Palestinian neighborhoods in Amman and the north.

The ensuing crisis had a drastic effect on the political situation and on the perception of it by the various parties. Hussein retained his throne, but only after anxious moments in Tel Aviv and Washington, where policy

52. Interview with Menachem Begin in *New York Times*, 2 May 1968; see Brecher, *Decisions in Israel's Foreign Policy*, pp. 487-88.

53. Brecher, p. 493.

54. *Ibid.*, pp. 495-98.

makers feared that the *fedayiin* would seize power in Jordan. The United States and Israel coordinated a careful contingency plan for joint military intervention should the king's rule appear to be in imminent danger: Israeli tanks would move into northern Jordan, while the United States assumed military responsibility for cordoning off the area and preventing the Soviets from assisting the Palestinians or the Syrians, whose tanks had entered northern Jordan in a half-hearted effort to aid the PLO. The United States was deeply impressed by the efficacy of the Israeli threat and by the advantage of having such a powerful ally on the scene. The nettlesome necessity of sending U.S. troops could be avoided, at a time when the country's military was already stretched thin by the burdens of the war in Indochina, and when the administration's political capacity to take on additional foreign adventures was severely limited by Congress and popular dissent. A message from the United States to Israel at the conclusion of the crisis asserted that "we believe that the steps Israel took have contributed immeasurably" to the withdrawal of Syrian troops and the positive resolution of the conflict.[55] Nadav Safran summed up the effect of Black September on the Nixon Administration:

> . . . the Jordanian episode drove home to the President and some of his advisers a crucial point which they previously saw only in the abstract. The crisis and its denouement demonstrated to them in a concrete and dramatic fashion the value for the United States of a strong Israel. At a time when the regional balance of forces among the Arab states, between the United States and the Soviet Union, as well as between Israel and the Arab states was seen to be imperiled and when the entire American position in the Middle East appeared, as a result, to be in jeopardy, the United States was able to retrieve the situation and turn it around only through the effective cooperation of a powerful Israel.[56]

The Jordanian crisis also turned the tide within the Nixon administration against Rogers and in favor of Kissinger and his perspective. By late November 1971, the State Department let it be known that it had abandoned efforts to seek a solution through the Rogers Plan.

Egypt was told, in no uncertain terms, that only the United States could bring peace and the return of occupied Egyptian territory, and that the United States was not prepared to undertake action to such ends on behalf of a country which it regarded as a Soviet client. Nasser had died in the

55. Kissinger, *White House Years*, p. 631.

56. Safran, *Israel: The Embattled Ally*, p. 455.

denouement of the Jordanian crisis, and Kissinger ultimately found in Nasser's successor, Anwar Sadat, a willing listener to his geopolitical argument. Sadat consequently expelled Soviet advisers from Egypt in July 1972. The United States, however, did not respond with any pressure on Israel to withdraw from Arab territory. The stage for the October War was set.

THE ALLON PLAN: ITS CONSEQUENCES

The Allon Plan had two basic kinds of provision: withdrawal from some areas and annexation of others. Although neither its proposal nor any other event has precipitated any withdrawal at all from the West Bank and Gaza Strip, the Allon Plan did facilitate progress towards the *de facto* annexation of parts of the West Bank and Gaza.

It is improbable that any very serious effort was ever made by Labor governments to obtain agreement from King Hussein to any variant of the plan, although it is equally improbable that it would have been politically possible for Hussein to assent. In any event, after Herut had come to power there was an effort on the part of some Labor officials to portray the Allon Plan as having been close to acceptance in the final phase of Labor's rule. This version, of course, had the advantage for Labor of suggesting that it – unlike Herut – had some real potential for bringing peace to Israel.

The major effect of the Allon Plan was to provide a "middle road" along which both minimalists and maximalists in Labor could proceed to practical annexation of parts of the West Bank and Gaza Strip, without the delay which would have been required by a thorough sorting out of alternatives and deciding amongst them. At the same time, the Allon Plan eased relations with the United States – even though that country did not accept the plan as a viable solution, and even though the Allon Plan was not formally adopted by the Israeli government – because it suggested that Israel was holding out the possibility of some withdrawal and some accord with King Hussein, even while it was gobbling up sections of the West Bank and Gaza.

The Allon Plan was able to serve such functions because its "operative section" was used by the government to determine the pattern of settlement although no formal determination was made in regard to its projection of future political arrangements. Labor's efforts to settle the "Allon territories" were in fact very serious: between June 1967 and May 1977, when Labor was defeated, the "official" settlements established numbered twenty-five in the Jordan Rift, seven elsewhere in the West Bank outside Jerusalem, and sixteen in Gaza-Rafiah.[57] In addition, a thick ring of settlements was beginning to close a circle around Jerusalem.

The settlements established during this period are extremely important for two reasons. First, the land and resources appropriated from the West Bank and Gaza were a significant loss to the Palestinian inhabitants. Second, the settlers ensconced therein included a significant group of zealots who were thereby provided with a base for mobilizing others of like mind and pressuring the government for expansion of settlement and eventual annexation of the areas.

The Gush Emunim is the preeminent case in point. It was formed after the October War by National Religious party activists within the Land of Israel movement. Amongst its early leaders were Rabbi Moshe Levinger of Kiryat Arba, an "Allon settlement," and Hanan Porat of Kfar Etzion, another "Allon settlement." The Gush undertook a movement of "illegal settlement" during the last few years of the Labor era, establishing three beachheads in the heavily populated West Bank highlands: Kaddum, Ofra, and Elon Moreh. Although Allon himself opposed this "illegal" settlement, various ministries provided material assistance to the settlers.

A further consequence of the Allon Plan was to erode the possibility of effective dissent from within the mainstream of Labor Zionism, and based on its own peculiar principles. The very fact of the massive settlement effort in the West Bank and Gaza tended to involve and implicate institutions associated with Labor and preempt their criticism. The stellar example of this is the Histadrut, the Israeli labor union which, through its enterprises, is also a major force in the Israeli economy. The Histadrut construction agencies became so deeply involved in lucrative contracts to build settlements that their deeds tended to belie any words of objection from the party once out of power. A Labor "dove," Member of Knesset Yossi Sarid, made a valiant effort at Histadrut and Labor conferences in 1983 to persuade those bodies to stop the Histadrut from contracting for such construction, but failed overwhelmingly, while leaders of Labor like Yitzhak Rabin and Shimon Peres observed silently.

57. Harris, *Taking Root.*

THE PLANS OF HERUT: THE BEGIN AND SHARON VERSIONS

The advent to power of the Herut in May 1977 was an event of incalculable significance in Israeli political life. Labor was defeated by the exhaustion of its own credibility, both by the reverses of the October War and by the corruption which permeated state and parastate institutions under its control. Herut's ascendancy was buttressed by a rising right-wing sentiment at the base, and by such small but highly mobilized and influential movements as Gush Emunim.

The Allon Plan was the only proposal for the future of the Palestinian occupied areas that was ever floated by those in power or close to power under Labor: Dayan's concepts of integration were underpinnings of a present policy rather than a formulated map for the future, as much as that policy was intended to frame the limits of future possibilities. Since the Herut's Likud bloc two plans – not mutually exclusive ones – have been presented. Both the Begin and Sharon plans are premised on continued Israeli control of the West Bank and Gaza Strip, with the open option of formal annexation.

THE BEGIN PLAN: ITS PROVISIONS

Israeli Prime Minister Menachem Begin developed the initial version of his plan for autonomy or "self-rule" in the West Bank and Gaza Strip not long after his election in May 1977. Following Sadat's peace initiative, pressure was mounting on the Israeli government to take a clear stand on an issue which Israeli governments had evaded since the conquests of June 1967: what territory would Israel yield for peace? What solution would Israel advance to the Palestinian issue? For Begin, the pressure was more intense than it had been for any of his predecessors. Both the U.S. and Egyptian governments appeared to be pressing for answers. Furthermore, the uproar in world public opinion that greeted Begin's election – particularly because of his party's extremist viewpoint on retaining the occupied Palestinian areas – created an awkward arena in which the Israeli leader would have to articulate his position.

In these circumstances, Begin called upon the concept of "autonomy," not exactly a new idea of his in relation to the Palestinians. He had floated a forerunner of his notion while still an opposition leader in 1975. "The Arab nation in the land of Israel, which we recognize," he then declared, "should be given cultural autonomy. We Jews, when we were a minority in different countries, always demanded cultural autonomy for ourselves. We must give them cultural autonomy – in other words, the education of their children in their tradition, in their tongue, and according to their religious precepts." He also averred that "a Likud government would guarantee to the Arab nation in the land of Israel a cultural autonomy, a fostering of their national culture, their religion and heritage."[58]

The historical roots of Begin's autonomy concept are the various systems that have accommodated the rights of minority communities to determine their own cultural and communal matters in a very restricted sense, for example in areas of personal status and education, while limiting their participation in matters of state, such as security, foreign policy, and resource allocation and development. The concept, of course, was a very thin one. It had probably served ideologically to protect the special position of Jewish nationality and culture in Israel, whose exclusivity the Herut and its predecessors in the Revisionist Zionist movement had so zealously sought to advance.

Begin developed a rather detailed plan for "autonomy" in the West Bank, projecting an administrative council sitting in Ramallah or Bethlehem, elected by the Palestinian inhabitants and exercising some management of internal affairs through various departments. Israelis would remain free to establish settlements in the West Bank, and the Israeli government would remain in control of foreign policy and military matters.[59]

For Begin, the autonomy plan had the virtue of evading both withdrawal from the West Bank – for no Likud politician could even hint at the possibility of leaving any part of the West Bank to Hussein, much less to the PLO – and also the requirement of foreswearing annexation of the area, which to the Likud is an integral part of Eretz Israel. The latter advantage Begin built into his plan by positing a five-year period of autonomy.

Begin developed this plan personally, working with two close aides, his Bureau Chief Yeheil Kadishai and Military Secretary Ephraim Poran. He presented the idea to his cabinet ministers only on the eve of a trip to Washington, during which he planned to propose the idea to President Jimmy Carter. Of the ministers only Dayan had been privy to the plan earlier.

58. Eitan Haber, Zeev Schiff, and Ehud Yaari, *The Year of the Dove* (New York: Bantam, 1979), p. 106.

59. *Ibid.*, p. 107. For text of Begin plan, see *Jerusalem Post*, 29 December 1977.

Begin and Dayan together presented the plan to Carter and major policy makers in his administration. There was reportedly an awkward moment when Carter's National Security Adviser Zbigniew Brzezinski likened Begin's proposed restrictions on linking the right to vote to choice of citizenship to the system prevailing in South Africa. Carter himself is said to have indicated that the proposal would be a fair basis for negotiation.[60]

Begin returned to Israel, and the plan became the subject of a seven-hour cabinet meeting. The cabinet members pointed to various matters which Begin in his haste and unilateral manner had overlooked – for example, the issue of water resources in the West Bank, which the Israeli government would not want to yield to the control of an autonomous administration. At the conclusion of the meeting, an urgent cable was sent to Israeli Ambassador Simcha Dinitz in Washington: the plan presented to Carter would have ten amendments regarding autonomy for the West Bank. By the time the cabinet formally ratified the plan on December 23, 1977, it had grown to twenty-six sections.[61] The process of adding official Israeli limitations to already inadequate offers of self-rule was to become a pattern. No sooner would a bad version of the plan be announced or adopted than Israeli interpretations or additions would be presented to render the plan still more opprobrious.

An extension to the Begin Plan exists which has received little attention but which sheds light on the underlying ideological assumptions and ambitions of the Begin policy. Begin continues to adhere to the old visions of Zeev Jabotinsky of power over both banks of the Jordan – and indeed Begin's supporters have been heard to serenade him at the opening of a new settlement in the West Bank with the old Revisionist hymn, "Two banks hath the Jordan, one is ours and so is the other."

Begin told an Israeli journalist in 1981,

> I want to tell you about the dream I am entertaining. We have learned that dreams sometimes come true and advance mankind. I dream of the day that peace will reign between us and the ruler of Transjordan to the east. And in the wake of that peace, we shall be able to give Transjordan – or to Jordan as it is called today – a free port to the Mediterranean, be it in Ashdod or in Haifa, and goods from both countries will be going to the East – our goods – and to the West – those of Jordan, and we shall be able to visit each other and we shall establish what I can term today a free confederation, and then really, perhaps the most beautiful and noble vision of Zeev Jabotinsky will materialize: there will be sated with wealth and plenty the son of Arabia, the son of Nazareth, and my own son.

60. Haber, Schiff, and Yaari, *Year of the Dove*, pp. 110-11.

61. *Ibid.*, pp. 111-12.

The reporter from *Maariv* asked Begin, "When you speak about a confederation, do you mean that there will be several authorities in several factors in Judea and Samaria, that is Israel and Transjordan?" Begin clarified:

No, I am talking about a confederation between western Eretz Israel and eastern Eretz Israel, a free and agreed confederation, living in peace and mutual respect, with a prosperous economy.[62]

THE BEGIN PLAN: ITS CONTEXT

The Begin Plan was formulated and announced in a context influenced by internal Israel political factors, by the acts and attitudes of other states, most especially of the United States but also in significant ways by Egypt, and by the growing international stature of the Palestine Liberation Organization, which was asserting the right of the Palestinians to a sovereign state. While the PLO continued to affirm the goal of the Palestinians as a secular democratic state in all of Palestine, the Palestinians were known to be seeking an independent Palestinian state in the West Bank and Gaza as a transitional step, and for this objective they had increasing diplomatic support from foreign governments.

The electoral victory of the Likud bloc (comprising Begin's Herut Party and the Liberals) in the spring of 1977 was a turning point in Israeli political history. From the establishment of the state until that point, Israeli politics had been dominated by the Labor party. Suddenly, for reasons having perhaps much more to do with Labor's perceived corruption and unfairness in distribution of state resources than a rightward turn in policy toward the Arabs, the Labor party was swept from power and those who had been their ideological enemies since the mandate period formed the cabinet. Begin's election campaign had been full of pledges to retain "Judea and Samaria" under Israeli sovereignty, and he solemnly renewed that promise on entering office.[63]

62. *Maariv,* 28 September 1981 (translated by Foreign Broadcast Information Service); see also *Jerusalem Post,* 1 October 1981.

63. For his oath on entering office, see *Jerusalem Post,* International Edition, 10-16 June 1981.

He perceived, however, that Israel might come under some pressure from the Carter administration to withdraw from at least parts of the territories occupied in 1967 and make some accommodation to Palestinian nationalism. While Kissinger dominated U.S. policy toward the Middle East, any such prospect appeared remote: his procedure was to deal first with the most manageable issues, and there was little prospect that the most intractable question of all would appear soon, if ever, on his agenda. With the coming of a new administration, however, hardliners in Israel had less assurance.

Shifts in U.S. Policy

The basis for a process away from the Kissingerian "step-by-step" approach was laid by a special study group established by the Brookings Institution, the Washington think tank, in late 1975. The assembled panel of "experts" argued in their report, released a year later, that the step-by-step approach was building up an ominous level of frustration in the Arab countries, and threatening an explosion which could seriously damage U.S. interests in the Middle East. Step-by-step diplomacy, they declared, should be replaced by a search for a "comprehensive solution."[64]

The Brookings panel did adjust the U.S. position a perceptible degree closer to reality: the United States had been maintaining the posture of an ostrich toward the Palestinian issue, whereas the Brookings report recognized it as "the heart of the Arab-Israeli conflict." But the Brookings experts failed to agree on the two crucial points that could have allowed the United States to make significant steps toward a solution: first, the group was unable to agree to affirm the representational status of the PLO; second, it did not agree on the nature of the Palestinian entity that was advocated. Whether the old "Jordanian option" should be resurrected and the Palestinian province be established as Hussein's "United Arab Kingdom" plan advocated, or whether the independent and sovereign state which the PLO demanded should be founded: the panel could agree on no recommendation to the U.S. government.

Whatever its lack of clarity and precision, the Brookings report did have a strong influence on the incoming Carter administration. Zbigniew Brzezinski, one signer of the report, became Carter's national security

---

64. *Toward Peace in the Middle East: Report of a Study Group* (Washington: Brookings Institution, 1975).

adviser; William Quandt, also a study group member, joined Brzezinski's staff.

Just as the first part of the Carter administration was marked by some vacillation in the setting of strategic policy for the Middle East as a whole, so too was there spectacular wavering on the subject of the Arab-Israeli issue and particularly on the subject of Palestinian rights. The most remarkable flip-flop came in October 1977: on the first of the month the United States and the Soviet Union issued a joint statement, calling for a comprehensive settlement through a new Geneva Conference, a settlement which would include Israeli withdrawal from territories occupied in 1967 and "resolution of the Palestinian question including ensuring the legitimate rights of the Palestinian people."[65] A PLO spokesperson welcomed the joint statement as a "positive step," but by the time that story hit the newswires, a U.S.-Israeli "working paper" had been reported that neatly undercut the U.S.-Soviet joint statement: U.S. Secretary of State Cyrus Vance and Moshe Dayan had agreed that acceptance of the joint statement was "not a prerequisite" for the reconvening of the Geneva Conference, and had reaffirmed United Nations resolutions 242 and 338 as "the agreed basis" for negotiations. Those resolutions, of course, refer to the Palestinians only as a "refugee" problem.[66] The Israeli government reacted to these ambiguous hints that the incoming Carter administration could be more open to the Palestinian point of view with grave and unnecessary alarm.[67]

It was not far into his term, on December 28, 1977, that Carter clarified earlier statements he had made on a Palestinian "homeland": he opposed, he declared, creation of a "radical, new independent nation" and specified that any Palestinian entity "ought to be associated with Jordan." He thus remained in strategic agreement with Henry Kissinger on this point, who had taken the opportunity of a speech to the World Jewish Congress on November 3 to reiterate his concern that a Palestinian state would be "destabilizing" and therefore by inference, inimical to U.S. interests in the Middle East: "A separate Arab state on the West Bank, whatever the

65. *U.S.-Soviet Joint Statement,* text, U.S. Department of State 1 October 1977; Palestinian response in WAFA, 2 October 1977.

66. For Vance-Dayan statement, see *Arab Record and Review* (1977), 19/20: 800-881.

67. For examples, see Abraham Ben-Zvi, *The United States and the Palestinians: The Carter Era* (Tel Aviv: Center for Strategic Studies, 1982, paper 16).

declaration, whatever the intention, inevitably must have as its objectives those that cannot be compatible with tranquility in the Middle East."[68]

The Sadat peace initiative increased the pressure on Begin to formulate a stance that could accommodate his political and ideological position of refusal to relinquish the West Bank and Gaza and at the same time avoid any immediate declaration of sovereignty, which would have created an awkward set of diplomatic circumstances.

In addition to these international and internal Israeli factors, Begin was confronted with a serious problem in the occupied West Bank. A year before Begin's election, the Labor government held municipal elections in the West Bank, apparently believing that Israeli and Hashemite machinations would result in a victory for a new West Bank leadership amenable to some form of future regularization of the occupation. In fact, the elected mayors and municipal council members were by and large nationalists, and in some cases public supporters of the PLO. To the Likud, this was fresh evidence of the bankruptcy of Labor's occupation policies.

THE BEGIN PLAN: ITS CONSEQUENCES

The Begin Plan eased the way toward the Camp David accords by providing a version of a conceptual basis on which the United States, Egypt, and Israel, all of which had different positions on an appropriate future for the West Bank and Gaza Strip, could claim that Camp David was not a mere separate peace treaty between Israel and Egypt, but a genuinely comprehensive agreement that had dealt with even the thorniest of issues, the Palestinian question, albeit in the absence of Palestinian representation.

Camp David

Camp David represented a turning point in regional affairs in the Middle East, and for United States policy toward the region. Although a comprehensive settlement for the Arab-Israeli conflict had been originally

68. *Palestine!* Bulletin, May 1978.

urged as a policy goal for the incoming Carter administration by strategists who believed that regional polarization was a dangerous phenomenon, the Camp David agreement, which was presented by its adherents as a comprehensive settlement, was in fact designed to sharpen the conflict in the region against what policy makers described as "Soviet influence."

Carter's first two years in office had been marked by an erratic vacillation in strategic planning: Some voices within the administration argued for a continuation of the kind of post-Vietnam military stance which had concentrated U.S. efforts in Europe, seen the decline of the troop strength of the armed forces by nearly 50 percent, and sharply limited the prospects of U.S. adventure abroad. Others were evincing a nostalgia for the days of protective reaction and triple-digit body counts. Near the beginning of the Carter administration, Samuel P. Huntington of Harvard University had prepared a memorandum for Zbigniew Brzezinski, Carter's national security adviser. Huntington suggested that the Gulf area was to become a prime arena of U.S.-Soviet confrontation, not the NATO area as the prevailing post-Vietnam wisdom in Washington had maintained.

Brzezinski's response included refurbishing the old concept of a "fire brigade," a military unit especially equipped and prepared for quick response to "brushfire war" in the third world. This counterinsurgent formation came to be called the Rapid Deployment Force, and Carter officially inaugurated it in Presidential Directive 18, in August 1977.

Early in his administration Carter also called for "demilitarization" of the Indian Ocean. But although practical measures were taken to prepare for the course of action urged by the more bellicose, the proposal for demilitarization was relegated to bureaucratic oblivion.

Much of the debate within the Carter administration on Middle Eastern policy focused on Iran. Brzezinski was a prominent advocate of the shah striking at dissidents and rebels with an iron fist; at the other pole Cyrus Vance, secretary of state, urged prudence and caution. When the shah fell in January 1979, the Nixon Doctrine fell with him, shattered into shards. The Carter administration took a decisive turn toward establishing its own military presence in the Middle East, strengthening military links with conservative regimes and adopting a confrontational stance with the Soviets *vis-à-vis* the Middle East.

The Camp David conference took place in this context. An anecdote that reflects the anxiety of the three principals over developments in Tehran relates that on September 9, the date on which the shah's troops opened fire on demonstrators, killing at least a hundred, Sadat telephoned the shah to offer help and reassurance. Sadat also prevailed on Carter to place a supportive call to the shah. Meanwhile, in New York, Israeli Foreign Minister Moshe Dayan told Barbara Walters that the crisis in Iran was even more serious than the matters under discussion at Camp David.[69]

In such a context, it is not surprising that Camp David was at least as much an armament agreement as it was a peace treaty. As a direct result, U.S. foreign military sales credits to Israel soared to $3.3 billion in 1979, higher even than the previous apex of $2.58 billion allotted in 1974 to resupply Israel after the October 1973 war.[70]

The Begin Plan for autonomy has yet to be implemented, of course, in the West Bank and Gaza Strip, and has been resoundingly rejected by the Palestinians of those areas and elsewhere as a method of denying their national rights. A preliminary attempt to move in the direction suggested by the Begin Plan was made by the Israeli government in the spring of 1982, when it appointed civil administrators of the West Bank and Gaza Strip. Mayors and other Palestinian officials refused to deal with the administrators. The Israeli authorities responded with a rash of dismissals of mayors and dissolutions of municipal councils, a harsh blow at significant Palestinian institutions.

THE SHARON PLAN: ITS PROVISIONS

Ariel Sharon has served as a member of the Israeli cabinet under Begin, for a time as minister of defense and later, when the recommendations of the Israeli commission investigating the massacres in the Sabra and Shatila refugee camps called for his resignation from the defense ministry for his "indirect responsibility" for the atrocities, as minister without portfolio. Sharon has advanced his own plan, without official sanction though with apparently more than mere official tolerance, for a resolution of the Palestinian issue.[71] He told *Time* magazine that:

69. Michael A. Ledeen and William Lewis, "Carter and the Fall of the Shah: The Inside Story," *Washington Quarterly* (Spring 1980).

70. See report by the Comptroller-General of the United States, *U.S. Assistance to the State of Israel* (Washington: General Accounting Office, 1983).

71. See Sheila Ryan and Muhammad Hallaj, *Palestine Is, But Not in Jordan* (Belmont, Mass.: Association of Arab-American University Graduates, 1983). Sharon's point of view has been reported a number of times in the Western press: Ranan B. Lurie, "Israel's General Sharon: As Tough as Ever," *Playboy,* March 1978; Sidney Zion and Uri Dan, "Israel's Peace Strategy," *New York Times Magazine,* 21 January 1979; and *The Economist,* 8 August 1981.

I believe that the starting point for a solution [to the problem of the Palestinians] is to establish a Palestinian state in that part of Palestine that was separated from what was to become Israel in 1922 and which is now Jordan. Some 80 percent of the population of Jordan is Palestinian. Most of the prominent members of the government are Palestinian Arabs – the same Arabs who are living in Galilee, in Nazareth, in Haifa. The only strangers are the members of the Hashemite Kingdom ruled by King Hussein.

In September 1970 there was a debate in the army over whether to respond to the Syrian invasion of Jordan. 1 was part of a minority who said that for the first time there was an opportunity to start solving the Palestinian problem. The solution was to let the Hashemite Kingdom disappear.

I don't mean that if we had a Palestinian state in Jordan we would have good neighbors. There would be a bitter conflict, but the conflict would be over territory, not over the right of Palestinians to exist as a nation. King Hussein is not a partner in the Camp David talks. I don't mind who takes over Jordan.[72]

During his tenure as foreign minister, Yitzhak Shamir expressed a very similar point of view. In a journal article, Shamir wrote that

On the subject of a political entity, a homeland for the Arabs of the former British-mandated territory of Palestine, the facts speak for themselves. The state known today as the Kingdom of Jordan is an integral part of what was once known as Palestine (77 percent of the territory); its inhabitants are therefore Palestinian – not different in their language, culture or religious and demographic composition from other Palestinians. . . . It is merely an accident of history that this state is called the Kingdom of Jordan and not the Kingdom of Palestine. . . . Reduced to its true proportions, the problem is clearly not the lack of a homeland for the Palestinian Arabs. That homeland is Trans-Jordan or eastern Palestine.[73]

Sharon and Shamir do not present a very original argument in claiming that the Palestinian demand for a homeland is redundant, as Jordan is already a "Palestinian state." Shamir's article in *Foreign Affairs,* in fact, is strongly reminiscent of a comment made by Yigal Allon in the same journal six years earlier. Allon argued that after all, the population of both banks, east and west, are Palestinian Arabs. The fact is that the great majority of Palestinians carry Jordanian passports whereas almost all of Jordan's inhabitants are Palestinians.[74]

72. *Time,* 5 October 1981.

73. Yitzhak Shamir, "Israel's Role in a Changing Middle East," *Foreign Affairs* (Spring 1982), 60(4): 791.

74. Allon, "Case for Defensible Borders," p. 47.

The Sharon Plan, perhaps more precisely the Sharon-Shamir Plan, has not been formally adopted by the Israeli government, though Menachem Begin while prime minister demonstrated quite a benign attitude toward it.[75] An extensive international publicity campaign has been waged on the premise of this plan, including a series of full-page advertisements in the *New York Times*.[76] Moreover, a number of disparate supporters of Israel have woven the principles of the plan into their public apologetics.[77]

The pretensions of the plan to a valid historical basis are of course absurd. When the British Mandate was imposed on Palestine after World War I, the Palestinians, like other neighboring peoples emerging from the Ottoman Empire, had not had the experience of living in a sovereign nation state. The national consciousness of the Palestinian people, and that of neighboring Arab peoples like the Syrians, had been developing during the final decades of the nineteenth century and opening decades of the twentieth. That national consciousness had primarily assumed the form of Arab nationalism; the hopes of this movement for establishment of a unified and independent Arab state were set back if not dashed by the action of the victorious European powers in dividing the Arab provinces of the Ottoman Empire amongst themselves as colonies.

This process of colonial division produced the Palestine Mandate. Although the mandate initially encompassed Transjordan, it is clear that British officials always planned a separate regime for it, and Transjordan was formally severed in 1922. More to the point than the British colonial attitude, however, is the reality that the development of Palestinian national consciousness is integrally linked to Palestinian land, Palestinian villages, and ancient Palestinian cities and towns including, among others, Jerusalem, Acre, Haifa, Jaffa, Gaza, Nazareth, Ramle, Lydda, Nablus, Ramallah, Bethlehem, and Hebron. In 1947-48, Zionist forces exiled three-quarters of a million Palestinians from many of these cities and from over 350 villages. Many of these refugees are indeed now living east of the Jordan, and the Sharon Plan assumes that their exile is not an exile at all, but an appropriate transfer to the portion of Palestine where they belong. It holds moreover that those Palestinians who are now living in the West Bank and Gaza Strip are dwelling outside their allotted "homeland" and therefore have no claim to national rights in the areas in which they live.

75. For example, in Begin's column in *The Jewish Press*, February 1981.

76. *New York Times*, 6 March 1983, for example.

77. New York City's Mayor Edward Koch, for example: see *Jerusalem Post*, 19 August 1981.

THE SHARON PLAN: ITS CONSEQUENCES

The articulation of the Sharon Plan may have given encouragement to those Israeli policy makers who advocated the invasion of Lebanon. More than three months before the invasion was launched, *Time* magazine reported that

> To bolster his military aims, Sharon with the backing of Foreign Minister Yitzhak Shamir is also touting a political rationale for such a maneuver [as the invasion of Lebanon]. He believes that the PLO would have no place to go after a defeat in Lebanon but Jordan, from which it was forcibly expelled in a brutal crackdown in 1970-71. With a little assistance from Israel, Sharon believes, the PLO could overthrow King Hussein and establish a Palestinian state in Jordan.[78]

This notion was not an entirely original strategic contribution of Sharon's: strategists to whose thinking Sharon has been attracted tend to regard the Palestinians as a factor that can be moved around at Israeli will on the chessboard of the Middle East. Illustrative of this mode of thought is the suggestion of Menachem Milson that the Palestinians living in Lebanon could perhaps be settled in east Jordan – a proposal set forth in *Commentary* magazine in an article written long before the invasion of Lebanon, the very article, in fact, that brought Milson to Sharon's attention and resulted in his appointment as civil administrator for Judea and Samaria, a post he did not long occupy.[79]

The Sharon Plan thus employed served the function of holding out the prospect that the invasion of Lebanon could not only deal with Israel's Palestinian problem in Lebanon, but also perhaps with Israel's Palestinian problem more generally.

There is a particular danger that the Sharon Plan could play a role in actualizing the implicit threat of expulsion of Palestinians from the West Bank and Gaza Strip. It is clear that the fear of such an expulsion is palpable among the Palestinian population of the occupied areas, and it is also clear that political forces in Israel far closer to the mainstream than Rabbi Meir Kahane, the title of whose book *They Must Go* succinctly states his view, would be pleased to see the departure of all Palestinians eastward across the Jordan River.

78. *Time*, 1 March 1981.

79. Menachem Milson, "How To Make Peace with the Palestinians," *Commentary* (May 1981), 70(5).

The Sharon Plan should be set in the conceptual context of a widening Israeli definition of areas of strategic concern. This development was indicated by a grandiose speech prepared for delivery by Sharon, in which Sharon revealed that Israel no longer limited its strategic goals to its own security, but was in fact prepared to combat what it regarded as Soviet clients from Turkey to the Gulf.[80] Israel now occupies much of and is deeply involved in the internal political and security affairs of Lebanon. Influential voices in Israel, including that of Sharon when he was at the apex of his power, have proposed war with Syria. Proposals and rough contingency plans have even been made for the division of Syria into five confessional statelets. There have also been occasional calls for invasion of the Hashemite Kingdom.

King Hussein not surprisingly regarded Sharon's plan as indirectly urging Israeli conquest of his kingdom. He stated in an interview that

> . . . Israel has begun to establish that the Palestinian cause is a Jordanian cause. This means that Israel considers itself on its own land and that the solution to the Palestinian cause is a Jordanian issue outside the territories occupied by Israel. . . .I will go further and say that if it, that is Israel, seeks to practically implement Begin's proposals, it can take place only through a military operation whose objective is the occupation of Jordan.[81]

The position of the United States in creating the context of strategy and policy for the Sharon Plan has been very ambiguous. There is abundant evidence of concern within the Reagan administration over the consequences of Israeli involvement in Lebanon, and particularly over the perils of Israeli occupation of central Lebanon. The prospect of an Israeli strike against the Hashemite Kingdom and/or Syria and a major displacement of Palestinians from the West Bank and Gaza Strip is one which no doubt would cause deep anxiety to the U.S. administration, both because in taking such actions Israel could stretch itself too thin and require a U.S. presence to stabilize the situation, as it did in Lebanon, and because Israeli aggression is potentially at least a complicating factor in U.S. relations with Arab regimes, even the most conservative among them.

On the other hand, there is also abundant evidence that the United States has taken a number of steps which have encouraged expansionist

80. In a speech prepared for delivery by Ariel Sharon to the World Zionist Organization.

81. *Al-Mustaqbal*, 5 September 1981, translated by the Foreign Broadcast Information Service.

tendencies within the Israeli government over the past several years. In regard to Lebanon, for example, the administration gave its famous "green light" for Israeli air strikes in Lebanon in the spring of 1981, and during a visit to Israel in the spring of 1982 Alexander Haig, then secretary of state, made declarations about the menace of "Soviet clients" in Lebanon which can only have been calculated to encourage those, including Sharon, who were publicly known to be urging an invasion.

Even more significantly, U.S. aid to Israel has continued to soar, and the administration has taken no steps to pressure Israel to withdraw from the West Bank and Gaza Strip. After Reagan announced his plan for the Middle East[82] and the Israeli government refused it on the following day, the United States carefully avoided any pressure on Israel to accept even the provisions of the Reagan Plan (which would have established a limited autonomy a la Camp David, while specifically disallowing any possibility of an independent Palestinian state). Instead, the administration ignored Israeli rejection of the plan, and allowed the brain-dead plan to respire on an artificial life support system for months, declaring it dead only after the Jordanian government announced that it would not proceed under the plan as it could not obtain the assent of the PLO.

CONCLUSION

The conditions of Palestinian life in the occupied West Bank and Gaza Strip have not been directly affected by the various plans offered by Israeli leaders for regularization of the occupation. Despite the Allon Plan, there has been no yielding of limited political authority over densely populated areas to any Jordanian or other Arab rule, nor has there been annexation of an Israeli "security zone" along the Jordan River and in parts of Gaza. Despite the Begin Plan, Palestinians are not living under the formalities of an "autonomy plan." Despite the objectives of the Sharon Plan, the Palestinians have not been relegated to a "Palestinian state" east of the Jordan River.

Nevertheless, each of these plans has played a role in shaping the configurations of oppression in the West Bank and Gaza Strip. The Allon Plan allowed Israeli authorities to initiate a far-reaching plan of settlement, despite their own differences of opinion on an ultimate peace agreement.

82. U.S. Department of State, *Current Policy*, no. 417.

The Begin Plan permitted the diffusion and intensification of settlement without causing a breakdown in the process of concluding a separate peace with Egypt at Camp David, and without incurring unnecessary difficulties in relations with the United States. The Sharon Plan, both in its use to encourage invasion of Lebanon and in its implicit proposal for extending Israeli power east of the Jordan, marks a new stage in integrating Israeli policy toward occupation of the West Bank with a growing regional bellicosity.

CHAPTER 21

Israel's Search for a Native Pillar:
The Village Leagues

Salim Tamari

One of the central dilemmas facing Israel, in its attempt to maintain control over the territories conquered in 1967, has been the inability of the successive Labor and Likud governments to establish a substantial group of collaborators to mediate its rule.[1] Nothing similar to the Zionist bond with the leaders of the Druze community in the Galilee (both in the prestate period and after 1948), with the Bedouins of the Naqab, or the military alliance with Saad Haddad's militias in southern Lebanon, existed during Israel's fifteen years of rule in the West Bank and Gaza.

The reasons for the absence of such native surrogates may be sought in current Israeli irreconcilability with any form of Palestinian nationalism, as well as in the relative ethnic homogeneity of the Palestinian population in the highlands – a condition that has made the traditional Israeli strategy of penetrating local power groups a rather formidable task. Moreover, whatever the failings of the Palestinian resistance movement in the occupied territories, it can be established as a tribute to its organizational abilities that it has, so far, limited the success of Israel's sponsorship of such collaborative elements to isolated quislings.

A similar version of this study appeared in the *Journal of Palestine Studies,* (Summer 1983) 12(4).

------

1. This is as much true of the Syrian Heights (the Golan), where the Druze population carried on one of the fiercest movements of resistance to the extension of Israeli law, as it is of Gaza and the West Bank.

Although it was possible for Israel to rule its subject Palestinian population through the direct apparatus of the military government, it has become increasingly difficult to do so after 1980-1981, when the Likud laid effective claims of Jewish sovereignty over the area. The absence of a surrogate power base for Israeli rule became an obstacle not only for the implementation of the Camp David accords, but also for the mediation of Israel's control over a progressively more unyielding civilian population. The significance of the emergence in 1980 of the Movement of Palestinian Leagues (*Harakat al-Rawabet al-Filastiniyya* – i.e. the Village Leagues) will be analyzed here in the context of these changed political circumstances.

The leagues represent the second attempt by the Zionist movement to establish a collaborative base among Palestinian peasants. The first took the form of *Hizb al-Zurra* (The Farmers Party) which the Jewish Agency played a crucial part in initiating in 1924 in the Nazareth, Nablus, and Hebron regions. The main objective of the party, then, was to add a rural base to the urban opposition to the Arab Executive, a committee of politicians who attempted to coordinate the struggle in the 1920s and 1930s under the anti-Zionist leadership of Haj Amin al-Husseini. The failure of *Hizb al-Zurra* to gather any momentum had as much to do with its weak organizational links with the Nashashibi-led opposition as with its inability to deal with the real needs of peasants under British rule.[2] [The Nashashibi family of Jerusalem began to gain political influence in the early 1900s as its rural landholdings increased – ed.]

Despite significant divergences between the Village Leagues of the 1980s and *Hizb al-Zurra* of 1924 in both political context and ideological contents, a stubborn historic continuity can be seen in the manner they have served a common ideological cause for their Zionist sponsors: the notion of mobilizing the "conservative peasantry" against its own urban-based nationalist movement. In both cases the Zionists, and now the Israelis, utilized all possible internal factions within the Palestinian camp: familial, religious, and regional.

BEGINNINGS IN HEBRON

The Village League of the Hebron District made its debut in the Jerusalem press on August 1, 1978 with an innocuous announcement

---

2. Y. Porath, *The Emergence of the Palestinian Arab National Movement* (London: Frank Cass, 1974), 12-30, 248-49.

declaring its main objectives to be "the resolution of local disputes among villagers in the most efficient and least costly method," and the encouragement "of rural cooperatives and social and charitable societies which will work for the benefit of all villagers."[3] The league local head at the time, Mustafa Dudin, declared on a number of occasions that his organization would desist from involvement in national politics, and strive to rectify decades of neglect that the Hebron villages had suffered at the hands of "town politicians."[4]

Four years later the same organization, (by then extended to the six regional districts of the West Bank), under the same leadership, announced itself in a public rally in the city of Hebron as "the vanguard of the peace forces in the West Bank and Gaza – whose historic task is to mobilize the Palestinian people in a peace movement . . . against bigotry and [Palestinian] terrorism."[5] Dudin, now the head of the renamed Movement of Palestinian Leagues, called for direct negotiations between Israel and "the Palestinian people" under the leadership of King Hussein.[6] Two months earlier Ariel Sharon, then minister of defense, had, at a cocktail party, presented the leaders of the leagues to American Defense Secretary Caspar Weinberger as the moderate leadership of the Palestinians in the West Bank. Before their meeting with Weinberger, Sharon had given Dudin and his associates the go-ahead "to set themselves up as the nascent administration of the 'self-governing authority' stipulated in the Camp David agreements."[7] By now the league of village folks, whose original aim had been the encouragement of rural cooperatives, had its own budget, its armed militias, its uniforms, its prison cells and interrogation centers, and its biweekly newspaper, *al-Mira* (the Mirror). Its main objective – according to leading ideologue Jawdat Sawalha – was to fight against the influence of the Palestine Liberation Organization and to negotiate on behalf of the Palestinians with the state of Israel.[8] How did this enigmatic organization emerge in the Palestinian arena, and what is its current role in the West Bank? This the question we will attempt to answer in the following analysis.

3. *Al-Quds*, 1 August 1978.

4. *Al-Fajr Weekly*, 26 July – 1 August 1981.

5. *Al-Anba*, 14 November 1982.

6. *Jerusalem Post*, 14 November 1982.

7. *Ibid.*, 2 September 1982.

8. *Maariv*, 17 July 1982.

MILSON'S STRATEGY

Israel's adoption of the Village Leagues as its instrument in the struggle against Palestinian nationalism had its roots in a peculiar interpretation which recalls – in a twisted manner – Lin Piao's theory of surrounding the cities with the (in this case, conservative) countryside. In 1981, in a widely noted article written for the American magazine *Commentary,* Professor Menachem Milson, the Arabist scholar-turned-supreme-ruler of the West Bank, enunciated his strategy for taming the Palestinians – a peculiar amalgam of Maoist dialectics and Orientalist conception of Arab social fabric. Palestinian society under Jordanian rule, as under Ottoman rule, functioned through a system of patronage, in which local notables and holders of power acted as intermediaries between their *protégés* and the central authority. The absence of a civic polity is seen as creating a form of bureaucratic feudalism which acts as the underpinning for Arab politics, whereby the provision of basic services and intercessions is exchanged for loyalty.[9] Moshe Dayan's policy in the West Bank and Gaza during the seventies, according to a Milson interpretor, had ruined this system: main objectives of the Dayan policy had been the ensuring of order and security, and the local Palestinians had been left to run their affairs by themselves – while the key positions of power had been kept in Israeli hands, behind the scenes. This policy of "non-intervention," according to Milson, allowed forces loyalist to the PLO to seize the main positions of power during the municipal elections of 1976, and to entrench themselves as a replacement for the old patronage system.[10] A combination of "terror, intimidation, and the dispensation of Joint Committee 'steadfastness' money" (allocated by the Arab states in 1978 to support Palestinians under occupation) succeeded in eroding whatever pockets of influence the Israeli military government had established. Thus Milson set himself in combat not only against the influence of the PLO, but against the ghost of Moshe Dayan as well.

The weak link in the post-1976 Palestinian nationalist hegemony, in this conception, was the systematic discrimination by the urban municipal councils against the villages in the allocation of development money and services. How to exploit this situation was quite simple: to storm the radical towns with the reactionary peasants. The instrument: the Village Leagues.

9. Milson, *Commentary* (May 1981), pp. 30-31.

10. Yochanan Manor, *Jerusalem Post,* 23 June 1982.

The key to the new policy was a distinction that Milson introduced, with the backing of Sharon and the Likud government, between the attempt at the physical elimination of the PLO power base in the West Bank (and Gaza) on the one hand, and the gradual political undermining of the social base for Palestinian nationalism on the other. The first task was now allocated to the military, the latter to the civil administration – of which Milson became the first head in November 1981. The thrust of his policy (contrary to the Dayan tradition) was one of *active intervention* in the daily life of West Bankers – through the offices of village potentates whose services and patronage rested directly on power delegated by the civil administration. Simultaneously the civil administration began to punish, and later administratively disqualify, any local leader or municipal head who did not collaborate with the new regime.

A SUPRALEGAL FORCE

From the beginning the powers of the Village Leagues rested on authority invested in them by the military government outside the context of the law. A careful reading of the internal bylaws of any of the seven original constituent leagues in the federation (those of Hebron, Bethlehem, Nablus, Ramallah, Silat al-Dhaher, Hibla, and Qabatya) reveals nothing of the wide powers delegated to them by the authorities – powers ranging from the processing of family reunion permits and driving licenses to the arrest and interrogation of political suspects. The basic bylaws (*nidham assasi*) of the Ramallah District Village Leagues, for example, are indistinguishable from the internal constitution of any rural cooperative dealing as they do with the development of scientific farming methods, the planning and execution of food processing enterprises, etc. – with the possible exception of the clause (art. 2a.) referring to the arbitration of local disputes.

Nevertheless the leagues did acquire extensive extralegal powers from a series of military orders that modified Jordanian law in the territories in such a way as to foster the growth of loyalist organizations such as the Village Leagues. Three such Military Orders stand out:

Military Order 378 (Article 53 A.1). This banned any resident of the region from carrying arms "except by official authorization," thus paving the way for the arming and training of "authorized" league militias.

Military Order 946 (Nov. 8, 1981). This replaced the term (West Bank) "region's commander" with that of "commander of IDF forces in the region." This seemingly innocuous change legitimized the dismantling of the military government of the West Bank and the integration of the whole region into the security system of Israel proper. The West Bank, in effect, is now ruled by the IDF command in the central region in all matters related to security. Civilian control became subject to the civil administration, headed first by Menachem Milson and later by acting head Yigal Karmon after the former's resignation in the aftermath of the Beirut massacres. It is no accident that the promotion of the Village Leagues and the arming of their militias date from this transfer of formal authority – in line with the provisions of the Camp David accords concerning the autonomous region in the West Bank and Gaza.

Military Order 999 (August 8, 1982). This modified the afore-mentioned M.O. 378 with an additional clause after "Every soldier is authorized . . . " which reads: " . . . or the proper authority appointed for that purpose . . . in all matters related to security in Judea and Samaria." This crucial order established for the first time the right of corporate bodies, such as the leagues, to intervene in matters of security, which had previously been the responsibility of the IDF and the police.

With the legal basis for the operation of the leagues thus secured, they were now allowed to operate on the basis of the patronage system envisioned by Menachem Milson. League heads in the various regions (often appointed *mukhtars* or those who replaced *mukhtars* who refused to cooperate with the civil administration) were now invested with sufficient intercessionary power to provide services most desired by villagers (and, increasingly, by urban residents). Among the most crucial services were the provision of family reunion permits for relatives residing abroad, travel permits for crossing the bridge to Jordan, appointments (and transfers) in the civil service, building permits and the cancellation of orders to demolish buildings illegally constructed, intercession on behalf of detained family members and reduction of prison terms for prisoners, and permits to acquire driving licenses.[11]

The civil administration allocated substantial sums, channeled through the Village League, to cooperating villages, and at the same time blocked even more substantial sums originating from the PLO-Jordanian Committee and from international agencies involved with development projects in the West Bank, thus enabling the leagues to wield more and more control over

---

11. Village League intercession is often needed not only to acquire a driving license, but also to have one's name removed from lists sent to driving schools prohibiting those named from taking driving lessons. Today, thousands of residents of the West Bank have their names on such lists.

such projects. The pages of *al-Mira* regularly feature the launching of new schemes for village electrification, piped drinking water, and the extension of internal roads – as if they were the league's own projects. These development schemes are seen by the civil administration as essential both to weaken the economic base for PLO legitimacy and to bolster the position of the leagues as champions of village progress. More sinister is the direction of "development" implied by these projects – which invariably have ended in linking undeveloped rural areas into Israel's regional electric and water network, thus fostering an irreversible process of integration and dependency on Israel in Palestinian rural areas. But this process has been hampered by two apparently unsurmountable obstacles: first by Israel's trimming of the civil administration development funds because of the low priority given to the West Bank (that is, to non-Jewish expenditures in the West Bank – funds are now diverted to the expansion of Jewish settlements in the area) and second, by the conflict in principle between the idea of developing the (Arab) rural hinterland and the quest for augmentation and territorial expansion of existing Jewish settlements given the limited water and land resources in the West Bank.

THE LEAGUES AS INSTRUMENTS OF CONTROL

The "developmental" function of the leagues has been superceded and, in many cases, sabotaged, by the original objective of smashing the PLO power base and creating an alternative local leadership. It is this objective that has dictated the social composition of league recruits, and the manipulation of factional and kinship loyalties within the villages.

Because both traditional village notables (often pro-Jordanian in sentiments) and the rural intelligentsia shied away from joining an organization whose declared aim was the combatting of Palestinian nationalism, the military government was compelled to rely on the socially marginal and politically ostracized elements among the peasantry as the backbone of Village League membership. Itinerant laborers, drifters, former members of the British police force and Jordanian *mukhabarat,* land brokers (for Himnuta – a land purchasing company for the Jewish Agency), and village transport workers constitute main sources for league recruits. The following occupational profile of the Village League full-time membership in the village of Sarr (Hebron District) is typical:

bus driver (chairman); former Arab Legion soldier; construction worker; construction worker and guard; part-time hotel worker; sheep trader; shopkeeper; hospital orderly; shepherd.[12]

Of the main league leaders in 1982 only three, aside from Dudin himself, are reputed to have any formal education at all (Muhammad Nasr, Jawdat Sawalha, and Yusef Hantuli, then editor of *al-Mira*). The assassinated head of the Ramallah league, Yusef al-Khatib, and Bishara Qumsiyyeh, head of the Bethlehem league, are known to be illiterates. Criminal and underworld figures abound in the membership. The present makeup of league membership does not seem to be a liability, from the Israeli point of view – rather it can serve as a means of control over their behavior. Moreover, the marginal social standing of members makes it possible for the civil administration to drop them in the event that they become politically dispensable – a situation likely to emerge if the Israeli government needs a politically more "respectable" group to collaborate with. In the meantime, the current social composition of league members ensures their insulation from nationalist influence and pressure.

REGIONAL VARIATIONS

Although the seven federated sections of the Village Leagues have shown a degree of unity in their opposition to the PLO and nationalist movements, they nevertheless display some significant regional differences. These differences are rooted in the social contexts from which they emerged, as well as in the local sentiments in favor of or opposed to the PLO. In Hebron, for example, the initial success of the league derives from the wide social base of the Dudin clan in the Dura region, coupled with the economic backwardness of the region and the preeminence of kinship and local identities over the national one. This social base was sustained even when the Dudin clan was divided in its support of its patrician – who was able to use kinship loyalties in sufficiently effective manner to neutralize the opposition. In Bethlehem, by contrast, the civil administration tried to combine Christian support with that of the Bedouin tribe of Taamreh – the resulting village league alliance was, and remains, weak and ineffective. Here the first head of the league, Bishara Qumsiyyeh, and later his son

12. From interview with A.B., a village resident.

Samir, of Beit Sahur (a nationalist and pro-PLO center), were forsaken by their own kin, and were increasingly compelled to depend on village thugs and their own militia to intimidate opponents, as for example in the series of attacks by league elements against university students, lecturers, and Beit Sahur residents during April 1982.[13]

In the north the situation is more complex. Nablus is the industrial and trading center of the West Bank, and the landlords of Nablus, Jenin, and Tulkarem control most of the irrigated cultivable land in the region. Trading links with Jordan are strong and consequently the Hashemite influence is considerable. The civil administration, according to Nablus informants, made several attempts to recruit Tahseen al-Faris (one of the leading pro-Jordanian figures, and chairman of the Agricultural Marketing Society) to head the Nablus Village Leagues. However the initial vacillation of the Jordanian government in its attitude towards the league, and its subsequent open attack on its leaders in March 1982, by which any formal association with them was made a treasonous act, played a decisive role in alienating the league from Hashemite elements, not only in Nablus but throughout the West Bank. Currently the main strongholds of the league in the north are Silat al-Dhaher, Qabatya (an important quarrying center with significant trade interests in Jordan), Hibla (in Tulkarem), and Assira al-Shamaliyyeh. The latter is one of the wealthiest villages in the Nablus district, and the home of Jawdat Sawalha (a reputed defector from Fatah) who is currently the head of the Nablus Village League and one of the ablest and most educated leaders of the movement.

In Ramallah, by contrast, league activity flourished in the villages adjoining the pre-1967 border with Israel. In 1980, Yusef al-Khatib, a land speculator from Bilin, established what was initially known as the Village League of Western Ramallah District.[14] Several of the eight villages involved in this league had lost substantial tracts of cultivable land in the armistice agreement of 1949 and are considerably poorer and more undeveloped than villages to the east of the Ramallah-Nablus highway. Poor terrain and a stagnant village economy forced many local farmers to work in Israel as day laborers.

The league made little headway in the eastern villages (with the possible exception of the village of Arura), where the remittances sent by emigrants to America and the Gulf, together with the relatively high

13. *Jerusalem Post,* 19 April 1982; *al-Fajr,* 30 April 1982.

14. For background information on al-Khatib and the Ramallah League, see Nura Sus, "The Village League — Part III, Ramallah," *al-Fajr,* 2-8 August 1981.

educational achievement of remaining villagers, buttressed a local peasant elite that succeeded in resisting economic integration with, and thus political dependence on, Israel. Whether this is the key factor in explaining the dramatic contrast in the political behavior of the eastern and western villagers requires further investigation. What can be claimed with some certainty is that the backwardness of the eastern villages had been reinforced by years of neglect by the Jordanian administration, and later by the corrupt manner of distributing Joint Committee funds for development. Both created an attitude of cynicism and frustration towards the urban municipalities and allied nationalist movements that administered the dispensation of "steadfastness" money. In Bilin – the center of the league's regional activity – the Khatib clan, or at least Yusef's branch within it, utilized kinship loyalties to mobilize one section of the village against another around the issue of land title claims. When Yusef al-Khatib was assassinated by the PLO underground after it was revealed that he fraudulently sold land belonging to the Samara clan (his political opponents) to Himnuta – the land purchasing arm of the Jewish Agency – Milson and Dudin used the occasion to justify the arming and training of the Village League militias in the spring of 1982. From then on, the Village Leagues went on the offensive.

WHAT ROLE FOR THE LEAGUES?

The new league offensive, as it turned out, was a matter mainly engineered by Ariel Sharon's defense ministry and the civil administration in the aftermath of the Lebanese campaign. Its primary objective was to preempt the mobilization of pro-Jordanian forces in the West Bank as a prelude to King Hussein's anticipated entry into the peace negotiations along the guidelines of the Reagan initiative. The directives of the new policy were laid out in a high-level (and presumably secret) conference held on October 24, 1982, in the Israeli defense ministry, in which the views of Milson's temporary successor, Col. Yigal Karmon, prevailed.[15] Karmon's directives, which were submitted to the (military) governors of the six districts in the West Bank, called, *inter alia,* for neutralization of pro-Jordanian elements in the territories; for continued repression of the radical

---

15. *Haaretz*, 16 November 1982. Karmon was reputedly sacked from his position by the defense ministry following the leakage of these directives to the Israeli press.

Palestinian leadership formerly associated with the National Guidance Committee; and for "massive support" of the Village Leagues.[16] The latter were referred to as "a group which we [the civil administration] started . . . these [forces] are not tied to outside, but are dependent on us." Israeli administrators were "directed to visit the appointed [i.e. collaborating] municipalities and the leagues and to report on the outcome of the visits."[17]

Following these directives the leagues held several authorized rallies (the only such rallies allowed in the occupied territories since 1967) in Ramallah and Hebron to promote their new political platform. The largest of those gatherings took place in Hebron in mid-November, 1982 – about two thousand supporters attended.[18] Karmon, Milson (now a "private citizen"), Dudin, and Muhammad Nasr (then head of the Hebron League) were the featured speakers. All called for direct negotiations between Israel and Jordan as the "only road to peace." Nasr stressed the leading role of the leagues as the indigenous bridge between the Jordanian regime and the Likud government. Milson called on the Palestinians to "resist the communists, the imperialists, and others who have sown strife and divisiveness in the area." Dudin attacked "Palestinian terrorism" and called on the Arab regimes to recognize Israel.[19]

The next step was to transform the leagues into a "national" party. So far the main weakness of the movement had been in its regional-familial character, and its strictly rural composition.[20] In an attempt to gain support from conservative elements in the urban centers of the West Bank the leagues moved their headquarters to the district centers with the full protection and support of the IDF. Moreover, the army assigned regular patrols to guard league offices.

16. *Al-Fajr*, 26 November 1982.

17. *Ibid.* See also *Haaretz*, 16 November 1982; *Jerusalem Post*, 17 November 1982; *New York Times*, 24 November 1982.

18. Estimated by J. Richardson, in the *Jerusalem Post* (14 November 1982). The pro-government *al-Anba* (November 14) reported the figure as 3,000, and the league's own paper, *al-Mira*, estimated 5,000.

19. *Al-Anba* and *Jerusalem Post*, 14 November 1982.

20. Only in the township of Jenin was the (military-appointed) mayor a league supporter.

Meanwhile, internal dissent began to appear within the ranks of the leagues. Muhammad Nasr, who had his own political ambitions and links with Israeli politicians independent of Dudin, began to mobilize younger members of the league with the aim of challenging Dudin's leadership. In the beginning of 1983 he took the opportunity of the latter's move to his winter residence in Jericho to announce the formation of the Democratic Movement for Peace.[21] The founding conference was announced on February 12, 1983 – three days before the announced convening of the sixteenth session of the Palestine National Council in Algiers. The proposed charter of the new party included a call for "internationally supervised elections in the West Bank and Gaza" to determine "the true leaders of the Palestinians," and the establishment of special relations between the future Palestinian "homeland" and the state of Jordan.[22] Both the timing and platform of the new party proved Nasr to be a man capable of strategic thinking lacking in other league bosses.

The founding conference of the new party, however, never took place. Instead, the newly appointed civil administrator, Shlomo Illya, had Nasr arrested and announced his expulsion from the leagues – replacing him with his deputy, Jamil al-Amleh. A few days later a number of league leaders, most notably Nasr himself and al-Khatib (of Ramallah), were accused of financial irregularities and of assault and murder.[23] The league's militia was "persuaded" to return 50 percent of its weapons to the army in order to "improve its image with the local population."[24] But Nasr later complained

21. See Zvi Bar-El's important article, "Politics 'Yuk,' : in *Haaretz, 11* February 1983.

22. *Jerusalem Post*, 2 February 1983.

23. *Al-Fajr*, 28 February 1983 and 1 March 1983; *al-Quds*, 1 March 1983; *Jerusalem Post*, 1 March 1983.

24. *Jerusalem Post*, 2 February 1983. The civil administration reorganized the leadership of the leagues along the following lines: Dudin was appointed chairman of the renamed Movement for Palestinian Leagues; Jamil al-Amleh replaced Nasr as head of the Hebron Village League; Riad al-Khatib replaced his brother Jamil as head of the Ramallah League; Samir Qumsiyyeh became head of the Bethlehem League; his father, Bishara Qumsiyyeh, was appointed second deputy to Dudin; Jawdat Sawalla, of Assira, became first deputy and (presumably) retained his former position as head of the Nablus Village League; Yusef Hantuli, who was chief editor of *al-Mira,* became secretary general (*al-amin al-am*) of the movement; Jamil al-Khatib, Riad's brother, was appointed "head of development programs," and Nasr was also removed from the editorship of *al-Mira* in favor of a certain Muhammad al-Raghib (for details see *al-Mira,* 3 March 1983.

to the Israeli press that only his followers were stripped of their arms, while Dudin's men kept their guns.[25]

The February coup against the league's young guards, as it transpired, was aimed at containing a revolt against Dudin in which both Col. Karmon and Muhammad Nasr played roles.[26] On the one hand, General Sharon and the civil administration, under Karmon's directives, were apparently upset by the league's support for the Reagan initiative and with Dudin's direct overtures to Egyptian and American officials concerning the league's possible role in the autonomy negotiations.[27] Nasr, on the other hand, attempted to take advantage of the Israeli fallout with Dudin's political moves in order to assert his own leadership against the "Dudin dictatorship," as he later called it. But he overplayed his cards by underestimating Dudin's power and by misjudging the military government's tolerance for his own statements against Jewish settlements and in support of a Palestinian state.[28] Ultimately Nasr's downfall reflected the Likud's ambivalence towards any attempt to expand the league's authority into that of an indigenous foundation for Israeli power, and indicated the government's preference for retaining its safer, and more restrictive, control functions.

CONCLUSION: FROM THE STICK TO THE CARROT AND BACK

We have traced the fortunes of the Village Leagues in response to the double strategy of the Israeli civil administration as articulated by the Sharon-Milson-Karmon team: that of destroying the infrastructure of the PLO in the West Bank and Gaza, while simultaneously fostering an alternative "moderate" local leadership capable of fulfilling the role of the Palestinian component in the autonomy negotiations.

25. *Jerusalem Post*, 25 April 1983.

26. Zvi Bar-El in *Haaretz*, 11 February 1983.

27. For the leagues' political program, see *al-Mira*, 13 March 1983.

28. See, for example, *Jerusalem Post*, 30 January 1983, and *al-Anba*, 14 November 1982.

As far as the first objective goes, the civil administration has been able to deal a severe blow, though by no means a decisive one, to several basic national institutions in the West Bank. This was accomplished through the dismantling of most of the elected municipal councils and replacing the mukhtarships of non-cooperating villages; by blocking Joint Committee funds for local projects; and by virtually paralyzing the activities of the National Guidance Committee and other national institutions – including the three universities.

The massive civil uprising that followed the removal of West Bank mayors from office and claimed twenty-two lives during April and May of 1982 was a significant barometer of mass sentiment but failed in thwarting Israel's declared objectives. But the league itself was not instrumental in playing a leading role in the implementation of these objectives. Rather, it confined itself – or was confined by its own limitations – to the role of intimidation in a war conducted by local thugs.

It is this "thuggishness" of the league – exemplified by the disreputable character of many in its membership and the narrow social base from which it recruits its supporters – that continues to obstruct the second objective intended for the league by the civil administration: that of an alternative Palestinian leadership. This failure was the product of several factors – not the least of which was a gut nationalist reaction against a group that was seen as a pliable instrument of an oppressive military government. To this must be added the overwhelming blow, administered by the Jordanian government ban and later by the initial Jordanian-PLO rapprochement, to the league's potential (traditional) base of recruitment. Finally, the league's creators displayed an astonishing ideological misconception of the relationship between town and village in the West Bank. The idea of mobilizing the dispossessed peasantry to rise against the privileged townsmen falters against the radical changes in social structure that have taken place in the last few decades in rural Palestine – the most significant of which is the complex occupational integration of rural labor and investments into the urban (and Israeli) economy. Politically, these changes are dramatically illustrated by the presence of proportionally higher numbers of "security" prisoners from rural, rather than urban, areas,[29] indicating an increasing politicization of the countryside.

Thus, the dilemma the Village League currently presents for the Israeli civil administration is the result of the mutually exclusive tasks it has demanded from it – that it be a repressive apparatus (against the national movement), and at the same time a base for a political alternative (requiring

---

29. Yehuda Litani, "Leaders by Proxy," *Haaretz*, 30 November 1981.

Menachem Milson, before the latter's resignation, to adopt a policy of freeing themselves from association with Menachem Begin's more extreme policies, especially those related to Israeli settlements and claims of Jewish sovereignty over the West Bank and Gaza. It was this political assertiveness, most notably when it took the "radical" line adopted by Muhammad Nasr, that brought about the league's downfall as a *political* organization, groomed to represent the West Bank in the autonomy negotiations. For in politics, dummies – as in the case of Pinocchio's nose – tend to have a life of their own, unforeseen by their creators. In this case, the league's attempt to distance itself from the Israeli embrace, however feeble it might have been, compelled the Israelis to redefine the league's arena of action.

But it would be wrong to underestimate the league's significance in performing its second function: that of acting as a medium of Israeli control over the occupied territories. In the current political stalemate engendered in Palestinian villages by the failure of the Jordanian-Palestinian rapprochement, it is most likely that the league will continue to grow and extend its institutional network as a broker of Israeli power, until either the Palestinian national movement works out an effective strategy of rural mobilization, *o r* until Israel resolves the final legal status of the territories.

POSTSCRIPT: 1989

The Palestinian uprising of December 1987 confirmed the final demise of the Village Leagues as a collaborationist institution. Several remnants of the league leadership publicly recanted their former roles at the height of the *intifada,* during March and April of 1988. The most prominent of those was Bishara Qumsiyyeh, who with his sons led the Bethlehem region Village League, who declared to the assembled congregation in the Beit Sahur Orthodox Church on March 26 that from today "I will be your servant and I swear never to betray you again."[30] This was followed by scores of such confessions in mosques, churches, and public halls from Jenin in the north to Hebron in the south. Other members remained dormant and on the payroll of the civil administration until the summer of 1988, when the military government compelled all Palestinians to acquire the stamp of the local Village League on all official papers (travel permits, driving licenses, etc.) as a countermeasure to the mass resignation of the civil service at the behest of the *intifada* leadership. But this was a mere formality. Both the citizens and the authorities knew that the act was devoid of renewed

30. *Al-Quds,* 26 March 1988; *The Jerusalem Post,* 28 March 1988; *The New York Times,* 26 March 1988.

legitimation for the leagues. None of the uprising circulars even made a public call for the boycott of the leagues, as they did with other official bodies of the civil administration. By mid-1989 about two dozen accused collaborators were liquidated by the underground movement, mostly during April and May. As far as I know none of these collaborators had been identified as members or former members against the Village Leagues.[31]

The theme of town against country had to reappear during the rebellion. One of the most intriguing commentaries on the Palestinian uprising appeared in a work entitled *The Intifada:Beginning or End?* (April 1988 – probably the first book about the uprising to be published) by Muhammad Nasr, former ideologue and head of the Hebron Village League. In it he makes the following remarkable analysis:

> "It is notable that the *intifada* manifests itself much more fiercely in the villages than in the traditional towns. This may be due to the task undertaken by the uprising [leaderships?] in fighting against social groups in power, where such groups are clearly visible in the small village community. Thus the violence of the uprising appears more intense in the rural sector because it is directed not only against the occupation forces, but also against all traditional controls and norms which attempted to immobilize the thrust and creativity of the new social forces. The *intifada* is thus a full scale political *and* social revolution. Those that follow the events note the fear which is consuming the hegemonic social groups today. Not wanting to surrender, these groups have mobilized themselves, and sought the intervention of certain regimes to help them regroup and regain their authority. . . . But unless we witness an external intervention in the uprising, their fall is inevitable.[32]

It is ironic that an essential interpretation of the uprising as a class war should come from a source that was originally groomed by the Israelis as a cornerstone for their structure of control.

A NOTE ON SOURCES

It is unfortunate that most of the people who provided me with material for this article will have to remain anonymous. I would like to express my gratitude, however, to Zvi Bar-El and Danny Rubenstein, correspondents for *Haaretz* and *Davar* respectively, for their valuable comments, and to Raja Shehadeh (of Law in the Service of Man, Ramallah) for information on military orders relevant to the Village Leagues.

31. See Joel Greenberg, "The Plight of the 'Collaborators,' " and Michal Sela, "Gazans Shun 'Collaborators,' " *The Jerusalem Post,* 5 May 1989.

32. Muhammad Nasr, *Al-intifada: Bidaya am nihava?* [Jerusalem?] April 1988, n.p., p. 18.

CHAPTER 22

The Development and Transformation of the Palestine National Movement

Sameer Y. Abraham

Since the creation of Israel in 1948, the Palestine national movement has undergone three distinct phases in its growth and development. For analytical purposes these developmental phases can be roughly characterized as 1) the underground period, from 1956 to 1967; 2) the formative years of revolutionary growth, from 1967 to 1973; and 3) the period of quasi-state development, from 1973 to 1982. The June 1982 Israeli invasion of Lebanon represents the beginning of a fourth phase. Of course, these historical phases are organically linked and overlap to a considerable extent. Within each period movements of quietude and slow organizational building are followed by periods of frantic growth, crisis, and transformation. The internal and external factors responsible for these developments are sometimes difficult to isolate. The purpose of this paper will be to outline each phase of development in the historical evolution of the Palestine national movement with the objective of linking the movement's development from one period to the next to shifts in political objectives and strategy.[1] Although reality is much more complex than this association would at first indicate, it is nevertheless possible to demonstrate a change from the early period of guerrilla warfare, in which the objective

An earlier version of this paper was presented at the 77th Annual Meeting of the American Sociological Association (San Francisco, California) September 6-10 1982.

1. No methodological attempt is made to separate "cause" and "effect" from one period to the next. The important fact to note is that these events have occurred simultaneously.

of the movement was the "liberation of all Palestine" through the use of "revolutionary armed struggle," to the recent and continuing quest for an "independent [i.e. partitioned] Palestinian state" through negotiated diplomatic means. Even the destructive results of the recent Israeli invasion of Lebanon, which was launched primarily to undermine the ability of the Palestine Liberation Organization (PLO) to achieve such an objective, does not appear to have significantly altered this situation.

THE UNDERGROUND PERIOD: 1956-1967

The decade between the Suez War (1956) and the June War (1967) marks the emergence (or reemergence) of the Palestine national movement through the establishment of Fatah.[2] The birth of the Palestine national movement during this period was a direct result of the inability of the Arab regimes and various political parties in the region to make any progress in the resolution of the Palestine problem. In fact, the emergence of Fatah corresponds in large measure to the military defeat of Egypt in the tripartite (Israeli-French- British) invasion of Egypt. At another level, the failure of the union between Egypt and Syria (1958-1961) pointed up the political shortcomings of Arab unity as a vehicle for the liberation of Palestine. So it was not without some irony that Fatah reversed the then dominant political slogan, "Arab unity is the road to the liberation of Palestine," and changed it to read: "The liberation of Palestine is the road to Arab unity." The reversal

2. Some authors date the emergence of Fatah in 1956: see Michael Hudson, "The Palestinian Resistance Movement: Its Significance in the Middle East Crisis," *Middle East Journal* (Summer 1969), 23(3): 299, Walter Laquer, *The Road to War* (Baltimore: Penguin Books, 1968), p. 68. Others contend that Fatah's birth took place a year later in 1957. See Abdullah Schleiffler, "The Emergence of Fatah," *Arab World* (May 1969), p. 16.

The leaders of the Palestinian resistance argue for the historical continuity of the movement from the early days of struggle against British imperialism and Zionism (1917-1948) to the present. In a few instances it is even possible to trace the activities of key individuals, like Yasir Arafat, who operated with Abd al-Qadir Husayni during the 1936-1939 rebellion. According to this view, the current resistance movement represents historical continuity and a reemergence of the struggle after an abrupt and short-lived lull (1948-1956). See, for example, Thomas Kiernan, *Arafat: The Man and the Myth* (New York: W.W. Norton, 1976), *passim;* Abu Iyad with Eric Rouleau, *My Home, My Land: A Narrative of the Palestinian Struggle* (New York: Times Books, 1978), *passim;* and Leila S. Kadi, "Origins of the Armed Resistance," in Russell Stettler, ed., *Palestine: The Arab-Israeli Conflict* (San Francisco: Ramparts Press, 1972), pp. 117-45.

of that slogan epitomized the fundamental difference between the Arab governmental view and the emerging Palestinian nongovernmental approach.

Fatah molded itself and has ultimately shaped the character of the entire Palestine national movement according to a set of core precepts. These include, first and foremost, *reasserting* Palestinian control over the destiny of the Palestinian people and struggle. Operationally this meant weaning the population away from the pan-Arab parties and governments which had come to dominate Palestinian affairs in the post-1948 period. In order to avoid coming into direct collision with the Arab governments, Fatah adhered to the policy of noninterference in the internal affairs of the Arab states so long as those states did not interfere in the Palestinian movement. Second, Fatah promulgated the view that a Palestinian movement would form the "vanguard" in the struggle to liberate Palestine; the Arab states and people were to be relegated to a supportive or secondary role. Third, "revolutionary armed struggle" was the method by which the Palestinian masses were to be mobilized and the struggle waged. A conventional military strategy was not ruled out, however, especially at a later date once the initial struggle had been successfully launched. Finally, the Fatah leadership defined itself as "nationalist" in outlook and devoid of any distinct (at least programmatic) ideological content.[3] In this respect, Fatah was heavily influenced by third world revolutions, especially the Algerian FLN and later the Chinese, Cuban, and Vietnamese experiences.

What has clearly distinguished the Fatah from its later rivals (Popular Front for the Liberation of Palestine, Popular Democratic Front for the Liberation of Palestine, etc.) was its acute disdain towards ideology. Fatah viewed the adoption of political and social ideologies as an obstacle to the liberation of Palestine, which had up until that time entangled the Palestine question in the murky depths of intra-Arab rivalries among competing political parties and personalities, be they Nasserism, the Arab Nationalist Movement, Baathism, the Muslim Brotherhood, communism, etc. Although members of the original Fatah leadership were influenced by the existing political currents of the day,[4] the failure of the Arab regimes and political parties to make any headway in the liberation of Palestine forced these

3. *Dialogue With Fateh* (Palestine National Liberation Movement, 1969), esp. pp. 52-56; and H. Al-Ayyubi, "Guide to Researchers: Fatah's Political and Military Ideas" (Arabic), *Shuun Filastiniya* (January 1974), 29: 116-26.

4. For a discussion of the various political currents which have influenced key Fatah leaders, see John W. Amos, *Palestinian Resistance: Organization of a Nationalist Movement* (New York: Pergamon Press, 1980), pp. 43-153.

leaders to look elsewhere for guidance. Their decision was to postpone adopting a political ideology until Palestine was liberated.[5] As the Palestine problem was a *national question,* they argued, the entire Palestinian nation and all social classes should be entitled to participate in the liberation struggle.[6] In other words, all social issues would be subordinated to the principal aim of national liberation. The Palestine national movement should not be directed in the interests of any single social class or political line. As Hani al-Hassan, a leading member of Fatah, stated, Fatah is not a movement of the right or left but rather one of "the new progressives – the movement which has gone beyond right and left."[7]

Although this viewpoint proved appealing, especially given the inability of the existing political parties to satisfy Palestinian grievances, the absence of an explicit social/political ideology made it easy for the basically middle class Palestinian leadership to dominate the movement. From another vantage point, a nonideological Palestinian nationalism would enable the leadership to maneuver through the many intra-Arab differences and rivalries without being branded as an agent of any single party or government. The absence of a distinct social/political ideology was aimed at maximizing support among the Arab states as well as among a broad coalition of Palestinians.

Most noteworthy during this period was the fact that the Palestinians took it upon themselves to form their own organization outside the existing political alignments of the day. An *independent* Palestinian leadership that could escape Arab governmental control remains an overriding goal today. But the lack of a territory from which Fatah could build a base of

5. One of the four key points repeatedly stressed by Fatah in its early newspaper, *Filastinuna,* stated ". . . the Palestinians must not embark upon unnecessary dialogue over the shape of the country after liberation." See Riad N. El-Rayyes and Dunia Naha, eds., *Guerrillas for Palestine: A Study of the Palestinian Commandos* (Beirut: An-Nahar Press, 1974), p. 21.

6. Fatah's lack of a social ideology is explained in Leila S. Kadi, *Basic Political Documents of the Armed Palestinian Resistance Movement* (Beirut: Palestine Liberation Organization Research Center, 1969), esp. pp. 103-6. See also "We Are in the Midst of a National Liberation Revolution and Not a Social Revolution" (Arabic), *Fatah*, 26 January 1970, p. 5; Naji Allush, *The Palestinian Revolution: Its Aims and Problems* (Arabic) (Beirut: Dar al-Taliah, 1970); Hani al Hassan, "Fatah between Theory and Practice: The Theoretical Framework" (Arabic), *Shuun Filastiniya* (March 1972), 7: 9-21; and Ehud Yaari, "Al Fatah's Political Thinking," *New Outlook* (November-December 1968), 2(9): 20-32.

7. *Ar Rai al-Am,* 23 April 1970, pp. 1-8.

operations, coupled with the fact that the Palestinian people were widely dispersed over a number of Arab countries, made it extremely difficult for the Fatah leadership to operate freely. On several occasions members of the leadership were imprisoned by Arab governments, some for months at a time.[8]

The evident weakness of the movement during this period of infancy led to its underground activity and forced it into direct cooperation with certain Arab governments, most notably Syria. Under the watchful eyes of the Syrian regime, Fatah began sporadic guerrilla operations against Israel on January 1, 1965.[9] Some of these actions were launched from Syrian territory, but most, it appears, were staged from Jordan and Lebanon in order to protect Syria from Israeli retaliation and to destabilize these regimes for Syrian political gain. In order to avoid falling victim to outright Syrian control, however, Fatah attempted to establish a base of operations in the West Bank of Jordan.[10] The West Bank appeared as a logical choice, as a large Palestinian community resided there along Israel's border and outside of direct Syrian control. Overall Palestinian military activity was limited and hampered by almost complete dependence upon the good will of Syria.[11]

By the mid-1960s, Fatah was still without widespread support among the Palestinian population. The pan-Arab movements and political personalities remained preeminent even with their many failings and shortcomings. In order to maintain their hold over the restive Palestinian population, the Arab states sponsored and controlled the newly formed Palestine Liberation Organization (PLO) in 1964. Fatah was now faced

8. In 1966, for example, the Baathist authorities in Syria imprisoned Yasir Arafat, Abu Jihad, Abu Ali Ayad, and Abu Sabri along with seven cadres of lesser importance. On the eve of the June 1967 war some 250 Palestinians suspected of being members and sympathizers of Fatah were languishing in Jordanian prisons. See Iyad, *My Home, My Land*, pp. 45-47; El-Rayyes and Nahas, eds., *Guerrillas for Palestine*, p. 22; and Ehud Yaari, *Strike Terror: The Story of Fatah* (New York: Sabra Books, 1970), p. 89.

9. At the time Fatah launched its first guerrilla raid, the organization, according to one leader, Farouq al-Qaddumi, had more men than arms. Amos, *Palestinian Resistance*, p. 204.

10. Fatah's underground organization in the West Bank proved to be a dismal failure; a firm base among the local population was never established during this period. See Yaari, *Strike Terror*, pp. 131-43; and *Arab World Daily*, 6 October 1967.

11. For a brief discussion of Fatah-Syrian relations, see William B. Quandt, et al., *The Politics of Palestinian Nationalism* (Berkeley: University of California Press, 1973), pp. 163-75.

with a direct challenge and competitor for the allegiance of (and recruits from) the Palestinian population. The PLO received official Arab government sanction and support, whereas Fatah operated mainly at Syria's sufferance and to a lesser extent received Algerian support. In general, Fatah's relations with the Arab states were antagonistic, forcing the movement to operate clandestinely, particularly in Jordan and Lebanon.[12] Syria remained the only "secure" base for Fatah, providing the movement with arms, training, and a political shield. But even this support was tenuous and dependent upon the political factions in power in a constantly changing government.[13] Early in its development, Fatah observed the necessity of avoiding dependence on any single Arab state for backing even if that state was "revolutionary" and "progressive" as Syria claimed to be. In order to become a truly independent Palestinian movement, Fatah would have to secure the backing of a number of sometimes opposing Arab states. Consequently, the rivalries which have fragmented and divided the Arab world have paradoxically worked to Fatah's advantage, at least at a tactical level.

Fatah's achievements during this stage of its development were limited, but not entirely insignificant by some accounts. Although the number of military operations launched between January 1956 and May 1967 did not exceed two hundred,[14] they did force the Israelis and Arab states to take the movement into account. In response, Israel carried out a series of retaliatory raids, the most serious of which were directed at the Jordanian towns of ash-Shunah, Jenin, Qalqilya (1965), villages in the Hebron district (1966), and es-Samu and neighboring areas on November 13, 1966.[15] Jordan and Lebanon attempted to secure their borders against such raids, while the Arab states in general moved toward more expressive support of the PLO.

Even with increasing military operations, the first decade of the Palestinian movement is most accurately characterized as a period of intense organization building, politicization, and propaganda work. These activities took precedence over military operations and laid the groundwork for the

12. Fuad Jabber, "The Arab Regimes and the Palestinian Revolution 1967-1971," *Journal of Palestine Studies* (Winter 1973). 2(2): 79-101.

13. Quandt, et al., *Politics of Palestinian Nationalism,* pp. 168-73.

14. *Ibid.,* p. 172.

15. A discussion of the es-Samu raid is contained in Fred J. Khouri, *The Arab-Israeli Dilemma* (Syracuse, N.Y,: Syracuse University Press, 1968). pp. 229-39.

military activities that began in 1965. A popular base among the Palestinian population was still lacking and only a core leadership of full-time members was active. The basic political aims of the movement were broadly articulated during this period, even though serious theoretical and strategic questions remained unanswered.[16] The goal was simply to liberate *all* Palestine, to free it of Zionist/Israeli colonialism and to return the Palestinian people to their homeland. "Revolutionary armed struggle" was the means by which these goals were to be achieved, even though guerrilla warfare was not viewed as an end in itself. The aim of guerrilla warfare was to "entangle" the Arab regimes into a wider war with Israel.

Fatah's declared political objectives and strategy appeared simplistic, inflexible, and even dogmatic. Scant attention, for example, was paid to developments in Israel or to the vision of a future Palestine and how relations between Arabs and Jews were to be defined once Palestine was liberated. Fatah spelled out its objective with regard to Israel/Zionism as entailing the "liquidation of the Zionist identity in all the occupied territory of Palestine, in its political, economic, and military forms."[17] In other words, Israel/Zionism was simply negated and the Palestinian-Arab indigenous character of the country and its inhabitants reaffirmed. This perspective can be attributed in part to the movement's infancy and its preoccupation with survival in an inhospitable Arab world. The antagonistic relationship with the main enemy, Israel, required little definition or analysis; the opponent was simply dealt with in the form of denial and nonrecognition. The major task for Fatah during this period was to define itself *vis-à-vis* the Arab states, party ideologies, and political personalities that had appropriated the mantle of the Palestine problem for themselves. To gain recognition and acceptance, Fatah must first differentiate itself from its Arab counterparts. The pages of *Filastinuna* ("Our Palestine"), Fatah's early publication, are filled with major criticisms of the prevailing governmental views. As a consequence of these attacks, the newspaper was banned in most countries and forced to circulate underground.

16. Two questions in particular appear to have been generally neglected. The first concerns an understanding of the nature and character of the Israeli state and society. The second has to do with the nature of the relationship between Israel and the United States, on the one hand, and the Arab regimes and the United States, on the other.

17. *The Palestine National Liberation Movement,* Al Fatah (mimeo, n.d.), pp. 13-14. See also *an-Nahar Report,* 11 February 1974.

Even while in its infancy, Fatah had succeeded in independently reintroducing a Palestinian element into the state level Arab-Israeli struggle. While still weak and hampered by severe governmental restrictions, the movement was able to begin the *re-Palestinization* of the conflict. At this stage Fatah was no more than a fledgling underground movement, but one determined to keep the Palestinian issue alive and at the center of regional events. Its clandestine existence was necessitated by the repression it encountered at the hands of the Arab states. Through its propaganda work and guerrilla raids it laid the groundwork for continuing tension and turmoil in the area. According to some accounts, the movement's military operations acted as a "catalyst" in triggering the June War (1967).[18] In any case, the movement was to benefit enormously from the consequences of the war. For in the war's aftermath, the movement would be able to transform itself from a dependent underground organization into an independent and open revolutionary movement.

THE FORMATIVE YEARS OF REVOLUTIONARY GROWTH: 1967-1973.

The six years between the June War (1967) and the October War (1973) represent the formative years in the growth and development of the Palestine national movement. Unlike the first phase, which is characterized by an emphasis on political activity and organization building, the second period is known for its emphasis on heightened military activity. Political objectives and strategy are further elaborated as the political objective of the "democratic state" is introduced as well as the military strategy of "peoples' war." It is during this time that the movement experienced its most stupendous growth in personnel, proliferation of organizations, and popular support. It is also during this period that the movement experienced its first major crisis and setback.

The astonishing collapse of the Arab armies in the June War vindicated Fatah's view that conventional means could not hope to defeat Israel, as the Arab masses could not play a direct role[19] The virtual vacuum created by the war provided Fatah with an opportunity to seize the initiative and

18. Quandt, et al., *Politics of Palestinian Nationalism*, p. 157.

19. See Leila S. Kadi, *Basic Political Documents*, p. 23.

propose itself as an alternative. Shortly after the war, Fatah resumed in earnest guerrilla raids against Israel. Fatah's objective was to make itself the nucleus around which resistance to Israel could be gathered. In less than a year, the Battle of Karameh (March 22, 1968) allowed Fatah to realize its long-sought-after dream beyond its wildest imaginings. In this battle, Fatah (with the assistance of the Jordanian army) broke with the rules of guerrilla warfare and defended the refugee camp of Karameh on the eastern bank of the Jordan against an Israeli retaliatory force dispatched to put an end to guerrilla incursions.[20] Although the camp was nearly leveled and the guerrillas "defeated" militarily, their determination to resist the invaders and capacity to inflict serious casualties against the Israeli army allowed Fatah to claim a political and psychological victory of major proportions. News of the "victory" electrified the Arab world. In their own way, the Palestinian guerrillas demonstrated the viability of guerrilla warfare: the once invincible Israeli army was shown to be mortal. The movement's leadership argued that the enemy could in fact be defeated if only the political will and determination were present.

Regardless of the varying interpretations of this battle,[21] it is now unquestioned that the Battle of Karameh represented a major turning point in the growth and development of the Palestinian movement. In a sense, it was the Palestinian equivalent of the Vietnamese success at Dien Bien Phu. The enlistment of thousands of recruits occurred so rapidly that a shortage of military instructors became readily apparent.[22] Funds, arms, supplies, and personnel flowed into the movement from all over the world. The number of military actions increased, as did the number of guerrilla

20. For a Resistance view of the battle, see "The Tale of Karameh," *Arab Palestinian Resistance* (March 1972), 4(3): 14-28. See also John Cooley, *Green March, Black September: The Story of the Palestinian Arabs* (London: Frank Cass, 1973), pp. 100-101; and Trevor N. Dupuy, *Elusive Victory: The Arab-Israeli Wars, 1947-1974* (New York: Harper and Row, 1978), pp. 350-56.

21. For an opposing view, see Paul A. Jureidini and William E. Hazen, *The Palestinian Movement in Politics* (Lexington, Massachusetts: Lexington Books, 1976), pp. 13-14; and Zeev Schiff and Raphael Rothstein, *Fedayeen: Guerrillas against Israel* (New York: David McKay, 1972), pp. 81-87.

22. Hisham Sharabi, *Palestine Guerrillas: Their Credibility and Effectiveness* (Beirut: Institute for Palestine Studies, 1970), p. 24.

casualties.[23] Dozens of new guerrilla groups were formed almost overnight.[24] Some were organized by Palestinians and others by Arab governments searching for a way to cleanse their regimes of the humiliating sting of the June War defeat. An organized presence in the Palestinian movement would allow the Arab regimes to keep a close watch over Palestinian activity while bestowing upon them the prestige of belonging to the movement without much corresponding responsibility.[25]

Unlike the previous period, in which Fatah faced repression from the Arab states and the rivalry of the Arab-sponsored PLO, the field was now wide open and the organization could conduct its activities unchecked. In fact, governmental collapse was so complete in Jordan that the movement no longer found it necessary to operate clandestinely.[26] As the Arab states receded into the background, a proliferation of Palestinian guerrilla groups of varying political persuasions competed with one another to dominate the movement. Although most groups were nationalist in outlook and generally agreed to the core precepts set down by Fatah, the Marxist-oriented groups such as the Popular Front for the Liberation of Palestine (PFLP) and the

23. According to a leading Fatah leader, Abu Iyad, the (average) number of military operations increased from "12 in 1967 to 52 in 1968, 199 in 1969, and 279 in the first eight months of 1970." Abu Iyad with Eric Rouleau, *My Home, My Land* p. 60.

According to Israeli military analysts Zeev Schiff and Raphael Rothstein, by 1969 the *fedayiin* casualty rate had reached ninety percent. *Fedayiin* losses between June 1967-January 1971 totaled 1,828. In comparison the total number of Israeli losses, civilian and military, during the same period was placed at 748, less than half the Palestinian casualties. See *Fedayeen*, pp. 80, 91-92. See also Bard E. O'Neill, *Armed Struggle in Palestine: A Political-Military Analysis* (Boulder, Colorado: Westview Press, 1978), pp. 237-49.

Another analyst argues that Israeli casualties are much higher than the Israelis officially claim. See Sharabi, *Palestine Guerrillas*, pp. 10-13.

24. By some estimates seventy new guerrilla groups were created in the immediate aftermath of Karameh. In fact, the plethora of organizations, many of which were no more than paper creations, became so great that Arab spokesmen began warning against the dangers of too many competing groups.

25. In addition to supporting select Palestinian organizations, some Arab governments created their own guerrilla organizations. Most of these organizations were short-lived. Currently only two Arab-sponsored organizations remain active: the Syrian-sponsored al-Saiqah and the Iraqi-sponsored Arab Liberation Front. For a discussion of the various commando organizations and their primary sources of aid, see Quandt, et al., *Politics of Palestinian Nationalism*, p. 66.

26. Kadi, *Basic Political Documents*, p. 25.

Popular Democratic Front for the Liberation of Palestine (PDFLP) stood at odds with the nonideological Fatah. Ideological differences sometimes proved difficult to surmount as some groups postulated conflicting political strategies and military tactics.[27] Part of this difficulty was surmounted when the PLO was freed of Arab state control in 1969. The entry of the *fedayiin* organizations into the PLO allowed it to operate as an umbrella organization through which coordination between groups could be established. With Yasir Arafat the elected chairman, the resistance movement was now operating "officially" in the Arab world, but it also inherited a bureaucracy not of its own making. Although the PLO had its political advantages, the burden of accepting government-level responsibilities at a time when the resistance was still in its early development posed serious questions about the future direction of the movement. Palestinian leaders were quick to point out that a PLO bureaucracy operating at a state level might be restricted in the revolutionary options which the movement could pursue.[28]

As the movement's numbers and political and military infrastructure expanded, a corresponding social apparatus emerged to meet other newly created needs. Hospitals, clinics, orphanages, childcare centers, and schools were opened and operated by the guerrilla organizations or at least were influenced by them. The Palestinian refugee camps were immediately liberated of Jordanian police control. An elaborate police and intelligence network was created to protect the camps. Newspapers, magazines, radio stations, and other facilities were organized to collect information, analyze, and disseminate it both within and outside the movement. Diplomatic missions and offices were established in various countries to win recognition of and support for the Palestinian struggle. In Jordan, the Palestinian movement began to form the nucleus of a reborn Palestinian society, one in the process of revolutionary reformation after almost two decades of dispersal, fragmentation, and stagnation. This reawakening placed a renewed emphasis on a Palestinian identity, an identity which had been submerged during the heady days of pan-Arab nationalism, Baathism, Syrianism, and all the other isms of the 1950s and 1960s.

Like most social upheavals, the Palestinian movement ignited vast energies and social forces, inevitably affecting the social organizational

27. For insight into the basic differences between Palestinian organizations, see El-Rayyes and Nahas, *Guerrillas for Palestine,* pp. 19-70; and Kadi, pp. 143-79.

28. The discussions ended in an attempt to "revolutionize" the PLO structure and utilize it to unify the competing commando organizations. See "Unity Formula," *Fatah* (29 May 1970), 2(9): 4.

patterns of the existing society. For the Palestinians, the movement represented an *immediate* transformation: they were now organized as a people, armed, and in command of their destiny. So pervasive was the impact of the movement that it was popularly referred to as a revolution (*thawra*). The role of the Palestinian revolution was interpreted differently by each guerrilla organization. The major division was between Fatah and the nationalist groups, on the one side, and the PFLP and PDFLP on the other. Even though all agreed that the principal aim of the movement was the liberation of Palestine, the Marxist organizations argued that such a goal was not only distant but that in order to reach it both Palestinian and Arab society would have to undergo a dramatic social transformation. Nothing short of an Arab liberation movement would have to be created to achieve the liberation of Palestine – as well as the Arab states – from "reactionary" control. As the PFLP noted, at first there would be an alliance between the Palestinian national and Arab liberation movement which in turn will "give rise to the Palestine-Arab force and the Palestine-Arab strategy which is [*sic*] capable of triumphing in a long and hard battle imposed by the nature of the enemy we are facing."[29] Fatah's position appeared more pragmatic, relegating the Arab states and masses to a supportive role in the struggle.

Differences also surfaced with regard to how social issues among the Palestinian and the Jordanian populations should be confronted. The "woman's question" was discussed and written about openly;[30] strikes by Jordanian and Palestinian workers were officially supported by the more "radical" guerrilla groups and sometimes instigated by them; in the countryside the peasantry was receiving increasing attention and support as some organizations attempted to build a solid rural base in the Maoist tradition.[31] The spread of these activities indicated that a revolutionary atmosphere was being fostered and authority relations at all levels were being thrown into question. The authority of the Jordanian police and army was routinely flouted-to such an extent that the PLO had to create a "unified

29. *A Strategy for the Liberation of Palestine* (Amman: Popular Front for the Liberation of Palestine, 1969), p. 49.

30. See Ghadi Karmi, "Liberation through Revolution for Palestinian Women," *The Guardian* (Manchester), 14 May 1976; Soraya Antonius, "Fighting on Two Fronts: Conversations with Palestinian Women," *Journal of Palestine Studies,* (Spring 1979), 8(3):26-45; "Interview with Leila Khalid," in Stetler, ed., *Palestine: The Arab-Israeli Conflict,* pp. 223-40; and Leila Khalid, *My People Shall Live: The Autobiography of a Revolutionary* (edited by George Hajjar) (London: Hodder and Stoughton, 1973).

31. Gerard Chaliand, *The Palestinian Resistance* (Middlesex, England: Penguin Books, 1972), pp. 84-96.

armed struggle command" (i.e. its own internal police) in order to regulate the behavior of some of its commandos and civilians.[32] These changes raised serious theoretical, strategic, and tactical questions for the movement's leadership. Whereas the Fatah leadership attempted to concentrate solely on military operations against Israel, the "radical" organizations were intent upon challenging the power and authority of the Jordanian monarchy.

By early 1970, the Palestinian movement had developed into a major force. Well funded, well armed, and buoyed with the support of the Palestinian and Arab people, the movement was now perhaps in its strongest position ever. Even if the impact of the revolution could be confined to the Palestinian population, which it could not, the developing contradiction between the Jordanian monarchy and the resistance would have emerged regardless. In less than three years, the Palestinian national movement was transformed from a weak, clandestine organization dependent on the Syrian regime which harbored it to an open, self-propelled national liberation organization in Jordan. The movement's rise was so spectacular that the Jordanian monarchy had to await changes in regional politics before it could attempt to curb the movement as it did.

In September 1970, the Palestinian movement and Jordanian government clashed militarily in what was to become a major civil war.[33] The Palestinian movement was defeated and forced to make a number of major concessions to the king regarding its presence in Jordan.[34] In June-

32. Originally created in April, 1969, the Palestine armed struggle command (PASC) was a loose coordinating body outside the framework of the PLO. It was enlarged a year later into the Unified Command under the auspices of a unity statement signed by all commando organizations. *Fatah* (29 May 1970), 2(9): 4.

33. See Sheila Ryan and Joe Stork, "U.S. and Jordan: Thrice-Rescued Throne," *MERIP Reports* (February 1972), pp. 3-11.

34. Sharp disagreements arose over the causes of the civil war and the defeat of the Resistance movement. For insights into these exchanges see *Arab World,* 3 March 1971; *al-Hurriyah,* 4 October 1971; *Arab World Weekly,* 23 January 1971: *LeMonde Weekly,* 27 January 1971; and "September: Counter-Revolution in Jordan" (Buffalo, New York: Palestine Solidarity Committee, n.d.).

The Jordanian civil war also led to a period of intense self-reflection within the movement. Of the many works which appeared, the following may be considered as representative of three broad ranges of opinion: Elias Murquss, *The Palestinian Resistance and the Present Situation* (Arabic) (Beirut: Dar al-Haqiqa, 1971); Sadiq Jalal al-Azm, *A Critical Study of the Thought of the Palestinian Resistance* (Arabic) (Beirut: Daral-Auda, 1973); Hussam-al-Kalib, *On the Palestinian Revolutionary Experience* (Arabic) (Damascus: Ministry of Culture, 1972).

July 1971, the two clashed again, this time in northern Jordan. The PLO was completely routed and forced to relocate in Syria and Lebanon. The Jordanian government was able to reestablish control over the Palestinian refugee camps and to entirely dominate if not dismantle the elaborate set of institutions which the PLO had built over the four-year period. Although defeated in Jordan, the Palestinian movement was not vanquished. And although attacks could no longer be launched against Israel from Jordanian soil, the Palestinians could still launch their raids from nearby Lebanon.

The beginning of an important *transition period* for the Palestinian movement can be dated from this time. There are two reasons for this: first, in 1970 and 1971 the movement suffered its first serious military and political setback not in a battle with Israel, but in a confrontation with an Arab government. The setback was critical enough to force the leadership to reassess its entire strategy and tactics. It was also a period when the unquestioned support of the Arab masses had begun to wane. Second, and perhaps just as important, 1970-1971 represented a turning point in the Arab world and the reentry of the Arab states into a primary role in the Arab-Israeli conflict.

The acceptance of the Rogers peace plan by Nasser in 1970, followed by Nasser's death later that year, signaled the beginning of a major policy shift in Egypt and in its role in the Arab-Israeli conflict. With Nasser's war of attrition with Israel along the banks of the Suez Canal and the acceptance of the American-sponsored peace plan ending the Suez Canal war, the Arab states were able to regain the political initiative. The successful Jordanian military action against the Palestinians acted to ensure that the PLO would only play a peripheral role in the conflict with Israel. To a certain extent, it was in the interests of some Arab regimes to "clip the wings" of the Palestinian movement so that the Arab states could be the dominant force in determining the outcome of the Arab-Israeli conflict. Of course, the extent to which the Palestinian movement was to be hampered or destroyed varied from one state to the next.

From its inception, the Palestinian movement possessed a revolutionary character even though some observers have questioned the validity of applying the term "revolution" to the movement.[35] To a certain extent, the debate is academic: regardless of intentions the *consequences* of the

---

35. See, for example, Samir Franjieh, "How Revolutionary is the Palestinian Resistance? A Marxist Interpretation," *Journal of Palestine Studies* (Winter 1972), 1(2): 52-60; and Sadik Al-Azm, "The Palestinian Resistance Movement Reconsidered," in Edward Said and Fuad Suleiman, eds., *The Arabs Today: Alternatives for Tomorrow* (Columbus, Ohio: Forum Associates, 1973), pp. 121-36.

movement have wide-ranging revolutionary implications. At the very minimum, the movement is determined to resist (i.e., defend Palestinian national rights against) continuing Israeli/Zionist colonialism and military occupation. At another level, the Palestinian movement seeks to rectify a historical injustice committed against the Palestinian people – it seeks to do this through the destruction of the Israeli/Zionist state (not people) and its replacement with a secular democratic state. By postulating the "democratic nonsectarian state" as a goal in 1969, the Palestinian movement invested itself with a revolutionary potential *vis-à-vis* its opponent. The more critical question has to do with the revolutionary impact of the movement with regard to the Palestinian population and Arab society.

In order to realize its aims, the Palestinian movement had to effect a radical rupture with the past. Palestinian thinking, relations, and behavior had been transformed under the pressure of the challenges posed by Israel. The extent of that transformation depends on the nature of the Palestinian-Israeli struggle and the role of external forces in the region. Should the struggle remain protracted, new social forces may emerge to meet the challenge. During the movement's brief development in Jordan, it was already apparent that Palestinian society was in the process of a revolutionary change. The movement's phoenix-like rise after 1967 provided a critical opening for the mobilization of vast social energies and the redirection of existing social forces. Before the future course could be charted, however, the movement's potential was dissipated when it was forced to defend itself against the Jordanian monarchy. Even though the movement pledged "noninterference" in the affairs of Arab states, the movement's very existence had revolutionary implications for all of Arab society. It is precisely that revolutionary possibility, coupled with the increasing friction with state authority, that triggered the confrontation with the Jordanian regime.

The transition period that began in 1970 was completed in the immediate aftermath of the October War (1973).[36] Not only had the Arab states seized the military initiative in the war, but they also seized political

36. The October War also represents an important transition period for the Arab world as a whole. In this regard, see Mohamed Sid-Ahmed, *After the Guns Fall Silent* (London: Croom Helm Ltd., 1976); Walid W. Kuzziha, *Palestine in the Arab Dilemma* (London: Croom Helm Ltd., 1979); Salah al-Din al-Bitar, "The Implications of the October War for the Arab World," *Journal of Palestine Studies* (Winter 1974), 3(2): 34-45; Ghassan Tueni, "After October: Military Conflict and Political Change in the Middle East," *Journal of Palestine Studies* (Summer 1974), 3(4): 114-30; and Munif al-Razzaz, "After the October War: New Historical Realities," *Arab Studies Quarterly* (Spring 1979), 1(2): 83-95.

initiative immediately following it. The American-mediated disengagement agreements with Israel in the Sinai and Golan Heights were seen as the beginning of a resolution to the "Arab-Israeli conflict." The introduction of the oil boycott (1973-1974) during this period gave the confrontation states of Egypt and Syria the support of the conservative oil-rich Gulf States and the entire Arab world. Although the PLO played an important role in the October War, its activities were completely overshadowed by the initial military successes – albeit limited – of the conventional Arab armies.[37] The October War had the effect of completely unifying the Arab states (if only momentarily) and forcing the Palestinian movement into the background. By the end of the war, the Arab regimes had become ascendant and the Palestinian movement subordinate. A new set of political and military conditions emerged that would ultimately transform the political objectives and character of the Palestinian movement.

During this period, the Palestinian movement continued its growth and development in all spheres. As the movement transformed itself from a weak underground organization into a fully developed national liberation movement, it also began to clarify its political objectives and strategy. The "Zionist state of Israel" was not simply to be destroyed. It was now to be *replaced* with a "democratic, nonsectarian state" that would equally recognize the rights of Jews, Muslims, and Christians in a "liberated" Palestine. The democratic state concept was introduced by Fatah theorists in late 1968.[38] One of its aims was to win the endorsement of Israelis while simultaneously keeping Palestinian aspirations in step with historical developments (i.e., Palestinians could not return to British Mandate Palestine). In other words, it was not enough to simply *negate* the Israeli/Zionist state, but it was now equally necessary to *affirm* – if only in a visionary manner – the alternative for which Arabs and Jews could jointly struggle. The incorporation into its policy of the democratic state as a goal of the PLO in 1969 represented a major political development and indicated the strength and maturity that the Palestinian movement had attained in such a short period of time.

37. In his narrative of the October War, General El-Shazly does not even mention the role of the Palestine Liberation Army on the Egyptian front or the role of PLO guerrillas on Israel's northern front. See Saad El-Shazly, *The Crossing of the Suez* (San Francisco: American Mideast Research, 1980). The Palestinian role in the fighting is described in *Filastin al-Thawra,* 14 November 1973.

38. The concept of the Palestinian Democratic State was first declared at the Second International Conference for Support of the Arab Peoples in Cairo (25-26 January 1969). It was later discussed and expounded in three articles in the *Fatah* (English-language) periodical, 10 November 1969 – 19 January 1970.

The strategy of "entanglement" of Arab states into war with Israel, which guided the underground guerrilla activity of the first period, was replaced by the concept of a "people's war" during this second phase of development.[39] Although many in the movement were of the opinion that the Palestinians should rely only upon themselves and the Arab people even if it meant developing a conventional military capability of their own, the leadership remained open and ready to receive conventional Arab support in any battle with Israel. The fact that Arab territories (Golan Heights, Sinai) were also occupied as a consequence of the June War made it inevitable that the Arab regimes would eventually rejoin the struggle. The war of attrition (1969-1970) along the Suez Canal was a clear indication that the Arab states would not remain militarily or politically idle while Israel occupied their lands.

However much the dominant wing of the PLO leadership attempted to confine the struggle to national goals,[40] the revolutionary *implications* for Arab society continued to manifest themselves. The more radical Palestinian organizations openly called for the overthrow of certain Arab regimes and for social revolution throughout the Arab world. But the actual revolutionary potential of the Palestinian movement came to an abrupt end in 1970 - 1971 before it had a chance to fully materialize. The defeat of the Palestinian movement by the Jordanian regime forced the leadership to relocate its main base to Lebanon and reevaluate its objectives and strategy. It had one of two strategic choices: 1) to widen the struggle and move in the direction of full-scale social revolution in the Arab world, as the radical groups called for; or 2) to continue along the narrow path of national liberation, as the dominant wing of the PLO demanded. Each choice required a different response from the Palestinian leadership and people. Either choice, however, would require the movement to undergo a major transformation during the next stage of its existence.

39. *Arab World Weekly,* 26 October 1968. See also Naji Allush, "The People's War – and the Arab People's War" (Arabic) *Dirasat Arabiya* (October 1973), No. 12, pp. 105-110.

40. Generally speaking the dominant wing of the PLO is represented by a nationalist current with Fatah at its core. This does not by any means imply that a consensus or monolithic political and ideological position exists either within Fatah or the PLO dominant wing. Differences of "right" or "left," "conservative" and "radical," appear to color all discussion. The fact remains that a strong nationalist *tendency* dominates Fatah and the PLO on most issues. For insights into current differences between Palestinian "moderates" and "rejectionists," see Muhammad Y. Muslih, "Moderates and Rejectionists within the Palestine Liberation Organization," *Middle East Journal* (Spring 1976), 30(2): 127-40; and M. Jafar. "The Ideological Divide in the Palestinian Resistance Movement," *Khamsin* (1978), pp. 115-24.

THE PERIOD OF QUASI-STATE DEVELOPMENT: 1973-1982

The third phase of development represents another historical departure for the Palestinian movement. This period began in the aftermath of the October War (1973) and ended with a U.S.-sponsored cease-fire (1981-1982) between Israel and the PLO. During these years, the PLO confronted a new series of political and military challenges, which propelled the movement into the realm of international diplomacy and away from "revolutionary armed struggle." In its pursuit of a negotiated settlement, the PLO proposed an "independent Palestinian state" in the West Bank and Gaza as its immediate objective. Concurrently, the PLO engaged in an intense period of institution building, which began to transform the organization into a quasi-state structure. Militarily encircled in Lebanon as a result of the civil war, the PLO adopted a policy of armed self-defense locally and political moderation internationally.

The October War shook the foundations upon which the relations of the post-June War period were constructed and upon which the political dynamics in the region rested. A direct result of the October War was the military and political ascendance of Egypt, Syria, and the Arab regimes, which combined to support the war effort and the negotiations which immediately followed. Radical and conservative regimes were united in their support of these countries. The disengagement agreements that were negotiated following the war completely neglected the Palestinians, however. By entering into these negotiations, the Arab states accorded Israel *de facto* recognition and, more importantly, paved the way for future negotiations toward a comprehensive Middle East peace. With the direct intervention of the United States as a mediator in the political process it was clear that the Arab-Israeli conflict had entered a new era. The October War had the effect of upsetting the previous "no war, no peace" situation that had catapulted the Palestinian movement onto center stage. A political resolution to the Arab-Israeli conflict was being pursued under the auspices of United States sponsorship and with United Nations Resolution 242 as the negotiating framework. The altered conditions of the post-October War period confronted the Palestinian movement with a new set of challenges that would lead to a major political and organizational transformation.

An immediate consequence of the October War was that it allowed the Arab states to reopen a diplomatic process to resolve the Arab-Israeli conflict politically. Following the celebrated Kissinger disengagement agreements, the United States, Arab states, and Israel were in principle agreed to reconvening a Geneva Conference to resolve all outstanding issues. A key stumbling block to convening the conference centered on Palestinian participation. The PLO would not accept UN Resolution 242 because it viewed Palestinians as "refugees" and completely ignored their national right to self-determination. On the other side, Israel refused to recognize and negotiate with the PLO in such a conference. A stalemate ensued and although various compromises were discussed, a reconvened Geneva Conference never materialized.[41]

The movement of the Arab states toward a negotiated settlement of the Arab-Israeli conflict forced the realization upon the PLO leadership that it could become politically isolated in the Arab world if it did not accept and work within the emerging consensus. The previous notion that "no Arab state could make peace with Israel without the Palestinians" held so long as the Arab states were incapable of posing a credible military threat to Israel and winning back occupied Arab territory. The October War overturned that notion, however, and permitted the Arab states to determine the nature and direction of a political settlement. And although most Arab states continued to reject UN Resolution 242 in principle, and the formal recognition of Israel which it entailed, their disengagement agreements, cease-fires, and plans to reconvene a Geneva Conference were tantamount to *de facto* recognition of Israel.

Given these circumstances, the PLO was faced with two choices in the post- October War period: either work within a unified Arab strategy or oppose it and suffer the myriad consequences associated with political isolation in the Arab world. The dominant, nationalist wing of the PLO leadership decided to pursue the common political strategy of the Arab states with the proviso that it would attempt to realize an "independent national state" in the West Bank and Gaza for itself.[42] This shift in political objectives emerged in the aftermath of the October War, although it had been discussed among the Palestinian left in the form of a "transitional program" even before the war.[43] By June 1974, the change in policy had

41. For insight into some of the compromise proposals offered, see Gideon Gottlieb, "Palestine: An Algerian Solution," *Foreign Policy* (Winter 1975-1976), No. 21, pp. 198-21; M. Cherif Bassiouni and Morton A. Kaplan, "A Mideast Proposal," *New Outlook* (June-July 1977), 20(4): 49-54. Other compromise solutions were raised in the Israeli press. See "The Diplomatic Scene," *Journal of Palestine Studies* (Winter 1978), 7(2): 139-45.

42. Sameer Y. Abraham, "The PLO at the Crossroads: Moderation, Encirclement, Future Prospects," *MERIP Reports* (September 1979), 9(7): 8.

43. A review of the elements contained in the "transitional program" can be found in Qais Salem, "Resistance and National Self-Determination in Palestine," *MERIP Reports* (1974), No. 28, pp. 3-10. See also "The Transitional Program of the Palestine Liberation Organization" (New York: PLO Office, 1974); and *An-Nahar Arab Report* (Backgrounder) (April 22, 1974), Vol. 5, No. 16.

become the accepted platform of the PLO majority. The Palestine National Council (PNC), the "parliament-in-exile" of the PLO, voted to accept the pursuit of a Palestinian state in "any part of Palestinian territory that is liberated.[44] The PLO had in mind the Palestinian territories occupied by Israel in June 1967, namely, east Jerusalem, the West Bank, and Gaza.

The October War and subsequent shift in Arab strategy had a significant effect on the Palestinian movement, an effect which was in some ways even more dramatic than that of the Jordanian civil war of 1970. As a result of the changing power relationships in the area, the PLO decided to pursue a policy directed toward a partial settlement of the Palestine problem. This decision required a major transformation of the PLO as a national liberation movement. The shift was most visible in the arena of international diplomacy, which the PLO energetically pursued through the following means:

1. There has been a substantial upgrading of the PLO diplomatic missions around the world. Wherever possible, the PLO has attempted to open offices in order to increase its visibility, recognition, and worldwide legitimacy. This strategy has been extremely successful; more countries today recognize the PLO (over 100) than they do Israel.

2. A concerted effort has been underway to have the PLO affirmed as the "sole legitimate representative of the Palestinian people." The Arab world officially accorded the PLO this status at the October 1974 Rabat Summit.[45] The PLO had already received a similar declaration from the Conference of Islamic Nations and the Conference of Non-Aligned Nations.[46]

3. A highly effective campaign was waged in the United Nations by key Arab states and third world allies to adopt a series of resolutions favorable to the PLO. In 1974, for example, the UN General Assembly invited the PLO to participate in the Assembly debate on Palestine by a

44. "Political Programme for the Present Stage of the PLO Drawn Up by the PNC," *Journal of Palestine Studies* (Summer 1974), 3(4): 224.

45. "The Palestine Resolution of the Seventh Arab Summit Conference," *Journal of Palestine Studies* (Winter 1975), 3(4): 224.

46. See *al-Nahar*, 24 February 1974; WAFA (Beirut), 22 March 1974. For excerpts of these two resolutions see *Journal of Palestine Studies* (Summer 1974) 3(4): 209-11.

resounding vote.[47] The debate ended in the adoption of two resolutions. Resolution 3236 reaffirmed that the Palestinian people are "indispensable for the solution of the Palestine question" and supported their right to "national independence and sovereignty." Resolution 3237 conferred "observer" status on the PLO. In 1975, the General Assembly invited the PLO to participate on an "equal footing" in any negotiations held under UN auspices, presumably meaning the Geneva Conference. A plethora of UN resolutions have followed as the UN has become a focal point for PLO diplomacy.[48]

4. On another diplomatic front, the PLO has begun a dialogue with influential Israelis and Zionists of various political persuasions. The most highly publicized contacts have been those between retired Major General Mattiyahu Peled's Israel-Palestine Peace Council, and PLO members and leaders in Europe.[49] These contacts, although occasionally denied by the PLO, received the official acknowledgement and approval of the PNC when during its thirteenth session (1977) they were openly discussed and encouraged to continue.[50]

Of course, contacts and exchanges with Israelis are not new to the Palestinian movement. Unlike past exchanges with Israeli socialists, communists, and radicals – for example Matzpen, Rakah, Redfront, groups that are staunchly anti-Zionist – these latest exchanges have

47. See United Nations Resolution 3120, October 14, 1974 in *Journal of Palestine Studies* (Spring 1975), 4(3): 188.

48. For a review of the key United Nations resolutions, see "The United Nations and Palestine: Major Resolutions of the General Assembly and the Security Council, 1947-1977," *Middle East International* (November 1977), pp. 17-20.

49. See, for example, "For Israeli-Palestinian Direct Talks," *New Outlook* (July-August 1975), 18(5): 51-52; "Israel Council for Israeli-Palestinian Peace Manifesto," *New Outlook* (February-March 1976), 19(2): 69-70; "Israeli-Palestinian Contact," *Israel and Palestine* (November-December 1976), No. 53/54, pp. 1-10; "Making Peace with the Enemy: Interview with Mattityahu Peled," *New Outlook* (January-February 1977), 20(1): 11-17; *Jerusalem Post,* 3 January 1977; *New York Times,* 2 January 1977.
See also Peter Mansfield, "Will the PLO Miss the Tide?" and "Peace and the Palestinians," *Middle East International* (November 1977), No. 77, pp. 6-7 and pp. 28-31.

50. Ibrahim Abu-Lughod, "PNC Maps Out Palestinian Strategy," *MERIP Reports* (May 1977), No. 57, p. 11. See also Godfrey Jansen, "The PLO after Cairo," *Middle East International* (May 1977), No. 71, p. 10.

been carried out with groups and individuals who explicitly state their commitment to a Jewish state and their continued adherence to Zionism, but who simultaneously seek a solution to the Palestine problem through the establishment of a West Bank-Gaza state with the PLO at its head.

5. Political diplomacy has also been directed at the United States. As early as September 1974, the PLO was reported to have conveyed to the United States its desire for a meeting between Kissinger and Arafat. In 1975, additional PLO messages were carried to the Ford administration by President Anwar Sadat of Egypt. The next year, two high-ranking members of the PLO entered the United States with the aim of opening a PLO information office in Washington and beginning a dialogue with government officials. These contacts have continued into the present and although the U.S. government has promised Israel that it will not recognize the PLO until it agrees to accept UN Resolution 242, a low-level U.S.-PLO dialogue of sorts has been in existence for some time.[51]

6. Along with third world countries and the socialist bloc, western European nations have moved progressively closer to recognizing the PLO. Austria and Greece have already accorded the PLO missions diplomatic status equivalent to the ambassadorial level. The 1980 "Venice Declaration" of the European community was another indication of the PLO's success in the diplomatic field.[52] These overtures to Western nations continue as the PLO has given high priority to winning the sympathy and support of the West for its cause.

51. Abraham, "PLO at the Crossroads," p. 6. See also Paul Findley, "An Opening for U.S.-PLO Talks?," *Journal of Palestine Studies* (Winter 1979), 8(2): 173-75; *New York Times*, 15 December 1976; *LeMonde*, 10 December 1973; and Mark Bruzonsky and Judith Kipper, "Washington and the PLO," *Middle East International* (February 1977), pp. 14-15.

52. The European Declaration (also known as the "Venice Declaration") was issued by the nine member states of the European Community following a two-day summit in Venice, June 13, 1981. While the declaration did not go far enough in expressing support for an independent state for the Palestinians, it did call for a "just solution" to the Palestinian problem based on a "comprehensive peace settlement" which would include the PLO as a party to the negotiations. See "The European Declaration," *American-Arab Affairs* (Summer 1982), No. 1, pp. 187-88. For insights into Palestinian views of the declaration, see "Nothing New from Venice," *Journal of Palestine Studies* (Autumn 1980), 10(1): 165-67.

The high point of the PLO's diplomacy was reached in 1977 when the PLO offered its own "peace plan" in order to restart the stalled Geneva Conference. The plan was submitted to the United States through the good offices of Syria.[53] Although the peace plan continued to reject UN Resolution 242, it further elaborated the PNC declaration of 1974 with regard to the establishment of an independent Palestinian state in the West Bank and Gaza. The key section of the plan states:

> It is to be assumed that a commitment would be made that, after the Palestinians secured the primary rights they are demanding, the means of achieving the aims of the [Palestine National] charter would become subject to change – such change in the *nature of the struggle* that these aims would be achieved by *peaceful means*. If a state came into being the body representing the Palestinian people would issue a constitution for the state, taking into account existing *realities and agreements*. . . . (emphasis added)

These proposals represent a major break with previous PLO thinking, objectives, and strategy. First, and above all else, there is a willingness to come to terms with Israel. Second, the PLO is prepared to alter its charter – a major point of contention with Israel[54] – so that the "nature of the struggle" (i.e. revolutionary armed struggle) is replaced by "peaceful means." Third, the newly formed Palestinian state would include in its constitution reference to the "existing realities and agreements" entered into by the PLO. In other words, the newly formed Palestinian state would be officially obligated to recognize Israel's existence, another major point of contention among Israelis. In so doing, the new Palestinian state would also officially endorse the historic partition of Palestine. Should such events

53. The plan first appeared in the Beirut daily *al-Nahar,* and although no mention of its origin was noted, it is generally reputed to be the "PLO memorandum" submitted to President Carter by President Hafez Assad during their May 9, 1977 meeting. See *Facts on File* (14 May 1977), 37(1905): 360. An abbreviated version of the plan also appeared in the *Guardian Weekly,* 7 August 1977 and is excerpted in the *Journal of Palestine Studies* (Autumn 1977), 7(1): 189-90.

54. The issue of the PLO covenant has been raised repeatedly by Israeli spokesmen: see Yehoshafat Harkabi, "The Palestinian National Covenant," in Michael Curtis, et al., eds., *The Palestinians: People, History, Politics* (New Brunswick, New Jersey: Transaction Books, 1975), pp. 143-53; Harkabi, "The Palestinians in the Israel-Arab Conflict," in Shlomo Avneri, ed., *Israel and the Palestinians* (New York: St. Martin's Press, 1971), pp. 1-21; Amos Elon and Sana Hassan, *Between Enemies: A Compassionate Dialogue between an Israeli and an Arab* (New York: Random House, 1974), esp. pp. 124-51; and Harkabi, *Palestinians and Israel* (New York: Wiley, 1974), *passim.*

come to pass, it is unlikely that the "demilitarized"[55] state envisioned by some leading Palestinian thinkers would ever be in a position to reclaim the remainder of historic Palestine. Hence, the proposal in effect gives legitimacy to a *two-state* solution to the Palestine problem. Such a plan not only relegates the "democratic state" concept to a distant "dream,"[56] but it also radically transforms the 1974 "ten-point program" of the PLO, and thus "in tone and substance it represents another landmark in the growth of Palestinian moderation."[57]

Clearly, then, during this period the PLO placed a great deal of emphasis on winning international recognition and legitimacy for its cause. Not only had the objectives changed – from the "total liberation of all Palestine" to the "establishment of an independent state on the West Bank and Gaza" – but the methods for achieving the new goals had changed as well. The commitment to "revolutionary armed struggle," although still a core precept of the PLO, was operationally relegated to a strategy of self-defense, as opposed to the preceding period when it was conceptualized as an *offensive* weapon. Terrorist activities had all but ceased by 1974 or were carried out by fringe groups outside the PLO's control.[58] Guerrilla raids into Lebanon were substantially decreased or undertaken only to coincide with clear political objectives or as retaliatory actions. (Israel's border security had also become more effective by this time.) By the mid-1970s it was apparent to most observers that the PLO had shifted to a political-diplomatic offensive that took precedence over military operations. The PLO's diplomatic activity in this period stood in glaring contrast to the militaristic activity that had dominated the movement in Jordan.

55. A demilitarized Palestinian state has been proposed by Walid Khalidi. See "Thinking the Unthinkable: A Sovereign Palestinian State," *Foreign Affairs* (July 1978), 61(4): 695-713. The director of the Palestine Research Center, Sabri Jiryis, has gone a step further by proposing that the PLO suspend guerrilla activity altogether and rely solely on political means for achieving its aims: see David Mandel, "A PLO Moderate Speaks Out: Interview with Sabri Jiryis," *New Outlook* (September 1975), 18(5): 12.

56. See Mandel, "PLO Moderate Speaks Out," pp. 11-17; and Abu Iyad, *My Home, My Land*, p. 225.

57. In the words of David Hirst, *Guardian Weekly,* 7 August 1977.

58. Some of the fringe groups have been supported by Arab states who have used them against the PLO. Perhaps the best known splinter group is that headed by the former Fatah member, Abu Nidal. Over the years Abu Nidal has been sheltered by Iraq, Syria, and Libya.

The emphasis on international diplomacy had the effect of completing the transformation of the PLO into an embryonic quasi-state structure, a process which had begun when the guerrilla groups accepted the mantle of the PLO in 1969. Not only were diplomatic missions opened throughout the world, but a significant political cadre and bureaucracy was organized to operate them. The political bureaucracy was supported by an elaborate research center, planning center, and information department in Beirut; by an expanded PNC; and by a burgeoning treasury to fund these programs. These funds were also used to increase social, educational, and cultural activities. In the short span of ten years (1969-1979), the PLO was transformed from an appendage of the Arab states to the nucleus of a Palestine government-in-exile in everything but name. Today, the PLO maintains its own 301-member parliament, the PNC, which is composed of representatives of the Palestine resistance organizations, representatives from virtually all Palestinian communities dispersed throughout the world, and representatives from organized sectors of Palestinian society including the General Union of Palestinian Writers and Journalists, Women's Union, Workers Union, Students Union, Teachers Union, Engineers Union, Lawyers Associations, Doctors Associations, Artists and Peasants Union.[59] Departments have been organized to care for the needs of the Palestinian people and to advance the Palestinian cause. In the area of health, for example, the PLO has established an elaborate system of hospitals, clinics, and medical centers to care for the injured and meet the health needs of the population. A social center has been established to meet the needs of families of deceased fighters and the blind and to deal with social affairs and welfare. In the economic sphere, the PLO has established its own factories, agricultural acreage, and even a cinema guild. The PLO maintains its own newspaper, *Filastin al-Thawra,* operates its own news agency, WAFA, radio stations, and a photography department. Its latest plans call for the establishment of a "Palestine Open University" to care for the higher education needs of Palestinians in the Arab world.[60] This intense institution building was encouraged by the leadership at all levels. Even the military wing of the movement began to develop a semiconventional force, shedding its previous *fedayi* image. Although the Western news media continue to

59. For additional insight into the PLO, see Rashid Hamid, "What is the PLO?," *Journal of Palestine Studies* (Summer 1975), 4(4): 90-109; Grace Halsell, "Yasser Arafat: The Man and His People," *The Link* (July-August 1982), 15(3): 1-14; Doyle McManus, *Los Angeles Times,* 21, 23, 25 June 1981 and 5 July 1981.

60. "Plans Advanced for Palestinian Open University," *Newsletter: Association of Arab-American University Graduates* (July 1979), 12(2): 1-3.

treat the PLO as simply a military organization, it is clear that the PLO has attempted to act as a government of the Palestinian people in the diaspora. By this time, the PLO had all the features of an emerging state with the exception of a territory to call its own.

One of the paradoxes of this period is that while the PLO was realizing major gains in international recognition and support, its survival as a movement in the region was being threatened by one event after another. The disengagement agreements of 1974-1975 were followed by the outbreak of the Lebanese civil war (1975), and Syria's military intervention in 1976.[61] The civil war forced the PLO into a destructive rear-guard action from which it could not easily disengage. Syria's entry into Lebanon and its confrontation with the PLO acted to further hamper the movement militarily and to pressure it to adhere to Syria's political outlook.[62] Meanwhile, Israel's intransigence in reconvening the Geneva Conference led to Sadat's path-breaking trip to Israel in 1977. In March 1978, Israel launched a major invasion of southern Lebanon, the culmination of which was the closure of the southern Lebanese border by Major Saad Haddad's renegade militia and UN (UNIFIL) peacekeeping troops. Just prior to the convening of Camp David in June 1978, the PLO found itself militarily surrounded in Lebanon. The right-wing Phalangists controlled east Beirut and most of Mt. Lebanon, Haddad and the UNIFIL forces patrolled the south and Syria, the PLO's ostensible ally, controlled west Beirut, the north, and the Biqa Valley. The challenges the PLO faced on the ground tended to coincide with the challenges the organization confronted in the political realm. The Camp David accords resulted in a peace treaty between Egypt and Israel and an autonomy plan for the Palestinians of the West Bank and Gaza. The plan was negotiated without Palestinian (or Arab) participation. Faced with a *fait accompli* and little alternative but to reject the scheme, the PLO and Arab world watched, much like bystanders, as Israel became more entrenched in the West Bank.

61. For a discussion of the Lebanese civil war, see in particular Kamal Salibi, *Crossroads to Civil War; Lebanon 1958-1976* (Delmar, New York: Caravan Books, 1976); Roger Owen, ed., *Essays on the Crisis in Lebanon* (London: Ithaca Press, 1976); Samih Farsoun and Walter Carroll, "The Civil War in Lebanon," *Monthly Review* (June 1976), 28(2): 12-38; Walid Khalidi, *Conflict and Violence in Lebanon: Confrontation in the Middle East* (Cambridge: Center for International Affairs, Harvard University, 1978); Hani A. Faris, "Lebanon and the Palestinians: Brotherhood or Fratricide?" *Arab Studies Quarterly* (Fall 1981), 3(4): 352-70.

62. Nigel Disney, "Why Syria Invaded Lebanon," *MERIP Reports* (October 1976), No. 51, pp. 3-10; Eric Rouleau, "Syria in the Quagmire," *SWASIA* (18 June 1976).

In the aftermath of the Camp David accords, the Palestinian confrontation with Israel shifted from southern Lebanon to the occupied West Bank. The election of a group of mayors openly supportive of the PLO in April 1976 led to an intensified campaign of Israeli repression aimed at subduing the population and destroying the indigenous leadership. The PLO launched intermittent artillery and rocket attacks against Israel — in reprisal, Israel mounted devastating assaults against Palestinian refugee camps and neighborhoods. The height of the destruction was reached in July 1981 when Israel undertook a retaliatory air raid against Beirut which resulted in over three hundred civilians killed and perhaps a thousand or more wounded. A historic American-sponsored cease-fire was agreed to between the PLO and Israel in the raid's aftermath.[63] That act pointed to all the contradictions within which the PLO has had to operate: the organization could enter into cease-fires and agreements with Israel (even though negotiated through third parties), but still remain unrecognized by the United States and Israel as a principal party to the conflict. In other words, the PLO could be treated as a government in upholding the cease-fire agreement, as it did, but could not be expected to behave responsibly in a future West Bank state.

During this third phase of its development, the PLO was transformed into a quasi-state organization, as it shifted its political objectives and strategy in correspondence with the changing political and military circumstances that emerged in the aftermath of the October War. The concept of total liberation and the "democratic secular state" were replaced with the immediate objective of an independent (i.e. partitioned) state in the West Bank and Gaza. Although the movement remains armed, political diplomacy has become the primary means through which the PLO has pursued its objectives during this period. Given its encirclement in Lebanon, "revolutionary armed struggle" no longer serves as an offensive weapon, but is used mainly for purposes of self-defense. With the exception of Lebanon, perhaps, the movement's potential for instigating revolutionary change in the Arab world, which was most apparent in Jordan, has been dramatically curbed. The focus of the Palestinians has turned inward, toward institution building and self-preservation in both Lebanon and the Israeli-occupied territories. These changes have produced a PLO that tends to behave more like a government than a revolutionary national liberation

63. *Washington Post,* 24 July 1981. See also *New York Times,* 24 July 1981; Jim Muir, "Begin Strikes Again to Undermine the Peace Plans," *Middle East International* (17 July 1981), No. 154, p. 2; Jim Muir, "Begin's Bloody Adventure Backfires," *Middle East International* (31 July 1981), No. 155, pp. 2-3.

movement. The net result is a leadership that is much more "moderately" inclined; one willing to engage in diplomacy rather than war. Even the Camp David accords and peace treaty between Egypt and Israel (1978) have been unable to alter this trend. The irony of this situation is that as the PLO was undergoing these changes and was preparing itself for negotiations with Israel, the latter has proven more intransigent and intent upon annexing the West Bank and Gaza. While encircled in Lebanon, the PLO had little choice but to continue to seek a diplomatic solution to the problem as Israel prepared for war.

A NEW PHASE OF STRUGGLE

Israel's full-scale invasion of Lebanon – which began on June 6, 1982 and continues in the form of a military occupation[64] –signals the beginning of a fourth phase in the brief history of the Palestine national movement. This war and its aftermath pose the gravest challenges to date for the Palestinian people and the PLO. Although Israel's war objectives were multiple, its principal aim was to destroy the PLO and Palestinian nationalism so that it could impose its version of "autonomy" on a defeated West Bank-Gaza population.[65] In declaring this as its main objective, the Israeli leadership implicitly confirmed the strength and legitimacy that the PLO and Palestinian nationalism have attained in world forums and among the Palestinian population.

64. This section draws upon an earlier paper delivered by the author at the 15th Annual Convention of the Association of Arab-American University Graduates, Inc. (Montreal, Quebec), 21-24 October 1982.

65. In the words of Israeli Defense Minister, Ariel Sharon, "The bigger the blow is and the more we damage the PLO infrastructure, the more the Arabs in [the West Bank] and Gaza will be ready to negotiate with us . . . I am convinced that the echo of this campaign is reaching into the house of every Arab family in [the West Bank] and Gaza." *Time,* 12 June 1982.

Amos Perlmutter summed up Begin and Sharon's objectives in these terms: "Begin and Sharon share the same dream: Sharon is the dream's hatchet man. That dream is to annihilate the PLO, douse any vestiges of Palestinian nationalism, crush PLO allies and collaborators in the West Bank and eventually force the Palestinians there into Jordan and cripple, if not end, the Palestinian movement." *Foreign Affairs* (Fall 1982), 61(1): 68. See also *The Times,* 19 June 1982; *Village Voice,* 22 June 1982; and *New Statesman,* 25 June 1982.

Even with the devastating consequences of the war, most of which have yet to be fully chronicled,[66] the PLO is far from having been vanquished. Although the PLO's evacuation from west Beirut to a number of distant Arab countries has created a new set of obstacles for the organization, the leadership appears committed to continuing its pursuit of an independent Palestinian state. The PLO's acceptance of the Fez peace plan[67] and its ongoing involvement with Jordan (and other Arab states) over the peace plan proposed by President Reagan[68] indicate that at least the dominant wing of the PLO leadership remains committed to a negotiated resolution to the conflict, a pattern which was firmly established during the previous decade. Many events can, of course, intervene to alter the PLO's direction. Israel's outright rejection of the Reagan initiative and its continuing military occupation of Lebanon have already prompted renewed guerrilla operations against Israeli troops in Lebanon.[69] These military engagements seem more indicative of Palestinian impatience with the slow pace of the peace process than of attempts to renew "revolutionary armed struggle" against Israel. In

66. Conflicting estimates of the killed, injured, and homeless have been reported during and after the fighting. By mid-July, Lebanese officials placed the number killed at 18,000 (*Washington Post*, 18 July 1982). By the end of the war Lebanese officials estimated that 27,000 had been killed, 40,000 wounded, and over 400,000 made homeless. These figures do not include the more than 1,000 Palestinian and Lebanese civilians massacred (and nearly 1,000 missing) in the Sabra and Shatila camps in mid-September. (*New York Times*, 19, 20, 26 September 1982). For a discussion of the various casualty figures, see Judith Tucker, "The War of Numbers," *MERIP Report s* (September-October 1982), 12(108/109): 47-50.

67. "Final Declaration of the Twelfth Arab Summit Conference," *Political Focus* (15 October 1982), 5(20): 2. See also Mohammed A. Salem, "Peace Signals from Fez," *Middle East International* (17 September 1982) No. 183, pp. 12-13; Jim Muir, "Peace Plans from Washington and Fez: Can the Twain Ever Meet?", *Middle East International* (17 September 1982) No. 183, pp. 2-4.

68. "Address by President Reagan: A New Opportunity for Peace in the Middle East," *American-Arab Affairs* (Fall 1982), No. 2, pp. 149-54. See also Jim Muir, "Target: The Reagan Plan," *Middle East International* (1 October 1982), No. 184, pp. 4-6; Hermann Fr. Eilts, "Reagan's Middle East Initiative," *American-Arab Affairs* (Fall 1982), No. 2, pp. 1-5; Emile A. Nakhleh, "A 'Fresh Start' toward Peace," *American-Arab Affairs* (Fall 1982), No. 2, pp. 6-10.

69. According to a recent report, "Since September 29, 1982 when Israelis pulled out of West Beirut, 17 Israelis have been killed and more than 90 wounded (apart from a building collapse in Tyre [ostensibly] due to a gas leak which took 76 Israeli lives and injured 27). Nine of the deaths and almost half of the injuries have occurred since December 1, with 13 incidents during the first week of January." *Christian Science Monitor*, 12 January 1983.

what follows, a preliminary attempt is made to assess the impact of this latest war on the Palestine national movement. For analytical purposes, four distinct, although interrelated, areas are isolated for evaluation, including 1) the PLO leadership; 2) the organization's military capability; 3) its socio-economic services sector; and 4) the PLO's political capability.

PLO Leadership

Perhaps the biggest defeat the Israelis suffered was their failure to capture or kill a single high-ranking member of the PLO political or military leadership. (Israel, on the other hand, lost two generals in the invasion.) In their race to Beirut, Begin and Sharon openly declared that one of their aims was to capture the PLO leadership in its "bunker."

The PLO leadership and its central command structure were able to escape the continuous Israeli "precision" bombing directed at it. When precision bombing failed, the Israeli high command turned to random, indiscriminate bombardment of Beirut in a desperate hope that the laws of probability would work in their favor – if they bombed wildly every part of the city they were bound to kill one or two leaders. That plan failed as well. Not only did the PLO leadership survive the ferocious bombardment and siege of Beirut, but the invasion had the effect of *strengthening* the resolve, effectiveness, and unity of the leadership. The PLO leadership emerged from the rubble of Beirut more united than ever, with PLO Chairman Yasir Arafat the undisputed leader of the PLO and Palestinian people. The Israelis not only failed miserably in their attempt to destroy the leadership, but they actually contributed to enhancing the prestige and image of the PLO as the only genuine combatant force in the Arab world worthy of the admiration of the Arab people. In some quarters Yasir Arafat is considered the most popular and respected leader in the Arab world. After the evacuation from Beirut, Arafat's stature was further enhanced when he was received by Greek Prime Minister Andreas Popendreaus, and accorded a reception as a world leader and "heroic struggler for freedom and independence." This meeting was followed by an audience with Pope John Paul II at the Vatican, a meeting with Italian President Pettrini and a presentation before the Interparliamentary Union during that visit. Arafat also met with French Foreign Minister Claude Cheysson. All of these meetings point to increasing world sympathy toward the Palestinian cause and to the failure of Israel to drive a wedge between the Western countries and the PLO.

In its new diaspora outside of Lebanon, the PLO leadership faces two problems, one logistical, the other political. From a logistical standpoint communication is now more difficult, as the leadership has been dispersed to a number of Arab host countries. Knowledge of the events on the battlefield in Lebanon must be communicated through second or even third parties rather than directly. Syria now appears to be the main headquarters of the leadership, but Arafat and other prominent leaders have resisted settling in any country permanently in order to avoid falling victim to the political pressures of the host. Consequently, the executive committee of the PLO met in Aden in January 1983; the PNC meeting was held in Algiers (February, 1983); and Arafat continues to shuttle between various countries.[70]

PLO Military Capability

With the exception of the PLO troops in the Biqa Valley and northern Lebanon, the PLO's forces have been dispersed to a number of distant Arab countries. These troops, separated from the battlefield, are now completely dependent on their Arab hosts for communication, transportation, supplies, and equipment. And although these forces remain under PLO command, *all* troops must now pass through Arab lines before engaging the Israelis.

The Israeli offensive forced the PLO to assume a defensive military posture. In southern Lebanon, the Palestinian detachments operated in a semiconventional manner, at first defending their positions and then withdrawing in classical guerrilla fashion to harass the enemy after regrouping. Some sites such as Beaufort Castle and Ein el-Hilwa and Rashidiyee refugee camps were defended until overrun by the Israeli army. Although some reports indicate that approximately 70 to 80 percent of the PLO fighters in the south were able to withdraw safely and regroup elsewhere, the fact remains that the PLO suffered a major military setback in southern Lebanon.[71] This fact should be viewed cautiously, however, as the PLO did not set out to defeat the enemy in the south or maintain a military presence in that area. Rather, their ultimate objective was to withdraw. Hence, the Israeli victory, if one can call it that, appears a

70. The PLO's official headquarters appears to be Tunisia while Syria remains the operations center for its troops stationed there and in northern Lebanon and the Biqa Valley.

71. While clearly hostile to the Palestinians, some of the ramifications of the PLO's setback are discussed by Robert W. Tucker, "Lebanon: The Case for the War," *Commentary* (October 1982), 7(4): 19-30.

superficial one, gained more through default than through a successful duel between two equal forces doing battle.

The defense of Beirut was another matter altogether. Whereas in the south, the PLO forces could eventually withdraw from their positions and begin operating in *mobile* guerrilla formations, the defense of Beirut demanded that the PLO operate in an urban environment and engage the enemy in static combat. The encirclement of Beirut meant that the PLO forces literally had their backs to the sea with no route of escape. Here the strategy was to hold out against intensifying bombardment by air, land, and sea and a siege designed to pressure the population into submission. An indefinite bombardment and intensifying siege of Beirut was unacceptable to the United States and even to part of the Israeli establishment. Consequently, the Israelis were forced to accept the American-sponsored negotiations leading toward the evacuation of greater Beirut by both parties. For the PLO, the decision to withdraw from Beirut was taken for many reasons, perhaps the most pressing being that the indiscriminate Israeli bombing was terrorizing the entire population of the city, and its inhabitants could not hold out indefinitely under such conditions.[72] Also, the PLO was able to extract certain political concessions from the United States and Arab countries in exchange for its agreement to evacuate the city. The Reagan Plan can be interpreted as one of those concessions, even though the plan as a whole does not answer all the demands of the PLO.

Only a small part of the PLO's military forces were actually destroyed, mainly in southern Lebanon, while those forces in Beirut, the Biqa Valley, and northern Lebanon remained basically intact or untouched. What the Israelis were able to achieve through the war was the *neutralization* of Palestinian military capability through encirclement and withdrawal. At every point, the contest was extremely unequal with the Israelis always fielding superior firepower and numbers against the PLO. Given such an unequal contest, the outcome of the Israeli invasion gives more evidence of the military prowess of the Palestinian fighters than of the "great victory" that Begin proclaimed.

72. The most succinct review of the battle of Beirut is found in Michael Jansen, *The Battle of Beirut: Why Israel Invaded Lebanon* (London: Zed Press, 1982). See also Jacobo Timmerman, *The Longest War* (New York: Alfred Knopf, 1982). See also "The War in Lebanon" (Special Issue) *Journal of Palestine Studies* (Summer/Fall 1982), 11(4)/12(1).

Social-Economic Services

The heavy toll of human suffering was, of course, the most serious consequence of the Israeli invasion.[73] Adding to this suffering is the damage done to the social-economic services sector of the PLO – damage beyond comprehension.[74] Palestine Red Crescent Society (PRCS) hospitals, clinics, nurseries, schools – in short, the entire social welfare infrastructure that the PLO had laboriously constructed over a fifteen-year period have been severely damaged or destroyed, as have the economic installations of SAMED, including factories, workshops, and rehabilitation and training centers. In cases in which the physical plant was only partially damaged, the Israelis and Lebanese authorities have denied school children, patients, employees, and staff access to their own facilities.[75] Physicians, nurses, attendants, and employees of the PRCS, SAMED (the PLO-run factories and workshops), and schools and other institutions have been killed, detained, are missing or are being held for possible deportation by the Lebanese authorities.

From the standpoint of monetary value and size, the PLO socioeconomic welfare apparatus represented a key area of growth for the Palestine national movement and for the Lebanese economy. SAMED, for example, was one of the largest employers in the country, with investments, payroll, and sales in the tens of millions of dollars. Similarly the PRCS was composed of an intricate complex of hospitals, clinics, field facilities, rehabilitation and training centers, pharmacies, nurseries and all that such an

73. The extent of the civilian suffering can be partially gleaned from the following news reports: Edward Coty, "After its Capture, Once Lively Sidon is Scene of Desolation, Destruction," *Washington Post,* 11 June 1982; David Shipler, "In Lebanon White Flags Fly Amid the Misery and Rubble," *New York Times,* 15 June 1982; David B. Ottaway, "War's Measure: Human Anguish," *Washington Post,* 16 June 1982; Richard Ben Cramer, "Following a Trail of Blood and Rubble in West Beirut," *Philadelphia Inquirer,* 24 June 1982; Simon Tisdall, "Lebanon Relief Worker Sees 'Colossal Destruction'," *The Guardian,* 25 June 1982; James Lemoyne, "Suffer the Children," *Newsweek,* 28 June 1982; and David Richardson, "Ein Hilwe – A Refugee Camp Reduced to Rubble by Bombing," *Jerusalem Post,* 9 July 1982.

74. Martin Birnstingle, et al., "After the Bombing and the Massacres . . . The Condition of the Palestinian People in the Camps of South Lebanon," *Report of a Visit by Mr. Martin Birnstingle, Professor Steven Rose and Dr. Pamela Zinkin* (London: Peace in Lebanon and Israel – Jewish Initiative, 1982). See also "Refugee Conditions in Lebanon," *Middle East International* (26 November 1982), No. 188, pp. 13-14.

75. Douglas Watson, "Israeli Aid Effort Leaves Palestinians Out," *The Sun,* 28 June 1982.

institution entails. The facilities and capabilities of the PRCS were considered up-to-date and effective in meeting the needs of the population. In many ways, the PRCS provided more and better services than did the health care facilities of the Lebanese government. PRCS facilities were usually better equipped and better staffed, and provided services free of charge to Palestinians and Lebanese alike. Tens of hundreds of millions of dollars were invested in building, maintaining, and staffing the PRCS.

The magnitude of the damage to both physical plant and institutional life cannot be gauged in monetary terms alone, however. The importance of these institutions to the Palestinian people extends well beyond buildings and financial investments. Above all else, these institutions represented the resolve of the Palestinian people to reassert control over their national destiny. Through them, the Palestinians demonstrated their self-reliance, and began constructing the nucleus of a Palestinian state apparatus. This socioeconomic welfare structure represented the reemergence of a Palestinian nation with a full complement of agencies and institutions to serve the needs of the population, and the population was provided with an opportunity to invest its energy, creativity, and skill in building a future. By serving the material and social needs of the population the PLO was in fact transforming a collection of refugees into the citizens of a reborn Palestinian nation. No monetary estimate can ever indicate the losses incurred by the destruction of so vital a component as this socioeconomic welfare mission. It will take many years to rebuild the physical infrastructure that was destroyed. The rebuilding assumes, of course, that the Israeli and Lebanese authorities will permit the normalization of institutional life among the Palestinians – recent reports from Lebanon indicate that both are opposed to Palestinians rebuilding their homes or reopening their institutions.[76] With the PLO command located outside of Lebanon, the socioeconomic services sector is deprived of its central authorizing and funding agency. Under the present circumstances, it is likely that the shattered infrastructure will remain inoperable and that the Palestinian population will be forced into greater dependence on the already overburdened facilities of the United Nations and other international relief agencies. Without an armed presence or a strong protector, Palestinian institutions simply cannot operate to fulfill the roles assigned them.

76. "Palestinians in Lebanon: Questions without Answers," *Middle East International* (26 November 1982), No. 188, p. 8; *New York Times*, 3 October 1982.

PLO Political Capability

The Israeli invasion also shattered the centralized political structure that the PLO had constructed in Lebanon over the past twelve years. Not only were offices demolished, personnel scattered, and lines of communication disrupted, but the political independence of the PLO was also thrown into jeopardy. Although Israel failed in completely destroying the military capability of the PLO, the organization suffered a *strategic political setback* when it was forced to abandon its central base of operations in Lebanon. The PLO was forced to concede its most precious and hard-won achievement: its political independence and freedom of movement. Even though Damascus has always been the "official" headquarters of the PLO, Lebanon was the living operations center of its political and military arm. Lebanon provided the PLO with greater freedom to conduct its activities than could be obtained from the surrounding Arab countries. In Lebanon there was relatively more room to maneuver, freed from the constraints, intrigues, and pressures of the Arab governments. The weakness of the Lebanese government proved a strength upon which to build an independent Palestine national movement. In the aftermath of the Jordanian civil war, the movement was able to establish an independent power base among the Palestinian and Lebanese populations. The so-called state-within-a-state that the PLO established was not meant to replace the Lebanese state, as so many observers implied. Rather, it was aimed at defending against the encroachments of the Israeli state. Ultimately, the quasi-state structure that the PLO had established represented the core of an emergent Palestinian state that was yet to set roots in Palestine. That is the context within which the Israeli invasion and subsequent removal of the PLO in Lebanon must be viewed. With the elimination of the Palestinian power center in Lebanon, and the dispersal of the PLO forces, leadership, and apparatus to distant Arab countries, the PLO is once again forced into an immediate dependence on the Arab regimes and the contradictions that may unite or divide them at any particular moment. Consequently, the PLO's capability to adopt independent political decisions is vulnerable and open to compromise. The response of the Arab states to the Reagan peace plan and the delicate position of the PLO in this matter is a good example of the events to come. Rather than confront Israel directly as in the past, the PLO now must pass through the Arab states (most notably Syria) or receive their official sanction before committing itself to any significant political (or military) action.[77]

In summary, the Israeli invasion of Lebanon culminated in the evacuation of the PLO to distant Arab countries. The PLO's socioeconomic services sector appears to have experienced the greatest damage. Although the PLO leadership remains intact, as does much of the political and military apparatus of the PLO, the organization is currently without a secure territorial base from which it can conduct its operations. Its dispersal has resulted in numerous logistical problems and a decentralized organization, the effectiveness of which is yet to be demonstrated.[78] Outside of Lebanon, the PLO's dependency on the Arab states is almost complete, and its political and military independence is in danger. Differences between Syria and the PLO leadership have already surfaced over the Reagan peace plan, and indicate that a major antagonism has developed. Political pressures are also being applied by other Arab states, as evidenced in a political communiqué issued by a group of former "rejectionist" PLO leaders meeting in Libya.[79] Given the present circumstances, the PLO leadership faces conflicting pressures from both conservative and radical regimes. The problem of possible response to the Reagan peace plan provides a good example of these cross-pressures at work: On the one hand, acceptance of the plan would probably lead to a major split in the Arab world and within the PLO leadership. On the other hand, rejection of the plan and the negotiating process leading to a Palestinian "entity" as envisioned in it would confront the PLO with the possibility of another force, namely Jordan, replacing it. In either case, the PLO faces a situation in which it has lost a great deal of control over its political destiny and events in the region.

77. Yezid Sayigh, "The Roots of Syrian-PLO Differences," *Middle East International* (29 October 1982), No. 186, pp. 15-16; Hugh Pope, "The PLO in Syria: Conflicting Views," *Middle East International*, (26 November 1982), No. 188, pp. 8-9; and *New York Times*, 1 October 1982.

78. The PLO's official newspaper, *Filastin al-Thawra*, is now located in Nicosia, Cyprus, its fighters dispersed to eight different Arab countries, while the Palestine Research Center remains in Beirut.

79. For the Tripoli communiqués, see *Middle East Economic Digest*, 21 January 1983. See also "Resolutions Adopted by the PLO Central Council at its Meeting on November 25, 1982 in Damascus," *Middle East International* (10 December 1982), No. 189, p. 19; Ibrahim AbuNab, "Confederation in All But Name?" and Hugh Pope, "The PLO: Arafat Goes His Own Way," *Middle East International* (10 December 1982), No. 189, pp. 3-4.

CONCLUSION

Since the creation of Israel, the brief history of the Palestine national movement spans twenty-five years. During that time, the movement's organizational structure and operation has changed, sometimes dramatically, as the mix of internal and external events demanded it. The ability of the PLO's leadership to adjust to rapidly changing events has proven a major asset in the organization's ability to survive the many forces poised against it. The leadership has been responsible for introducing a series of changes in the movement's political objectives and military strategy. During the underground period (1956-1967), when Fatah was still a fledgling clandestine guerrilla movement, it sought the "liberation of all Palestine," which was to be achieved through a process of revolutionary armed struggle culminating in the "entanglement" of the Arab states in a decisive war with Israel. (The June War [1967] ended decisively, but in Israel's favor.) The devastating consequences of the war provided the movement with a historic opportunity, during the formative years that followed (1967 - 1973), to develop into an open, revolutionary movement in Jordan. As the movement grew in strength, it further refined its vision of the future by introducing the concept of a "democratic, nonsectarian state" as its political objective. In parallel fashion, the military strategy was also further elaborated to include the notion of "people's war," a concept that tended to reveal a loss of faith in the ability of the Arab states to wage a successful conventional war against Israel. Just as the movement's revolutionary potential surfaced, the movement confronted its first major crisis and defeat in the Jordanian civil war (1970 - 1971). In the nine years that followed, the PLO established itself as the "sole legitimate representative of the Palestinian people" and transformed its organization into a quasi-state apparatus. The movement toward a comprehensive peace settlement in the aftermath of the October War (1973) influenced the PLO to modify its goals and strategy once again. An "independent Palestinian state" in the West Bank and Gaza appeared as the accepted platform of the PLO and remains so today. International diplomacy rather than armed struggle is now seen as the principal means of realizing this goal. As the PLO evolved from an uncompromising and military revolutionary organization to a diplomatic and governmental one, Israeli policy became more intransigent and aggressive.

The Israeli war in Lebanon has left the PLO shattered. Palestinians and Lebanese alike suffered tens of thousands of casualties in one of the most destructive of Arab-Israeli wars. As for the Palestine national movement, the socioeconomic services sector sustained the greatest damage. And although the PLO leadership escaped unharmed, the military capability of the movement has been neutralized and its political independence is currently in question. Completely dependent on the Arab states that harbor it, the PLO faces a situation reminiscent of its early clandestine period when almost every action of Fatah required the consent of Syria. The developing antagonism between the PLO leadership and the current Syrian regime over the Reagan peace plan is a sign of the many challenges the PLO confronts in trying to maintain control over its political destiny. In a sense, the entire history of the Palestine national movement can be read as a single attempt by Palestinians to regain control over their lives and their struggle. The Israeli war in Lebanon has substantially undermined that process and leaves the movement more vulnerable to the conflicting pressures of the Arab states.*

* Editor's Note: the impact of the *intifada* on the Palestine national movement and its relationship with the Arab States, Israel and the big powers are discussed in Chapter 1., pp. 42-48.

CHAPTER 23

Alternatives to the Occupation

Muhammad Hallaj

INTRODUCTION

The occupation of Palestine, largely accomplished in 1948 and completed in 1967, signified more than anything else the dismantlement and dispersion of Palestinian society. It not only violated the inalienable rights of the Palestinian people, but also clashed with the prevailing political ethics of our age. For that reason, the occupation was bound to inspire both the resistance of the Palestinian people and the repugnance of the international community.

In the 1960s and 1970s it became evident that the destruction of Palestine did not become, as it was intended to be, an irreversible historic reality. Palestine, "in one of history's greatest surprises,"[1] emulated its most illustrious son and defied death with resurrection. Within one generation after the catastrophe of 1948, the Palestinians recovered from their trauma, regained their identity, regenerated their national movement, and resumed the struggle for their denied national rights. Under the leadership of the Palestine Liberation Organization they recreated their shattered society. They established political, military, economic, cultural, and social institutions, and they made unparalleled advances in education. Consequently, they became active participants in the affairs of the Middle East.

---

1. *Search for Peace in the Middle East* (Philadelphia, Pa.: American Friends Service Committee, 1970), p. 36.

In occupied Palestine itself, the Palestinians managed to maintain a significant presence. Although half of them were forced into exile, Israel's effort to "absentify" them completely from their homeland was resisted, and they continue to make up about 40 percent of Palestine's total population.[2] They increasingly acquired the characteristics of a coherent and viable community. They built universities and factories; they reclaimed land and operated hospitals; they created journalism and an art movement; they revived their folklore and resisted the occupation. Inside and outside Palestine, they reaffirmed their common identity and struggled for shared aspirations.[3]

This Palestinian revival, which frustrated Israel's attempt to make the destruction of Palestine irrevocable, was reinforced by international developments supportive of Palestinian rebirth. The decolonization process brought to the world's political arena an increasing number of nations that shared with the Palestinian people the colonial experience, and the international community became increasingly sensitive to Palestinian grievances and aspirations. An international consensus began to emerge and crystallize which saw the destruction of Palestine as repugnant and supported the reconstruction of Palestine.[4]

The Palestinian reawakening and the emerging supportive international consensus threatened the Israeli design to recreate a Middle East without Palestine or Palestinians. Israel reacted with a two-pronged attack to discredit the idea of Palestinian nationhood and to undermine the material foundations of Palestinian society. It argued that the whole Palestinian question was a fictitious issue, and advocated policies designed to offer substitutes and alternatives to Palestinian self-determination.[5]

2. "Absentify" is a Palestinian expression (*taghyib*, in Arabic) that connotes the variety of methods used by Israel to diminish Palestinian presence and to render it inconsequential.

3. On Palestinian institutions in the occupied territories and outside, respectively, see Emile Nakhleh, *The West Bank and Gaza: Toward the Making of a Palestinian State* (Washington: American Enterprise Institute, 1979), and Cheryl Rubenberg, *The Palestine Liberation Organization: Its Institutional Infrastructure* (Belmont, Mass.: Institute of Arab Studies, 1983).

4. On the nature of the emerging international consensus see Ghayth Armanazi, "The Rights of the Palestinians: The International Dimension," *Journal of Palestinian Studies* (Spring 1974), 3(3):88-96.

5. Yehuda Z. Blum, Israel's ambassador to the UN, called the Palestine question "one of the phoniest issues in modern political history." See Blum's "Israel, the U.N. and Middle East Peace," *Middle East Focus*, September 1980, p. 18.

Simultaneously, Israel stepped up its attack against the Palestinian people, their leadership, and institutions inside and outside the occupied territories. Inside occupied Palestine, it maintained a generally oppressive policy that sporadically escalated into waves of violent repression, as was the case in the spring of 1982. It speeded up the confiscation of Arab land and the erection of Jewish settlements. It dynamited homes and expelled people. It dismissed mayors, dissolved municipal councils, and closed down universities and newspapers. It organized and armed a band of quislings – the Village Leagues – to terrorize the population and to masquerade as representatives of the people, and it proceeded with functional annexation by integrating the socioeconomic infrastructure of the West Bank and Gaza with that of Israel.[6]

Israel also escalated its war against the Palestinian people in the diaspora. In the summer of 1982 this war reached the proportions of a genocidal onslaught against the Palestinian community and its supporters in Lebanon.[7]

Israel's Palestinian policy is motivated by its determination to monopolize Palestine as a "Jewish homeland," and is blinded by the fatal assumption that its conflict with the Palestinians is a zero sum game and that Palestinian and Israeli interests are utterly irreconcilable. It has rejected all proposals based on the need for a reciprocal compromise with the Palestinian people and has resisted all the alternatives to its total occupation of Palestine.

Notwithstanding this intransigent Israeli attitude, alternatives to continued occupation and conflict have been proposed during the past fifteen years. They have in common a belief in the reconcilability of the Arab-Israeli conflict on the basis of sharing the contested land, united or divided, as the homeland of both Palestinians and Israelis. The three basic alternatives that have been proposed are the following:

1. The United Arab Kingdom. This proposal envisions Israeli withdrawal from the occupied West Bank (and possibly from the Gaza Strip), which would become an autonomous Palestinian region, federated with the east bank of Jordan into a United Arab Kingdom.

2. The secular, democratic state. This proposal envisions the reconsititution of Palestine as a unified nonsectarian republic for its Arab

---

6. On Israel's *de facto* annexation of the West Bank and Gaza see William Claiborne and Edward Cody, *The West Bank: Hostage of History* (Washington: Foundation for Middle East Peace, 1980).

7. An Israeli soldier in Lebanon told Robert Fisk, the correspondent of *The Times* of London: "I would like to see all the Palestinians dead because they are a sickness wherever they go." *The Times,* 17 June 1982.

and Israeli inhabitants, who would share sovereignty over the country as their common homeland.

3. The two-state solution. The Arab-Israeli conflict and the Palestinian problem would be resolved on the basis of partition, by the establishment of an independent Palestinian state alongside Israel.

THE UNITED ARAB KINGDOM

On March 15, 1972, Jordan's King Hussein proposed the replacement of Israeli occupation with an autonomous "Palestinian region" consisting of the West Bank and any other Palestinian territory from which Israel withdrew (an obvious reference to the Gaza Strip), linked to a "Jordanian region" consisting of the east bank, in a federated state to be known as the United Arab Kingdom. The two regions of the kingdom would have their own regional governments, including a governor, a legislature, a cabinet, and a court system, and would exercise jurisdiction over local affairs. The central government, headed by the king, would have a federal legislature in which both regions would be equally represented, a council of ministers, and a federal supreme court, and would exercise authority over "matters emanating from the status of the kingdom as one international entity, as well as matters which ensure the safety, stability, and prosperity of the kingdom." The country would have unified armed forces, and the king would be their supreme commander. Jerusalem would be the capital of the Palestinian region, and Amman would be the capital of the Jordanian region as well as the federal capital.[8]

The United Arab Kingdom proposal was presented by King Hussein as a formula intended to reconcile the main conflicting positions that fuel the Arab-Israeli conflict and, thus, as a way for a just and lasting peace in the Middle East. By withdrawing from the West Bank, Israel would comply with Security Council Resolution 242 and remove Arab apprehensions about its intention to annex the occupied territories. By the establishment of an "autonomous Palestinian region" the Palestinians would enjoy a measure of self-government. And by linking the Palestinian region with Jordan Hussein sought to appease Israel's adamant opposition to an independent Palestinian state. He saw his proposal as a reconciliation of Arab and Israeli positions within the framework of international sanction.

8. Text of the proposal in *Palestinian Arab Documents, 1972,* (Beirut: Institute for Palestine Studies, 1975, document 115), pp. 115-19 (in Arabic).

King Hussein's proposal came too late. The bloody conflict between the Jordanian regime and the Palestinian Liberation Organization (PLO) in 1970-7 I reinforced the Palestinians' traditional distrust of the Hashemites and their resolve to resist the reimposition of Jordanian rule over them. Israel, which had annexed Jerusalem and its surroundings and embarked on a massive program of land confiscation and settlement, did not experience adequate Arab or international pressure to induce it to accept the return of occupied territory in exchange for an accommodation with its neighbors. Furthermore, a decision to withdraw was not politically feasible for an Israeli government whose survival depended on coalition partners ideologically committed to maximalist Zionist goals. Even the international community had begun to realize the inadequacy of Resolution 242, which ignored the national aspirations of the Palestinian people, and had begun to move in the direction of supporting Palestinian statehood not only to redress the injustice suffered by the Palestinian people, but also as a requirement for a lasting peace in the Middle East.[9] Consequently, the United Arab Kingdom proposal was vehemently rejected by Israel and the Palestinians, was opposed by the majority of the Arab states and public opinion, and met with a cool reception from the international community in general.

It is important to explore the reasons for Israeli and Palestinian opposition to the United Arab Kingdom proposal, because they not only explain its failure but also define the most basic issues in the conflict. Hussein's proposal failed because it was based on two erroneous assumptions: that Israel was prepared to withdraw from occupied Palestinian territories, and that the Palestinians were willing to forfeit their right to political independence.

The king's proposal occasioned debate and elicited definite policy positions from those on the highest levels of the Israeli political system. On March 16, 1972, the day after the king made his proposal public in Amman, the Israeli prime minister, Golda Meir, opened a parliamentary debate on the Jordanian proposal with a severe attack on King Hussein in which she said that the king spoke of "territories not his and not under his control." She derided him for imagining himself to be "the liberator of territories and the founder of kingdoms," and concluded that his proposal "cannot be a basis for an agreement with Israel."[10] The Israeli position crystallized in a

9. For example, see UN resolutions 2792 D (XXVI), 6 December 1971; 2963 E (XXVII), 13 December 1972; and 3089 (XXVIII), 7 December 1973.

10. Ahmad Khalifah, "Israeli Reaction to King Hussein's Proposal," *Shuun Filastiniya* (May 1972), 9:261. This is a part of a seven-part report on King Hussein's United Arab Kingdom proposal and the reaction of various parties to it.

resolution passed by the Knesset, which affirmed that "the historic rights of the Jewish people in the Land of Israel are not subject to doubt."[11]

Israel was telling King Hussein that the occupied territories belonged to Israel, that they were not contested territories, and that he had no right to speak about their future. The Israeli position was a reaffirmation of maximalist Zionist territorial ambitions and demonstrated the fact that Israel sought not an appropriate formula for divesting itself of the occupied territories but Arab acquiescence in indefinite Israeli control over them.

The Palestinians also rejected Hussein's proposal. Although he said that his proposal was based on "absolute adherence to the legitimate rights of the Palestinian people and aims to enable them to recover and preserve these rights,"[12] the Palestinians thought otherwise. They saw the proposal as a denial rather than a fulfillment of their national rights and aspirations. The Palestinian rejection was nearly unanimous and, without a doubt, was intensified by Hussein's war against the PLO in 1970-71.

On March 16, 1972, the day immediately following Hussein's public announcement of his proposal, the Executive Committee of the PLO issued a formal statement of its position, which it described as "a decisive and final response to King Hussein's proposal." This statement characterized the Jordanian plan as a usurpation of the Palestinian people's right to determine their own future.[13]

All major Palestinian resistance groups also rejected the United Arab Kingdom proposal. The Popular Democratic Front for the Liberation of Palestine, in a statement issued by its official spokesman on March 15, condemned Hussein's plan, calling it a Hashemite-Zionist scheme "to liquidate the Palestinian cause," and called on all resistance groups to oppose the plan.[14] The following day, the Popular Front for the Liberation of Palestine declared its rejection of the proposal,[15] and in a follow-up statement published on March 18 described it as an attempt "to Arabize the

11. *Ibid.*

12. King Hussein's speech in *Palestinian Arab Documents,* 1972, p. 117.

13. Text of statement in *ibid.,* document 121, pp. 133-35. Direct quotation from p. 133.

14. PDFLP statement in *ibid.,* document 117, p. 120.

15. PFLP statement in *ibid.,* document 118, p. 121.

occupation."[16] The head of the political department of the PLO prepared a memorandum in which he analyzed Hussein's proposal, its motives, and consequences. He not only condemned it but also linked it to the Hashemite family's long-standing and persistent betrayal of the Palestinian people and their struggle.[17]

Fatah, the largest of the Palestinian resistance groups, rejected the United Arab Kingdom proposal and characterized it as a conspiratorial scheme against the Palestinian people.[18] Yasir Arafat, Fatah's leader and the chairman of the PLO Executive Committee, in an interview with an Iraqi newspaper on March 19, called Hussein's project a carbon copy of the Israeli Allon Plan.[19]

The Jordanian plan was also rejected by Palestinian popular organizations. In a joint statement issued by six associations on March 25, at the conclusion of a week-long convention, the project was described as "another link in the chain of conspiracies against the Palestinian revolution to liquidate our cause."[20] King Hussein even failed to secure acceptance of his proposal by the Palestinians living under his jurisdiction, in the east bank of Jordan. In an attempt to secure such an endorsement, he summoned a number of prominent leaders of the Palestinian community to his palace, but they refused to issue the endorsement he sought. Instead, they sent a written message to the president of the Palestine National Council (PNC), dated April 3, 1972, in which they warned of the "extreme seriousness" of the proposal, which they said was detrimental to the national aspirations of the Palestinian people.[21]

Furthermore, the Palestinians in the occupied West Bank and Gaza expressed their opposition through written messages, dated April 6, 1972, addressed to the Palestinian Popular Assembly which convened in Cairo

16. *Ibid.,* document 126, p. 138.

17. *Ibid.,* document 120, pp. 126-33.

18. Fatah's statement in *ibid.,* document 124, pp. 136-37.

19. Text of interview in *ibid.,* document 133, pp. 145-47.

20. Text of statement in *ibid.,* document 146, pp. 162-63. The six organizations were the General Union of Palestinian Workers, the General Union of Palestinian Women, the General Union of Palestinian Students, the Union of Palestinian Lawyers, the General Union of Palestinian Teachers, and the High Council of Palestinian Youth.

21. Text of letter in *ibid.,* document 158, pp. 190-91.

between April 6 and 10 in conjunction with the tenth (emergency) session of the Palestine National Council. The memorandum from the West Bank rejected the United Arab Kingdom proposal and said that "the king has no right to speak in our name or to represent us."[22] The message from the Gaza Strip called the proposal "the Hussein-Allon project" and said "we refuse to be driven to the butcher who slaughtered thousands of our sons."[23]

The Popular Assembly responded to such expressions and, in its final communiqué, expressed its rejection of the United Arab Kingdom proposal, and called on the Arab states to sever their relations with Jordan and impose sanctions against it.[24] The assembly also passed a special resolution dealing with the United Arab Kingdom plan which included the following condemnation of King Hussein:

> The Jordanian king appointed himself guardian of the Palestinian people, issuing decisions regarding their fate, ignoring and even denying their right to determine their own future through their own legal institutions [PLO] which enjoy their confidence.[25]

The resolution also called on the Palestine National Council to transmit this Palestinian position to all states and international organizations, to seek the expulsion of Jordan from the Arab League, and to seek the imposition of Arab sanctions against it. The PNC adopted the resolution of the Popular Assembly.[26]

Thus, the Palestinians inside and outside the occupied territories expressed a consensus against the United Arab Kingdom project. This Palestinian position was broadly supported by the Arab world, through official governmental decisions as well as positions of political parties and popular organizations. The most unequivocal opposition to King Hussein's proposal came from President Anwar Sadat of Egypt, who announced in his opening speech to the tenth session of the PNC that his government decided "to sever all relations with the Jordanian regime."[27] The Syrian president

22. Text of message in *ibid.*, document 172, pp. 206-7.

23. Text in *ibid.*, document 173, p. 207.

24. Text of communiqué in *ibid.*, document 186, p. 231.

25. Text in *ibid.*, document 183, pp. 222-25. Quotation from p. 222.

26. Text of PNC decision in *ibid.*, document 186, p. 231.

27. Text of Sadat's speech in *ibid.*, document 168, pp. 201-2.

and the national leadership of the ruling Ba'ath party also condemned Hussein's proposal.[28] So did the president of Iraq and its ruling party.[29] The proposal was considered and rejected by the government of Kuwait[30] and by the Presidential Council of the Union of Arab Republics.[31] Libya refused to receive King Hussein's emissary who sought to present the plan to the Libyan government.[32]

Numerous Arab popular organizations also expressed opposition to the United Arab Kingdom proposal. It was rejected by the General Union of Jordanian Students[33] and by the Progressive Forces and Parties in Lebanon.]The representatives of twenty-three Arab political parties and organizations from Algeria, Iraq, Syria, Egypt, Lebanon, Morocco, Jordan, Oman, and South Yemen also issued a joint statement rejecting Hussein's United Arab Kingdom proposal.[35] The project was also opposed by the Union of Arab Journalists,[36] and by the Federation of Arab Trade Unions, which called on affiliated organizations to pressure their governments to institute a political and economic boycott of Jordan.[37]

28. For the Ba'ath party statement see *ibid.*, document 139, pp. 141-43; for President Assad's position see text of his speech in *ibid.*, document 174, pp. 208-9.

29. For President Bakr's statement see *ibid.*, document 136, pp. 148-49; for the position of the leadership of the Iraq Baath party see *ibid.*, document 132, pp. 144-45.

30. Statement of the Minister of State for Cabinet Affairs in *ibid.*, document 137, p. 149.

31. Text in *ibid.*, document 128, pp. 140-41.

32. *The Yearbook of the Palestine Question, 1972* (Beirut: Institute for Palestine Studies, 1976), p. 154 (in Arabic).

33. For statement see *Palestinian Arab Documents, 1972*, document 122, pp. 135-36.

34. See *ibid.*, document 125, pp. 137-38.

35. For the list of the groups and text of the statement see *ibid.*, document 175, pp. 209-10.

36. *Yearbook of the Palestine Question, 1972*, pp. 196-97.

37. *Ibid.*, pp. 193-94.

The United Arab Kingdom proposal was presented as a method to resolve the Arab-Israeli deadlock by offering a formula for the termination of the Israeli occupation. It evoked Palestinian and Arab opposition because it played into Israel's resolve to veto political independence for the Palestinian people. And it ran afoul of Israel's preference for territorial aggrandizement. For these reasons, it failed as an alternative to continued occupation and conflict.[38]

THE DEMOCRATIC SECULAR STATE

The most daring and imaginative formula for the resolution of the Palestine question and the settlement of the Arab-Israeli conflict was proposed by the PLO in the late 1960s. The PLO proposed the reconsititution of Palestine as a geographically and politically unified state in which Palestinian Arabs and Israeli Jews would share sovereignty over a common homeland as citizens enjoying equal rights and obligations. The Palestinians who proposed this formula saw in it an act of civilized and historic reconciliation, superior to the political compromises motivated by acquiescence with the imposed *faits accomplis* of the recent past. Dr. Fayez Sayegh explained the rationale of this vision for the future of Palestine this way:

> What is needed is a principled and courageous vision. The required vision must do precisely what a "compromise" cannot. A compromise takes its departure from the actual positions of the contending parties and seeks to find a solution somewhere *between* them. The needed vision transcends those starting points and looks for a solution *above* them both.
>
> Men who cannot or will not surrender to one another may be inspired to surrender together to a higher vision – and in that surrender find freedom and fulfillment, as well as reconciliation.[39]

38. It should be pointed out that the more recent proposal by President Ronald Reagan (September 1, 1982) is a modified version of Hussein's 1972 plan. In that sense, the project is being revived by the U.S. government, a fact which appears to support views, expressed after King Hussein initially announced his proposal, that it "was American inspired. For this view see Clovis Maksoud, "American-Israeli Dimensions of King Hussein's Project," *Shuun Filastiniya* (May 1972), 9:5-19; and Ahmad Bahauddin, "The Roots of King Hussein's Project," *ibid.* (June 1972), 10:45-50.

39. Fayez A. Sayegh, "A Palestinian View," *The Arab World* (February 1970), 16(2): 18. Emphasis in original.

These Palestinians saw other proposed solutions as being at best compromises with injustice, as deceptive shelters between the crushing pressures of opposing claims. They saw their vision of a democratic secular Palestine as a synthesis that would ensure the greater security of historic reconciliation. As the director of the PLO Planning Office put it, the idea of a nonsectarian Palestinian state "represents the only progressive humanitarian solution. . . . This solution seeks to deal with the problem from its inception, permanently, equitably, and progressively"[40] Establishment of such a state was seen as the ideal way to a just and durable Arab-Israeli peace, because this solution addressed the basic issues of the conflict and the essential grievances and aspirations of the parties. It was envisioned as the only way possible for both the Jewish community that developed in Palestine and the Palestinians to live in the country as self-governing communities with equal rights and responsibilities.

Until the PLO adopted the concept of the democratic secular state in the late 1960s, the Palestinian national movement was primarily preoccupied with the Zionist threat to the Palestinian people's status as the majority indigenous community in Palestine. Jewish immigrants were perceived as an invasionary force, and the Palestinian national movement struggled for an independent Arab Palestine as the only feasible safeguard against domination. After the creation of the state of Israel and the consequent destruction of Palestine, the Palestinians continued, with understandably intensified conviction, to see the Jewish presence in Palestine as the root cause of their tragedy and to see the restoration of the *status quo ante* (usually described in Palestinian rhetoric as the liberation of Palestine) as the essential condition for the recovery of their lost rights. The Palestinians were overwhelmed by the sense of their loss, and their thoughts were preoccupied with the redress of injustice, which would be accomplished by the reversal of recent past history. The Jewish presence in Palestine was an injustice to be redressed, rather than an issue to be addressed.

In the 1950s the Palestinians dreamed of "the return" and gradually reorganized their national movement to struggle for the prerequisite liberation of their homeland. Both "liberation" and "return" had, for the Palestinians, mystical rather than practical political connotations. The vision did not accord with the new realities and, therefore, remained abstract and did not mature into the basis of a plan for the future of the country.

The idea of the democratic secular state began to germinate in 1968. By 1969 it had gained sufficient support among the Palestinians to appear on the agenda of their highest policy-making body, the Palestine National

40. Muhammad Rasheed (Nabil Shaath), *Towards a Democratic State in Palestine* (Beirut: Palestine Research Center, 1970), p. 7.

Council, and to gain its endorsement. In its fifth session, held from February 1 to 4, 1969, the PNC resolved that "the bitter struggle of the Palestinian people to liberate their homeland and to return aims at the establishment in Palestine of a free democratic society for all Palestinians: Muslims, Christians, and Jews."[41] In its sixth session, convened between September 1 and 6, 1969, the PNC formally adopted the concept of the democratic secular state as the operational meaning of the outcome of the liberation of Palestine and as the political objective of Palestinian struggle for self-determination. It endorsed the recommendation of its political committee, which included the following provision:

> Palestinian struggle aims to end the Zionist entity in Palestine, to enable the Palestinian people to return to their homeland and to establish in all of Palestine a democratic state free of all types of racial discrimination and religious bigotry.[42]

The PLO continued to affirm this policy in subsequent PNC sessions. It did so in its seventh session (May 30-June 3, 1970) and in its eighth session (February 28-March 5, 1971), in which it resolved that:

> Palestinian armed struggle is not an ethnic or religious struggle against the Jews. Therefore, the future state in a Palestine freed from Zionist colonization is the Palestinian democratic state in which all those willing to live in peace will enjoy the same rights and obligations.[43]

The PLO not only endorsed the democratic secular state but also made great efforts to secure widespread popular support for it. As a spokesman for one of the main resistance groups put it, through the idea of the democratic secular state, "the Palestinian revolution achieved the total defeat of traditional chauvinistic thinking."[44] The idea of a democratic secular state in Palestine offered an alternative to what a PLO leader called "Arab chauvinism and Zionist racism."[45] and by doing so it changed the

41. Text of resolution in Rashid Hamid, *Resolutions of the Palestine National Council, 1964-1974* (Beirut: Palestine Research Center, 1975), p. 139 (in Arabic).

42. *Ibid.*, p. 151.

43. *Ibid.*, p. 178.

44. Interview with Jamil Hilal, DFLP, conducted by the author in Beirut, 9 March 1982.

45. Interview with Bassam Abu Sharif, PFLP, conducted by the author in Beirut, 10 March 1982.

Arab-Israeli conflict from a zero sum game to a reconcilable contest and made possible a break in "the dialectics of oppression" that fueled the conflict.[46]

The Israelis reacted instinctively and fiercely against the proposal of a Palestinian democratic secular state. They questioned the sincerity of the desire for Arab-Jewish coexistence which it entailed, they characterized it as a public relations ploy, and they rejected it as a "euphemism" for the destruction of Israel. In fact they found genocidal implications in the proposal. Professor Y. Harkabi said the idea required "turning back the wheels of history and erasing the Jewish state." This political position, he said, "was bound to have genocidal implications."[47]

The Israeli reaction and intervening events convinced the PLO that the democratic secular state was not a practical political objective for the foreseeable future. It was set aside as the long-range, strategic objective of Palestinian struggle. Like Plato's ideal state, it was honored as a model *sub specie aeternitatis,* for men to imitate if not attain. When Yasir Arafat addressed the United Nations General Assembly on November 13, 1974, he spoke of it as the Palestinian dream.[48]

The Palestinian national movement began to search for a more attainable alternative. Although convinced of the superiority of its vision for the future of Palestine, it felt the need for interim, confidence-building measures. In 1974, the Palestine National Council opted for the two-state solution and redefined the objectives of Palestinian struggle as the establishment of a Palestinian state in a divided Palestine.

46. Afif Safieh, "Three Steps to Middle East Peace," *Al-Fajr* (Jerusalem), 13-19 September 1981, p. 8.

47. Y. Harkabi, "The Meaning of 'A Democratic Palestinian State,'" in *Palestinians and Israel* (New York: Wiley, 1974), pp. 70-106, direct quotation from p. 70. Emphasis in original. It is interesting to note that Harkabi weakens his own argument by admitting the attractiveness of the idea. He wrote: "Arabs brandish the slogan of a 'Democratic State' as a means of psychological warfare against us [Israelis] in order to weaken our determination, and we should be aware of this." *Ibid.,* p. 81.

48. Text of Arafat's speech in *International Documents on Palestine, 1974* (Beirut: Institute for Palestine Studies, 1977), pp. 134-44.

THE PALESTINIAN STATE

When the United Nations General Assembly recommended the partition of Palestine in 1947, the Arabs objected to the recommendation on the grounds that it was both illegal and unfair to the indigenous Arab community. It was illegal because it was beyond the authority of the General Assembly to recommend the division of a country against the expressed will of the majority of its population, and unfair because it allocated the larger part of the country to a minority of recent immigrants who owned less than 6 percent of the land.[49]

The Zionist movement, and later the state of Israel, used this Arab rejection of the partition plan of 1947 to justify the forceful occupation of all of Palestine and the denial of the right to self-government to the Palestinian people. The partition of Palestine and the coexistence of the Arab and the Jewish state it envisioned was thus rejected by both Arabs and Israelis. Arab and Israeli expectations appeared to be totally and mutually exclusive.

In the late 1960s, the Palestinians began to search for a solution that could transcend the competing and clashing claims and provide a resolution above them, as Fayez Sayegh put it in a passage cited earlier. The result of that search was the vision of the democratic secular state, but this was rejected by Israel and remained an unreciprocated ideal. The vision did, however, inform the further quest for a way to reconcile the Palestinian people's right to a homeland with the reality of Jewish presence in Palestine. The Palestinians, in the 1970s, came to accept the idea of the coexistence of two independent states in Palestine through the establishment of a Palestinian state in a part of the country. In its twelfth session (1974), the Palestine National Council approved a ten-point political program that sanctioned the two-state solution by identifying the aim of Palestinian struggle to be the establishment of a Palestinian "national authority" in any part of Palestine from which the Israeli occupation was withdrawn.[50]

In the 1960s, the Palestinians reconciled their rights to the fact of the presence of a Jewish *community* in Palestine by proposing the democratic

49. Henry Cattan, *Palestine, the Arabs and Israel: The Search for Justice* (London: Longmans, 1969), pp. 25-30.

50. Text of the ten-point program in Hamid, *Resolutions,* pp. 247-48. English translation in *International Documents on Palestine, 1974,* pp. 449-50.

secular state for both peoples. In the 1970s, they reconciled themselves to the fact of the existence of a Jewish *state*. By accepting the two-state solution, the Palestinians were responding to Israeli criticism of the democratic state idea: that the Israelis "do not want to become Palestinians of Jewish faith; they intend to remain Israelis."[51]

But Palestinian acceptance of the two-state solution, implied in the ten-point program of 1974, was not simply a concession to the Israeli rejection of the democratic secular state. On the contrary, the Palestinians tended to see the two-state solution as an interim solution and as a prelude to the reunification of the country as a democratic secular state. The establishment of an independent Palestinian state in a part of Palestine was seen as a measure that would build confidence and enhance the prospects of future unification. As the PLO representative in Lebanon put it, the emergence of the Palestinian state would do away with the need for armed struggle against Israel, but the quest for the democratic secular state would continue. "Israel will be within sight of the Palestinian citizen, and the Palestinian state within sight of the Israeli citizen," he said. "We will respond to bigotry with openness ... we will give the Israeli citizen a model to challenge the existing Israeli system. We will create a pole to attract future Jewish generations, because they will certainly be attracted away from the Zionist ghetto to the open, pluralistic society we will create."[52]

Obviously, the adoption of the two-state solution by the PLO in 1974 did not signify Palestinian abandonment of the vision of the democratic secular state. It did, however, signify two important modifications of the Palestinian conception of the conditions for Arab-Jewish coexistence in Palestine: It brought the Palestinians closer to the form of coexistence which Israel since its inception professed to seek, namely Arab coexistence with an Israeli *state;* and it indicated Palestinian willingness to strive by peaceful means for the eventual fulfillment of their vision of a reunified Palestine.

Palestinian acceptance of the two-state solution, then, served as an interlude to provide a needed opportunity for mutual reassurance. It also served to answer questions, posed by the 1973 Arab-Israeli war and the consequent political moves, regarding the future of the Palestinian territories from which Israel might be induced to withdraw. The disengagement agreements between Israel on one hand and Syria and Egypt on the other, and the possibility of similar moves in the West Bank, challenged the

51. Harkabi, "Meaning of 'A Democratic Palestinian State,' " p. 102.

52. Interview with Shafiq al-Hout, conducted by the author in Beirut, 8 March 1982.

Palestinians to clarify their position on the future government of the Palestinian territories from which Israel would withdraw, and the decision of the twelfth PNC to establish a Palestinian "national authority" on such territories was in response to this eventuality.

Furthermore, the Palestinian acceptance of the two-state solution was encouraged by an emerging international consensus in favor of the creation of a Palestinian state in a part of Palestine alongside the state of Israel. A series of resolutions passed by the United Nations General Assembly throughout the 1970s made clear that the international community saw partition as the solution most likely to succeed in reconciling Palestinian and Israeli aspirations. Some Palestinians believed that the international community did not find the democratic secular state to be unacceptable. The secretary of the Revolutionary Council of Fatah pointed out that "increasing international support for the PLO came after Abu Ammar's speech to the United Nations, in which he proposed the democratic secular state as the Palestinian dream."[53] Prevailing Palestinian opinion, however, seemed to agree with the assessment of the director of the PLO Planning Office, who said that the PLO had to respond to the prevailing international environment "which does not go in its support of the Palestinian people beyond supporting their right to establish an independent state in a part of Palestine to coexist with a Jewish state in the rest of the country."[54]

After the PLO came to accept the establishment of a Palestinian state in the portion of the country from which Israel might be induced to withdraw, it gradually firmed up this position until it became an explicit and broadly based Palestinian consensus. In its thirteenth session in 1977, the PNC not only reaffirmed the PLO's willingness to accept a partitioned Palestine, but made that acceptance more explicit by replacing the earlier term "national authority" with the less ambiguous "state," making it more clear that the PLO sought to resolve the Arab-Israeli conflict by the establishment of a Palestinian state in a part of Palestine.[55] Furthermore, the resistance groups that had dissented from the two-state solution in 1974, and thus had come to be known as the rejection front, supported the ten-point program in 1978, thereby giving the PNC resolution a broader base of support. For the first time since the establishment of Israel, the Palestinian national movement

53. Interview with Sakher Abu Nizar, conducted by the author in Beirut, 16 March 1982.

54. Interview with Munir Shafiq, conducted by the author in Beirut, 8 March 1982.

55. *Palestinian Arab Documents,* 1977, document 71 (Beirut: Institute for Palestine Studies, 1978), pp. 96-98.

saw the attainment of Palestinian national rights and the resolution of the Arab-Israeli conflict to be reconcilable with the existence of Israel.

The Arab states also moved in the same direction. By accepting Security Council Resolution 242 of 1967, they accepted the existence of Israel in exchange for its withdrawal from the territories it occupied in the war of June 1967. After the Palestinians accepted the two-state solution, the Arab states proposed and endorsed plans to resolve the conflict on the basis of the partition of Palestine. In 1980 a Saudi proposal, the Fahed Plan, expressed Arab readiness to conclude peace on the basis of partition.[56] In September 1982, the Arab states unanimously approved, in a summit conference at Fez, Morocco, a similar Saudi-Tunisian plan which proposed Arab-Israeli peace on the basis of creating a Palestinian state in the territories Israel occupied in 1967.[57] Israel categorically rejected this alternative to continued occupation and conflict. Its foreign minister called this formula for coexistence "a new declaration of war on Israel."[58]

CONCLUSION

Israel's rejection of all alternatives to its continued occupation confirms its preference for territorial aggrandizement to peaceful accommodation with its neighbors. The common denominator among all the rejected proposals for Arab-Israeli peace is that they require an end to Israeli occupation. And that is precisely what Israel is determined to avoid. Israel's rejection of proposals that do not envision the replacement of its occupation with an independent Palestinian state (its typical justification for rejecting other peace plans) indicates that it is the withdrawal of its occupation that it really rejects.

The unavoidable conclusion is that Israel, in its dealings with the Palestinian people, seeks to displace rather than to replace injustice and oppression. Israel's insensitive and shortsighted reliance on the great power its alliance with the United States enables it to maintain can neither

---

56. For text of the Fahed proposal see Congressional Research Service, Library of Congress, *Middle East Peace Proposals* (Washington, D.C.), p. 16.

57. For text of the plan see *The Times* (London), 11 September 1982.

58. *Los Angeles Times*, 11 September 1982.

legitimize nor normalize its existence. It only confirms the judgment that Israel "is a small country, armed to the teeth, strong in national spirit, but sorrowfully lacking in foresight."[59] Israel must understand that its long-range interests, as well as the national rights of the Palestinians, require not substitutes for Palestinian freedom, but alternatives to Israeli occupation.

59. E.H. Hutchinson, *Violent Truce* (New York: Devin-Adair, 1956), p. 142.

CHAPTER 24

THE UNITED STATES AND PALESTINE IN THE 1980s*

Naseer Aruri

The Dialectics Of Unilateralism

Since the end of the 1967 Middle East war, two approaches have emerged for settling the Arab-Israeli conflict: a comprehensive settlement under international auspices and a "peace process" conducted under United States supervision. The first approach envisions an international framework with authority to shape a settlement in accordance with recognized legal principles and accepted practices.[1] The international consensus, associated with this approach, embodied an historic compromise, based on the exchange of territory for peace: The Arab states and the Palestinians would recognize the permanence of Israel within the 1967 borders in return for the recognition of the right of the Palestinians to self-determination. This approach is based on U.N. Resolutions 242 and 338, which have been universally accepted as the cornerstone of a proper settlement.

This approach was championed by the Soviet Union and promoted by the great majority of third world countries, including the Arab states. It was endorsed by Arab summit conferences from Algiers and Rabat in 1973 and 1974, to Fez and Amman in 1982 and 1987. It received an implicit sanction

* A revised and updated version of an article which appeared in *Journal of Palestine Studies* (Spring 1989) 18(3):3-21.

1. These would include the inadmissibility of territorial acquisition, hence resolutions 242 and 338; and equal rights for the Palestinian people, hence General Assembly resolutions 3236 of November 22, 1974, which recognized the rights of the Palestinian people to self-determination, national independence and sovereignty. That resolution also requested the U.N. Secretary-General to establish contacts with the PLO on all matters concerning Palestine.

from the 1977 Palestine National Council session in Cairo and an explicit acknowledgment from the 1988 PNC session in Algiers, which was made even more explicit by Yasir Arafat's statements to the UN General Assembly session in Geneva, his subsequent press conference and the "Stockholm Document", all in December 1988.

The second approach also claimed resolutions 242 and 338 as a foundation for a reasonable settlement, but endorses the concept of direct bilateral negotiations between states in a step-by-step process, leading towards a comprehensive settlement. The exchange of territory for peace dimension of this approach remained unclear and seemed to allow for Israel's retaining some parts of occupied Arab land.

The diplomatic history of the Middle East for the past two decades reveals that five United States administrations consistently followed the second approach, thereby thwarting an international settlement. Between 1969 and 1973, U.S. diplomacy succeeded in tipping the balance against the international consensus.[2] It undermined the international pressure exerted between June 1967 and March 1969 to effect Israeli withdrawal, by channeling diplomatic efforts towards a separate peace between Egypt and Israel. It subsequently used the "Big Four" talks on the Middle East to advocate the Rhodes formula, and succeeded in limiting those talks to the "Big Two" in 1969, excluding Britain and France. U.S. diplomatic hegemony was further enhanced by Kissinger's shuttle diplomacy in the aftermath of the October 1973 war, which succeeded in interrupting the superpowers' condominium in the Middle East. Henceforth, the peace process was reduced, in effect, to an exclusive American undertaking, which shielded Israel from the international scrutiny and succeeded in permitting Israel to consolidate its occupation of Palestinian and other Arab territories. At the same time, Israel succeeded in rejecting every U.S. peace initiative involving withdrawal from any part of Palestine, starting with Secretary of State William Rogers' plan in 1969 and ending with that of George Shultz in 1988.[3]

2. For a discussion of United States opposition to the international consensus on Palestine, see the author's article "United States Opposition to An International Peace Conference on the Middle East, 1967-1985" *International Journal of Islamic and Arabic Studies,* (Winter 1985) 2(1) 87-98.

3. The basic features of the Shultz initiative were:

1. Negotiations between an Israeli and Jordanian-Palestinian delegation will begin on arrangements for a transitional period. These negotiations were to continue for six months.

2. Seven months after transitional negotiations begin, final status negotiations will begin and proceed for one year.

Alleging that the Reagan Plan contradicted Camp David and undermined Israeli security, the Israeli Cabinet "resolved" on September 2, 1982 not to "enter into any negotiations with any party."[4] And following the submission of the Shultz Plan in March 1988, Prime Minister Shamir declared "Shultz's signature" as the "only acceptable" part of that plan, which he also denounced as "bad", "unwelcomed" and "unpractical."[5] And yet, the American posture towards Israel, before and after the Shultz Plan, was one of excessive generosity. At the time that the Reagan administration was expressing concern about Israeli excesses in dealing with the insurrection in the West Bank and Gaza, it granted Israel a debt relief of approximately $2 billion, bidding rights on U.S. military contracts equal to those of NATO allies, and 80 percent financing of a new short range ballistic missile system as part of the SDI, better known as Star Wars.[6] The administration's request of $3.6 billion in military aid for Israel in fiscal 1989 represented an increase of $1.8 billion. Estimating that the increase matched the direct cost of putting down the Palestinian *intifada* over a twelve month period, Donald Neff wrote in *Middle East International* that Israel was "already practically assured compensation for its direct costs even if the uprising lasts a full year."[7]

Moreover, a Memorandum of Agreement, which was signed into law by President Reagan on April 22, 1988, after Shamir's rejection of the Shultz plan, institutionalized the U.S.- strategic relationship. A State Department official expressed the dismay of the government officials who disagreed with Shultz's decision by saying that this grant of Shamir's request for the

———

3. The transitional period will be three months.

4. An international conference will launch the negotiations but will not approve solutions or veto agreements. Palestinians will be represented in a joint Jordanian-Palestinian delegation. Negotiations between this joint delegation and Israel will proceed independently of any other negotiations.

See, State Department Bureau of Public Affairs, "U.S. Policy in the Middle East" *(Selected Document no. 27)*, June 1988, p.2.

4. Text distributed in English by Israel's Government Press Office was printed in *New York Times*, 3 September 1982.

5. *Boston Globe*, 12 March 1988.

6. *New York Times*, 24 December 1987.

7. Donald Neff, "Funding the Intifada Bill," *Middle East International*, 14 May 1988, pp. 7-8.

Memorandum, "may be seen by his opponents [in Israel] as a reward for not being serious about the peace process." A senior Israeli official confirmed this by saying "it almost looks like Shultz gave him [Shamir] a reward for not cooperating."[8]

Why was Israel allowed to treat its patron and benefactor with such defiance and contempt? The answer to this question relates to the manner in which the U.S.-Israel special relationship came to be viewed by both parties. The ensuing fifteen years, since the October 1973 war, witnessed the emergence of the United States as the *de facto* superpower of the region, its principal custodian and sole arbiter of peace. Unlike other regions of the world, the Middle East was deprived of the natural and inevitable competition between the two superpowers; and Israel took the credit for the strategic coup and expected to reap the benefits. The suspension of peace in the Middle East was the price of unilateralism.

THE SPECIAL RELATIONSHIP

The Sinai accord of 1975 and Camp David of 1979 embody the principle that the final settlement of the Palestine question will not be premised on the "faulty assumption" that Israel violated Palestinian rights.[9] Hence, the matter of sovereignty in the West Bank and Gaza was to be included in the category of negotiable items. That, in reality, was the true meaning of America's diplomatic blockade against the PLO, which was decreed by Henry Kissinger in 1975, and lifted by the Reagan administration on its way out of office. Columnist David Wilson of the *Boston Globe* correctly observed that the purpose of the Kissinger formula was to "protect Israel and its American ally from having to deal with the 1.7 million Palestinians under occupation."[10]

Such moves required a tacit reinterpretation of Resolution 242. Given that resolution's broad acceptance as a foundation for a settlement, it was necessary to keep it at diplomatic center stage. Its failure to mention Palestinian rights appealed to Israel, yet its withdrawal clause contradicted Israeli goals. To reconcile these conflicting components, the U.S. allowed 242 to be understood in such a way as to allow for a certain accommodation of the Israeli position. For example, despite the fact that Camp David

8. *New York Times*, 22 April 1988.

9. Jimmy Carter's phrase as reported in *New York Times*, 1 April 1976.

10. *Boston Globe*, 20 December 1988.

promised a comprehensive settlement on the basis of 242, it in effect altered the status of the West Bank and Gaza from occupied territory, according to international law, to a disputed territory whose sovereignty was to be a matter for negotiations. Moreover, the Egyptian-Israeli agreement, brokered by the United States, granted Israel a virtual veto over the final disposition of these Palestinian territories occupied since 1967. Thus, Israel's withdrawal from the Sinai Peninsula, which took place in April 1982 in accordance with these agreements, was considered by Israeli leaders as its final territorial "concession"; a fulfillment of its obligations under Security Council Resolution 242. "There will never again be a redivision of Western Eretz Israel," said Menachem Begin at that time, asserting "eternal sovereignty" over the West Bank and Gaza, and consequently blocking off the Camp David option for these territories.[11]

A political settlement thus became intertwined with the United States-Israel special relationship, which was bolstered by the anti-Soviet thrust of the first Reagan Administration, and in turn, reinforced by the antiterrorist dimension of America's global strategy.[12] The more intense the cold war with the Soviet Union grew, the stronger the special relationship with Israel became. The more inroads perceived to have been made in the third world by local forces allied with the Soviet Union, the more pronounced became Israel's counter-revolutionary role at a global level, and consequently the less urgent became a Middle East settlement. By the same token, the more dependent the Arab countries became on the United States for regime security and financial stability and the less coherent the Arab position became, due to inter-Arab strife and Palestinian internecine conflict, the less responsive was the U.S. to their general concerns.

Although the United States strategic calculations did not totally side-step the role of conservative Arab states, under Reagan the U.S.-Israel special relationship was the favored one, thus giving much greater weight to a hard-line Israeli position. The special relationship became a principal impediment to a global settlement and a means to the marginalization of the Palestine question and the containment of Palestinian nationalism.

Together, these aspects of post-1973 American policy accelerated the disenfranchisement of the Palestinians from the "peace process" and tried to insure their national exclusion from the new order that would emanate from

11. *New York Times*, 22 April 1988.

12. For a discussion of Reagan's antiterrorist policies, see Naseer Aruri and John Carroll, "U.S. Policy and Terrorism," *American-Arab Affairs* (Fall 1985), 14:59-70; also by the same authors, "The Anti-Terrorist Crusade," *Arab Studies Quarterly* (Spring 1987), 4(2):173-87.

it. Aside from the 1977 aberration under Carter, U.S. policy continued to denigrate the Palestine question until it became a secondary, if not even a tertiary, issue during Reagan's presidency. That transformation of Israel from client to strategic ally and the corresponding marginalization of the Palestine question made the "peace process" more responsive to strategic calculation and the exigencies of the cold war than to basic international legal principles and the requirements for regional harmony.

The Rationale for Strategic Cooperation

The period between September 1982, when the Reagan Plan was unveiled,[13] and May 1983, when the ill-fated Shultz plan for Lebanon was proposed, was a period of reflection in U.S. Middle East policy circles. The foreign policy establishment was considering whether U.S. strategic interests in the region (oil, trade and investment), which required a stable sphere of influence, would be better promoted by a measure of even-handedness, or by near total reliance on Israel, as the only reliable pillar for U.S. interests. A principal difficulty stemmed from the fact that both Israel and conservative Arab states shared Reagan's concern about a Soviet "threat"; however, they disagreed on issues of priority and causality. The Arabs and their dwindling number of supporters in the Washington policy apparatus argued that regional stability was a safeguard against revolution and Soviet influence, and that required a durable solution of the Palestine problem. Israeli supporters dismissed the Palestine question and highlighted the Gulf as the source of instability.

13. The salient features of the Reagan Plan were:

1. Palestinian and Israeli sovereignties over the West Bank and Gaza are precluded.
2. Final peace will be sought in association with Jordan.
3. Resolution 242 applies to all fronts but the actual withdrawal depends on the "extent of true peace and normalization."
4. Jerusalem remains one city.
5. Israeli settlements in the West Bank and Gaza will be placed under the new Jordanian-Palestinian government.
6. The Palestinians will have "full autonomy" including authority over the "land and its resources, subject to fair safeguards on water."

For a discussion of the Reagan Plan, see Naseer Aruri and Fouad Moughrabi, "The Reagan Middle East Initiative," *Journal of Palestine Studies* (Winter 1983), 12(2):10-30.

By mid-1983, the Reagan administration, which was embarrassed by the devastation in Lebanon and its own role in the war, was no longer defensive about its special relationship with Israel. It felt no special obligation to act as if a Palestinian settlement was necessary and proper, and launched an offensive against Arab states whom it accused of having stalled the "peace process." Saudi Arabia was blamed for the failure to arrange a Jordanian-Palestinian formula and Syria for refusing to accept the Shultz attempted diktat of May 17, 1983 in Lebanon.[14] The Reagan plan was thus laid to rest.

The special relationship was transformed into a strategic alliance between the United States and Israel. In October 1983, President Reagan signed National Security Decision Directive 111, thus fulfilling his campaign promise that Israel, as a "unique strategic asset," would receive major concessions in the areas of weapons, trade, aid, and technology. Aid from the United States was converted to outright grants and was no longer earmarked for special projects. Israel was given unique access to U.S. military technology and markets, and as previously stated, it was accorded a NATO-like status.

Secretary of State Shultz became the Reagan administration's chief proponent of close strategic cooperation with Israel, going much beyond his predecessor Alexander Haig. Haig's framework for a Middle East policy had been the "consensus of strategic concerns," which was to bring together a conservative constellation of regional powers that would *include* Israel.[15] Shultz's framework instead assigned Israel a pivotal, global role in addition to its regional duties on behalf of the status quo in the Middle East. With Shultz in power, the United States conducted its Middle East policy on the basis of the "consensus of strategic concerns" plus the special relationship with Israel. Israel's value to the U.S. national interest, defined in global cold war terms, began to outweigh the importance to U.S. interests of an Israeli-Palestinian settlement. By 1983, the Reagan administration had accepted the Israeli view that the Palestine question is not the principal cause of instability in the Middle East. Henceforth, that issue would not be allowed to interfere in the special relationship between a superpower and its strategic ally.

14. For a discussion of the "Shultz Agreement" on Lebanon, see the author's "The United States Intervention In Lebanon," *Arab Studies Quarterly* (Fall 1985), 7(4):59-77.

15. Haig's strategy was outlined in a testimony before the Senate Foreign Relations Committee on September 17, 1981: "Secretary Haig: U.S. Strategy In The Middle East," U.S. Department of State, Bureau of Public Affairs, *Current Policy No. 312.*

The strengthening of the special relationship between the United States and Israel and the corresponding marginalization of the Palestine question in the aftermath of the 1982 invasion of Lebanon was based on several factors.

First, Israel's war aims in 1982 were not incompatible with U.S. policy objectives in the region. The reduction of Syrian influence in the region as well as the destruction of the PLO infrastructure were seen as positive developments by an administration that considered these forces to be Soviet clients. For Nixon and Kissinger, the PLO had been simply a Soviet surrogate, which had to be nipped in the bud. Unable to accomplish that objective, however, the United States was satisfied to see Israel complete the mission in the summer or 1982.

Second, the political map of Lebanon produced by the Israeli invasion had the potential to produce a pro-Western regime with a U.S. trained military, capable of knitting the heterogeneous factions into a political community. An anti-Syrian right-wing government in Lebanon with normal ties to Israel, was seen as a natural extension of the Sadat-Mubarak regime in Egypt, a vindication of the Camp David diplomatic approach to the Arab-Israeli conflict, and a testimony to the ascendancy of the United States and the erosion of Soviet influence in the Middle East.

Third, the Israeli invasion was expected to afford an opportunity to implement the politics of "moderation." Jordan was to be equipped with a rapid deployment force for use in the Gulf region, while Saudi Arabia would help arrange postwar conditions in the region. Specifically, the invasion was relied upon to produce Syrian acquiescence in a Pax Americana-Israelica.

Washington felt free to revive strategic cooperation with Israel without embarrassment and without fear of Arab reprisal, given the defeat of the "radical" forces.

Antiterrorism

The peculiar emphasis which was placed on combating international terrorism in Reagan's foreign policy reinforced the special relationship and further marginalized and de-legitimized the Palestinian national movement. The Reagan administration readily and uncritically accepted Israel's premises about conflict and stability in the region: that Palestinian "terrorism" (rather than legitimate Palestinian demands), together with Islamic fundamentalism constituted the great threats to the Middle East. The United States, whose global position was undermined during the 1970s in Angola, Ethiopia, Iran, Afghanistan, Nicaragua, and Cambodia, allegedly because of a Vietnam syndrome, which inhibited U.S. military commitments abroad, was declared ready to resume intervention. The Reagan

Administration would proceed on the assumption that Carter's "wimpish" policies were a mere aberration that would be replaced by a renewed effort to roll back Soviet gains in the third world. Hence the pursuit of strong-arm policies in Grenada, Lebanon, and Nicaragua, as well as the launching of a crusade against international "terrorism," with Libya, Iran, Syria and the PLO as primary targets were all designed to rally a reluctant U.S. public around the resumption of interventionism.

Reagan's perception of Israel as a "unique strategic asset" was reinforced by that foreign policy climate, which was dominated by the political thought of neo-conservatives such as Norman Podhoretz, Jeanne Kirkpatrick, Richard Pipes and Irving Kristol. It was also promoted by such right-wing journalists as William Safire and George Will and anticommunist politicians and hawkish strategists as Richard Allen, Robert McFarlane, Alexander Haig, Elliot Abrams and above all George Shultz. The foreign policy consensus they shaped was premised on the notion that a "legacy of restraint," known also as the Vietnam syndrome, had to be eradicated, lest the United States lose its position as the preeminent superpower. They challenged America to rehabilitate intervention and to "stand tall" against communists, terrorists and would-be challengers of U.S. domination. Israel's rhetoric about terrorism was, therefore, accepted by the administration without question. Israel also became a conduit for channeling U.S. money and weapons to a variety of unsavory regimes and movements.[16] Over the last eight years, the secret mining of Nicaraguan harbors, the ill-defined military mission in Lebanon, the double dealings with Iran to subsidize the Contras, the campaign of disinformation about Libya, and the transfer of advanced military technology to South Africa in contravention of the 1986 U.S. Anti-Apartheid Act constitute but a modest portion of the Reagan administration's global agenda that had an Israeli connection. Given, therefore, Israel's role as a bastion of anticommunism and a catalyst in Mr. Reagan's post-Vietnam formula for U.S. military intervention, it was rather unseemly to bring up an issue as insignificant as that of the West Bank into the relations of the strategic allies.

As long as that foreign policy climate prevailed, Israel was insulated from the pressure for a territorial settlement. Its utility in U.S. global strategy far outweighed its obligations to peace in the region. Thus, the

16. On Israel's role in the U.S., global strategy see Noam Chomsky, *The Fateful Triangle* (Boston: South End Press, 1983); Jane Hunter, *Israeli Foreign Policy: South Africa and Central America* (Boston: South End Press, 1988); Israel Shahak, *Israel's Global Role: Weapons for Repression* (Belmont, Mass.: AAUG Press, 1982); Milton Jamail and Margo Gutierrez, *It's No Secret: Israel's Military Involvement in Central America* (Belmont, Mass.: AAUG Press, 1986).

continuation of the untenable *status quo* in the occupied Arab territories was linked to heightened conflict in the world. By the same token, the urgency for reconsideration of the *status quo* would be likely to develop only in the context of detente.

ALTERED REALITIES OF THE CONFLICT

The latter period of the Reagan presidency was one of profound change in the Middle East and in the world at large. This change has altered the three levels of the Arab-Israeli conflict, the local, regional and international, in such a manner that the assumptions of the U.S.-Israeli convergence of interests can no longer avoid reconsideration. The anti-cold war thinking and foreign policy reforms adopted by Mikhail Gorbachev in 1985 were bound to have an impact on the Middle East impasse. The new Soviet policies are clearly designed to maximize influence on all sides of major regional issues. The pursuit of a middle ground has given Soviet diplomacy a pragmatic thrust calculated to develop broad acceptability. The emphasis on cooperation, collective security and political instead of military solutions, has already given Mr. Gorbachev and the Soviet Union a new international image as an arbiter of peace.

Judging that American hegemony in the Middle East was undiminished by Brezhnev's policies; that the Soviet Union lacked any influence in Israel and enjoyed little influence in the Arab world, which remained generally pro-West, Gorbachev decided to redress the imbalance. Largely absent from the Middle East "peace process" since its 1972 ouster by Kissinger, the Soviet Union is now returning to the region – not as the sponsor of local surrogates or the archenemy of reactionary Arab states or Zionist Israel, but as a superpower eager to play the role of a moderator. Moscow has already taken initiatives aimed at restoring diplomatic contacts with Israel, establishing diplomatic relations with conservative Arab states in the Gulf, improving relations with Egypt – all as part of a strategy calculated to broaden its diplomatic options. Moscow was instrumental in bringing about the unity session of the Palestine National Council in April 1987 in Algiers and in persuading the PLO to revise its position on the nature of the international peace conference and other preconditions for peace, such as the controversial issue of Israel's right to exist. Soviet policy under Gorbachev has, in effect, revised the 1981 Brezhnev plan to make accommodations to U.S. and Israeli demands.

The new Soviet approach is likely to restrain further developments in the U.S.-Israel special relationship, having gone a long way towards meeting the U.S. position, and bringing with it a regional alignment, most of whose components are normally pro-West. This alignment including Egypt,

Jordan, Saudi Arabia, Iraq, and the PLO, conceives of a framework that envisages the exchange of territory for peace, a solution which the U.S., Europe and the Soviet Union have urged to varying degrees. Furthermore, the Soviet Union, having just concluded or brokered agreements ending regional conflicts in Afghanistan, southern Africa, Cambodia, and Central America, will be in a strong position to argue that the imperatives for an international settlement in the Middle East are not less urgent than elsewhere.

Supporting this endeavor will be the countries of Western Europe, which warmly received Arafat's peace initiatives. A case in point was the opportunity granted him by the Socialist members of the European Parliament in September 1988 to give a major address on the Palestinian perspective on peace. The invitation to Strassbourg emphasized a new European readiness to participate in a peace process based on the concept of mutual recognition. Another European contribution was made by Sweden, whose foreign minister Sten Andersson played a crucial role in bridging U.S.-PLO differences which culminated in the U.S. historic decision to open talks with the PLO on December 15, 1988. Considerable European pressure was exerted upon Washington to reciprocate Arafat's conciliatory statements made in Stockholm and in Geneva in December 1988. Even British Prime Minister Margaret Thatcher commented that Arafat's statements qualified the PLO to take part in a peace conference.[17] And when Secretary of State Shultz finally declared the end of the no-talk policy with the PLO, the British Foreign office issued a statement welcoming the fact that "the Americans share our analysis that the PLO has moved to positions that represent real progress."[18]

Differences between the United States and EEC countries over the Palestine question constitute an implicit pressure on the United States to abandon its isolation from the global consensus. The universality of that consensus was vividly expressed on December 2, 1988 when every single European nation joined an almost unanimous General Assembly in the vote to hold its session in Geneva after Arafat was subjected to a U.S. visa denial. The U.S. and Israel cast the only dissenting votes. And when the Assembly censured the U.S. for the visa denial, only Britain abstained in a vote of 151 against 2 - Israel and the United States.[19] The tide in favor of the PLO in Europe was further demonstrated in January 1989 when Yasir

17. *Boston Globe,* 16 December 1988.

18. *Ibid.*

19. *Boston Globe*, 1 December 1988.

Arafat was received in Madrid by outgoing, present, and next presidents of the EEC's foreign affairs committee. Such visits together with the papal audience demonstrate the huge gap between the U.S. and its European allies. The juxtaposition of the visa affair with the high level at which Arafat is received in Europe, reveals the extent to which Washington had painted itself into a corner.

Moreover, the EEC countries have also demonstrated their willingness and capacity to exert pressure on Israel to modify its hard-line stance on the Palestine question. For example they used the threat of withholding trade privileges in 1988 to force Israel to allow Palestinians growers to export farm products to Europe directly bypassing Israeli firms. The concept of mutual recognition, as a requisite for durable peace in the Middle East, has become so entrenched into the European and Soviet perspectives, that would make it rather difficult for U.S. policy-makers to ignore.

Domestic Environment

Washington's sudden awakening to the fact that the *status quo* in the West Bank and Gaza was untenable came in February 1988, after five years of total diplomatic inactivity. The United States' fifteen-year monopoly of the stalled "peace process" had effectively prevented other actors from participating in a serious search for a negotiated settlement. Consistent with that posture, Secretary Shultz embarked in 1988 on a series of visits to the region, which failed to produce a settlement. His plan was a confirmation of the U.S. custodianship over the Middle East, a reminder that the region is United States turf. As such, it was designed to pre-empt any serious international proposals for peace.

It almost seemed as if Mr. Shultz was trying to save Israel in spite of itself, to protect Israel's tarnished image *inside* the United States. He endorsed Israel's right to contain the *intifada*, but differed with the Likud leadership over the proper means of suppression. Hence his assistant secretary for human rights, Richard Schifter, told a congressional panel:

> In our view, Israel clearly has not only the right, but the obligation, to preserve or restore order in the occupied territories and to use appropriate levels of force to accomplish that end.[20]

This statement, which coincided with unprecedented Israeli measures including banning the press and sealing off the entire West Bank and Gaza,

---

20. David Ottoway, "State Department Official Defends Israel's Use of Force," *Washington Post*, 30 March 1988, p. A-21.

differed from Henry Kissinger's famous counsel to Israel only in tone, not in substance.[21]

While Schifter was giving Israel a green light to restore "law and order," State Department spokesman Charles Redman was expressing "regrets" over the Israeli restrictions and its balancing of "harsh security measures" with "violent demonstrations."[22] The State Department's approach reflected an attempt to sanitize Israeli practices, which the U.S. government was finding difficulty in defending *inside* the United States. Hence the seemingly erratic reactions of the administration to Israeli excesses, which consisted of soft criticism and reassurances of support, of using the veto to protect Israel in the Security Council and then abstaining or supporting the universal condemnation. For example, the United States abstained from voting on a Security Council resolution which "strongly deplored the opening of fire by the Israeli army, resulting in the killing and wounding of defenseless Palestinian civilians" on the pretext that it was "unacceptably harsh."[23] The U.S. then supported a resolution which called on Israel on January 5, 1988 "to refrain from deporting any Palestinian civilians from the occupied territories" but abstained when a second resolution on January 14 expressed "deep regret that Israel ... has deported Palestinian civilians."[24] Two weeks later, the United States vetoed a resolution which called on Israel to "desist forthwith from its policies and practices which violate the human rights of the Palestinian people."[25]

21. According to a confidential memorandum by Julius Berman, a former chairman of the Conference of Presidents of Major American Jewish Organizations, Henry Kissinger told eight Jewish leaders at a breakfast in early February 1988 the following:

> Israel should bar the media from entry into the territories involved in the present demonstrations, accept the short-term criticism of the world press for such conduct, and put down the insurrection as quickly as possible — overwhelmingly, brutally and rapidly.

Letter dated February 3, 1988 typed on stationary imprinted with Kaye, Scholer, Fireman, Hays & Handler. Also news story by Robert McFadden in *New York Times.*, 5 March 1988.

22. Ottoway, "State Department Official."

23. Resolution 605. (December 22, 1987).

24. Resolutions 607 (January 5, 1988) and 608 (January 14, 1988).

25. Resolution s/19466 (January 29, 1988).

Secretary Shultz warned against drawing conclusions from the previous abstention. Immediately after that, he said:

> I think it's important for everyone to understand that the United States regards its friendship and the strength of its relationship with Israel as key and unshakable... Occasionally we disagree, but through all of that,this relationship, as I said, is unshakable – that's what that means.[26]

And yet, the United States warned Israel about possible damage to the "unshakable" relationship when orders were issued on August 18, 1988 for the expulsion of twenty–five Palestinians in addition to thirty–seven already expelled in 1988. Deputy Secretary of State John Whitehead warned Israeli minister Oded Eran that American public opinion does not tolerate expulsions:

> You have heard our position before but now the issue has reached the point that an increasing number of Americans are wondering what Israel is doing. If this attitude persists, damage to our bilateral relations will occur. We will oppose Israel in the U.N. and elsewhere. We urge you to reconsider the expulsion orders, or, at a minimum, to refrain from carrying them out.[27]

Although public opinion is passive, its role in the formulation of public policy in participatory systems is crucial. There are strong indications that a gap has been growing recently between public opinion and the content of public policy in the United States with respect to the Palestine-Israel conflict, largely due to the *intifada*. Yet Palestine, as already shown, has never been high on the official agenda. As long as it did not interfere in America's policy objectives in the region, peace initiatives seemed unnecessary. Despite its deficiencies and the lack of resolve to assure its success, the Shultz plan was, in part, a response to altered domestic realities. The subsequent U.S. decision to talk with the PLO, in response to Arafat's acceptance of U.S. conditions, also seemed to accord with the views of a majority of Americans.

A public opinion poll conducted in January 1988 revealed that 36 percent of Americans believed that Israel had reacted to the Palestinian uprising too harshly.[28] A June 1987 poll showed that 61 percent, labeled by

26. Donald Neff, "Diplomatic Isolation," *Middle East International.* (23 January 1988), pp. 7-8.

27. *Jerusalem Post.* 24 August 1988.

28. Mark J. Penn and Douglas E. Schoen, "American Attitudes towards the Middle East, " *Public Opinion,* (May/June 1988), p. 47.

the *Los Angeles Times* as a "vast majority," favored the exchange of territory for peace.[29] Another poll conducted in January 1988 found that 31 percent of Americans favored a Palestinian state federated with Jordan.[30] By March 1988, a Gallup poll determined that 41 percent favored the "establishment of an independent Palestinian state," without reservation.[31] Prior to the uprising, a June 1987 poll revealed that 50 percent favored PLO participation in peace negotiations.[32]

In January 1988, a general call for peace was endorsed by 74 percent, of whom 74 percent favored a PLO role in the negotiations.[33] The same poll showed that 48 percent favored "direct contact" between the U.S. and the PLO, of whom 56 percent did not even stake their approval on PLO recognition of Israel's right to exist, as required by the Kissinger formula. This percentage increased in March, when a Gallup poll showed that a substantial 57 percent of Americans (versus 27 percent who disagreed) favored direct negotiations between the U.S. and the PLO, while 66 percent favored direct negotiations between Israel and the PLO.[34] A *Los Angeles Times* poll, conducted during the spring of 1988, found that 34 percent of non-Jews favored a reduction of military aid to Israel and 65 percent thought that there was "an element of racism in the attitude of Israelis towards Arabs."

These figures do not, of course, imply that while the U.S. government has been on a collision course with the Palestinians for years, the U.S. public has been sympathetic to their aspirations. Analysis of public opinion polls ranging from a neutral base comparison year of 1981 through mid-1988 reveals a consistent trend of U.S. public support for Israel. When asked in 1981 whom the U.S. should support in the Arab-Israeli conflict, 47 percent favored Israel and only 11 percent favored the Arabs. In January 1988, 43 percent favored Israel while only 11 percent favored the Arabs.[35]

29. *Los Angeles Times*, 3 June 1987.

30. Penn and Schoen, p. 46.

31. Gallup Organization, "A Gallup Survey Regarding the West Bank and Gaza Conflict between Israel and the Palestinians," Princeton, N.J.: 11 March 1988.

32. *Los Angeles Times*, 3 June 1987.

33. Penn and Schoen, p. 46.

34. Gallup Organization, "Survey".

35. Penn and Schoen, p. 45.

The new factor in the equation is the *intifada*, which is seen as a non-violent insurrection juxtaposed against Israeli repression that reminds Americans of Chile or South Africa. Moreover, the conflict is now seen in the U.S. more in *Palestinian*-Israeli, rather than in *Arab*-Israeli terms.

Although support for Israel held steady in 1988, it also rose dramatically for the Palestinians. A Gallup Poll showed that the percentage of those expressing sympathy with Israel was 43 percent in May 1988 and 46 percent in December 1988. The corresponding figures for the Palestinians were 20 percent and 24 percent, respectively.[36] If we compare these figures with the 11 percent support for the "Arabs" in January 1988, the roughly 100 percent increase of support for the Palestinians can be accounted for by the fact that the question, which produced 11 percent support in January, referred to "Arabs," while that, which produced 20 percent and 24 percent later in 1988, referred to "Palestinians." That increase, we should point out, resulted largely from a change in the category of the uncommitted, and thus did not reflect an erosion of public support for Israel.

The beginning of a shift in public opinion was also visible in media coverage. ABC *Nightline's* week-long series from Jerusalem, in which three Palestinians and four Israelis participated in a "town meeting" setting in that city was perhaps the first Palestinian-Israeli debate of the conflict on national television. Millions of viewers in the United States saw the Palestinians, perhaps for the first time, as a national group with normal aspirations for a dignified existence, and a determination to pursue their goals in a reasonable manner.

The American press reacted to Israeli repression with uncharacteristic criticism. A survey of twenty newspaper editorials revealed this trend during the month of December 1987. One theme of the criticism focused on Israel's special moral obligation given the history of Jewish persecution. For example, the *St. Petersburg Times* of Florida wrote:

> As a nation whose very existence was meant to atone for two millenniums of persecution culminating in the holocaust, Israel inherited the burden of conducting itself according to high moral principles.[37]

The *Omaha World Herald* said that "Israel, of all nations, should be sensitive about oppression."[38] The *Arizona Republic* went as far as

---

36. George Gallup Jr. and Alec Gallup, "Talks with PLO Support," *San Francisco Chronicle,* 16 January 1989.

37. *St. Petersburg Times,* 29 December 1987.

38. *Omaha World Herald,* 21 December 1987.

implying a prohibited analogy with Nazi behavior:

> Israel has evolved from a nation founded by the remnants of Hitler's death camps into a country dependent on forced labor. . . . The inmates, have become the guards . . . who could have imagined that one day the survivors of Auschwitz would . . . strap young Arabs to the fronts of jeeps as human shields.[39]

Other newspapers compared Israeli behavior to that of the apartheid regime in South Africa, normally considered taboo in the discourse on the Middle East. The *Miami Herald* wrote that "Thoughtful Israelis foresee and shudder at their nation becoming analogous to South Africa."[40]

The *Sun Reporter* of San Francisco made an analogy between the two settler states in rather explicit language:

> South Africa and Israel are both republics, . . . both aggressively make claims of being democracies. . . . The U.S. regards both nations as being firm allies in the secret war against communism. . . . Both are engaged in hostilities against indigenous people who were already in residence. Arabs living in the West Bank do not live any better than Blacks in Soweto. . . . The Arabs have no arms. Like the Blacks. . . . they throw rocks.[41]

Some editorials placed the blame for Israeli intransigence, which led to the present deadlock, on the Reagan administration. For example, the *Grand Rapids Press* accused the administration of having been "almost servile in its deference to the Israeli government," asserting that "the U.S. has let the Mideast peace process sit idle and has done nothing to discourage Israeli provocations in the occupied territories or hasten the establishment of a homeland for the Palestinians."[42] Other editorials reminded Israel of its obligations under the special relationship. The *Charlotte Observer* wrote that "Israel, which depends so heavily on American money and support, must take appropriate steps toward achieving peace so as to maintain its critically important international image."[43]

Another domestic arena for U.S. policy towards Palestine is the American Jewish community, which continues to supply the major

39. *Arizona Republic* , 17 December 1987.

40. *Miami Herald*, 21 December 1987.

41. *Sun Reporter*, 23 December 1987.

42. *Grand Rapids Press*, 25 December 1987.

43. *The Charlotte Observer*, 28 December 1987.

organized political force behind the strategic alliance and against Palestinian rights. Endowed with organizational skills, financial resources, privileged access to decision making and the mass media and overlapping membership with business, trade unions and the Democratic Party, the Jewish community supplies the leverage which has so far enabled the Israeli lobby to assure unquestioning support of Israeli policies.

Expressions of discontent with Israeli practices began to surface in the U.S. Jewish community in the latter part of 1987 and became somewhat more frequent in 1988. The American Jewish Congress adopted a resolution in September 1987 which labeled the occupation as "benign," but warned that its continuation would lead to

> repressive measures that, in the long run, cannot but distort and corrupt the values we associate with a Jewish state. . . . The Jewish commitment to personal dignity, to human freedom, to social justice and to the rule of law all argue against the permanent governance of another people by a Jewish state.[44]

Rabbi Alexander Schindler, president of the Union of American Hebrew Congregations, cabled the Israeli president saying that Israel's policy was "an offense to the Jewish spirit" and it "threatens to erode the support of Israel's friends here in the U.S."[45] Albert Vorspan, the senior vice-president of the organization, warned Shamir that "Israel should not always expect reflexive support from American Jews."[46] Vorspan wrote that "American Jews are traumatized by the events in Israel" and that the occupied territories have become "Israel's Vietnam, Kent State and Watts rolled into one."[47] S. Hyman Bookbinder, a spokesperson for the American Jewish Committee, expressed similar sentiments and concerns about an anti-Israel backlash in the United States, when he said that Rabin's policy of might, power and blows "has caused great chagrin, great dismay among their best Jewish supporters."[48] In a letter to the *New York Times*, prominent

44. "Resolution of the Jewish Congress on the Middle East Peace Process," *American-Arab Affairs* (Fall 1987), 22:120-123.

45. *New York Times*, 25 January 1988.

46. *New York Times*, 21 March 1988.

47. *New York Times*, 8 May 1988.

48. *New York Times*, 26 January 1988. See also James Franklin "U.S. Jewish Leader Criticizes Israelis For Crackdown on Press," *Christian Science Monitor*, 5 March 1988. Reference is to Theodore Ellenoff, president of the American Jewish Committee; see also Linda Feldmann, "U.S. Jews in Turmoil over Violence in Israel," *Christian Science Monitor*, 4 March 1988.

Jewish intellectuals Irving Howe, Arthur Hertzberg, Michael Walzer, and Henry Rosovsky called upon Israel to express readiness "to end the occupation in such a way that, with necessary territorial adjustments, Israeli security and Palestinian national aspirations can be satisfied."

In Congress as well, Israel's supporters seemed troubled by the consequences of the Israeli policy of "might, force and blows." For example, senators known to be ardent supporters of Israeli policies, such as Carl Levin (D) of Michigan and Rudy Boschwitz (R) of Minnesota initiated the process which led thirty of their colleagues to sign a letter critical of Shamir's summary rejection of Shultz's initiative in the spring of 1988. The letter expressed the view that "peace negotiations have little chance of success if the Israeli government's position rules out territorial compromise."[49]

Another group of well-known supporters of Israel in the House of Representatives such as Barney Frank of Massachusetts, James Scheur of New York and Howard Berman, Henry Waxman, and Tom Lantos of California attempted to follow up with another letter, which did not materialize.[50] Apparently, Shultz himself intervened so that the administration would not appear to be behind these efforts to pressure Israel. The *New York Times* quoted a State Department official as saying that "what we don't want is the appearance that we are orchestrating pressure, because we're not."[51]

On another front, progressive groups like the Jewish Peace Fellowship and the New Jewish Agenda held many demonstrations outside the Israeli Embassy in Washington and many Israeli consulates around the country. The split in the Jewish community over Israel was dramatized by the New York conference, which was sponsored by *Tikkun* in December 1988. Among the themes voiced in that meeting were: "Wake up Israel; negotiate now; break the lock of AIPAC; and create J-PAC: A Jewish Peace Action Committee that would support Israel by affirming the Palestinian right to establish an independent state."[52] What is perhaps more interesting was the absence of any campaigns by the Israeli lobby in the U.S. in support of

49. *Washington Post*, 8 March 1988.

50. *New York Times*, 25 March 1988; see also Rob Wright, "Rep. Frank Urges Israel to Withdraw From Territories," *Boston Globe*, 9 March 1988.

51. *New York Times*, 11 March 1988; see also Joseph Harsch, "Shultz's Slow Steady Mideast Moves Builds on U.S. Jews' Support," *Christian Science Monitor.*, 18 March 1988.

52. See article by Mark Muro. "And Now: A Jewish Intifadah," *Boston Globe* (Focus Section) 25 December 1988, p. A-24.

Israel's opposition to the opening of a dialogue by the U.S. with the PLO. The public remarks of representatives of the major Jewish organizations have been rather low-keyed and reticent in their acquiescence in the U.S. decision.

CONFLICT AND CONVERGENCE IN U.S.-ISRAELI RELATIONS

The preceding does not imply that we are on the verge of a new era of international cooperation, which will render the cold war a relic of a by-gone era, as some euphoric journalists would have us believe. Nor does it imply that the U.S. has abandoned its general hostility to the fundamental rights of the Palestinian people.

For example, Secretary of State George Shultz's 1988 proposal for a "comprehensive settlement" in the Middle East envisaged a final resolution of the Palestine question that precludes the Palestinian people's rights to "self-determination without external interference," to "national independence and sovereignty," to "return to their homes and property," and to select and designate their own representatives.[53] It referred to these basic issues in vague terms. For example, it stated that "Palestinians must achieve control over political and economic decisions affecting their lives." This constitutes neither sovereignty nor administrative autonomy. Likewise, the Shultz plan adds that "Palestinians must be active [but not necessarily independent] participants in negotiations to determine their future." Also "Legitimate [but not necessarily national] Palestinian rights can be achieved in a manner which protects Israeli security."[54]

In the second major development of 1988, the U.S. has done no more than agree to talk to the PLO, and George Shultz emphasized that "the first item of business on our agenda in that dialogue will be the subject of terrorism."[55] Reaffirming the U.S. position on direct negotiations and the role of the PLO in these negotiations, he said:

53. These elementary rights are enshrined in many United Nations resolutions, including Resolution 3236 (XXIX), November 22, 1974; Resolution 181 (11), November 29, 1947, known generally as the "Partition Resolution," and Resolution 194 (111), December 11, 1948.

54. From the statement by Secretary of State George Shultz addressed to the Palestinians in the occupied territories in east Jerusalem, February 26, 1988. Washington, D.C.: Department of State, Bureau of Public Affairs (*Current Policy No.. 1055*).

55. Text of Shultz's news conference in *New York Times*, 15 December 1988, p. 18-A.

We hope that the dialogue may help bring about direct negotiations that will lead to peace. How those negotiations are structured, who is there to speak on behalf of the Palestinians, is a subject that's a difficult one; we've worked on it a long time, and I imagine it will continue to be difficult.[56]

Recent diplomatic history of the region, however, reveals a number of so-called reassessments, undertaken by successive administrations, including Reagan's. These were intended to remind Israel that occasional historical changes may alter the context and forces affecting U.S. and Israeli interests in the region, provoking divergence in their styles, conceptions of security, and the cost and nature of alliances. Such divergences are not atypical of those between colonial settler regimes, which must survive on the land, labor, and resources of indigenous people, and the more mobile and flexible metropolitan interests, which must accommodate shifting alliances and emerging political and economic forces. In other words, the U.S. is more capable of adapting to shifting alignments than Israel.

The rhetoric of U.S. policy towards Israel began to shift in response to this emerging gap between the two countries, which surfaced as a result of the *intifada*. For example, on June 11, 1988 in an address before the New York Council on Foreign Relations, Under-secretary of State Richard Murphy raised the issue of supporting the *intifada*. His speech was appropriately titled, "Middle East Peace: Facing Realities and Challenges."[57] He noted a glaring disparity between Israel's defense expenditure, which amounts to 19 percent of Gross National Product and the average, which is 5 percent for other countries in the world. Such disparity can be maintained only by a permanent U.S. subsidy, which will impose severe burdens on an economy that is already burdened by the largest budget and trade deficits in U.S. history and by a defense budget approaching $300 billion a year. Israel's diplomatic rigidity and lack of sensitivity to altered realities was succinctly described by Hebrew University Professor Yaron Ezrahi in the following way:

Israel has been jarred into reality... our leaders were living in the most incredible and unrealistic universe, constructed entirely by their own hands. In this universe, American support was treated as though it were a divine right. Israel did not invest seriously in political initiatives vis-a-vis the Palestinians, and it was indifferent to the changes in American public opinion. Now we are paying the price.[58]

56. *Ibid.*

57. Richard W. Murphy, "Middle East Peace: Facing Realities and Challenges," U.S. Department of State, Bureau of Public Affairs, *Current Policy No. 1082.*

58. *New York Times*, 19 December 1988.

Divergence between Israeli and American perceptions of security is another result of altered realities in the Middle East. Secretary of State Shultz challenged Israel on June 5, 1988, upon his arrival there to save his ill-fated plan, to reassess its concept of security:

> The location of borders is less significant today in ensuring security than the political relations between neighbors. Peace is the real answer to the problem of security.[59]

He urged Israel and the Arabs to reexamine their definitions of political rights, boundaries and sovereignty, which he considered as "out-dated" in view of emerging global realities:

> Borders today are permeable and porous, indifferent to the ballistic missile, and indifferent to the desire of any sovereign to shut out the outside world.[60]

Richard Murphy, under-Secretary of State for Near Eastern and South Asian Affairs lectured Israel about the new meanings of security, given the regional and global realities of 1988. He asked:

> Are peace and normalization essential to satisfy the necessity for security? The answer is yes, because geography and conventional military strategy can no longer ensure security.[61]

And again, he challenged Israel to "accept and act upon the understanding that legitimate political rights and democratic self-expression for Palestinians are compatible with Israeli security." He added: "In the long run, they are the key to real security for an Israel at peace with its neighbors."[62]

The altered realities have also moved the U.S. towards a public re-examination of the concept of rights and an updating of the adjectives that describe these rights. In addition, the belated discovery of the damaging consequences of an impasse impelled Washington to sound the proper warning about prolonged occupations. Thus, Secretary Shultz challenged Israel on June 5, 1988 to see that "continued occupation of the West Bank

59. State Department, "U.S. Policy In The Middle East," p. 8.

60. *Ibid.*

61. Murphy, "Middle East Peace: Facing Realities and Challenges." *op.cit.*

62. *Ibid.*

and Gaza and frustration of Palestinian rights is a dead-end street."[63] His discourse during his 1988 shuttles, while conforming to the linguistic parameters of diplomacy, did not conceal U.S. anxiety about the consequences of the impasse. A seemingly even-handed terminology[64] was sprinkled about to lend credibility to U.S. mediation: He promised an "equitable settlement of the land issue" and tried to assure the Arabs that resolution 242 calls for the "exchange of territory for peace." The settlement must address "legitimate Palestinian political rights" so that Palestinians and Israelis "learn to treat each other decently, respect their mutual right to live in security, and fulfill their political aspirations." Palestinian-Israeli accommodation is not consistent with a "winner-take-all" approach; Israelis and Palestinians "will realize that the fulfillment of their own dreams is impossible without the fulfillment of the other side's dream." While Shultz promised the Palestinians "control over political and economic decisions that affect their lives" and active participation in the peace process, he spoke of the necessity to call off their uprising: "For Palestinians, the challenge is to forge an effective political program to replace slogans and violence."

If we judge the emerging U.S. approach to the Palestine-Israel conflict by Mr. Shultz's prose, we might conclude that we are approaching a new chapter in United States Middle East diplomacy – one that is more credible and more even-handed. Although it signifies some departures from the uncritical support of the general Israeli position, deemed necessary because of strategic considerations, it still maintains opposition to fundamental Palestinian rights and to real international supervision of the negotiations. And yet the Reagan-Shultz legacy to George Bush will probably include a need for a change, not only surrounding definitions of security and conceptions of rights and significance of costs, but also of existing peace frameworks. For example, Camp David has been treated by many politicians, who felt comfortable with the pre-*intifada status quo,* as a sacred principle. It was invoked by Israel and her supporters as the basis for rejecting the Shultz plan. Under-secretary of State Richard Murphy was probably the first U.S. official to publicly downgrade Camp David in the forthcoming stage of negotiations. He asked rhetorically:

63. "U.S. Policy In The Middle East."

64. Secretary Shultz, "The Administration's Approach to Peacemaking." Speech before the Washington Institute for Near East Policy, Wye Plantation, Queenstown, Maryland, September 16, 1988. U.S. Department of State, *Current Policy No. 1104.*

> Can these people really believe that the clock can be turned back to 1978 and that
> negotiations can start from a basis which Jordan, Syria, and others rejected
> categorically? This is an illusion which cannot and will not be fulfilled.[65]

Murphy added the factors of "demography, tools of war and extremism" to
the emerging realities which are changing the diplomatic landscape of the
Middle East.

BUSH'S POLICY AND FUTURE PROSPECTS

The Reagan-Shultz legacy to the Bush administration may not have
been reversed by the decision to open a dialogue with the PLO. And it
should be made clear that the PLO paid a high price for the dialogue, having
met not only Kissinger's conditions for it but also Reagan's codicils. The
latter included accepting Israel's "right" to exist rather than merely its right
"to live in peace," as well as the "renunciation" rather than a
"condemnation" of terrorism. Both of these additions, which impelled
Shultz to boast, that "I did not change my mind, they changed theirs," could
be used by the legal minds of the new governments in Washington and Tel
Aviv to extract new concessions from the Palestinians: If Israel had the
moral and legal right to exist, then why did the Palestinians wage a "war"
against it for forty years? By the same logic, the Zionist movement would
have to be seen, not as a colonial–settler phenomenon, which resulted in
Palestinian dispersal and dispossession, but as a national liberation
movement. It may also be argued that the *intifada* is a form of violence and
would have to be "renounced" along with the National Charter, which
negates Israel's "right" to exist. In fact, according to the first disclosure in
the West of the classified protocol of the initial negotiations between the
United States and the PLO in Tunis, the United States apparently considers
the *intifada* a form of terrorism. The *Jerusalem Post,* citing the Egyptian
magazine *al-Musawwar* as its source, quotes the U.S. delegation as saying
to the PLO:

> Undoubtedly, the internal struggle that we are witnessing in the occupied
> territories aim to undermine the security and stability of the State of Israel, and we
> therefore demand cessation of those riots, which we view as terrorist acts against
> Israel. This is especially true as we know you are directing from outside the
> territories those riots which are sometimes very violent . . . we want to emphasize
> that the word 'terrorism,' as we understand it includes all Palestinian military action
> against Israel, whether against Israeli targets, installations or people... This concept
> includes military action undertaken by Palestinians inside the occupied territories.[66]

65. Murphy, p. 3.

66. *Jerusalem Post,* 6 January 1989.

The Bush administration adhered to this position when it explained its first veto of a Security Council resolution deploring Israel's treatment of Palestinians in the occupied territories. The U.S. deputy representative Herbert Okun told the fourteen members of the Council, who voted in favor of the resolution, that it was flawed:

> It does not take into sufficient account the context in which they occur or the excesses of the other side. . . . Palestinian acts of violence, no more than those committed by Israel, cannot be condoned.[67]

Washington's root difficulty with the Palestinians is not terrorism or their refusal to grant Israel the right to exist, but rather the perception of their destabilizing potential in a region over which the United States claims tutelage. This chapter has shown that the Kissinger conditions and Reagan's codicils for talks with the PLO were part of a conscious political decision meant to obstruct a negotiated settlement, out of deference to a strategic relationship with Israel. Such a settlement, in turn, was intended to fulfill the strategic aim of defeating the last vestiges of Arab "radicalism." The acceptance by the PLO of the U.S. conditions is thus seen by the United States as a vindication of its steadfastness and a fulfillment of the primary goals of its Middle East policy.

The firm commitment of George Bush to the strategic alliance with Israel is not likely to erode in the near future. His party's platform during the 1988 campaign commits him to opposing the creation of an independent Palestinian state, deemed as "inimical to the security interests of Israel, Jordan and the U.S." Such opposition, however, will not necessarily lead the Bush administration to stop the Palestinians from pursuing that option. Although the Reagan plan of 1982 perceived peace as being achievable neither on the basis of the formation of an independent Palestinian state, nor on the basis of Israeli sovereignty in the West Bank and Gaza, Camp David, on the other hand, left both options open for negotiations. Given that these two documents form the cornerstone of the U.S. diplomatic framework for the Palestine-Israel conflict, any new initiatives by the Bush administration were expected to fall somewhere along that spectrum, which is capable of accommodating the post-1988 Palestinian minimalist position as well as the post-*intifada* Likud position.

The common denominators of the Camp David/Reagan Plan framework consist of "full autonomy," transitional periods, elections for a "self-governing authority," and some kind of association with Jordan, none of which is likely to cause serious disagreement between Israel and the Bush

---

67. *New York Times*, 18 February 1989.

administration. The *intifada* has already impelled Israel to advance a plan incorporating phraseology and invoking principles taken right out of the American diplomatic and political dictionary, no doubt intended to provide Congress with the necessary arsenal for maintaining the *status quo*. Concepts such as "free, democratic elections," a sacrosanct concept in liberal America, "lull in violence," "interim stage" and "final solution" decorate the 20-point program approved by the Israeli cabinet on May 4, 1989.[68] And yet, the four "basic premises" of the plan ensure its non-workability. These are: Direct negotiations based on the Camp David Accords; "no" to a Palestine State; "no" to negotiations with the PLO; "no" to any change in the status of Judea, Samaria and Gaza other than in accordance with the basic guidelines of the Government."[69]

The "free and democratic" elections, which impressed Secretary of State James Baker III as a good idea, were offered to the Palestinians in the West Bank and Gaza in the manner of either accept or risk the consequences. "Harsh measures" were threatened by Defense Minister Rabin as punishment for rejecting the plan. As an example of what may lay ahead for the Palestinians, Rabin placed the entire Gaza strip with its 650,000 residents under total curfew for a whole week, an experiment which was to be repeated and which included, for the first time in twenty-two years, an enforced recall of all Gazans employed in Israel.[70]

Michael Lerner, editor of *Tikkun* magazine, wrote the following about Mr. Shamir's elections plan:

> Shamir has made it clear that these elections will be no freer than those held in some totalitarian countries.[71]

Neither international supervision of the elections, nor even a limited redeployment of the Israeli army away from urban centers in the occupied territories, was envisaged under this plan. Candidates would be expected to refrain from raising the issue of Palestinian statehood during the campaign., and the Arab sector of Jerusalem, with 10 percent of the Arab population in the West Bank, and Gaza, with the most prominent Palestinian leaders,

68. "A Peace Initiative: Document," *Jerusalem Post*, 15 May 1989.

69. *Ibid.*

70. Peretz Kidron, "Shamir's Plan in Trouble at Home and Abroad," *Middle East International* (26 May 1989), 351:3.

71. Michael Lerner, "Barker's Mideast Speech," *Miami Herald* (section 5c), 28 May 1989.

would be barred from participation in those elections, as a demonstration that Israel considers its annexation of east Jerusalem final and irrevocable. Beyond all these limitations, the Israeli plan envisions the emergence of elected Palestinian representatives for negotiations, commencing no later than the third year of the five-year interim period of self-rule. Those negotiations would end in a "final solution" and an Israeli-Jordanian peace treaty.

Such contemplated arrangements are not different from what had been attempted by the United States, Israel, and Egypt between 1979 and 1982. And yet, the Bush administration embraced the elections idea with such enthusiasm that it has already become the centerpiece of United States Middle East diplomacy. David Korn, a United States delegate to the so-called autonomy talks between 1979 and 1981, explained the Bush administration's endorsement of this "warmed-over" version of Camp David in the following words:

> [It] chose to center its Middle East peace efforts on elections because elections are a safe issue: besides being a sacrosanct principle of democracy, they were agreed to by Israel all the way back in 1978 when it signed the Camp David frameworks. But playing safe is not playing successfully. The media and the public should not be misled: elections are almost certain to be a dead-end street.[72]

A clear illustration of "playing safe" was a major policy address by President Bush's secretary of state, James Baker, before the American Israel Public Affairs Committee (AIPAC) on May 22, 1989. The speech was widely interpreted in the United States as the first statement of the Bush administration and was generally described as even-handed. The Secretary of State admonished Israel, the Arabs, the Palestinians, and the Soviets to make concessions, leaving Washington comfortably in the position of arbiter. And as such, his speech offered a "middle-ground," defined as "self-government for Palestinians in the West Bank and Gaza in a manner acceptable to Palestinians, Israel and Jordan."[73] In fact, Mr. Baker's demands on the Palestinians and the Arabs were more specific than those made on Israel, and they went beyond those made by his predecessor, George Shultz. He urged them to produce a "constructive" response to the initiative which the "Israeli government *has* offered." He commanded the

72. *New York Times,* 14 June 1989 (Letter to the Editor).

73. Secretary Baker, United States Department of State, Bureau of Public Affairs, "Principles and Pragmatism: American Policy toward the Arab-Israeli Conflict," *Current Policy No. 1176.*

Palestinians to "renounce the policy of phrases in all languages. . . . Amend the Covenant. Translate the dialogue of violence in the *intifada* into a dialogue of politics and diplomacy."[74] He asked them to accept a transitional period of autonomy prior to a final settlement. He warned them not to "distort international organization" by seeking admission to membership in the United Nations specialized agencies. He wanted them to convince the Israelis of their peaceful intentions, to accept as a real opening the elections proposed by the Shamir government and to "understand that no one is going to deliver Israel for you."

As for Israel, the new element in Mr. Baker's AIPAC speech was merely the language:

> Now is the time to lay aside, once and for all, the unrealistic vision of a greater Israel. . . . .Forswear annexation. Stop settlement activity. Allow schools to reopen. Reach out to the Palestinians as neighbors who deserve political rights.

Mr. Baker clearly placed the onus for breaking the impasse on the Arab world, which he admonished to "take concrete steps towards accommodation with Israel," and insisted that such steps cannot be outside the framework of the so-called peace process. He, therefore, ignored previous Arab efforts on behalf of accommodation made through U.N. mediator Gunnar Jarring in 1970 and continuing throughout the seventies and eighties in numerous resolutions adopted by Arab summit conferences. He bade the Arabs to "end the economic boycott; stop the challenges to Israel's standing in international organizations; repudiate the odious line that Zionism is racism." He then turned to the Soviet Union, which, unlike the United States, recognizes the right of self-determination for both Arabs and Jews in Palestine, and challenged it to extend the "new thinking" to the Middle East. After recognizing Soviet concessions in matters affecting Jewish life and immigration rights in the USSR and noting that Moscow considers Shamir's election proposal "worthy of consideration," he told the Soviets to go further by restoring diplomatic ties with Israel and stopping the supply of weapons to "countries like Libya."

On the whole, the first major policy statement of the Bush Administration introduced very little, if any, in terms of substance. But the sensational phraseology, reaffirming the U.S. perspective on Israel's obligations under Resolution 242, marked a stylistic change in Washington's dealing with Israel. The only new element in the speech, however, is Washington's open support for Shamir's elections plan. And to the extent that the plan represents the latest form of Israeli procrastination, ongoing

74. *Ibid.*

since 1968 for the purpose of gaining time to consolidate the occupation, ward off international criticism and maintain the impasse, Washington's support for it is consistent with its strategy of the past two decades. The *Boston Globe*, which titled its editorial reaction to Baker's speech "A Realistic Mideast Vision," nevertheless recognized "a blatant contradiction in the diplomatic posture of the Bush Administration . . . qualified support to Shamir's plan for elections." The editorial goes on to offer the following analysis of the plan:

> The text of the Shamir plan makes it plain that elections are intended as a means to avoid negotiations with the PLO, consideration of a Palestinian state, or ceding Israeli sovereignty over conquered land. In other words, the Shamir plan is a tactic to preserve the possibility of realizing the dream of a greater Israel, just as Begin hoped the separate peace with Egypt and his 1982 invasion of Lebanon would give Israel a free hand to impose its sovereignty in the West Bank and Gaza.[75]

The authors of the elections plan intended it to be a public relations exercise designed to throw the diplomatic ball back in the court of the PLO. And yet neither the Likud Party nor the Bush Administration accepts the PLO as negotiator. What Washington wants from the PLO, having exhausted all means of promoting Jordan as interlocutor, is to deliver the Palestinian leadership in the occupied territories, i.e. to acquiesce in the ongoing process aiming to substitute self-government for Palestinian statehood.

At the time of this writing, in the early summer of 1989, the PLO refused to reject the elections plan out of hand, as it had done ten years ago with regard to Camp David. In fact, it encouraged Palestinian leaders in the occupied territories to meet with the Bush administration's first high-ranking delegation in May 1989, while its own contacts with the United States were limited to the level of the ambassador to Tunisia. In doing so, the PLO wanted to avoid being seen as the spoiler and to push the United States to take seriously what the Shamir government had started as a public relations exercise.

The final outcome of Mr. Bush's renewed "peace process," however, is not difficult to predict. Mr. Baker's AIPAC speech found symmetry in a non-symmetrical situation: it equated the dream of an independent state on but 25 percent of the land of pre-1948 Palestine with the dream of a greater Israel on 100 percent of Palestine and possibly in other Arab areas, including southern Lebanon and the Syrian Golan heights. It aimed to find the compromise between the minimal Palestinian position and the maximal Israeli position. But even this myopic vision conflicts with the plans of Mr.

75. *Boston Globe*, 27 May 1989.

Shamir who was elected on a party plank of non-withdrawal from the West Bank and Gaza. His latest interview confirms this unwillingness to cede even one inch of territory. When asked by the *Miami Herald* "will any territory whatsoever be given back?" he replied:

> You know my view, that we have to work for peace and not to seek solutions on the territorial plane.[76]

To bolster this curious separation between peace and a territorial settlement, he added:

> I know many great experts in international law who say that by our withdrawal from Sinai we have already implemented Resolutions 242 and 338.[77]

Herein lay the likely disagreement between the Bush administration and Israel. According to Abba Eban, this interpretation by Shamir is what had led to the collapse of the Shultz Plan of 1988 and the Jordan disengagement from the West Bank.[78] From the Israeli vantage point, the elections plan is designed to prevent "foreign sovereignty west of the River Jordan." On the other hand, the Bush agenda is bound to include the restoration of Resolution 242 to an acceptable interpretation given the new local, regional and international imperatives discussed above. From the American vantage point, however, the sovereignty issue must be discussed in terms of Resolution 242, which considers the West Bank and Gaza as occupied territories. The projected elections would then be designed to contribute to this objective by reconfirming the geographic character and accentuating the status of these occupied territories under international law.

This analysis is contingent on the constancy of the local, regional, and international imperatives discussed in this chapter. The maintenance of the *status quo* in the occupied territories, in Israel, and with the PLO; the present Arab alignment whose principal actors are Jordan, Egypt, the PLO, and Iraq; and the current level of relations between the superpowers. The U.S.-PLO substantive dialogue has added to the improvement in U.S.-Arab relations, but it may have also created unrealistic expectations from the Bush administration. The next phase in U.S. Middle East diplomacy is likely to include more pressure on the Palestinians and Arab states than on Israel. The U.S. has not yet committed itself to accepting the PLO as the

---

76. *Miami Herald*, 21 May 1989.

77. *Ibid.*

78. Abba Eban, "242 Revisited," *Jerusalem Post*, 25 November 1989.

representative of the Palestinians, to accepting the Soviet Union as cosponsor of negotiations or to initiating the convening of an international conference. These procedural items will no doubt have a price. There are already signs that indicate the reappearance of Kissinger's men at the top foreign policy level in Washington. Not only has Lawrence Eagleburger been appointed to the position of Undersecretary of State, next only to James Baker; he was also the cochair (with Walter Mondale) of a 1988 seminar held under the auspices of the pro-Israel Washington Institute for Near East Policy. The recommendations of that seminar, entitled *Building for Peace*, counseled caution with regard to any early initiatives and to the convening of an international conference as the proper forum for negotiations.[79]

The Bush Administration was afforded by its predecessor some maneuverability, which could be used to open a dialogue with Israel for the purpose of bridging a perceptual gap regarding the limits and obligations of the special relationship and the dictates of U.S. and Israeli interests in the region. The debate will not center on the rationale and substance of that relationship but on its manifestations and procedural requirements. The Palestinian uprising has reshaped and clarified the Arab-Israeli conflict in 1988; Mr. Bush's challenge is to reconcile the U.S. and Israeli responses.

79. Mary Curtius, "Israel Wary of Path Bush Will Take," *Boston Globe,* 27 January 1989.

BIBLIOGRAPHY

Abboushi, Wasif F. *The Unmaking of Palestine.* Cambridgeshire, England: Middle East and North African Studies Press, 1985.

Abu-Ghazaleh, A. *Arab Cultural Nationalism in Palestine during the British Mandate.* Beirut: Institute for Palestine Studies, 1973.

Abu-Iyad. *Palestinien sans patrie: Entretiens avec Eric Rouleau.* Paris: Fayolle, 1978.

Abu-Lughod, I., ed. *The Arab-Israeli Confrontation of June 1967: An Arab Perspective.* Evanston, Ill.: Northwestern University Press, 1970.

—— *The Transformation of Palestine.* Evanston, Ill.: Northwestern University Press, 1971.

—— *Palestinian Rights: Affirmation and Denial.* Wilmette, Ill.: Medina University Press, 1983.

Amiri, M. *Jerusalem: Arab Origin and Heritage.* London: Longman, 1978.

Antonius, G. *The Arab Awakening.* 1938. Reprint. New York: Putnam, 1948.

The Arabs under Israeli Occupation. Beirut: Institute for Palestine Studies (Annual documentary since 1974).

Aronson, G. *Creating Facts: Israel, Palestinians and the West Bank.* Washington, D.C.: Institute of Palestine Studies, 1987.

Aruri, N. *Jordan: A Study in Political Development 1921-1965.* The Hague: Martinus Nijhoff, 1972.

Aruri, N., ed. *The Palestinian Resistance to Israel's Occupation.* Wilmette, Ill.: Medina University Press, 1970.

—— ed. *Middle East Crucible: Studies on the Arab-Israeli Confrontation of October 1973.* Wilmette, Ill.: Medina University Press, 1970.

Aruri, N., and E. Ghareeb. *Enemy of the Sun: Poems of Palestinian Resistance.* Washington: Drum and Spear Press, 1970.

Aruri, N., F. Moughrabi, and J. Stork. *Reagan and the Middle East.* Belmont, Mass.: AAUG Press, 1983.

al-Asmar, F. *To Be an Arab in Israel.* London: Frances Pinter, 1975.

Ata, I.W. *The West Bank Palestinian Family.* New York: Routledge & Kegan Paul, 1987.

Avnery, U. *My Friend, The Enemy.* London: Zed Books, 1986.

Awartani, H. *West Bank Agriculture: A New Outlook.* Nablus: Najah University, 1978.

Begin, M. *The Revolt: The Story of the Irgun.* New York: Henry Shuman, 1951.

Bell, J. *Terror Out of Zion.* New York: St. Martin's, 1977.

Bendt, I., and J. Downing. *We Shall Return: Women of Palestine.* London: Zed Press, 1982.

Benvenisti, M. *1986 Report: Demographic, Economic, Legal, Social, and Political Developments in the West Bank.* Jerusalem: The West Bank Data Project, 1986.

—— *Conflict and Contradiction.* New York: Villard Books, 1986.

Bober, A., ed. *The Other Israel: The Radical Case against Zionism.* New York: Doubleday, 1972.

Bonds, J., et al. *Our Roots Are Still Alive: The Story of the Palestinian People.* San Francisco: People's Press, 1977.

Brenner, L. *Zionism in the Age of Dictators: A Reappraisal.* Westport, Conn.: Lawrence Hill & Co., 1983.

Bull, V. *The West Bank: Is It Viable?* Lexington, Mass.: Lexington Books, 1975.

Carter, J. *The Blood of Abraham: Insights into the Middle East.* Boston: Houghton Mifflin Company, 1985.

Cattan, H. *Palestine and International Law.* London: Longman, 1973.

—— *Jerusalem.* London: Croom Helm, 1981.

Chaliand, G. *The Palestinian Resistance.* Harmondsworth: Penguin, 1972.

Chomsky, N. *Peace in the Middle East?* New York: Vintage Books, 1974.

—— *The Fateful Triangle: The United States, Israel and the Palestinians.* Boston: South End Press, 1984.

Cobban, H. *The Palestinian Liberation Organization: People, Power and Politics.* Cambridge: Cambridge University Press, 1984.

Cohen, A. *Political Parties in the West Bank under the Jordanian Regime 1949 -1967.* Ithaca, New York: Cornell University Press, 1982.

Cohen, E. A. *Human Rights in the Israeli Occupied Territories. Dover N.H.:* Manchester University Press, 1986.

—— *A Compassionate Peace: Future for the Middle East.* Report prepared for the American Friends Service Committee. New York: Hill & Wang, 1982.

Cooley, J. *Green March, Black September: The Story of the Palestinian Arabs.* London: Cass, 1973.

Cossali, P., and C. Robson. *Stateless In Gaza.* London and New Jersey: Zed Books, 1986.

Council for the Advancement of Arab-British Understanding. *Punishing the Innocent: House Demolitions as Collective Punishment on the West Bank.* London: CAABU, 1987.

Curtiss, R. *A Changing Image: American Perceptions of the Arab-Israeli Dispute.* Washington, D.C.: American Educational Trust, 1986.

Davis, J. *The Evasive Peace: A Study of the Zionist Arab Problems.* Cleveland: Dillion, 1976.

Davis, U. *Israel: An Apartheid State.* London: Zed Books, 1987.

Dhaher, A. *The Palestinian Experience.* Menas Press, 1986. Dist. by Lynne Rienner Publishers, Inc., Boulder, Colo.

Drobles, M. *Master Plan for the Development of Settlement in Judea and Samaria 1979-83.* Jerusalem: World Zionist Organization, Department of Rural Settlement, 1978.

Ekin, L. *Enduring Witnesses: The Churches and the Palestinians.* Geneva: World Council of Churches, 1985.

Epp, F. *Whose Land Is Palestine?* Grand Rapids, Mich.: Eerdmans, 1970.

—— *The Israelis: Portrait of a People in Conflict.* Scottsdale, Pa.: Herald Press, 1980.

Fahmy, I. *Negotiating for Peace in the Middle East.* Baltimore: Johns Hopkins, 1983.

Falloon, V. *Excessive Secrecy, Lack of Guidelines: A Report on Military Censorship in the West Bank.* Ramallah, West Bank: Al-Haq – Law in the Service of Man, 1986.

Feinberg, N. *Studies in International Law: With Special Reference to the Arab-Israel Conflict.* Jerusalem: Magnes Press, 1979.

Flapan, S. *Zionism and the Palestinians.* London: Croom Helm, 1979.

Genet, J. *Un Captive Amoureux.* Paris: Gallimard, 1986.

Gharaibeh, F. *The Economies of the West Bank and Gaza Strip.* Boulder, Colo.: Westview Press, 1985.

Giacaman, R. *Life and Health in Three Palestinian Villages. Lowell, Mass.:* Ithaca Press, 1987.

Gilmour, D. *Dispossessed: The Ordeal of the Palestinians 1917-1980.* London: Sidgwick & Jackson, 1980.

Gonen, J. *A Psychohistory of Zionism.* New York: Mason/Charter, 1975.

Goodwin-Gill, G. *The Refugee in International Law.* Oxford: Clarendon Press, 1983.

Gorny, Y. *The Arab Question and the Jewish Problem.* Tel Aviv: Am Oved Publishers, 1986.

Graham-Brown, S. *Palestinians and Their Society, 1880-1946: A Photographic Essay.* London: Quartet, 1980.

—— *Education, Repression, Liberation: Palestinians.* London: World University Service, 1984.

Granott, A. *The Land System in Palestine.* London: Eyre and Spottiswoode, 1952.

Green, S. *Living by the Sword: American and Israel in the Middle East.* Brattleboro, Vt.: Amana Books, 1988

Gresh, A. *The PLO, the Struggle Within: Towards an Independent Palestinian State.* Translated by A.M. Berrett. London: Zed Books, 1985.

Grossman, D. *Jewish and Arab Settlements in the Tulkarm Sub-District.* Jerusalem: The West Bank Data Project, 1986.

Hadawi, S. *Bitter Harvest, Palestine 1914-67.* New York: New World Press, 1967.

Halsell, G. *Journey to Jerusalem.* New York: Macmillan, 1981.

Harris, W. *Taking Root: Israeli Settlement in the West Bank, the Golan and Gaza-Sinai, 1967-1980.* Chichester and New York: Wiley, 1980.

Hassan Bin Talal. *Palestinian Self-Determination: A Study of the West Bank and Gaza Strip.* Salem, N.H.: Quartet, 1982.

Heller, M. *A Palestinian State: The Implication for Israel.* Cambridge: Harvard University Press, 1983.

Heydemann, S., ed. *Issues in Contemporary Israel: The Begin Era.* Boulder, Colo.: Westview Press, 1984.

Hillal, J. *Al-Daffa al-Gharbiya: Al-Tarkib al-Ijtimai wa al-Iqtisadi* (West Bank Economic and Social Structure 1948-1974). Beirut: PLO Research Center, 1974.

Hiltermann, J. *Israel's Deportation Policy in the Occupied West Bank and Gaza.* Occasional Paper #2. Ramallah, West Bank: Al-Haq – Law in the Service of Man, 1986.

Hirst, D. *The Gun and the Olive Branch.* London: Faber, 1977.

Hopkins, J. *Jerusalem: A Study in Urban Geography.* Grand Rapids, Mich.: Baker, 1971.

International Christian Committee for the Relief of Arab Refugees, West Bank Area Council, Middle East Council Churches. *Annual Report, of 1978.* Jerusalem, 1979.

—— *Self-Help Village Development Program.* Jerusalem, 1979.

International Labor Organization. *Report of the Director General, 1982.* Appendix, "Report of the Situation of Workers of the Occupied Arab Territories." Geneva, 1982.

Israel in Lebanon: *Report of the International Commission.* London: Ithaca, 1982.

al-Jafari, W. *Al-Mustamarat al-Istitaniya al-Israiliya fi al-Aradi al-Muhtala 1967-1980* (Colonial Settlements in the Occupied Territories 1967-1980). Beirut: Institute for Palestine Studies, 1981.

Jansen, J. *The Battle of Beirut: Why Israel Invaded Lebanon.* Boston: South End Press, 1983.

Jeffries, J. *Palestine: The Reality.* Westport, Conn.: Hyperion Press, 1976.

Jiryis, S. *The Arabs in Israel.* New York: Monthly Review Press, 1976.

——— *Al-Quds: al-Mukhattatat al-Sahyuniya, al-Ihtilal, al-Tahwid* (Jerusalem: Zionist Schemes, Occupation, Judaization). Beirut: Institute for Palestine Studies, 1981.

Kahane, M. *They Must Go.* New York: Grosset & Dunlap, 1981.

Kahhaleh, S. *The Water Problem in Israel and Its Repercussions on the Arab-Israeli Conflict.* Beirut: Institute for Palestine Studies, 1981.

Kanaana, S. *Socio-Cultural and Psychological Adjustment of the Arab Minority in Israel.* San Francisco: R & E Research Associates, 1976.

Kapeliouk, A. *Israel: La fin des mythes.* Paris: Albin Michel, 1975.

The Karp Report: *An Israeli Government Inquiry into Settler Violence against Palestinians on the West Bank.* Washington, D.C.: Institute for Palestine Studies, 1984.

Kazziha, W. *Palestine in the Arab Dilemma.* London: Croom Helm, 1979.

Khalidi, R. *The Arab Economy in Israel.* London: Croom Helm, 1987. Distributed by Longwood Publishing Group.

Khalidi, W., ed. *From Haven to Conquest: The Origins and Development of the Palestine Problem 1897-1948.* Beirut: Institute for Palestine Studies, 1971.

al-Khatib, R. *The Judaization of Jerusalem.* Beirut: PLO Research Center, 1970.

Khouri, F. *The Arab-Israeli Dilemma.* 3d ed. Syracuse: Syracuse University Press, 1985.

Kirisci, K. *The PLO and World Politics: A Study of the Mobilization of Support for the Palestinian Cause.* New York: St. Martin's Press, 1987.

el-Kodsy, A., and E. Lobel. *The Arab World and Israel.* New York: Monthly Review Press, 1970.

Kubursi, A. *The Economic Consequences of the Camp David Agreements.* Beirut: Institute for Palestine Studies, and Kuwait Chamber of Commerce and Industry, 1981.

Kutcher, A. *The New Jerusalem: Planning and Politics.* Cambridge: M.I.T. Press, 1975.

Kuttab, J., and R. Shehadeh. *Civilian Administration in the Occupied West Bank: Analysis of Israel Military Order No. 947.* Wapakoneta, Ohio: Law in the Service of Man, 1982.

Langer, F. *With My Own Eyes: Israel and the Occupied Territories.* Part 1. London: Ithaca Press, 1981.

—— *These Are My Brothers: Israel and the Occupied Territories.* Part 2. London: Ithaca Press, 1981.

Lesch, A. *Arab Politics in Palestine 1917-1939: The Frustration of a Nationalist Movement.* Ithaca, New York: Cornell University Press, 1979.

—— *Political Perceptions of the Palestinians on the West Bank and Gaza Strip.* Washington, D.C.: Middle East Institute, 1980.

Lilienthal, A. *The Zionist Connection. II: What Price Peace?* New Brunswick, N.J.: North American, 1982.

Locke, R., and A. Stewart. *Bantustan Gaza.* London: Zed Press, 1985.

Lukacs, Y. *Documents on the Israeli-Palestinian Conflict, 1907- 1983.* Cambridge: Cambridge University Press, 1984.

Lustick, I. *Arabs in the Jewish State: Israel's Control of a National Minority.* Austin: University of Texas Press, 1980.

Mallison, S., and W. T. Mallison. *The Palestine Problem in International Law and World Order.* New York: Longman, 1983.

Mansour, A., with a preface by Michel Chatelus. *Palestine: An Economy of Resistance in the West Bank and Gaza.* Paris: Editions L'Harmattan, 1983.

Ma'oz, M. *Palestinian Leadership on the West Bank: The Changing Role of the Mayors under Jordan and Israel.* London and Totowa, N.J.: F. Cass, 1984.

Mason, H., ed. *Reflections on the Palestine Crisis.* The Hague: Mouton, 1970.

Metzger, J., M. Orth, and C. Sterzing. *This Land Is Our Land: The West Bank under Israeli Occupation.* London: Zed Press, 1985.

Mikedadi, L. *Surviving the Siege of Beirut.* London: Onyx Press, 1983.

Miller, Y. *Government and Society in Rural Palestine, 1920-1948.* Austin: University of Texas Press, 1985.

Mishal, S. *West Bank East Bank: The Palestinians in Jordan 1949- 1967.* New Haven: Yale University Press, 1976.

—— *The PLO under Arafat: Between Gun and Olive Branch.* New Haven and London: Yale University Press, 1986.

Nakhleh, E. *The West Bank and Gaza: Toward the Making of a Palestinian State.* Washington, D.C.: American Enterprise Institute, 1979.

Nakhleh, E., ed. *A Palestinian Agenda for the West Bank and Gaza.* Washington, D.C.: American Enterprise Institute, 1980.

Nakhleh, K. *Palestinian Dilemma: Nationalist Consciousness and University Education in Israel.* Detroit: AAUG, 1979.

Nakhleh, K., and E. Zureik, eds. *The Sociology of the Palestinians.* London: Croom Helm, 1980.

Nashef, T. *The Palestine Arab and Jewish Political Leadership.* New York: Asia Publishing House, 1979.

Nassib, S., and C. Tisdall. *Beirut: Front Line Story.* London: Pluto, 1983.

National Lawyers Guild. *Treatment of Palestinians in Israeli-Occupied West Bank and Gaza.* New York: National Lawyers Guild, 1978.

Neff, D. *Warriors of Jerusalem.* Brattleboro, Vt.: Amana Books, 1987.

Nijim, B., ed. and Bishara Muammar, researcher. *Toward The De-Arabization of Palestine/Israel.* Dubuque, Iowa: Kendall & Hunt, 1984.

Nuseibeh, H. *Palestine and the United Nations.* Salem, N.H.: Quartet, 1982.

Nuwayhid, A. *Rijal min Filastin* (Men from Palestine). Beirut: Manshurat Filastin al-Muhtalla, 1981.

O'Neil, B. *Armed Struggle in Palestine: A Political-Military Analysis.* Boulder, Colo.: Westiren Press, 1978.

Ott, D. *Palestine in Perspective: Politics, Human Rights, and the West Bank.* London: Quartet, 1980.

Oz, A. *In the Land of Israel.* New York: Harcourt Brace Jovanovich, 1983.

Palestine National Fund. *Statistical Yearbook of Palestine.* Damascus, 1981.

Peck, J. *The Reagan Administration and the Palestinian Question.* Washington, D.C.: Institute for Palestine Studies, 1984.

Perry, G., ed. *Palestine: Continuing Dispossession.* Belmont, Mass: AAUG Press, 1986.

Playfair, E. *Administrative Detention in the Occupied West Bank.* Ramallah, West Bank: Al-Haq – Law in the Service of Man, 1985.

Polk, W. *The Elusive Peace: The Middle East in the Twentieth Century.* New York: St. Martin's Press, 1979.

Polk, W., D. Stamler, and E. Asfour. *Backdrop to Tragedy.* Boston: Beacon, 1957.

Quandt, W. *Decade of Decision: American Policy toward the Arab-Israeli Conflict.* Berkeley: University of California Press, 1977.

—— *Camp David: Peacemaking and Politics.* Washington, D.C.: Brookings Institute, 1986.

Quandt, W., F. Jabber, and A. Lesch. *The Politics of Palestinian Nationalism.* Berkeley: University of California Press, 1973.

Randall, J. *Going All the Way: Christian Warlords, Israeli Adventures and the War in Lebanon.* New York: Viking, 1983.

Richardson, J. *The West Bank: A Portrait.* Washington, D.C.: Middle East Institute, 1984.

Rodinson, M. *Israel: A Colonial Settler State?* New York: Monad, 1973.

—— *Israel and the Arabs.* Harmondsworth: Penguin, 1968.

Rokach, L. *Israel's Sacred Terrorism.* Belmont, Mass.: AAUG Press 1980.

Roy, S. *The Gaza Strip Survey.* Jerusalem: The West Bank Data Project and The Jerusalem Post, 1986.

Rubenberg, C. *The Palestine Liberation Organization: Its Institutional Infrastructure.* Belmont, Mass.: Institute of Arab Studies, 1983.

—— *Israel and the American National Interest: A Critical Examination.* Urbana and Chicago: University of Illinois Press, 1986.

Rubenstein, S. *The Communist Movement in Palestine and Israel, 1919-1984.* Boulder, CO.: Westview Press,1985.

Said, E. *The Question of Palestine.* New York: Times Books, 1979.

—— *After the Last Sky: Palestinian Lives.* Photographs by Jean Mohr. New York: Pantheon, 1986.

Saraste, L., *For Palestine.* translated by Greg Coogen. London: Zed Press, 1985.

Schleifer, A. *The Fall of Jerusalem.* New York: Monthly Review Press, 1972.

Scholch, A. ed. *Palestinians over the Green Line: Studies on the Relations between Palestinians on Both Sides of the 1949 Armistice Line since 1967.* London: Ithaca Press, 1983.

Seger, K., ed. *Portrait of a Palestinian Village: The Photographs of Hilma Granqvist.* London: Third World Center for Research and Publishing, 1981.

Sella, A., and Y. Yishai. *Israel the Peaceful Belligerent, 1967-79.* St. Martin's Press, 1986.

Semyonov, M., and N. Lewin-Epstein. *Hewers of Wood and Drawers of Water: Noncitizen Arabs in the Israeli Labor Market.* Ithaca, New York: ILR Press, 1987.

Shadid, M. *The United States and the Palestinians.* London: Croom Helm, 1981.

Shahak, I., trans. and ed. *The Zionist Plan for the Middle East.* Belmont, Mass.: AAUG Press, 1982.

Shavit, D. *The United States in the Middle East: A Historical Dictionary.* Westport, Conn.: Greenwood Press, 1988.

Shbib, S. *Hizb al-Istiqlal al-Arabi fi Filastin 1932-1933* (The Arab Independence Party in Palestine). Beirut: PLO Research Center, 1981.

Shehadah, R. *The Third Way: A Journal of Life in the West Bank.* London: Quartet, 1982.

—— *Samed: Journal of a West Bank Palestinian.* New York: Adama Books, 1984.

—— *Occupier's Law: Israel and the West Bank.* Washington, D.C.: Institute for Palestine Studies, 1985.

Shehadeh, R., and J. Kuttab. *The West Bank and the Rule of Law.* New York: International Commission of Jurists and Law in the Service of Man, 1980.

Shinar, D. *Palestinian Voices: Communication and Nation Building in the West Bank.* Boulder, Colo.: Lynne Rienner Publishers, 1986.

Shipler, D. *Arabs and Jews: Wounded Spirits in a Promised Land.* New York: Times Books, 1986.

Smith, G. *Zionism: The Dream and the Reality: A Jewish Critique.* London: David and Charles (Holdings), 1974.

Smith, P. *Palestine and the Palestinians, 1876-1983.* New York: St. Martin's Press, 1984.

Stewart, D. *Palestinians: Victims of Expediency.* London: Quartet, 1982.

Sykes, C. *Crossroads to Israel.* Cleveland: World, 1959.

Tamari, S., and R. Giacaman. *Zbeidat: The Social Impact of Drip Irrigation on a Palestinian Peasant Community in the Jordan Valley.* Bir Zeit: Bir Zeit University, 1980.

Tarbush, T. *Reflections of a Palestinian.* Washington, D.C.: American-Arab Affairs Council, 1986.

Tibawi, A. *British Interests in Palestine.* London: Oxford University Press, 1961.

Timmerman, J. *The Longest War.* London: Chatto and Windus, 1980.

Tschirgi, D. *The Politics of Indecision: Origins and Implications of American Involvement with the Palestine Problem.* New York: Praeger, 1983.

Turki, F. *The Disinherited: Journal of a Palestinian Exile.* New York: Monthly Review Press, 1972.

United Nations. Committee on the Exercise of the Inalienable Rights of the Palestinian People. *The International Status of the Palestinian People.* New York, 1979.

—— *Israel's Policy on the West Bank.* New York, 1979.

—— *The Question of the Observance of the Fourth Geneva Convention of 1949 in Gaza and the West Bank including Jerusalem Occupied by Israel in June 1967.* New York, 1979.

—— *The Question of Palestine.* New York, 1979.

—— *The Status of Jerusalem.* New York, 1979.

—— *Acquisition of Land in Palestine.* New York, 1979.

United Nations Relief and Works Agency for Palestinian Refugees. *Report of the Commissioner General 1 July 1980-30 June 1981.* New York, 1981.

Uris, L. *The Haj.* New York: Doubleday, 1984.

Van Arkadie, B. *Benefits and Burdens: A Report on the West Bank and Gaza Strip Economies since 1967.* New York/Washington: Carnegie Endowment for International Peace, 1977.

Waines, D. *A Sentence of Exile: The Palestine/Israel Conflict 1897- 1977.* Wilmette, Ill.: Medina University Press, 1977.

Weiler, J. *Israel and the Creation of a Palestinian State: A European Perspective.* Croom Helm, 1985. Dist. by Longwood Publishing Group.

Weinstock, N. *Zionism: False Messiah.* Edited and translated by A. Adler. London: Ink Links, 1979.

Woolfson, M. *Bassam Shaka: Portrait of a Palestinian.* London: Third World Center for Research and Publishing, 1981.

Wright, Claudia. *The Politics of Liquidation: The Reagan Administration Policy towards the Arabs.* Belmont, Mass.: AAUG Press., 1986.

Young, R. *Missed Opportunities for Peace: U.S. Middle East Policy – 1981-1986.* Philadelphia: The American Friends Service Committee, 1987.

Yunis, M. *Community Development versus Personal Property: Israel's Pacification Policy in the Occupied West Bank and Gaza Strip.* Amman: Yarmonk University Center of Hebraic Studies, 1987.

Zeadey, F., ed. *Camp David: A New Balfour Declaration.* Detroit: AAUG, 1979.

Zuaiter, A. *Al-Haraka al-Wataniya al-Filastiniya, 1935-1939: Yawmiyat Akram Zuaiter* (The Palestinian National Movement 1935-1939: The Diaries of Akram Zuaiter). Beirut: Institute for Palestine Studies, 1980.

Zureik, E. *The Palestinians in Israel: A Study in Internal Colonialism.* London: Routledge and Kegan Paul, 1979.

Zureik, E., and F. Moughrabi, eds. *Public Opinion and the Palestine Question.* New York: St. Martin's Press, 1987.

INDEX